English Legal System

Eleventh Edition

Catherine Elliott

and

Frances Quinn

Longman
is an imprint of

PEARSON

Harlow, England • London • New York • Boston • San Francisco • Toronto
Sydney • Tokyo • Singapore • Hong Kong • Seoul • Taipei • New Delhi
Cape Town • Madrid • Mexico City • Amsterdam • Munich • Paris • Milan

Pearson Education Limited

Edinburgh Gate
Harlow
Essex CM20 2JE
England

and Associated Companies throughout the world

Visit us on the World Wide Web at:
www.pearsoned.co.uk

First published 1996
Second edition 1998
Third edition 2000
Fourth edition 2002
Fifth edition 2004
Sixth edition 2006
Seventh edition 2006
Eighth edition 2007
Ninth edition 2008
Tenth edition 2009
Eleventh edition 2010

ISBN: 978-1-4082-3056-5

British Library Cataloguing-in-Publication Data
A catalogue record for this book is available from the British Library

Library of Congress Cataloging-in-Publication Data
Elliott, Catherine.
   English legal system / Catherine Elliott and Frances Quinn. – 11th ed.
        p.   cm.
   ISBN 978-1-4082-3056-5 (pbk.)
    1. Law–Great Britain.   2. Justice, Administration of–Great Britain.
3. Courts–Great Britain.   I. Quinn, Frances.   II. Title.
     KD662.E45 2010
     349.42—dc22
                                                            2009047335

10   9   8   7   6   5   4   3   2   1
14   13   12   11   10

Typeset by 35
Printed and bound in Great Britain by Ashford Colour Press Ltd, Gosport, Hants

The publisher's policy is to use paper manufactured from sustainable forests.

Brief contents

Part 4 DISPUTE RESOLUTION

Part 5 CONCEPTS OF LAW

Contents

Visit mylawchamber at **www.mylawchamber.co.uk/ElliottELS** to access a wealth of resources to support your studies and teaching in English legal system. These include:

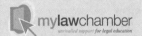 **my**lawchamber
unrivalled support for legal education

FOR STUDENTS
Companion website support

● Access to the accompanying **Pearson eText** – an electronic version of *English Legal System, eleventh edition*, which you can personalise with your own notes. Extensive links are provided to the Pearson eText from all of the resources listed below, and it is fully searchable.

● **Multiple-choice questions**, **flashcards** and **practice exam questions** to test yourself on each topic throughout the course.

● **Updates** to major changes in the law to make sure you are ahead of the game by knowing the latest developments.

● Live **weblinks** to help you read more widely around the subject, and really impress your lecturers.

Use your access card to activate the unrivalled support for your studies. Online purchase is also available at **www.mylawchamber.co.uk/register**.

Guided tour

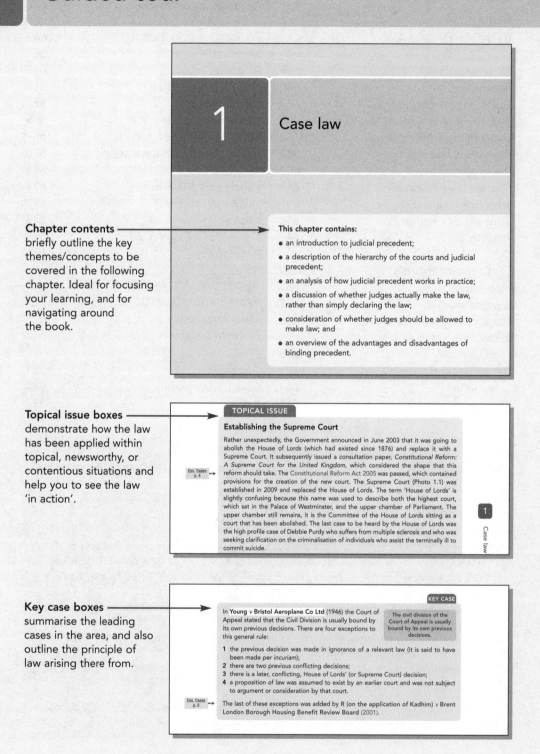

1

Case law

This chapter contains:

- an introduction to judicial precedent;
- a description of the hierarchy of the courts and judicial precedent;
- an analysis of how judicial precedent works in practice;
- a discussion of whether judges actually make the law, rather than simply declaring the law;
- consideration of whether judges should be allowed to make law; and
- an overview of the advantages and disadvantages of binding precedent.

Chapter contents briefly outline the key themes/concepts to be covered in the following chapter. Ideal for focusing your learning, and for navigating around the book.

Topical issue boxes demonstrate how the law has been applied within topical, newsworthy, or contentious situations and help you to see the law 'in action'.

TOPICAL ISSUE

Establishing the Supreme Court

Rather unexpectedly, the Government announced in June 2003 that it was going to abolish the House of Lords (which had existed since 1876) and replace it with a Supreme Court. It subsequently issued a consultation paper, *Constitutional Reform: A Supreme Court for the United Kingdom*, which considered the shape that this reform should take. The Constitutional Reform Act 2005 was passed, which contained provisions for the creation of the new court. The Supreme Court (Photo 1.1) was established in 2009 and replaced the House of Lords. The term 'House of Lords' is slightly confusing because this name was used to describe both the highest court, which sat in the Palace of Westminster, and the upper chamber of Parliament. The upper chamber still remains, it is the Committee of the House of Lords sitting as a court that has been abolished. The last case to be heard by the House of Lords was the high profile case of Debbie Purdy who suffers from multiple sclerosis and who was seeking clarification on the criminalisation of individuals who assist the terminally ill to commit suicide.

Ess. Cases p. 4

1

Case law

Key case boxes summarise the leading cases in the area, and also outline the principle of law arising there from.

KEY CASE

In **Young v Bristol Aeroplane Co Ltd** (1946) the Court of Appeal stated that the Civil Division is usually bound by its own previous decisions. There are four exceptions to this general rule:

> The civil division of the Court of Appeal is usually bound by its own previous decisions.

1 the previous decision was made in ignorance of a relevant law (it is said to have been made *per incuriam*);
2 there are two previous conflicting decisions;
3 there is a later, conflicting, House of Lords' (or Supreme Court) decision;
4 a proposition of law was assumed to exist by an earlier court and was not subject to argument or consideration by that court.

Ess. Cases p. 8

The last of these exceptions was added by R (on the application of Kadhim) v Brent London Borough Housing Benefit Review Board (2001).

Diagrams and flow charts are used throughout to highlight complex legal processes.

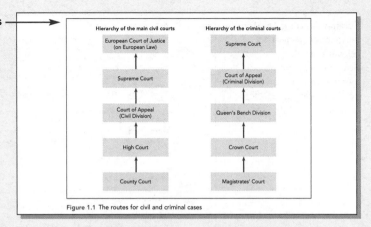

Hierarchy of the main civil courts

European Court of Justice (on European Law)

↑

Supreme Court

↑

Court of Appeal (Civil Division)

↑

High Court

↑

County Court

Hierarchy of the criminal courts

Supreme Court

↑

Court of Appeal (Criminal Division)

↑

Queen's Bench Division

↑

Crown Court

↑

Magistrates' Court

Figure 1.1 The routes for civil and criminal cases

Exam style question and answer guidance help you to test your understanding and successfully prepare for assessments.

Answering questions

1 What do we mean when we say that the English Legal System is a common law system? *London External LLB*

The meaning of 'common law' is discussed at p. 12. The term 'common law' has different meanings depending on the context in which it is being used. In the context of this question the focus is on common law being a product of England's legal history. It can be contrasted to the civil law systems which can be found in Continental Europe (for example, France) and countries which were influenced by Continental Europe. This essay is not concerned with the distinction between equity and 'common law' which is discussed at p. 122.

One approach to this essay would be to first provide a historical analysis of the common law (found on p. 12). Secondly, contrast the common law systems which emphasise judge-made law and the doctrine of judicial precedent, with the civil law systems which place a greater emphasis on legislative codes. Finally, provide some examples of the common law working in practice. For example, the fact that the definition of murder can be found in case law and the way that definition has been developed by the courts.

2 Judicial reasoning in case law 'consists in the applying to new combinations of circumstances those rules of law which we derive from legal principles and judicial precedents . . . and we are not at liberty to reject them, and to abandon all analogy to them'. (Mr Justice Peak, 1833)
Does this statement reflect the operation of precedent today? *London External LLB*

Your answer could be divided into two parts. The first part could discuss how the statement of Mr Justice Peak fits within the classic declaratory theory of law provided by William Blackstone (p. 24). The basic rules that underpin judicial precedent with the hierarchy of the courts, and the ways that cases can be followed, distinguished, overruled and reversed support this view (p. 23).

1

Case law

Chapter summaries enable you to identify, recap and focus on the key points from the chapter you've just read.

Summary of Chapter 9: Law reform

The law needs to change to reflect the changes in society. Changes in the law can be made through the process of case law or by Parliament. The four ways in which Parliament can change the law are:

- repeal;
- creation;
- consolidation; and
- codification.

Pressures for reform
The inspiration for reform may come from a variety of sources, including:

- pressure groups;
- political parties;
- the civil service;
- treaty obligations; and
- public opinion and media pressure.

Agencies of law reform
There are a number of agencies set up to consider the need for reform in areas referred to them by the Government. These agencies are:

- the Law Commission;
- Royal Commissions;
- public inquiries; and
- other temporary inquiries.

The level of success of these agencies has varied considerably. Governments have no obligation to follow their recommendations. Some of the recommendations involve too many compromises and, where lawyers dominate, the resulting reforms may be under-ambitious.

Further reading sections contain references to relevant articles, government papers and internet resources which you may wish to use for further study.

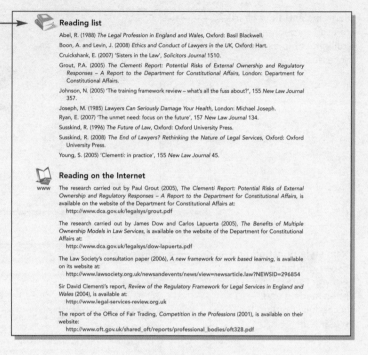

The boxes in the margin direct you to the relevant pages in the accompanying book *English Legal System: Essential Cases and Materials, 2nd edition* where you can find extensive extracts of key cases, statutes, government reports and reform proposals.

Ess. Cases p. 7

it represented a possible interpretation of th
only concerned a temporary transitional peri
There are, however, a range of cases where
apply the 1966 Practice Statement. For exa
within marriage is a crime, overturning a leg
In **Hall v Simons** (2000), the House of L
Rondel v Worsley (1969), which had given b
ligence in their presentation of cases.

Visit the Companion Website at **www.mylawchamber.co.uk/ ElliottELS**, where you can find a number of valuable resources to aid your study, including: multiple-choice questions; exam-style questions with answer guidance; an online glossary; interactive flashcards of key terms and links to useful web resources.

Preface

This book is designed to provide a clear explanation of the English legal system and how it works in practice today. As ever, the legal system and its operation are currently the subject of heated public debate, and we hope that the material here will allow you to enter into some of that debate and develop your own views as to how the system should develop.

One of our priorities in writing this book has been to explain the material clearly, so that it is easy to understand, without lowering the quality of the content. Too often, law is avoided as a difficult subject, when the real difficulty is the vocabulary and style of legal textbooks. For that reason, we have aimed to use 'plain English' as far as possible, and explain the more complex legal terminology where it arises. There is also a glossary of difficult words at the back of the book. In addition, chapters are structured so that material is in a systematic order for the purposes of both learning and revision, and clear subheadings make specific points easy to locate.

Although we hope that many readers will use this book to satisfy a general interest in law and the legal system, we recognise that the majority will be those who have to sit an examination on the subject. Therefore, each chapter features typical examination questions, with detailed guidance on answering them, using the material in the book. This is obviously useful at revision time, but we recommend that when first reading the book, you take the opportunity offered by the questions sections to think through the material that you have just read and look at it from different angles. This will help you both understand and remember it. You will also find a section at the end of the book which gives useful general advice on answering examination questions on the English legal system.

This book is part of a series that has been written by the same authors. The other books in the series are *Criminal Law*, *Contract Law* and *Tort Law*. There is also a companion book entitled *English Legal System: Essential Cases and Materials, 2nd edition*, which brings together relevant primary source material on the subject. Helpful cross-references to the cases and materials book are provided in the margin to the text.

We have endeavoured to state the law as at 1 January 2010.

Catherine Elliott and Frances Quinn
London, 2010

Acknowledgements

We are grateful to the following for permission to reproduce copyright material:

Figures

Figure 2.1 from *Criminal Defence Service (Advice and Assistance) Act*, The Stationery Office (2001), Figure 10.1 from *Judicial and Court Statistics*, Her Majesty's Stationery Office (2007) p. 177, Figure 11.3 from *Annual Report of the Legal Services Ombudsman for England and Wales*, Her Majesty's Stationery Office (2004/5) p. 56, Figure 13.1 from *Judicial and Statistics* Her Majesty's Stationery Office (2007) p. 175, Figure 13.2 from *Crown Prosecution Service Annual Report* (2005–6) p. 80, Figure 18.1 from Policing and the criminal justice system – public confidence and perceptions, *Findings from the 2004/5 British Crime survey*, p. 16 (2004–5), Figure 18.3 from *Criminal Statistics 2007 England and Wales* (2007) p. 51 (Fig.3.7), Figure 19.1 from *Criminal Statistics 2007 England and Wales* (2007) p. 12 (Fig.1.2), Figure 19.3 from *Crown Prosecution Service Annual Report 2008 (Annex B – Casework Statistics)*, p. 82, www.cps.gov.uk/publications/reports/2008/annex_b.html, Figure 20.2 from *Criminal Statistics: England and Wales 2001*, p. 18 (Fig. 1.3), Figure 20.3 from *Criminal Statistics: England and Wales 2001*, p. 81 (Fig. 7.4), Figure 20.5 from *Criminal Statistics in England and Wales 2007* (2007) p. 10 (Fig. 1.1), Figure 21.1 from *Criminal Statistics 2007 England and Wales*, p. 45 (Fig.3.3), Figure 21.3 from *Criminal Statistics: England and Wales 2002*, p. 90 (Fig. 4.10), Figure 21.4 from *Crown Prosecution Service Annual Report 2002–2003*, p. 14, Figure 22.2 from *Judicial Statistics Annual Report 2005 (revised)*, p. 44, Figure 22.3 from Court service website, www.mcsi.gov.uk, Figure 22.4 from *Civil Justice Reform Evaluation Further Findings* (2002), Fig. 22.12, Figure 22.5 from *Civil Justice Reform Evaluation Further Findings* (2002) Fig. 2, Figure 22.6 from *Civil Justice Reform Evaluation Further Findings* (2002) Fig. 1, Figure 22.7 from *Civil Justice Reform Evaluation Further Findings* (2002) Fig. 6, Figure 22.8 from *Civil Justice Reform Evaluation Further Findings* (2002) Fig. 10, Figure 23.1 from *Judicial Statistics Annual Report 2005*, p. 106, Figure 24.1 from *Judicial Statistics Annual Report 2005*, p. 6, Figure 24.2 from *Judicial Statistics Annual Report 2004*, p. 3, Crown Copyright material is reproduced with permission under the terms of the Click-Use License; Figure 11.1 from Trends in the solicitors' profession, *Annual Statistical Report* (2008), www.lawsociety.org.uk, © The Law Society; Figure 25.1 from Association of British Travel Agents.

Tables

Table 10.3 from Department of Constitutional Affairs, Table 11.1 from *Annual Report of the Legal Services Ombudsman for England and Wales*, Her Majesty's Stationery Office (2004/5) p. 15, Tables 13.1, 13.2 from The Judiciary in the Magistrates' Courts, *Home Office RDS Occasional Paper*, no. 66 (Morgan and Russell 2000), Table 19.1 from *Crime in England and Wales 2006–07*, p. 105 (Table 19.5d), Crown Copyright material is reproduced with permission under the terms of the Click-Use License.

Text

Exam Board Questions: chapter 5, p. 111; chapter 10, p. 183; chapter 12, p. 265; chapter 17, p. 372; chapter 17, p. 373; chapter 18, p. 419; chapter 22, p. 566; chapter 25. p. 633 from London External LLB.

Photographs

Alamy Images: 67 Photo 483 (Photo 20.2), Alex Segre/Alamy 180 (Photo 10.4), Justin Kase zelevenz/Alamy 13 (Photo 1.1), Alex Segre/Alamy 533 (Photo 22.1), David Hoffman Photo Library/Alamy 137 (Photo 9.1), Photofusion Picture Library/Alamy 512 (Photo 21.2); **nisyndication.com:** 139 (Photo 9.3 (front cover)) © *News of the World*/23 July 2000/nisyndication.com; **Hawgood, David:** 476 (Photo 20.1); **Getty Images:** Ian Waldie/Getty Images 138 (Photo 9.2), Dan Kitwood/Getty Images 171 (Photo 10.3); Scott Barbour/Getty Images 551 (Photo 22.2); **Hampshire Constabulary:** Jan Brayley/Hampshire Constabulary 385 (Photo 18.2); **HMSO:** 159 (Photo 10.1) © Copyright 2002 Parliamentary Education Unit 48; **iStockphoto:** © iStockphoto/Leah-Anne Thompson 406 (Photo 18.3), © iStockphoto/Luke Daniek 94 (Photo 5.2); **John Conner Press Associates:** 139 (Photo 9.3 (photo of Sarah Payne)); **Jupiter Unlimited:** 93 (Photo 5.1), 235 (Photo 12.1), 312 (Photo 15.1); **Mercury Press:** 509 (Photo 21.1); **Mirrorpix:** © Trinity Mirror/Mirrorpix 455 (Photo 19.1); **Press Association Images:** 380 (Photo 18.1); © Press Association Images/Tony Harris 144 (Photo 9.5); PA Archive/Press Association Images 17 (Photo 1.2); **Rex Features:** 140 (Photo 9.4); Eddie Mulholland/Rex Features 314 (Photo 15.2); **Richard Croft:** 190 (Photo 11.1); **The Law Society of England and Wales:** 211 (Photo 11.2) © The Law Society; www.judiciary.gov.uk: 165 (Photo 10.2).

Every effort has been made to trace the copyright holders and we apologise in advance for any unintentional omissions. We would be pleased to insert the appropriate acknowledgement in any subsequent edition of this publication.

Table of cases

Cases in **bold** are included in *English Legal System: Essential Cases and Materials, second edition*. This book provides fuller extracts from key documents for more in-depth study.

Table of statutes

Table of statutory materials

Statutory materials in **bold** are included in *English Legal System: Essential Cases and Materials, second edition.* This book provides fuller extracts from key documents for more in-depth study.

Cases, law reports and case references: a guide

In order to understand the table of cases and the reference to cases in this book generally, you need to know about the naming of cases, law reports and case references.

Case names

Each legal case that is taken to court is given a name. The name of the case is usually based on the family name of the parties involved. Where there are more than two parties on each side, the case name tends to be shortened to just include one name for each side. In essays, the name of the case should normally be put into italics or underlined, though in this book we have chosen to put them in bold. The exact case names in civil law and criminal law are slightly different so we will consider each in turn.

Criminal law case names

If Ms Smith steals Mr Brown's car then a criminal action is likely to be brought by the state against her. The written name of the case would then be **R v Smith**. The letter 'R' stands for the Latin *Rex* (King) or *Regina* (Queen) depending on whether there was a king or queen in office at the time of the decision. Sometimes the full Latin terms are used rather than the simple abbreviation R, so that the case **R v Smith** if brought in 2004 while Queen Elizabeth is in office could also be called **Regina v Smith**. The idea is that the action is ultimately being brought by the state against Ms Smith.

The 'v' separating the two parties' names is short for 'versus', in the same way as one might write **Nottingham Forest Football Club v Arsenal Football Club** when the two teams are going to play a match against each other. When speaking, instead of saying 'R versus Smith' one should really say 'The Crown against Smith'.

If Ms Smith is only 13, and therefore still a minor, the courts cannot reveal the identity of the child to the public and therefore the case will be referred to by her initial rather than her full name: **R v S**.

Occasionally criminal prosecutions are brought by the Government's law officers. If an action was brought by the Attorney General against Ms Smith it would be called **A G v Smith**. If it was brought by the Director of Public Prosecutions it would be called **DPP v Smith**. Should the state fail to bring an action at all, Mr Brown might choose to bring a private prosecution himself and the case would then be called **Brown v Smith**.

Civil law case names

In civil law if Mr Brown is in a neighbour dispute with Ms Smith and decides to bring an action against Ms Smith the name of the case will be **Brown v Smith**. This is orally expressed as 'Brown and Smith', rather than 'Brown versus Smith'. At the original trial, the first name used is the name of the person bringing the action (the claimant) and the second name used is that of the defendant. If there is an appeal against the original decision, then the first name will usually be the name of the appellant and the second name that of the respondent, though there are some exceptions to this.

In civil law the state can have an interest in what are described as judicial review cases. For example, Mr Brown may be unhappy with his local council, Hardfordshire City Council, for failing to take action against his neighbour. He may bring an action against the Council and the action would be called **R *v* Hardfordshire City Council, ex parte Brown**.

In certain family and property actions a slightly different format may be used. For example, if Ms Smith's child, James Smith, is out of control and needs to be taken into care, a resulting legal action might be called **Re Smith** or **In re Smith**. 'Re' is Latin and simply means 'in the matter of' or 'concerning'. So the name **Re Smith** really means in the matter of James Smith.

As with civil cases there is sometimes a need to prevent the public from knowing the name of the parties, particularly where children are involved. The initials of the child are then used rather than their full name. So the above case might be called **Re S** rather than **Re Smith** to protect James.

The Law Reports

Because some cases lay down important legal principles, over 2,000 each year are published in law reports. Some of these law reports date back over 700 years. Perhaps the most respected series of law reports are those called *The Law Reports*, because before publication the report of each case included in them is checked for accuracy by the judge who tried it. It is this series that should be cited before a court in preference to any other. The series is divided into several sub-series depending on the court which heard the case, as follows:

Appeal Cases (containing decisions of the Court of Appeal, the former House of Lords, the Supreme Court and the Privy Council).

Chancery Division (decisions of the Chancery Division of the High Court and their appeals to the Court of Appeal).

Family Division (decisions of the Family Division of the High Court and their appeals to the Court of Appeal).

Queen's Bench (decisions of the Queen's Bench Division of the High Court and their appeals to the Court of Appeal).

Neutral citation

Following the Practice Direction (Judgments: Form and Citation), a system of neutral citation was introduced in 2001 in the Court of Appeal and the High Court. This form of citation was introduced to facilitate reference to cases reported on the Internet and in CD-ROMs. Unlike reports in books, these reports do not have fixed page numbers and volumes. A unique number is now given to each approved judgment and the paragraphs in each judgment are numbered. The system of neutral citation is as follows:

Civil Division of the Court of Appeal: [2004] EWCA Civ 1, 2, 3, etc.
Criminal Division of the Court of Appeal: [2004] EWCA Crim 1, 2, 3, etc.
Administrative Court: [2004] EWHC Admin 1, 2, 3, etc.

The letters 'EW' stand for England and Wales. For example, if **Brown v Smith** is the fifth numbered judgment of 2004 in the Civil Division of the Court of Appeal, it would be cited: **Brown v Smith** [2004] EWCA Civ 5. If you wished to refer to the fourth paragraph of the judgment, the correct citation is [2004] EWCA Civ 5 at [4]. The neutral citation must always be used on at least one occasion when the judgment is cited before a court.

Case reference

Each case is given a reference(s) to explain exactly where it can be found in a law report(s). This reference consists of a series of letters and numbers that follow the case name. The pattern of this reference varies depending on the law report being referred to. The usual format is to follow the name of the case by:

A year Where the date reference tells you the year in which the case was decided, the date is normally enclosed in round brackets. If the date is the year in which the case is reported, it is given in square brackets. The most common law reports tend to use square brackets.

A volume number Not all law reports have a volume number, sometimes they simply identify their volumes by year.

The law report abbreviation Each series of law reports has an abbreviation for its title so that the whole name does not need to be written out in full. The main law reports and their abbreviations are as follows:

All England Law Reports   (All ER)
Appeal Cases   (AC)
Chancery Division   (Ch D)
Criminal Appeal Reports   (Cr App R)
Family Division   (Fam)
King's Bench   (KB)
Queen's Bench Division   (QB)
Weekly Law Reports   (WLR)

A page number This is the page at which the report of the case commences. For example, **Cozens v Brutus** [1973] AC 854 means that the case was reported in the Appeal Cases law report in 1973 at page 854; **DPP v Hawkins** [1988] 1 WLR 1166 means that the case was reported in the first volume of the Weekly Law Reports of 1988 at page 1166; and **R** *v* **Angel** (1968) 52 Cr App R 280 means that the case was reported in the 52nd volume of the Criminal Appeal Reports at page 280.

These references can be used to go and find and read the case in a law library which stocks the relevant law reports. This is important as a textbook can only provide a summary of the case and has no legal status in itself, it is the actual case which contains the law.

Where a case has been decided after the Practice Direction of 2001 introducing neutral citations for the Court of Appeal and Administrative Court, the neutral citation will appear in front of the law report citation. For example: **Brown** *v* **Smith** [2004] EWCA Civ 5, [2004] QB 432, [2004] 3 All ER 21.

Introduction

This introduction discusses three key characteristics of the unwritten constitution of the United Kingdom:

- the principle that too much power should not be invested in the hands of a single person or body (known as the separation of powers);

- the supremacy of Parliament; and

- the rule of law, which means that the state should govern according to agreed rules.

This book examines the legal system of England and Wales, looking at how our law is made and applied. To understand the legal system, however, you first need to know something about the context in which this legal system is operating: the constitution. A constitution is a set of rules which details a country's system of government; in most cases it will be a written document, but in some countries, including Britain, the constitution cannot be found written down in one document, and is known as an unwritten constitution.

Constitutions essentially set out broad principles concerning who makes law and how, and allocate power between the main institutions of the state – government, Parliament and the judiciary. They may also indicate the basic values on which the country should expect to be governed, such as the idea that citizens should not be punished unless they have broken the law, or that certain rights and freedoms should be guaranteed, and the state prevented from overriding them.

The unwritten constitution

Britain is very unusual in not having a written constitution – every other Western democracy has one. In many cases, the document was written after a major political change, such as a revolution or securing independence from a colonial power. The fact that the British constitution is not to be found in a specific document does not mean that we do not have a constitution: if a country has rules about who holds the power to govern, what they can and cannot do with that power, and how that power is to be passed on or transferred, it has a constitution, even though there is no single constitutional document. In our constitution, for example, it is established that the Government is formed by the political party which wins a general election, and that power is transferred from that party when they lose an election.

Having said that, the exact details of some areas of our constitution are subject to debate. This is because its sources include not only Acts of Parliament and judicial decisions, which are of course written down (although not together in one document), but also what are known as conventions. Conventions are not law, but are long-established traditions which tend to be followed, not because there would be any legal sanction if they were not, but because they have simply become the right way to behave. In this respect they are a bit like the kind of social rules that most people follow – for example, it is not against the law to pick your nose in public, but doing so usually invites social disapproval, so we generally avoid it. In the same way, failing to observe a constitutional convention is not against the law, but provokes so much political disapproval that conventions generally are followed, and most people concerned would see them as binding. Some well-established examples of conventions are that the Queen does not refuse to give her consent to Acts of Parliament; judges do not undertake activities associated with a political party; and the Speaker of the House of Commons does his or her job impartially, despite being a member of one of the parties represented in the House.

Because conventions are not law, they are not enforced by the courts; but someone who has broken a convention may end up being forced to resign from their post as a result of the disapproval it causes.

Three basic principles underlying the British constitution are the separation of powers, the supremacy of Parliament and the rule of law.

The separation of powers

One of the fundamental principles underlying our constitution is that of the separation of powers. According to this principle, developed by the eighteenth-century French philosopher Montesquieu, all state power can be divided into three types: executive, legislative and judicial. The executive represents what we would call the Government and its servants, such as the police and civil servants; the legislative power is Parliament; and judicial authority is exercised by the judges.

The basis of Montesquieu's theory was that these three types of power should not be concentrated in the hands of one person or group, since this would give them absolute control, with no one to check that the power was exercised for the good of the country. Instead, Montesquieu argued, each type of power should be exercised by a different body, so that they can each keep an eye on the activities of the other and make sure that they do not behave unacceptably.

Montesquieu believed that England, at the time when he was writing, was an excellent example of this principle being applied in practice. Whether that was true even then is debatable, and there are certainly areas of weakness now, as we shall see in later chapters.

The supremacy of Parliament

A second fundamental principle of our constitution has traditionally been the supremacy of Parliament (also called parliamentary sovereignty). This means that Parliament is the highest source of English law; so long as a law has been passed according to the rules of parliamentary procedure, it must be applied by the courts. The legal philosopher, Dicey, famously explained that according to the principle of parliamentary sovereignty Parliament has 'under the English Constitution, the right to make or unmake any law whatever; and, further, that no person or body is recognised by the law of England as having a right to override or set aside the legislation of Parliament'. So if, for example, Parliament had passed a law stating that all newborn boys had to be killed, or that all dog owners had to keep a cat as well, there might well be an enormous public outcry, but the laws would still be valid and the courts would, in theory at least, be obliged to uphold them. The reasoning behind this approach is that Parliament, unlike the judiciary, is democratically elected, and therefore ought to have the upper hand when making the laws that every citizen has to live by.

This approach is unusual in democratic countries. Most comparable nations have what is known as a Bill of Rights. This is a statement of the basic rights which citizens can expect to have protected from state interference; it may form part of a written constitution, or be a separate document. In many countries, the job of a Bill of Rights is done by incorporating into national law the European Convention on Human Rights, an international Treaty which was agreed after the Second World War, and seeks to protect basic human rights such as freedom of expression, of religion and of movement. A Bill of Rights takes precedence over other laws and the courts are able to refuse to apply legislation which infringes any of the rights protected by it.

Ess. Cases
p. 202 →
Although Britain is one of the original signatories of the European Convention on Human Rights, for many years it was not incorporated into English law. Parliament has now passed the Human Rights Act 1998, which came into force in October 2000. This Act at last incorporates the Convention into domestic law, but it does not give the Convention superiority over English law. It requires that, wherever possible, legislation should be interpreted in line with the principles of the Convention, but it does not allow the courts to override statutes that are incompatible with it, nor does it prevent Parliament from making laws that are in conflict with it.

Section 19 of the Act requires that when new legislation is made, a Government Minister must make a statement before the second reading of the Bill in Parliament, saying either that in their view the provisions of the Bill are compatible with the Convention or that, even if they are not, the Government wishes to proceed with the Bill anyway. Although the implication is obviously that, in most cases, Ministers will be able to say that a Bill conforms with the Convention, the Act's provision for the alternative statement confirms that parliamentary supremacy is not intended to be overridden. The Act does make one impact on parliamentary supremacy, though a small one: s. 10 allows a Minister of the Crown to amend by order any Act which has been found by the courts to be incompatible with the Convention, whereas normally an Act of Parliament could only be changed by another Act. However, there is no obligation to do this and a piece of legislation which has been found to be incompatible with the Convention would remain valid if the Government chose not to amend it.

By contrast, a definite erosion of parliamentary supremacy has been brought about by Britain's membership of the European Union (EU). The EU can only make laws concerning particular subject areas, but in those areas, its law must take precedence over laws made by Parliament, and in this respect Parliament is no longer, strictly speaking, the supreme source of law in the UK. In areas of law not covered by the EU, however, Parliament remains supreme. For further discussion of this issue see pp. 107–8.

An interesting and unusual view of the present constitutional position has been put forward by John Laws (1998), writing in the academic journal *Public Law*. He suggests that, even without a Bill of Rights, it can be argued that Parliament is not quite so all-powerful as traditional constitutional doctrine would suggest. His point is that Parliament draws its power from the fact that it is democratically elected: we accept its authority to make law because we all have a say in who makes up Parliament. Therefore, says Laws J, it must follow that Parliament's power is restricted to making laws which are consistent with democracy, and with the idea that if we are all entitled to a vote, we must also be entitled to a certain minimum level of treatment. That would mean that our example of a law that all newborn boys had to be killed, which would clearly conflict with this entitlement, might actually be beyond Parliament's law-making powers and, according to Laws J, the courts would therefore be constitutionally entitled to refuse to uphold it. This view has not been tested by the courts, but it certainly provides an interesting contribution to the debate.

In 1998 some important constitutional changes were made which passed some of the powers of the Westminster Parliament to new bodies in Scotland and Northern Ireland. The new Scottish Parliament, created by the Scotland Act 1998, can make laws affecting Scotland only, on many important areas, including health, education, local government, criminal justice, food standards and agriculture, though legislation on foreign affairs, defence, national security, trade and industry and a number of other areas will still be made for the whole of the UK by the Westminster Parliament. The Northern Ireland Act 1998 similarly gives the Northern Ireland Assembly power to make legislation for Northern Ireland in some areas, though again, foreign policy, defence and certain other areas are still to be covered by Westminster.

In the same year, the Government of Wales Act established a new body for Wales, the Welsh Assembly but, unlike the other two bodies, the Welsh Assembly does not have the power to make primary legislation; legislation made in Westminster will continue to cover Wales. However, the Welsh Assembly is able to make what is called delegated legislation (discussed at p. 79).

The rule of law

The third basic principle of our constitution is known as the rule of law. It is developed from the writings of the nineteenth-century writer Dicey. According to Dicey, the rule of law had three elements. First, that there should be no sanction without breach, meaning that nobody should be punished by the state unless they had broken a law. Secondly, that one law should govern everyone, including both ordinary citizens and state officials. Thirdly, that the rights of the individual were not secured by a written constitution, but by the decisions of judges in ordinary law.

The real importance of the rule of law today lies in the basic idea underlying all three of Dicey's points (but especially the first) that the state should use its power according to agreed rules, and not arbitrarily. The issue has arisen frequently in the context of the state's response to terrorism. For example, opposition to an alleged shoot to kill policy by the armed forces in Northern Ireland against suspected terrorists was based on the principle that suspected criminals should be fairly tried, according to the law, and punished only if convicted.

The pressure group JUSTICE issued a manifesto for the rule of law in 2007. This suggests that the rule of law can be broken down into a set of values that governments should accept as matters of constitutional principle which should not be breached. Thus JUSTICE suggests that under the rule of law, governments should:

- adhere to international standards of human rights;
- uphold the independence of judges and the legal profession;
- protect the right to a fair trial and due process;
- champion equality before the law;
- ensure access to justice;
- accept rigorous powers of scrutiny by the legislature;

● ensure that greater cooperation between governments within Europe is matched by increased rights for citizens.

A practice that has recently come to light which appears to breach the rule of law is that of 'extraordinary rendition'. This describes the kidnapping of people by state representatives and their subsequent detention, without recourse to established legal procedures (such as a formal request for the extradition of a suspect). The US intelligence service has kidnapped a large number of foreign nationals suspected of involvement with the terrorist organisation, Al Qaeda, from around the world and removed them to secret locations without following any established legal procedures. It has been alleged that the UK has provided the US with some assistance in this practice through, in particular, the provision of information about suspects and the use of UK airports.

The Constitutional Reform Act 2005 introduced some major reforms to the British constitution. This Act expressly states in its first section that it 'does not adversely affect . . . the existing constitutional principle of the rule of law'.

A written constitution?

There has been much debate in recent years about whether the UK should have a written constitution. The main reasons put forward in favour of this are that it would clear up some of the grey areas concerning conventions, make the constitution accessible to citizens, and, some argue, provide greater protection of basic rights and liberties, such as freedom of speech.

Written constitutions can be changed, but usually only by means of a special procedure, more difficult than that for changing ordinary law. Thus, it might be necessary to hold a referendum on the proposed change, or gain a larger than usual majority in Parliament, or both. This contrasts with our unwritten constitution, which can be altered by an ordinary piece of legislation. So, some people have argued that the right of people suspected of committing a crime to remain silent when questioned, without this being taken as evidence of guilt, was part of our constitution; nevertheless, that right was essentially abolished by the Criminal Justice and Public Order Act 1994. If the UK had had a written constitution then this right would probably have been contained in it and a special procedure would have had to be followed to amend the constitution to remove that right. The integration of the European Convention on Human Rights into domestic law may prove to be the first step towards a fully fledged written constitution.

Those in favour of our unwritten constitution argue that it is the product of centuries of gradual development, forming part of our cultural heritage which it would be wrong to destroy. They also point out that the lack of any special procedural requirements for changing it allows flexibility, so that the constitution develops along with the changing needs of society.

Reading list

Dicey, A. (1982) *Introduction to the Study of the Law of the Constitution*, Indianapolis: Liberty Classics.

Horowitz, M.J. (1977) 'The Rule of Law: An Unqualified Good?', 86 *Yale Law Journal* 561.

Montesquieu, C. (1989) *The Spirit of the Laws*, Cambridge: Cambridge University Press.

Raz, J. (1972) 'The Rule of Law and Its Virtue', 93 *Law Quarterly Review* 195.

Reading on the Internet

www   The manifesto for the rule of law prepared by JUSTICE is available on their website:
http://www.justice.org.uk

Visit **www.mylawchamber.co.uk/ElliottELS** to access multiple-choice questions, flashcards and practice exam questions to test yourself on this chapter.

SOURCES OF LAW

The word 'source' can mean several different things with regard to law, but for our purposes it primarily describes the means by which the law comes into existence. English law stems from eight main sources, though these vary a great deal in importance:

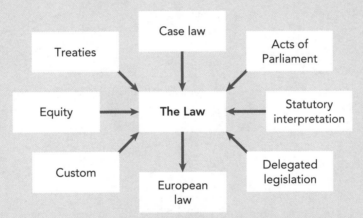

The basis of our law today is case law, a mass of judge-made decisions which lay down rules to be followed in future court cases. For many centuries case law was the main form of law and it is still very important today. However, Acts of Parliament (also known as statutes) are the most important source of law, in the sense that they prevail over most of the other sources. As well as being a source of law in their own right, Acts of Parliament contribute to case law, since the courts occasionally have to interpret the Acts, and such decisions lay down new precedents. Delegated legislation is made by the administration rather than the legislature, and lays down detailed rules to implement the broader provisions of Acts of Parliament.

An increasingly important source of law is the legislation of the European Union, which is the only type of law that can take precedence over Acts of Parliament in the UK. Finally, custom, equity and international treaties are minor sources of law.

Part 1 concludes with a discussion of the process of law reform, whereby these sources of law can be changed to reflect the changes taking place in society.

1

Case law

This chapter contains:

- an introduction to judicial precedent;

- a description of the hierarchy of the courts and judicial precedent;

- an analysis of how judicial precedent works in practice;

- a discussion of whether judges actually make the law, rather than simply declaring the law;

- consideration of whether judges should be allowed to make law; and

- an overview of the advantages and disadvantages of binding precedent.

Historical background

Before the Norman conquest, different areas of England were governed by different systems of law, often adapted from those of the various invaders who had settled there; roughly speaking, Dane law applied in the north, Mercian law around the midlands, and Wessex law in the south and west. Each was based largely on local custom and, even within the larger areas, these customs, and hence the law, varied from place to place. The king had little control over the country as a whole, and there was no effective central government.

When William the Conqueror gained the English throne in 1066, he established a strong central government and began, among other things, to standardise the law. Representatives of the king were sent out to the countryside to check local administration, and were given the job of adjudicating in local disputes, according to local law.

When these 'itinerant justices' returned to Westminster, they were able to discuss the various customs of different parts of the country and, by a process of sifting, reject unreasonable ones and accept those that seemed rational, to form a consistent body of rules. During this process – which went on for around two centuries – the principle of *stare decisis* ('let the decision stand') grew up. Whenever a new problem of law came to be decided, the decision formed a rule to be followed in all similar cases, making the law more predictable.

The result of all this was that by about 1250, a 'common law' had been produced, that ruled the whole country, would be applied consistently and could be used to predict what the courts might decide in a particular case. It contained many of what are now basic points of English law – the fact that murder is a crime, for example.

The principles behind this 'common law' are still used today in creating case law (which is in fact often known as common law). From the basic idea of *stare decisis*, a hierarchy of precedent grew up, in line with the hierarchy of the modern court system, so that, in general, a judge must follow decisions made in courts which are higher up the hierarchy than his or her own (the detailed rules on precedent are discussed later in this section). This process was made easier by the establishment of a regular system of publication of reports of cases in the higher courts. The body of decisions made by the higher courts, which the lower ones must respect, is known as case law.

The English common law system was exported around the world wherever British influence dominated during the colonial period. These countries, including the US and many Commonwealth countries, are described as having common law systems. They are often contrasted with civil law systems, which can be found in Continental Europe and countries over which European countries have had influence. The best-known civil law system is the French legal system, whose civil code has been highly influential.

Establishing the Supreme Court

Rather unexpectedly, the Government announced in June 2003 that it was going to abolish the House of Lords (which had existed since 1876) and replace it with a Supreme Court. It subsequently issued a consultation paper, *Constitutional Reform: A Supreme Court for the United Kingdom*, which considered the shape that this reform should take. The Constitutional Reform Act 2005 was passed, which contained provisions for the creation of the new court. The Supreme Court (Photo 1.1) was established in 2009 and replaced the House of Lords. The term 'House of Lords' is slightly confusing because this name was used to describe both the highest court, which sat in the Palace of Westminster, and the upper chamber of Parliament. The upper chamber still remains, it is the Committee of the House of Lords sitting as a court that has been abolished. The last case to be heard by the House of Lords was the high profile case of Debbie Purdy who suffers from multiple sclerosis and who was seeking clarification on the criminalisation of individuals who assist the terminally ill to commit suicide.

The Government was anxious to point out that the reform did not imply any dissatisfaction with the performance of the House of Lords as the country's highest court of law:

Ess. Cases
p. 4

Photo 1.1 The Supreme Court in Parliament Square
Source: © Justin Kase Zelevenz/Alamy

1

Case law

On the contrary its judges have conducted themselves with the utmost integrity and independence. They are widely and rightly admired, nationally and internationally. The Government believes, however, that the time has come to establish a new court regulated by statute as a body separate from Parliament.

Six of the current Law Lords opposed the reform, considering the change unnecessary and harmful.

Separation from Parliament

The consultation paper stated that this reform was necessary to enhance the independence of the judiciary from both the legislature and the executive. It pointed to the growth of judicial review cases and the passing of the Human Rights Act 1998 as two key reasons why this reform was becoming urgent. Article 6 of the European Convention on Human Rights requires not only that the judges should be independent, but also that they should be seen to be independent. The fact that the Law Lords sat as a Committee of the House of Lords raised issues about whether it appeared to be dependent on the legislature rather than independent.

The new Supreme Court is completely separate from Parliament. Its judges have no rights to sit and vote in the upper chamber. Only the Law Lords who sat in the House of Lords before it was abolished have the right to sit and vote in the House of Lords in its legislative capacity after their retirement from the judiciary.

One advantage of this change is that the court no longer sits in the Palace of Westminster, where there is a shortage of space. The Supreme Court is based in a refurbished neo-gothic building opposite Parliament in Parliament Square.

Jurisdiction

The Supreme Court can hear appeals from the whole of the United Kingdom. Its jurisdiction is the same as that of the former House of Lords, except in relation to devolution cases. In the past the Privy Council, not the House of Lords, had the jurisdiction to hear cases concerning the devolution of Scotland, Wales and Northern Ireland. This jurisdiction has been transferred to the Supreme Court. The reason for this transfer is to remove any perceived conflict of interest in which the UK Parliament, with an obvious interest in a dispute about devolution, appears to be sitting in judgment over the case.

The Supreme Court does not have the power to overturn legislation, a power enjoyed by the Supreme Court in America. It is not a purely constitutional court (like the *Conseil constitutionnel* in France), partly because we do not have a written constitution so it would be difficult to determine the jurisdiction of a constitutional court for the United Kingdom. The new court does not have the power to give preliminary rulings on difficult points of law because English courts do not traditionally consider issues in the abstract, so giving such a power to the Supreme Court would sit uneasily with our judicial traditions, though we are becoming accustomed to this procedure for the European Court of Justice.

Membership

The 12 full-time Law Lords from the former House of Lords are the first judges of the Supreme Court. The Government wants to keep the same number of full-time judges, but to continue to allow the court to call on the help of other judges on a part-time basis. Members of the Supreme Court are called 'Justices of the Supreme Court'. The Lord Chancellor was a member of the Appellate Committee of the House of Lords, but does not have a right to sit in the Supreme Court. The judges no longer automatically become Lords.

Qualifications for membership have remained the same as for the House of Lords. The Government rejected the idea that changes should be made to make it easier for distinguished academics to be appointed in order to enhance the diversity of the court. This is disappointing, as the Government itself acknowledges that the current pool of candidates for the court is very narrow, and the Government's statistics show that the current senior judiciary are not representative of society.

The appointment process is discussed on p. 164. Candidates are not subjected to confirmation hearings before Parliament as these would risk politicising the appointment process.

In the Supreme Court five judges normally sit together as they did in the House of Lords. An option for serious cases would be to allow all 12 judges to hear the case, but this would be an expensive procedure. The rules for permission to appeal have remained largely unchanged, so the range and number of cases is likely to be similar to those of the House of Lords. The senior Law Lord, Baroness Hale, has predicted that the opening of the Supreme Court will amount to 'business as usual'.

1

Case law

Judicial precedent

Case law comes from the decisions made by judges in the cases before them (the decisions of juries do not make case law). In deciding a case, there are two basic tasks: first, establishing what the facts are, meaning what actually happened; and secondly, how the law applies to those facts. It is the second task that can make case law, and the idea is that once a decision has been made on how the law applies to a particular set of facts, similar facts in later cases should be treated in the same way, following the principle of *stare decisis* described above. This is obviously fairer than allowing each judge to interpret the law differently, and also provides predictability, which makes it easier for people to live within the law.

The judges listen to the evidence and the legal argument and then prepare a written decision as to which party wins, based on what they believe the facts were, and how the law applies to them. This decision is known as the judgment, and is usually long, containing quite a lot of comment which is not strictly relevant to the case, as well as an explanation of the legal principles on which the judge has made a decision. The explanation of the legal principles on which the decision is made is called the *ratio decidendi* – Latin for the 'reason for deciding'. It is this part of the judgment, known as binding precedent, which forms case law.

All the parts of the judgment which do not form part of the *ratio decidendi* of the case are called *obiter dicta* – which is Latin for 'things said by the way'. These are often discussions of hypothetical situations: for example, the judge might say 'Jones did this, but if she had done that, my decision would have been . . .'. None of the *obiter dicta* forms part of the case law, though judges in later cases may be influenced by it, and it is said to be a persuasive precedent.

In deciding a case, a judge must follow any decision that has been made by a higher court in a case with similar facts. The rules concerning which courts are bound by which are known as the rules of judicial precedent, or *stare decisis*. As well as being bound by the decisions of courts above them, some courts must also follow their own previous decisions; they are said to be bound by themselves.

The hierarchy of the courts

The European Court of Justice

Decisions of the European Court of Justice (ECJ) on interpretation of the European Treaties, validity of the acts of Community institutions and interpretation of the statutes of Council bodies are binding on all English courts. It appears not to be bound by its own decisions.

The Supreme Court

Apart from cases concerning European law, the Supreme Court is the highest appeal court on civil and criminal matters, and all other English courts are bound by it. The Supreme Court replaced the long-established House of Lords in 2009 and the rules of precedent are expected to be exactly the same for the Supreme Court as they were for the House of Lords before it. The House of Lords was traditionally bound by its own decisions, but in 1966 the Lord Chancellor issued a Practice Statement saying that the House of Lords was no longer bound by its previous decisions. In practice the House of Lords only rarely overruled one of its earlier decisions, and this reluctance is illustrated by the case of **R v Kansal (No. 2)** (2001). In that case the House of Lords held that it had probably got the law wrong in its earlier decision of **R v Lambert** (2001). The latter case had ruled that the Human Rights Act 1998 would not have retrospective effect in relation to appeals heard by the House of Lords after the Act came into force, but which had been decided by the lower courts before the Act came into force. Despite the fact that the majority thought the earlier judgment of **Lambert** was wrong, the House decided in **Kansal** to follow it. This was because **Lambert** was a recent decision, it represented a possible interpretation of the statute that was not unworkable and it only concerned a temporary transitional period.

Ess. Cases
p. 7 → There are, however, a range of cases where the House of Lords had been prepared to apply the 1966 Practice Statement. For example, in **R v R** (1991), it held that rape within marriage is a crime, overturning a legal principle that had stood for centuries.

In **Hall v Simons** (2000), the House of Lords refused to follow the earlier case of **Rondel v Worsley** (1969), which had given barristers immunity against claims for negligence in their presentation of cases.

In **R v G and another** (2003), the House of Lords overruled an established criminal case of **R v Caldwell** (1981). Under **R v Caldwell**, the House had been prepared to convict people for criminal offences where the prosecution had not proved that the defendant personally had intended, or seen the risk of causing, the relevant harm, but had simply shown that a reasonable person would have had this state of mind on the facts. This was particularly harsh where the actual defendant was incapable of seeing the risk of harm, because, for example, they were very young or of low intelligence. **Caldwell** had been heavily criticised by academics over the years, but when the House of Lords originally reconsidered the matter in 1992, in **R v Reid** (1992), it confirmed its original decision. However, when the matter again came to the House of Lords in 2003, the House dramatically admitted that it had got the law wrong. It stated:

> The surest test of a new legal rule is not whether it satisfies a team of logicians but how it performs in the real world. With the benefit of hindsight the verdict must be that the rule laid down by the majority in **Caldwell** failed this test. It was severely criticised by academic lawyers of distinction. It did not command respect among practitioners and judges. Jurors found it difficult to understand; it also sometimes offended their sense of justice. Experience suggests that in **Caldwell** the law took a wrong turn.

Ess. Cases p. 98 → In **Re Pinochet Ugarte** (1999), the House of Lords stated that it had the power to reopen an appeal where, through no fault of his or her own, one of the parties has been subjected to an unfair procedure. The case was part of the litigation concerning

Photo 1.2 Demonstrators celebrate the House of Lords' decision for the deportation of the former Chilean President, Augusto Pinochet

Source: PA Archive/Press Association Images

General Augusto Pinochet, the former Chilean head of state. The Lords reopened the appeal because one of the Law Lords who heard the original appeal, Lord Hoffmann, was connected with the human rights organisation Amnesty International, which had been a party to the appeal. This meant that there was a possibility of bias and so the proceedings could be viewed as unfair. The Lords stressed, however, that there was no question of them being able to reopen an appeal because the decision made originally was thought to be wrong; the Pinochet appeal was reopened because it could be said that there had not been a fair hearing, and not because the decision reached was wrong (although at the second hearing of the appeal, the Lords did in fact come to a slightly different decision).

Privy Council

The Privy Council was established by the Judicial Committee Act 1833. It is the final appeal court for many Commonwealth countries. The judges of the Supreme Court have become the judges of the Privy Council and its other members have remained the same. The Privy Council sits in the new buildings of the Supreme Court but remains a separate entity.

Ess. Cases
p. 12

Under the traditional rules of precedent, the decisions of the Privy Council do not bind English courts, but have strong persuasive authority because of the seniority of the judges who sit in the Privy Council (**de Lasala v de Lasala** (1980)). This well-established rule of precedent has been thrown into doubt by the recent Court of Appeal judgment of **R v James and Karimi** (2006). The Court of Appeal held that, in exceptional circumstances, a Privy Council judgment can bind the English courts and effectively overrule an earlier House of Lords' judgment. This conflicts with the traditional approach to such judgments (and the expected approach to judgments of the Supreme Court), confirmed by the House of Lords in **Miliangos v George Frank (Textiles) Ltd** (1976) that 'the only judicial means by which decisions of this House can be reviewed is by this House itself'.

TOPICAL ISSUE

Increased influence of the Privy Council

Recent developments in criminal law suggest that Privy Council decisions can occasionally make important changes to the common law, even indirectly overruling an earlier House of Lords' decision and therefore also decisions of the Supreme Court. The cases which highlighted the potential power of the Privy Council were concerned with the partial defence of provocation in criminal law which if successful can reduce a defendant's liability from murder to manslaughter. The defence is laid down in s. 3 of the Homicide Act 1957. This section has been interpreted as laying down a two-part test. The first part of the test requires the defendant to have suffered from a sudden and temporary loss of self-control when he or she killed the victim. The second part of the test provides that the defence will only be available if a reasonable person would have reacted as the defendant did. This is described as an objective test, because it is judging the defendant's conduct according to objective standards, rather than their own standards. However, in practice reasonable people almost never kill, so if this second requirement was interpreted strictly, the defence would rarely succeed. As a result, in **R** v **Smith (Morgan James)** (2001) the House of Lords held that, in determining whether a reasonable person would have reacted in this way, a court could take into account the actual characteristics of the defendant. So if the defendant had been depressed and was of low intelligence, then the test would become whether a reasonable person suffering from depression and of low intelligence would have reacted by killing the victim.

Ess. Cases
p. 10 →

In an appeal from Jersey on the defence of provocation, Attorney General for Jersey v Holley (2005), the Privy Council refused to follow the case of **Smith (Morgan James)**, stating that the case misinterpreted Parliament's intention when it passed the Homicide Act 1957. It considered that the only characteristics that should be taken into account when considering whether the defendant had reacted reasonably were characteristics that were directly relevant to the provocation itself, but not general characteristics which simply affected a person's ability to control him or herself.

Ess. Cases
p. 12 →

The Court of Appeal in James and Karimi decided to apply the Privy Council's judgment in **Holley** rather than the House of Lords' judgment in **Smith (Morgan James)**. The Court of Appeal acknowledged that this went against the established rules of judicial precedent. It gave various justifications for treating this as an exceptional case in which those established rules should not apply. It pointed out that the Privy Council had realised the importance of its judgment and had chosen to have an enlarged sitting of nine judges, all drawn from the House of Lords:

> The procedure adopted and the comments of members of the Board in **Holley** suggest that a decision must have been taken by those responsible for the constitution of the Board in **Holley** . . . to use the appeal as a vehicle for reconsidering the decision of the House of Lords in **Morgan Smith**, not just as representing the law of Jersey but as representing the law of England. A decision was taken that the Board hearing the appeal to the Privy Council should consist of nine of the twelve Lords of Appeal in Ordinary.

The emphasis on the enlarged formation of the Privy Council potentially leaves the status of its judgments dependent upon an administrative decision as to how many judges should sit, a decision which has never been the subject of any legal controls.

The judges in **Holley** were divided in their verdict six to three. The start of the first judgment of the majority stated:

> This appeal, being heard by an enlarged board of nine members, is concerned to resolve this conflict [between the House of Lords and the Privy Council] and clarify definitively the present state of English law, and hence Jersey law, on this important subject.

The dissenting judges stated:

> We must however accept that the effect of the majority decision is as stated in paragraph 1 of the majority judgment.

Thus, even the dissenting judges appear to accept that the majority decision lays down the law in England. The Court of Appeal also considered that if an appeal was taken to the House of Lords, the outcome was 'a foregone conclusion' and the House would take the same approach as **Holley**:

> Half of the Law Lords were party to the majority decision in **Holley**. Three more in that case accepted that the majority decision represented a definitive statement of English

1

Case law

law on the issue in question. The choice of those to sit on the appeal might raise some nice questions, but we cannot conceive that, whatever the precise composition of the Committee, it would do other than rule that the majority decision in **Holley** represented the law of England. In effect, in the long term at least, **Holley** has overruled **Morgan Smith**.

This argument would be more convincing if the **Holley** case had been decided by a unanimous verdict. In fact, there are still potentially six House of Lords' judges who could prefer the **Smith (Morgan James)** approach: the three dissenting judges and the three House of Lords judges who did not hear the **Holley** case.

Lord Woolf recognised in **R v Simpson** (2003) that the rules of judicial precedent must provide certainty but at the same time they themselves must be able to evolve in order to do justice:

> The rules as to precedent reflect the practice of the courts and have to be applied bearing in mind that their objective is to assist in the administration of justice. They are of considerable importance because of their role in achieving the appropriate degree of certainty as to the law. This is an important requirement of any system of justice. The principles should not, however, be regarded as so rigid that they cannot develop in order to meet contemporary needs.

The Court of Appeal presumably concluded in **James and Karimi** that this was a situation where justice could only be achieved by shifting the established rules of judicial precedent. The actual outcome of the case makes it more difficult for a partial defence to murder, reducing liability to manslaughter, to succeed. This may be considered to achieve justice for victims' families, but it may be an injustice to the mentally ill defendant.

The Court of Appeal

This is split into Civil and Criminal Divisions; they do not bind each other. Both are bound by decisions of the old House of Lord, and the new Supreme Court.

KEY CASE

In **Young v Bristol Aeroplane Co Ltd** (1946) the Court of Appeal stated that the Civil Division is usually bound by its own previous decisions. There are four exceptions to this general rule:

> The civil division of the Court of Appeal is usually bound by its own previous decisions.

1 the previous decision was made in ignorance of a relevant law (it is said to have been made *per incuriam*);
2 there are two previous conflicting decisions;
3 there is a later, conflicting, House of Lords' (or Supreme Court) decision;
4 a proposition of law was assumed to exist by an earlier court and was not subject to argument or consideration by that court.

Ess. Cases p. 8 →

The last of these exceptions was added by **R (on the application of Kadhim) v Brent London Borough Housing Benefit Review Board** (2001).

In the Criminal Division, the results of cases heard may decide whether or not an individual goes to prison, so the Criminal Division takes a more flexible approach to its previous decisions and does not follow them where doing so could cause injustice.

The High Court

This court is divided between the Divisional Courts and the ordinary High Court. All are bound by the Court of Appeal, the old House of Lords and the new Supreme Court.

The Divisional Courts are the Queen's Bench Division, which deals with criminal appeals and judicial review, the Chancery Division and the Family Division, which both deal with civil appeals. The two civil Divisional Courts are bound by their previous decisions, but the Divisional Court of the Queen's Bench is more flexible about this, for the same reason as the Criminal Division of the Court of Appeal. The Divisional Courts bind the ordinary High Court.

The ordinary High Court is not bound by its own previous decisions. It can produce precedents for courts below it, but these are of a lower status than those produced by the Court of Appeal, the old House of Lords or the new Supreme Court.

The Crown Court

The Crown Court is bound by all the courts above it. Its decisions do not form binding precedents, though when High Court judges sit in the Crown Court, their judgments form persuasive precedents, which must be given serious consideration in successive cases, though it is not obligatory to follow them. When a circuit or district judge is sitting no precedents are formed. Since the Crown Court cannot form binding precedents, it is obviously not bound by its own decisions.

Magistrates' and county courts

These are called the inferior courts. They are bound by the High Court, Court of Appeal, the old House of Lords and the new Supreme Court. Their own decisions are not reported, and cannot produce binding precedents, or even persuasive ones; like the Crown Court, they are therefore not bound by their own decisions.

European Court of Human Rights

The European Court of Human Rights (ECtHR) is an international court based in Strasbourg. It hears cases alleging that there has been a breach of the European Convention on Human Rights. This court does not fit neatly within the hierarchy of the courts. Under s. 2 of the Human Rights Act 1998, an English court is required to 'take account of' the cases decided by the ECtHR, though its decisions do not bind the English courts. In practice, when considering a Convention right, the domestic courts try to follow the same interpretation as that given by the ECtHR. In **R (on the application of Alconbury Developments Ltd)** *v* **Secretary of State for the Environment, Transport and the Regions** (2001), the House of Lords said:

1

Case law

> In the absence of some special circumstances it seems to me the court should follow any clear and constant jurisprudence of the European Court of Human Rights. If it does not do so there is at least a possibility the case will go to that court which is likely in the ordinary case to follow its own constant jurisprudence.

Despite this, the House of Lords has refused to follow an earlier decision of the ECtHR. In **Morris** *v* **UK** (2002), the ECtHR ruled that the courts martial system (which is the courts system used by the army) breached the European Convention on Human Rights as it did not guarantee a fair trial within the meaning of Art. 6 of the Convention. Subsequently, in **Boyd** *v* **The Army Prosecuting Authority** (2002), three soldiers who had been convicted of assault by a court martial argued before the House of Lords that the court martial had violated their right to a fair trial under the Convention. Surprisingly, the argument was rejected and the House of Lords refused to follow the earlier decision of the ECtHR. It stated:

> While the decision in **Morris** is not binding on the House, it is of course a matter which the House must take into account [s. 2(1)(a) of the Human Rights Act 1998] and which demands careful attention, not least because it is a recent expression of the European Court's view on these matters.

The House considered that the European Court was given 'rather less information than the House' about the courts martial system, and in the light of this additional information it concluded that there had been no violation of the Convention.

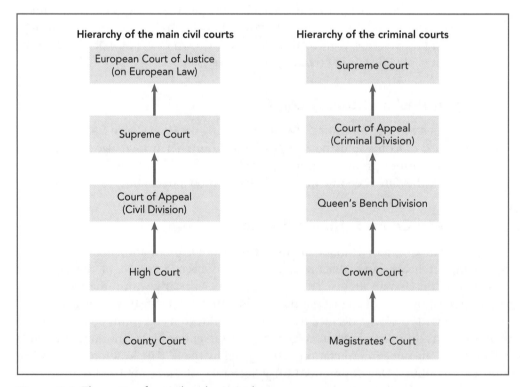

Figure 1.1 The routes for civil and criminal cases

Where there is a conflict between a decision of the ECtHR and a national court which binds a lower court, then the lower court should usually follow the decision of the binding higher national court, but give permission to appeal. Thus, in **Kay v Lambeth London Borough Council** (2006) the Court of Appeal had been faced with a binding precedent of the House of Lords which conflicted with a decision of the ECtHR. The Court of Appeal had applied the House of Lords' decision but given permission to appeal. In the subsequent appeal the House had agreed that this was the appropriate course of action. We can expect to see similar tensions in the relationship between the Supreme Court and the ECtHR.

How judicial precedent works

When faced with a case on which there appears to be a relevant earlier decision, the judges can do any of the following:

Follow If the facts are sufficiently similar, the precedent set by the earlier case is followed, and the law applied in the same way to produce a decision.

Distinguish Where the facts of the case before the judge are significantly different from those of the earlier one, then the judge distinguishes the two cases and need not follow the earlier one.

Overrule Where the earlier decision was made in a lower court, the judges can overrule that earlier decision if they disagree with the lower court's statement of the law. The outcome of the earlier decision remains the same, but will not be followed. The power to overrule cases is only used sparingly because it weakens the authority and respect of the lower courts.

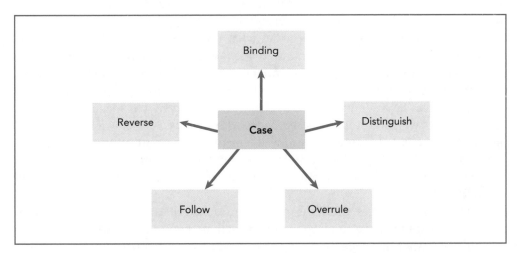

Figure 1.2 How judicial precedent works

Reverse If the decision of a lower court is appealed to a higher one, the higher court may change it if they feel the lower court has wrongly interpreted the law. Clearly when a decision is reversed, the higher court is usually also overruling the lower court's statement of the law.

In practice the process is rather more complicated than this, since decisions are not always made on the basis of only one previous case; there are usually several different cases offered in support of each side's view of the question.

How do judges really decide cases?

The independence of the judiciary was ensured by the Act of Settlement 1700, which transferred the power to sack judges from the Crown to Parliament. Consequently, judges should theoretically make their decisions based purely on the logical deductions of precedent, uninfluenced by political or career considerations.

The eighteenth-century legal commentator, William Blackstone, introduced the declaratory theory of law, stating that judges do not make law, but merely, by the rules of precedent, discover and declare the law that has always been: '[the judge] being sworn to determine, not according to his private sentiments . . . not according to his own private judgment, but according to the known laws and customs of the land: not delegated to pronounce a new law, but to maintain and expound the old one'. Blackstone does not accept that precedent ever offers a choice between two or more interpretations of the law: where a bad decision is made, he states, the new one that reverses or overrules it is not a new law, nor a statement that the old decision was bad law, but a declaration that the previous decision was 'not law', in other words that it was the wrong answer. His view presupposes that there is always one right answer, to be deduced from an objective study of precedent.

Today, however, this position is considered somewhat unrealistic. If the operation of precedent is the precise science Blackstone suggests, a large majority of cases in the higher courts would never come to court at all. The lawyers concerned could simply look up the relevant case law and predict what the decision would be, then advise whichever of the clients would be bound to lose not to bother bringing or fighting the case. In a civil case, or any appeal case, no good lawyer would advise a client to bring or defend a case that they had no chance of winning. Therefore, where such a case is contested, it can be assumed that, unless one of the lawyers has made a mistake, it could go either way, and still be in accordance with the law. Further evidence of this is provided by the fact that one can read a judgment of the Court of Appeal, argued as though it were the only possible decision in the light of the cases that had gone before, and then discover that this apparently inevitable decision has promptly been reversed by the House of Lords.

In practice, then, judges' decisions may not be as neutral as Blackstone's declaratory theory suggests: they have to make choices which are by no means spelt out by precedents. Yet, rather than openly stating that they are choosing between two or more equally relevant precedents, the courts find ways to avoid awkward ones, which give the impression that the precedents they do choose to follow are the only ones that could possibly apply. In theory, only the Supreme Court, which can overrule its own decisions as well as those of other courts, can depart from precedent: all the other courts must follow the precedent that applies in a particular case, however much they dislike it. In fact, there are a number of ways in which judges may avoid awkward precedents that at first sight might appear binding:

- By distinguishing the awkward precedent on its facts – arguing that the facts of the case under consideration are different in some important way from those of the previous case, and therefore the rule laid down does not apply to them. Since the facts are unlikely to be identical, this is the simplest way to avoid an awkward precedent, and the courts have made some extremely narrow distinctions in this way.
- By distinguishing the point of law – arguing that the legal question answered by the precedent is not the same as that asked in the present case.
- By stating that the precedent has been superseded by more recent decisions, and is therefore outdated.
- By giving the precedent a very narrow *ratio decidendi*. The only part of a decision that forms binding precedent is the *ratio*, the legal principle on which the decision is based. Since judges never state 'this is the *ratio decidendi*', it is possible to argue at some length about which bits of the judgment actually form the *ratio* and therefore bind courts in later cases. Judges wishing to avoid an awkward precedent may reason that those parts of the judgment which seem to apply to their case are not part of the *ratio*, and are only *obiter dicta*, which they are not obliged to follow.
- By arguing that the precedent has no clear *ratio decidendi*. There are usually three judges sitting in Court of Appeal cases, and five in the Supreme Court. Where each judge in the former case has given a different reason for coming to the same decision, or where, for example, two judges of the Supreme Court take one view, two more another, and the fifth agrees with none of them, it can be argued that there is no one clear *ratio decidendi* for the decision.
- By claiming that the precedent is inconsistent with a later decision of a higher court, and has been overruled by implication.
- By stating that the previous decision was made *per incuriam*, meaning that the court failed to consider some relevant statute or precedent. This method is used only rarely, since it clearly undermines the status of the court below.
- By arguing that the precedent is outdated, and no longer in step with modern thinking. The best-known example of this approach (which is not frequently used) is the case of **R** *v* **R** (1991), when the House of Lords overturned a centuries-old common law rule that rape within marriage was not a crime (see p. 16).

We can see that there is considerable room for manoeuvre within the doctrine of precedent, so what factors guide judicial decisions, and to what extent? The following are some of the answers that have been suggested.

Dworkin: a seamless web of principles

Ronald Dworkin argues that judges have no real discretion in making case law. He sees law as a seamless web of principles, which supply a right answer – and only one – to every possible problem. Dworkin reasons that although stated legal rules may 'run out' (in the sense of not being directly applicable to a new case) legal principles never do, and therefore judges never need to use their own discretion.

In his book *Law's Empire* (1986), Professor Dworkin claims that judges first look at previous cases, and from those deduce which principles could be said to apply to the case before them. Then they consult their own sense of justice as to which apply, and also consider what the community's view of justice dictates. Where the judge's view and that of the community coincide, there is no problem, but if they conflict, the judges then ask themselves whether or not it would be fair to impose their own sense of justice over that of the community. Dworkin calls this the interpretive approach and, although it may appear to involve a series of choices, he considers that the legal principles underlying the decisions mean that in the end only one result could possibly surface from any one case.

Dworkin's approach has been heavily criticised as being unrealistic: opponents believe that judges do not consider principles of justice but take a much more pragmatic approach, looking at the facts of the case, not the principles.

Critical theorists: precedent as legitimation

Critical legal theorists, such as David Kairys (1998), take a quite different view. They argue that judges have considerable freedom within the doctrine of precedent. Kairys suggests that there is no such thing as legal reasoning, in the sense of a logical, neutral method of determining rules and results from what has gone before. He states that judicial decisions are actually based on 'a complex mixture of social, political, institutional, experiential and personal factors', and are simply legitimated, or justified, by reference to previous cases. The law provides 'a wide and conflicting variety' of such justifications 'from which courts pick and choose'.

The process is not necessarily as cynical as it sounds. Kairys points out that he is not saying that judges actually make the decision and then consider which precedents they can pick to justify it; rather their own beliefs and prejudices naturally lead them to give more weight to precedents which support those views. Nevertheless, for critical legal theorists, all such decisions can be seen as reflecting social and political judgments, rather than objective, purely logical deductions.

Critical theory argues that the neutral appearance of so-called 'legal reasoning' disguises the true nature of legal decisions which, by the choices made, uphold existing power relations within society, tending to favour, for example, employers over employees, property owners over those without, men over women, and rich developed countries over poor undeveloped ones.

Griffith: political choices

In similar vein, Griffith (1997) argues in his book *The Politics of the Judiciary* that judges make their decisions based on what they see as the public interest, but that their view of this interest is coloured by their background and their position in society. He suggests that the narrow social background – usually public school and Oxbridge – of the highest judges (see p. 170), combined with their position as part of established authority, leads them to believe that it is in the public interest that the established order should be maintained: in other words, that those who are in charge – whether of the country or, for example, in the workplace – should stay in charge, and that traditional values should be maintained. This leads them to 'a tenderness for private property and dislike of trade unions, strong adherence to the maintenance of order, distaste for minority opinions, demonstrations and protests, the avoidance of conflict with Government policy even where it is manifestly oppressive of the most vulnerable, support of governmental secrecy, concern for the preservation of the moral and social behaviour [to which they are] accustomed'.

As Griffith points out, the judges' view of public interest assumes that the interests of all the members of society are roughly the same, ignoring the fact that within society, different groups – employers and employees, men and women, rich and poor – may have interests which are diametrically opposed. What appears to be acting in the public interest will usually mean in the interest of one group over another, and therefore cannot be seen as neutral.

Waldron: political choices, but why not?

In his book, *The Law* (1989), Waldron agrees that judges do exercise discretion, and that they are influenced in those choices by political and ideological considerations, but argues that this is not necessarily a bad thing. He contends that while it would be wrong for judges to be biased towards one side in a case, or to make decisions based on political factors in the hope of promotion, it is unrealistic to expect a judge to be 'a political neuter – emasculated of all values and principled commitments'.

Waldron points out that to be a judge at all means a commitment to the values surrounding the legal system: recognition of Parliament as supreme, the importance of precedent, fairness, certainty, the public interest. He argues that this itself is a political choice, and further choices are made when judges have to balance these values against one another where they conflict. The responsible thing to do, according to Waldron, is to think through such conflicts in advance, and to decide which might generally be expected to give way to which. These will inevitably be political and ideological decisions. Waldron argues that since such decisions have to be made 'the thing to do is not to try to hide them, but to be as explicit as possible'. Rather than hiding such judgements behind 'smokescreens of legal mystery . . . if judges have developed particular theories of morals, politics and society, they should say so up front, and incorporate them explicitly into their decision-making'.

Waldron suggests that where judges feel uncomfortable about doing this, it may be a useful indication that they should re-examine their bias, and see whether it is an appropriate consideration by which they are to be influenced. In addition, if the public know the reasoning behind judicial decisions 'we can evaluate them and see whether we want to rely on reasons like that for the future'.

Some support for Waldron's analysis can be found in Lord Hoffmann's judgment in **Arthur JS Hall & Co** *v* **Simons** (2000). In that case the House of Lords dramatically removed the established immunity of barristers from liability in negligence for court work. Lord Hoffmann stated:

I hope that I will not be thought ungrateful if I do not encumber this speech with citations. The question of what the public interest now requires depends upon the strength of the arguments rather than the weight of authority.

Do judges make law?

Although judges have traditionally seen themselves as declaring or finding rather than creating law, and frequently state that making law is the prerogative of Parliament, there are several areas in which they clearly do make law.

In the first place, historically, a great deal of our law is and always has been case law, made by judicial decisions. Contract and tort law are still largely judge-made, and many of the most important developments – for example, the development of negligence as a tort – have had profound effects. Even though statutes have later been passed on these subjects, and occasionally Parliament has attempted to embody whole areas of common law in statutory form, these still embody the original principles created by the judges.

Secondly, the application of law, whether case law or statute, to a particular case is not usually an automatic matter. Terminology may be vague or ambiguous, new developments in social life have to be accommodated, and the procedure requires interpretation as well as application. As we have suggested, judicial precedent does not always make a particular decision obvious and obligatory – there may be conflicting precedents, their implications may be unclear, and there are ways of getting round a precedent that would otherwise produce an undesirable decision. If it is accepted that Blackstone's declaratory theory does not apply in practice, then clearly the judges do make law, rather than explaining the law that is already there. The theories advanced by Kairys, Griffith and Waldron all accept that judges do have discretion, and therefore they do to some extent make law.

Where precedents do not spell out what should be done in a case before them, judges nevertheless have to make a decision. They cannot simply say that the law is not clear and refer it back to Parliament, even though in some cases they point out that the decision before them would be more appropriately decided by those who have been elected to make decisions on changes in the law. This was the case in **Airedale NHS Trust** *v* **Bland** (1993), where the House of Lords considered the fate of Tony Bland, the football supporter left in a coma after the Hillsborough stadium disaster. The court had to decide whether it was lawful to stop supplying the drugs and artificial feeding that were keeping Mr Bland alive, even though it was known that doing so would mean his death soon afterwards. Several Law Lords made it plain that they felt that cases raising 'wholly new moral and social issues' should be decided by Parliament, the judges' role being to 'apply the principles which society, through the democratic process, adopts, not to impose their standards on society'. Nevertheless, the courts had no option but to make a decision one way or the other, and they decided that the action was lawful in the circumstances, because it was in the patient's best interests.

Thirdly, our judges have been left to define their own role, and the role of the courts generally in the political system, more or less as they please. They have, for example, given themselves the power to review decisions of any public body, even when Parliament has said those decisions are not to be reviewed. And despite their frequent pronouncements that it is not for them to interfere in Parliament's law-making role, the judges have made it plain that they will not, unless forced by very explicit wording, interpret statutes as encroaching on common law rights or judge-made law (see p. 64). They also control the operation of case law without reference to Parliament: an obvious example is that the 1966 Practice Direction announcing that the House of Lords would no longer be bound by its own decisions, which made case law more flexible and thereby gave the judges more power, was made on the court's own authority, without needing permission from Parliament.

The House of Lords has explained its approach to judicial law-making (which is likely to be the same for the Supreme Court) in the case of **C (A Minor)** *v* **DPP** (1995) which raised the issue of children's liability for crime. The common law defence of *doli incapax* provided that a defendant aged between 10 and 14 could be liable for a crime only if the prosecution could prove that the child knew that what he or she did was seriously wrong. On appeal from the magistrates' court, the Divisional Court held that the defence was outdated and should no longer exist in law. An appeal was brought before the House of Lords, arguing that the Divisional Court was bound by precedent and not able to change the law in this way. The House of Lords agreed, and went on to consider whether it should change the law itself (as the 1966 Practice Direction clearly allowed it to do), but decided that this was not an appropriate case for judicial law-making. Explaining this decision, Lord Lowry suggested five factors were important:

- where the solution to a dilemma was doubtful, judges should be wary of imposing their own answer;
- judges should be cautious about addressing areas where Parliament had rejected opportunities of clearing up a known difficulty, or had passed legislation without doing so;
- areas of social policy over which there was dispute were least likely to be suitable for judicial law-making;
- fundamental legal doctrines should not be lightly set aside;
- judges should not change the law unless they can be sure that doing so is likely to achieve finality and certainty on the issue.

This guidance suggests that the judges should take quite a cautious approach to changing the law. In practice, however, the judges do not always seem to be following these guidelines. For example, in an important criminal case of **R** *v* **Dica** (2004) the Court of Appeal overruled an earlier case of **R** *v* **Clarence** (1888) and held that criminal liability could be imposed on a defendant for recklessly infecting another person with HIV. This change in the law was made despite the fact that the Home Office had earlier decided that legislation should not be introduced which would have imposed liability in this situation (*Violence: Reforming the Offences Against the Person Act 1861* (1998)). The Home Office had observed that 'this issue had ramifications going beyond the criminal law into wider considerations of social and public health policy'.

Some commentators feel that the judiciary's current approach is tending to go too far, and straying outside its constitutional place. Writing in the *New Law Journal* in 1999, Francis Bennion, a former parliamentary counsel, criticised what he called the 'growing appetite of some judges for changing the law themselves, rather than waiting for Parliament to do it'. Bennion cites two cases as examples of this. The first, **Kleinwort Benson Ltd** *v* **Lincoln City Council** (1998), concerns contract law, and in particular, a long-standing rule, originating from case law, that where someone made a payment as a result of a mistake about the law, they did not have the right to get the money back. The rule had existed for nearly two centuries, and been much criticised in recent years – so much so that a previous Lord Chancellor had asked the Law Commission to consider whether it should be amended by legislation, and they had concluded that it should. This would normally be taken by the courts as a signal that they should leave the issue alone and wait for Parliament to act, but in this case the Lords decided to change the rule. In doing so, Lord Keith expressed the view that 'a robust view of judicial development of the law' was desirable. Bennion argues that, in making this decision, the Lords were usurping the authority which constitutionally belongs to Parliament. He also points out that judicial, rather than parliamentary, change of the law in this kind of area causes practical difficulties, because it has retrospective effect; a large number of transactions which were thought to be settled under the previous rule can now be reopened. This would not usually be the case if Parliament changed the law.

The second case Bennion criticises is **DPP** *v* **Jones** (1999), which concerned a demonstration on the road near Stonehenge. In that case the Lords looked at another long-held rule, that the public have a right to use the highway for 'passing and repassing' (in other words, walking along the road), and for uses which are related to that, but that there is no right to use the highway in other ways, such as demonstrating or picketing. In **Jones**, the House of Lords stated that this rule placed unrealistic and unwarranted restrictions on everyday activities, and that the highway is a public place that the public has a right to enjoy for any reasonable purpose. This decision clearly has major implications for the powers of the police to break up demonstrations and pickets.

Bennion argues that, in making decisions like these, the judiciary are taking powers to which they are not constitutionally entitled, and that they should not extend their law-making role into such controversial areas.

When should judges make law?

Again, this is a subject about which there are different views, not least among the judiciary, and the following are some of the approaches which have been suggested.

Adapting to social change

In 1952, Lord Denning gave a lecture called 'The Need for a New Equity', arguing that judges had become too timid about adapting the law to the changing conditions of society. They were, he felt, leaving this role too much to Parliament, which was too slow and cumbersome to do the job well (by 1984, he felt that judges had taken up the task again).

Lord Scarman, in **McLoughlin v O'Brian** (1982), stated that the courts' function is to adjudicate according to principle, and if the results are socially unacceptable Parliament can legislate to overrule them. He felt that the risk was not that case law might develop too far, but that it stood still and did not therefore adapt to the changing needs of society.

Paterson's (1982) survey of 19 Law Lords active between 1967 and 1973 found that at least 12 thought that the Law Lords had a duty to develop the common law in response to changing social conditions. A case where the judges did eventually show themselves willing to change the law in the light of social change is **Fitzpatrick v Sterling Housing Association Ltd** (2000). The case concerned a homosexual man, Mr Fitzpatrick, who had lived with his partner, Mr Thompson, for 18 years, nursing and caring for him after Mr Thompson suffered an accident which caused irreversible brain damage and severe paralysis. Mr Thompson was the tenant of the flat in which they lived and, when he died in 1994, Mr Fitzpatrick applied to take over the tenancy, which gave the tenant certain protections under the Rent Acts. The landlords refused. The Rent Act 1977 states that when a statutory tenant dies, the tenancy can be taken over by a spouse, a person living with the ex-tenant as wife or husband, or a member of the family who was living with the tenant. Mr Fitzpatrick's case sought to establish that he was a member of Mr Thompson's family, by virtue of their close and loving relationship.

The Court of Appeal agreed that 'if endurance, stability, interdependence and devotion were the sole hallmarks of family membership', there could be no doubt that the couple were a family. They also pointed out that discriminating against stable same-sex relationships was out of step with the values of modern society. However, they recognised that the law on succession to statutory tenancies was firmly rooted in the idea that families were based on marriage or kinship, and this had only ever been relaxed in terms of heterosexual couples living together, who were treated as if married. As a result, the court concluded that it would be wrong to change the law by interpreting the word family to include same-sex couples; all three judges agreed that such a change should be made, in order to reflect modern values, but it should be made by Parliament. The House of Lords, however, overturned the Court of Appeal's decision. It ruled that the appellant could not be treated as the spouse of the deceased tenant, but as a matter of law a same-sex partner could establish the necessary familial link for the purposes of the legislation.

Types of law

Lord Reid has suggested that the basic areas of common law are appropriate for judge-made law, but that the judges should respect the need for certainty in property and contract law, and that criminal law, except for the issue of *mens rea*, was best left to Parliament.

Consensus law-making

Lord Devlin (1979) has distinguished between activist law-making and dynamic law-making. He saw new ideas within society as going through a long process of acceptance. At first society will be divided about them, and there will be controversy, but eventually such ideas may come to be accepted by most members of society, or most members will at least become prepared to put up with them. At this second stage we can say there is a consensus. We can see this process in the way that views have changed over recent decades on subjects such as homosexuality and sex before marriage.

Law-making which takes one side or another while an issue is still controversial is what Devlin called dynamic law-making, and he believed judges should not take part in it because it endangered their reputation for independence and impartiality. Their role is in activist law-making, concerning areas where there is a consensus. The problem with Devlin's view is that in practice the judges sometimes have no choice but to embark on dynamic law-making. In **Gillick v West Norfolk and Wisbech Area Health Authority** (1985), the House of Lords was asked to consider whether a girl under 16 needed her parents' consent before she could be given contraceptive services. It was an issue on which there was by no means a consensus, with one side claiming that teenage pregnancies would increase if the courts ruled that parental consent was necessary, and the other claiming that the judges would be encouraging under-age sex if they did not. The House of Lords held, by a majority of three to two, that a girl under 16 did not have to have parental consent if she was mature enough to make up her own mind. But the decision did not end the controversy, and it was widely suggested that the judges were not the right people to make the choice. However, since Parliament had given no lead, they had no option but to make a decision one way or the other, and were therefore forced to indulge in what Devlin would call dynamic law-making.

Respecting parliamentary opinion

It is often stated that judges should not make law where there is reason to believe Parliament does not support such changes. In **President of India v La Pintada Compañia Navigación SA** (1984), the House of Lords felt that there was a strong case for overruling a nineteenth-century decision that a party could receive no interest on a contract debt, but they noted that the Law Commission had recommended that this rule should be abolished and the legislators specifically decided not to do so. Lord Brandon said that to make new law in these circumstances would be an 'unjustifiable usurpation of the function which properly belongs to Parliament'.

Similarly, it is sometimes argued that judges should avoid making law in areas of public interest which Parliament is considering at the time. Lord Radcliffe suggested that, in such areas, judges should be cautious 'not because the principles adopted by Parliament are more satisfactory or more enlightened, but because it is unacceptable constitutionally that there should be two independent sources of law-making at work at the same time'.

Protecting individual rights

In a 1992 lecture, the human rights lawyer Anthony Lester QC argued that while judges must have regard to precedent, they could still use their discretion within the system of precedent more effectively. He argued that, in the past, judges have abdicated responsibility for law-making by surrounding themselves with self-made rules (such as the pre-1966 rule that the House of Lords was bound by its own decisions). Since the 1960s, however, he feels that this tendency has gradually been reduced, with judges taking on more responsibility for developing the common law in accordance with contemporary values, and being more willing to arbitrate fairly between the citizen and the state. Lester praises this development, arguing that the judges can establish protection for the individual against misuse of power, where Parliament refuses to do so.

Advantages of case law

Certainty

Judicial precedent means litigants can assume that like cases will be treated alike, rather than judges making their own random decisions, which nobody could predict. This helps people plan their affairs.

Detailed practical rules

Case law is a response to real situations, as opposed to statutes, which may be more heavily based on theory and logic. Case law shows the detailed application of the law to various circumstances, and thus gives more information than statute.

Free market in legal ideas

The right-wing philosopher Hayek (1982) has argued that there should be as little legislation as possible, with case law becoming the main source of law. He sees case law as developing in line with market forces: if the *ratio* of a case is seen not to work, it will be abandoned; if it works, it will be followed. In this way the law can develop in response to demand. Hayek sees statute law as imposed by social planners, forcing their views on society whether they like it or not, and threatening the liberty of the individual.

Flexibility

Law needs to be flexible to meet the needs of a changing society, and case law can make changes far more quickly than Parliament. The most obvious signs of this are the radical changes the House of Lords made in the field of criminal law, following announcing in 1966 that its judges would no longer be bound by their own decisions.

Disadvantages of case law

Complexity and volume

There are hundreds of thousands of decided cases, comprising several thousand volumes of law reports, and more are added all the time. Judgments themselves are long, with many judges making no attempt at readability, and the *ratio decidendi* of a case may be buried in a sea of irrelevant material. This can make it very difficult to pinpoint appropriate principles.

A possible solution to these difficulties would be to follow the example of some European systems, where courts hand down a single concise judgment with no dissenting judgments. However, some of these decisions can become so concise that lawyers are required to do considerable research around the specific words used to discover the legal impact of the case, because no detailed explanation is provided by the judges.

Rigid

The rules of judicial precedent mean that judges should follow a binding precedent even where they think it is bad law, or inappropriate. This can mean that bad judicial decisions are perpetuated for a long time before they come before a court high enough to have the power to overrule them.

Illogical distinctions

The fact that binding precedents must be followed unless the facts of the case are significantly different can lead to judges making minute distinctions between the facts of a previous case and the case before them, so that they can distinguish a precedent which they consider inappropriate. This in turn leads to a mass of cases all establishing different precedents in very similar circumstances, and further complicates the law.

Unpredictable

The advantages of certainty can be lost if too many of the kind of illogical distinctions referred to above are made, and it may be impossible to work out which precedents will be applied to a new case.

Dependence on chance

Case law changes only in response to those cases brought before it, so important changes may not be made unless someone has the money and determination to push a case far enough through the appeal system to allow a new precedent to be created.

Unsystematic progression

Case law develops according to the facts of each case and so does not provide a comprehensive code. A whole series of rules can be built on one case, and if this is overruled the whole structure can collapse.

Lack of research

When making case law the judges are only presented with the facts of the case and the legal arguments, and their task is to decide on the outcome of that particular dispute. Technically, they are not concerned with the social and economic implications of their decisions, and so they cannot commission research or consult experts as to these implications, as Parliament can when changing the law. In the US litigants are allowed to present written arguments containing socio-economic material, and Lord Simon has recommended that a law officer should be sent to the court in certain cases to present such arguments objectively. However, Lord Devlin considered that allowing such information would encourage the judges to go too far in making law.

Retrospective effect

Changes made by case law apply to events which happened before the case came to court, unlike legislation, which usually only applies to events after it comes into force. This may be considered unfair, since if a case changes the law, the parties concerned in that case could not have known what the law was before they acted. US courts sometimes get round the problems by deciding the case before them according to the old law, while declaring that in future the new law will prevail: or they may determine with what degree of retroactivity a new rule is to be enforced.

KEY CASE

In **SW v United Kingdom** (1995), two men, who had been convicted of the rape and attempted rape of their wives, brought a case before the European Court of Human Rights, alleging that their convictions violated Art. 7 of the European Convention on Human Rights, which provides that criminal laws should not have retrospective effect. The men argued that when the incidents which gave rise to their convictions happened, it was not a crime for a man to force his wife to have sex; it only became a crime after the decision in **R v R** (1991) (see p. 16). The court dismissed the men's argument: Art. 7 did not prevent the courts from clarifying the principles of criminal liability, providing the developments could be clearly foreseen. In this case, there had been mounting criticism of the previous law, and a series of cases which had chipped away at the marital rape exemption, before the **R v R** decision.

> There is no breach of the European Convention when courts clarify the law provided legal developments can be foreseen.

The same issue came before the courts again in **R v C** (2004). In that case the defendant was convicted in 2002 of raping his wife in 1970. On appeal, he argued that this conviction breached Art. 7 of the European Convention and tried to distinguish the earlier case of **SW v United Kingdom** (1995). He said that while in **SW v United Kingdom** the defendant could have foreseen in 1989 when he committed the offence that his conduct would be regarded as criminal, this was not the case in 1970. This argument was rejected by the Court of Appeal. It claimed, rather unconvincingly, that a husband in 1970 could have anticipated this development in the law. In fact, the leading textbooks at the time clearly stated that husbands were not liable for raping their wives.

Recent criminal cases have shown that the retrospective effect of case law can also work to the benefit of the defendant. In **R v Powell and English** (1999) the House of Lords clarified the law that should determine the criminal liability of accomplices. An earlier controversial case that had involved the criminal liability of an accomplice was that of **R v Bentley** (1953), whose story was made into the Hollywood film *Let Him Have It*. Bentley was caught and arrested after being chased across rooftops by police. Craig had a gun and Bentley is alleged to have said to Craig, 'Let him have it'. Craig then shot and killed a policeman. Craig was charged with murdering a police officer (at that time a hanging offence) and Bentley was charged as his accomplice. In court Bentley argued that when he shouted, 'Let him have it', he was telling Craig to hand over his gun rather than, as the prosecution claimed, encouraging him to shoot the police officer. Nevertheless both were convicted. Craig was under the minimum age for the death sentence, and was given life imprisonment. Bentley, who was older, was hanged. The conviction was subsequently overturned by the Court of Appeal in July 1998, following a long campaign by his family. In considering the trial judge's summing up to the jury, the Court of Appeal said that criminal liability 'must be determined according to the common law as now understood'. The common law that applied in 1998 to accomplice liability was more favourable than the common law that applied in 1952. The danger in practice is that every time the common law shifts to be more favourable to defendants, the floodgates are potentially opened for defendants to appeal against their earlier convictions. To try to avoid this problem, the Criminal Justice and Immigration Act 2008 provides that the Court of Appeal can reject as out of time references made to it by the Criminal Cases Review Commission which are based purely on a change in the common law. The court is likely to do this where a rejection of the appeal will not cause substantial injustice.

Undemocratic

Lord Scarman pointed out in **Stock v Jones** (1978) that the judge cannot match the experience and vision of the legislator; and that unlike the legislator the judge is not answerable to the people. Theories, like Griffith's, which suggest that precedent can actually give judges a good deal of discretion, and allow them to decide cases on grounds of political and social policy, raise the question of whether judges, who are unelected, should have such freedom.

Answering questions

1 **What do we mean when we say that the English Legal System is a common law system?**
London External LLB

The meaning of 'common law' is discussed at p. 12. The term 'common law' has different meanings depending on the context in which it is being used. In the context of this question the focus is on common law being a product of England's legal history. It can be contrasted to the civil law systems which can be found in Continental Europe (for example, France) and countries which were influenced by Continental Europe. This essay is not concerned with the distinction between equity and 'common law' which is discussed at p. 122.

One approach to this essay would be to first provide a historical analysis of the common law (found on p. 12). Secondly, contrast the common law systems which emphasise judge-made law and the doctrine of judicial precedent, with the civil law systems which place a greater emphasis on legislative codes. Finally, provide some examples of the common law working in practice. For example, the fact that the definition of murder can be found in case law and the way that definition has been developed by the courts.

2 **Judicial reasoning in case law 'consists in the applying to new combinations of circumstances those rules of law which we derive from legal principles and judicial precedents . . . and we are not at liberty to reject them, and to abandon all analogy to them'. (Mr Justice Peak, 1833)**
   Does this statement reflect the operation of precedent today? *London External LLB*

Your answer could be divided into two parts. The first part could discuss how the statement of Mr Justice Peak fits within the classic declaratory theory of law provided by William Blackstone (p. 24). The basic rules that underpin judicial precedent with the hierarchy of the courts, and the ways that cases can be followed, distinguished, overruled and reversed support this view (p. 23).

The second part of your answer could point to theories and practice which undermine this view so that it may not 'reflect the operation of precedent today'. Thus, you could discuss the work of the critical theorists (p. 26), and Griffith (p. 26). The material under the subheadings 'Do judges make law?' (p. 28) would also be useful to answer this part of the essay.

You might conclude that while Mr Justice Peak's statement might suggest that the judges are simply applying existing legal principles and judicial precedents to a particular set of facts, there may be some flexibility in the way in which those principles and precedents can be applied, and there may be other factors that help determine the outcome of a case.

3 **Precedent must, on the one hand, provide certainty, but on the other hand, it must be flexible in adapting to social change. In view of the so-called binding nature of precedent, how are judges able to reconcile these seemingly contradictory characteristics in their use of precedent?**

You should begin by explaining what precedent is and how *stare decisis* operates, drawing on the materials in the sections on 'Judicial precedent' (p. 15) and 'How judicial precedent works' (p. 23). Certainty and flexibility are two of the advantages of precedent. Preoccupation with certainty could lead to an overly-rigid system where bad decisions have to be followed. However, there are a number of ways in which judges can exercise flexibility, and indeed, are permitted to do so. Examples that could be given include:

- Use of the 1966 Practice Statement. An illustration of the Practice Statement being applied is **R v R** (1991) discussed on p. 16.
- The rules in **Young v Bristol Aeroplane Co Ltd** (1946) (relevant material can be found under the heading 'The Court of Appeal' p. 20);
- The practice of distinguishing earlier cases on their facts (see the section entitled 'How do judges really decide cases?' on p. 24).

You could argue that this flexibility involves judges in 'making law', as opposed to applying the law, and you could express your view as to whether you think this is acceptable.

You might conclude with your view on how effectively (or not) you think judges balance certainty and flexibility, and indeed, whether you think they have to.

4 Critically evaluate the extent to which the doctrine of binding precedent inhibits judicial creativity.

The phrase 'judicial creativity' is a reference to the judges' ability to create or make law. Your essay could start by explaining the rules relating to judicial precedent including a clear explanation of the judicial hierarchy, and the exceptional rules relating to both the Court of Appeal and the Supreme Court (drawing upon material contained under the headings 'Judicial precedent' and 'How judicial precedent works'. The relevance of the distinction between *ratio decidendi* and *obiter dicta* should be explained and the importance of decisions of the European Court and the European Court of Human Rights could also be mentioned. Explain some of the arguments in favour of precedent, such as certainty and consistency. This part of your answer would aim to show how far the rules of judicial precedent inhibit judicial freedom.

The second part of your essay could then explore how far, despite the rules of judicial precedent, 'judicial creativity' still exists. You might discuss some of the material contained under the heading 'Do judges make law?' in this chapter. You could discuss:

- the sheer amount of case law in our system (especially in contract and tort);
- applying the law is not usually an automatic matter in practice;
- judges have been left to define their own role in the system, in the context of the principle of the separation of powers; and
- the increased availability of reported material can afford significant judicial opportunities to distinguish cases, and thus to influence the future direction of case law.

You should finish with a conclusion, drawing on the points you have made, that states how far you think precedent does inhibit judicial creativity.

5 Evaluate the advantages of abolishing the doctrine of binding judicial precedent.

You first need to describe the doctrine of binding precedent, but do not spend too much time on this, as pure description is not what the question is asking for.

You should then consider what the law would lose if precedent were abandoned – the material on the advantages of precedent is relevant here. Then talk about the disadvantages of the system of precedent, and what might be gained by abolishing it. You could bring in the effects of the 1966 Practice Direction as an example of the relaxation of precedent, and talk about whether you feel it has benefited the law or not, mentioning appropriate cases.

You might mention innovations which would lessen the role of precedent, such as codification, and say whether you feel they would be desirable and why.

Your conclusion could state whether or not you feel precedent serves a useful role, and outline any changes which you feel should be made to its operation.

Summary of Chapter 1: Case law

Judicial precedent
In deciding a case, a judge must follow any decision that has been made by a higher court in a case with similar facts. Judges are bound only by the part of the judgment that forms the legal principle that was the basis of the earlier decision, known as the *ratio decidendi*. The rest of the judgment is known as *obiter dicta* and is not binding.

The hierarchy of the courts
The European Court of Justice is the highest authority on European law, in other matters the Supreme Court is the highest court in the UK. Under the 1966 Practice Direction, the Supreme Court is not bound by its previous decisions.

How do judges really decide cases?
According to the traditional declaratory theory laid down by William Blackstone, judges do not make law but merely discover and declare the law that has always been. Ronald Dworkin also accepts that the judges have no real discretion in making case law, but he bases this view on his concept that law is a seamless web of principles.

Very different views have been put forward by other academics. Critical theorists argue that judicial decisions are actually influenced by social, political and personal factors and that the doctrine of judicial precedent is merely used to legitimate the judges' decisions. Griffith also thinks that judges are influenced by their personal background. Waldron accepts that judges make political choices but sees no fundamental problem with this.

When should judges make law?
There is no doubt that on occasion judges make law. There is some debate as to when judges ought to make law. When judges make law they can adapt it to social change, but Francis Bennion has highlighted the danger that if the courts are too willing to make law, they undermine the position of Parliament.

Advantages of binding precedent
The doctrine of judicial precedent provides:

- certainty;
- detailed practical rules;
- a free market in legal ideas; and
- flexibility.

Disadvantages of binding precedent
Case law has been criticised because of its:

- complexity and volume;
- rigidity;
- illogical distinctions;
- unpredictability;
- dependence on chance;
- retrospective effect; and
- undemocratic character.

1

Case law

Reading list

Hale, Sir M. (1979) *The History of the Common Law of England*, Chicago: University of Chicago Press.

Hohfeld, W.N. and Cook, W.W. (1919) *Fundamental Legal Concepts as Applied in Judicial Reasoning*, London: Greenwood Press.

Kairys, D. (1998) *The Politics of Law: A Progressive Critique*, New York: Basic Books.

Lawson, C.M. (1982) 'The family affinities of common law and civil law legal systems', 6 *Hastings International Comparative Law Review* 85.

MacCormick, N. (1978) *Legal Rules and Legal Reasoning*, Oxford: Clarendon.

Summers, R. (1992) *Essays on the Nature of Law and Legal Reasoning*, Berlin: Duncker & Humblot.

Weinreb, L. (2004) *Legal Reason: The Use of Analogy in Legal Argument*, Cambridge: Cambridge University Press.

Reading on the Internet

www   Decisions of the Supreme Court can be found on the website of the Supreme Court at:
http://www.supremecourt.gov.uk/decided-cases/index.html

The former House of Lords' judgments are available on the House of Lords' judicial business website at:
http://www.publications.parliament.uk/pa/ld/ldjudgmt.htm

Some important judgments are published on the Court Service website at:
http://www.hmcourts-service.gov.uk

Visit www.mylawchamber.co.uk/ElliottELS to access multiple-choice questions, flashcards and practice exam questions to test yourself on this chapter.

2

Statute law

This chapter discusses:

- the House of Commons;
- the House of Lords;
- how an Act of Parliament is made; and
- post-legislative scrutiny.

Introduction

Statutes are made by Parliament, which consists of the House of Commons, the House of Lords and the Monarch. Another term for a statute is an Act of Parliament. In Britain, Parliament is sovereign, which has traditionally meant that the law it makes takes precedence over law originating from any other source though, as we shall see, membership of the European Union (EU) has compromised this principle. EU law aside, Parliament can make or cancel any law it chooses, and the courts must enforce it. In other countries, such as the United States of America, the courts can declare such legislation unconstitutional, but our courts are not allowed to do that.

House of Commons

The House of Commons is the democratically elected chamber of Parliament. Every four to five years Members of Parliament (MPs) are elected in a general election. There are 646 MPs who discuss the big political issues of the day and proposals for new laws.

House of Lords

The House of Lords acts as a revising chamber for legislation and its work complements the business of the Commons. Members of the House of Lords are not elected by the general public, instead the majority are appointed by the Queen on the recommendation of the House of Lords Appointments Commission. The House of Lords currently has about 750 members, divided into four different types:

- life peers,
- retired judges of the former House of Lords' judicial committee,
- bishops, and
- elected hereditary peers.

Life peers are appointed for their lifetime only, so the right to sit in the House of Lords is not passed on to their children.

TOPICAL ISSUE

Modernising the House of Lords

Traditionally, hereditary peers have sat in the House of Lords and this right was passed down from father to son. Membership of the House is currently undergoing a major reform to remove the role of the hereditary peers. Their right to sit and vote in the House of Lords was ended in 1999 by the House of Lords Act, but 92 members were elected internally to remain until the next stage of the Lords reform process.

The Royal Commission for the Reform of the House of Lords, chaired by Lord Wakeham, published its report in January 2000. It recommended that there should be a chamber of about 550 members. Only a minority would be elected, to represent the regions; the remainder would be appointed by an independent Appointments Commission. It would be responsible for selecting members who were broadly representative of British society. Approximately 20 per cent of the House of Lords' members would be politically independent and the others would reflect the political balance as expressed by the last general election. The Appointments Commission would be under a statutory duty to ensure that at least 30 per cent of new members were women and that minorities were represented in numbers at least proportionate to their representation in the total population. The powers of the new chamber would be broadly comparable with the present House of Lords.

In 2001 the Government White Paper, *The House of Lords – completing the reform*, proposed an adapted version of the Wakeham reforms. These were highly criticised, and the Government withdrew them and decided to refer the matter to a Joint Committee of both Houses to examine the issue afresh. In 2007 the Government published another White Paper, *The House of Lords: Reform*, suggesting that the House should be a hybrid chamber with 50 per cent of its members elected and the rest appointed. In the same year the Commons voted in favour of a completely elected House of Lords, while the Lords itself voted for a purely appointed membership, though these votes will not in themselves change the law. Later that year, the Government Green Paper *The Governance of Britain* (2007) committed itself to enacting the will of the Commons, including the removal of the remaining hereditary peers. The Government introduced into Parliament in 2009 the Constitutional Reform and Governance Bill which contains provisions for the abolition of the remaining hereditary peers.

This reform might partly reflect public discontent at the 'cash for honours' controversy, when there were suggestions that individuals had been made Lords in return for donations to political parties. Such a reform could also provide a response to the recent scandal that some members of the Lords appear to have arranged for legislation to be amended in return for receiving large sums of money from private companies.

Making an Act of Parliament

Policy development

Before the parliamentary legislative process begins, usually a policy objective will have been identified by the Government. This policy objective may have been set out in an election manifesto or included in an official consultation document, known as a Green Paper. The latter document puts forward tentative proposals, which interested parties may consider and give their views on. The Green Paper will be followed by a White Paper, which contains the specific reform plans.

ELIZABETH II   c. 4

Criminal Defence Service (Advice and Assistance) Act 2001

2001 CHAPTER 4

An Act to clarify the extent of the duty of the Legal Services Commission under section 13(1) of the Access to Justice Act 1999.   [10th April 2001]

B E IT ENACTED by the Queen's most Excellent Majesty, by and with the advice and consent of the Lords Spiritual and Temporal, and Commons, in this present Parliament assembled, and by the authority of the same, as follows: —

1   Extent of duty to fund advice and assistance

(1) Subsection (1) of section 13 of the Access to Justice Act 1999 (c. 22) (duty of Legal Services Commission to fund advice and assistance as part of Criminal Defence Service) shall be treated as having been enacted with the substitution of the following for paragraph (b) and the words after it—

"(b) in prescribed circumstances, for individuals who—

   (i)   are not within paragraph (a) but are involved in investigations which may lead to criminal proceedings,

   (ii) are before a court or other body in such proceedings, or

   (iii) have been the subject of such proceedings;

and the assistance which the Commission may consider appropriate includes assistance in the form of advocacy."

(2) Regulations under subsection (1) of section 13 (as amended above) may include provision treating them as having come into force at the same time as that subsection.

2   Short title

This Act may be cited as the Criminal Defence Service (Advice and Assistance) Act 2001.

Figure 2.1 Criminal Defence Service (Advice and Assistance) Act 2001
Source: The Stationery Office. © Crown Copyright 2001.

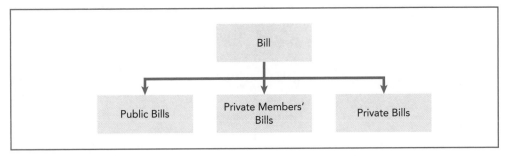

Figure 2.2 Parliamentary Bills

Bills

All statutes begin as a Bill, which is a proposal for a piece of legislation. There are three types of Bill:

Public Bills These are written by parliamentary counsel who specialise in drafting legislation. They are presented to Parliament by Government ministers and change the general law of the whole country.

Private Members' Bills These are prepared by an individual backbench MP (someone who is not a member of the Cabinet). MPs wanting to put forward a Bill have to enter a ballot to win the right to do so, and then persuade the Government to allow enough parliamentary time for the Bill to go through. Consequently very few such Bills become Acts, and they tend to function more as a way of drawing attention to particular issues. Some, however, have made important contributions to legislation, an example being the Abortion Act 1967 which stemmed from a Private Member's Bill put forward by David Steel.

Private Bills These are usually proposed by a local authority, public corporation or large public company, and usually only affect that sponsor. An example might be a local authority seeking the right to build a bridge or road.

The actual preparation of Bills is done by expert draftsmen known as Parliamentary Counsel.

First reading

The title of the prepared Bill is read to the House of Commons. This is called the first reading, and acts as a notification of the proposed measure.

Second reading

At the second reading, the proposals are debated fully, and may be amended, and members vote on whether the legislation should proceed. In practice, the whip system (party officials whose job is to make sure MPs vote with their party) means that a Government with a reasonable majority can almost always get its legislation through at this and subsequent stages.

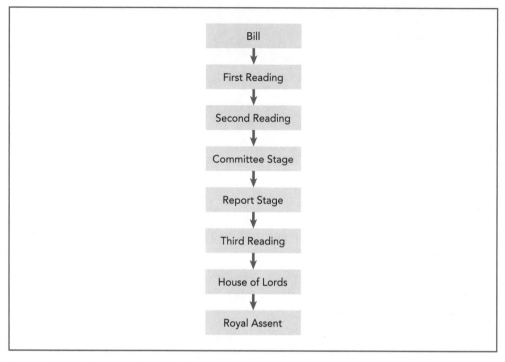

Figure 2.3 Making an Act of Parliament

Committee stage

The Bill is then referred to a committee of the House of Commons for detailed examination, bearing in mind the points made during the debate. At this point further amendments to the Bill may be made.

Report stage

The committee then reports back to the House, and any proposed amendments are debated and voted upon.

Third reading

The Bill is re-presented to the House. There may be a short debate, and a vote on whether to accept or reject the legislation as it stands.

House of Lords

The Bill then goes to the House of Lords, where it goes through a similar process of three readings. If the House of Lords alters anything, the Bill returns to the Commons for further consideration. The Commons then responds with agreement, reasons for disagreement, or proposals for alternative changes.

At one time legislation could not be passed without the agreement of both Houses, which meant that the unelected House of Lords could block legislation put forward by the elected House of Commons. The Parliament Acts of 1911 and 1949 lay down special procedures by which proposed legislation can go for Royal Assent without the approval of the House of Lords after specified periods of time. These procedures are only rarely used, because the House of Lords usually drops objections that are resisted by the Commons, though their use has increased in recent years. Four Acts of Parliament have been passed to date relying on the Parliament Act 1949:

- War Crimes Act 1991;
- European Parliamentary Elections Act 1999;
- Sexual Offences (Amendment) Act 2000;
- Hunting Act 2004.

KEY CASE

It is of particular note that the procedures were used to pass the controversial Hunting Act 2004. This Act bans hunting wild animals with dogs and a form of hunting known as hare coursing. It was passed despite the House of Lords' opposition, by using the Parliament Act 1949.

> The Parliament Acts of 1911 and 1949 cannot be used to enact major constitutional reforms.

Ess. Cases p. 24 Members of the pressure group the Countryside Alliance brought a legal challenge to the Act in R (on the application of Jackson and others) v Attorney General (2005). They argued that the Parliament Act 1949 was itself unlawful and that therefore the Hunting Act, which was passed relying on the procedures it laid down, was also unlawful. The initial Act of 1911 had required a two-year delay between the first vote in the House of Commons and reliance on the special procedures in the Act. The 1949 Act reduced this delay to one year and was itself passed using the special procedures in the 1911 Act. The Countryside Alliance claimed that the 1949 Act was unlawful because it had been passed relying on the procedures laid down in the 1911 Act, when the 1911 Act was not drafted to allow its procedures to be used to amend itself. This argument was rejected by the courts. The Law Lords stated that the 1911 and 1949 Acts could not be used to enact major constitutional reforms, such as the abolition of the House of Lords. Since the 1949 Act was simply reducing the House of Lords' delaying power from two years to one, this did not amount to a major constitutional reform and so the 1949 Act was lawful and so also, therefore, was the Hunting Act.

Royal Assent

In the vast majority of cases, agreement between the Lords and Commons is reached, and the Bill is then presented for Royal Assent. Technically, the Queen must give her consent to all legislation before it can become law, but in practice that consent is never refused.

The Bill is then an Act of Parliament, and becomes law, though most do not take effect from the moment the Queen gives her consent, but on a specified date

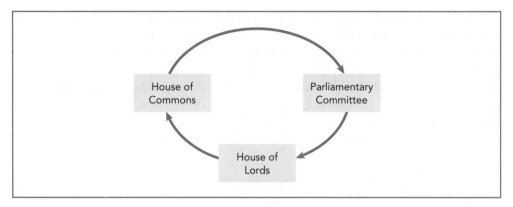

Figure 2.4 Legislative process

Photo 2.1 Houses of Parliament
Source: © Copyright 2002 Parliamentary Education Unit

in the near future or when a commencement order has been issued by a Government minister.

Accelerated procedures

In the case of legislation about which there is no controversy, the procedure may be simplified, with the first three readings in the Lords, then three in the Commons, with the Bill passing back to the Lords only if there is disagreement. Private Bills technically go through the above procedure, and are examined to make sure that adequate warning has been given to anyone affected by the provisions, but there is little debate on them. Consolidating Acts, which simply bring together all the existing law on one topic, also go through an accelerated procedure, with no debate, because they do not change the law; codification bills, on the other hand, go through the normal process (see p. 133).

Post-legislative scrutiny

The Law Commission (a body responsible for looking at how the law needs to be reformed) has considered whether a formal procedure should be introduced to scrutinise legislation after it has been passed. Following a consultation process the Commission issued a report on the subject entitled *Post-Legislative Scrutiny* (2006). This report strongly supports the creation of a joint parliamentary committee on post-legislative scrutiny which would routinely check whether new legislation – both Acts of Parliament and delegated legislation (discussed in Chapter 4) – is working effectively. These recommendations were accepted by the Government in its report *Post-legislative scrutiny – The Government's approach* (2008).

Ess. Cases p. 28

2

Statute law

Answering questions

1 There has been some disagreement as to the way in which the House of Lords should be reformed. What are the various options, and how do these differ from its present composition?

You could start by setting out the present composition and role of the House of Lords (as a second unelected chamber), before going on to describe the conflicting proposals (p. 42) and how these would affect the power of the House of Lords. Note that the Parliament Acts had effectively reduced the House of Lords' power, but if its members were elected it could develop the authority to exercise greater control over the House of Commons. You could give an opinion as to whether or not making the House of Lords into an elected (i.e. more democratic) chamber with greater powers would be a good or a bad thing.

2 Describe the stages of the law-making process in Parliament: to what extent is approval of the House of Lords always required?

The first part of your essay could contain a fairly full but essentially descriptive account of the legislative process, starting with the Green and White Papers and through to Royal Assent, and emphasising the principle that consent of both Houses and the Crown is usually required.

The second part of the question focuses upon the exceptional provisions of the Parliament Acts 1911 and 1949 allowing legislation to proceed to Royal Assent without the approval of the House of Lords. Mention should be made of the recent and highly publicised case of **R (on the application of Jackson and others)** v **Attorney General** concerning the validity of the Hunting Act 2004. In that case the House of Lords stated that the Parliament Acts could be used for ordinary legislation but not for major constitutional reforms; and as the Hunting Act was not a major constitutional reform, the Parliament Acts had been correctly used.

Additional marks would be secured by mentioning the Law Commission Report *Post-Legislative Scrutiny*.

Summary of Chapter 2: Statute law

Introduction
Statutes are made by Parliament, which consists of the House of Commons, the House of Lords and the Monarch.

House of Commons
The House of Commons is the democratically elected chamber of Parliament.

House of Lords
Following the House of Lords Act 1999, membership of the House of Lords is currently undergoing a major reform to remove the role of the hereditary peers. The Government is considering removing the remaining 92 hereditary peers. An independent Appointments Commission selects some non-party members for the upper House and vets party appointments.

Making an Act of Parliament
All statutes begin as a Bill. There are three types of Bill:

- Public Bills;
- Private Members' Bills; and
- Private Bills.

The legislative process usually starts in the House of Commons and proceeds as follows:

- First reading;
- Second reading;
- Committee stage;
- Report stage;
- Third reading;
- House of Lords;
- Royal Assent.

Role of the House of Lords
The Parliament Acts of 1911 and 1949 lay down special procedures by which proposed legislation can go for Royal Assent without the approval of the House of Lords after specified periods of time. These procedures are only rarely used, because the House of Lords usually drops objections that are resisted by the Commons, though their use has increased in recent years.

 ### Reading list

Renton, D. (1975) *The Preparation of Legislation*, London: HMSO.

Royal Commission for the Reform of the House of Lords (2000) *A House for the Future*, Cm 4534, London: HMSO.

Reading on the Internet

Copies of Public Bills currently being considered by Parliament can be found at:
http://www.parliament.uk/business/bills_and_legislation.cfm

Copies of recent legislation can be found at:
http://www.opsi.gov.uk/acts.htm

Useful explanatory notes prepared by the Government to explain the implications of recent legislation can be found at:
http://www.opsi.gov.uk/legislation/uk-expa.htm

The Law Commission's consultation paper, *Post-Legislative Scrutiny* (2006), is available on its website at:
www.lawcom.gov.uk/docs/cp178.pdf

Visit www.mylawchamber.co.uk/ElliottELS to access multiple-choice questions, flashcards and practice exam questions to test yourself on this chapter.

2

Statute law

3

Statutory interpretation

When judges are faced with a new piece of legislation, its meaning is not always clear and they have to interpret it. Often, when interpreting the Act, the judges say that they are looking for Parliament's intention. In this chapter we will consider:

- the meaning of parliamentary intention;

- the rules of statutory interpretation;

- internal aids to statutory interpretation;

- external aids to statutory interpretation, including the Human Rights Act 1998 and the official record of what was said in Parliament (known as *Hansard*); and

- theories about how judges interpret statutes in practice.

Introduction

Although Parliament makes legislation, it is left to the courts to apply it. The general public imagine that this is simply a case of looking up the relevant law and ruling accordingly, but the reality is not so simple. Despite the fact that Acts of Parliament are carefully written by expert draftsmen, there are many occasions in which the courts find that the implications of a statute for the case before them are not at all clear.

Bennion (2005) has identified a number of factors that may cause this uncertainty:

- A word is left out because the draftsman thought it was automatically implied. For example, a draftsman writing a statute banning men with facial hair from parks might write that 'men with beards or moustaches are prohibited from parks'. Does this mean that a man who has a beard **and** a moustache would be allowed in? If the words 'and/or' were used it would be clear, but the draftsman may have thought this was automatically implied.
- A broad term was used, leaving it to the user to decide what it includes. Where a statute bans vehicles from the park, this obviously includes cars and lorries, but the courts would have to decide whether it also prohibited skateboards, bikes or roller skates, for example.
- An ambiguous word or phrase was used on purpose, perhaps because the provision is politically contentious. The European Communities Act 1972 was ambiguous about the position of UK legislation.
- The wording is inadequate because of a printing, drafting or other error.
- The events of the case before the court were not foreseen when the legislation was produced. In the example given above regarding vehicles, skateboards might not have been invented when the statute was drafted, so it would be impossible for Parliament to say whether they should be included in the term 'vehicles'.

In any of these cases, the job of the courts – in theory at least – is to discover how Parliament intended the law to apply and put that into practice. This is because, as you know, in our constitution, Parliament is the supreme source of law (excluding EU law, which will be discussed later), and therefore the judiciary's constitutional role is to put into practice what they think Parliament actually intended when it made a particular law, rather than simply what the judges themselves might think is the best interpretation in the case before them. However, as we shall see, the practice is not always as straightforward as the constitutional theory suggests.

What is parliamentary intention?

The idea of parliamentary intention is a very slippery concept in practice. The last example above is one illustration of this: how could Parliament have had any intention at all of how skateboards should be treated under the legislation, if skateboards were not invented when the legislation was passed?

More problems are revealed if we try to pin down precisely what parliamentary intention means. Is it the intention of every individual Member of Parliament at the time the law was passed? Obviously not, since not every member will have voted for the legislation or even necessarily been present when it was passed. The intention of all those who did support a particular piece of legislation is no easier to define either, since some of those are likely to be acting from loyalty to their party, and will not necessarily have detailed knowledge of the provisions, much less have thought hard about how they might apply in as yet unseen circumstances. Even among those MPs who have considered the detailed provisions, there may be many different opinions as to how they should apply in different situations. And even if one of these groups was taken to represent true parliamentary intention, how are their views to be assessed? It is hardly feasible to conduct a poll every time a legislative provision is found to be unclear.

In fact, the people who will have paid most attention to the wording of a statute are the Ministers who seek to get them through Parliament, the civil servants who advise the Ministers and the draftsmen who draw up the legislation. None of these can really be said to amount to Parliament.

Statutory interpretation and case law

Once the courts have interpreted a statute, or a section of one, that interpretation becomes part of case law in just the same way as any other judicial decision, and subject to the same rules of precedent. A higher court may decide that the interpretation is wrong, and reverse the decision if it is appealed, or overrule it in a later case but, unless and until this happens, lower courts must interpret the statute in the same way.

How are statutes interpreted?

Parliament has given the courts some sources of guidance on statutory interpretation. The Interpretation Act 1978 provides certain standard definitions of common provisions, such as the rule that the singular includes the plural and 'he' includes 'she', while interpretation sections at the end of most modern Acts define some of the words used within them – the Police and Criminal Evidence Act 1984 contains such a section. A further source of help has been provided since the beginning of 1999: all Bills passed since that date are the subject of special explanatory notes, which are made public. These detail the background to the legislation and explain the effects particular provisions are intended to have.

Apart from this assistance, it has been left to the courts to decide what method to use to interpret statutes, and four basic approaches have developed, in conjunction with certain aids to interpretation.

Rules of interpretation

The literal rule

This rule gives all the words in a statute their ordinary and natural meaning, on the principle that the best way to interpret the will of Parliament is to follow the literal meaning of the words they have used. Under this rule, the literal meaning must be followed, even if the result is silly; for example, Lord Esher stated, in **R** *v* **City of London Court Judge** (1892): 'If the words of an Act are clear, you must follow them, even though they lead to a manifest absurdity. The court has nothing to do with the question of whether the legislature has committed an absurdity.'

Examples of the literal rule in use are:

Whitely *v* **Chapell** (1868) A statute aimed at preventing electoral malpractice made it an offence to impersonate 'any person entitled to vote' at an election. The accused was acquitted because he impersonated a dead person and a dead person was clearly not entitled to vote!

London and North Eastern Railway Co *v* **Berriman** (1946) A railway worker was knocked down and killed by a train, and his widow attempted to claim damages. The relevant statute provided that this was available to employees killed while engaging in 'relaying or repairing' tracks; the dead man had been doing routine maintenance and oiling, which the court held did not come within the meaning of 'relaying and repairing'.

Ess. Cases
p. 31 → **Fisher** *v* **Bell** (1961) After several violent incidents in which the weapon used was a flick-knife, Parliament decided that these knives should be banned. The Restriction of Offensive Weapons Act 1959 consequently made it an offence to 'sell or offer for sale' any flick-knife. The defendant had flick-knives in his shop window and was charged with offering these for sale. The courts held that 'offers for sale' must be given its ordinary meaning in law, and that in contract law this was not an offer for sale but only an invitation to people to make an offer to buy. The defendant was therefore not guilty of a crime under the Act, despite the fact that this was obviously just the sort of behaviour that Act was set up to prevent.

Advantages of the literal rule

It respects parliamentary sovereignty, giving the courts a restricted role and leaving law-making to those elected for the job.

Disadvantages of the literal rule

Where use of the literal rule does lead to an absurd or obviously unjust conclusion, it can hardly be said to be enacting the will of Parliament, since Parliament is unlikely to have intended absurdity and injustice. The case of **London and North Eastern Railway Co** *v* **Berriman** (above) is an example of literal interpretation creating injustice where Parliament probably never intended any – the difference in the type of work being done does not change the degree of danger to which the workers were exposed.

In addition, the literal rule is useless where the answer to a problem simply cannot be found in the words of the statute. As Hart (1994) has pointed out, some terms have a core of very clear meaning, but it may still be unclear how far that word stretches: the example above of an imaginary law banning 'vehicles' from the park clearly illustrates this. Where such a broad term is used, the answer is simply not there in the words of the statute, and the courts have to use some other method.

The Law Commission in 1969 pointed out that interpretation based only on literal meanings 'assumes unattainable perfection in draftsmanship'; even the most talented and experienced draftsmen cannot predict every situation to which legislation may have to be applied. As Ingman (1987) notes, it also expects too much of words in general, which are at best 'an imperfect means of communication'. The same word may mean different things to different people, and words also shift their meanings over time.

Zander, in his book *The Law-Making Process* (2004), describes the literal approach as 'mechanical, divorced both from the realities of the use of language and from the expectations and aspirations of the human beings concerned . . . in that sense it is irresponsible'.

In **R (on the application of Haw)** *v* **Secretary of State for the Home Department** (2006), the Court of Appeal refused to apply a literal interpretation to a new piece of legislation, as it considered that this would not reflect the intention of Parliament. The case concerned Brian Haw, who had been holding a protest in Parliament Square, opposite Parliament, against the war in Iraq since June 2001. He lived on the pavement and displayed a large number of placards protesting about Government policy in Iraq. The demonstration had earlier been held to be lawful, since it neither caused an obstruction nor gave rise to any fear that a breach of the peace might arise. The Serious Organised Crime and Police Act 2005, s. 133(1) was subsequently passed, which required any person who intended to organise a demonstration in the vicinity of Parliament to apply to the police for authorisation to do so. Section 132(1) provided that a person who carried on a demonstration in the designated area was guilty of an offence if, when the demonstration started, appropriate authorisation had not been given:

(1) Any person who –
(a) organises a demonstration in a public place in the designated area, or
(b) takes part in a demonstration in a public place in the designated area, or
(c) carries on a demonstration by himself in a public place in the designated area,
is guilty of an offence if, when the demonstration **starts**, authorisation for the demonstration has not been given under section 134(2).

Haw argued that the Act did not apply to his demonstration because it had started before the Act came into force. The Court of Appeal held that the Act did in fact apply to Haw's demonstration: 'Any other conclusion would be wholly irrational and could fairly be described as manifestly absurd.' Construing the statutory language in context, Parliament's intention was clearly to regulate all demonstrations in the designated area, whenever they began. Thus, rather than following a literal interpretation of the legislation, the courts looked at its context to determine the intention of Parliament. The court gave particular weight to the fact that the 2005 Act repealed a provision in the Public Order Act 1986. That provision had provided for controls to be placed on public demonstrations and would have applied to demonstrations which had been started since 1986. The Court of Appeal thought it was inconceivable that Parliament would have intended to repeal that power to control demonstrations started before 2005 and replace it with legislation which could only control demonstrations started after 2005, as this would leave a significant gap in the power of the state to control demonstrations.

Conditions have now been imposed on Haw's demonstration in accordance with the provisions of the 2005 Act, aimed primarily at restricting the size of the demonstration. It is accepted that Haw's demonstration in itself does not pose a security risk, but if a large number of people joined his demonstration this could be an opportunity for terrorists to join in and conceal an explosive device. Reform proposals contained in the Draft Constitutional Renewal Bill would remove the 2005 statutory restrictions on protests near Parliament.

The golden rule

This provides that if the literal rule gives an absurd result, which Parliament could not have intended, then (and only then) the judge can substitute a reasonable meaning in the light of the statute as a whole. It was defined by Lord Wensleydale in **Grey v Pearson** (1857): 'The grammatical and ordinary sense of the words is to be adhered to, unless that would lead to some absurdity, or some repugnance or inconsistency with the rest of the instrument, in which case the grammatical and ordinary sense of the words may be modified so as to avoid that absurdity and inconsistency, but no further.'

Examples of the golden rule in use are:

R v Allen (1872) Section 57 of the Offences Against the Person Act 1861 stated that 'Whosoever being married shall marry any other person during the life of the former husband or wife . . . shall be guilty of bigamy.' It was pointed out that it was impossible for a person already married to 'marry' someone else – they might go through a marriage ceremony, but would not actually be married; using the literal rule would make the statute useless. The courts therefore held that 'shall marry' should be interpreted to mean 'shall go through a marriage ceremony'.

Maddox v Storer (1963) Under the Road Traffic Act 1960, it was an offence to drive at more than 30 mph in a vehicle 'adapted to carry more than seven passengers'. The vehicle in the case was a minibus made to carry 11 passengers, rather than altered to do so, and the court held that 'adapted to' could be taken to mean 'suitable for'.

Adler v George (1964) The defendant was charged under s. 3 of the Official Secrets Act 1920, with obstructing a member of the armed forces 'in the vicinity of any prohibited place'. He argued that the natural meaning of 'in the vicinity of' meant near to, whereas the obstruction had actually occurred in the prohibited place itself, an air force station. The court held that while in many circumstances 'in the vicinity' could indeed only be interpreted as meaning near to, in this context it was reasonable to construe it as including being within the prohibited place.

Inco Europe Ltd v First Choice Distribution (2000) The House of Lords stated that words could be added to a statute by a judge to give effect to Parliament's intention where an obvious error had been made in drafting a statute.

Advantages of the golden rule

The golden rule can prevent the absurdity and injustice caused by the literal rule, and help the courts put into practice what Parliament really means.

Disadvantages of the golden rule

The Law Commission noted in 1969 that the 'rule' provided no clear meaning of an 'absurd result'. As in practice that was judged by reference to whether a particular interpretation was irreconcilable with the general policy of the legislature, the golden rule turns out to be a less explicit form of the mischief rule (discussed below).

The mischief rule

KEY CASE

The mischief rule was laid down in **Heydon's Case** in the sixteenth century, and provides that judges should consider three factors:

- what the law was before the statute was passed;
- what problem, or 'mischief', the statute was trying to remedy;
- what remedy Parliament was trying to provide.

The judge should then interpret the statute in such a way as to put a stop to the problem that Parliament was addressing.

Judges can interpret a statute so that it effectively tackles the problem that Parliament wanted to deal with: the mischief rule.

Examples of the mischief rule in use are:

Ess. Cases p. 33 → **Smith v Hughes** (1960) The Street Offences Act 1959 made it a criminal offence for a prostitute to solicit potential customers in a street or public place. In this case, the prostitute was not actually in the street, but was sitting in a house, on the first floor, and tapping on the window to attract the attention of the men walking by. The judge decided that the aim of the Act was to enable people to walk along the street without being solicited, and since the soliciting in question was aimed at people in the street, even though the prostitute was not in the street herself, the Act should be interpreted to include this activity.

Elliott v Grey (1960) The Road Traffic Act 1930 provided that it was an offence for an uninsured car to be 'used on the road'. The car in this case was on the road, but jacked up, with its battery removed, but the court held that, as it was nevertheless a hazard of the type which the statute was designed to prevent, it was covered by the phrase 'used on the road'.

Royal College of Nursing v DHSS (1981) The Abortion Act 1967 stated that terminations of pregnancy were legal only if performed by a 'registered medical practitioner'. By 1972, surgical abortions were largely being replaced by drug-induced ones, in which the second stage of the process (attaching the patient to a drip), was carried out by nurses, under the instructions of a doctor. The House of Lords ruled that the mischief which the Act sought to remedy was the uncertain state of the previous law, which drove many women to dangerous back-street abortionists. It sought to do this by widening the grounds on which abortions could be obtained, and ensuring that they were carried out with proper skill in hygienic conditions, and the procedure in question promoted this aim, and was not unlawful. It was a controversial decision, with Lords Wilberforce and Edmund Davies claiming that the House was not interpreting legislation but rewriting it.

Advantages of the mischief rule

The mischief rule helps avoid absurdity and injustice, and promotes flexibility. It was described by the Law Commission in 1969 as a 'rather more satisfactory approach' than the other two established rules.

Disadvantages of the mischief rule

Heydon's Case was the product of a time when statutes were a minor source of law, compared to the common law. Drafting was by no means as exact a process as it is today, and the supremacy of Parliament was not really established. At that time too, what statutes there were tended to include a lengthy preamble, which more or less spelt out the 'mischief' with which the Act was intended to deal. Judges of the time were very well qualified to decide what the previous law was and what problems a statute was intended to remedy, since they had usually drafted statutes on behalf of the king, and Parliament only rubber-stamped them. Such a rule may be less appropriate now that the legislative situation is so different.

The purposive approach

Historically, the preferred approach to statutory interpretation was to look for the statute's literal meaning. However, over the last three decades, the courts have accepted that the literal approach can be unsatisfactory. Instead, the judges have been increasingly influenced by the European approach to statutory interpretation which focuses on giving effect to the purpose of the legislation. During his judicial career, Lord Denning was at the forefront of moves to establish a more purposive approach, aiming to produce decisions that put into practice the spirit of the law, even if that meant paying less than usual regard to the letter of the law – the actual words of the statute. He felt that the mischief rule could be interpreted broadly, so that it would not just allow the courts to look at the history of the case, but it would also allow them to carry out the intention of Parliament, however imperfectly this might have been expressed in the words used. In reality, the purposive approach that has developed takes a more liberal approach to statutory interpretation than is traditionally associated with the mischief rule. Denning stated his views in **Magor and St Mellons Rural District Council v Newport Corporation** (1952):

> We do not sit here to pull the language of Parliament to pieces and make nonsense of it . . . we sit here to find out the intention of Parliament and carry it out, and we do this

better by filling in the gaps and making sense of the enactment than by opening it up to destructive analysis.

On appeal, the House of Lords described this approach as 'a naked usurpation of the judicial function, under the guise of interpretation . . . If a gap is disclosed, the remedy lies in an amending Act.'

In fact, over time, the House of Lords has come to accept that a purposive approach to statutory interpretation can, in certain cases, be appropriate. The move towards a purposive approach has been particularly marked in relation to the interpretation of European legislation and national legislation that is designed to implement European legislation, as the European Court of Justice (like most civil law countries) tends itself to adopt a purposive approach to statutory interpretation. Thus in **Pickstone** *v* **Freemans** (1988) the House of Lords held that it had to read words into inadequate domestic legislation in order to give effect to European legislation which was intended to tackle the problem of women being paid less than men for the same work.

But the purposive approach has not been restricted to the context of European law, and has been applied to pure domestic legislation. In **Pepper** *v* **Hart** (1993) the House of Lords stated:

> The days have long passed when the court adopted a strict constructionist view of interpretation which required them to adopt the literal meaning of the language. The courts now adopt a purposive approach which seeks to give effect to the true purpose of legislation and are prepared to look at much extraneous material that bears on the background against which the legislation was enacted.

KEY CASE

Ess. Cases
p. 35 ➡

In R (Quintavalle) *v* Secretary of State for Health (2003) the House of Lords was required to interpret the Human Fertilisation and Embryology Act 1990. Section 1 of this Act defines an embryo as 'a live human embryo where fertilisation is complete' and their use was regulated by the Human Fertilisation and Embryology Authority (HFEA). After the Act had been passed, scientists developed a cloning technique whereby embryos were not created by fertilising an egg, but by replacing the nucleus of an egg with a cell from another person. The Government had issued a statement saying that medical research involving cloned embryos did fall within the Act and could be regulated by HFEA. The pressure group, Pro-Life Alliance, was opposed to such research and sought a declaration of the courts that HFEA was acting outside its statutory powers. The House of Lords gave the Act a purposive interpretation to give effect to the intention of Parliament. It observed that under the influence of European legal culture 'the pendulum has swung towards purposive methods of construction':

> The basic task of the court is to ascertain and give effect to the true meaning of what Parliament has said in the enactment to be construed. But that is not to say that attention should be confined and a literal interpretation given to the particular provisions which give rise to difficulty . . . The court's task, within the permissible bounds of interpretation, is to give effect to Parliament's purpose. So the

Legislation can be interpreted using a purposive approach.

controversial provisions should be read in the context of the statute as a whole, and the statute as a whole should be read in the historical context of the situation which led to its enactment.

It concluded that Parliament could not have intended to exclude cloned embryos from being regulated by HFEA.

ss. Cases
p. 202

TOPICAL ISSUE

The Human Rights Act 1998

The Human Rights Act 1998 incorporates into UK law the European Convention on Human Rights, which is an international treaty signed by most democratic countries, and designed to protect basic human rights. In much of Europe, the Convention has been incorporated into national law as a Bill of Rights, which means that the courts can overrule domestic legislation which is in conflict with it. This is not the case in the UK. Instead, s. 3(1) of the Human Rights Act requires that: 'So far as it is possible to do so, primary and subordinate legislation must be read and given effect in a way which is compatible with the Convention rights.' Section 2 further requires that, in deciding any question which arises in connection with a right protected by the Convention, the courts should take into account any relevant judgments made by the European Court of Human Rights. If it is impossible to find an interpretation which is compatible with the Convention, the court concerned can make a declaration of incompatibility under s. 4 of the Act. This does not affect the validity of the statute in question, but it is designed to draw attention to the conflict so that the Government can change the law to bring it in line with the Convention (although the Act does not oblige the Government to do this). There is a special 'fast track' procedure by which a Minister can make the necessary changes.

When new legislation is being made, the relevant Bill must carry a statement from the relevant Minister, saying either that its provisions are compatible with the Convention, or that, even if they are not, the Government wishes to go ahead with the legislation anyway. In the latter case, the Government would be specifically saying that the legislation must override Convention rights if there is a clash, but clearly any Government intent on passing such legislation would be likely to face considerable opposition and so would have to have a very good reason, in the eyes of the public, for doing so.

If the courts consider that a literal interpretation of an Act would render the legislation in breach of the European Convention, under s. 3 the precise wording of the Act may in certain circumstances be ignored and the Act given an interpretation which conforms with the Convention. In **R v A** (2001) the House of Lords noted that:

> Under ordinary methods of interpretation a court may depart from the language of the statute to avoid absurd consequences: section 3 goes much further . . . In accordance with the will of Parliament as reflected in section 3 it will sometimes be necessary to adopt an interpretation which linguistically may appear strained.

This case was concerned with the prosecution of rape. Evidence of a complainant's past sexual experience is sometimes admissible as evidence in court in rape trials.

Such evidence has in the past been used to give the jury a bad impression of the victim and make it appear that she was not a credible witness – the insinuation being that a woman who has had an active sex life with men other than a husband is immoral and cannot be trusted generally. The Government was concerned that rape victims were not being adequately protected in court proceedings and legislation was passed on the matter. The Youth Justice and Criminal Evidence Act 1999, s. 41 provided that evidence of the complainant's past sexual behaviour could only be given if 'a refusal of leave might have the result of rendering unsafe a conclusion of the jury or . . . the court on any relevant issue in the case'. The clear intention of Parliament was to significantly restrict the use of past sexual history evidence in rape trials. Unfortunately, in the first case to reach the House of Lords concerning this section, the House relied on the Human Rights Act 1998 in order to ignore the clear intention of Parliament. It ruled that a defendant had to be given the opportunity to adduce evidence as to the complainant's past sexual behaviour with the defendant which had taken place over a week before the purported rape. It considered that otherwise this section would be in breach of Art. 6 of the European Convention on Human Rights guaranteeing a fair trial. The interpretation of the legislation ran contrary to Parliament's intention when it passed that Act, though it is arguable that Parliament's ultimate intention was being respected as provided for in the Human Rights Act 1998.

Ess. Cases
p. 45 →

In Ghaidan v Godin-Mendoza (2004) the House of Lords encouraged the courts to use s. 3 to interpret statutes in accordance with the European Convention. Lord Steyne noted that, at the time of the judgment, ten declarations of incompatibility had been made under s. 4, of which five had been overturned on appeal, and s. 3 had only been relied on ten times. He concluded from these statistics that s. 4 was being relied on too often, when it should only be used as a last resort, and that instead the courts should make greater use of s. 3 to interpret legislation in accordance with the Convention.

The House felt that, in the context of s. 3, the courts should be prepared to move away from the 'semantic lottery' of the words used by the draftsman and interpret the statute in the light of Convention rights:

> [O]nce it is accepted that section 3 may require legislation to bear a meaning which departs from the unambiguous meaning the legislation would otherwise bear, it becomes impossible to suppose Parliament intended that the operation of section 3 should depend critically upon the particular form of words adopted by the parliamentary draftsman in the statutory provision under consideration.

The House simply requires the courts to make sure that the meaning given to the legislation is consistent with the 'fundamental features' of the statute and the judges must avoid deciding issues calling for legislative deliberation. This potentially gives the courts considerable flexibility when relying on s. 3 to interpret a statute which risks breaching the European Convention.

The Court of Appeal went too far in Re S (2002). It attempted to interpret the Children Act 1989 by adding a new procedure requiring the local authority to contact the guardian of a child subjected to a care order in particular circumstances. The House of Lords allowed an appeal as it considered that the Court of Appeal had crossed the boundary between interpretation and amendment. The new procedure created by the Court of Appeal conflicted with a fundamental feature of the 1989 Act that judicial supervision of care orders was very restricted.

Thus, there are certain limits on the courts' powers of interpretation when applying s. 3 of the Human Rights Act 1998, but they still appear to have greater powers of interpretation in this context than when they are exercising their ordinary powers of statutory interpretation.

Interpreting European legislation

Section 2(4) of the European Communities Act 1972 provides that all parliamentary legislation (whether passed before or after the European Communities Act) must be construed and applied in accordance with European law. The case of **R** v **Secretary of State for Transport, ex parte Factortame** (1990) makes it clear that the English courts must apply European law which is directly effective even if it conflicts with English law, including statute law (these issues are discussed more fully in Chapter 5: European law).

Aids to interpretation

Whichever approach the judges take to statutory interpretation, they have at their disposal a range of material to help. Some of these aids may be found within the piece of legislation itself, or in certain rules of language commonly applied in statutory texts – these are called internal aids. Others, outside the piece of legislation, are called external aids. Since 1995, a very important new external aid has been added in the form of the

s. Cases
p. 202 → Human Rights Act 1998.

Internal aids

The literal rule and the golden rule both direct the judge to internal aids, though they are taken into account whatever the approach.

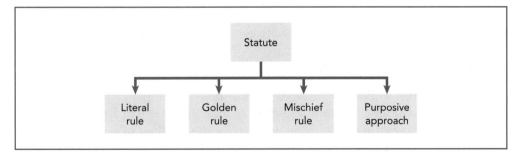

Figure 3.1 Approaches to statutory interpretation

The statute itself

To decide what a provision of the Act means the judge may draw a comparison with provisions elsewhere in the statute. Clues may also be provided by the long title of the Act or the subheadings within it.

Explanatory notes

Acts passed since the beginning of 1999 are provided with explanatory notes, published at the same time as the Act.

Rules of language

Developed by lawyers over time, these rules are really little more than common sense, despite their intimidating names. As with the rules of interpretation, they are not always precisely applied. Examples include:

Ejusdem generis General words which follow specific ones are taken to include only things of the same kind. For example, if an Act used the phrase 'dogs, cats and other animals' the phrase 'and other animals' would probably include other domestic animals, but not wild ones.

Expressio unius est exclusio alterius Express mention of one thing implies the exclusion of another. If an Act specifically mentioned 'Persian cats', the term would not include other breeds of cat.

Noscitur a sociis A word draws meaning from the other words around it. If a statute mentioned 'cat baskets, toy mice and food', it would be reasonable to assume that 'food' meant cat food, and dog food was not covered by the relevant provision.

Presumptions

The courts assume that certain points are implied in all legislation. These presumptions include the following:

- statutes do not change the common law;
- the legislature does not intend to remove any matters from the jurisdiction of the courts;
- existing rights are not to be interfered with;
- laws which create crimes should be interpreted in favour of the citizen where there is ambiguity;
- legislation does not operate retrospectively: its provisions operate from the day it comes into force, and are not backdated;
- statutes do not affect the Monarch.

It is always open to Parliament to go against these presumptions if it sees fit – for example, the European Communities Act 1972 makes it clear that some of its provisions are to be applied retrospectively. But, unless the wording of a statute makes it absolutely clear that Parliament has chosen to go against one or more of the presumptions, the courts can assume that the presumptions apply.

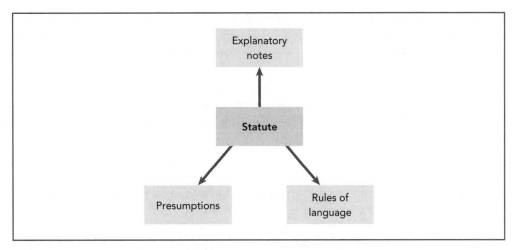

Figure 3.2 Internal aids to interpretation

Some indication of the weight which judges feel should be attached to presumptions can be seen in the case of **L'Office Cherifien des Phosphates Unitramp SA** *v* **Yamashita-Shinnihon Steamship Co Ltd** (*The Boucraa*) (1994), which concerned the presumption against retrospective effect. The House of Lords stated that the important issue was 'simple fairness': if they read the relevant statute as imposing the suggested degree of retrospective effect, would the result be so unfair that Parliament could not have intended it, even though their words might suggest retrospective effect? This could be judged by balancing a number of factors, including the nature of the rights affected, the clarity of the words used and the background to the legislation.

What remains unclear is how judges decide between different presumptions if they conflict, and why certain values are selected for protection by presumptions, and not others. For example, the presumption that existing rights are not to be interfered with serves to protect the existing property or money of individuals, but there is no presumption in favour of people claiming state benefits.

External aids

The mischief rule directs the judge to external aids, including the following:

Historical setting

A judge may consider the historical setting of the provision that is being interpreted, as well as other statutes dealing with the same subjects.

Dictionaries and textbooks

These may be consulted to find the meaning of a word, or to gather information about the views of legal academics on a point of law.

Reports

Legislation may be preceded by a report of a Royal Commission, the Law Commission or some other official advisory committee (see p. 136). The House of Lords stated in

Black Clawson International Ltd *v* **Papierwerke Waldhof-Aschaffenburg AG** (1975) that official reports may be considered as evidence of the pre-existing state of the law and the mischief that the legislation was intended to deal with.

Treaties

Treaties and international conventions can be considered when following the presumption that Parliament does not legislate in such a way that the UK would be in breach of its international obligations.

Previous practice

General practice and commercial usage in the field covered by the legislation may shed light on the meaning of a statutory term.

Hansard

This is the official daily report of parliamentary debates, and therefore a record of what was said during the introduction of legislation. For over 100 years, the judiciary held that such documents could not be consulted for the purpose of statutory interpretation. During his career, Lord Denning made strenuous efforts to do away with this rule and, in **Davis** *v* **Johnson** (1978), justified his interpretation of the Domestic Violence and Matrimonial Proceedings Act 1976 by reference to the parliamentary debates during its introduction. The House of Lords however rebuked him for doing so, and maintained that the rule should stand.

KEY CASE

Ess. Cases
p. 40 →

In 1993, the case of **Pepper** *v* **Hart** overturned the rule against consulting *Hansard*, and such consultation is clearly now allowed. The case was between teachers at a fee-paying school (Malvern College) and the Inland Revenue, and concerned the tax which employees should have to pay on perks (benefits related to their job). Malvern College allowed its teachers to send their

> When interpreting a statute the courts can consult *Hansard* to see what a Minister had said about a piece of legislation in order to decide what Parliament had intended.

sons there for one-fifth of the usual fee, if places were available. Tax law requires employees to pay tax on perks, and the amount of tax is based on the cost to the employer of providing the benefit, which is usually taken to mean any extra cost that the employer would not otherwise incur. The amount paid by Malvern teachers for their sons' places covered the extra cost to the school of having the child there (in books, food and so on), but did not cover the school's fixed costs, for paying teachers, maintaining buildings and so on, which would have been the same whether the teachers' children were there or not. Therefore the perk cost the school little or nothing, and so the teachers maintained that they should not have to pay tax on it. The Inland Revenue disagreed, arguing that the perk should be taxed on the basis of the amount it saved the teachers on the real cost of sending their children to the school.

The reason why the issue of consulting parliamentary debates arose was that, during the passing of the Finance Act 1976 which laid down the tax rules in question, the then Secretary to the Treasury, Robert Sheldon, had specifically mentioned the kind of situation that arose in **Pepper v Hart**. He had stated that where the cost to an employer of a perk was minimal, employees should not have to pay tax on the full cost of it. The question was, could the judges take into account what the Minister had said? The House of Lords convened a special court of seven judges, which decided that they could look at *Hansard* to see what the Minister had said, and that his remarks could be used to decide what Parliament had intended.

The decision in **Pepper v Hart** was confirmed in **Three Rivers District Council v Bank of England (No. 2) (1996)**, which concerned the correct interpretation of legislation passed in order to fulfil obligations arising from an EC directive. Although the legislation was not itself ambiguous, the claimants claimed that, if interpreted in the light of the information contained in *Hansard*, the legislation imposed certain duties on the defendants, which were not obvious from the legislation itself. The defendants argued that *Hansard* could only be consulted where legislation contained ambiguity, but the court disagreed, stating that where legislation was passed in order to give effect to international obligations, it was important to make sure that it did so, and consulting legislative materials was one way of helping to ensure this. The result would appear to be that *Hansard* can be consulted not just to explain ambiguous phrases, but to throw light on the general purpose of legislation.

In **R v Secretary of State for the Environment, Transport and the Regions, ex parte Spath Holme Ltd** (2001), the House of Lords gave a restrictive interpretation of the application of **Pepper v Hart**. The applicant was a company that was the landlord of certain properties. It sought judicial review of the Rent Acts (Maximum Fair Rent) Order 1999, made by the Secretary of State under s. 31 of the Landlord and Tenant Act 1985. The applicant company contended that the 1999 Order was unlawful as the Secretary of State had made it to alleviate the impact of rent increases on certain categories of tenants, when a reading of *Hansard* showed that Parliament's intention was that such orders would only be made to reduce the impact of inflation. On the use of *Hansard* to interpret the intention of Parliament, the House of Lords pointed out that the case of **Pepper v Hart** was concerned with the meaning of an expression used in a statute ('the cost of a benefit'). The Minister had given a statement on the meaning of that expression. By contrast, the present case was concerned with a matter of policy, and in particular the meaning of a statutory power rather than a statutory expression. Only if a Minister were, improbably, to give a categorical assurance to Parliament that a power would not be used in a given situation would a parliamentary statement on the scope of a power be admissible.

KEY CASE

ss. Cases
p. 40 →

In Wilson v Secretary of State for Trade and Industry (2003) the House of Lords again gave a restrictive interpretation to **Pepper v Hart**. It held that only statements in *Hansard* made by a Minister or other promoter of legislation could be looked at by the court; other statements recorded in *Hansard* had to be ignored.

When interpreting a statute, only statements in *Hansard* made by a Minister or other promoter of legislation can be looked at by the court.

Under the British constitution, Parliament and the courts have separate roles. Parliament enacts legislation, the courts interpret and apply it. Due to the principle of the separation of powers (see p. 3), neither institution should stray into the other's domain. Thus, Art. 9 of the Bill of Rights 1689 provides that 'the freedom of speech and debates or proceedings in Parliament ought not to be impeached or questioned in any court or place out of Parliament'. In **Wilson v Secretary of State for Trade and Industry**, the House of Lords emphasised the importance of the courts not straying into Parliament's constitutional role. It concluded from this that *Hansard* could only be used to interpret the meaning of words in legislation; it could not be used to discover the reasons for the legislation. The Court of Appeal in **Wilson** had used *Hansard* to look at the parliamentary debates concerning a particular Act. It was not trying to discover the meaning of words, as their meaning was not in doubt, but to discover the reason which led Parliament to think that it was necessary to pass the Act. The House of Lords held that the Court of Appeal had been wrong to do this. Referring to *Hansard* simply to check the meaning of enacted words supported the principle of parliamentary sovereignty (see p. 3). Referring to *Hansard* to discover the reasoning of Parliament, where there was no ambiguity as to the meaning of the words, would go against the sovereignty of Parliament.

The Human Rights Act 1998 requires the courts to exercise a new role in respect of Acts of Parliament. This new role is fundamentally different from interpreting and applying legislation. The courts are now required to determine whether the legislation violates a right laid down in the European Convention on Human Rights. If the Act does violate the Convention, the courts have to issue a declaration of incompatibility. In order to determine this question, the House of Lords stated in **Wilson** that the courts can only refer to *Hansard* for background information, such as the social policy aim of the Act. Poor reasoning in the course of parliamentary debate was not a matter which could count against the legislation when determining the question of compatibility.

Although it is now clear that *Hansard* can be referred to in order to find evidence of parliamentary intention, there is still much debate as to how useful it is, and whether it can provide good evidence of what Parliament intended. The following three sub-sections cover some of the arguments for use of this source.

Usefulness

Lord Denning's argument, advanced in **Davis v Johnson** (1978), was that to ignore it would be to 'grope in the dark for the meaning of an Act without switching on the light'. When such an obvious source of enlightenment was available, it was ridiculous to ignore it – in fact Lord Denning said after the case that he intended to continue to consult *Hansard*, but simply not say he was doing so.

Other jurisdictions

Legislative materials are used in many foreign jurisdictions, including many other European countries and the US. In such countries, these materials tend to be more accessible and concise than *Hansard* – it is difficult to judge whether they are consulted because of this quality, or whether the fact that they are consulted has encouraged those who produce them to make them more readable. It is argued that the latter might be a useful side-effect of allowing the judges to consult parliamentary materials.

Media reports

Parliamentary proceedings are reported in newspapers and on radio and television. Since judges are as exposed to these as anyone else, it seems ridiculous to blinker themselves in court, or to pretend that they are blinkered.

The arguments against the use of this source are detailed in the next three subsections.

Lack of clarity

The House of Lords, admonishing Lord Denning for his behaviour in **Davis** *v* **Johnson**, and directing that parliamentary debates were not to be consulted, stated that the evidence provided by the parliamentary debates might not be reliable; what was said in the cut and thrust of public debate was not 'conducive to a clear and unbiased explanation of the meaning of statutory language'.

Time and expense

Their Lordships also suggested that, if debates were to be used, there was a danger that the lawyers arguing a case would devote too much time and attention to ministerial statements and so on, at the expense of considering the language used in the Act itself.

> It would add greatly to the time and expense involved in preparing cases involving the construction of a statute if counsel were expected to read all the debates in *Hansard*, and it would often be impracticable for counsel to get access to at least the older reports of debates in select committees in the House of Commons; moreover, in a very large proportion of cases such a search, even if practicable, would throw no light on the question before the court . . .

This criticism of the use of *Hansard* was highlighted by Lord Steyn, a judge in the House of Lords, in his article 'Pepper v Hart: A Re-examination' (2001). He suggests that much of the work of the appellate courts is now concerned with the interpretation of documents, such as statutes, rather than the examination of precedents.

Parliamentary intention

The nature of parliamentary intention is difficult, if not impossible, to pin down. Parliamentary debates usually reveal the views of only a few members and, even then, those words may need interpretation too.

Lord Steyn (2001) criticised the way the use of *Hansard* in **Pepper** *v* **Hart** gives pre-eminence to the Government Minister's interpretation of the statute and ignores any dissenting voices by opposition MPs. The Minister only spoke in the House of Commons and the detail of what he said was unlikely to have been known by the House of Lords. He therefore queries how the Minister's statement can be said to reflect the intention of Parliament, which is made up of both Houses. He points to the nature of the parliamentary process:

> The relevant exchanges sometimes take place late at night in nearly empty chambers. Sometimes it is a party political debate with whips on. The questions are often difficult

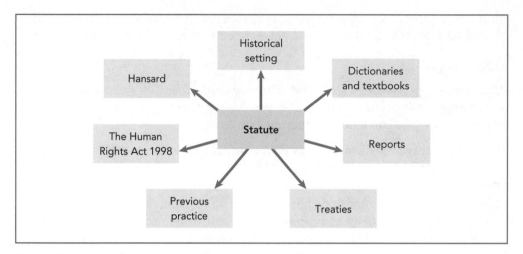

Figure 3.3 External aids to interpretation

but political warfare sometimes leaves little time for reflection. These are not ideal conditions for the making of authoritative statements about the meaning of a clause in a Bill. In truth a Minister speaks for the Government and not for Parliament. The statements of a Minister are no more than indications of what the Government would like the law to be. In any event, it is not discoverable from the printed record whether individual members of the legislature, let alone a plurality in each chamber, understood and accepted a ministerial explanation of the suggested meaning of the words.

This criticism has been partly tackled by the House of Lords in **Wilson** *v* **Secretary of State for Trade and Industry** (2003). The House stated that the courts must be careful not to treat the ministerial statement as indicative of the intention of Parliament:

Nor should the courts give a ministerial statement, whether made inside or outside Parliament, determinative weight. It should not be supposed that members necessarily agreed with the Minister's reasoning or his conclusions.

The House emphasised that the will of Parliament is expressed in the language used in its enactments.

How do judges really interpret statutes?

This question has much in common with the discussion of case law and the operation of precedent (p. 23); in both cases, discussion of rules conceals a certain amount of flexibility. The so-called 'rules of interpretation' are not rules at all, but different approaches. Judges do not methodically apply these rules to every case and, in any case, the fact that they can conflict with each other and produce different results necessarily implies some choice as to which is used. There is choice too in the relative weight given to internal and external aids, and rules of language, and approaches have varied over the years.

Just as with judicial precedent, the idea that statutory interpretation is an almost scientific process that can be used to produce a single right answer is simply nonsense. There is frequently room for more than one interpretation (otherwise the question would never reach the courts) and judges must choose between them. For clear evidence of this, there is no better example than the litigation concerning Augusto Pinochet, the former head of state of Chile. He had long been accused of crimes against humanity, including torture and murder and conspiracy to torture and to murder. When he made a visit to the UK, the Spanish Government requested that he should be extradited to Spain so that they could put him on trial. This led to protracted litigation concerning whether it was legal for Britain to extradite him to Spain, and eventually the question came before the House of Lords. Pinochet's defence argued on the basis of the State Immunity Act 1978, which gives other states immunity from prosecution in English courts; the Act provides that 'states' includes heads of state. The Lords were therefore asked to decide whether this immunity extended to Pinochet's involvement in the acts he was accused of and, by a majority of three to two, they decided that it did not. Yet when the appeal was reopened (because one of the judges, Lord Hoffmann, was found to have links with Amnesty International, who were a party to the case), this time with seven Law Lords sitting, a different decision was reached. Although the Lords still stated that the General did not have complete immunity, by a majority of six to one, they restricted his liability to those acts which were committed after 1978, when torture committed outside the UK became a crime in the UK. This gave General Pinochet immunity for the vast majority of the torture allegations, and complete immunity for the allegations of murder and conspiracy to murder.

The reasoning behind both the decisions is complex and does not really need to concern us here; the important point to note is that in both hearings the Lords were interpreting the same statutory provisions, yet they came up with significantly different verdicts. Because of the way it was reopened, the case gives us a rare insight into just how imprecise and unpredictable statutory interpretation can be, and it is hard to resist the implication that if you put any other case involving statutory interpretation before two separate panels of judges, they might well come up with different judgments too.

Given then that judges do have some freedom over questions of statutory interpretation, what influences the decisions they make? As with case law, there are a number of theories.

Dworkin: fitting in with principles

Dworkin (1986) claims that, in approaching a case, the job of judges is to develop a theory about how the particular measure they are dealing with fits with the rest of the law as a whole. If there are two possible interpretations of a word or phrase, the judge should favour the one that allows the provision to sit most comfortably with the purpose of the rest of the law and with the principles and ideals of law and legality in general. This should be done, not for any mechanical reason, but because a body of law which is coherent and unified is, just for that reason, a body of law more entitled to the respect and allegiance of its citizens.

Cross: a contextual approach

Sir Rupert Cross (1995) suggests that the courts take a 'contextual' approach in which, rather than choosing between different rules, they conduct a progressive analysis, considering first the ordinary meaning of the words in the context of the statute (taking a broad view of context), and then moving on to consider other possibilities if this provides an absurd result. Cross suggests that the courts can read in words that are necessarily implied, and have a limited power to add to, alter or ignore words that would otherwise make a provision unintelligible, absurd, totally unreasonable, unworkable or completely inconsistent with the rest of the Act.

Willis: the just result

John Willis's influential article 'Statute Interpretation in a Nutshell' (1938) was cynical about the use of the three 'rules'. He points out that a statute is often capable of several different interpretations, each in line with one of the rules. Despite the emphasis placed on literal interpretation, Willis suggests that the courts view all three rules as equally valid. He claims they use whichever rule will produce the result that they themselves believe to be just.

Griffith: political choices

As with case law (see p. 23), Griffith (1997) claims that, where there is ambiguity, the judiciary choose the interpretation that best suits their view of policy. An example of this was the 'Fares Fair' case, **Bromley London Borough Council v Greater London Council** (1983). The Labour-controlled GLC had enacted a policy – which was part of their election manifesto – to lower the cost of public transport in London, by subsidising it from the money paid in rates (what we now call Council Tax). This meant higher rates. Conservative-controlled Bromley Council challenged the GLC's right to do this.

The powers of local authorities (which then included the GLC) are defined entirely by statute, and there is an assumption that if a power has not been granted to a local authority by Parliament, then it is not a power the authority is entitled to exercise. The judges' job then was to discover what powers Parliament had granted the GLC, and to determine whether their action on fares and rates was within those powers.

Section 1 of the Transport (London) Act 1969 stated: 'It shall be the general duty of the Greater London Council to develop policies, and to encourage, organise and where appropriate, carry out measures which will promote the provision of integrated, efficient and economic transport facilities and services in Greater London.' The key word here was 'economic', with each side taking a different view of its meaning.

The GLC said 'economic' meant 'cost-effective', in other words, giving good value for money. They stated that good value covered any of the policy goals that transport services could promote: efficient movement of passengers, reduction of pollution and congestion, possibly even social redistribution. Bromley Council, on the other hand, said that 'economic' meant 'breaking even': covering the expenses of its operation out of the fares charged to the passengers and not requiring a subsidy.

It is not difficult to see that both sides had a point – the word 'economic' could cover either meaning, making the literal rule more or less useless. Because of this, Lord Scarman refused to consult a dictionary, stating that: 'The dictionary may tell us the several meanings the word can have but the word will always take its specific meaning (or meanings) from its surroundings.' Lord Scarman stressed that those surroundings meant not just the statute as a whole, but also the general duties of the GLC to rate-payers; that duty must co-exist with the duty to the users of public transport.

Lord Scarman concluded:

'Economic' in s. 1 must, therefore, be construed widely enough to embrace both duties. Accordingly, I conclude that in s. 1(1) of the Act 'economic' covers not only the require-ment that transport services be cost-effective but also the requirement that they be provided so as to avoid or diminish the burden on the ratepayers so far as it is practicable to do so.

Griffith has argued that the idea of a 'duty' to ratepayers as explained in the case is entirely judge-made, and that the Law Lords' ruling that the interests of transport users had been preferred over those of ratepayers is interfering with the role of elected authorities. He suggests that 'public expenditure can always be criticised on the ground that it is excessive or wrongly directed', but that it is the role of elected bodies to make such decisions, and if the public does not like them 'the remedy lies in their hands at the next election'.

It is certainly odd that when the judges make so much play of the fact that Parliament should legislate because it is elected and accountable, they do not con-sider themselves bound to respect decisions made in fulfilment of an elected body's manifesto. What the Lords were doing, argues Griffith, was making a choice between two interpretations, based not on any real sense of what Parliament intended, but 'primarily [on] the Law Lords' strong preference for the principles of the market economy with a dislike of heavy subsidisation for social purposes' – in other words a political choice.

The judiciary would argue against this proposition, but it is certainly difficult to see where any of the 'rules of interpretation' fitted into this case: none of the rules of interpretation or the aids to interpretation forced the judges to favour Bromley Council's interpretation of the law over that of the GLC. They could have chosen either interpretation and still been within the law, so that choice must have been based on something other than the law.

Reform of statutory interpretation

The problems with statutory interpretation have been recognised for decades but, despite several important reports, little has changed. The Law Commission examined the interpretation of statutes in 1967 and had 'little hesitation in suggesting that this is a field not suitable for codification'. Instead, it proposed certain improvements within the present system.

3

Statutory interpretation

- More liberal use should be made of internal and external aids.
- In the event of ambiguity, the construction which best promoted the 'general legislative purpose' should be adopted. This could be seen as supporting Denning's approach.

The Renton Committee on the Preparation of Legislation produced its report in 1975, making many proposals for improving the procedure for making and drafting statutes, including the following:

- Acts could begin with a statement of purpose in the same way that older statutes used to have preambles.
- There should be a move towards including less detail in the legislation, introducing the simpler style used in countries such as France.
- More use could be made in statutes of examples showing the courts how an Act was intended to work in particular situations.
- Long, un-paragraphed sentences should be avoided.
- Statutes should be arranged to suit the convenience of the ultimate users.
- There should be more consolidation of legislation.

In 1978, Sir David Renton, in a speech entitled 'Failure to Implement the Renton Report' noted that there had been a small increase in the number of draftsmen and increased momentum in the consolidation process, but that Parliament had continued to pass a huge amount of legislation, with no reduction in the amount of detail and scarcely any use of statements of purpose. Fifteen years later, in 1992, a Commission appointed by the *Hansard* Society for Parliamentary Government reported that little had changed. Having consulted widely, it concluded that there was widespread dissatisfaction with the situation, and suggested that the drafting style adopted should be appropriate for the main end users of legislation, with the emphasis on clarity, simplicity and certainty. There should be some means of informing citizens, lawyers and the courts about the general purpose behind a particular piece of legislation, and unnecessary detail should be avoided. The Commission suggested that an increase in the number of draftsmen might be necessary to achieve these aims: since its report, four more draftsmen have been recruited, but otherwise there was little response from the previous Government. The current Government, however, has placed a high priority on making the workings of law and government accessible to ordinary people, and the introduction of explanatory notes to Bills passed from 1999 is an important step forward.

Answering questions

1 **Using appropriate examples, explain three judicial rules of statutory interpretation.**

The three traditional rules of statutory interpretation are the literal rule, the golden rule and the mischief rule. The literal rule gives the words of a piece of legislation their ordinary and natural meaning. Thus, in **Whitely v Chappell** the accused was acquitted of impersonating a person entitled to vote as he had impersonated a person who was dead and therefore not so entitled.

In **Fisher** v **Bell**, the offence of **offering** for sale was not committed where there had been merely an invitation to treat.

The golden rule applies where the literal rule produces an absurd result, and allows for the modification of words to avoid that absurdity but no further. Thus in **R** v **Allen** the supposed offence of marrying when already married was in fact impossible, and so the courts interpreted 'shall marry' to mean 'shall go through a marriage ceremony'.

The mischief rule was established in **Heydon's Case** and provides that the judges should look at the law before the statute was passed, look at the mischief it was trying to remedy and look at the remedy Parliament provided. Thus, in **Elliott** v **Grey**, the offence of an uninsured car being 'used on the road' was committed even when it was jacked up as it did create a hazard.

2 The four approaches to statutory interpretation are so inconsistent with each other that a different result could be reached in the same case if the judges simply followed a different approach. Discuss.

A starting point would be to set out, briefly, the requirements/meaning of the four approaches. Then, in order to discuss the comment directly, you could take a number of case examples, such as **Royal College of Nursing** v **DHSS** (1981) (p. 58); **Smith** v **Hughes** (1960) (p. 58); and **Berriman** (1946) (p. 55) and apply each of the four approaches to the disputed words in each case. This would clearly demonstrate how a different result could be reached depending on the approach taken.

You could close by expressing a preference for one of the approaches and explain why you prefer this approach – for example, if you thought the purposive approach was preferable, this might be because it does try to give effect to parliamentary intention and it responds to events not foreseen when the legislation was produced.

3 Why do judges sometimes refer to *Hansard*?

Your essay could start by observing that the application of the three traditional rules of statutory interpretation – the literal rule, the golden rule and the mischief rule – may not provide a clear answer as to the meaning of a piece of legislation. Moreover, despite the extensive use of both internal and external aids to statutory interpretation, the meaning of a term or phrase may continue to remain unclear.

In **Davis** v **Johnson**, the House of Lords rejected Lord Denning's attempts to use *Hansard* to aid statutory interpretation; but later in **Pepper** v **Hart** the House of Lords accepted that reference to *Hansard* could be made. This was later confirmed by their Lordships' opinions in **Three Rivers District Council** v **Bank of England**. However, in **Wilson** v **SS Trade and Industry**, the Law Lords emphasised that *Hansard* could only be looked at to consider statements made by a Minister or the promoter of a Bill.

You could conclude by noting that the need to refer to *Hansard* to interpret statutes would be reduced if legislation was clearly drafted so that the aims of its promoters could be clear to the courts without the need to look at parliamentary debates.

Summary of Chapter 3: Statutory interpretation

Parliamentary intention
In interpreting statutes the courts are looking for the intention of Parliament, but this intention is frequently difficult to find.

Rules of statutory interpretation
There are four approaches to statutory interpretation:

- the literal rule;
- the golden rule;
- the mischief rule; and
- the purposive approach.

Human Rights Act 1998
Under s. 3 of the 1998 Act the courts are required to read legislation in a way that is compatible with Convention rights.

Interpreting European legislation
Under s. 2(4) of the European Communities Act 1972, all parliamentary legislation must be construed in accordance with European law.

Internal aids to statutory interpretation
Internal aids consist of the statute itself and rules of language.

External aids to statutory interpretation
These include:

- dictionaries and textbooks;
- the explanatory notes;
- reports that preceded the legislation;
- treaties; and
- *Hansard*, following the decision of **Pepper v Hart**.

How do judges really interpret statutes?
Different academics have put forward arguments as to how judges really interpret statutes. John Willis argues that the courts use whichever rule will produce the result that they themselves believe to be just. Griffith thinks that judges interpret statutes in a way that coincides with their political preferences, referring to the case of **Bromley London Borough Council v Greater London Council** to support his arguments.

Reform of statutory interpretation
The Renton Committee on the Preparation of Legislation in 1975 recommended reforms of the procedure for making and drafting statutes, but little has changed.

 ### Reading list

Bennion, F.A.R. (2005) *Statutory Interpretation*, London: Butterworths.

Bennion, F.A.R. (2007) 'Executive estoppel: *Pepper v Hart* revisited', *Public Law* (2007) Spring 1.

Cross, Sir R. (1995) *Statutory Interpretation*, Bell, J. and Engle, G. (eds), London: Butterworths.

Manchester, C., Salter, D., and Moodie, P. (2000) *Exploring the Law: The Dynamics of Precedent and Statutory Interpretation* (2nd edn), London: Sweet & Maxwell.

Steyn, J. (2001) 'Pepper v Hart: A Re-examination', *Oxford Journal of Legal Studies* 59.

Willis, J. (1938) 'Statute interpretation in a nutshell', 16 *Canadian Bar Review* 1.

Reading on the Internet

Hansard is available at:

http://www.publications.parliament.uk/pa/pahansard.htm

Visit **www.mylawchamber.co.uk/ElliottELS** to access multiple-choice questions, flashcards and practice exam questions to test yourself on this chapter.

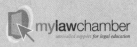

3

Statutory interpretation

4

Delegated legislation

This chapter discusses:

- the three forms of delegated legislation;
- why delegated legislation is necessary;
- how delegated legislation is controlled; and
- criticism made of delegated legislation.

Introduction

In many cases, the statutes passed by Parliament lay down a basic framework of the law, with creation of the detailed rules delegated to Government departments, local authorities, or public or nationalised bodies. There are three main forms of delegated legislation:

Statutory instruments These are made by Government departments.

Bye-laws These are made by local authorities, public and nationalised bodies. Bye-laws have to be approved by central Government.

Orders in Council These are made by Government in times of emergency. They are drafted by the relevant Government department, approved by the Privy Council and signed by the Queen.

On an everyday basis, delegated legislation is an extremely important source of law. The output of delegated legislation far exceeds that of Acts of Parliament, and its provisions include rules that can substantially affect the day-to-day lives of huge numbers of people – safety laws for industry, road traffic regulations and rules relating to state education, for example.

The power to make delegated legislation

Ordinary members of the public cannot decide on a whim to make delegated legislation. Instead, usually an Act of Parliament is required, known as an enabling Act, which gives this power to a branch of the state. The Act can be quite specific, giving a limited power to make legislation on a very narrow issue, or it can be quite general and allow for a wide range of delegated legislation to be made. An example of such a general provision is the European Communities Act 1972, s. 2, which allows the executive to make delegated legislation to bring into force in the UK relevant European legislation. Local authorities have been given a general power to make bye-laws under s. 235 of the Local Government Act 1972. Recent years have seen a move towards centralised government and therefore a reduced role for bye-laws. The current Government, however, has been favouring the use of local bye-laws to strengthen community involvement in regulating behaviour in their local areas. To facilitate the use of bye-laws the Local Government and Public Involvement in Health Act 2007 has been passed containing provisions for a faster legislative process for some bye-laws.

Ess. Cases p. 53 →

TOPICAL ISSUE

An attack on democracy?

Parliament has recently passed an Act which gives the executive very wide powers to make delegated legislation, the Legislative and Regulatory Reform Act 2006. This Act was introduced following a report of the Better Regulation Task Force, *Regulation – Less is More* (2005). The official aim of the Act is to make it simpler and faster to

Ess. Cases p. 55 →

4

Delegated legislation

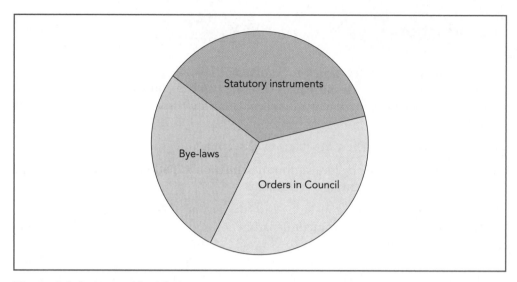

Figure 4.1 Delegated legislation

amend existing legislation. It allows Ministers to issue statutory instruments to amend legislation or implement recommendations of the Law Commission (with the possibility of some changes being added by the Government). No vote in Parliament would be required, though the statutory instrument could be blocked by a new parliamentary committee. The first draft of the Bill was severely criticised by a panel of MPs for giving excessive powers to make delegated legislation which were disproportionate to the Bill's stated aims. In the light of these criticisms some amendments were made, but concerns remain that this is an unnecessary shift of power from a democratically elected Parliament, to the executive. The director of the pressure group JUSTICE has commented:

> In its original form, the Bill went well beyond what the Government says it wanted and was one of the most appallingly drafted Bills I've ever seen. It was just amazingly wide. Either that was the Government's intention, in which case they really were trying to accumulate a major increase in power, or it wasn't, in which case it's pretty incompetent.

Why is delegated legislation necessary?

Delegated legislation is necessary for a number of reasons:

Insufficient parliamentary time Parliament does not have the time to debate every detailed rule necessary for efficient government.

Speed It allows rules to be made more quickly than they could by Parliament. Parliament does not sit all the time, and its procedure is slow and cumbersome; delegated legislation often has to be made in response to emergencies and urgent problems.

Technicality of the subject matter Modern legislation often needs to include detailed, technical provisions – those in building regulations or safety at work rules for example. MPs do not usually have the technical knowledge required, whereas delegated legislation can use experts who are familiar with the relevant areas.

Need for local knowledge Local bye-laws in particular can only be made effectively with awareness of the locality. Recognition of the importance of local knowledge can be found with the devolved assemblies for Scotland, Wales and Northern Ireland. These democratic bodies have important powers to make delegated legislation.

Flexibility Statutes require cumbersome procedures for enactment, and can only be revoked or amended by another statute. Delegated legislation, however, can be put into action quickly, and easily revoked if it proves problematic.

Future needs Parliament cannot hope to foresee every problem that might arise as a result of a statute, especially concerning areas such as health provision or welfare benefits. Delegated legislation can be put in place as and when such problems arise.

Control of delegated legislation

Because it is not directly made by elected representatives, delegated legislation is subject to the following range of controls, designed to ensure that the power delegated is not abused.

Consultation

Those who make delegated legislation often consult experts within the relevant field, and those bodies which are likely to be affected by it. In the case of road traffic regulations, for example, Ministers are likely to seek the advice of police, motoring organisations, vehicle manufacturers and local authorities before making the rules. Often the relevant statute makes such consultation obligatory and names the bodies which should be consulted. Under the National Insurance Act 1946, for example, draft regulations must be submitted to the National Insurance Advisory Committee. In other cases there may be a general statutory requirement for 'such consultation as the minister thinks appropriate with such organisations as appear to him to represent the interest concerned'.

Publication

All delegated legislation is published, and therefore available for public scrutiny. Alongside the statutory instrument, the Government now publishes an explanatory memorandum detailing the statutory instrument's policy objective and legislative context. The importance of publishing legislation was emphasised in a European case

4

Delegated legislation

in 2009. A man had been prevented from getting on a plane with a tennis racket as hand luggage. The airline had pointed to some European regulations that prohibited certain articles from being taken on board the plane for security reasons. The relevant items were listed in an appendix which had been published but when the appendix was amended the amended version was not published. The passenger claimed that the amended regulations could not be enforced against him because they had never been published. This argument was accepted by the court because governments should not be allowed to pass secret legislation; the public should be able to ascertain the scope of their rights and obligations under the law.

Supervision by Parliament

There are a number of ways in which Parliament can oversee delegated legislation.

Revocation

Parliamentary sovereignty means that Parliament can at any time revoke a piece of delegated legislation itself, or pass legislation on the same subject as the delegated legislation.

The affirmative resolution procedure

Enabling Acts dealing with subjects of special, often constitutional, importance may require Parliament to vote its approval of the delegated legislation. This is called the affirmative resolution procedure, whereby delegated legislation is laid before one or both Houses (sometimes in draft), and becomes law only if a motion approving it is passed within a specified time (usually 28 or 40 days). Since a vote has to be taken, the procedure means that the Government must find parliamentary time for debate, and opposition parties have an opportunity to raise any objections. In practice, though, it is very rare for the Government not to achieve a majority when such votes are taken.

The negative resolution procedure

Much delegated legislation is put before Parliament for MPs under the negative resolution procedure. Within a specified time (usually 40 days), any member may put down a motion to annul it. An annulment motion put down by a backbencher is not guaranteed to be dealt with, but one put down by the Official Opposition (the party with the second largest number of MPs) usually will be. If, after debate, either House passes an annulment motion, the delegated legislation is cancelled.

Committee supervision

Several parliamentary committees monitor new delegated legislation. The Joint Committee on Statutory Instruments watches over the making of delegated legislation and reports to each House on any delegated legislation which requires special consideration, including any regulations made under an Act that prohibit challenge by the courts, or which seem to make unusual or unexpected use of the powers granted by the enabling Act. However, the Committee may not consider the merits of any piece of delegated legislation. This is the responsibility of the House of Lords' Merits of Statutory Instruments Committee. In addition, the House of Lords' Select Committee on Delegated Powers and Deregulation looks at the extent of legislative powers proposed to be delegated by Parliament to Government Ministers. It is required to report on whether the provision of any Bill inappropriately delegates legislative power, or subjects the exercise of legislative power to an inappropriate level of parliamentary scrutiny.

Questions from MPs

MPs can ask Ministers questions about delegated legislation at a ministerial question time, or raise them in debates.

The House of Lords

Although the House of Lords cannot veto proposed Acts, the same does not apply to delegated legislation. In 1968 the House of Lords rejected an order imposing sanctions against the Rhodesian Government made under the Southern Rhodesia Act 1965.

Control by the courts: judicial review

While the validity of a statute can never be challenged by the courts because of parliamentary sovereignty, delegated legislation can. It may be challenged on any of the following grounds under the procedure for judicial review.

Procedural *ultra vires*

Here the complainant claims that the procedures laid down in the enabling Act for producing delegated legislation have not been followed. In **Agricultural, Horticultural and Forestry Industry Training Board** *v* **Aylesbury Mushrooms Ltd** (1972), an order was declared invalid because the requirement to consult with interested parties before making it had not been properly complied with.

Substantive *ultra vires*

This is usually based on a claim that the measure under review goes beyond the powers Parliament granted under the enabling Act. In **Customs and Excise Commissioners** *v* **Cure & Deeley Ltd** (1962), the powers of the Commissioners to make delegated legislation under the Finance (No. 2) Act 1940 were challenged. The Act empowered them to produce regulations 'for any matter for which provision appears to them necessary for the purpose of giving effect to the Act'. The Commissioners held that this included allowing them to make a regulation giving them the power to determine the amount of tax due where a tax return was submitted late. The High Court invalidated the regulation on the ground that the Commissioners had given themselves powers far beyond what Parliament had intended; they were empowered only to collect such tax as was due by law, not to decide what amount they thought fit.

R *v* **Secretary of State for Social Security, ex parte Joint Council for the Welfare of Immigrants** (1996) concerned the Asylum and Immigration Appeals Act 1993 which provided a framework for determining applications for asylum, and for appeals after unsuccessful applications. It allowed asylum seekers to apply for social security benefits while they were waiting for their applications or appeals to be decided, at a cost of over £200 million per year to British taxpayers. This led to concern from some quarters that the provisions might attract those who were simply seeking a better lifestyle than that available in their own countries (often called economic migrants), as opposed to those fleeing persecution, whom the provisions were actually designed to help.

In order to discourage economic migrants, the then Secretary of State for Social Security exercised his powers to make delegated legislation under the Social Security (Contributions and Benefits) Act 1992, and produced regulations which stated that social security benefits would no longer be available to those who sought asylum after they had entered the UK, rather than immediately on entry, or those who had been refused leave to stay here and were awaiting the outcome of appeals against the decision.

The Joint Council for the Welfare of Immigrants challenged the regulations, claiming that they fell outside the powers granted by the 1992 Act. The Court of Appeal upheld their claim, stating that the 1993 Act was clearly intended to give asylum seekers rights which they did not have previously. The effect of the regulations was effectively to take those rights away again since, without access to social security benefits, most asylum seekers would either have to return to the countries from which they had fled, or live on nothing while their claims were processed. The court ruled that Parliament could not have intended to give the Secretary of State powers to take away the rights it had given in the 1993 Act: this could only be done by a new statute, and therefore the regulations were *ultra vires*.

The decision was a controversial one, because the regulations had themselves been approved by Parliament, and overturning them could be seen as a challenge to the power of the legislature, despite the decision being explained by the court as upholding that power.

Unreasonableness

If rules are manifestly unjust, have been made in bad faith (for example by someone with a financial interest in their operation) or are otherwise so perverse that no reasonable official could have made them, the courts can declare them invalid.

Confirmation by Government Minister

Under s. 235(2) of the Local Government Act 1972, bye-laws passed by local authorities often need to be confirmed by the relevant Government Minister. This confirmation process checks that:

- the local authority had the power to make the legislation;
- the consultation process was undertaken;
- there is no duplication or conflict with existing legislation;
- the bye-law deals with a genuine and specific local problem (rather than a national issue);
- there is no conflict with Government policy.

Following the passing of the Local Government and Public Involvement in Health Act 2007, regulations can be passed allowing bye-laws dealing with specified issues to be made under an accelerated procedure which does not require confirmation by a Government Minister.

Criticism of delegated legislation

Lack of democratic involvement

This argument is put forward because delegated legislation is usually made by civil servants, rather than elected politicians. This is not seen as a particular problem where the delegated legislation takes the form of detailed administrative rules, since these would clearly take up impossible amounts of parliamentary time otherwise. However, in the latter years of the last Conservative Government there was increasing concern that delegated legislation was being used to implement important policies.

The role of the Privy Council in passing delegated legislation is particularly sensitive because it is not a democratic body. The civil rights group, JUSTICE, published a report in 2009 pointing out that orders in Council made by the Privy Council had been used to abolish the right of trade union membership for some civil servants and to force residents of the Chagos Islands to leave their homes and prevent them from returning.

Overuse

Critics argue that there is too much delegated legislation; this is linked to the point above, as there would be little problem with increasing amounts of delegated legislation if its purpose was merely to flesh out technical detail.

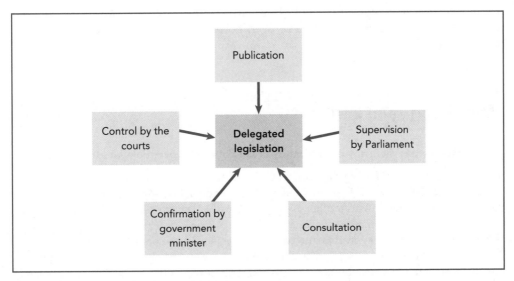

Figure 4.2 Control of delegated legislation

4

Delegated legislation

Sub-delegation

Delegated legislation is sometimes made by people other than those who were given the original power to do so.

Lack of control

Despite the above list of controls over delegated legislation, the reality is that effective supervision is difficult. First, publication has only limited benefits, given that the general public are frequently unaware of the existence of delegated legislation, let alone on what grounds it can be challenged and how to go about doing so. This in turn has an effect on the ability of the courts to control delegated legislation, since judicial review relies on individual challenges being brought before the courts. This may not happen until years after a provision is enacted, when it finally affects some-one who is prepared and able to challenge it. The obvious result is that legislation which largely affects a class of individuals who are not given to questioning official rules, are unaware of their rights, or who lack the financial resources to go to court, will rarely be challenged.

A further problem is that some enabling Acts confer extremely wide discretionary powers on Ministers; a phrase such as 'the Minister may make such regulations as he sees fit for the purpose of bringing the Act into operation' would not be unusual. This means that there is very little room for anything to be considered *ultra vires*, so judicial review is effectively frustrated.

The main method of control over delegated legislation is therefore parliamentary, but this too has its drawbacks. Although the affirmative resolution procedure usually ensures that parliamentary attention is drawn to important delegated legislation, it is rarely possible to prevent such legislation being passed. The Select Committee on the Scrutiny of Delegated Powers makes an important contribution, and has been able to secure changes to a number of important pieces of legislation. However, it too lacks real power, as it is unable to consider the merits of delegated legislation (as opposed to whether the delegated powers have been correctly used) and its reports have no binding effect.

Answering questions

1 To what extent is there any parliamentary or judicial control over delegated legislation?

Your introduction could explain that delegated legislation normally takes the form of statutory instruments, bye-laws and Orders in Council. The authority to make such legislation usually derives from an enabling Act, in other words, an Act which enables an individual or organisation to make legislation on a specific issue.

Your essay could then be divided into two parts: parliamentary controls and judicial controls. Considering first parliamentary controls, parliament exercises control over delegated legislation through requiring a consultation process, the publication of all draft legislation, Parliamentary supervision through the affirmative or negative resolution process, and the scrutiny by relevant Parliamentary committees.

Looking secondly at the judicial controls, the courts exercise scrutiny through the process of judicial review which will check whether the delegated legislation has met the procedural and substantive requirements. In respect of procedural *ultra vires*, the courts ensure that the correct procedure has been followed; see for example **Agricultural, Horticultural and Forestry Industry Training Board** *v* **Aylesbury Mushrooms Ltd**. They check that the delegated legislation does not go beyond the provisions of the enabling Act – see **CEC** *v* **Cure & Deeley Ltd**, where the court held that the Commissioners could not give themselves powers that went significantly beyond those intended by Parliament.

2 **The effect that delegated legislation has on daily life is significantly greater than that of primary legislation (Acts of Parliament). What are the benefits of delegated legislation? In your view, do its benefits outweigh its weaknesses?**

You need to begin by setting out what the benefits and criticisms of delegated legislation are, which are discussed on pages 80–1 and 85–6 respectively. In order to answer the question properly though, you must then express your view as to whether or not the former outweigh the latter, and explain your reasoning. You could certainly use the democracy argument raised in the 'Topical issue' section on p. 79.

3 Read the source material below and answer parts (a), (b) and (c) which follow.

Exercise on Delegated Legislation

Source A

Police and Criminal Evidence Act 1984
(1984 c.60)
Section 60
Tape-recording of Interviews

(1) It shall be the duty of the Secretary of State –

. . .

(b) to make an order requiring the tape-recording of interviews of persons suspected of the commission of criminal offences, or of such descriptions of criminal offences as may be specified in the order . . .

(2) An order under subsection (1) above shall be made by statutory instrument and shall be subject to annulment in pursuance of a resolution of either House of Parliament.

Source B

Statutory Instrument
1991 No. 2687
The Police and Criminal Evidence Act 1984
(Tape-recording of Interviews) (No. 1) Order 1991

Made	29th November 1991
Laid before Parliament	6th December 1991
Coming into force	1st January 1992

Now, therefore, in pursuance of the said section 60(1)(b), the Secretary of State hereby orders as follows:

. . .

2. This Order shall apply to interviews of persons suspected of the commission of indictable offences which are held by police officers at police stations in the police areas specified in the schedule to this Order and which commence after midnight on 31st December 1991.

3(1) Subject to paragraph (2) below, interviews to which this Order applies shall be tape-recorded in accordance with the requirements of the code of practice on tape-recording which came into operation on 29th July 1988 . . .

3(2) The duty to tape-record interviews under paragraph (1) above shall not apply to interviews –

(a) where the offence of which a person is suspected is one in respect of which he has been arrested or detained under section 14(1)(a) of the Prevention of Terrorism (Temporary Provisions) Act 1989; . . .

(a) Using Sources A and B to illustrate your answer, compare the legislative process in relation to an Act of Parliament on the one hand and delegated legislation on the other.

(b) What are the advantages and disadvantages of delegated legislation?

(c) Each of the following interviews was conducted by police officers and took place at a police station covered by SI 1991/2687, but none of the interviews was tape-recorded.
    (i)   On 30th November 1991 Alice was charged with an indictable offence and interviewed;
    (ii)   Bertie, who was suspected of an indictable offence, was interviewed on 1st April 1998;
    (iii)   Cedric, detained under s. 14(1)(a) of the Prevention of Terrorism (Temporary Provisions) Act 1989 was interviewed in April 1998.

Discuss interviews (i), (ii) and (iii) with reference to Source B.

(a) For material on the legislative process in relation to an Act of Parliament see p. 43 and for delegated legislation pp. 79–81. You could point out that the Police and Criminal Evidence Act 1984 was an enabling Act which allowed the Secretary of State to make the Statutory Instrument 1991/2687. You could mention that statutory instruments are made by Government departments and contrast this with bye-laws and Orders in Council (p. 79). When explaining the negative resolution procedure (p. 82) you could refer to the fact that the statutory instrument on tape-recording interviews was laid before Parliament on 6 December 1991 and that s. 60(2) of PACE refers to this process.

(b) Material on the advantages of delegated legislation can be found on p. 80 under the heading 'Why is delegated legislation necessary?' Criticisms can be found on pp. 85–6.

(c) (i) As Statutory Instrument 1991/2687 provides that its provisions only apply to interviews that take place after midnight on 31st December 1991, the police were under no obligation to tape-record Alice's interview.

(ii) Bertie's interview should have been tape-recorded as he was suspected of committing an indictable offence and the interview took place after the provisions of the statutory instrument came into force. You could look at possible remedies, particularly the exclusion of the evidence obtained, which is discussed at p. 400.

(iii) There was no obligation to tape-record Cedric's interview as he had been detained under the Prevention of Terrorism (Temporary Provisions) Act 1989.

Summary of Chapter 4: Delegated legislation

There are three main forms of delegated legislation:

- statutory instruments;
- bye-laws; and
- Orders in Council.

The power to make delegated legislation

Usually an Act of Parliament is required giving the power to make delegated legislation to a branch of the state.

Why is delegated legislation necessary?

Delegated legislation is necessary because it saves parliamentary time, constitutes a quick form of legislation, and is suited to technical subject areas or where local knowledge is needed.

Control of delegated legislation

Delegated legislation is controlled through:

- the consultation of experts;
- publication of the legislation;
- supervision by Parliament;
- the courts with the judicial review procedure; and
- confirmation by a Government Minister.

Criticism of delegated legislation

Delegated legislation has been criticised due to:

- lack of democratic involvement;
- overuse;
- sub-delegation; and
- lack of controls.

Reading list

Burns, S. (2006) 'Tipping the balance', *New Law Journal* 787.

McHarg, A. (2006) 'What is delegated legislation?', *Public Law* 539.

Reading on the Internet

www   Statutory instruments are published on the website of the Office of Public Sector Information at:
    http://www.opsi.gov.uk/stat.htm

Visit **www.mylawchamber.co.uk/ElliottELS** to access multiple-choice questions, flashcards and practice exam questions to test yourself on this chapter.

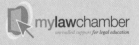

4

Delegated legislation

5

European law

This chapter discusses:

- the six key institutions of the European Union: the Council of Ministers, the European Council, the Commission, the European Parliament, the Court of Justice of the European Union and the European Central Bank;

- how European law is made;

- the four main sources of European law: treaties, regulations, directives and decisions; and

- the impact of European Union law on the UK.

Introduction

The European Union (EU) currently comprises 27 European countries. The original members – France, West Germany, Belgium, Luxembourg, Italy and The Netherlands – laid the foundations in 1951, when they created the European Coal and Steel Community (ECSC). Six years later, they signed the Treaty of Rome, creating the European Economic Community (EEC) and the European Atomic Energy Community (Euratom). The original six were joined by the UK, Ireland and Denmark in 1973, Greece in 1981 and Spain and Portugal in 1986 and, in the same year, the member countries signed the Single European Act, which developed free movement of goods and people within the Community (the single market), and greater political unity. Finland, Austria and Sweden joined in 1995. Following the Nice summit in 2004, the EU increased its membership from 15 to 27, with most of the new members coming from eastern Europe.

In 1993 the Maastricht Treaty renamed the European Economic Community the European Community and also created the European Union (EU). Following the Lisbon Treaty in 2009 the European Community has now been totally replaced by the European Union.

The aims of the European Union

The original aim of the first treaty signed, the Treaty of Paris (1951), was to create political unity within Europe and prevent another world war. The ECSC placed the production of steel and coal in all the member states under the authority of a single community organisation, with the object of indirectly controlling the manufacture of arms and therefore helping to prevent war between member states. The ECSC ceased to exist in 2002. Euratom was designed to produce cooperative nuclear research, and the EEC to improve Europe's economic strength.

It is the EEC (now known as the EU) that has had the most significance, particularly for law. Its object now is to weld Europe into a single prosperous area by abolishing all restrictions affecting the movement of people, goods and money between member states, producing a single market of over 370 million people, available to all producers in the member states. This, it is hoped, will help Europe to compete economically with countries such as the US, Japan, China and India, the member states being stronger as a block than they could possibly be alone. The Single European Act 1986 was a major step towards this goal, setting a target of 1992 for the abolition of trade barriers between member states. The practical effect is that, for example, a company manufacturing rivets in Leeds, with an order from a company in Barcelona, can send the rivets all the way there by lorry without the driver having to fill in customs forms as he or she crosses every border. The rivets will be made to a common EU standard, so the Spanish firm will know exactly what they are going to receive, while any trademarks or other rights over the design of the rivets will be protected throughout the member states. Just as goods can now move freely throughout the EU, so can workers: for example, a designer from Paris can go and work in London, or Milan, or Dublin, with no need for a work permit and no problem with immigration controls.

Table 5.1 Membership of Europe

Year	Country
1951	Belgium France Italy Luxembourg Netherlands West Germany
1973	Denmark Ireland United Kingdom
1981	Greece
1986	Portugal Spain
1995	Austria Finland Sweden
2004	Cyprus Czech Republic Estonia Hungary Latvia Lithuania Malta Poland Slovakia Slovenia
2007	Bulgaria Romania

Along with these closer economic ties, it is intended that there should be increasing political unity, though there is some disagreement – particularly, though not exclusively, in Britain – as to how far this should go. Nevertheless, progress is being made: the Treaty on European Union (TEU, also known as the Maastricht Treaty), signed in 1992, was the first major move in this direction, establishing the aims of a single currency (the Euro), joint defence and foreign policies, and inter-governmental cooperation on justice and home affairs. The introduction of the Euro began in 1999 (though not in the UK, which had negotiated the right to opt out of the programme), and the Amsterdam Treaty, signed in 1997, gave more precise definition to the common foreign and security policy and cooperation in justice and home affairs. These matters now fall within the scope of the EU.

Photo 5.1 The European Flag
Source: Jupiter Unlimited

Modernising the European Union

The European institutions and decision-making structures were originally designed 50 years ago for a small community of six countries. These structures became out-of-date and inadequate to cope with the expanded membership of Europe. A new European Constitution was drawn up with a view to modernising the European institutions, making them more democratic and efficient. However, referendums in the Netherlands and France rejected this Constitution. After a two-year period of reflection, the Lisbon Treaty was agreed in 2007 which adopts the most important of the planned reforms of the failed Constitution in a pragmatic and minimalist format, rather than the more grandiose presentation of the Constitution (which would have got rid of all the previous EU treaties and replaced them with a single Constitution). The Lisbon Treaty leaves all the existing European treaties in place and simply makes key amendments. It was ratified by all the members states and came into force in December 2009.

The institutions of the European Union

There are six key European institutions: the Commission, the Council of Ministers, the European Council, the European Parliament of the European Union, the European

Photo 5.2 The European Commission
Source: © iStockphoto/Luke Daniek

Court of Justice and the European Central Bank. Each of these institutions will be considered in turn.

The Commission

The Commission is composed of 27 members, called Commissioners, who are each appointed by the member states, subject to approval by the European Parliament, for five years. During the preparation of the Lisbon Treaty, efforts were made to include provisions to reduce the number of commissioners to make the organisation more streamlined and potentially more efficient, but these efforts proved unsucessful. They must be nationals of a member state, and in practice there tend to be two each from the largest states – France, Germany, Italy, Spain and the UK – and one each from the rest. However, the Commissioners do not represent their own countries: they are independent, and their role is to represent the interests of the EU overall. The idea is that the Commission's commitment to furthering EU interests balances the role of the European Council, whose members represent national interests.

In addition to its part in making EU legislation (see p. 101), the Commission is responsible for ensuring that member states uphold EU law, and has powers to investigate breaches by member states and, where necessary, bring them before the Court of Justice. It also plays an important role in the relationship of the EU with the rest of the world, negotiating trade agreements and the accession of new members, and draws up the annual draft budget for the EU. It is assisted in all these functions by an administrative staff, which has a similar role to that of the civil service in the UK.

The reputation of the Commission was seriously damaged in 1999 when an independent report found evidence of fraud, mismanagement and nepotism, forcing all the Commissioners to resign.

European Council

The members of the European Council are the president of the European Commission and the 27 heads of state of the member countries (for example, the Prime Minister of the United Kingdom, the President of France and the Chancellor of Germany). The European Council meets twice a year and has the same powers as the Council of Ministers, though the two are technically separate institutions. Many of the key decisions affecting the future direction of Europe are taken at these meetings. The Presidency of the Council is held by each member state, in rotation, for a period of six months.

Following the Lisbon Treaty, the President of the European Council will be elected by a qualified majority for a term of two-and-a-half years (renewable once), replacing the six-monthly rotating presidency. The newly defined role of the President includes ensuring the 'external representation of the Union on issues concerning its common foreign and security policy', which has led those opposed to a stronger Europe to be concerned that the President could effectively become a head of state for Europe – a move towards a president of the United States of Europe. The former British Prime Minister, Tony Blair, was considered for this position, but was found to be too controversial a figure due to his involvement in instigating the Iraq War. Instead, a former Prime Minister of Belgium was selected for this prestigious position.

The Council of Ministers

The Council of Ministers represents the interests of individual member states. It is a very powerful body in Europe and plays an important role in the passing of legislation. It does not have a permanent membership – in each meeting the members, one from each country, are national government ministers chosen according to the subject under discussion (so, for example, a discussion of matters relating to farming would usually be attended by the Ministers for Agriculture of each country). The Council meets most weeks to agree legislation and policy.

The Council may be questioned by the European Parliament, but the chief control is exercised by the national governments controlling their ministers who attend the Council.

The European Parliament

The Parliament is composed of 736 members (MEPs), who are directly elected in their own countries. In Britain they are elected to represent a geographical area which is much larger than for MPs, since there are only 72 MEPs for the whole country. Elections are held every five years.

The individual member countries are each allocated a number of seats, roughly according to population, though on this basis the smaller countries are over-represented. Members sit in political groupings rather than with others from their own country.

The Treaty of Lisbon has increased the powers of the European Parliament, to try and strengthen the democratic process within Europe. As well as taking part in the legislative process (discussed below) the Parliament has a variety of roles to play in connection with the other institutions. Over the Commission, it exercises a supervisory power. It has a right of veto over the appointment of the Commission as a whole, and can also sack the whole Commission by a vote of censure. In 1999 the entire Commission resigned during a crisis over fraud and mismanagement within the Commission, to avoid a vote of censure. The Commission must make an annual report to Parliament, and Parliament can also require Commissioners to answer written or oral questions. The Commission has to submit each proposed budget of the European Union to the European Parliament for its approval.

The Council is not accountable to Parliament in the same way, but the Parliament reports on it three times a year, and the President of the Council is obliged to address the Parliament once a year, followed by a debate. The Parliament can also bring actions against other EU institutions for failure to implement EU law.

The Parliament appoints an Ombudsman, who investigates complaints of maladministration by EU institutions from individuals and MEPs. It can also be petitioned by any natural or legal person living or having an office within a member state, on any issue within the EU field which affects that person directly.

Court of Justice of the European Union

The whole court system of the European Union is known as the Court of Justice of the European Union. This, in fact, consists of three courts: the European Court of Justice, the General Court, and the Civil Service Tribunal.

The European Court of Justice (ECJ)

The ECJ has the task of supervising the uniform application of EU law throughout the member states, and in so doing it can create case law. It is important not to confuse it with the European Court of Human Rights, which deals with alleged breaches of human rights by countries who are signatories to the European Convention on Human Rights. That court is completely separate, and not an institution of the EU.

The ECJ, which sits in Luxembourg, has 27 judges, appointed for a period of six years (which may be renewed). The judges are assisted by eight Advocates General, who produce opinions on the cases assigned to them, indicating the issues raised and suggesting conclusions. These are not binding, but are nevertheless usually followed by the court. Both judges and Advocates General are chosen from those who are eligible for the highest judicial posts in their own countries.

Most cases are heard in plenary session, that is with all the judges sitting together. Only one judgment will be delivered, giving no indication of the extent of agreement between the judges, and these often consist of fairly brief propositions, from which it can be difficult to discern any *ratio decidendi*. Consequently, lawyers seeking precedents often turn to the opinions written by the Advocates General. Since September 1989 the full ECJ has been assisted by a new Court of First Instance to deal with specialist economic law cases. Parties in such cases may appeal to the full ECJ on a point of law.

The majority of cases heard by the ECJ are brought by member states and institutions of the Community, or are referred to it by national courts. It has only limited power to deal with cases brought by individual citizens, and such cases are rarely heard.

The ECJ has two separate functions: a judicial role, deciding cases of dispute; and a supervisory role.

The judicial role of the ECJ

The ECJ hears cases of dispute between parties, which fall into two categories: proceedings against member states, and proceedings against European institutions.

Proceedings against member states may be brought by the Commission, or by other member states, and involve alleged breaches of European law by the country in question. For example, in **Re Tachographs: EC Commission v UK** (1979), the ECJ upheld a complaint against the UK for failing to implement a European regulation making it compulsory for lorries used to carry dangerous goods to be fitted with tachographs (devices used to record the speed and distance travelled, with the aim of preventing lorry drivers from speeding, or from driving for longer than the permitted number of hours). The Commission usually gives the member state the opportunity to put things right before bringing the case to the ECJ.

Proceedings against EU institutions may be brought by member states, other EU institutions and, in limited circumstances, by individual citizens or organisations. The procedure can be used to review the legality of EU regulations, directives or decisions, on the grounds that proper procedures have not been followed, the provisions infringe a European Treaty or any rule relating to its application, or powers have been misused. In **United Kingdom v Council of the European Union** (1996) the UK sought to have the Directive on the 48-hour working week annulled on the basis that it had been unlawfully adopted by the Council. The application was unsuccessful.

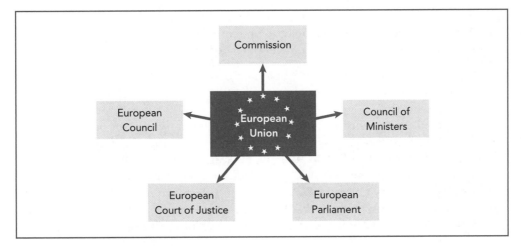

Figure 5.1 Institutions of the European Union

In the past there was no machinery for enforcing judgments against states. Following the Maastricht Treaty, there is now provision for member states to be fined.

Decisions made in these kinds of cases cannot be questioned in UK courts.

The supervisory role of the ECJ

Article 267 of the Treaty on the Functioning of the European Union provides that any court or tribunal in a member state may refer a question on EU law to the ECJ if it considers that 'a decision on that question is necessary to enable it to give judgment'. The object of this referral system is to make sure that the law is interpreted in the same way throughout Europe.

A reference must be made if the national court is one from which there is no further appeal – so in Britain, the Supreme Court must refer such questions, while the lower courts usually have some discretion about whether or not to do so. About 20 references a year are made from UK courts. The Art. 267 procedure is expensive and time consuming, often delaying a decision on the case for a long time (about nine months), and so lower courts have been discouraged from using it. Consequently attempts have been made to set down guidelines by which a court could determine when a referral to the ECJ would or would not be necessary.

KEY CASE

In **Bulmer** v **Bollinger** (1974), the Court of Appeal was asked to review a judge's exercise of discretion to refer a question under what is now Art. 267. They pointed out that the European Court could not interfere with the exercise of a judge's discretion to refer, and Lord Denning set down guidelines on the points which should be taken into account in considering whether a reference was necessary. He emphasised the cost and delay that a reference could cause, and stated that no reference should be made:

> Lord Denning laid down guidance on when courts should make references to the European Court of Justice under Art. 267.

- where it would not be conclusive of the case, and other matters would remain to be decided;
- where there had been a previous ruling on the same point;
- where the court considers that point to be reasonably clear and free from doubt;
- where the facts of the case had not yet been decided.

Unless the point to be decided could be considered 'really difficult and important', said Lord Denning, the court should save the expense and delay of a reference and decide the issue itself.

Denning's view has since been criticised by academics, who point out that it can be cheaper and quicker to refer a point at an early stage, than to drag the case up through the English courts first. In addition, the clear and consistent interpretation of EU law can come to depend on whether individual litigants have the resources to take their cases all the way up to the Supreme Court. Critics also note that the apparent importance of the case should not be decisive, as many important decisions of the ECJ have arisen from cases where the parties actually had little at stake.

Although the judiciary still use Denning's **Bulmer** guidelines, there now appears to be a greater willingness to refer cases under the Art. 267 procedure. In **Customs and Excise Commissioners** *v* **APS Samex** (1983), Bingham J pointed out that, in interpreting European law, the Court of Justice has certain advantages over national courts: it can take a panoramic view of the whole of European law, compare the legislation as it is written in different member states' languages, and it is experienced in the purposive approach to interpretation for which European legislation was designed. In addition, it has the facility to allow member states to make their views on an issue known. As a result, it is better placed than a national court to decide issues of interpretation. In a later case, **R** *v* **International Stock Exchange, ex parte Else** (1993), the same judge (by then Master of the Rolls), said that if, once the facts have been found, it is clear that an issue of European law is vital to a court's final decision, that court should normally make an Art. 267 referral: English courts should only decide such issues without referral if they have real confidence that they can do so correctly, without the help of the ECJ.

Where a case is submitted, proceedings will be suspended in the national court until the ECJ has given its verdict. This verdict does not tell the national court how to decide the case, but simply explains what EU law on the matter is. The national court then has the duty of making its decision in the light of this.

Regardless of which national court submitted the point for consideration, a ruling from the ECJ should be followed by all other courts in the EU – so, theoretically, a point raised by a county court in England may result in a ruling that the highest courts in all the member states have to follow. Where a ruling reveals that national legislation conflicts with EU law, the national Government usually enacts new legislation to put the matter right.

The court's decisions can be changed only by its own subsequent decision or by an amendment of the Treaty, which would require the unanimous approval of member states through their own Parliaments. Decisions of the European Court cannot be questioned in English courts. This principle has limited the jurisdiction of the Supreme Court as a final appellate court.

5

European law

Table 5.2 Membership of the European institutions

Commission	27 Commissioners
European Council	The president of the European Commission and 27 heads of state
Council of Ministers	It does not have a permanent membership. For each meeting one minister is chosen from each country according to the subject of the meeting
European Parliament	A maximum of 751 Members of the European Parliament (MEPs)
European Court of Justice	27 judges

An illustration of the use of Art. 267 is the case of **Marshall *v* Southampton and South West Hampshire Area Health Authority** (1986). Miss Marshall, a dietician, was compulsorily retired by the Authority from her job when she was 62, although she wished to continue to 65. It was the Authority's policy that the normal retiring age for its employees was the age at which state retirement pensions became payable: for women this was 60, though the Authority had waived the rule for two years in Miss Marshall's case. She claimed that the Authority was discriminating against women by adopting a policy that employees should retire at state pension age, hence requiring women to retire before men. This policy appeared to be legal under the relevant English legislation but was argued to be contrary to a Council directive providing for equal treatment of men and women. The national court made a reference to the ECJ asking for directions on the meaning of the directive. The ECJ found that there was a conflict with UK law, and the UK later changed its legislation to conform.

It is important to note that the ECJ is not an appeal court from decisions made in the member states. It does not substitute its own decisions for those of a lower court (except those of its own Court of First Instance, discussed below). It will assist a national court at any level in reaching a decision, but the actual decision remains the responsibility of the national court. When parties in an English case talk of taking the case to Europe, the only way they can do this is to get an English court to make a referral for an Art. 267 ruling, and they may have to take their case all the way to the Supreme Court to ensure this.

General Court

This court was originally known as the European Court of First Instance and was established in 1988 to reduce the workload of the European Court of Justice. It was renamed by the Lisbon Treaty in 2009, becoming the General Court. It primarily hears direct actions against EU institutions. Appeals on points of law are heard by the European Court of Justice.

Civil Service Tribunal

The Civil Service Tribunal hears disputes between the European Union and its civil servants.

European Central Bank

The European Central Bank (ECB) gained the official status of being an institution of the European Union under the Lisbon Treaty in 2009. The ECB was established in 1998 and has its headquarters in Frankfurt in Germany. It is responsible for the economic and monetary policy of the 16 Member States that have adopted the Euro as their national currency, known together as the Eurozone. The primary objective of the ECB is to maintain price stability within the Eurozone, in other words to keep inflation below 2 per cent. It has responsibility for fixing the interest rate within the Eurozone. It takes its decisions independently of governments and the other European institutions.

Making European legislation

The Council of Ministers (often called simply 'the Council'), the Commission and the European Parliament all play a role in making EU legislation. A complicated range of different procedures has been developed to make these laws. All legislation starts with a proposal from the Commission and the Council enjoys the most power in the legislative process.

Parliament's legislative role was historically purely advisory, with the Commission and the Council having a much more powerful role in the legislative process. This led to concern over the lack of democracy within Europe, for while Parliament is directly elected by the citizens of Europe, the Commission and Council members are not. The role of the European Parliament in the passing of European legislation has gradually been increased by the Single European Act, the Maastricht Treaty, the Amsterdam Treaty and the Lisbon Treaty. Increasingly, the passing of EU legislation requires the approval of the European Parliament as well as the Council, through the co-decision process.

The Council continues to play an important role in the passing of European legislation. There are three systems of voting in the Council:

- **unanimity**, where proposals are only passed if all members vote for them;
- **simple majority**, where proposals only require more votes for than against; and
- **qualified majority**, which allows each state a specified number of votes (the larger the state, the more votes it has), and provides that a proposal can only be agreed if there are a specified number of votes in its favour.

These voting procedures have been controversial, because where unanimity is not required a member state can be forced to abide by legislation for which it has not voted, and which it believes is against its interests. This is seen as compromising national sovereignty. However, requiring unanimity makes it difficult to get things done quickly (or sometimes at all) and, as a result, initial progress towards the single market was very slow. The need to speed progress up led to both the Single European Act and the Maastricht Treaty requiring only qualified majority voting more often. The Amsterdam Treaty and the Lisbon Treaty extended its use a little more, and it is now the norm for many areas.

Types of European legislation

There is a range of different forms of European legislation: treaties, regulations, directives and decisions. In considering the impact of this legislation on UK law a distinction has to be drawn between direct applicability and direct effect. Direct applicability refers to the fact that treaty articles, regulations and some decisions immediately become part of the law of each member state. Directives are not directly applicable.

Where European legislation has direct effect, it creates individual rights which national courts must protect without any need for implementing legislation in that member state. In the UK the national courts were given this power under s. 2(1) of the European Communities Act 1972.

There are two types of direct effect: vertical direct effect gives individuals rights against Governments; and horizontal direct effect gives rights against other people and organisations.

Provisions of treaties, regulations and directives only have direct effect if they are clear, unconditional and their implementation requires no further legislation in member states. These conditions were first laid down in the context of treaties in **Van Gend en Loos v Nederlandse Tariefcommissie** (1963).

The ability of individuals to rely on European law before their national courts greatly enhances its effectiveness. National courts can quickly apply directly effective legislation and can draw on a wide range of remedies. Where legislation does not have direct effect, the only method of enforcement available in the past was an action brought by the Commission or a member state against a member state before the ECJ. This process can be slow and provides no direct remedy for the individual.

However, in the 1990s the ECJ recognised the right of individuals to be awarded damages by their national courts for breach of European legislation by a member state, even where the legislation did not have direct effect. Originally, in **Francovich v Italy** (1992), this right was applied where directives had not been implemented but it has been developed to extend to any violation of European law. In **Francovich**, an Italian company went into liquidation, leaving its employees, including Francovich, unpaid arrears of salary. Italy had not set up a compensation scheme for employees in such circumstances as was required by a European directive. Francovich sued in the Italian courts. The court held that although the directive was not sufficiently precise to have direct effect it gave a right to damages.

Liability will be imposed on a member state if:

- the legislation was intended to confer rights on individuals;
- the content of those rights is clear from the provisions of the legislation;
- there is a direct causal link between the breach of the member state's obligation and the damage sustained by the individual.

In addition, a fourth condition was added by **Brasserie du Pecheur SA v Germany** (1996) and **R v Secretary of State for Transport, ex parte Factortame** (1990):

- there was a serious breach of European law.

The four different types of European law will now be examined in turn.

Treaties

The Treaties of the European Union are international treaties agreed between all the member states. They effectively constitute the European constitution, establishing the six key European institutions and the aims of the European Union. The founding treaties are the Treaty on European Union (also known as the Maastricht Treaty) and the Treaty on the Functioning of the European Union (historically known as the Rome Treaty). These treaties have been amended over the years and their article numbers changed as the European Union has evolved. Treaty provisions can create rights and obligations.

KEY CASE

The case of **Van Gend en Loos** (1963) decided that a treaty provision has direct effect if it is unconditional, clear and precise as to the rights or obligations it creates, and leaves member states no discretion on implementing it. Treaty provisions which are unconditional, clear and precise, and allow no discretion on implementation, have both horizontal and vertical direct effect.

Treaty provisions have direct effect if they are unconditional, clear and precise and impose an obligation on member states to implement them.

An example of a directly effective treaty provision is Art. 157 of the Treaty on the functioning of the European Union. This provides 'equal pay for male and female workers for equal work of equal value'. In **Macarthys Ltd** *v* **Smith** (1979), Art. 157 was held to give a woman in the UK the right to claim the same wages as were paid to the male predecessor in her job, even though she had no such right under the UK equal pay legislation passed in 1970, before the UK joined Europe.

Treaty provisions which are merely statements of intent or policy, rather than establishing clear rights or duties, require detailed legislation to be made before they can be enforced in the member states.

Regulations

A regulation is the nearest European law comes to an English Act of Parliament. Regulations apply throughout the EU, usually to people in general, and they become part of the law of each member nation as soon as they come into force, without the need for each country to make its own legislation.

Regulations must be applied even if the member state has already passed legislation which conflicts with them. In **Leonesio** *v* **Italian Ministry for Agriculture and Forestry** (1973), a regulation to encourage reduced dairy production stated that a cash premium should be payable to farmers who slaughtered cows and agreed not to produce milk for five years. Leonesio had fulfilled this requirement, but was refused payment because the Italian constitution required legislation to authorise government expenditure. The ECJ said that once Leonesio had satisfied the conditions, he was entitled to the payment; the Italian Government could not use its own laws to block that right.

Directives

Directives are less precisely worded than regulations, because they aim to set out broad objectives, leaving the member states to create their own detailed legislation in order

5

European law

to put those objectives into practice (within specified time limits). As a result, it was originally assumed by most member states that directives could not have direct effect, and would not create individual rights until they had been translated into domestic legislation. However, the ECJ has consistently refused to accept this view, arguing that direct effect is an essential weapon if the EU is to ensure that member states implement directives.

KEY CASE

Ess. Cases p. 60 →

The case which initially established direct effect for directives was Van Duyn v Home Office (1974). The Home Office had refused Van Duyn permission to enter the UK because she was a member of a religious group, the Scientologists, which the Government wanted to exclude from the country at the time. Van Duyn argued that her exclusion was contrary to provisions in the Treaty of Rome on freedom of movement. The Government responded by pointing out that the Treaty allowed exceptions on public policy grounds, but Van Duyn then relied on a later directive which said that public policy could only be invoked on the basis of personal conduct, and Van Duyn herself had done nothing to justify exclusion. The case was referred to the ECJ, which found that the obligation conferred on the Government was clear and unconditional, and so created enforceable rights.

Directives have direct effect where they impose clear and unconditional obligations on a government.

The reasoning behind the approach taken in **Van Duyn** was explained in **Pubblico Ministero v Ratti** (1979), where the ECJ pointed out that member states could not be allowed to rely on their own wrongful failure to implement directives as a means of denying individual rights.

Directives have vertical direct effect but not horizontal direct effect. This means that they impose obligations on the state and not individuals. Thus, they have direct effect in proceedings against a member state (vertical) but not in proceedings between individuals (horizontal). A directive with direct effect can be utilised by an individual against the state when the state has failed to implement the directive properly or on time.

The issue of direct effect was important in the high-profile case of **R (on the application of Mayor and Citizens of Westminster City Council) v Mayor of London** (2002). Westminster Council had applied for judicial review of the decision to introduce a £5 congestion charge to enter central London. The decision had been taken by the Mayor of London, Ken Livingstone. The High Court rejected the application. Westminster Council had sought to rely on a provision of a directive. The High Court stated that the Council could not do this, as when directives had direct effect they only gave rights to individuals and not to Government institutions.

The ECJ has found a number of ways to widen access where the principle of vertical direct effect applies. First, it has defined 'the state' very broadly to include all public bodies, including local authorities and nationalised industries. This meant, for example, that in **Marshall v Southampton Area Health Authority** (1986), discussed at

p. 99, Miss Marshall was able to take advantage of the relevant directive even though she was not suing the Government itself, because her employer was a health authority and therefore considered to be a public body.

Secondly, in **Von Colson v Land Nordrhein-Westfalen** (1984), the court introduced the principle of indirect effect, stating that national courts should interpret national law in accordance with relevant directives, whether the national law was designed to implement a directive or not. The principle was confirmed in Marleasing SA v La Comercial Internacional de Alimentación SA (1990). Here, Marleasing alleged that La Comercial, a Spanish company, had been formed with the express purpose of defrauding creditors (of which they were one) and sought to have its articles of association (the document under which a company is formed) declared void. Spanish contract law allowed this, but the EU had passed a directive which did not. Which should the member state court follow? The ECJ held that where a provision of domestic law was 'to any extent open to interpretation', national courts had to interpret that law 'as far as possible' in line with the wording and purpose of any relevant directive. This would apply whether the domestic law was passed before or after the directive, except that domestic law passed before a directive would only be affected once the time limit for implementation of the directive had expired.

ss. Cases
p. 50 →

Marleasing has been much discussed by academics, but it is still unclear quite how far national courts are expected to go in implementing directives having indirect effect. EU law experts Craig and de Búrca (2007) suggest, however, that the principle of indirect effect probably only applies where national law is sufficiently ambiguous to allow it to be interpreted in line with directives; where there is a conflict, but the national law is clear, member state courts are unlikely to be required to override that law.

Thirdly, some recent cases have allowed an unimplemented directive to act as a shield, though not as a sword, to the benefit of private individuals. In other words, the directive could be relied upon to provide a defence but not to provide a right of action. For example, **CIA Security International SA v Signalson** (1996) concerned the failure by the Belgian Government to notify the Commission of its law on security systems in accordance with a European directive on the subject (Notification Directive 98/34).

Table 5.3 Impact of European legislation

Impact	Meaning of term
Direct applicability	Legislative provisions immediately become part of the law of each member state.
Direct effect	Legislation creates individual rights which national courts must protect without any need for implementing legislation in the member state.
Horizontal direct effect	Legislation gives rights against governments, individuals and private organisations.
Vertical direct effect	Legislation gives rights against governments.
Indirect effect	National courts should interpret national law in accordance with relevant European legislation.

Litigation arose between two private companies, CIA Security and Signalson. Signalson tried to prevent CIA from marketing an alarm system which had not been approved under Belgian law. CIA successfully argued that the Belgian law did not apply because the Commission had not been notified about it in accordance with the European directive. Thus, CIA were able to rely on the directive to provide a defence in the litigation between two private individuals. On the surface it looked as if the directive was being given horizontal direct effect in breach of established principles of European law, but in fact the case has been interpreted as merely allowing a directive to give private individuals a defence. Another interpretation of the case was that Signalson was effectively acting as an agent of the state, bringing proceedings for the withdrawal of a product which potentially did not conform with Belgian law.

In **R (on the application of Wells) *v* Secretary of State for Transport, Local Government and the Regions** (2005), there was a plan by a private company to reopen a quarry in an environmentally sensitive area. No environmental impact assessment had been carried out by the state in accordance with the Environmental Impact Assessment Directive (Directive 85/337). A local resident asked the Secretary of State to remove or modify the planning permission pending the carrying out of the assessment, but he refused. In the subsequent litigation, the court had to consider whether the local resident could rely on the directive. The court acknowledged that a directive cannot be used as a sword to impose obligations on a private individual. But a directive could be used as a shield, even if in doing so there would be a negative impact on a private individual: in this case the quarry owners would have to stop work on the quarry until the completion of the environmental impact assessment. As the quarry owners were not required to carry out an obligation, this did not amount to the imposition of direct horizontal effect.

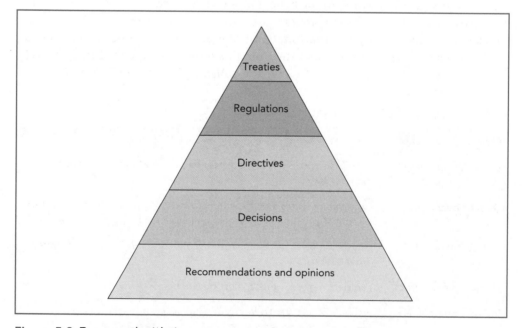

Figure 5.2 European legislation

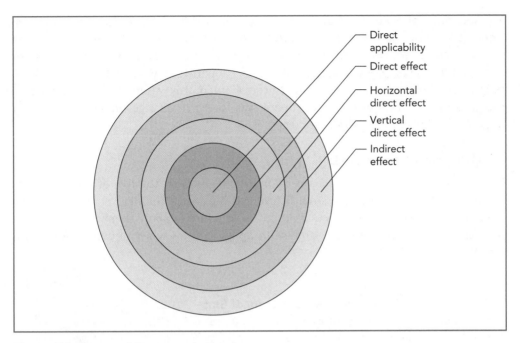

Figure 5.3 Impact of European legislation

Decisions

A decision may be addressed to a state, a person or a company and is binding only on the recipient. Examples include granting, or refusing, export licences to companies from outside the EU.

Recommendations and opinions

The Council and the Commission may issue recommendations and opinions which, although not to be disregarded, are not binding law.

How does EU law affect the UK?

Membership of the EU has had a number of effects on UK law and our legal system.

New sources of law

Joining the original EEC created new and very important sources of law for the UK. Section 2(4) of the European Communities Act 1972 provides that English law should be interpreted and have effect subject to the principle that European law is supreme; this means that European law now takes precedence over all domestic sources of law. As a result, it has had a profound effect on the rights of citizens in this country and, in particular, on the rights of employees, especially female workers. For example, in

R v Secretary of State for Employment, ex parte Equal Opportunities Commission (1994), the House of Lords found that parts of the Employment Protection (Consolidation) Act 1978 were incompatible with European law on equal treatment for male and female employees, because the Act gave part-time workers fewer rights than full-timers. Since most part-time workers were women, this was held to discriminate on the basis of sex, and the UK Government was forced to change the law, and greatly improve the rights of part-time workers.

The role of the courts

Because EU law takes precedence over domestic legislation, the role of the courts has changed as a result of membership. Before the UK joined the EEC, statutes were the highest form of law, and judges had no power to refuse to apply them. Now, however, they can – in fact they should – refuse to apply statutes which are in conflict with directly effective EU law.

KEY CASE

The leading case in this area is **R v Secretary of State for Transport, ex parte Factortame** (1990). It arose from the fishing policy decided by member states in 1983, which allowed member states to limit fishing within 12 miles of their own shores to boats from their

> Judges should refuse to apply statutes which are in conflict with directly effective EU law.

own country, and left the remainder of the seas around the European Community open to fishing boats from any member state. In addition, to preserve stocks of fish, each state was allocated a quota of fish, and required not to exceed it. Soon after the new rules were in place, the UK Government became concerned that Spanish fishing boats were registering as British vessels, so that their catches counted against the British quota rather than the Spanish, and genuine British fishermen were as a result getting a smaller share. The Government therefore passed the Merchant Shipping Act 1988, which contained provisions to prevent the Spanish trawlers taking advantage of the British quota.

Spanish boat owners challenged the Act, claiming it was in conflict with EU law on the freedom to set up business anywhere in Europe, and the House of Lords agreed. They stated that s. 2(4) of the European Communities Act 'has precisely the same effect as if a section were incorporated in . . . [the 1988 Act, saying] that the provisions with respect to registration of British fishing vessels were to be without prejudice to the directly enforceable Community rights of nationals of any member state . . .'.

The decision was criticised as compromising the rights of the UK Parliament to make law for this country, as the House of Lords rendered effectively unenforceable the Merchant Shipping Act. But the House of Lords was firm in dismissing such complaints, pointing out that it was very clear before the UK joined Europe that doing so would mean giving up some degree of sovereignty over domestic law, and that this was accepted voluntarily when the UK joined the Community. 'Under . . . the Act of 1972, it has always been clear that it was the duty of a United Kingdom court, when delivering final judgment, to override any rule of national law found to be in conflict with any directly enforceable rule of Community law . . .'

Lord Justice Laws stated in **Thoburn** *v* **Sunderland City Council** (2002) that the European Communities Act 1972 was a constitutional Act which could only be repealed by express provisions of an Act of Parliament (and not by implication). The case concerned a group of market stall holders who became known in the tabloid press as the 'metric martyrs'. They had refused to sell their fruit and vegetables in kilos and grammes, preferring to stick to the old weighing system of pounds and ounces. They argued that they had not breached the law because part of the 1972 Act had been impliedly repealed by a later Act of Parliament: the Weights and Measures Act 1985, which allowed for the use of the old imperial measures.

In his judgment Lord Justice Laws stated that Acts of Parliament should be divided between 'ordinary' statutes and 'constitutional' statutes. The European Communities Act was a constitutional Act and could only be repealed if Parliament used express words to show its intention to do so.

The role of the courts is also affected by the principle stated in **Marleasing** (see p. 105), which effectively means that the courts now have a new external aid to consider when interpreting statutes, and should take notice of it wherever they can do so without straining the words of the statute.

The UK courts are subjected to the supervisory jurisdiction of the ECJ, as explained (on p. 97), and this gives a further source of law, since the courts of all member states are bound by ECJ decisions on the interpretation and application of EU law.

The future

One view of the influence of UK membership of Europe on our national law was given by Lord Denning, in poetic mood, in **Bulmer** *v* **Bollinger**: 'The Treaty is like an incoming tide. It flows into the estuaries and up the rivers. It cannot be held back.' Lord Scarman, obviously in an equally lyrical frame of mind, commented:

> For the moment, to adopt Lord Denning's imagery, the incoming tide has not yet mingled with the home waters of the common law: but it is inconceivable that, like the Rhone and the Arve where those two streams meet at Geneva, they should move on, side by side, one grey with the melted snows and ice of the distant mountains of our legal history, the other clear blue and clean, reflecting modern opinion. If we stay in the Common Market, I would expect to see its principles of legislation and statutory interpretation, and its conception of an activist court whose role is to strengthen and fulfil the purpose of statute law, replace the traditional attitudes of English judges and lawyers to statute law and the current complex style of statutory drafting.

What Lord Scarman was referring to was the difference in approach between the English legal system and those in mainland Europe. When drafting statutes, for example, English law has tended towards tightly written, very precise rules, whereas the continental style is looser, setting out broad principles to be followed. As a result, the continental style of statutory interpretation takes a very purposive approach, paying most attention to putting into practice the spirit of the legislation, and filling in any gaps in the wording if necessary, as opposed to the more literal style traditionally associated with English judges. The ECJ tends to take the continental approach, and it

5

European law

has been suggested that, as time goes on, this will influence our own judges more and more, leading to more creative judicial decision-making, with corresponding changes in the drafting of statutes.

Following the **Factortame** litigation there was concern that Europe was threatening the sovereignty of the UK Parliament, as the ECJ ruling had caused an Act of Parliament to be set aside. Lord Denning revised his description of European law as like an 'incoming tide' and stated:

> No longer is European law an incoming tide flowing up the estuaries of England. It is now like a tidal wave bringing down our sea walls and flowing inland over our fields and houses – to the dismay of all. (*The Independent*, 16 July 1996)

The academic Seamus Burns (2008) has suggested that, in the light of subsequent legal developments, Lord Denning 'might have to revise his image of EU law being like an incoming tide permeating our existing legal order, and more realistically compare it to a tsunami, enveloping everything in its path with irresistible force'.

In **R v Secretary of State for Foreign and Commonwealth Affairs, ex parte Lord Rees-Mogg** (1994) an unsuccessful attempt was made to demonstrate that the UK could not legally ratify the Maastricht Treaty. In rejecting this claim, the court pointed out that the Treaty did not involve the abandoning or transferring of powers, so that a Government could choose to later denounce the Treaty, or fail to honour its obligations under it.

Answering questions

1 **What have been the major consequences of the United Kingdom's membership of the European Union for the character of the English legal system?** *London External LLB*

Some of the relevant material that you need to answer this question can be found under the subheading 'How does EU law affect the UK?' (pp. 107–8). A possible answer to this question could be broken up into four parts which would look at:

- parliamentary sovereignty;
- the influence of civil legal systems;
- practical impact of membership;
- future impact.

You could use these subheadings in your essay, to show clearly to the reader your essay structure.

Parliamentary sovereignty
The greatest impact of membership of the European Union has been on the principle of the sovereignty of Parliament (discussed at p. 3) with the courts having the power to refuse to apply statutes which are in conflict with directly effective EU law (see p. 105).

The influence of civil legal systems
Most of the other members of the European Union have a civil legal system, as opposed to a common law system (see p. 12). Because the UK was not a member of the European Union at the time of its creation (when it was known as the European Economic Community), it was the institutions from the civil legal systems that had the greatest impact on the institutions of the European Union. The European Union is therefore a means by which the English legal system has been influenced by the civil legal systems. It provides an opportunity for the English legal practitioners to see alternative ways of functioning and to consider whether they wish changes to be made to the English legal system in the light of these alternatives. The Government considered adopting some of the procedures used in the European Court of Justice (ECJ) for its new Supreme Court, but has rejected them (see p. 597). For example, abstract questions of law can be referred to the ECJ under Art. 267. The British Government has decided that this sits uncomfortably with the English legal tradition of deciding issues of law in the context of specific factual cases and has not given the new Supreme Court the power to hear such cases. Also all the judges sit in the ECJ to hear each case. While there were 12 full-time House of Lords' judges, these usually divided up, and sat as panels of five. The Supreme Court is continuing this practice rather than following the ECJ model.

Practical impact
Through its legislation, the European Union has a direct impact on the content and form of English law. The courts have also been forced to take a different approach to the interpretation of European legislation, which has influenced generally the courts' approach to statutory interpretation (see p. 63).

Future impact
You could conclude your essay with a discussion of the likely increased impact of membership of the European Union on the English legal system in the future. Material for this section can be found at pp. 109–10.

5

European law

2 European law provisions have had a profound impact on UK law. In particular, explain how it has affected the use of precedent by judges in UK courts.

You should begin by explaining what precedent is and what it means (refer back to Chapter 1). Then, you could divide your answer into five main parts:

- A discussion of s 2(4) of the European Communities Act 1972, which is considered under the heading 'New sources of law' on pp. 107–8. The impact of this provision can be illustrated by the case of **Factortame** (1990) (see p. 108) as judges should refuse to apply domestic legislation which conflicts with directly effective EU law.
- The effect of **Marleasing** (1990) (p. 105) in providing a new external aid to statutory interpretation.
- In cases against other member states, decisions cannot be questioned by UK courts (see p. 97).
- UK courts are subject to the supervisory jurisdiction of the ECJ since the courts of all member states are bound by ECJ decisions on the interpretation and application of EU law. See in particular the section entitled 'The supervisory role of the ECJ' on p. 98.
- You could argue that in reality EU provisions only have a limited effect, because they apply only to the interpretation of EU law.

There may be evidence to suggest that UK courts are adopting a more purposive continental approach to statutory interpretation (see Chapter 3).

3 To what extent has the English legal system irrevocably accommodated European Union Law?

An introduction to this essay could observe that the principle of parliamentary sovereignty gives parliament an unfettered discretion to enact laws, and foreign treaties do not automatically become part of domestic law. When the United Kingdom became a member of what is now the European Union, the European Communities Act 1972 provided authority for the application of EU law over UK domestic law. This has led to the courts refusing to apply domestic legislation inconsistent with EU law as occurred in **R v Secretary of State for Transport, ex parte Factortame** (1990). Your essay could point to the different sources of European Law and give specific examples of European law which now form an integral part of UK law.

As the application of EU law derives from the 1972 Act, Parliament could, in theory, revoke it and so the principle of parliamentary sovereignty remains intact. In **Thoburn v Sunderland City Council**, Lord Justice Laws emphasised that revocation would have to be explicit and not by implication. However, even if the 1972 Act were to be revoked, whilst new European laws would no longer override domestic law, the substantive principles of EU law are now strongly embedded within the English legal system.

4 Explain the role of the European Court of Justice.

Although the responsibility of applying EU law falls upon the domestic courts of the respective EU member states, the ECJ is responsible for the uniform application of EU law throughout Europe. In fulfilling this duty, the ECJ has both a judicial and a supervisory role.

In its judicial role it hears disputes between parties – against either member states (for example, **Re Tachographs: EC Commission v UK**) or European institutions (for example, **UK v Council of the European Union**). Following the Maastricht Treaty, members can be fined for failing to enforce judgments.

In its supervisory role, under Art. 267 the ECJ receives cases from domestic courts where a piece of European legislation needs to be interpreted to enable the domestic court to give judgment (for example, **Bulmer** v **Bollinger**). In **Customs and Excise Commissioners** v **APS Samex**, Bingham J emphasised that the ECJ can take a panoramic view of EU law and apply a purposive approach.

A ruling from the ECJ has application throughout the EU, and so its decisions promote cohesion and certainty whilst leaving individual domestic courts to apply its principles in their decisions.

Summary of Chapter 5: European law

Introduction
The European Union currently has 27 members. It was established to create political unity within Europe and to prevent another world war.

The institutions of the European Union
There are six key institutions of the European Union: the Commission, the Council of Ministers, the European Council, the European Parliament, Court of Justice of the European Union and the European Central Bank. The European Court of Justice has two separate functions: a judicial role where it decides cases of dispute and a supervisory role under Art. 267 of the Treaty on the Functioning of the European Union.

Making European legislation
The Council of Ministers, the Commission and the European Parliament all play a role in making European legislation. All legislation starts with a proposal from the Commission, though the Council enjoys the most power in the legislative process. Increasingly, the qualified majority system of voting is being used by the Council in agreeing new legislation.

Types of European legislation
The different forms of European legislation are:

- treaties;
- regulations;
- directives; and
- decisions.

How does EU law affect the UK?
Membership of the EU has had a number of effects on UK law and on our legal system. Joining the original EEC created new and very important sources of law for the UK. Because EU law takes precedence over domestic legislation, the role of the courts has changed as a result of membership of the Union. Now judges should refuse to apply statutes which are in conflict with directly effective European law. The impact of membership of the EU is likely to increase in the future.

Reading list

Booth, A. (2002) 'Direct effect', *Solicitors Journal* 924.

Burns, S. (2008) 'An incoming tide', 158 *New Law Journal* 44.

5

European law

Levitsky, J. (1994) 'The Europeanization of the British Legal Style', 42 *American Journal of Comparative Law* 347.

Reading on the Internet

www   Access to the homepages of the European institutions can be obtained from the following website:
http://europa.eu/institutions/index_en.htm

European legislation is available at:
http://eur-lex.europa.eu/en/index.htm

Visit www.mylawchamber.co.uk/ElliottELS to access multiple-choice questions, flashcards and practice exam questions to test yourself on this chapter.

6

Custom

This chapter discusses:

- the history of custom as a source of law; and
- when custom can be a source of law today.

Introduction

As we have seen, the basis of the common law was custom. The itinerant justices sent out by William the Conqueror (see p. 12) examined the different local practices of dealing with disputes and crime, filtered out the less practical and reasonable ones, and ended up with a set of laws that were to be applied uniformly throughout the country. As Sir Henry Maine, a nineteenth-century scholar who studied the evolution of legal systems, has pointed out, this did not mean that custom itself was ever law – the law was created by the decisions of judges in recognising some customs and not others.

Custom still plays a part in modern law, but a very small one. Its main use is in cases where a traditional local practice – such as fishermen being allowed to dry their nets on a particular piece of land, or villagers holding a fair in a certain place – is being challenged. Custom was defined in the **Tanistry Case** (1608) as 'such usage as has obtained the force of law' and, in these cases, those whose practices are being challenged assert that the custom has existed for so long that it should be given the force of law, even though it may conflict with the general common law.

When can custom be a source of law?

To be regarded as conferring legally enforceable rights, a custom must fulfil several criteria.

'Time immemorial'

It must have existed since 'time immemorial'. This was fixed by a statute in 1275 as meaning 'since at least 1189'. In practice today claimants usually seek to prove the custom has existed as far back as living memory can go, often by calling the oldest local inhabitant as a witness. However, this may not always be sufficient. In a dispute over a right to use local land in some way, for example, if the other side could prove that the land in question was under water until the seventeenth or eighteenth century, the right could therefore not have existed since 1189. In **Simpson** v **Wells** (1872), a charge of obstructing the public footway by setting up a refreshment stall was challenged by a claim that there was a customary right to do so derived from 'statute sessions', ancient fairs held for the purpose of hiring servants. It was then proved that statute sessions were first authorised by the Statutes of Labourers in the fourteenth century, so the right could not have existed since 1189.

Reasonableness

A legally enforceable custom cannot conflict with fundamental principles of right and wrong, so a customary right to commit a crime, for example, could never be accepted. In **Wolstanton Ltd** v **Newcastle-under-Lyme Corporation** (1940) the lord of a manor claimed a customary right to take minerals from under a tenant's land, without paying compensation for any damage caused to buildings on the land. It was held that this was unreasonable.

Certainty and clarity

It must be certain and clear. The locality in which the custom operates must be defined, along with the people to whom rights are granted (local fishermen, for example, or tenants of a particular estate) and the extent of those rights. In **Wilson v Willes** (1806) the tenants of a manor claimed the customary right to take as much turf as they needed for their lawns from the manorial commons. This was held to be too vague, since there appeared to be no limit to the amount of turf which could be taken.

Locality

It must be specific to a particular geographic area. Where a custom is recognised as granting a right, it grants that right only to those specified – a custom giving fishermen in Lowestoft the right to dry their nets on someone else's land would not give the same right to fishermen in Grimsby. Custom is only ever a source of local law.

Continuity

It must have existed continuously. The rights granted by custom do not have to have been exercised continuously since 1189, but it must have been possible to exercise them at all times since then. In **Wyld v Silver** (1963), a landowner, wishing to build on land where the local inhabitants claimed a customary right to hold an annual fair, argued that the right had not been exercised within living memory. The court nevertheless granted an injunction preventing the building.

Exercised as of right

It must have been exercised peaceably, openly and as of right. Customs cannot create legal rights if they are exercised only by permission of someone else. In **Mills v Colchester Corporation** (1867) it was held that a customary right to fish had no legal force where the right had always depended on the granting of a licence, even though such licences had traditionally been granted to local people on request.

Consistency

It must be consistent with other local customs. For example, if a custom is alleged to give the inhabitants of one farm the right to fish in a lake, it cannot also give the inhabitants of another the right to drain the lake. The usual course where a conflict arises is to deny that the opposing custom has any force, though this is not possible if it has already been recognised by a court.

6

Custom

Obligatory

Where a custom imposes a specific duty, that duty must be obligatory – a custom cannot provide that the lord of a manor grants villagers a right of way over his land only if he likes them, or happens not to mind people on his land that day.

Conformity with statute

A custom which is in conflict with a statute will not be held to give rise to law.

TOPICAL ISSUE

Custom in international law

Ess. Cases
p. 74 →

Custom is particularly important in the context of international law where fixed legal rules (for example in treaties and the Geneva Conventions) are less developed. In 2005 the International Committee of the Red Cross published a study aimed at promoting customary international humanitarian law. It identified 161 rules of customary international humanitarian law, which provide legal protection for people affected by armed conflict. These customs derive from the practice of states as expressed, for example, in military manuals, national legislation and diplomatic statements. They are considered to be binding custom in international law if they reflect the widespread, representative and uniform practice of states and are accepted as law.

These customs are particularly important during civil wars as treaty law is primarily concerned with international conflicts. The study showed that customary international humanitarian law applicable in non-international armed conflict goes beyond the rules of treaty law. While treaty law covering internal armed conflict does not expressly prohibit attacks on civilians, international customs do. Customs are particularly important in this context because, while only states are bound by international treaties, all those involved in internal fighting, including rebel groups, are bound by international customs.

Answering questions

1 Custom is one of the sources of UK law. In reality, how useful is it as such a source?

Start by listing the sources of law, which include custom (as covered in Part 1 of the book). Arguments that could be put forward on the limited usefulness of custom include that:

- custom plays only a small part;
- custom is not, of itself, 'law' (p. 116);
- the criteria applied – including proof of its existence since time immemorial – is very restrictive.

However, custom may be important in international law.

Summary of Chapter 6: Custom

Introduction
The basis of the common law was custom. Custom still plays a part in modern law, but a very small one. Its main use is in cases where a traditional local practice is being challenged.

When can custom be a source of law?
To be regarded as conferring legally enforceable rights, a custom must fulfil several criteria:

'Time immemorial'
It must have existed since 'time immemorial'. This was fixed by a statute in 1275 as meaning 'since at least 1189'.

Reasonableness
A legally enforceable custom cannot conflict with fundamental principles of right and wrong.

Certainty and clarity
It must be certain and clear.

Locality
It must be specific to a particular geographic area.

Continuity
It must have existed continuously.

Exercised as of right
It must have been exercised peaceably, openly and as of right.

Consistency
It must be consistent with other local customs.

Obligatory
Where a custom imposes a specific duty, that duty must be obligatory.

Conformity with statute
A custom which is in conflict with a statute will not be held to give rise to law.

Reading list

Maine, Sir H. (2001) *Ancient Law*, London: Dent.

Visit **www.mylawchamber.co.uk/ElliottELS** to access multiple-choice questions, flashcards and practice exam questions to test yourself on this chapter.

mylawchamber
unrivalled support for legal education

7 Equity

This chapter looks at:

- how equity became a source of law;
- the difference between common law and equity;
- reforms introduced by the Judicature Acts 1873–75;
- equity today; and
- the future of equity as a source of law.

Introduction

In ordinary language, equity simply means fairness, but in law it applies to a specific set of legal principles, which add to those provided in the common law. It was originally inspired by ideas of fairness and natural justice, but is now no more than a particular branch of English law. Lawyers often contrast 'law' and equity, but it is important to know that when they do this they are using 'law' to mean common law. Equity and common law may be different, but both are law. Equity is an area of law which can only be understood in the light of its historical development.

How equity began

As we have seen, the common law was developed after the Norman Conquest through the 'itinerant justices' travelling around the country and sorting out disputes. By about the twelfth century, common law courts had developed which applied this common law. Civil actions in these courts had to be started by a writ, which set out the cause of the action or the grounds for the claim made, and there grew up different types of writ. Early on, new writs were created to suit new circumstances, but in the thirteenth century this was stopped. Litigants had to fit their circumstances to one of the available types of writ: if the case did not fall within one of those types, there was no way of bringing the case to the common law court. At the same time, the common law was itself becoming increasingly rigid, and offered only one remedy, damages, which was not always an adequate solution to every problem – if a litigant had been promised the chance to buy a particular piece of land, for example, and the seller then went back on the agreement, damages might not be an adequate remedy since the buyer really wanted the land, and may have made arrangements on the basis that it would be acquired.

Consequently, many people were unable to seek redress for wrongs through the common law courts. Many of these dissatisfied parties petitioned the king, who was thought of as the 'fountain of justice'. These petitions were commonly passed to the Chancellor, the king's chief minister, as the king did not want to spend time considering them. The Chancellor was usually a member of the clergy, and was thought of as 'keeper of the king's conscience'. Soon litigants began to petition the Chancellor himself and, by 1474, the Chancellor had begun to make decisions on the cases on his own authority, rather than as a substitute for the king. This was the beginning of the Court of Chancery.

Litigants appeared before the Chancellor, who would question them, and then deliver a verdict based on his own moral view of the question. The court could insist that relevant documents be disclosed, as well as questioning the parties in person, unlike the common law courts which did not admit oral evidence until the sixteenth century, and had no way of extracting the truth from litigants. Because the court followed no binding rules, relying entirely on the Chancellor's view of right and wrong, it could enforce rights not recognised by the common law, which, restricted by precedent, was failing to adapt to new circumstances. The Court of Chancery could provide whatever remedy best suited the case – the decree of specific performance, for example, would have meant that the seller of land referred to above could be forced to honour the promise. This type of justice came to be known as equity.

Common law and equity

Not surprisingly, the Court of Chancery became popular, and caused some resentment among common lawyers, who argued that the quality of decisions varied with the length of the Chancellor's foot – in other words, that it depended on the qualities of the individual Chancellor. Because precedents were not followed and each case was considered purely on its merits, justice could appear arbitrary, and nobody could predict what a decision might be.

On the other hand, this very flexibility was seen as the great advantage of equity – where any rules are laid down, there will always be situations in which those rules produce injustice. The more general the rule, the more likely this is, yet it is impossible to foresee and lay down all the specific exceptions in which it should not apply. Equity dealt with these situations by applying notions of good sense and fairness, but in doing so laid itself open to the charge that fairness is a subjective quality.

The common lawyers particularly resented the way in which equity could be used to restrict their own jurisdiction. Where the common law gave a litigant a right which, in the circumstances, it would be unjust to exercise, the Court of Chancery could issue a common injunction, preventing the exercise of the common law right. An example might be where a litigant had made a mistake in drawing up a document. Under common law the other party could enforce the document anyway, even if they were aware of the mistake but failed to draw attention to it. This was considered inequitable, and a common injunction would prevent the document being enforced.

KEY CASE

Tensions between equity and the common law came to a head in 1615 in **The Earl of Oxford's Case**, where conflicting judgments of the common law courts and the Court of Chancery were referred to the king for a decision; he advised that where there was conflict, equity should prevail. Had this decision not been made, equity would have been worthless – it could not fulfil its role of filling in the gaps of the common law unless it was dominant.

> Where there is a conflict between equity and the common law, then equity should prevail.

Nevertheless, the rivalry continued for some time, but gradually abated as equity too began to be ruled by precedent and standard principles, a development related to the fact that it was becoming established practice to appoint lawyers rather than clergy to the office of Lord Chancellor. By the nineteenth century, equity had a developed case law and recognisable principles, and was no less rigid than the common law.

The Judicature Acts

Once equity became a body of law, rather than an arbitrary exercise of conscience, there was no reason why it needed its own courts. Consequently the Judicature Acts of 1873–75, which established the basis of the court structure we have today, provided that equity and common law could both be administered by all courts, and that there would no longer be different procedures for seeking equitable and common law remedies. Although the Court of Chancery remained as a division of the High Court, like all other courts it can now apply both common law and equity.

Equity today

It is important to note that the Judicature Acts did not fuse common law and equity, only their administration. There is still a body of rules of equity which is distinct from common law rules, and acts as an addition to it. Although they are implemented by the same courts, the two branches of the law are separate. Where there is conflict, equity still prevails.

Equitable maxims

Although both the common law and equity lay down rules developed from precedents, equity also created maxims which had to be satisfied before equitable rules could be applied. These maxims were designed to ensure that decisions were morally fair. The following are some of them.

'He who comes to equity must come with clean hands'

This means that claimants who have themselves been in the wrong in some way will not be granted an equitable remedy. In **D&C Builders** *v* **Rees** (1966) a small building firm did some work on the house of a couple named Rees. The bill came to £732, of which the Reeses had already paid £250. When the builders asked for the balance of £482, the Reeses announced that the work was defective, and they were only prepared to pay £300. As the builders were in serious financial difficulties (as the Reeses knew), they reluctantly accepted the £300 'in completion of the account'. The decision to accept the money would not normally be binding in contract law, and afterwards the builders sued the Reeses for the outstanding amount. The Reeses claimed that the court should apply the doctrine of equitable estoppel, which can make promises binding when they would normally not be. However, Lord Denning refused to apply the

7

Equity

doctrine, on the grounds that the Reeses had taken unfair advantage of the builders' financial difficulties, and therefore had not come 'with clean hands'.

'He who seeks equity must do equity'

Ess. Cases
p. 76

Anyone who seeks equitable relief must be prepared to act fairly towards their opponent. In **Chappell** *v* **Times Newspapers Ltd** (1975), newspaper employees who had been threatened that they would be sacked unless they stopped their strike action applied for an injunction to prevent their employers from carrying out the threat. The court held that, in order to be awarded the remedy, the strikers should undertake that they would withdraw their strike action if the injunction was granted. Since they refused to do this, the injunction was refused.

'Delay defeats equity'

Ess. Cases
p. 76

Where a claimant takes an unreasonably long time to bring an action, equitable remedies will not be available. The unreasonableness of any delay will be a matter of fact to be assessed in view of the circumstances in each case. In **Leaf** *v* **International Galleries** (1950) the claimant bought a painting of Salisbury Cathedral described (innocently) by the seller as a genuine Constable. Five years later, the buyer discovered that it was nothing of the sort, and claimed the equitable remedy of rescission, but the court held that the delay had been too long.

These maxims (there are several others) mean that where a claimant's case relies on a rule of equity, rather than a rule of common law, that rule can only be applied if the maxims are satisfied – unlike common law rules which have no such limitations.

▓ Equitable remedies

Equity substantially increased the number of remedies available to a wronged party. The following are the most important:

Injunction This orders the defendants to do or not to do something.

Specific performance This compels a party to fulfil a previous agreement.

Rectification This order alters the words of a document which does not express the true intentions of the parties to it.

Rescission This restores parties to a contract to the position they were in before the contract was signed.

Equitable remedies are discretionary. A claimant who wins the case is awarded the common law remedy of damages as of right, but the courts may choose whether or not to award equitable remedies. They are very much an addition to common law remedies, and usually only available if common law remedies are plainly inadequate.

Equitable principles have had their greatest impact in the development of the law of property and contract, and remain important in these areas today. The two best-known contributions come from property law, and are the developments of the law of trusts, and the basis of the rules which today govern mortgages. The creation of alternative remedies has also been extremely important.

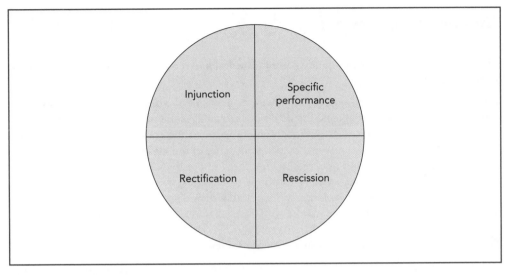

Figure 7.1 Equitable remedies

TOPICAL ISSUE

Equity's future?

Equity has shown itself capable of adapting and expanding to meet new needs, and so creating law reform. During the 1950s and 1960s, it responded to increasing marital breakdown by stating that a deserted wife could acquire an equitable interest in the family home, providing an interim solution to a growing problem until legislation could be passed in the form of the Matrimonial Homes Act 1967. And in the 1970s, two important new remedies were created by extending the scope of injunctions: the Anton Piller order, by which the court can order defendants to allow their premises to be searched and relevant documents to be removed, and the Mareva injunction, a court order to a third party, such as a bank, to freeze the assets of a party to a dispute where there is a danger that they may be removed from the court's jurisdiction (by being taken out of the country, for example, and therefore made unavailable if damages were ordered by the court).

However, more recent attempts to extend equitable jurisdiction, notably in **Scandinavian Trading Tanker Co AB** v **Flota Petrolera Ecuatoriana** (1983) and **Sport International Bussum BV** v **Inter-Footwear Ltd** (1984), have been firmly resisted by the House of Lords.

The availability of discretionary remedies means that equity still fulfils the traditional function of supplementing the common law, providing just and practical remedies where the common law alone is not enough, but restricting itself to cases where those remedies are felt to be genuinely and justly deserved.

Answering questions

1 Critically analyse the role of equity – both historical and modern – in the English and Welsh legal system today.

The historical background of equity and how it came about as a separate source of law is discussed on p. 121. Today, equity and the common law remain separate bodies of law, albeit they are dealt with by the same courts. Although equity supports the common law, in the event of a conflict, equity prevails. Your answer should set out some of the maxims and explain that equity implies notions of fairness and good sense. You should note the wide range of remedies available under equity and equity's ability to adapt to changing needs ('Topical issue', p. 125). However, you should also acknowledge that equitable remedies are only discretionary and that they are mostly useful in a limited number of fields, such as in contract and property law.

2 To what extent does equity remain a separate source of law?

Historically equity developed separately from the common law to remedy the shortcomings of the common law and was dispensed from separate courts (the Court of Chancery). The **Earl of Oxford's Case** in 1615 established that where common law and equity judgments conflicted, equity prevailed. Equity continued to evolve into a set of principles. The Judicature Acts 1873–75 abolished different procedures and provided that equity and common law be administered by all courts; but these measures did not fuse common law and equity.

Equity remains distinct from the common law and is epitomised in the equitable maxims such as 'delay defeats equity' – as illustrated by **Leaf v International Galleries**. Equity also provides remedies not available at common law (for example, injunctions and specific performance) but these are in addition to remedies available at common law.

Thus today equity can be accessed through the normal courts but remains a separate, supplementary strand of law, although in cases such as **Sport International Bussum BV v Inter-Footwear Ltd**, the House of Lords has firmly resisted extension of equitable principles.

Summary of Chapter 7: Equity

Introduction
In law the term 'equity' refers to a specific set of legal principles, which add to those provided in the common law.

How equity began
By the thirteenth century the common law had become inflexible and, in order to obtain justice in specific cases, individuals petitioned the king who passed the cases to the Lord Chancellor to consider. By 1474, the Chancellor had begun to make decisions on the cases on his own authority, rather than as a substitute for the king. This was the beginning of the Court of Chancery.

Common law and equity
Tensions developed between the common law and the Court of Chancery. Matters came to a head in 1615 in **The Earl of Oxford's Case**, where conflicting judgments of the

common law courts and the Court of Chancery were referred to the king for a decision; he advised that where there was conflict, equity should prevail. By the nineteenth century, equity had a developed case law and recognisable principles, and was no less rigid than the common law.

The Judicature Acts

The Judicature Acts of 1873–75 provided that there would no longer be separate courts administering equity and common law.

Equity today

Although equity and the common law are implemented by the same courts, the two branches of the law are separate. Where there is conflict, equity still prevails.

Equitable maxims

Equity developed maxims to ensure that decisions are morally fair. The following are some of them.

- 'He who comes to equity must come with clean hands.'
- 'He who seeks equity must do equity.'
- 'Delay defeats equity.'

Equitable remedies

The following are the most important equitable remedies, all of which are available at the discretion of the court:

- injunction;
- specific performance;
- rectification;
- rescission.

Reading list

Burrows, A. (2002) 'We Do This At Common Law But That In Equity', 22 *Oxford Journal of Legal Studies* 1.

Millett, L. (2000) 'Modern equity: a means of escape', *Judicial Studies Board Journal* 21.

Salter, M. and Doupe, M. (2006) 'Concealing the past? Questioning textbook interpretations of the history of equity and trusts', 22 *Liverpool Law Review* 253.

Visit **www.mylawchamber.co.uk/ElliottELS** to access multiple-choice questions, flashcards and practice exam questions to test yourself on this chapter.

8

Treaties

This chapter discusses:

- treaties as an important source of international and national law; and

- the implementation of treaties.

Introduction

When the UK enters into treaties with other countries, it undertakes to implement domestic laws that are in accordance with the provisions of those treaties. For the purposes of the legal system, probably the most important treaties signed by the UK Government are those setting up and developing the European Union, and the European Convention on Human Rights (discussed on p. 301).

Implementation of treaties

In many countries, treaties automatically become part of domestic law when the country signs them. However, in the UK, the position is that signing treaties usually does not instantly make them law, so citizens cannot rely on them in proceedings brought in UK courts. Only when Parliament produces legislation to enact its treaty commitments do those commitments become law – the Taking of Hostages Act 1982 is an example of legislation incorporating the provisions of international treaties. Until such legislation is produced, individuals cannot usually take advantage of the protections envisaged by treaties.

However, there are some treaties which do not precisely follow this rule. Parts of the treaties setting up the European Communities are directly applicable in British courts, and can be relied on to create rights and duties just like an English statute (this subject is discussed in the chapter on European law).

TOPICAL ISSUE

Treaties under a modern constitution

In 2008 the Minister of Justice published a White Paper looking at ways to improve the current constitution: *The Governance of Britain: Constitutional Renewal* (2008). The Constitutional Reform and Governance Bill was presented to Parliament in 2009. It contains provisions to put on a statutory footing the procedures followed for the ratification of a treaty. In essence, it provides for treaties to be ratified by following a negative resolution procedure (see p. 82). The relevant Government Minister would have to lay a copy of the treaty before parliament and 21 days would have to pass without either of the parliamentary Houses resolving that the treaty should not be ratified. If either House did resolve that the treaty should not be ratified, a further condition would be triggered requiring the Secretary of State to lay a statement before Parliament explaining why he or she was of the opinion that the treaty should nevertheless be ratified. Should it be the House of Commons that had resolved the treaty should not be ratified, the Minister would have to wait a further 21 days after the above statement had been laid, and the treaty could not be ratified if the Commons again resolved to oppose it within that period. In exceptional circumstances these procedures would not have to be followed.

Ess. Cases p. 81

Ess. Cases p. 82

8

Treaties

Answering questions

1 **In what way can treaties be said to be a source of law?**

In order to answer this question you should read this chapter in conjunction with Chapter 5 'European law'. Start by explaining what treaties are and give some important examples, such as the Treaty of Rome and the Maastricht Treaty. You need to explain that some provisions in treaties can be directly applicable and that they can have direct effect. Use of cases such as **Van Gend en Loos** (1963) will illustrate this and will also help to show in what way treaties form a source of law (see p. 101 onwards).

Remember that in the UK, to maintain the sovereignty of Parliament, treaties must be implemented into UK law by the passing of an Act of Parliament. This applied even to the Treaty of Rome and the European Convention on Human Rights (see Chapter 15).

Reading on the Internet

www The European Convention on Human Rights is available on the website of the European Court of Human Rights at:

http://www.echr.coe.int/echr

Visit www.mylawchamber.co.uk/ElliottELS to access multiple-choice questions, flashcards and practice exam questions to test yourself on this chapter.

9

Law reform

This chapter discusses:

- judicial and parliamentary law reform in practice;

- the impetus for law reform from pressure groups, political parties, the civil service, treaty obligations, public opinion and media pressure;

- the different agencies that have been set up to consider the need for reform in areas referred to them by the Government, including the Law Commission, Royal Commissions and public inquiries; and

- the success of these agencies of law reform.

Introduction

An effective legal system cannot stand still. Both legal procedures and the law itself must adapt to social change if they are to retain the respect of at least most of society, without which they cannot survive. Many laws which were made even as short a time ago as the nineteenth century simply do not fit the way we see society today – until the early part of the twentieth century, for example, married women were legally considered the property of their husbands, while, not much earlier, employees could be imprisoned for breaking their employment contracts.

Most legislation in this country stands until it is repealed – the fact that it may be completely out of date does not mean it technically ceases to apply. The offences of challenging to fight, eavesdropping and being a common scold for example, which long ago dropped out of use, nevertheless remained on the statute book until they were abolished by the Criminal Law Act 1967. In practice, of course, many such provisions simply cease to be used, but where it becomes clear that the law may be out of step with social conditions, or simply ineffective, there are a range of ways of bringing about change.

Judicial change

Case law can bring about some reform – one of the most notable recent examples was the decision in **R v R** (1991), in which the House of Lords declared that a husband who has sexual intercourse with his wife without her consent may be guilty of rape. Before this decision, the law on rape within marriage was based on an assertion by the eighteenth-century jurist Sir Matthew Hale, that 'by marrying a man, a woman consents to sexual intercourse with him, and may not retract that consent'. This position had been found offensive for many years before **R v R**. In 1976, Parliament considered it during a debate on the Sexual Offences Act, but decided not to make changes at that time, and it was not until 1991 that the Court of Appeal and then the House of Lords held that rape within marriage should be considered an offence.

Lord Keith stated that Hale's assertion reflected the status of women within marriage in his time, but since then both the status of women and the marriage relationship had completely changed. The modern view of husband and wife as equal partners meant that a wife could no longer be considered to have given irrevocable consent to sex with her husband; the common law was capable of evolving to reflect such changes in society, and it was the duty of the court to help it do so.

In practice, however, major reforms like this are rarely produced by the courts, and would not be adequate as the sole agency of reform. Norman Marsh's article 'Law Reform in the United Kingdom' (1971) puts forward a number of reasons for this.

1 First, as we saw in the chapter on case law, there is no systematic, state-funded process for bringing points of law in need of reform to the higher courts. The courts can only deal with such points as they arise in the cases before them, and this depends on the parties involved having sufficient finance, determination and interest to take their case up through the courts. Consequently, judge-made reform proceeds not on the basis of which areas of law need changes most, but on a haphazard presentation of cases.

2   Secondly, judges have to decide cases on the basis of the way the issues are presented to them by the parties concerned. They cannot commission research, or consult with interested bodies to find out the possible effects of a decision on individuals and organisations other than those in the case before them – yet their decision will apply to future cases.

3   Thirdly, judges have to recognise the doctrine of precedent, and for much of the time this prohibits any really radical reforms.

4   Marsh's fourth point is that reforming decisions by judges have the potential to be unjust to the losing party. Law reforms made by Parliament are prospective – they come into force on a specified date, and we are not usually expected to abide by them until after that date. Judicial decisions, on the other hand, are retrospective, affecting something that happened before the judges decided what the law was. The more reformatory such a decision is, the less the likelihood that the losing party could have abided by the law, even if they wanted to.

5   Finally, Marsh argues, judges are not elected, and therefore feel they should not make decisions which change the law in areas of great social or moral controversy. They themselves impose limits on their ability to make major changes and will often point out to Parliament the need for it to make reforms, as happened in the **Bland** case concerning the Hillsborough stadium disaster victim (see p. 28).

9

Law reform

Reform by Parliament

The majority of law reform is therefore carried out by Parliament. It is done in four ways:

- **Repeal** of old and/or obsolete laws.
- **Creation** of completely new law, or adaptation of existing provisions, to meet new needs. The creation of the offence of insider dealing (where company officials make money by using information gained by virtue of a privileged position) in the Companies Act 1980 was a response to public concern about 'sharp practice' in the city.
- **Consolidation**. When a new statute is created, problems with it may become apparent over time, in which case further legislation may be enacted to amend it. Consolidation brings together successive statutes on a particular subject and puts them into one statute. For example, the legislation in relation to companies was consolidated in 1985.
- **Codification**. Where a particular area of the law has developed over time to produce a large body of both case law and statute, a new statute may be created to bring together all the rules on that subject (case law and statute) in one place. That statute then becomes the starting point for cases concerning that area of the law, and case law, in time, builds up around it. The Criminal Attempts Act 1981 and the Police and Criminal Evidence Act 1984 are examples of codifying statutes. Codification is thought to be most suitable for areas of law where the principles are well worked out; areas that are still developing, such as tort, are less suitable for codifying.

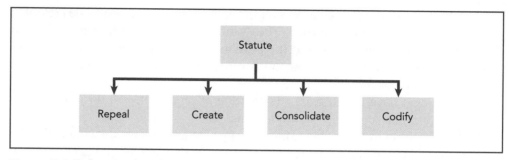

Figure 9.1 Reforming legislation

These types of reform often happen together – the Public Order Act 1986, for example, created new public order offences designed to deal with specific problems of the time, such as football hooliganism and, at the same time, repealed out-of-date public order offences.

Some significant law reforms have come about as a result of Private Members' Bills (see p. 45) – an example is the Abortion Act 1967 which resulted from a Private Members' Bill put forward by David Steel.

Pressures for reform

The inspiration for reform may come from a variety of sources, alone or in combination. As well as encouraging Parliament to consider particular issues in the first place, they may have an influence during the consultation stage of legislation.

Pressure groups

Groups concerned with particular subjects may press for law reform in those areas – examples include charities such as Shelter, Help the Aged and the Child Poverty Action Group; professional organisations such as the Law Society and the British Medical Association; business representatives such as the Confederation of British Industry. JUSTICE is a pressure group specifically concerned with promoting law reform in general.

Pressure groups use a variety of tactics, including lobbying MPs, gaining as much publicity as possible for their cause, organising petitions, and encouraging people to write to their own MP and/or relevant Ministers. Some groups are more effective than others: size obviously helps, but sheer persistence and a knack for grabbing headlines can be just as productive – the anti-porn campaigner Mary Whitehouse almost single-handedly pressurised the Government to create the Protection of Children Act 1978, which sought to prevent child pornography. The amount of power wielded by the members of a pressure group is also extremely important – organisations involved with big business tend to be particularly effective in influencing legislation, and there is a growing industry set up purely to help them lobby effectively, for a price. On the other hand, pressure groups made up of ordinary individuals can be very successful, particularly if the issue on which they are campaigning is one which stirs up strong emotion in the general public. An example was the Snowdrop Petition, organised after the shooting of 16 young children and their teacher in Dunblane, Scotland. Despite enormous opposition from shooting clubs, it managed to persuade the then Government to ban most types of handguns.

Political parties

Some of the most high-profile legislation is that passed in order to implement the Government party's election manifesto, or its general ideology – examples include the privatisations of gas and water and the creation of the Poll Tax by the Conservative Government which began in 1979.

The civil service

Although technically neutral, the civil service nevertheless has a great effect on legislation in general. It may not have party political goals, but various departments will have their own views as to what type of legislation enables them to achieve departmental goals most efficiently – which strategies might help the Home Office control the prison population, for example, or the Department of Health make the NHS more efficient. Ministers rely heavily on senior civil servants for advice and information on the issues of the day, and few would consistently turn down their suggestions.

Treaty obligations

The UK's obligations under the treaties establishing the EU and the European Convention on Human Rights both influence changes in British law.

Public opinion and media pressure

As well as taking part in campaigns organised by pressure groups, members of the public make their feelings known by writing to their MPs, to Ministers and to newspapers. This is most likely to lead to reform where the ruling party has a small majority. The media can also be a very powerful force for law reform, by highlighting issues of concern. In 1997, media pressure helped secure a judicial inquiry into the racially motivated killing of South London teenager Stephen Lawrence. The inquiry was authorised to look not only at the Lawrence case itself, but at the general issue of how racially motivated killings are investigated.

Public opinion and media pressure interact; the media often claims to reflect public opinion, but can also whip it up. What appears to be a major epidemic of a particular crime may in fact be no more than a reflection of the fact that once one interesting example of it hits the news, newspapers and broadcasting organisations are more likely to report others. An example of this is the rash of stories during 1993 about parents going on holiday and leaving their children alone, which caught the headlines largely because of a popular film about just such a situation, *Home Alone*. Leaving children alone like this may have been common practice for years, or it may be something done by a tiny minority of parents, but the media's selection of stories gave the impression of a sudden epidemic of parental negligence. In 2000 there was a high-profile campaign by the *News of the World* to 'name and shame' paedophiles. The Government subsequently introduced a limited reform of the law.

9

Law reform

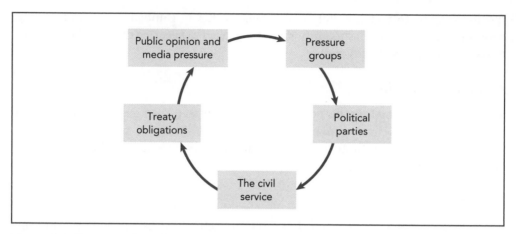

Figure 9.2 Pressures for reform

Agencies of law reform

Much law reform happens as a direct response to pressure from one or more of the above sources, but there are also a number of agencies set up to consider the need for reform in areas referred to them by the Government. Often problems are referred to them as a result of the kind of pressures listed above – the Royal Commission on Criminal Justice 1993 was set up as a result of public concern and media pressure about high-profile miscarriages of justice, such as the Birmingham Six and the Guildford Four.

The Law Commission

Established in 1965 (along with another for Scotland), the Law Commission is a permanent body, comprising five people drawn from the judiciary, the legal profession and legal academics. In practice, the chairman tends to be a High Court judge, and the other four members to include a QC experienced in criminal law, a solicitor with experience of land law and equity, and two legal academics. They are assisted by legally qualified civil servants.

Under the Law Commissions Act 1965 the Law Commission's task is to:

- codify the law;
- remove anomalies in the law;
- repeal obsolete and unnecessary legislation;
- consolidate the law;
- simplify and modernise the law.

The Commission works on reform projects referred to it by the Lord Chancellor or a Government department, or on projects which the Commission itself has decided would be suitable for its consideration. At any one time the Commission will be engaged on between 20 and 30 projects of law reform.

A typical project will begin with a study of the area of law in question, and an attempt to identify its defects. Foreign legal systems will be examined to see how they deal with similar problems. The Commission normally publishes a consultation paper inviting comments on the subject. The consultation paper describes the present law and its shortcomings and sets out possible options for reform. The Commission's final recommendations are set out in a report which contains a draft Bill where legislation is proposed. It is then essentially for the Government to decide whether it accepts the recommendations and to introduce any necessary Bill in Parliament.

Royal Commissions

These are set up to study particular areas of law reform, usually as a result of criticism and concern about the relevant area. They are made up of a wide cross-section of people: most have some expertise in the area concerned, but usually only a minority are legally qualified. The Commissions are supposed to be independent and non-political.

A Royal Commission can commission research, and also take submissions from interested parties. It produces a final report detailing its recommendations, which the Government can then choose to act upon or not. Usually a majority of proposals are acted upon, sometimes in amended form.

Important recent Royal Commissions include the 1981 Royal Commission on Criminal Procedure, the Royal Commission on Criminal Justice, which reported in 1993, and the Royal Commission on Reform of the House of Lords, which reported in 2000.

Public inquiries

Photo 9.1 Brixton riots
Source: © David Hoffman Photo Library/Alamy

9

Law reform

Where a particular problem or incident is causing social concern, the Government may set up a one-off, temporary committee to examine possible options for dealing with it. Major disasters, such as the Hillsborough football stadium disaster, the sinking of the ferry *Herald of Free Enterprise* and railway accidents; events such as the Brixton riots during the 1980s; and advances in technology, especially medical technology (such as the ability to fertilise human eggs outside the body and produce 'test tube babies') may all be investigated by bodies set up especially for the job. In recent years inquiries have been set up following the BSE crisis, the murder of Victoria Climbié (a young girl living away from her parents), and the conviction of the serial killer Harold Shipman. These inquiries usually comprise individuals who are independent of Government, often with expertise in the particular area. Academics are frequent choices, as are judges – Lord Scarman headed the inquiry into the Brixton riots and Lord Hutton (2004) headed the inquiry into the suicide of Dr David Kelly following the war in Iraq.

Public inquiries consult interested groups, and attempt to reach a consensus between them, conducting their investigation as far as possible in a non-political way. Inquiries publish their findings and make recommendations as to how practices can be improved.

Photo 9.2 Dr David Kelly's death was the subject of Lord Hutton's inquiry
Source: Ian Waldie/Getty Images

NAMED
SHAMED

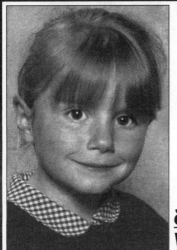

News of the World — JULY 23, 2000 — PLUS YOUR SUNDAY MAGAZINE — Price 60p

IF YOU ARE A PARENT YOU MUST READ THIS

There are 110,000 child sex offenders in Britain.. one for every square mile. The murder of Sarah Payne has proved police monitoring of these perverts is not enough. So we are revealing WHO they are and WHERE they are..starting today

FACE OF AN ANGEL: Sarah has inspired our crusade

FOR SARAH CAMPAIGN: PAGES 2, 3, 4, 5 AND 6

Photo 9.3 *News of the World*: its campaign to name and shame paedophiles

Source: Remember When, The Newspaper Archive. The *News of the World*, London, 23 July 2000.
© *News of the World*/23 July 2000/nisyndication.com (front cover); © John Conner Press Associates Ltd. (photograph of Sarah Payne)

Photo 9.4 Victoria Climbié

Source: Rex Features

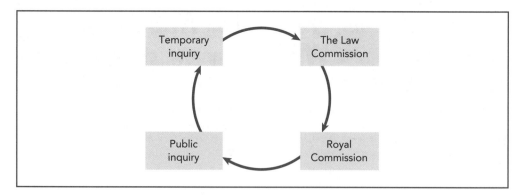

Figure 9.3 Agencies of law reform

Other temporary inquiries

From time to time, various Government departments set up temporary projects to investigate specific areas of law. One of the most important examples is the inquiry by Lord Woolf into the Civil Justice System (p. 534).

Performance of the law reform bodies

The Law Commission

One of the principal tasks of the Commission at its inception was codification, and this programme has not on the whole been a success. The Commission's programme was ambitious: in 1965 it announced that it would begin codifying family law, contract, landlord and tenant, and evidence. Attempts in the first three were abandoned – family in 1970, contract in 1973 and landlord and tenant in 1978. Evidence was never begun.

Zander (1988) suggests the reasons for the failure are 'a mixture of conservatism and a realisation on the part of draftsmen, legislators and even judges that [codification] simply did not fit the English style of lawmaking'. The draftsmen were not keen on the idea that codes would have to be drawn up in a broader manner than was normal for traditional statutes. Legislators were doubtful of the concept of a huge Bill which would attempt to state the law in a vast area such as landlord and tenant. The judges objected to the vision promoted by Lord Scarman, the Commission's first chairman, of the code coming down like an iron curtain making all pre-code law irrelevant. As Zander explains, this appeared to the judges like 'throwing the baby out with the bathwater – losing the priceless heritage of the past and wasting the fruits of legislation and litigation on numerous points which would still be relevant to interpret the new code'.

The Law Commission is particularly concerned with the Government's failure to codify the criminal law. Between 1968 and 1974 the Commission produced a series of working papers, but in 1980 announced that its shortage of resources would not allow it to continue, and appealed for help with the task. The Society of Public Teachers of Law responded, and set up a four-person committee, which by 1985 had produced a draft code. But this has never been legislated as law. In most countries criminal law is contained in a single code so that it is accessible to the people against whom it will be applied. The Commission has now embarked upon a programme to produce a series of draft Bills, based on the code but incorporating appropriate law reform proposals, which will in themselves make substantial improvements in the law. If enacted, these Bills will form a criminal code. But at the moment there is no tangible sign of progress in implementation of any of their major reports dating back to 1993. Decisions of the courts continue to draw attention to defects in the substantive law in areas on which they have already reported. One ray of hope has been the passing of legislation consolidating the sentencing regime, and further impetus for codification has been given by the review of criminal procedure under Lord Justice Auld (2001). In the Home Office White Paper, *Criminal Justice: the Way Ahead* (2001) it stated that it did intend to codify the criminal law as part of its modernisation process.

9

Law reform

However, opinions are mixed on whether codification would prove to be of very great value even if it ever becomes possible. Supporters say it would provide accessibility, comprehensibility, consistency and certainty. A code allows people to see their rights and liabilities more clearly than a mixture of case law and separate statutes could, and should encourage judges and others who use it to look for and expect to find answers within it. Lord Hailsham has said that a good codification would save a great deal of judicial time and so reduce costs, and the academic Glanville Williams (1983) makes the point that criminal law is not like the law of procedure, meant for lawyers only, but is addressed to all classes of society, and so the greater accessibility and clarity of a code should be particularly welcomed in this area.

Critics say a very detailed codification could make the law too rigid, losing the flexibility of the common law. And if it were insufficiently detailed, as Zander (2004) points out, it would need to be interpreted by the courts, so creating a new body of case law around it, which would defeat the object of codification and make the law neither more accessible nor more certain. It may be that the Law Commission's failure to codify the law signifies a problem with codification, not with the Law Commission.

Instead of proceeding with large-scale codification, the Law Commission has chosen to clarify areas of law piece by piece, with the aim of eventual codification if possible. Family law in particular has been significantly reformed in this way, even if the results are, as Zander points out, a 'jumble of disconnected statutes rather than a spanking new code'.

As far as general law reform is concerned, as well as the major family law reforms, the Commission has radically changed contract law by recommending control of exclusion clauses which led to the passing of the Unfair Contract Terms Act 1977. Its report, *Criminal Law: Conspiracy and Criminal Law Reform* (1976), helped shape the Criminal Law Act 1977 and its working paper, *Offences Against Public Order* (1982), was instrumental in creating the Public Order Act 1986. Following its recommendations, the Computer Misuse Act 1990 introduced new criminal offences relating to the misuse of computers; and the Family Law Act 1996 changed the law on domestic violence and divorce.

In recent years, however, there has been a major problem with lack of implementation of Law Commission proposals. By 1999, 102 law reform reports had been implemented, which represented two-thirds of their final reports. There is a better chance of proposals from the Law Commission becoming legislation if the subject concerned comes within the remit of the Ministry of Justice; there is less chance if they concern other departments, particularly the Home Office. In any case, it has been pointed out that implementation of proposals is not the only benefit of a permanent law reform body. Stephen Cretney (1998), a legal academic who has been a Law Commissioner, suggests that one of its most important contributions has simply been getting law reform under discussion and examination, and drawing attention to the needs of various areas of law.

In its White Paper, *Governance of Britain: Constitutional Renewal* (2008), the Government laid out plans to strengthen the Law Commission's role. The Law Commission Act 2009 has now been passed which places a statutory duty on the Lord Chancellor to report annually to Parliament on the Government's intentions regarding outstanding Law Commission recommendations.

Royal Commissions

These have had mixed success. The 1978 Royal Commission on Civil Liability and Compensation for Personal Injury produced a report that won neither public nor Government support, and few of its proposals were implemented.

The Royal Commission on Criminal Procedure has most of its recommendations implemented by the Police and Criminal Evidence Act 1984 (PACE), but subsequent criticisms of PACE mean this is less of a success than it appears. The Royal Commission stated that the aim behind its proposals was to secure a balance between the rights of individuals suspected of crime, and the need to bring guilty people to justice. PACE has, however, been criticised by the police as leaning too far towards suspects' rights, and by civil liberties campaigners as not leaning far enough.

Perhaps the most successful Royal Commission in recent years has been the Royal Commission on Assizes and Quarter Sessions, which reported in 1969. Its proposals for the reorganisation of criminal courts were speedily implemented.

As regards the 1993 Royal Commission on Criminal Justice, this has met with mixed results. Some of its recommendations were introduced in the Criminal Justice and Public Order Act 1994 and the Criminal Appeal Act 1995, which created the Criminal Cases Review Commission (see p. 590) in response to the Commission's criticism of the criminal appeals system. On the other hand, the Government has ignored some of its proposals and has proceeded to introduce changes that the Royal Commission was specifically opposed to, for example the abolition of the right to silence.

Public inquiries and other temporary committees

These rely to a great extent on political will, and the best committees in the world may be ineffective if they propose changes that a Government dislikes. Lord Scarman's investigation into the Brixton riots is seen as a particularly effective public inquiry, getting to the root of the problem by going out to ask the people involved what caused it (his Lordship, then retired, shocked his previous colleagues by taking to the streets of Brixton and being shown on television chatting to residents and cuddling their babies). His proposals produced some of the steps towards police accountability in PACE. But the subsequent inquiry into the case of Stephen Lawrence shows that the progress made was not sufficient. The Civil Justice Review was also instrumental in bringing about reform, though views on the success of the changes are mixed and the area has subsequently been tackled again by Lord Woolf.

Public inquiries are often set up after a major disaster or matter of controversy, where there is suspicion on the part of the community involved. For example, an inquiry was set up after Harold Shipman was convicted of murdering a large number of his elderly patients. People demanding an inquiry are usually looking for an independent and open examination of the facts to determine what exactly happened and to prevent this happening again. In practice, public inquiries can put forward a large number of recommendations that the government may appear to accept but then nothing is done to implement these recommendations, so that the risks of reoccurrence remain. For example, Dame Janet Smith's inquiry into the Shipman case made many recommendations that have not been acted upon.

9

Law reform

Photo 9.5 Scene outside the Lawrence Inquiry, Elephant and Castle, London

Source: PA Photos. Photograph © Tony Harris

Ess. Cases
p. 91 →

Ess. Cases
p. 92 →

TOPICAL ISSUE

Streamlining public inquiries

The Government has been concerned by the inefficiency and cost of recent public inquiries. For example, the inquiry into Bloody Sunday in Ireland took seven years and is reported to have cost £155 million. The Government therefore decided to introduce legislation to improve the inquiry process, partly in an attempt to keep costs down. In 2004 a consultation paper was issued on the subject called *Effective Inquiries*. Following this consultation process, the Inquiries Act 2005 was passed. The stated aim of the Government in passing this legislation was to modernise procedures, control costs and give more effective powers to those chairing the inquiries. Despite this, the legislation has been criticised; Amnesty International has claimed that any inquiries established under this legislation would be a 'sham' and urged judges to refuse appointments to them. It is worried that the legislation fails to allow adequate public scrutiny and 'undermines the rule of law, the separation of powers and human rights protection'. The Act arguably gives too much power to the executive, as the executive will be able to decide whether or not to publish the final report of any inquiry, whether to exclude evidence if this is deemed 'in the public interest', and whether the inquiry, or part of it, will be held in public or private.

The first inquiry to be set up under this legislation looked at allegations of state collusion in the murder of Patrick Finucane, who was an outspoken human rights lawyer in Northern Ireland. Amnesty International was concerned that this inquiry was ineffective because of the limitations of the Inquiries Act 2005.

Governments can refuse to hold a public inquiry which they feel may prove politically embarrassing. The parents of four soldiers killed in Iraq wanted there to be a public inquiry into whether the war in Iraq was illegal. The Government refused to establish such an inquiry and the families sought a judicial review of this decision, arguing that they have a right to a public inquiry under Art. 2 of the European Convention on Human Rights which guarantees the right to life: **R (on the application of Gentle)** *v* **the Prime Minister** (2008). Their application was rejected by the House of Lords, which held that Art. 2 could not restrict a nation's decision to go to war. Ultimately, the decision as to whether or not to hold a public inquiry is a political one, not a legal one.

Problems with law reform agencies

Lack of power

There is no obligation for Government to consult the permanent law reform bodies, or to set up Royal Commissions or other committees when considering major law reforms. Mrs Thatcher set up no Royal Commissions during her terms of office, despite the fact that important and controversial legislation – such as that abolishing the GLC – was being passed.

Political difficulties

Governments also have no obligation to follow recommendations, and perfectly well-thought-out proposals may be rejected on the grounds that they do not fit in with a Government's political position. An example was the recommendation of the Law Commission in 1978 that changes be made to the rule that interest is not payable on a contract debt unless the parties agreed otherwise. The idea was supported by the House of Lords in **President of India** *v* **La Pintada** (1984), but the Government was persuaded not to implement the proposals after lobbying from the CBI and consumer organisations.

Even where general suggestions for areas of new legislation are implemented, the detailed proposals may be radically altered. The recommendations of law reform agencies may act as justification for introducing new legislation yet, as Zander (2004) points out, often when the Bill is published it becomes clear that the carefully constructed proposal put together by the law reform agency 'has been unstitched and a new and different package has been constructed'.

Lack of influence on results

Where proposals are implemented, ideas that are effective in themselves may be weakened if they are insufficiently funded when put into practice – a matter on which law reform bodies can have little or no influence. The 1981 Royal Commission on Criminal Procedure's recommendations were largely implemented in the Police and

Criminal Evidence Act 1984, and one of them was that suspects questioned in a police station should have the right to free legal advice, leading to the setting up of the duty solicitor scheme. While the idea of the scheme was seen as a good one, underfunding has brought it close to collapse, and meant that in practice relatively small numbers of suspects actually get advice from qualified, experienced solicitors within a reasonable waiting time. This has clearly frustrated the aims of the Royal Commission's recommendation.

Too much compromise

Royal Commissions and temporary committees have the advantage of drawing members from wide backgrounds, with a good spread of experience and expertise. However, in some cases this can result in proposals that try too hard to represent a compromise. The result can be a lack of political support and little chance of implementation. It is generally agreed that this was the problem with the Pearson Report, the report of the Royal Commission on Civil Liability and Compensation for Personal Injury.

Influence of the legal profession

Where temporary law reform committees have a high proportion of non-lawyers, the result can be more innovative, imaginative ideas than might come from legally trained people who, however open-minded, are within 'the system' and accustomed to seeing the problems in a particular framework. However, this benefit is heavily diluted by the fact that the strong influence of the legal profession on any type of reform can defeat such proposals even before they reach an official report.

An example was the suggestion of the Civil Justice Review in its consultation paper that the county courts and High Court might merge, with some High Court judges being stationed in the provinces to deal with the more complex cases there. Despite a warm welcome from consumer groups and the National Association of Citizens' Advice Bureaux, the proposals were effectively shot down by the outcry from senior judges who were concerned that their status and way of life might be adversely affected, and the Bar, which was worried that it might lose too much work to solicitors. In the event the proposal was not included in the final report.

Waste of expertise

Royal Commissions and temporary committees are disbanded after producing their report, and take no part in the rest of the law-making process. This is in many ways a waste of the expertise they have built up.

Lack of ministerial involvement

There is no single ministry responsible for law reform so that often no Minister makes it his or her priority.

Answering questions

1 **To what extent is the English Law Commission effective?**

Here you are basically being asked how well the Law Commission has done its job. Your introduction might state what the Commission was set up to do, and then the rest of your essay can consider whether it has fulfilled that function and thereby given an important impetus to law reform. You could start by explaining that the Law Commission is a permanent body drawing personnel from the judiciary, the legal professions and academia. It puts forward proposals for

- codification,
- the removal of anomalies,
- repealing obsolete laws,
- consolidation,
- simplification, and
- modernisation.

With regard to how effective the Law Commission has been, its original ambitions of codifying the law – particularly criminal, family, contract, landlord and tenant and evidence law – has not been achieved. Zander has suggested that this failure is due to conservatism and that codification fits uneasily into the English legal system. More recently the Law Commission has been dogged by a lack of resources and it has focused upon draft bills addressing relatively narrow topics, such as unfair contract terms. Finish by summing up what you think the Commission's contribution has been – it has certainly managed to promote discussion of law reform and drawn attention to the need to amend certain areas of law.

2 **Critically evaluate the agencies of law reform in England and Wales.**

Note that this question can apply not only to the official bodies such as the Law Commission, but also to informal ones such as pressure groups, and you need to discuss both types. It may be a good idea to divide your answer into official and unofficial law reform bodies: taking each in turn, you can describe how they operate and assess their effectiveness, pointing out any problems in the way they work. Do not forget that what is needed is a critical account – just listing the bodies and what they do will get you very few marks. What the examiners want to know is not just what the bodies do, but how well they do it.

Your discussion of the formal bodies of law reform could include the Law Commission, Royal Commissions and public inquiries. Your discussion of the informal bodies of law reform could include pressure groups, the media, academics through their research showing how the law is working in practice and the judiciary who might highlight problems with the law in their judgments in the hope that Parliament might take note.

Your conclusion might generally sum up the effect of these multiple bodies, saying whether, taken together, you feel they do an adequate job in reforming the law. The success of these agencies depends essentially upon the Parliamentary willingness to accept their findings and act thereon.

3 **Despite the influence of, for example, pressure groups, public opinion and the media, numerous problems with law reform agencies have resulted in a lack of implementation of reform proposals, especially those advanced by the Law Commission. What factors have contributed towards this lack of implementation?**

You could start by setting out what influence pressure groups, public opinion and the media do have on proposed reforms to the law (p. 134). The main part of your answer should then concentrate on the material contained in the section entitled 'Problems with law reform agencies' (p. 145), explaining why reform proposals are often not implemented. You could also note that, although there has been a lack of implementation of Law Commission proposals in recent years, those proposals do nonetheless perform the useful function of highlighting areas of law needing reform (p. 142).

Summary of Chapter 9: Law reform

The law needs to change to reflect the changes in society. Changes in the law can be made through the process of case law or by Parliament. The four ways in which Parliament can change the law are:

- repeal;
- creation;
- consolidation; and
- codification.

Pressures for reform
The inspiration for reform may come from a variety of sources, including:

- pressure groups;
- political parties;
- the civil service;
- treaty obligations; and
- public opinion and media pressure.

Agencies of law reform
There are a number of agencies set up to consider the need for reform in areas referred to them by the Government. These agencies are:

- the Law Commission;
- Royal Commissions;
- public inquiries; and
- other temporary inquiries.

The level of success of these agencies has varied considerably. Governments have no obligation to follow their recommendations. Some of the recommendations involve too many compromises and, where lawyers dominate, the resulting reforms may be under-ambitious.

 Reading list

Cretney, S. (1998) *Law, Law Reform and the Family*, Oxford: Clarendon Press.

Hutton, Lord (2004) *Report of the Inquiry into the Circumstances Surrounding the Death of Dr David Kelly C.M.G.*, London: Stationery Office.

Marsh, N. (1971) 'Law reform in the United Kingdom: A new institutional approach', 13 *William and Mary Law Review* 263.

Reading on the Internet

www The Law Commission's website is:
   http://www.lawcom.gov.uk

John Halliday has produced a report on the work of the Law Commission which has been published on the Law Commission's website:
   http://www.dca.gov.uk/majrep/lawcom/halliday.htm

Visit www.mylawchamber.co.uk/ElliottELS to access multiple-choice questions, flashcards and practice exam questions to test yourself on this chapter.

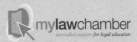

9

Law reform

PART 2

PEOPLE WORKING IN THE LEGAL SYSTEM

This Part of the book looks at the different people involved in the English legal system. Some of these are in paid employment, such as the professional judges, barristers, solicitors and legal executives. Others are essentially unpaid and include jurors and magistrates.

10 The judges

This chapter discusses:

- the role of the judges;
- the different types of judges, known as the 'judicial hierarchy';
- how judges are appointed and trained;
- the five ways that a judge may cease to be a judge;
- the independence of the judiciary;
- criticisms of the judiciary and options for reform.

The role of the judges

The judges play a central role under the British constitution. A basic principle of our constitution is known as the rule of law, discussed at p. 5. Under the rule of law judges are expected to deliver judgments in a completely impartial manner, applying the law strictly, without allowing any personal preferences to affect their decision-making.

The judges play a vital but sensitive role in controlling the exercise of power by the state. They do this in particular through the procedure of judicial review. The passing of the Human Rights Act 1998 significantly increased the powers of the judges to control the work of Parliament and the executive. A controversial judicial decision which highlights the tension between the roles of the judges, Parliament and the executive is

Ess. Cases p. 208 → **A and X and others** *v* **Secretary of State for the Home Department** (2004). Following fear over the increased risks of terrorism, Parliament had passed the Anti-Terrorism, Crime and Security Act 2001. This allowed the Government to detain in prison suspected terrorists without trial. The subsequent detention of nine foreign nationals was challenged through the courts and the House of Lords ruled that their detention was unlawful because it violated the Human Rights Act. As a result, the relevant provisions within the legislation were repealed and replaced by the Prevention of Terrorism Act 2005. This established control orders, which can potentially amount to house arrest – the first time we have seen this measure in the UK.

Judicial hierarchy

The judges are at the centre of any legal system, as they sit in court and decide the cases. At the head of the judiciary is the President of the Courts of England and Wales. This position was created by the Constitutional Reform Act 2005. Before that Act was passed, the Lord Chancellor had been the head of the judiciary. The new President of the Courts of England and Wales (in practice the Lord Chief Justice, discussed below) is now the head of the judiciary, being officially the president of the Court of Appeal, the High Court, the Crown Court, the county courts and the magistrates' courts. He or she is technically allowed to hear cases in any of these courts, though in practice he or she is only likely to choose to sit in the Court of Appeal. Under s. 7 of the Act, the President's role is to represent the views of the judiciary to Parliament and to Government Ministers. He or she is also responsible for the maintenance of appropriate arrangements for the welfare, training and guidance of the judiciary and for arranging where judges work and their workload.

The most senior judges are the 12 Justices of the Supreme Court. They sit in the Supreme Court and the Privy Council.

At the next level down, sitting in the Court of Appeal, are 38 judges known as Lord Justices of Appeal and Lady Justices of Appeal. The Criminal Division of the Court of Appeal is presided over by the Lord Chief Justice who, following the Constitutional

Table 10.1 The hierarchy of the judiciary

Judge	Usual court
Justice of the Supreme Court	Supreme Court and Privy Council
Lord Chief Justice	Criminal Division of the Court of Appeal
Master of the Rolls	Civil Division of the Court of Appeal
Lord Justice of Appeal	Court of Appeal
High Court judge	High Court and Crown Court
Circuit judge	County Court and Crown Court
District judge	Crown Court
District judge (magistrates' court)	Magistrates' court
Recorder	County Court and Crown Court

Reform Act 2005, is also known as the President of the Courts of England and Wales (discussed above). He or she can at the same time act as the Head of Criminal Justice or appoint another Court of Appeal judge to take this role.

The Civil Division of the Court of Appeal is presided over by the Master of the Rolls. There is also a Head of Civil Justice and a Head of Family Justice.

In the High Court, there are 107 full-time judges. As well as sitting in the High Court itself, they hear the most serious criminal cases in the Crown Court. Although – like judges in the Court of Appeal and the Supreme Court – High Court judges receive a knighthood, they are referred to as Mr or Mrs Justice Smith (or whatever their surname is), which is written as Smith J.

The next rank down concerns the circuit judges, who travel around the country, sitting in the county court and also hearing the middle-ranking Crown Court cases. The Criminal Justice and Public Order Act 1994 added a further role, allowing them occasionally to sit in the Criminal Division of the Court of Appeal.

The slightly less serious Crown Court criminal cases are heard by district judges, and then there are recorders, who are part-time judges dealing with the least serious Crown Court criminal cases. Recorders are usually still working as barristers or solicitors, and the role is often used as a kind of apprenticeship before becoming a circuit judge. Because of the number of minor cases coming before the Crown Court, there are now assistant recorders as well, and at times retired circuit judges have been called upon to help out. Finally, in larger cities there are district judges (magistrates' courts), who were previously known as stipendiary magistrates, and are full-time, legally qualified judges working in magistrates' courts.

In practice, there is some flexibility between the courts, so that judges sometimes sit in more senior courts than their status would suggest. This practice is illustrated by the diagram below.

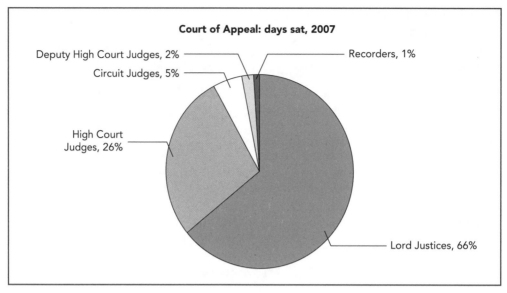

Figure 10.1 Court of Appeal: days sat, 2007

Source: Judicial and Court Statistics 2007, p. 177

A reduced role for the Lord Chancellor

The position of Lord Chancellor has existed for over 1,400 years. He (there has never actually been a female Lord Chancellor) has played a central role in the English legal system, but the position is currently being reformed following persistent criticism. This criticism is based on the constitutional doctrine of the separation of powers. Under this doctrine, the power of the state has to be divided between three separate and independent arms: the judiciary (comprising the judges), the legislature (Parliament in the UK); and the executive (the Government of the day). The idea is that the separate arms of the state should operate independently, so that each one is checked and balanced by the other two, and none becomes all-powerful. The doctrine of the separation of powers was first put forward in the eighteenth century by the French political theorist Montesquieu. Montesquieu argued that if all the powers were concentrated in the hands of one group, the result would be tyranny. Therefore, the doctrine requires that individuals should not occupy a position in more than one of the three arms of the state – judiciary, legislature and executive; each should exercise its functions independently of any control or interference from the others; and one arm of the state should not exercise the functions of either of the others.

The Lord Chancellor has had such wide powers, which extended to all three arms of the state, that his existence was a clear breach of the doctrine of the separation of powers. We will look first at his judicial powers. He has been at the head of the whole judiciary, and effectively appointed all the other judges. He has been President of the High Court, the Crown Court and the Court of Appeal. He has also officially been

President of the Chancery Division of the High Court, although in practice the Vice-Chancellor usually performed this role. When the Lord Chancellor sat as a judge, it was in the House of Lords or the Privy Council, but recent Lord Chancellors chose only to do this occasionally or not at all, and the House of Lord, has now been abolished.

As regards his political role, the Lord Chancellor has been a Cabinet Minister and Speaker of the House of Lords. Although technically appointed by the Queen, the Lord Chancellor is actually chosen by the Prime Minister and goes out of office when that party loses an election, as well as being eligible for removal by the Prime Minister, just like any other Minister.

In relation to his executive functions, he was at the head of the Lord Chancellor's Department. He had powers to give directions about the business of the courts, and responsibility for the Law Commission and the state funding of legal services. Most controversially, he has had control over judicial appointments. Politically, the most important judicial appointment is that of the Master of the Rolls; as president of the Court of Appeal his or her view on the proper relationship between the executive government and the individual is crucial. The appointment of Lord Donaldson in 1982 was seen as a strongly political appointment and one which the then Prime Minister favoured: he had been a Conservative councillor, and was not promoted during the years of the previous Labour Government, 1974–79. There was some publicity concerning Lord Donaldson's political views at the time of the high-profile GCHQ union membership case, **Council of Civil Service Unions _v_ Minister for the Civil Service** (1985) and, as a result, his Lordship declined to preside over the Court of Appeal when it considered the Government's appeal in that case.

So the position of the Lord Chancellor as a member of the judiciary, the executive and the legislature clearly went against the idea that no individual should be part of all three arms of the state. The conflicting roles of the Lord Chancellor were highlighted in 2001 when the media drew attention to the fact that the Lord Chancellor had been involved in political fundraising. Guests to a dinner he had organised were invited to make donations to the Labour Party and there were concerns that lawyers might seek promotion by giving substantial donations. Legal Action Group, a pressure group, has argued that the various roles of the Lord Chancellor put him in breach of the European Convention on Human Rights.

In June 2003 the Government announced that it intended to abolish the office of Lord Chancellor. At the same time it established a Minister for Constitutional Affairs, with significantly fewer powers than his or her predecessor. The new Minister was intended to be a more traditional member of the executive, with no right to sit as a judge, no role in the judicial appointments process and not the Speaker of the House of Lords. The first person to be appointed Minister for Constitutional Affairs was Lord Falconer.

There was considerable criticism of the hasty way in which this reform was commenced and much of the detail about who would fulfil many of the previous powers of the Lord Chancellor had not been decided before some of the changes were introduced. The new Minister for Constitutional Affairs, therefore, had to be Lord Chancellor as well and was forced to fulfil some of the old functions of the Lord Chancellor, though he stated he would not choose to sit as a judge in the House of Lords.

10

The judges

Table 10.2 Past role of the Lord Chancellor

Branch of Government	Role of the Lord Chancellor
Legislature	Speaker of the House of Lords
Executive	Government Minister
Judiciary	Judge in the House of Lords and Privy Council. He was also President of the group of courts formerly known as Supreme Court and President of the Chancery Division of the High Court.

The Government introduced to Parliament the Constitutional Reform Bill, which in its original form would have abolished the office of Lord Chancellor and given his powers to a range of individuals including the Minister for Constitutional Affairs. The passage of this Bill through Parliament proved to be complicated. Many people were unhappy with the speed at which these important reforms were being introduced with only a limited consultation process. Following opposition in the House of Lords, the Government agreed to amend the Constitutional Reform Bill. The position of Lord Chancellor was retained, though his or her role was significantly reduced. With the passing of the Constitutional Reform Act 2005, four major changes to the role of the Lord Chancellor have been made. As a result he or she no longer:

- sits as a judge;
- heads the judiciary;
- takes a central role in the judicial appointment process; or
- automatically becomes the Speaker of the House of Lords.

He or she remains as the head of a Government department (now called the Ministry of Justice), but his or her powers and links to the judges have been removed to satisfy the principle of the separation of powers. The Lord Chancellor has become a more traditional Cabinet Minister, responsible, in particular, for legal aid, the Law Commission and the court system. At pp. 162–4 we look at how the Lord Chancellor's powers have been replaced as regards judicial appointments. A new position of President of the Court of England and Wales has been created by s. 7 of the Constitutional Reform Act 2005. This person (in practice the Lord Chief Justice) is at the head of the judiciary and the Lord Chancellor's judicial functions are transferred to him or her.

The Lord Chancellor retains a constitutional obligation to uphold the rule of law under s. 1 of the 2005 Act (discussed at p. 169). Under s. 3, he also has a duty to uphold the independence of the judiciary (discussed at p. 169).

In 2006 the Government replaced the Ministry for Constitutional Affairs with a Ministry of Justice, so that the Lord Chancellor is no longer the Minister for Constitutional Affairs, but the Minister for Justice (see p. 292).

As regards the Lord Chancellor's historical function as Speaker of the House of Lords, it is now up to the House of Lords in its parliamentary capacity to determine who will be the Speaker of the House. The Lord Chancellor is no longer required to be a

Photo 10.1 The Right Honourable Jack Straw MP, Lord Chancellor and Secretary of State for Justice

Source: www.justice.gov.uk

member of the House of Lords, but could be a member of the House of Commons instead. This could lead to the position becoming more political.

In the past, the Lord Chancellor had to be a lawyer, but under s. 2 of the Constitutional Reform Act 2005, the Lord Chancellor must simply appear to the Prime Minister to be qualified 'by experience'. Subsection (2) states that this experience could have been gained as a Government Minister, a member of either Houses of Parliament, a qualified lawyer, a teacher of law in a university or 'other experience that the Prime Minister considers relevant'. Thus, in future, the Lord Chancellor may not be a lawyer.

Appointments to the judiciary

The way in which judges are appointed has been radically reformed by provisions in the Constitutional Reform Act 2005. In order to evaluate the new appointment procedures, it is useful to understand how judges were appointed before these reforms were introduced. We will therefore look first at the old procedures before looking at the new ones.

The old appointment procedures

Prior to the 2005 Act, the Lord Chancellor played a central role in the appointment of judges. The Lords of Appeal in Ordinary (the judges in the House of Lords) and the Lord Justices of Appeal were appointed by the Queen on the advice of the Prime

Minister, who in turn was advised by the Lord Chancellor. High Court judges, circuit judges and recorders were appointed by the Queen on the advice of the Lord Chancellor.

Over the years there had been considerable criticism of the way in which judges were appointed and, as a result, changes had been made even before the more radical reforms of the 2005 Act. In the past only barristers could become senior judges. The Courts and Legal Services Act 1990 widened entry to the judiciary, reflecting the changes in rights of audience (see p. 191), and (at least in theory) opening up the higher reaches of the profession to solicitors as well as barristers. The selection process for judges in the High Court involved the old Department for Constitutional Affairs gathering information about potential candidates over a period of time by making informal inquiries (known as 'secret soundings') from leading barristers and judges.

The normal procedure for recruiting for a job is to place an advertisement in a newspaper and to allow people to apply. By contrast, until recently, there were no advertisements for judicial office, you simply waited to be invited to the post. Advertisements have more recently been placed for junior and High Court judges, but still not for positions in the Court of Appeal and above.

At the Government's request, an inquiry into the system for judicial appointments was undertaken by Sir Leonard Peach, a senior civil servant. His report was published in December 1999. Sir Leonard was generally happy with the quality of the work and the professionalism of the civil servants involved in the appointments process. One of the key recommendations of the report was that a Commissioner for Judicial Appointments should be appointed to provide independent monitoring of the procedures for appointing judges and Queen's Counsel (for an explanation of Queen's Counsel, see p. 201). This recommendation was accepted by the Government and the first Commissioner was appointed in 2001. Sir Leonard Peach did not recommend any changes to the system of secret soundings.

In the past, the final selection process consisted of a traditional job interview. For the appointment of most judges, this was replaced in 2003 with the attendance at an assessment centre for a whole day. The centres require judicial applicants to sit through an interview, participate in role-play and pass a written examination and are meant to offer applicants a fairer opportunity to demonstrate their knowledge and skills and thereby reduce the danger of subjective judgments and resulting discrimination. Research carried out for the Government has found that these assessment centres are, indeed, a fairer method of judicial selection than one relying solely on an interview process.

The Law Society, the professional body representing solicitors, considered the limited reforms made following Sir Leonard Peach's report in 1999 'inadequate', particularly as the new Commissioner was merely responsible for monitoring the existing system, rather than having any direct involvement in the appointments process itself.

The three main criticisms of the old system of selecting judges were that it was dominated by politicians, secretive and discriminatory. On the first issue, the Lord Chancellor and the Prime Minister played central roles in this process but they were politicians and could be swayed by political factors in the selection of judges. The Lord Chancellor presented the Prime Minister with a shortlist of two or three names listing them in the order of his or her own preference. Mrs Thatcher is known to have selected Lord Hailsham's second choice on one occasion.

On the second issue, the constitutional reform organisation Charter 88, among others, criticised the old selection process for being secretive and lacking clearly defined selection criteria. The process was handled by a small group of civil servants who, although they consulted widely with judges and senior barristers, nevertheless wielded a great deal of power. This process was considered to be unfair because it favoured people who had a good network of contacts, perhaps because of their school and family, rather than focusing on the individual's strength as a future judge. There was also a danger that too much reliance was placed on a collection of anecdotal reports from fellow lawyers, with candidates being given no opportunity to challenge damning things said about them.

Since 1999 the Law Society had refused to participate in the secret soundings process. The president of the Law Society described the system as having 'all the elements of an old boys' network', and being inconsistent with an open and objective recruitment process. 'We suspect we were being used to legitimise a system where other people's views were more important than ours. It didn't really matter what we thought, it was the views of the senior judiciary and the Bar which counted.' The highest ranking solicitor among the judiciary is a single High Court judge.

The first report of the Commission for Judicial Appointments was published in 2002. The secret soundings system was found to be poorly understood by both the applicants and the people who were consulted. The Lord Chancellor's Department was criticised for the way it administered the 'sifting' process, where officials weeded out weak applicants at an early stage. In addition, the report concluded that the Department's lack of detailed records of how decisions were reached meant that it was impossible to determine whether applicants had been fairly assessed.

As regards the third criticism, that the old appointments process was discriminatory, a 1997 study commissioned by the Association of Women Barristers is of interest. It found that there was a strong tendency for judges to recommend candidates from their own former chambers. The study looked at appointments to the High Court over a ten-year period (1986–96) and found that of the 104 judges appointed, 70 (67.3 per cent) came from a set of chambers which had at least one ex-member among the judges likely to be consulted. In addition, a strikingly high percentage of appointments came from the same handful of chambers: 28.8 per cent of new judges from chambers which represented 1.8 per cent of the total number of chambers in England and Wales. The fact that those who advised on appointments were already well established within the system could make it unlikely that they would encourage appointment from a wider base: Lord Bridge, the retired Law Lord, commented in a 1992 television programme that they tend to look for 'chaps like ourselves'. As Helena Kennedy QC (1992) has put it, 'the potential for cloning is overwhelming', and the outlook for potential female judges and those from the ethnic minorities not promising.

The process of 'secret soundings' gave real scope for discrimination, with lawyers instinctively falling back on gender and racial stereotypes in concluding whether someone was appropriate for judicial office. For example, individuals were asked whether they thought candidates showed 'decisiveness' and 'authority'. But these are

10

The judges

very subjective concepts and Kamlesh Bahl has argued (*The Guardian*, 10 April 1995) that, as the judiciary is seen as a male profession, perceptions of judicial characteristics, such as 'authority', are also seen as male characteristics. 'Authority' is dependent more on what others think than on the person's own qualities. Indeed, research published by the Bar Council in 1992 concluded:

> It is unlikely that the judicial appointment system offers equal access to women or fair access to promotion to women judges . . . The system depends on patronage, being noticed and being known. (*Without Prejudice? Sex Equality at the Bar and in the Judiciary*, 1992, para. 48(1))

However, in his book *The Judge*, Lord Devlin (1979) says that, while it would be good to open up the legal profession, so that it could get the very best candidates from all walks of life, the nature of the job means that judges will still be the same type of people whether they come from public schools and Oxbridge or not, namely those 'who do not seriously question the status quo'.

In its second annual report, published in 2003, the Commission for Judicial Appointments concluded that there was systemic bias in the way that the judiciary and the legal profession operated. This bias prevented women, ethnic minorities and solicitors from applying successfully for judicial office. The Commission was fundamentally unhappy with the appointment process for High Court judges and recommended that it should be stopped immediately because it was 'opaque, out-dated and not demonstrably based on merit'.

The new appointment procedures

The Government published a consultation paper, *Constitutional Reform: a new way of appointing judges* (2003). While some improvements had been made in recent years to the appointment procedures, the Government concluded that:

> The most fundamental features of the system . . . remain rooted in the past. Incremental changes to the system can only achieve limited results, because the fundamental problem with the current system is that a Government minister, the Lord Chancellor, has sole responsibility for the appointments process and for making or recommending those appointments. However well this has worked in practice, this system no longer commands public confidence, and is increasingly hard to reconcile with the demands of the Human Rights Act.

Following a limited consultation process, the Constitutional Reform Act 2005 was passed containing provisions for the establishment of a Judicial Appointments Commission responsible for a new judicial appointments process. It is hoped that its creation will help to put an end to the breaches of the principle of the separation of powers and reinforce judicial independence.

Under Schedule 12 to the Act, the Commission has 14 members: five lay members (including the chair), five judges, two legal professionals, a tribunal member and a lay magistrate. The members are appointed by the Queen on the recommendation of the Lord Chancellor. Candidates must be selected on the basis of merit and be of good character. Part 2 of the Tribunals, Courts and Enforcement Act 2007 contains provisions to try to widen the pool of lawyers eligible to become judges. In the past, to be eligible for appointment as a judge a person needed to have experience as a judge in a more junior court or rights of audience in a court (which effectively limited judicial appointments to barristers and solicitors). If these professions were dominated by white men from an upper-middle class background, then the judiciary would inevitably share this profile. Under the 2007 Act, eligibility is no longer based on the number of years candidates have had rights of audience before a court, but instead on their number of years' post-qualification experience. The latter is a much broader concept but equally reflects a person's experience of the law. The required number of years' experience has been reduced from seven to five years and ten to seven years, depending on the seniority of the judicial office. In order to be considered for judicial office a person must have a relevant qualification. Following the 2007 Act the Lord Chancellor has issued regulations stating that the qualification of a legal executive is sufficient for judicial appointment in the magistrates' courts and tribunals. As 60 per cent of legal executives are women, this should help to increase the number of female judges.

Government lawyers are now allowed to become judges. These lawyers are people employed in the Crown Prosecution Service, Serious Fraud Office and the Government Legal Service. They will be able to sit as civil recorders (part-time judges) and deputy district judges in the magistrates' court, provided their own department is not involved in the case. This is a major development, as such lawyers have a wide range of backgrounds, with women and ethnic minorities well represented and the majority state educated. Their recruitment as junior judges will hopefully make the profession at this level more representative of society, but it is not clear that there is any real justification for not making the more senior judicial posts open to these lawyers.

In performing its functions the Judicial Appointments Commission must have regard to the need to encourage diversity in the range of persons available for selection (s. 64). It is allowed to encourage people it believes should apply for judicial posts to apply. The Minister is able to issue guidance which the Commission must have regard to. This guidance can include directions on increasing diversity in the judiciary.

The Commission evaluates candidates and recommends, on the basis of merit only, one individual for each vacancy. The Minister is not able to choose someone who has not been recommended to him or her by the Commission. He or she is, however, able to ask for a candidate who is not initially recommended by the Commission to be reconsidered, and can refuse the appointment of someone recommended and ask for a new name to be put forward. The Minister has the ability to reject a candidate once, and to ask the Commission to reconsider once. Having rejected once, the Minister must accept whichever subsequent candidate is selected.

There is special provision for the appointment of the Lord Chief Justice, the heads of Division and the Lord Justices of Appeal. The Commission establishes a selection panel of four members, consisting of two senior judges (normally including the Lord Chief Justice) and two lay members of the Commission.

Appointments of Lords Justices and above are currenty still formally made by the Queen on the advice of the Prime Minister, after the Commission has made a recommendation to the Minister. However, provisions are contained in the Constitutional

Reform and Governance Bill which, if passed, will remove the role of the Prime Minister altogether.

The Appointments Commission is not involved in the appointment of judges to the Supreme Court. Instead, when there is a vacancy, the Minister will appoint a temporary Commission. This Commission will include the President and Deputy President of the Supreme Court, as well as one member of each of the three judicial appointing bodies of England and Wales, Scotland and Northern Ireland. The temporary Commission will put forward between two and five recommended candidates to the Minister, according to prescribed criteria. The Minister must then consult with the senior judges, the First Minister in Scotland, the National Assembly for Wales, and the First Minister and deputy First Minister in Northern Ireland. The Minister will afterwards notify the name of the selected candidate to the Prime Minister who must recommend this candidate to the Queen for appointment.

The Law Society thinks that a choice of up to five gives too much scope for political interference, and thinks that only one name should be put forward for each job vacancy.

The Commission for Judicial Appointments has been abolished. A Judicial Appointments and Conduct Ombudsman now oversees the recruitment process and has the power to investigate individual complaints about judicial appointments.

Judicial selection in other countries

In civil law systems, such as France, there is normally a career judiciary. Individuals opt to become judges at an early stage, and are specifically trained for the job, rather than becoming lawyers first as they do here. The judiciary is organised on a hierarchical basis, and judges start in junior posts, dealing with the least serious cases, and work up through the system as they gain experience. One drawback is that they can be viewed as part of the civil service, rather than as independent of Government.

In the US there are two basic methods of selection, appointment and election, although a compromise between the two methods is often made. All federal judges are appointed by the President, subject to confirmation by the Senate, which may include examining a prospective judge's character and past life, as the confirmation of Clarence Thomas, the judge accused of sexual harassment, did in the 1990s. Most state and local judges are elected, although genuine competition for a post is rare. In a number of states elections are used to confirm in office judges who have been in their posts for a limited period.

The Bill of Rights leads Americans to favour single-issue pressure groups which mount legal campaigns – most famously in the case of the 1954 decision to end racial segregation in schools – to achieve political aims. These groups realise the vital importance of the person who decides such cases and therefore spend a lot of time and money researching potential candidates to see if their views fit and, if not, whether there is any damaging information which could be used to prevent their appointment. There are also associations which are interested simply in enhancing the reputation of the court, so that the American Bar Association, in particular, launches extensive inquiries of every nominee involving hundreds of interviews with judges and academics, and commissioning studies of a candidate's opinions.

Although most US judicial nominations are confirmed, 20 per cent of nominees are rejected and, more importantly, Presidents are discouraged from proposing people who might fall at this hurdle. The knowledge that one will have to submit oneself to such public examination might affect the way in which judges behave earlier in their careers.

Wigs and gowns

ss. Cases
p. 127 → Traditionally judges have been required to wear a wig made of horse hair and a gown when sitting in court. The Government became concerned that this tradition could make the judges appear old-fashioned to court users. Following a consultation process, it has been decided that from 2008 onwards judges hearing civil court cases are no longer required to wear a wig. Judges hearing criminal cases will continue to wear a wig because the wig provides a degree of anonymity for judges, so that they are less likely to be recognised by defendants or their associates outside court, and also an important element of dignity to the court proceedings.

10

The judges

Photo 10.2 The new style robes for male judges

Source: www.judiciary.gov.uk

Training

Although new judges have the benefit of many years' experience as barristers or solicitors, they have traditionally received a surprisingly small amount of training for their new role, limited until recently to a brief training period, organised by the Judicial Studies Board. In the last few years, this has been supplemented in several ways: the advent of the Children Act 1989 has meant that social workers, psychiatrists and paediatricians have shared their expertise with new judges, while concern about the perception of judges as racist, or at best racially unaware, has led to the introduction of training on race issues. The reforms to the civil justice system and the passing of the Human Rights Act 1998 have led to the provision of special training to prepare for these legal reforms.

Pay

Judges are paid large salaries – £170,000 at High Court level – which are not subject to an annual vote in Parliament. The official justification for this is the need to attract an adequate supply of candidates of sufficient calibre for appointment to judicial office, and in fact some top barristers can earn more by staying in practice. One of the attractions for a barrister of becoming a judge is the security of a pensionable position after years of self-employment.

Table 10.3 Judicial salaries

Judge	Pay
Justices of the Supreme Court	£203,000–£211,000
Lord Chief Justice	£236,000
Master of the Rolls	£211,000
Lord Justice of Appeal	£193,000
High Court judge	£170,000
Circuit judge	£126,000
District judge	£101,000
District judge (magistrates' court)	£101,000

Source: Department for Constitutional Affairs.

Promotion

The traditional view has been that there is no system of promotion of judges, on the ground that holders of judicial office might allow their promotion prospects to affect their decision-making. In practice, judges are promoted from lower courts to higher courts: potential recorders generally have to have proved themselves as assistant recorders; circuit judges as recorders. Those appointed to the High Court have usually served as a recorder or deputy High Court judge. The process is the same as for an initial judicial appointment, with the involvement of the Judicial Appointments Commission.

Termination of appointment

There are five ways in which a judge may leave office:

Dismissal

Judges of the High Court and above are covered by the Act of Settlement 1700, which provides that they may only be removed from office by the Queen on the petition of both Houses of Parliament. The machinery for dismissal has been used successfully only once, when in 1830 Sir Jonah Barrington, a judge of the High Court of Admiralty in Ireland, was charged with appropriating £922 to his own use. Proceedings against the judge were conducted in each House and each passed a resolution against the judge calling for his dismissal, which was then confirmed by the king. No judge has been removed by petition of Parliament during the twentieth or twenty-first centuries.

Under the Courts Act 1971, circuit judges and district judges can be dismissed by the Lord Chancellor, if the Lord Chief Justice agrees, for 'inability' or 'misbehaviour'. In fact this has occurred only twice since the passing of the Act: Judge Bruce Campbell (a circuit judge) was sacked in 1983 after being convicted of smuggling spirits, cigarettes and tobacco into England in his yacht; Judge Margaret Short was sacked in 2009 following complaints that she had been petulant and rude towards solicitors. Misbehaviour can include a conviction for drink-driving or any offence involving violence, dishonesty or moral turpitude. It would also include any behaviour likely to cause offence, particularly on religious or racial grounds or behaviour that amounted to sexual harassment.

In dismissing a judge, s. 108(1) of the Constitutional Reform Act 2005 provides that the Lord Chancellor will have to comply with any procedures that have been laid down to regulate this process. Judges who have been sacked for breaching the judicial code of conduct will, since 2009, have their names and the reasons for their removals made public.

In addition to dismissal there is, of course, also the power not to reappoint those who have been appointed for a limited period only.

10

The judges

Discipline

In practice the mechanisms for disciplining judges who misbehave are more significant than those for dismissal, which is generally a last resort. There was concern in the past that there were no formal disciplinary procedures for judges. Over the years there had been a few judges whose conduct had been frequently criticised, but who had nevertheless remained on the Bench, and the lack of a formal machinery for complaints was seen as protecting incompetent judges. The pressure group JUSTICE had recommended the establishment of a formal disciplinary procedure in its report on the judiciary in 1972. The Constitutional Reform Act 2005 contains provision for the establishment of such procedures. The Act gives the Lord Chancellor and the Lord Chief Justice joint responsibility for judicial discipline. Section 108(3) states:

> The Lord Chief Justice may give a judicial office holder formal advice, or a formal warning or reprimand, for disciplinary purposes (but this section does not restrict what he may do informally or for other purposes or where any advice or warning is not addressed to a particular office holder).

The Office for Judicial Complaints was set up in 2006 to handle complaints about judges and provide advice and assistance to the Lord Chancellor and Lord Chief Justice in the performance of their joint role in this context under the Constitutional Reform Act. The Office for Judicial Complaints will dismiss a complaint if it fails to meet the criteria set out in the judicial discipline regulations. If the case is not dismissed by that Office, the Lord Chancellor and the Lord Chief Justice will consider the evidence and decide what action, if any, is appropriate. In certain complex cases the matter may be referred to a senior judge for a judicial investigation. If the complaint is upheld the Lord Chief Justice and the Lord Chancellor may decide that disciplinary action is required.

A person can be suspended from judicial office for any period when they are subject to criminal proceedings, have been convicted, are serving a criminal sentence, are subject to disciplinary procedures or where it has been determined under prescribed procedures that a person should not be removed from office, but it appears to the Lord Chief Justice, with the agreement of the Lord Chancellor, that the suspension is necessary for maintaining public confidence in the judiciary.

The Judicial Appointments and Conduct Ombudsman is able to review the handling of complaints about judicial conduct.

The Office for Judicial Complaints received 1,437 complaints about judicial office holders from April 2007 to March 2008. Of those, 61 per cent related to the judicial decision itself and were therefore dismissed because they were outside the scope of the complaint system. Disciplinary action was taken in 49 cases. Nineteen magistrates and two tribunal office holders were removed from office, three for committing criminal offences. A Crown Court judge was suspended by the Office for Judicial Complaints pending its investigations into accusations published in the *News of the World* newspaper that he allowed a male prostitute with whom he was having a relationship to sit beside him on the bench, pretending that he was a law student.

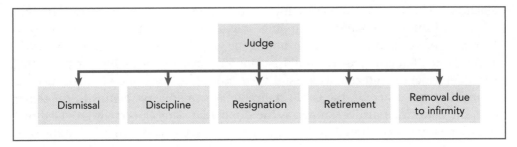

Figure 10.2 Termination of appointment

As well as the formal procedures discussed above, judges may be criticised in Parliament, or rebuked in the appellate courts, and are often censured in the press. There may be complaints from barristers, solicitors or litigants, made either in court or in private to the judge personally. 'Scurrilous abuse' of a judge may, however, be punished as contempt of court.

Resignation

Serious misbehaviour has on occasion been dealt with not by dismissal, but by the Lord Chancellor suggesting to the judge that he or she should resign.

Retirement

Judges usually retire at 70.

Removal due to infirmity

The Lord Chancellor has powers to remove a judge who is disabled by permanent infirmity from the performance of his or her duties and who is incapacitated from resigning his or her post.

Independence of the judiciary

In our legal system great importance is attached to the idea that judges should be independent and be seen to be independent. In addition to the commonsense view that they should be independent of pressure from the Government and political groups, and in order to decide cases impartially, judicial independence is required by the constitutional doctrine known as the separation of powers (discussed on p. 3).

In the past, the broad role of the Lord Chancellor was seen as both a threat to judicial independence and as the protector of judicial independence. He was a threat because he breached the doctrine of the separation of powers, but, at the same time as the head of the judiciary, he was responsible for defending judges from Government

10

The judges

influence. When the Government announced in 2003 that it planned to introduce major constitutional changes, including the abolition of the position of Lord Chancellor, this caused some concern among the judges. They were worried that, without the Lord Chancellor, there would be nobody with responsibility for protecting their independence, and that as a result their independence could be threatened. In response to these concerns, the Lord Chancellor signed an agreement with the senior judge, the Lord Chief Justice, known as the Concordat. This agreement provided that some of the key judicial functions of the Lord Chancellor would be handed to the Lord Chief Justice when the constitutional reforms were introduced and that key aspects of this agreement would be incorporated into the legislation which was subsequently done. Following political negotiations, the post of Lord Chancellor was not actually abolished, though the role of the Lord Chancellor has significantly changed. With the changes in the role of the Lord Chancellor introduced by the Constitutional Reform Act 2005, the Government sought to reassure judges that their independence would still be guaranteed, by introducing a statutory guarantee of the independence of the judiciary. Section 3 states:

> The Lord Chancellor, other Ministers of the Crown and all with responsibility for matters relating to the judiciary or otherwise to the administration of justice must uphold the continued independence of the judiciary.

It also provides that:

> The Lord Chancellor and other Ministers for the Crown must not seek to influence a particular judicial decision through any special access to the judiciary.

Other safeguards of judicial independence include the security of tenure given to judges, which ensures they cannot be removed at the whim of one of the other branches of power; the fact that their salaries are not subject to a parliamentary vote; and the rule that they cannot be sued for anything done while acting in their judicial capacity. Independence in decision-making is provided through the fact that judges are only accountable to higher judges in appellate courts.

The importance of the independence of the judiciary can be seen, for example, in judicial review, where the courts can scrutinise the behaviour of the executive, and in some cases declare it illegal. However, there are a number of problems with the idea of the judiciary as independent (see p. 174). In addition, litigation that raises the question of judicial bias is discussed on p. 607.

Criticisms of the judiciary

Background, ethnic origin, sex and age

Judges are overwhelmingly white, male and middle to upper class, and frequently elderly, leading to accusations that they are unrepresentative of, and distanced from, the majority of society. In 1995, 80 per cent of Lords of Appeal, Heads of Division, Lord Justices of Appeal and High Court judges were educated at Oxford or Cambridge. Over

50 per cent of the middle-ranking circuit judges went to Oxbridge but only 12 per cent of the lower-ranking district judges did. Eighty per cent of judges appointed since 1997 were educated at a public school. The appointments made by the current Labour Government have not broken this mould. The narrow background of the judges does mean that they can be frighteningly out of touch with the world in which they are working. Mr Justice Harman, who resigned in 1998, said in three different cases that he had not heard of the footballer Paul Gascoigne, the rock band Oasis and the singer Bruce Springsteen.

In 2004 only 16 per cent of judges were women; and only 9 per cent of senior judges (High Court or above) were women. There are still no women sitting as judges in the European Court of Justice. The first female judge was appointed to the House of Lords in 2004, Lady Justice Hale. She now sits in the Supreme Court. There are only two female judges in the Court of Appeal and ten female High Court judges. In 2006, the Equal Opportunities Commission warned that at the current rate it will take 40 years

Ess. Cases p. 111 →

for women to achieve equality in the senior judiciary. Just 3 per cent of court judges in 2004 came from an ethnic minority, with one member of the Court of Appeal coming from an ethnic minority and one High Court judge. By comparison, 8 per cent of the population of England and Wales come from an ethnic minority. Lord Lane, the former Lord Chief Justice, said after his retirement that his regret at being forced off the bench was due, at least partly, to the fact that his colleagues were 'a jolly nice bunch of chaps'. This remark reinforces the view of many that the judiciary is actually a sort of rarefied gentlemen's club.

Photo 10.3 Lady Justice Hale
Source: Dan Kitwood/Getty Images

10

The judges

The age of the full-time judiciary has remained constant over many years with the average age of a judge being 58. With a retirement age of 70, judges are allowed to retire five years later than most other professions. David Pannick (1987) has written in his book, *Judges*, that 'a judiciary composed predominantly of senior citizens cannot hope to apply contemporary standards or to understand contemporary concerns'.

Before the Courts and Legal Services Act 1990, judges were almost exclusively selected from practising barristers. Since it is difficult for anyone without a private income to survive the first years of practice, successful barristers have tended to come from reasonably well-to-do families, who are of course more likely to send their sons or daughters to public schools and then to Oxford or Cambridge. Although the background of the Bar is gradually changing, the age at which judges are appointed means that it will be some years before this is reflected in the ranks of the judiciary.

The new opportunities provided for solicitors to join the judiciary, provided by the Courts and Legal Services Act 1990, and the new right of Government lawyers to become junior judges may in time help to alter the traditional judicial background, since there are larger numbers of women, members of the ethnic minorities and those from less privileged backgrounds working as solicitors and Government lawyers than in the barrister's profession. Since April 2005 judges below High Court level are able to sit part time, which may prove attractive to women combining work with childcare responsibilities.

Section 64 of the Constitutional Reform Act 2005 provides that the Judicial Appointments Commission 'must have regard to the need to encourage diversity in the range of persons available for selection for appointments'. The Lord Chancellor can issue guidance for the Commission in order to encourage a range of persons to be available for selection (s. 65). The Government issued a consultation paper, *Increasing Diversity in the Judiciary* (2004). At the launch of this paper, the Minister for Constitutional Affairs stated:

> It is a matter of great concern that the judiciary in England and Wales – while held in high regard for its ability, independence and probity, is not representative of the diverse society it serves. A more diverse judiciary is essential if the public's confidence in its judges is to be maintained and strengthened.
>
> We need to find out why people from diverse backgrounds and with disabilities are not applying for judicial appointment in the numbers we might expect and, once we have identified the barriers, we need to do something about removing them. Judicial appointments will continue to be made on merit. But I do not believe that there is any conflict between merit and diversity.

Ess. Cases p. 124 A diversity strategy was launched by the Lord Chancellor in 2006 which aims to increase the number of women and black and ethnic minority judges. The strategy seeks to achieve this by promoting fair and open selection processes based solely on merit and by ensuring that the culture and working environment for judicial office holders encourages and supports a diverse judiciary. The Lord Chancellor is considering introducing flexible working hours for judges, career breaks, a work-shadowing programme and changes to age limits in order to try to attract a more diverse range of people to a judicial career. Part 2 of the Tribunals, Courts and Enforcement Act 2007 aims to widen the pool of lawyers eligible for the judiciary (see p. 163).

Unfortunately, the appointments made by the Judicial Appointments Commission have failed to increase diversity in the judiciary. In 2008, of the seven solicitors who applied to be High Court judges, none were appointed. Ethnic minority candidates made up 13 per cent of applicants, but only 8 per cent were selected. Although the statistics show a rise in women and ethnic minority judicial appointments these are mostly at low or part-time levels. The Commission has argued that the legal profession itself must become more diverse if further progress is to be made.

Research has been carried out by Dame Hazel Genn into why senior lawyers are not seeking judicial office (*The attractiveness of senior judicial appointments to highly qualified practitioners* (2009)). Her research concluded that:

> Female solicitors who had reached partnership in magic circle firms, and who felt that their professional journey had been something of a struggle, were reluctant to begin again, and perhaps have to struggle to re-establish their credibility, in a world that they perceived to be even more antediluvian than City commercial law practice.

An important practical obstacle to attracting a wider range of people to become judges is the general requirement that individuals work at least three weeks a year as a part-time judge for a probationary period of at least two years before they are considered for a permanent position. This can be problematic for solicitors and single parents and reflects the flexibility of the barrister profession rather than other potential candidates. Hazel Genn's research identified this requirement to undertake part-time work as a particular obstacle for women solicitors. She noted:

> First, the time commitment might be more than their co-partners felt could be spared from the practice. Second, they would have to forego a significant amount of salary to compensate for the time out of practice. Third, they would have to work very hard to make up the time spent while sitting. Finally, they were concerned that taking a part-time judicial appointment might be interpreted by their partners as reflecting a lack of commitment to the practice.

This requirement to work part time before being considered for a permanent position could simply be abolished, as it does not exist for appointments to other senior professional positions.

Training

Considering the importance of their work, judges receive very little training, even with recent changes. They may be experienced as lawyers, but the skills needed by a good lawyer are not identical to those required by a good judge. Unlike the career judge system seen on the Continent, where judges cut their judicial teeth in the lower courts, and gain experience as they move up to more serious cases, our judges often begin their judicial careers with cases that may involve substantial loss of liberty for the individual. Nor are they required to have shown expertise in the areas of law they will be required to consider: it is perfectly possible for a High Court judge to try a serious criminal case, and possibly pass a sentence of a long term of imprisonment, without ever having done a criminal case as a lawyer in practice.

The most serious cases of all in the civil courts are not being heard by High Court judges but by deputy High Court judges. These deputies are circuit judges spending a few days in London or, more likely, barristers filling time between cases. The only thing to be said about this system is that it is cheaper for the Treasury.

Problems with judicial independence

While the Constitutional Reform Act 2005 has now given statutory recognition to the independence of the judiciary, there remain a number of threats to judicial independence.

Supremacy of Parliament

Apart from where European law is involved, it is never possible for the courts to question the validity of existing Acts of Parliament. In the UK all Acts of Parliament are treated as absolutely binding by the courts, until such time as any particular Act is repealed or altered by Parliament itself in another statute or by a Minister under the special fast-track procedure provided for under the Human Rights Act 1998. The judiciary are therefore ultimately subordinate to the will of Parliament – unlike, for example, judges in the US, who may declare legislation unconstitutional. Dworkin (1978) has argued that if judges had the power to set aside legislation as unconstitutional, judicial appointments would become undesirably political, and judges would be seen as politicians themselves. He points to the political character of high judicial appointments in the US.

Treasury counsel

Those barristers retained to represent the Government in court actions in which the Government are involved – called Treasury counsel – are very likely to be offered High Court judgeships in due course.

Non-judicial work

Judges also get involved in non-judicial areas with political implications, for example, chairing inquiries into events such as Bloody Sunday in Londonderry, the Brixton riots or the Zeebrugge ferry disaster. Thus, Lord Justice Scott chaired the high-profile inquiry into the arms-to-Iraq affair and the High Court Judge, Sir William Macpherson, headed the inquiry into the handling of the police investigation of the death of the black teenager Stephen Lawrence, who was murdered in South London. This function can often be seen to undermine the political neutrality of the judiciary – in the early 1970s, for example, Lord Diplock headed an inquiry into the administration of justice in Northern Ireland, the report of which led to the abolition of jury trials for terrorist offences in the region. To this day such hearings are known as Diplock courts, which does nothing to uphold the reputation for independence of the judiciary.

The Hutton inquiry, following the war against Iraq and David Kelly's death, raised questions about the future role of judges in public inquiries. There was wide public dissatisfaction with the Hutton Report (2004), and a general unease as to how independent the judge and chair, Lord Hutton, had been. As a result, the former Lord Chief Justice, Lord Woolf, wrote a memo to the House of Commons Public Administration Select Committee expressing concern that Lord Hutton had been used as a political tool by the Government: 'I have no doubt that Lord Hutton was drawn into the most difficult area after he gave his report. He found himself being criticised.'

Cases with political implications

Although judges generally refrain from airing their political views, they are sometimes forced to make political decisions, affecting the balance between individuals and the state, the allocation of resources, and the relative powers of local and national government. Despite the official view of judges as apolitical, the fact that these decisions have political ramifications cannot be avoided; judges do not have the option of refusing to decide a case because it has political implications, and have to make a choice one way or the other.

However, concerns have been expressed that too often such decisions defend the interests of the Government of the day, sometimes at the expense of individual liberties. In the wartime case of **Liversidge v Anderson** (1942), Lord Atkin voiced concern about the decision by a majority of judges in the House of Lords that the Home Secretary was not required to give reasons to justify the detention of a citizen, commenting that the judges had shown themselves 'more executive minded than the executive'.

Certain cases have borne out this concern. In **McIlkenny v Chief Constable of the West Midlands** (1980), Lord Denning dismissed allegations of police brutality against the six men accused of the Birmingham pub bombings with the words:

> Just consider the course of events if this action were to go to trial . . . If the six men fail, it will mean that much time and money and worry will have been expended by many people for no good purpose. If the six men win, it will mean that the police were guilty of perjury, that they were guilty of violence and threats, that the confessions were involuntary and were improperly admitted in evidence: and that the convictions were erroneous. That would mean that the Home Secretary would have either to recommend they be pardoned or he would have to remit the case to the Court of Appeal under section 17 of the Criminal Appeal Act 1968. This is such an appalling vista that every sensible person in the land would say: it cannot be right that these actions should go any further. They should be struck out.

In other words, Lord Denning was saying, the allegations should not be addressed because, if proved true, the result would be to bring the legal system into disrepute.

In **R v Ponting** (1985), the civil servant Clive Ponting was accused of leaking documents revealing that the Government had covered up the circumstances in which the Argentine ship the *General Belgrano* was sunk during the Falklands war. Ponting argued that he had acted 'in the interests of the state' (a defence laid down in the Official Secrets Act at the time), but Mr Justice McGowan directed the jury that 'interests of the state' meant nothing more or less than the policies of the Government of the day. Nevertheless the jury acquitted Ponting (see p. 252).

The danger of political bias has been increased as a result of the Human Rights Act 1998 coming into force. While judges have already decided some politically sensitive cases, the number is likely to increase, with litigation directly accusing Government actions and legislation of breaching fundamental human rights. The journalist Hugo Young argues that we will see the emergence of the 'political judge'. He observes:

> The Convention will require domestic judges to involve themselves in matters of principle, as Irvine was the first to understand. Not long ago, he lucidly described the emergence of what sounds like the 'political judge'. The presence of the Convention, he said, would sometimes require judges to give a decision on the morality of the conduct, and not simply its compliance with the bare letter of the law. (*The Guardian*, 18 July 1998)

Over time the changing role of the judiciary is most likely to be visible in the Supreme Court. The House of Lords' judges decided about 100 cases a year, usually on technical commercial and tax matters, though with the implementation of the Human Rights Act 1998, it was increasingly hearing cases raising human rights issues. The Supreme Court is likely to move closer to the US Supreme Court, deciding fundamental issues on the rights of the individual against the state.

At the moment there appear to be the greatest tensions between the judges and the Government with regard to the application of the terrorist legislation and the judges' approach to sentencing. In 2006, the Attorney General published a list of more than 200 judges who have given 'unduly lenient' sentences to criminals. The list was drawn up by looking at successful appeals against lenient sentences made by the Attorney General to the Court of Appeal. In response, a spokesperson from the Judicial Communications Office stated:

> Figures on successful appeals against a judge's sentencing can only begin to have relevance if they are set against the total number of sentencing decisions made by the judge in question, and those where there has been no appeal or an appeal has been rejected. It should also be borne in mind that some judges have caseloads involving more complex and serious cases, so they might be more likely to feature in appeal cases. In any event, there are many cases where the Court of Appeal reduces sentences without implying any criticism of the sentencing judges, sometimes indeed because of changes of circumstances – such as new evidence – after the original sentencing decision.

At the same time, the then Constitutional Affairs Minister, Vera Baird, criticised the judiciary during an appearance on BBC Radio 4's *Any Questions* programme. Baird attacked a trial judge for giving a convicted paedophile, Craig Sweeney, a sentence which potentially allowed him to be released after six years' imprisonment. The Lord Chancellor came to the defence of the trial judge and pointed out that he had simply applied the relevant sentencing guidelines to the case. Vera Baird subsequently apologised for her remarks in a letter to the Lord Chancellor.

The pressure group, JUSTICE, has issued a *Manifesto for the rule of law*. This document seeks to remind politicians that there is a constitutional convention that the government should refrain from criticising the judiciary in any manner that would diminish public confidence. This convention was repeatedly breached by the former Home Secretaries John Reid and David Blunkett. Under their own rules of professional conduct, judges are not usually allowed to publicly respond to criticisms so such criticisms do not lead to a constructive debate. In addition, it is in everyone's interests that the judges who enforce the law are respected in society.

TOPICAL ISSUE

The media and freedom of expression

The media (including newspapers, television and radio) hold considerable power and their role depends on them having the right to inform the public. Any restriction on their freedom of expression is an irritation to the media and it is the judges who are required to police the scope of this freedom. In recent years the right to privacy has been extended by the courts. This was highlighted in the judgment of Mr Justice Eady in the High Court when he ruled that the *News of the World* had been wrong to publish a story about Max Mosley (the president of the body that regulates Formula I racing), paying prostitutes to act out sadomasochistic activities. Mosley's parents were well-known fascist sympathisers who had reportedly been friends and supporters of Adolph Hitler. The newspaper suggested that the sexual activities had a Nazi-style theme. This judgment of Mr Justice Eady was publicly criticised by the editor of the *Daily Mail* in 2009, who made a very personal attack on the judge himself, and the tone of this attack raises questions about how far the independence of the judiciary is sufficiently protected from the pressures of the media. In 1900 a newspaper editor was convicted for contempt of court for calling a judge an 'impudent little man in horsehair', but such a response would seem disproportionate today. The Judicial Communications Office acts as the press office for the judiciary and it issued the following statement in response to the editor's speech:

> Judges determine privacy cases in accordance with the law and the particular evidence presented by both parties. Any High Court judgment can be appealed to the Court of Appeal.

It is understandable that the judges would not want to enter into a public dispute with a newspaper editor, but it is also noteworthy that Government Ministers, and in particular the Lord Chancellor who under the Constitutional Reform Act 2005 is responsible for protecting the independence of the judiciary, did not speak up in support of the judges. As a politician the Lord Chancellor will be anxious to keep the media on his or her side ready for the next general election.

10

The judges

Right-wing bias

In addition to their alleged readiness to support the Government of the day, the judiciary have been accused of being particularly biased towards the interests traditionally represented by the right wing of the political spectrum. In his influential book *The Politics of the Judiciary*, Griffith states that: 'in every major social issue which has come before the courts in the last thirty years – concerning industrial relations, political protest, race relations, government secrecy, police powers, moral behaviour – the judges have supported the conventional, settled and established interests' (1997).

Among the cases he cites in support of this theory is **Bromley London Borough Council v Greater London Council** (1982). In this case the Labour-run GLC had won an election with a promise to cut bus and tube fares by 25 per cent. The move neces-sitated an increase in the rates, levied on the London boroughs, and one of those boroughs, Conservative-controlled Bromley, challenged the GLC's right to do this. The challenge failed in the High Court, but succeeded on appeal. The Court of Appeal judges condemned the fare reduction as 'a crude abuse of power', and quashed the supplementary rate that the GLC had levied on the London boroughs to pay for it. The House of Lords agreed, the Law Lords holding unanimously that the GLC was bound by a statute requiring it to 'promote the provision of integrated, efficient and economic transport facilities and services in Greater London', which they interpreted to mean that the bus and tube system must be run according to 'ordinary business principles' of cost-effectiveness. The decision represented a political defeat for the Labour leaders of the GLC and a victory for the Conservative councillors of Bromley.

Other cases cited by Griffith include **Council of Civil Service Unions *v* Minister for the Civil Service** (1984) – the 'GCHQ' case in which the House of Lords supported the withdrawal of certain civil servants' rights to belong to a trade union; **Attorney General *v* Guardian Newspapers Ltd** (1987), which banned publication of *Spycatcher*, a book on the security services, even though it was generally available in America and Australia; and several cases arising out of the 1984 miners' strike, such as **Thomas *v* NUM (South Wales Area)** (1985), in which injunctions were sought to prevent pro-testers collecting at pit gates and shouting abuse at those going to work. The judge in that case, according to Griffith, had some difficulty in finding the conduct illegal, but eventually decided that it amounted to 'a species of private nuisance, namely unreasonable interference with the victim's right to use the highway'; Griffith describes the decision as 'judicial creativity at its most blatant'.

Commentators have also noted that the great advances in judicial review in the 1960s and 1970s came almost entirely at the expense of Labour policies, and that judi-cial reluctance to review Government decisions of the executive is most likely to be decisive in cases where the Government in question is a Conservative one. However, the past few years have seen a shift; the decisions of the last Conservative Home Secretary, Michael Howard, were several times found illegal by the courts. Legal journalist and writer Joshua Rozenberg argued that the bias at least in favour of the establishment has broken down. He has written:

> Much of the responsibility for the rift between judiciary and government must fall on the shoulders of the Lord Chancellor. By shaking up the legal profession and paving the way for solicitors – and probably, before long, Crown Prosecution Service lawyers – to appear in the higher courts, and by his lack of support for judges on the key issues of pay, hours and pensions, Lord McKay has fashioned a fundamental shift in the natural order: a judi-ciary which can no longer be relied on to support the establishment. (*The Guardian*, Tuesday 12 April 1994)

The previous Home Secretary, David Blunkett, expressed displeasure on a number of occasions with the decisions of the courts, particularly where these decisions ran counter to his policies on sentencing and immigration.

Bias against women

In her book *Eve was Framed*, Helena Kennedy (1992) argues that the attitude of many judges to women is outdated, and sometimes prejudiced. The problems are particularly apparent in cases involving sexual offences: Kennedy cites the comments of Cassell J in 1990, that a man who had unlawful intercourse with his 12-year-old stepdaughter was understandably driven to it by his pregnant wife's loss of interest in sex.

Kennedy alleges that women are judged according to how well they fit traditional female stereotypes. Because crime is seen as stepping outside the feminine role, women are more severely punished than men, and women who do not fit traditional stereotypes are treated most harshly.

The Judicial Studies Board, responsible for the training of judges, has issued judges with the *Equal Treatment Bench Book*. This advises judges on equal treatment of people in court and the appropriate use of language to avoid causing offence by, for example, being sexist.

Influence of Freemasonry

Freemasonry is a secret society, which does not allow women to join. Among its stated aims is the mutual self-advancement of members and there has long been concern about the extent of membership among the police as well as the judiciary, on the basis that loyalty to other masons – who might be parties in a case, or colleagues seeking promotion or other favours – could have a corrupting influence. Josephine Hayes, chair of the Association of Women Barristers, told newspapers that anecdotal evidence suggested that there was public concern about the influence that masonic membership might have on judges: clients whose opponents were Freemasons had been known to express worries that the judge might also be one. She pointed out that, although fears of actual influence might be unfounded, the concern that it might exist weakened confidence in the legal system.

The Association of Women Barristers also suggests that Freemasonry may have a discriminatory effect on women lawyers' chances of appointment to the Bench. It points out that because the current system of appointment depends on recommendation by existing judges, men benefited by the opportunities which Freemasonry provides to meet senior judges. Such opportunities, it points out, have become even more valuable now that the practising Bar has grown to over 8,000, so that judges no longer necessarily know all candidates for the judiciary personally. The Association has argued that judges should be obliged to resign from the Freemasons on appointment to the bench. The previous Lord Chancellor, Lord McKay, opposed such a rule, arguing that as a matter of principle individuals should be free to join any lawful organisation they wished. He pointed out that the judicial oath requires all judges to swear 'to do right to all manner of people . . . without fear or favour, affection or ill will'. He suggested that this meant there was no conflict of interest between membership of the Freemasons and judicial office.

10

The judges

Photo 10.4 The offices of the Freemasons in central London
Source: Alex Segre/Alamy

In an attempt to introduce greater transparency, a questionnaire was sent in 1998 to all members of the judiciary asking them to declare their 'Masonic status'. Five per cent of those who responded admitted to being Freemasons.

Lack of specialisation

A very distinctive feature of the English system is that judges tend not to specialise: instead, they are organised in terms of the hierarchy of the courts in which they work. In France, for example, every region has its own court structure, and there will be hundreds of judges of equal status, instead of the elite group that form the pinnacle of our judiciary. It has been argued that this arrangement prevents our judiciary from developing the kind of expertise that, in France, has contributed to the development of specialist courts such as the *Conseil d'Etat*, which deals with administrative law; the development of our administrative law is said to have suffered as a result. However, it can also be argued that the English model gives the highest judges an overview of the whole system, which helps ensure that different branches of law remain fundamentally consistent with each other.

In any case, there are some signs that the system is changing. First, the growth of tribunals has removed many specialist areas from the ordinary courts: most tribunals are presided over by people with specialist knowledge of the relevant areas. The growth of mediation systems as an alternative method of dispute resolution (see Chapter 25) has also contributed to this. Secondly, Lord Woolf's report on the civil justice system recommends that High Court and circuit judges should concentrate on fewer areas of work, though he did not suggest that they actually became specialists in particular subjects.

Shortage of time

There is a growing concern that judges currently have insufficient time allocated for them to read the papers for a case. Court of Appeal judges are only allocated four reading days a month when they can do legal research. The rest of the time they are expected to be sitting hearing court cases. This is in striking contrast with some appellate judges in the US who only hear cases four days per month.

Reform of the judiciary

The appointment process

The judicial appointment process has undoubtedly been improved by the reforms introduced by the Constitutional Reform Act 2005. However, there are some weaknesses in those reforms and the Government could have gone much further in removing itself from the appointment process. The pressure group Civil Liberties is concerned that the Act only creates an advisory panel for judicial appointments, as the ultimate decision to appoint will still be made by the Government Minister (or effectively the Prime Minister for Court of Appeal and Supreme Court judges).

The Government's consultation paper, *Constitutional Reform: a new way of appointing judges* (2003), considered the creation of three possible types of commission:

- an Appointing Commission,
- a Recommending Commission,
- a Hybrid Commission.

An Appointing Commission would itself make the decision who to appoint with no involvement of a Minister at any stage. This is similar to the arrangements that exist in some Continental European countries.

A Recommending Commission would make recommendations to a Minister as to who he or she should appoint (or recommend that the Queen appoints). The final decision on who to appoint would rest with the Minister.

A Hybrid Commission would act as an Appointing Commission in relation to the more junior appointments and as a Recommending Commission for the more senior appointments.

Ultimately, the Government favoured the creation of a Recommending Commission, but an Appointing Commission would have more effectively removed Government interference in the judicial appointment process.

Ess. Cases
p. 121 →

TOPICAL ISSUE

Judicial appointments under a modern constitution

In 2008 the Minister for Justice published a White Paper looking at ways to improve the current constitution: *The Governance of Britain: Constitutional Renewal* (2008). The Constitutional Reform and Governance Bill was presented to Parliament in 2009. This contains provisions for the removal of the Prime Minister from the appointment process for the judges of the Court of Appeal and Supreme Court. The White Paper had suggested that other changes to the appointment process should be made including removing the Lord Chancellor from the appointment process for judges below High Court level and allowing the Lord Chancellor to lay down additional appointment criteria and set performance targets for the Judicial Appointments Commission. Ultimately the Government accepted that the new appointment system has not been in operation long enough to justify major changes to the balance achieved by the 2005 reforms.

The 2007 consultation paper on judicial appointments considered whether selection should be subject to the advice and consent of Parliament to increase accountability if the role of Government Ministers was reduced. It concluded:

> To adopt such an approach in this country could lead to the strong perception that judicial appointments were being politicised, and such a perception could have an impact on confidence in the independence of the judiciary . . . [T]here would . . . be the risk that the decision to confirm or reject could be based on factors other than the candidate's ability to do the job effectively.

The consultation paper also pointed out that such a process would lead to delays, discourage some candidates from applying, use up scarce resources of parliamentary time and damage the status of the judges appointed because they could have been publicly criticised by Parliament during the appointment process.

Training

It has been widely suggested that judges should receive more training, not just at the beginning of their careers, but at frequent intervals throughout. Helena Kennedy (1992) suggests that judges might also benefit from sabbaticals, in which they could study the practices of other jurisdictions, and the work of social agencies and reform groups.

Judge Pickles (1988) has put forward the view that the judiciary needs more training in sociology, psychology, penology and criminology, and to learn more about how criminals are dealt with in other systems. Lord Woolf (1996) has proposed that judges should receive training in information technology so that they can make greater use of computers in their work.

Organisation

The Court Service issued a consultation document entitled *Transforming the Crown Court* (1999). This document proposes that judges should have planned work which begins at 9 am and finishes not before 5 pm, including an increase of their daily court sittings from five to six hours. It also suggests that it would be more efficient for some High Court judges to be based permanently outside London, rather than occasionally going on circuit in the provinces. These recommendations had earlier been made by Lord Woolf's Civil Justice Review.

Answering questions

Questions about the judiciary generally focus on their independence, but as this is closely related to appointments, background and selection, you need to know more than just the information under the heading of independence of the judiciary, as the following example shows.

1 **What are the roles and responsibilities of the judiciary? Does the selection process in England and Wales ensure that appropriate people are selected to carry these out?** *London External LLB*

The question clearly divides into two parts:

● What are the roles and responsibilities of the judiciary?
● Does the selection process in England and Wales ensure that appropriate people are selected to carry these out?

It would be a good idea to divide your essay into these two parts to show the examiner that you are answering the exact question asked. Your introductory paragraph should state clearly that this is the structure you have followed.

Looking in the first part of the essay at the roles and responsibilities of the judiciary, this is asking you about the work undertaken by the judiciary. You could point out that they are primarily associated with hearing and deciding trials, but their functions are actually more extensive than this. Their work can be divided between civil and criminal matters. In civil matters their role has been changing, as the Woolf reforms have pushed them into case management and many cases never reach trial. In criminal matters you could contrast the role of the judges in the Crown Court with the role of the jury – see the subheading 'The function of the jury' at p. 234. You could also look specifically at the work of the magistrates at pp. 276–9. In addition to being involved in litigation, the judges also have an important role in the law reform process, hearing inquiries of public importance (see p. 136). The Lord Chancellor was considered to have too many 'roles and responsibilities' and his or her functions have been reduced by the Constitutional Reform Act 2005.

The second part of this essay raises the controversial issue of the appointment of the judiciary. It is important that you are bang up to date on this subject, as the appointment process is currently being reformed – see p. 181. You are asked whether the appointment system ensures that 'appropriate people' are selected. In considering this, you could discuss the problem that the judges are not representative of the society in which they work (see p. 170) and the reforms to the appointment process are one effort to tackle this problem. The Government recognises that a reform of the appointment process alone will not be sufficient to broaden access to the profession.

2 The position of Lord Chancellor in the past clearly breached the doctrine of separation of powers. How have the reforms contained in the Constitutional Reform Act 2005 addressed this breach of a fundamental constitutional principle? In your view, have these reforms been successful?

The first part of this question deals specifically with the separation of powers and how that has been addressed in the reforms contained in the Constitutional Reform Act 2005, while the second part of the question asks about the success (or not) of the reforms generally.

You must describe what the doctrine of separation of powers is and how the Lord Chancellor's former role extended into all three arms of the state (p. 156). Then you should look at the provisions of the 2005 Act that changed (not abolished – although that was the original proposal) the Lord Chancellor's role. For example, the Act reduces the Lord Chancellor's powers of judicial appointment, and he or she is no longer the head of the judiciary or Speaker of the House of Lords. You should point out that while this ostensibly maintains the independence of the judiciary, this is not, however, guaranteed in practice (pp. 174–81).

Finally, you should examine some of the provisions set out in the 2005 Act (you could select, perhaps, the provisions relating to the Judicial Appointments Commission as an example) to see if the reforms have been successful.

3 'For nearly 300 years, the English judge has been guaranteed his independence.' How far is this true? In your opinion, can the decisions of our judges be regarded as satisfactory to all members of society?

Your introduction should place the reference to 300 years by mentioning the provisions of the Act of Settlement (p. 167). After that the question seems to need answering in two parts: has the English judge been guaranteed independence and, in the light of the answer, can his or her judgments properly be regarded as satisfactory to all members of society?

In the first part, you should look at the factors that are supposed to guarantee the independence of the judiciary. These include the new statutory guarantee contained in the Constitutional Reform Act 2005, security of tenure, separation of powers, salaries not subject to a parliamentary vote and so on (see p. 170). Then go on to examine the problems with independence that suggest it is not guaranteed.

In the second part of your answer, you can give examples of cases where the lack of judicial independence has resulted in decisions that are not satisfactory to certain members of society – again, the material on right-wing and executive bias is useful here.

If you have time you could add that the lack of independence is not the only reason that their decisions are not satisfactory to all members of society, and bring in the material about the background of judges and their alleged bias against women.

NB If you happen to have swotted up on judges, you will naturally be looking for a question in which you can show off this knowledge, but beware: questions which at first sight look as though they concern the judiciary may actually be about statutory interpretation and the law-making role of judges.

4 What measures have been taken to make the judiciary more representative of society?

Until recently, the statutory eligibility for judicial appointment was based exclusively upon the exercise of rights of audience; and consequently the pool of eligible judicial appointees was limited. A good response will quote appropriate statistics to demonstrate that senior judges were predominantly male, white, middle-class and Oxbridge educated; and over half of the circuit judges had attended Oxbridge. Women and ethnic minorities were substantially under-represented. Consideration might be given to the reasons for this: historically experience as a barrister was required which often reflected family support in the early stages of the career. These problems have been addressed by encouraging solicitors to progress to become judges (for example, through provisions in the Courts and Legal Services Act 1990 allowing solicitors to secure rights of audience in all courts) and allowing part-time judicial appointments at certain levels. In addition, the Constitutional Reform Act 2005 requires the Judicial Appointments Commission to have regard to the need to encourage diversity. In 2006 a diversity strategy was introduced and flexible working hours and career break schemes are being considered. The Tribunals, Courts and Enforcement Act 2007 contains further provisions to widen the pool of those eligible for judicial appointment.

Summary of Chapter 10: The judges

10

The judges

The role of the judges

The judges play a central role under the British Constitution, playing a vital but sensitive role in controlling the exercise of power by the state.

Judicial hierarchy

At the head of the judiciary is the President of the Courts of England and Wales. The most senior judges are the Justices of the Supreme Court. At the next level down, sitting in the Court of Appeal, are 38 judges known as Lord Justices of Appeal and Lady Justices of Appeal.

A reduced role for the Lord Chancellor

With the passing of the Constitutional Reform Act 2005, four major changes to the role of the Lord Chancellor have been introduced. As a result he or she no longer:

- sits as a judge;
- heads the judiciary;
- takes a central role in the judicial appointment process; or
- automatically becomes the Speaker of the House.

He or she will remain as the head of a government department (now called the Ministry of Justice), but his or her powers and links to the judges have been removed to satisfy the principle of the separation of powers.

Appointing the judges

The way in which judges are appointed has been radically reformed by provisions in the Constitutional Reform Act 2005. The Act contains provisions for the establishment of a new Judicial Appointments Commission. It is hoped that the creation of this body will help to put an end to the breaches of the principle of separation of powers and reinforce judicial independence. Depending on their rank, judges are appointed by the Queen on the advice of the Prime Minister or by the Lord Chancellor.

Training

Training is provided by the Judicial Studies Board.

Termination of appointment

There are five ways in which a judge may leave office:

- dismissal;
- discipline;
- resignation;
- retirement; and
- removal due to infirmity.

Independence of the judiciary

In our legal system great importance is attached to the idea that judges should be independent and be seen to be independent. Section 3 of the Constitutional Reform Act 2005 states:

> The Lord Chancellor, other Ministers of the Crown and all with responsibility for matters relating to the judiciary or otherwise to the administration of justice must uphold the continued independence of the judiciary.

Criticisms of the judiciary

Judges are overwhelmingly white, male and middle to upper class, and frequently elderly, leading to accusations that they are unrepresentative of the society they serve. The appointments process has been criticised for being dominated by politicians, secretive and discriminatory. Judges receive very little training. There are real concerns that the independence of the judiciary is not sufficiently protected. The academic, Griffith, has accused judges of being biased towards the interests traditionally represented by the right wing of the political spectrum. The lawyer, Baroness Helena Kennedy, has argued that the attitude of many judges to women is outdated and sometimes prejudiced. There is also concern that some judges are members of the Freemasons.

Reading list

Devlin, P. (1979) *The Judge*, Oxford: Oxford University Press.

Griffith, J.A.G. (1997) *The Politics of the Judiciary*, London: Fontana Press.

Hailsham, Lord (1989) 'The Office of Lord Chancellor and the Separation of Powers', 8 *Civil Justice Quarterly* 308.

Kennedy, H. (1992) *Eve was Framed: Women and British Justice*, London: Chatto.

Malleson, K. (1997) 'Judicial training and performance appraisal: the problem of judicial independence', 60 *Modern Law Review* 655.

Malleson, K. (1999) *The New Judiciary – The Effect of Expansion and Activism*, Aldershot: Ashgate.

Malleson, K. (2000) 'Factors affecting the decision to apply for silk and judicial office', London: Lord Chancellor's Department.

Pannick, D. (1987) *Judges*, Oxford: Oxford University Press.

Partington, M. (1994) 'Training the judiciary in England and Wales' 144 *Civil Justice Quarterly* 319.

Paterson, A. (1982) *The Law Lords*, London: Macmillan.

Peach, Sir L. (1999) *Appointment Processes of Judges and Queen's Counsel in England and Wales*, London: HMSO.

Pickles, J. (1988) *Straight from the Bench*, London: Coronet.

Windlesham, Lord (2005) 'The Constitutional Reform Act 2005: Ministers, judges and constitutional change, Part 1' [2005] *Public Law* 806.

Woodhouse, D. (2007) 'The Constitutional Reform Act 2005 – defending judicial independence the English way' (2007) *International Journal of Constitutional Law* 5 (1) 153.

Reading on the Internet

www

The White Paper on constitutional reform *The Governance of Britain: Constitutional Renewal* (2008) is available on the website of the Ministry of Justice at:
http://www.justice.gov.uk/whatwedo/governance.htm

The report of the House of Lords Parliamentary Committee *Relations Between the Executive, the Judiciary and Parliament* (2007) is available on Parliament's website at:
http://www.parliament.the-stationery-office.co.uk/pa/ld200607/ldselect/ldconst/151/151.pdf

The consultation paper *The Governance of Britain: Judicial Appointments* (2007) is available on the website of the Ministry of Justice at:
http://www.justice.gov.uk/publications/cp2507.htm

The website of the Judicial Appointments Commission is available at:
http://www.judicialappointments.gov.uk/index.htm

The consultation paper *Constitutional reform: a new way of appointing judges* is available on the website for the former Department for Constitutional Affairs at:
http://www.dca.gov.uk/consult/jacommission/index.htm

The consultation paper *Court working dress in England and Wales* is available on the website for the old Department for Constitutional Affairs at:
http://www.dca.gov.uk/consult/courtdress

The report by Hazel Genn (2009) *The attractiveness of senior judicial appointment to highly qualified practitioners – Report to the Judicial Executive Board* has been published on the Judicial website:
http://www.judiciary.gov.uk/docs/report-sen-jud-appt.pdf

Sir Leonard Peach's report into judicial appointments is available on:
http://www.dca.gov.uk/judicial/peach/indexfr.htm

General information on the judiciary is available on:
http://www.judiciary.gov.uk

The booklet *Judicial Appointments in England and Wales: Policies and Procedure* is available on the Department for Constitutional Affairs' website at:
http://www.dca.gov.uk/judicial/appointments/jappinfr.htm

The website of the Judicial Studies Board can be found at:
http://www.jsboard.co.uk

10

The judges

Visit **www.mylawchamber.co.uk/ElliottELS** to access multiple-choice questions, flashcards and practice exam questions to test yourself on this chapter.

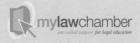

11

The legal professions

This chapter discusses:

- solicitors – their work, qualifications and training;
- the handling of complaints against solicitors;
- barristers – their work, qualifications and training;
- senior barristers, known as Queen's Counsel;
- the handling of complaints against barristers;
- the background of barristers and solicitors;
- attempts to increase diversity in the legal professions through educational reforms;
- the regulation of the professions;
- changes to the business structures in which the professions are organised;
- moves towards fusing the solicitor and barrister professions into a single profession; and
- legal executives – their work, qualifications and training.

Introduction

The British legal profession, unlike that of most other countries, includes two separate branches: barristers and solicitors (the term 'lawyer' is a general one which covers both branches). They each do the same type of work – advocacy, which means representing clients in court, and paperwork, including drafting legal documents and giving written advice – but the proportions differ, with barristers generally spending a higher proportion of their time in court.

In addition, some types of work have traditionally been available to only one branch (conveyancing to solicitors, and advocacy in the higher courts to barristers, for example), and barristers are not usually hired directly by clients – their first point of contact will usually be a solicitor, who then engages a barrister on their behalf if it proves necessary. As we shall see, though, these divisions are beginning to break down.

In the past, the two branches of the profession have been fairly free to arrange their own affairs but, over the past 20 years, this situation has changed significantly with the Government directly and indirectly exercising increased controls over the profession, most recently with the passing of the Legal Services Act 2007.

Solicitors

There are around 98,000 solicitors of which 75,000 work in a solicitor's office. The solicitor profession has been growing rapidly, so that since 1970 it has more than trebled in size. Their governing body is the Law Society. Until recently, the Law Society acted both as the representative of solicitors and as the solicitor's regulator.

 A Government commissioned report by Sir David Clementi (**2004**) raised concerns that this dual function could cause a conflict of interests with the Law Society putting the solicitor first, rather than the consumer, when making decisions regarding the regulation of the profession. In response to these concerns, in 2005 membership of the Law Society became voluntary and the Law Society decided to separate its representative function from its regulatory function. The profession is now regulated by the Solicitors Regulation Authority. This Authority has seven lay members and nine solicitor members. It deals with all regulatory and disciplinary matters, setting monitoring and enforcing standards for solicitors. Its stated purpose is to set, promote and secure in the public interest standards of behaviour and professional performance necessary to ensure that clients receive a good service and that the rule of law is upheld. As a result of these changes, the Law Society has shifted from being a mandatory governing body for solicitors to a voluntary trade association. It aims to protect and promote solicitors by, for example, lobbying Government.

Work

For most solicitors, paperwork takes up much of their time. It includes conveyancing (legal aspects of the buying and selling of houses and other property) and drawing up wills and contracts, as well as giving written and oral legal advice. Until 1985, solicitors

Ess. Cases
p. 139

Photo 11.1 The Law Society
Source: © Richard Croft

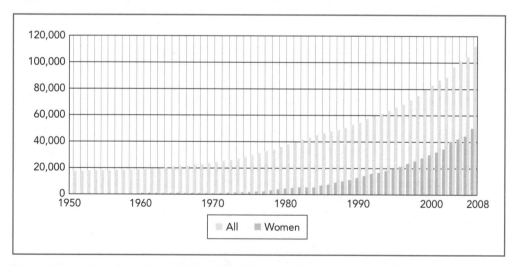

Figure 11.1 Growth in the numbers of solicitors with practising certificates
Source: Law Society website. Trends in the solicitors' profession, Annual statistical report 2008 [www.lawsociety.org.uk].
© The Law Society

were the only people allowed to do conveyancing work, but this is no longer the case – people from different occupations can qualify as licensed conveyancers, and the service is often offered by banks and building societies. Probate work (which concerns wills) can now also be done by banks, building societies, insurance companies and legal executives, and consequently the proportions of work done by solicitors are changing.

Solicitors have traditionally been able to do advocacy work in the magistrates' court and the county court, but not generally in the higher courts. This situation was changed by the Courts and Legal Services Act 1990 and the Access to Justice Act 1999. These Acts put in place the mechanics for equalising rights of audience between barristers and solicitors. Now all barristers and solicitors acquire full rights of audience when they are admitted to the Roll (an official register of qualified lawyers entitled to practice), though they will only be able to exercise these rights on completion of the necessary training. When undertaking advocacy work, solicitors can, since 2008, wear wigs in court, just like barristers, which reinforces the fact that they are of equal status. There are currently 4,500 solicitor-advocates. Many firms are sending their solicitors on courses, making advocacy training compulsory and designating individuals as in-house advocates. Thus, solicitors are increasingly doing the advocacy work themselves rather than sending it to a barrister. Where Government funding has established fixed fees for work, solicitors are faced with a simple choice: keep the money or give it away. Even those solicitors who do not have full rights of audience can appear in the High Court in bankruptcy proceedings, or to read out a formal, unchallenged statement; and in the Crown Court if the case is an appeal from the magistrates' court, or has been committed to the Crown Court for sentence, and they appeared in the same case in the magistrates' court. They can also appear before a single judge of the Court of Appeal, and in High Court proceedings held in chambers.

Traditionally, an individual solicitor did much less advocacy work than a barrister but, as more solicitors gain the necessary training to become solicitor-advocates, this is changing. In any case, solicitors as a group do more advocacy than barristers, simply because 98 per cent of criminal cases are tried in the magistrates' court, where the advocate is usually a solicitor. The amount of advocacy done by solicitors is also growing as a result of the removal of many contract and tort cases from the High Court to the county court, following the Courts and Legal Services Act 1990.

Solicitors can, and usually do, form partnerships with other solicitors. Alternatively, since 2001, they can form a Limited Liability Partnership. Under an ordinary partnership a solicitor can be personally liable (even after retirement) for a claim in negligence against the solicitor firm, even if he or she was not involved in the transaction giving rise to the claim. Under the Limited Liability Partnership (LLP) a partner's liability is limited to negligence for which he or she was personally responsible. Law firms are increasingly converting into LLPs, though some are reluctant to do so as it would require them to be more open about how much senior staff earn.

Solicitors work in ordinary offices, with, in general, the same support staff as any office-based business, and have offices all over England and Wales and in all towns. Practices range from huge London-based firms dealing only with large corporations, to small partnerships or individual solicitors, dealing with the conveyancing, wills, divorces and minor crime of a country town. The top City law firms are known as

11

The legal professions

the 'Magic Circle' and a Sweet and Maxwell survey found nearly a quarter of all law students wanted to join one when they qualified, though in practice a much smaller percentage will succeed in doing do. Most law firms are small, with 85 per cent of them having four or fewer partners, and nearly half having only one partner. Some solicitors work in law centres and other advice agencies, Government departments, private industry and education rather than in private practice.

Figures published in the journal *Commercial Lawyer* in September 2000 show that an elite group of 100 City solicitors working in central London are earning more than £1 million per year. But this figure has to be seen in the context of a profession that has over 80,000 members. The average annual salary for a solicitor is £51,463.

Qualifications and training

Almost all solicitors begin with a degree, though not necessarily in law. A number of law schools introduced an admissions test in 2004, the National Admissions Test for Law, to help select students onto their popular law degrees. Although no minimum degree classification is laid down, increased competition for entry to the profession means that most successful applicants now have an upper second class degree, and very few get in with less than a lower second.

Students whose degree is not in law have to take a one-year course leading to the Common Professional Examination (CPE). It is possible for non-graduate mature students, who have demonstrated some professional or business achievements, to enter the profession without a degree. They take a broad, two-year CPE course. Only a very small number of people take this route and it is not a route the Law Society encourages – they suggest that, for most people, it is worth putting in the extra year to do a law degree and enter in the conventional manner, especially bearing in mind that many universities and colleges now offer mature students law degrees which can be studied part time, so that students do not have to give up paid employment. It is also possible for legal executives (discussed at p. 224) to become solicitors without first taking a degree course.

The next step, for law graduates and those who have passed the CPE, is a one-year Legal Practice Course, designed to provide practical skills, including advocacy, as well as legal and procedural knowledge. Since 2009 the LPC is divided into two stages. Stage one covers the core areas: business law and practice; property law and practice; litigation; professional conduct and regulation; taxation; wills and administration of estates; and skills elements (writing, drafting, interviewing, advising, advocacy and practical legal research). Stage two consists of three vocational electives which can be studied at different institutions if wished. The two stages will normally be completed within a year, but students can take breaks in their studies as long as they complete the course within five years. Fees for the LPC are between £5,000 and £9,000, yet both the CPE and the Legal Practice Course are eligible only for discretionary LEA grants, and are not covered by the Government's student loan scheme. The Law Society provides a very small number of bursaries, and has also negotiated a loans scheme with certain high street banks, which offers up to £5,000, that students do not begin paying back until they have finished studying; a few large London firms also offer assistance to those students they wish to attract into employment. The vast majority of students, however, are obliged to fund themselves or rely on loans.

After passing the Legal Practice exams, the prospective solicitor must find a place, usually in a firm, to serve a two-year apprenticeship. There can be intense competition for these places, especially in times of economic difficulty when firms are reluctant to invest in training; in 1995–96, there were only 4,170 traineeships on offer, for the almost 7,000 LPC students. Formally known as articles, the two-year period is now called a training contract, and includes a 20-day practical skills course, building on subjects studied during the Legal Practice Course. The work of a trainee solicitor can be very demanding, and a survey carried out for the Law Society found that a third work more than 50 hours a week. Trainee solicitors should receive a minimum salary of £15,332 outside London and £17,110 in London. In practice, the average salary for a trainee solicitor is £20,925.

It is possible to become a solicitor without a degree, by completing the one-year Solicitors' First Examination Course, and the Legal Practice Course, and having a five-year training contract. Legal executives (see p. 224) sometimes go on to qualify in this way.

The majority of solicitors qualifying each year are still law graduates – in 1993–94, 64 per cent of those admitted to the Law Society Roll had a law degree, with only 19 per cent being graduates in subjects other than law. However, the Law Society say that the non-law degree and CPE route is becoming more popular, with a third of places on Legal Practice Courses currently being taken by people aiming to qualify this way. Legal academics have expressed some concern about this, but the Law Society point out that, in some years, pass rates for non-law graduates in Solicitors' Finals have been higher than those for law graduates. Making up the remaining 17 per cent are Fellows

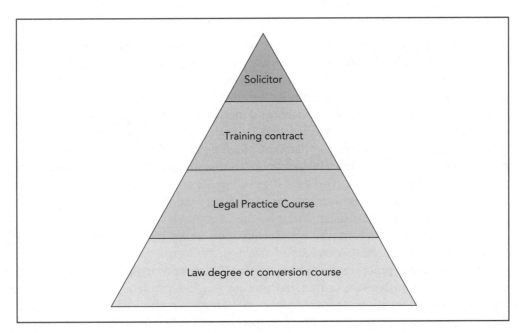

Figure 11.2 Qualifying as a solicitor

11

The legal professions

of the Institute of Legal Executives, lawyers from overseas, solicitors transferring from Scotland or Northern Ireland and ex-barristers.

All solicitors are required to participate in continuing education throughout their careers. They are required to do 16 hours a year, with the subjects covered depending on each individual's areas of interest or need. Records must be kept of courses attended.

Lord Woolf has observed that the solicitor profession is becoming 'increasingly polarised' depending on the nature of the work carried out, with lawyers working in City firms earning significantly more than those in high street practices. Specialist LPC courses are now being offered for City law firms. Lord Woolf has criticised this development, as he fears it could undermine the concept of a single-solicitor profession with a single professional qualification. Such courses may, over time, create a barrier which prevents students from other colleges from entering a big commercial practice. Lord Woolf has observed that, given the quality of the trainees attracted by the City firms, it should be possible for them to provide any enhanced training they require after the end of the Legal Practice Course.

Certain lawyers qualified abroad, particularly Europe, and English barristers can convert to become English solicitors by passing the Qualified Lawyers Transfer Test (QLTT).

Complaints

Complaints can be made to the Legal Complaints Service, to the Legal Services Ombudsman and/or by an action in negligence.

Legal Complaints Service

There have been ongoing problems with the way complaints against solicitors are handled. The body responsible for dealing with these complaints has undergone numerous reforms and name changes over the years to deal with these problems. Until 1996, complaints about solicitors were handled by the Solicitors Complaints Bureau (SCB). The Bureau was widely criticised for delay and inefficiency, and a report by the National Consumer Council in 1994 suggested that its policy of attempting to conciliate the parties favoured solicitors over complainants, tending in many cases to impose a settlement or dismiss the complaint. The maximum compensation available to complainants was £1,000, and this was criticised as being too low. Another issue of concern was that the Solicitors Complaints Bureau was not sufficiently independent of the profession, as its powers were merely delegated to it by the Law Society.

Worried by these criticisms, the Law Society looked into the problems and in 1995 produced a report entitled *Supervision of Solicitors; the Next Decade*. The report found that the complaints process needed to be more efficient and customer-friendly, with a greater role for non-lawyers so that the process was independent of the profession. Its main recommendation was acted upon in 1996, when the Solicitors Complaints Bureau was replaced by the Office for the Supervision of Solicitors (OSS). This body was renamed the Consumer Complaints Service (CCS) in 2004.

However, the problems associated with the Solicitors Complaints Bureau remained and the complaints process has been repeatedly criticised by the Legal Services Ombudsman (discussed below).

In 2007 the CCS was abolished and replaced by the Legal Complaints Service. This should provide an independent complaints handling service. It is also intended to be more efficient and consumer-friendly. Unfortunately, spectators of this endlessly changing organisation may well be cynical as to whether this latest reform will succeed where its predecessors have failed. In 2007 the Solicitors Regulation Authority issued a new Code of Conduct for solicitors which states at rule 2.05 that a solicitor firm must have 'a written complaints procedure and that complaints are handled promptly, fairly and effectively in accordance with it'.

If the Legal Complaints Service considers that the complaint raises an issue of professional standards the case can be referred to the Solicitors Disciplinary Tribunal to consider whether disciplinary action is required.

Ess. Cases p. 136 → Problems with the handling of complaints have been highlighted by the fallout from the Coal Health Compensation Scheme. This scheme was set up by the Government in 1999 to compensate miners for respiratory disease and vibration white finger suffered as a result of working for the national coal industry. The scheme was expected to cost the Government £1 billion. Solicitors were criticised for deducting large sums of money as legal fees from money that was intended to be paid to their clients as compensation. In 65 per cent of the cases that had been settled by March 2008, the solicitors' legal fees had been greater than the compensation received by the client. Many complaints were made to the Legal Complaints Service but the Legal Services Complaints Commissioner has criticised the inconsistent way these complaints have been handled.

The problem of complaints handling was considered in Sir David Clementi's review of the legal professions in 2004. He recommended that an independent Office for Legal Complaints should be established which would handle all consumer complaints against any legal service provider (including solicitors and barristers). It would be supervised by a new Legal Services Board. The Legal Services Complaints Commissioner would be abolished. While the Law Society was happy with this proposal, the Bar Council is concerned that the new body may prove slower and more expensive than the existing arrangements. It commented:

Table 11.1 Investigations where the Ombudsman found that complaint handling was satisfactory

	Apr 2004 to Mar 2005	Apr 2003 to Mar 2004	Apr 2002 to Mar 2003	Apr 2001 to Mar 2002
Solicitors/Law Society	62.0%	53.3%	67.2%	57.9%
Barristers/GCB	78.7%	86.8%	88.4%	92.9%
Licensed Conveyancers/CLC	33.3%	66.7%	61.5%	60.0%
All cases	**63.8%**	**57.5%**	**69.2%**	**60.9%**

Source: Annual report of the Legal Services Ombudsman for England and Wales 2004/2005, p. 15

We have an extremely good record on complaints as confirmed by the Legal Services Ombudsman. We do not want the service provided to the public to be diminished by being sucked into a large bureaucratic Office for Legal Complaints.

Ess. Cases
p. 144

The Government has however accepted Sir David Clementi's recommendation, and provisions to establish this new body are contained in the Legal Services Act 2007. It has started to recruit people to work in the Office for Legal Complaints, as the first step in the process of setting up the Office itself in October 2010. The Legal Complaints Service will be closed down once it is replaced by the Office for Legal Complaints. Eighty per cent of the staff currently employed by the Legal Complaints Service are expected to be employed by the new Office for Legal Complaints. This does raise questions about how different the new Office will be.

Legal Services Ombudsman

The Office of the Legal Services Ombudsman was established in 1990. Its role is to oversee the handling of complaints by the professional regulatory bodies, and offers the final appeal regarding complaints against lawyers. Complainants who are dissatisfied with the way their grievances are handled by the Legal Complaints Service can ask the Legal Services Ombudsman to investigate. If he or she is dissatisfied with the way the relevant professional body has handled the complaint, the Ombudsman can recommend that the relevant professional body reconsiders the complaint and/or order compensation to be paid.

Due to the Government's dissatisfaction with the solicitors' complaints handling process, it has also created a Legal Services Complaints Commissioner (LSCC). The role of the LSCC is to oversee the operation of the Legal Complaints Service, partly by setting its targets. He or she has the power to impose large fines on the Law Society if these targets are not met. Ms Zahida Manzoor, the current Legal Services Ombudsman, has been formally appointed to hold this post as well. Her two roles, however, remain distinct: as Ombudsman she is concerned with individual complaints, as LSCC she supervises the complaints handling process as a whole. Manzoor's dual role does create a certain tension, as she both sets the targets for the Legal Complaints Service in her role as complaints commissioner and polices their performance as Ombudsman. The Law Society has argued that this allows her to act as police, judge and jury and was very unhappy when, in 2006, she imposed a £220,000 fine for failings in the complaints system.

The Office of the Legal Services Ombudsman is expected to cease to exist in 2010 and the Office of Legal Services Complaints Commissioner in 2011, when the Office for Legal Complaints has been established.

Action for negligence

Solicitors can also be sued for negligent work like most other professionals. Following the House of Lords' judgment of **Arthur JS Hall & Co** v **Simons** (2000) solicitors no longer enjoy any immunity from liability for work connected to the conduct of a case in court.

Promotion to the judiciary

In the past, solicitors were only eligible to become circuit judges, but the Courts and Legal Services Act 1990 has opened the way for them to become judges in the higher courts (see Chapter 10: The judges).

Claims management companies

Claims management companies are companies that find people who have a legal problem (for example by placing adverts on the television and radio asking whether you have suffered an accident in the last three years). They then refer these people to solicitors, who pay the company for the referral. There has been concern that some of these companies have behaved inappropriately, for example, by encouraging members of the public to start litigation when they do not have a genuine claim, or by pushing people to take out expensive loans to pay for legal insurance premiums they cannot really afford. The Law Society relaxed its restrictions on advertising in 1986, but law firms have been slow to take up this opportunity, and relied heavily on the advertising of claims management companies instead. To try to put an end to unscrupulous practices by these companies, they are now required to have a licence and are regulated in accordance with provisions in Part 2 of the Compensation Act 2006. They have to comply with new rules of conduct covering advertising, marketing, soliciting of business and complaints procedures. Any unauthorised provision of claims services is punishable by up to two years' imprisonment. There are a number of exceptions from the requirement for authorisation under the 2006 Act to cover professions whose conduct is already regulated, for example, insurance companies and trade unions. Once the Legal Services Board has been established (provided for in the Legal Services Act 2007), it will

ss. Cases p. 152 →

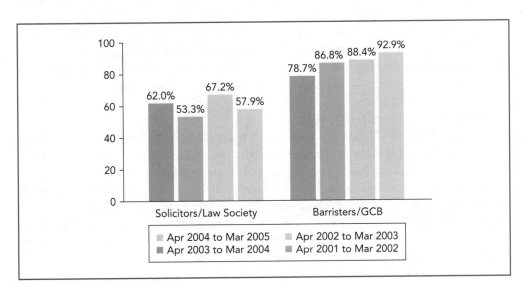

Figure 11.3 Investigations where Ombudsman complaint handling was satisfactory

Source: Annual report of the Legal Services Ombudsman for England and Wales 2004/2005, p. 56

monitor the new regulatory body to see whether it is effectively tackling the problem of bad practice among claims management companies.

Barristers

There are around 14,000 barristers in independent practice, known collectively as the Bar. Their governing body is the Bar Council, which acts as a kind of trade union, safe-guarding the interests of barristers. The Bar Council, like the Law Society, has tried to separate its representative functions from its regulatory functions, and has therefore established a Bar Standards Board responsible for regulating the Bar. The Board makes the rules and takes the decisions affecting entry to, training for, and practice at the Bar, including disciplinary issues.

Work

Advocacy is the main function of barristers, and much of their time will be spent in court or preparing for it. Until the changes made under the Courts and Legal Services Act in 1990, barristers were, with a few exceptions, the only people allowed to advocate in the superior courts – the Supreme Court, the Court of Appeal, the High Court, the Crown Court and the Employment Appeal Tribunal. We have seen that this has now changed, and they are increasingly having to compete with solicitors for this work. Barristers also do some paperwork, drafting legal documents and giving written opinions on legal problems.

Barristers must be self-employed and, under Bar rules, cannot form partnerships, but they usually share offices, called chambers, with other barristers. All the barristers in a particular chambers share a clerk, who is a type of business manager, arranging meetings with the client and the solicitor and also negotiating the barristers' fees. Around 70 per cent of practising barristers are based in London chambers, though they may travel to courts in the provinces; the rest are based in the other big cities.

Not all qualified barristers work as advocates at the Bar. Like solicitors, some are employed by law centres and other advice agencies, Government departments or private industry, and some teach. Some go into these jobs after practising at the Bar for a time, others never practise at the Bar.

Traditionally, a client could not approach a barrister directly, but had to see a solici-tor first, who would then refer the case to a barrister. In 2004 the ban on direct access to barristers was abolished. Members of the public can now contact a barrister without using a solicitor as an intermediary. Barristers are today able to provide specialist advice, drafting and advocacy without a solicitor acting as a 'middleman', although the management of litigation will still generally be handled by solicitors. Direct access to the client is permitted where the barrister has been in practice for three years, and has undertaken a short course preparing them for this new mode of operation.

Barristers work under what is called the 'cab rank' rule. Technically, this means that if they are not already committed for the time in question, they must accept any case which falls within their claimed area of specialisation and for which a reasonable fee is offered. In practice, barristers' clerks, who take their bookings, may manipulate the rule to ensure that barristers are able to avoid cases they do not want to take. The cab rank rule does not apply where a barrister is approached directly by a potential client, rather than being referred to them by a solicitor. In these circumstances, barristers must follow a principle of non-discrimination, under which they must not refuse work because of the way it is funded or because the client is unpopular.

Barristers' pay varies considerably. Average earnings of barristers are apparently very high at £178,000 a year. But those working in the legal aid sector are earning much less than those relying on private clients. The Bar Council has suggested that some recently qualified junior barristers who practise in crime can be earning as little as £10,000 a year and even those with established practices may be earning around £40,000 a year.

Qualifications and training

The starting point is (at least) an upper second class degree. If this degree is not in law, applicants must do the one-year course leading to the Common Professional Examination (the same course taken by would-be solicitors with degrees in subjects other than law). Mature students may be accepted without a degree, but applications are subject to very stringent consideration, and this is not a likely route to the Bar.

All students then have to join one of the four Inns of Court: Inner Temple; Middle Temple; Gray's Inn; and Lincoln's Inn, all of which are in London. The Inns of Court first emerged in the thirteenth century and their role has evolved over time. Their main functions now cover the provision of professional accommodation for barristers' chambers and residential accommodation for judges, discipline, the provision of law libraries and the promotion of collegiate activities.

Students take the year-long Bar Vocational Course: until 1996, this was only available at the Inns of Court School of Law in London, but can now be taken at eight different institutions around the country. The course includes oral exercises, and tuition in interviewing skills and negotiating skills, and, as with solicitors' training, more emphasis has been laid on these practical aspects in recent years.

Ess. Cases p. 133 → The Bar Vocational Course has been reviewed by the Bar Standards Board which published a report, *Entry to the Bar,* in 2007. Changes to the content of the course will be introduced in 2010 and the course will be renamed the Bar Professional Training Course (BPTC). This report has suggested that consideration should be given as to whether students should be required to have a 2:1 degree in order to undertake the course and pass an entrance examination checking their aptitude for the barrister profession, by looking in particular at their communication and written skills. It recommends that there should be a single, unified final examination, set and marked externally and overseen by a board of examiners, to deal with the perceived differences in standards between different providers.

Only discretionary Local Education Authority grants are available for this year and the Common Professional Examination, and neither are covered by the Student Loan Scheme. The Inns of Court between them provide around £4 million in sponsorship. Approximately 25 per cent of students will receive assistance from their Inn, with about half of these obtaining a sum of between £3,000 and £6,000. Around 2,000 people take the Bar Vocational Course each year, and each one has to pay approximately £12,000 for the course alone, and then find living expenses on top.

Students have to dine at their Inn 12 times. This rather old-fashioned and much-criticised custom stems from the idea that students will benefit from the wisdom and experience of their elders if they sit among them at mealtimes. The dinners are linked to seminars, lectures and training weekends, in order to provide genuine educational benefit.

After this, the applicant is called to the Bar, and must then find a place in a chambers to serve his or her pupillage. This is a one-year apprenticeship in which pupils assist a qualified barrister, who is known as their pupil master. In the past funding for pupillage has been a problem. But pupils should now normally be paid a minimum of £10,000 a year. Competition for pupillage places can be fierce, with only 500 pupillage vacancies available each year. Pupillage is usually done in two six-month blocks, with different pupil masters and usually in different chambers. Pupils are required to take courses on advocacy, advice to counsel and forensic accountancy, as part of the increased emphasis on practical skills.

Pupillage completed, the newly qualified barrister must find a permanent place in a chambers, known as a tenancy. This can be the most difficult part, and some are forced to 'squat' – remaining in their pupillage chambers for as long as they are allowed, without becoming a full member – until they find a permanent place. There are only around 300 tenancies available each year – one to every two pupils.

In 1993, the Royal Commission on Criminal Justice recommended that barristers should have to undertake further training during the course of their careers, after noting that both preparation of cases and advocacy were failing to reach acceptable standards. In response, the Bar Council introduced a continuing education programme. Barristers must now complete a minimum of 45 hours of continuing education in the prescribed subjects by the end of their first three years of practice. They have to study four subjects:

- Case Preparation and Procedure;
- Substantive Law or Training relating to Practice;
- Ethics; and
- Advocacy Training.

The Bar Council has also introduced an established practitioners' programme under which all barristers who have been qualified for over three years must undertake each year a minimum of 12 hours' study.

Complaints

Until recently barristers enjoyed an immunity from liability for negligent work in court. This immunity had been recognised by the courts in the case of **Rondel v Worsley** (1969). The main justification for the immunity was that a negligence action would effectively result in a retrial of the case that gave rise to the allegation of negligence, which would damage the certainty and finality of the original verdict. In other words, clients would seek to use litigation against their barrister to reopen indirectly litigation that had already been lost.

KEY CASE

The immunity of barristers from liability for negligence was dramatically abolished by the House of Lords in **Arthur JS Hall & Co** *v* **Simons** (2000). There was no longer any good reason to treat barristers differently from other professionals – their negligence could give rise to liability in tort.

> Barristers can be liable for negligent work.

Despite this judgment, in the most recent House of Lords case on the point, **Moy** *v* **Pettman Smith** (2005), the House proceeded to treat a barrister more leniently than other professionals. A barrister had been sued for negligently failing to settle a case. The House concluded that she had not been negligent, and in reaching this conclusion it repeatedly referred to what could be expected from a barrister of her 'seniority and purported experience'. This is notably different from the way the work of other professionals has been judged in comparable situations. A doctor's work, for example, in a case of alleged negligence is usually judged by the standards of 'reasonably competent practitioners' and the courts ignore their level of seniority.

The Bar Standards Board (BSB) has responsibility for complaints against barristers. Complaints are considered first by a Complaints Commissioner, who is an independent non-lawyer employed by the BSB. The Commissioner will investigate and where he or she believes there is a case to answer the matter will be referred to the Complaints Committee. If the BSB believes there has been a serious breach of the Bar's Code of Conduct the case can be referred to a Disciplinary Tribunal. The Disciplinary Tribunal has the power to fine, suspend or permanently prevent the individual from practising as a barrister.

The Legal Services Ombudsman oversees the Bar's handling of complaints in the same way as with complaints about solicitors (see p. 194). In 1999, the Ombudsman's annual report praised the Bar's complaints handling, commenting that 'a more modern and consumerist mentality is starting to prevail'. However, a MORI poll carried out in 2003 suggests there is still considerable room for improvement. The survey found that three-quarters of people who make complaints about their barrister are unhappy with the investigation process. By contrast, three-quarters of barristers were very satisfied with how complaints were investigated and the outcome of investigations. Most complainants thought the system was designed by lawyers, for lawyers. Once established, the new office for Legal Complaints (see p. 195) will take over responsibility for dealing with complaints against barristers.

Promotion to the judiciary

Suitably experienced barristers are eligible for appointment to all judicial posts, and the majority of current judges have practised at the Bar (for details of appointments, see Chapter 10: The judges).

Queen's Counsel

After 10 years in practice, barristers and solicitors may apply to become a Queen's Counsel, or QC (sometimes called a silk, as they wear gowns made of silk). This usually

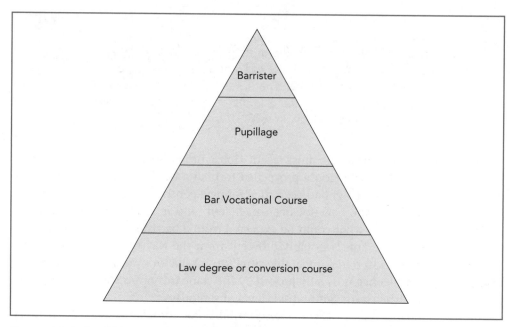

Figure 11.4 Qualifying as a barrister

means they will be offered higher-paid cases, and need do less preliminary paperwork. The average annual earnings of a QC are £270,000, with a small group earning over £1 million a year. At the moment most QCs are barristers, though not all barristers attempt or manage to become QCs – those that do not are called juniors, even up to retirement age. Juniors may assist QCs in big cases, as well as working alone. Since 1995, solicitors can also be appointed as QCs, but there are currently only eight QCs who come from the solicitor profession.

The future of the QC system was put in doubt when the Office of Fair Trading in 2001 suggested the system was merely a means of artificially raising the price of a barrister's services. The Bar Council counter-argued that, actually, the system was an important quality mark which directs the client to experienced, specialist lawyers where required.

In the past the appointment process for QCs was similar to that for senior judges, including the system of secret soundings, and with civil servants, a Cabinet Minister and the Queen all involved. In 2003 the appointment process was suspended, following criticism of the QC system. Appointments were recommended in 2004 but relying on a new appointment process. The Government is no longer involved. Instead, responsibility for appointments has been placed in the hands of the two professional bodies: the Bar Council and the Law Society. They select candidates on the basis of merit, following an open competition. The secret soundings system has been abolished and replaced by structured references from judges, lawyers and clients who have seen the candidate in action. The title of QC has been retained for the time being, though the Law Society would like to see it replaced with another name, to mark a clean break from the past, when the system clearly favoured barristers. Commenting on the new appointment procedures, the Law Society president stated:

> Consumers can be assured that holders of the QC designation under the new scheme have been awarded it because of what they know not who they know, and that their superior expertise and experience has been evaluated by an independent panel on an objective basis.

The Government's current view is that the badge of QC is a well-recognised and respected 'kitemark' of quality both at home and abroad. The existence of QCs helps enhance London's status as the centre of international litigation and arbitration.

Background of barristers and solicitors

Lawyers have, in the past, come from a very narrow social background, in terms of sex, race and class; there have also been significant barriers to entrants with disabilities. In recent years the professions have succeeded in opening their doors to a wider range of people, so that they are more representative of the society in which they work.

White, middle-class men dominate in most professions, excluding many people who would be highly suited to such careers. A narrow social profile created particular problems for the legal professions in the past. First, it meant that the legal professions have been seen as unapproachable and elitist, which put off some people from using lawyers and thereby benefiting from their legal rights (this issue is examined in Chapter 17). Secondly, the English judiciary is drawn from the legal professions and, if their background is narrow, that of the judiciary will be too (this issue is examined in Chapter 10). Increasingly, the professions are becoming representative of the society in which they function.

The Ministry of Justice has set up a research project called 'Barriers leading into law'. This project will track 32 law students for a year to help understand the barriers to becoming lawyers faced by people from different backgrounds.

Women

Women were only allowed to become lawyers with the passing of the Sex Disqualification (Removal) Act 1919, which allowed women to enter all professions. Up to then, the Law Society had been anxious to keep women out to protect the financial interests of the existing male solicitors. Thirty-five years later there were still only 350 practising women solicitors. At that time, many male solicitors with their own practices saw training for the legal profession as an easy way to educate and provide for their daughters and their own retirement. Thus these female solicitors tended to work in family firms.

The number of women in the professions has increased dramatically since the 1970s. In 1987 women accounted for less than 20 per cent of all solicitors; now 44 per cent of solicitors are women. Today there are more women qualifying for the solicitor profession than men.

For the barrister profession in 2002, equal numbers of men and women qualified to practise and 32 per cent of barristers are women.

The problem now, for women, is less about entry into the professions and more about pay, promotion and working conditions. Female solicitors earn less than male solicitors. Research carried out for the Legal Services Commission in 2008 suggests that on average men earned £100,000 more than women. Statistics published by the Law Society show that male solicitors are earning on average 50 per cent more than female solicitors: on average a male solicitor is earning £60,000 compared with £41,000 for a female solicitor.

Fewer women are being promoted to become partners in their law firm. Over 50 per cent of male solicitors are partners in their firm, compared to only 23 per cent of female solicitors. This cannot simply be explained by the fact that the average age of women solicitors is younger: 88 per cent of male solicitors in private practice with 10–19 years of experience were partners, compared with 63 per cent of female solicitors with the same experience. There is a similar problem in the barrister profession. In 2003, 112 men were made Queen's Counsel, but only nine women.

A growing problem exists of women choosing to leave the profession early. This is either because they find it impossible to combine the demands of motherhood with a legal career or because they are frustrated at the 'glass ceiling' which seems to prevent women lawyers from achieving the same success as their male counterparts. Solicitor firms do not tend to have provisions in place for flexible or part-time working for solicitors. Those that do, tend to discourage solicitors from taking advantage of them (*Research Study No. 26 of the Law Society Research and Policy Planning Unit* (1997)). The Law Society has recognised that in order to retain women and to ensure that the investment in their training is not lost, the profession must consider more flexible work arrangements (including career breaks) to allow women (and men) to continue to work alongside caring responsibilities.

The legal profession also needs to tackle the long hours culture to stem the flow of women lawyers leaving the profession. The macho culture of working long hours forces women, who often have to juggle work and family, out of the legal world.

The solicitor, Elizabeth Cruickshank (2007), has commented:

> We have been encouraged to think that there would be a 'trickle up' effect because of the sheer numbers of women entering the profession, so that we would no longer be held back by the 'sticky floor', bump our heads against the 'glass ceiling' or fall off the 'glass cliff'. Reflection shows that apparently the floor, the ceiling and the cliff are still in place and that the trickle upwards is almost inexorably slowed by social gravity.

Ethnic minorities

Again, the picture is improving. The number of solicitors from ethnic minority groups has increased recently. In 2003, 8 per cent of practising solicitors came from an ethnic minority. This compares with 4 per cent in 1995. In 2003, 17 per cent of trainee solicitors were from a minority ethnic group. There are still, however, very few male Afro-Caribbean solicitors.

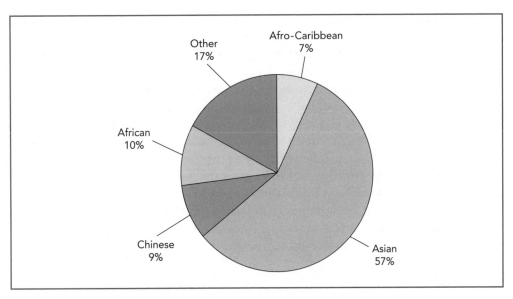

Figure 11.5 The ethnic origin of solicitors from minority ethnic groups, 2006

Source: Law Society. Fact Sheet: Minority ethnic group solicitors 2006 [www.lawsociety.org.uk]

As regards the Bar, in 1989, 5 per cent of practising barristers came from an ethnic minority; in 2003 they made up 11 per cent of practising barristers and 20 per cent of pupils. This compares favourably with other professions.

Regrettably, there have in the past been reports in the media of black candidates doing less well in legal examinations than white candidates, particularly at the Bar. It has been suggested that oral examinations may be particularly vulnerable to subjective marking.

The Law Society has recognised that obstacles still exist for ethnic minorities in the solicitor profession. This is because most solicitor firms do not follow proper recruitment procedures, do not have an equal opportunities policy and practice, and the levels of discrimination within society at large are reflected in the perception of solicitors and their clients. Only 23 per cent of black and minority ethnic solicitors are partners in their firms, compared to 39 per cent of white solicitors. Research carried out for the Legal Services Commission in 2008 suggests that ethnic minority barristers were earning on average £50,000 less than their white counterparts. Statistics published by the Law Society show that white solicitors are earning 25 per cent more than black solicitors: on average a white solicitor is earning £60,000 compared with £41,000 for a black solicitor.

Class

The biggest obstacle to a career in law now seems to be a person's social background. Law degree students are predominantly middle class, with less than one in five coming from a working class background. In 2009 a Government report, *Unleashing Aspiration: The Final Report of the Panel on Fair Access to the Professions*, identified that lawyers were increasingly coming from wealthy families. Lawyers born in 1958 tended to come

11

The legal professions

from families whose income was 40 per cent higher than average. Lawyers born in the 1970s grew up in households whose income was 64 per cent higher than average, so the problem is getting worse rather than better, with even average middle class students finding it difficult to build a career in law. A 1989 Law Society Survey found that over a third of solicitors had come from private schools, despite the fact that only 7 per cent of the population attend such schools. In recent years, more lawyers have been educated in the state sector, but this progress could soon be reversed. This is because the lack of funding for legal training has made it very difficult for students without well-off parents to qualify, especially as barristers.

One possible source of change for the future is the number of part-time law degrees and Legal Practice Courses now available to mature students, who tend to come from a much broader range of backgrounds than those who attend university straight from school. Students on part-time courses can support themselves by continuing to work while they study in the evenings and at weekends.

Disability

Much attention has been paid to the under-representation of working class people, ethnic minorities and women in the legal profession, but disabled people are less often discussed. Skill as a lawyer requires brains, not physical strength or dexterity, yet it seems there are still significant barriers to entry for disabled students, particularly to the Bar. Part of the problem is simply practical: a quarter of court buildings are over 100 years old and were never designed to offer disabled access. Most now have rooms adapted for disabled people, but need notice if they are to be used, which is hardly feasible for junior barristers, who often get cases at very short notice. The other main barrier is effectively the same as that for ethnic minorities, working-class people and women: with fierce competition for places, 'traditional' applicants have the advantage.

Steps are being taken to address the problems of disabled applicants to the Bar. In 1992, the Bar's Disability Panel was established. This offers help to disabled people who are already within the profession or are hoping to enter it, by matching them to people who have overcome or managed to accommodate similar problems. The Inner Temple also gives grants for reading devices, special furniture and other aids, with the aim of creating a 'level playing field' for disabled and able-bodied people.

TOPICAL ISSUE

Increasing diversity through educational reforms

The Solicitors Regulation Authority is considering changing the way people qualify as solicitors to try to broaden access to the profession for a more diverse range of students. The Law Society has observed:

> The existing training pathway – a degree in law, one year on a Legal Practice Course and a two-year training contract – has worked well, and will continue to be the route to qualification for many. But it is a system that favours the young school leaver with a traditional academic education who is prepared to take on a five figure debt. It makes law a difficult career choice for the rest. That is discriminatory – and not good for the profession.

In 2005 the Law Society published a consultation paper, *Qualifying as a solicitor – a framework for the future*. The consultation paper suggested that it should no longer be necessary for a future solicitor to complete a Legal Practice Course or, in fact, to have any academic legal qualifications (such as a law degree). Instead, candidates would simply need to demonstrate they had acquired the necessary skills and knowledge by passing assessments set by the Law Society.

These proposals were the subject of considerable criticism, in particular that, without the course structure of the Legal Practice Course, consistent standards would not be maintained. As a result, a further consultation paper has been issued, *A new framework for work based learning* (2006). This paper recommends that the current academic and vocational training qualifications should essentially remain the same. Changes would be made, instead, to the work experience aspect of the qualification process. At the moment, when a person completes the Legal Practice Course, they can only become a fully qualified solicitor if they are able to find a training contract. Thousands of people each year fail to find such a position. The Solicitors Regulation Authority is considering establishing an alternative route to qualifying. Instead of having a training contract, individuals would be able to work in any legal environment and have that work supervised and accredited directly by the Authority. People taking this route could gain their work experience at any stage, including while they were actually studying on the Legal Practice Course. There would no longer be a requirement that the trainee solicitor gain their experience over two years; instead, the emphasis would be on the student demonstrating through a portfolio of their work that they had attained the relevant skills. In practice, this arrangement would allow paralegals to qualify as solicitors without having a training contract. Qualifying in this way is likely to take longer than the two-year training contract, and there is a risk that it might create a two-tier profession, with solicitors qualifying by the new route being viewed as inferior to those qualifying by the traditional route. However, this reform could help those people who pass their Legal Practice Course but are then unable to secure a training contract.

Changes would also be made to the training contract route to qualification, though it would still be necessary for these trainees to do the Legal Practice Course first. Law firms would have to apply to become accredited training organisations. The accredited firm would assess the work of trainee solicitors four times at regular six-monthly intervals. The Solicitors Regulation Authority is currently carrying out a small pilot scheme of its proposals and intends to review these proposals in 2010 in the light of the success (or otherwise) of the pilot.

Sadly, the new proposals fail to tackle the problem of the cost of getting the academic and vocational qualifications, which will continue to act as a barrier to students from lower income families. It is undoubtedly important that the legal profession should be a career option for all able students from a wide range of backgrounds, and that people should not be prevented from entering the profession because their family is not rich. The Charter 88 constitutional reform pressure group has argued that students should be funded throughout their legal training. The Law Society and the Bar Council have made representations to the Government, pointing out that training for other professions, such as medicine and teaching, is paid or involves reduced fees. In her book *Eve was Framed* (1992), Helena Kennedy QC argues that selection

s. Cases
p. 130

11

The legal professions

for the Bar in particular has always been based too much on 'connections' and financial resources than on ability. She recommends public funding for legal education and that there should be incentives for barristers' chambers to take on less conventional candidates.

Michael Zander (1988) argued that both the academic and the vocational stages of training could be improved, with a consequent rise in professional standards. Law degrees should include at least preliminary training in areas such as drafting documents and developing interviewing skills. Both pupillage and training contracts can be 'infinitely variable' in quality, according to Zander, 'ranging from excellent to deplorable' depending on where they are undertaken. He suggested a more integrated training was needed, like that undertaken by medical students, with better links between academic and vocational stages.

The former Advisory Committee on Legal Education and Conduct (ACLEC) examined the whole issue of legal training. Its 1996 report suggested that the two branches should no longer have completely separate training programmes at the postgraduate stage. Instead, after either a law degree or a degree in another subject plus the CPE, all students would take a Professional Legal Studies course, lasting around 18 weeks. Only then would they decide which branch of the profession to choose, going on to a Legal Practice Course (for solicitors) or Bar Vocational Course (for barristers) which would be only 15–18 weeks long. This, the ACLEC suggested, would prevent the problem of students having to specialise too early. It also recommended that funding should be made available for the CPE course and the vocational stage of training.

Performance of the legal professions

Over the past 30 years, the performance of lawyers has come in for a great deal of criticism. The last good report was given by the 1979 Royal Commission on Legal Services, which found that 84 per cent of clients were satisfied with the work done by their lawyers, and only 13 per cent were actually dissatisfied. The Commission interpreted this as a vote of confidence for the profession, but as Zander (1988) pointed out, the research was not entirely reliable, since ordinary individuals are unlikely to have sufficient knowledge or experience to make informed judgments about the service they received – they might recognise very bad legal work, but were unlikely to know whether they had received the best advice or help for their situation. Significantly, a similar survey among corporate clients, who use lawyers more frequently, reported a higher level of dissatisfaction.

Since the 1979 Royal Commission, many different criticisms of the profession have been made, from many different quarters. In 1995, the Consumers' Association magazine *Which?* caused a stir with a survey of the standards of advice provided by solicitors. Its researchers phoned a number of solicitors, posing as members of the public seeking advice about simple consumer problems, and the advice given was assessed by the Association's own legal team. The verdict was not good, with much of the advice given being assessed as inadequate or simply wrong. Two years later, the magazine repeated the test and, once again, the results were bad: of the 79 solicitors approached by researchers, the majority gave advice which was incomplete, or in some cases incorrect. In several cases, researchers were incorrectly told that their situation gave them no claim in law; the magazine points out that real-life clients told this would probably not pursue the matter further and would therefore not take advantage of their full legal rights. *Which?* accepted that lawyers cannot be expected to be experts in every area of law, but argued that, if asked something outside their area of expertise, they should admit that and either find out the answer or refer the client to someone else. The Law Society criticised both surveys, arguing that the methods employed were not realistic; and after complaints about the first survey, *Which?* admitted that its allegations against one firm had proved to be wrong.

The number of complaints made about lawyers continues to rise, according to the 2003 annual report from the Legal Services Ombudsman. Figures from the Consumer Complaints Service seem to suggest that the problem is not spread throughout its branch of the profession, however; it claims 80 per cent of complaints made to the Consumer Complaints Service concern the same 950 firms, out of the 8,500 in practice.

A survey undertaken for the Law Society in 2001 found that the public perceive lawyers as formal, expensive and predatory. It may be that they are now being accused of being predatory because of the intensive television advertising by companies who pass work on to solicitors.

One of the most common areas for complaint is costs. The Law Society's Written Practice Standard requires solicitors to give clients written information about all aspects of financing their case, including how the fee is calculated, arrangements for payment and liability for the other side's costs. However, a 1995 report by the National Association of Citizens' Advice Bureaux (NACAB), *Barriers to Justice*, concluded that few clients actually received clear information about costs, and that this was part of the reason why fees were so often the cause of complaints. NACAB recommended that solicitors should have to agree with clients a timetable for regular updates on costs, confirm the arrangement in writing and provide leaflets giving information about costs. Research carried out in 2005 for the consumer group *Which?* showed that three out of ten people did not feel they got value for money from solicitors and a third did not feel they received a good service.

Barristers' prices have also been the subject of considerable criticism and, in particular, the fees charged by what the press have called 'super silks' – QCs whose annual earnings can top £1 million. As a result of this criticism, the House of Lords looked into the issue, and reported in October 1998 that the fees being charged in some cases were excessive. The report accused barristers' clerks of 'deliberately pitching fees at a very high level' (a conclusion which was not all that surprising, since securing the best possible fee for his or her barrister is part of a clerk's job). The report was welcomed by the Legal Action Group, which said that the excessively high fees charged by some QCs were undermining public confidence in the legal system.

The legal profession suffers from a negative public image. A survey of over 1,000 consumers and 100 lawyers carried out in 2005 found that while most lawyers consider themselves forward-thinking and up to date, the public think quite the opposite. The consumers said the main attributes they associated with lawyers were that they were good with people but also ruthless and ambitious. The Law Society launched a national advertising campaign in 2005 to try to change the public's view of the profession. The adverts portrayed solicitors as heroes to encourage the public to consult solicitors about their legal problems.

The future of the professions

A number of Government reports have been published in recent years pushing for changes in the professions. In 2001 the Office of Fair Trading (OFT) issued a report entitled *Competition in the Professions* (2001). This looked primarily at the restrictive practices of barristers and solicitors. These professions were criticised for imposing unjustified restrictions on competition and were urged to take prompt action to put an end to these practices.

Professor Zander (2001b) criticised the report, stating:

> What is deplorable about these developments is the simplistic belief that equating the work done by professional people to business will necessarily improve the position of the consumer, when the reality is that sometimes it may rather worsen it. Certainly one wants competition to ensure that professional fees are no higher than they need to be and that the professional rules did not unnecessarily inhibit efficiency. But what one looks for from the professional even more is standards, integrity and concern for the client of a higher order than that offered in the business world. To damage those even more important values in the name of value for the consumer in purely economic terms may be to throw out the baby with the bath water.

The Government accepted that the legal professions should be subject to competition law. It subsequently issued a consultation paper, *In the Public Interest?*, which questioned the competitiveness of legal services given primarily by solicitors working in solicitor firms.

The Bar Council has made some changes in the light of the OFT report, but has rejected many of its key recommendations. Direct access to the Bar has been increased (see p. 199).

In July 2003, the Government established an independent review into the regulation of legal services. The review was chaired by Sir David Clementi and considered which regulatory framework 'would best promote competition, innovation and the public and consumer interest in an efficient, effective and independent legal sector'.

Ess. Cases
p. 139

Sir David Clementi published his final report in 2004, *Review of the regulatory framework for legal services in England and Wales*. The Government subsequently published a White Paper in 2005 entitled *The Future of Legal Services – Putting Consumers First*, in which it accepted most of Sir David Clementi's recommendations. The Legal Services Act 2007 contains the key reforms, which will be considered in turn below.

11

Photo 11.2 'My solicitor: my hero'

Source: The Law Society of England and Wales

Regulation of the legal professions

Regulation is the process by which the standards of the profession are set and maintained, protecting both the interests of the members of the profession and the clients of the professionals. When clients are using a regulated professional they should be able to trust the work of that professional.

Sir David Clementi looked at how improvements in the provision of legal services could be made through changes to the regulation of the professions. Historically the professions regulated themselves. Sir David Clementi considered that the established regulatory arrangements did not prioritise the public's interest. He therefore looked at whether the professions should be stripped of their right to regulate themselves and whether instead an independent regulator should be created. The professional bodies would merely represent their professions and not regulate them. Clementi commented:

> Among the suggested advantages of this approach are the clear independence of the regulator, clarity of purposes for both regulator and representative bodies and consistency of rules and standards across the profession and services. An independent regulator would be well placed to make tough, fair enforcement decisions and to facilitate lay/consumer input into the decision making processes.
>
> Disadvantages might include creating an overly bureaucratic and inefficient organisation, with consequent issues of costs and unwieldy procedure. A further argument is that it fails to recognise the significance of strong roots within the profession and their importance on the international stage. Divorcing the regulatory functions from the profession might lessen the feeling of responsibility professionals have for the high standard of their profession and their willingness to give time freely to support the system.

Ess. Cases
p. 144 → Ultimately, Clementi concluded that an independent Legal Services Board should be set up and provisions for the establishment of this Board are contained in the Legal Services Act 2007. The Legal Services Board was established in 2009.

The new Board oversees the way the existing professional bodies regulate the professions. It has a duty to promote the public and consumer interests as well as protecting the independence of the legal profession and supporting access to justice. It has statutory responsibility to ensure standards of regulation, training and education of the legal professions. It is led by a part-time chair and a full-time chief executive, who are both non-lawyers, as are the majority of the Board's members. All the members of the Board are selected on merit by the Lord Chancellor after consultation with the Lord Chief Justice. It is hoped that the involvement of the Lord Chief Justice in the appointment process will support the Board's independence from the Government. Politicians must not have too much control over the lawyers whose challenges to possible abuses of power are essential in a free and democratic society. For example, lawyers represent members of the public in criminal cases, when children are being taken into care and when local authorities seek to evict anti-social tenants. The Law Society had unsuccessfully argued that members of the Legal Services Board should be appointed by an independent appointment panel.

The professional bodies are now required by the 2007 Act to separate their regulatory and representative functions. As an immediate response to Sir David Clementi's report on the regulation of the professions, the professional bodies went ahead and separated their regulatory functions from their representative functions. Thus the Law Society set up the Solicitors Regulation Authority and the Bar Council set up the Bar Standards Board.

While the Legal Services Board does not replace the Bar Standards Board and the Solicitors Regulation Authority, it holds them to account for the work they do. The new Board takes only a light-touch, supervisory approach to regulation (as recommended by Sir David Clementi), intervening merely when it is in the public interest. This light-touch approach will avoid costly duplication of effort, stifling innovation and burdening the front-line regulators. The Legal Services Act 2007 gives the Legal Services Board the power to set targets for front-line regulators and it has the power to remove a body's authorisation to regulate if these targets are not met. Front-line regulators have to apply to the Legal Services Board for permission to carry out regulatory functions, such as the regulation of alternative business structures.

The aim of this reform is to achieve consistency and transparency, while keeping costs down and leaving day-to-day regulation close to those who provide the services. The reform has been generally well received, though the Bar is unhappy that it has lost the power to regulate itself.

Since its creation, the Solicitors Regulation Authority has had quite difficult relations with the Law Society itself and the large corporate law firms based in the City of London (often known as the 'Magic Circle'). The Law Society still wants to retain some control over the broader issues concerning regulation, while the Solicitors Regulation Authority is anxious to enjoy complete independence from the Law Society. The Solicitors Regulation Authority considers that if the regulation of the solicitor profession is to be credible in the eyes of the public, it must be genuinely independent of pressures from solicitors via the Law Society. The chair of the Solicitors Regulation Authority has stated: 'We need to bury for ever the damaging perception that lawyers are regulated by lawyers purely for the benefit of lawyers.' Section 30 of the Legal Services Act 2007 requires the Legal Services Board to make rules which create adequate separation of the various professional bodies' representative and regulatory functions.

In 2009 the Law Society announced that it had established a review of the regulation of law firms. When asked why the Law Society rather than the Solicitors Regulation Authority were conducting this review, the chief executive of the Law Society stated:

> The Solicitors Regulation Authority is not a legal person, it is a body of the Law Society. The obligation of the Law Society is to make sure the Solicitors Regulation Authority is properly dealing with those tasks delegated to it.

This statement would seem to suggest that the Law Society does not wish to view the Solicitors Regulation Authority as completely independent. The Legal Services Board appears to be unhappy with the level of control being exercised over the Solicitors Regulation Authority by the Law Society. The Board issued a consultation paper entitled *Boosting Public Confidence in Legal Regulation* (2009) containing draft rules that would strip the Law Society of virtually all its remaining powers over the Solicitors Regulation Authority. The consultation paper suggests that the Law Society should 'ring-fence' the Solicitors Regulation Authority, with the function of regulation being delegated completely to the Authority. Under the proposals the Solicitors Regulation Authority would have the freedom to pursue its own business plan, to appoint its own staff and set its own budget, free from control or veto by the Law Society: 'The representative arm [in other words, the Law Society] should always have a voice but it should not exercise control, or interfere in the day-to-day business of regulation.'

The review set up by the Law Society will be carried out by Lord Hunt (a solicitor and former Government Minister) and will advise on what effective modern regulation means in the context of the legal profession. It will look at how to ensure legal services are regulated in ways that are effective for consumers, businesses and the legal sector, taking account of the very different requirements of diverse parts of the legal services market. A particular issue that this review will consider is how the Magic Circle law firms should be regulated. This was partly in response to signs that some of the biggest corporate law firms were considering alternatives to the existing system of regulation and representation. As these firms were increasingly opening offices overseas, their representation nationally by the Law Society was becoming less important. They are anxious to remain competitive at an international level and they do not want a heavy-handed regulatory system to obstruct their global expansion.

The review will consider whether the large corporate law firms need to be regulated separately by a new regulator, which would work alongside the Solicitors Regulation Authority, or whether a specialist City group should be set up within the Solicitors Regulation Authority. The review will consider the appropriate structures for regulating corporate law firms. It will examine whether the regulatory issues and risks associated with such firms are different from those of small firms and firms with significant private client work rather than corporate client work. It has been argued that corporate purchasers of legal services do not need the same regulatory protections as a private individual. At least on the surface, a large City law firm is a very different work environment from a small high street firm of solicitors. The review will consider whether the same rules and approach to compliance apply to all firms, irrespective of the nature of their clients, or whether a one-size-fits-all approach is outmoded. The Solicitors Regulation Authority has stated that: 'While the way in which we regulate big and small firms may require different approaches, ultimately the same ethical standards must apply and we must regulate all sectors fairly.' In his interim report Lord Hunt suggests City law firms should be self-regulated, with careful checks being imposed to make sure this is being carried out effectively. It looks unlikely that Lord Hunt will recommend a different regulatory regime for corporate law firms as he has stated:

> I am well aware of the competing interests who argue for different standards for different parts of an industry. But I think the legal profession is very different because our standards are set in codes of practice which have statutory force and which have endured for generations. Nevertheless I think the review is timely when there are many changes taking place in that statutory structure.

In the meantime, the Law Society in 2009 published a report by a former civil servant, Nick Smedley, linked to this review stating that the Solicitors Regulation

Authority is not up to the job of regulating corporate law firms and needs to be fundamentally restructured to equip it for the task. It recommends the creation of a 'quasi-autonomous' body called the Corporate Regulation Group within the Solicitors Regulation Authority, based not in the Authority's premises in the Midlands but in a separate building in London, to regulate the big corporate law firms. Employees of this group would have to be better paid than other employees of the Authority so that it could recruit and retain staff with knowledge and experience of the corporate law sector. Smedley has rejected the more radical option of a completely separate regulator for corporate firms.

Smedley (2009) warns that if his recommendations are not accepted then the City law firms might themselves set up a separate regulator. This is a serious risk. It would amount to a split away from the Law Society and the established solicitor profession, effectively creating a new City legal profession. This would constitute a public divorce in what is already in practice quite a divided profession. The current financial crisis and in particular the problems in the banking sector have partly arisen due to weak regulation. It has highlighted that a careful balance needs to be reached between protecting consumers from risk and the freedom needed to grow businesses. The City law firms are anxious to remain competitive during the worst world recession since the 1930s, but it would seem to be in nobody's interests for the regulation of City law firms to be weakened, though it is understandable that their regulation needs to be appropriate to their international work and their risks. In the current economic climate any change to the regulation of City lawyers needs to be perceived as a strengthening in professional regulation and not a weakening. The current economic environment would not seem to be the right time for City lawyers to be seen to be breaking away from the historical controls of the Law Society and the new Solicitors Regulation Authority.

Business structures

Currently, most legal services can be delivered to the public only by solicitors working in a law firm or by barristers in independent practice at the Bar. Sir David Clementi considered two new business structures through which legal services could be delivered to the public: legal disciplinary practices and multi-disciplinary partnerships. The Government has decided to go one step further, with the introduction of 'alternative business structures' provided for in the Legal Services Act 2007. The first legal disciplinary practices were established in 2009 and are seen as an interim step before the introduction of alternative structures.

Legal disciplinary practice

Legal disciplinary practices (LDPs) have been permitted since 2009. Under a legal disciplinary practice up to 25 per cent of the partners can be non-lawyers alongside solicitors, barristers and legal executives and thereby share ownership in the legal practice. The LDP must have a minimum of one solicitor partner. The OFT report, Sir David Clementi's report and the Government's consultation document, *In the public interests?*, all came out in favour of the creation of LDPs.

11

The legal professions

Of the 14 LDPs initially established, 13 involved the promotion of a non-lawyer to become a partner. They were people who were already senior employees in solicitor firms, such as finance directors, HR managers and IT managers. The other LDP involved the promotion of a legal executive to the position of partner. Thus, this business structure should make it easier to retain and reward high-quality staff in firms who are not solicitors, as they can now become partners. One of the reasons that more non-lawyers are seeking to become partners by this means is that barristers and legal executives have had the option of re-qualifying as solicitors to become partners under the traditional solicitor firm structure. There have been fewer applications to set up LDPs than expected, partly because of the current recession.

LDPs are regulated by the Solicitors Regulation Authority and it will carry out character and suitability tests for non-lawyer partners.

Multi-disciplinary partnerships

Multi-disciplinary partnerships would bring together lawyers with other professionals, such as accountants, surveyors and estate agents. These organisations would be able to provide legal and non-legal services, so that they could be described as a 'one-stop shop', offering a range of services to their clients. Sir David Clementi did not recommend that these should be allowed. He was cautious about them and said the Government should only consider introducing multi-disciplinary partnerships once some experience had been gained from the introduction of legal disciplinary practices. The Bar Council was opposed to their introduction, stating:

> The unravelling Enron case should remind us all of the strong public interest that resides in independent professions. Multi-disciplinary partnerships would be dominated by accountancy mega-firms, hungry for corporate consultancy work, and who would regard the independence of the Bar as a matter of secondary importance.

In fact, the Government has gone one step further with the provisions in the Legal Services Act 2007 for the creation of alternative business structures.

Alternative business structures

The Government's 2005 White Paper and the Legal Services Act 2007 go much further than Sir David Clementi on the subject of business structures for legal services. The relevant provisions of the Act are likely to be brought into force in 2011 and will allow legal services to be provided to the public through a wide range of alternative business structures, which would include multi-disciplinary partnerships. A key difference between legal disciplinary practices which were introduced in 2009 and the planned alternative business structures is that the latter will allow external ownership (for example a law business could be owned by Tesco) while the former must be owned by the partners to the practice. As a result, under an alternative business structure potentially a large amount of external funding could be invested into a law business. The aim is to increase competition to the benefit of consumers and to increase investment in legal service providers, so that they can improve such areas as the use of IT for the delivery of legal services and expand to provide a better quality of service to the consumer. The impact of these changes has been considered by research commissioned by the Government – James Dow and Carlos Lapuerta (2005) *The Benefits of Multiple Ownership Models in Law Services*. A central conclusion of this research was that external investment would lead to an increased use of IT for the delivery of legal services.

The Chair of the Solicitors Regulation Authority, Peter Williamson, has suggested that the establishment of alternative business structures 'could well be the legal profession's equivalent of the financial world's Big Bang' with big business getting involved in the provision of legal services. The Co-op, Halifax and the AA publicly announced that they intended to offer legal advice and assistance directly to the public, once the legislation had been brought into force. The Co-op plans to establish 'Co-operative Legal Services', offering a range of legal services, including conveyancing and will writing. It will be based in Bristol and employ approximately 150 people, including a team of 30 lawyers. It already offers a free Legal Services helpline to its customers which has been praised by consumer groups but criticised by the Law Society for not offering face-to-face advice to its clients.

The Co-op's research into the legal market found that there was a general distrust of legal service providers. This is exacerbated by the media's portrayal of the legal system, but it also stems from clients' experiences. Unlike many other businesses, the solicitor profession has often not moved with the times to take into account the development of Internet services and mobile phones. The Co-op considers it can succeed in this market because people like to deal with a business which they feel is a trusted brand, with which they have an existing relationship, and where they know what to expect. They want this combined with the professionalism, skill and *gravitas* of a properly qualified lawyer.

Halifax is proposing to launch 'Halifax Legal Solutions' which will provide a service whereby the public pay an annual membership fee of £89 for access to a 24-hour legal helpline. Additional services, such as conveyancing, will be available at fixed prices. Halifax has recognised that the banks and building societies, with their network of branded, highly visible shop fronts on every high street, have a huge advantage over local solicitors operating in isolation.

The Government considers that bigger organisations might provide advice more efficiently than the existing business structures for lawyers. The reform has become known as the 'Tesco Law' because big organisations will be able to buy law firms. The Bar Council is unhappy with this reform proposal. It has pointed out that outside commercial involvement does not always mean better and cheaper services. Large, wealthy companies would be allowed to employ a few solicitors and lots of paralegals (individuals with more limited legal qualifications) to offer these services. This could be primarily a telephone service, offered from a centralised location and focused at only the better paid work. Just as out of town supermarkets have forced the closure of local greengrocers and chemists, alternative business structures for legal advisers could lead to the closure of many high street solicitor firms. The Lord Chancellor has admitted that the new business structures could affect the future of small high street solicitor firms, but the Government does not seem keen on small firms, pointing out in its 2005 White Paper that research by Paul Grout (2005) found that complaints of dishonest practice are disproportionately generated by smaller law firms.

The Bar Council has stated that the historical ban on barristers forming partnerships actually promoted competition between the 10,000 barristers in private practice, and preserved their fundamental independence, which is at the core of the justice system. It is unhappy that non-lawyers could become owners and investors in legal practices. The Bar has argued that non-lawyers would not be bound by the ethical codes of standard that apply to legal professionals and that the independence of the legal practice would be put at risk. It considers that the current proposed safeguards would be inadequate to prevent improper interference by external investors with the delivery of legal services.

While the professions have been quick to attack the planned introduction of alternative business structures, it may be that the quality of their current services has made them vulnerable to this type of reform. Most people would be perfectly happy to go through life without ever having to instruct a solicitor. They only turn to a legal professional out of necessity and frequently at times of distress: for example, to get a divorce, or because they have been in an accident or have been arrested by the police. The Lord Chancellor's introduction to the White Paper, *The Future of Legal Services: Putting the Consumer First* (2005), observes:

> The professional competence of lawyers is not in doubt. The calibre of many of our legal professionals is among the best in the world. But despite this, too many consumers are finding that they are not receiving a good or a fair deal.

In practice, much of the work in solicitor firms is already being done by paralegals rather than solicitors themselves. The personal contact between the solicitor and client

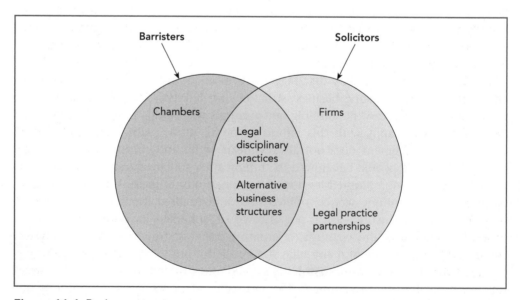

Figure 11.6 Business structures

has been reduced through the use of claims management companies, who refer cases to solicitors at a fee and the solicitor will have never met the client personally but merely receive a paper file on the case. Thus solicitors themselves are not always providing a personal face-to-face service.

A parliamentary joint committee looked at the proposed introduction of alternative business structures contained in the then Legal Services Bill. The committee was concerned that there was a risk of a conflict of interest between the different participants in alternative business structures and inappropriate pressure could be placed on lawyers within such structures to sell products, such as insurance policies, from other branches of the organisation. The evidence presented to the committee suggested that alternative business structures might not be allowed to practise in America and some European countries.

Office for Legal Complaints

The Legal Services Act 2007 contains provisions for the establishment of an Office for Legal Complaints to hear complaints against all legal professions. This reform is discussed on p. 195.

Fusion of the professions

The divided legal profession dates from the nineteenth century, when the Bar agreed to give all conveyancing work and all direct access to clients to the solicitors, in return for sole rights of audience in the higher courts and the sole right to become senior judges for barristers. However, since the late 1960s, there have been a series of moves towards breaking down this division. Following the Access to Justice Act 1999, solicitors automatically have rights of audience, though they still have to undertake training in order to exercise these rights. It is likely that an increasing number of solicitors will undertake this training to become solicitor-advocates.

There has been much discussion over recent years as to whether the professions will eventually fuse. When the Courts and Legal Services Act 1990 was passed, it was thought that it might be the first step in Government plans to fuse the two professions by legislation. Until 1985, the two branches had been largely left alone to divide work between themselves, and had made their own arrangements for this; the abolition of the solicitors' monopoly on conveyancing was the first major Government interference in this situation, and the Courts and Legal Services Act was obviously a much bigger step towards regulation by Government rather than the professions themselves. Even if the Government did not force fusion, it has been suggested, it could happen anyway if large numbers of solicitors take up rights of audience.

Alternatively, it has been suggested that the Bar might survive, but in a much reduced form, and there is much debate about which areas would suffer most. Barristers generally fall into two groups: those who specialise in commercial fields, such as company law, tax and patents; and those who have what is called a common law practice, which means that they deal with a fairly wide range of common legal issues, such as crime, housing and family law. Some legal experts believed that commercial lawyers would be most likely to survive, since they have a specialist knowledge that solicitors cannot provide. However, for several years now, solicitors in City firms have been becoming more specialist themselves and, if able to combine specialist knowledge with rights of audience, they would clearly be a threat to the commercial Bar. In addition, such firms offer high incomes, without the insecurity of self-employment at the Bar, and therefore they are able to attract first-rate students who once would have automatically been attracted to the more prestigious Bar. As these entrants work their way up through law firms, the Bar's traditional claim to offer the best expertise in high-level legal analysis will be difficult to sustain.

Others have suggested that common law barristers have a better chance of surviving competition from solicitors. They cater for the needs of ordinary high street solicitors, who generally have a wide-ranging practice, and spend much of their time seeing clients and gathering case information. This leaves little opportunity to swot up on the finer details of every area of law with which clients need help so, where specialist legal analysis is needed, they refer the client to a barrister with experience in the relevant area.

The Inns of Court (discussed on p. 199) set up a Working Party on the future of the Inns of Court which reported in 2000. The aim of the Working Party was to review the impact of the Access to Justice Act 1999, which has made it easier for more solicitors and employed barristers to qualify to appear in the higher courts. It recommended that membership of the Inns should be offered to solicitors entitled to appear in the higher courts, on payment of an entrance fee of £1,000. The report warns that if the Inns cease to be of relevance to the profession they run the risk of decline. The Inns are financially dependent on rents from their properties, which are priced at the very top of the market. If the Bar does decline in numbers – as many predict – they could well find themselves left with property they cannot let at rents no one wants to pay. One of the greatest threats to the future of the Bar is the fact that employed lawyers' rights of audience have increased. Much of the work that the Bar currently gets from the Crown Prosecution Service in particular is likely to disappear as the advocacy will be done 'in-house'.

When Sir David Clementi was appointed in 2003 to review the legal professions, there were fears that this might be the moment when the Government forced the two professions to fuse and abolished the Bar Council and Law Society. In fact these fears proved ill-founded. Below we look at some of the arguments for and against fusion of the two professions.

Arguments for fusion of the professions

Expense

With the divided profession a client often has to pay both a solicitor and a barrister, sometimes a solicitor and two barristers and, as Michael Zander (2001a) puts it, 'To have one taxi meter running is less expensive than to have two or three.' However, the Bar Council prepared a report called *The Economic Case for the Bar. A comparison of the*

Table 11.2 Moves towards fusion

Year	Moves towards fusion
1969	Following the Royal Commission on Assizes and Quarter Sessions, the Lord Chancellor was given the power to allow solicitors extended rights of audience where there were not enough barristers.
1972	A Practice Direction from the Lord Chancellor's Department stated that solicitors could appear in appeals or committals for sentencing from the magistrates' to the Crown Court, where they had appeared for that client in the magistrates' court.
1979	The Royal Commission on Legal Services unanimously rejected a proposal for the fusion of the professions.
1985	A Practice Direction permitted solicitors to appear in the Supreme Court in formal or unopposed proceedings, and when judgment is given in open court.
1986	The Law Society document, *Lawyers and the Courts: Time for Some Changes*, proposed that all lawyers should undergo the same training, work two or three years in 'general practice', and then choose to go on to train as barristers if they wished. The Bar Council rejected this idea.
1988	The Marre Committee was set up by the Bar Council and the Law Society to look at, among other things, whether any changes were needed in the structure of the profession. It largely advocated maintaining the status quo.
1990	The Courts and Legal Services Act contained the following provisions: • direct access to barristers by certain professional clients; • access to the higher levels of the judiciary for solicitors; • multi-disciplinary partnerships to be allowed, subject to the agreement of the professions' ruling bodies; • rights of audience in all courts should be extended to 'suitably qualified' persons, not necessarily barristers or solicitors. Applications for this right had to be made to the Lord Chancellor's Advisory Committee and then approved by the Lord Chancellor and four judges.
1992	Solicitor-advocates were introduced (discussed on p. 191).
1999	Following the Lord Chancellor's report, *Modernising Justice* (1998), the Access to Justice Act 1999 was passed. This replaces the Lord Chancellor's Advisory Committee with the new Legal Services Consultative Panel, which takes over the role of regulating rights of audience. The procedure for approving changes to the rules on rights of audience is simplified and the Lord Chancellor has a new power, subject to parliamentary approval, to change rules which are unduly restrictive. This last power is designed to ensure that the legal professions themselves cannot cling on to restrictive rules and prevent reform. All barristers and solicitors now automatically acquire full rights of audience, though they are only able to exercise them by successfully completing the necessary training.
2001	The Office of Fair Trading issued its report on anti-competitive practices in the professions, which is discussed on p. 210.
2004	The Clementi Committee issued its report into the regulation of the professions.
2007	The Legal Services Act 2007, containing provisions for alternative business structures, receives Royal Assent.

11

The legal professions

costs of barristers and solicitors (2000). This paper claimed that it was generally more economical to employ the services of a barrister, particularly a junior, for work within his or her area of expertise than to use a solicitor. In broad terms it stated that the differences in charge-out rates make it from 25 per cent to 50 per cent cheaper to employ the services of a junior barrister than an assistant solicitor in London. A major factor is that barristers' overheads are approximately half those of solicitors. However, the paper is misleading, as without direct access to clients for barristers it is not an either/or situation. The reality is that a client does not pay for either a solicitor or a barrister, but if they employ a barrister they must pay for both, along with the cost of the solicitor preparing the papers for the barrister.

Inefficiency

A two-tier system means work may be duplicated unnecessarily, and the solicitor prepares the case with little or no input from the barrister who will have to argue it in court. Barristers are often selected and instructed at the last moment – research by Bottoms and McLean in Sheffield revealed that in 96 per cent of cases where the plea was guilty, and 79 per cent where it was not guilty, clients saw their barrister for the first time on the morning of the trial. In this situation important points may be passed over or misunderstood.

Waste of talent

Prospective lawyers must decide very early on which branch of the profession they wish to enter, and if, having chosen to be a solicitor, the lawyer later discovers a talent for advocacy, they may be denied the chance to use it to the full.

Other countries

All common law countries have bodies of specialist advocates, and possibly need them, but no other country divides its legal profession in two as England does.

Arguments against fusion

Specialisation

Two professions can each do their different jobs better than one profession doing both.

Independence

The Bar has traditionally argued that its cab rank principle guarantees this, ensuring that no defendant, however heinous the charges, goes undefended; and that no individual should lack representation because of the wealth or power of the opponent. The fact that barristers operate independently, rather than in partnerships, also contributes. However, the Courts and Legal Services Act 1990 does provide for solicitors with advocacy certificates to operate on a cab rank basis, which has somewhat weakened the Bar's argument. In addition, successful barristers do get round the cab rank rule in practice.

Table 11.3 Comparison of barristers and solicitors

	Barrister	Solicitor
Number	14,000	98,000
Professional organisation	Bar Council	Law Society
Professional course	Bar Vocational Course (BVC)	Legal Practice Course (LPC)
Apprenticeship	Pupillage	Training contract

Importance of good advocacy

Our adversarial system means that the presentation of oral evidence is important; judges have no investigative powers and must rely on the lawyers to present the case properly.

The 1979 Royal Commission suggested that fusion would lead to a fall in the quality of the advocacy, arguing that although many solicitors were competent to advocate in the magistrates' and county courts, arguing before a jury required different skills and greater expertise, and if rights were extended it was unlikely that many solicitors would get sufficient practice to develop these.

Access to the Bar

Critics of moves towards fusion argued that it may result in many leading barristers joining the large firms of commercial solicitors, so making their specialist skills less accessible to the average person. Smaller practices might generate insufficient business to justify partnership with a barrister and find it difficult to secure a barrister of equal standing to the opponent's; they would be reluctant to refer a client to a large firm, for fear of losing them permanently. A major drift towards large firms could worsen the already uneven distribution of solicitors throughout the country.

The judiciary

A reduction in the number of specialist advocates might make it more difficult to make suitable appointments to the Bench; although the potential candidates would increase, they would not be as well known to those carrying out the selection process. On the other hand this might eventually mean appointments would have to be made on a more open, regulated system, and from a wider social base.

Use of court time

Court cases are not given a fixed time, only a date; depending on the progress of previous cases they may appear at any time during a morning or afternoon session, or be held over until another day – the idea behind this is that the clients and their lawyers should wait for courts, rather than the other way round. It has been suggested that barristers are best organised for this, though there seems no reason why, within a united profession, those lawyers who specialise in court work could not organise themselves accordingly.

11

The legal professions

Other legal personnel

Legal executives

Most firms of solicitors employ legal executives, who do much of the same basic work as solicitors. Their professional body is the Institute of Legal Executives. Although technically they are under the supervision of their employers, in practice many experienced executives specialise in particular areas – such as conveyancing – and take almost sole charge of that area. From the firm's point of view, they are a cheaper option than solicitors for getting this work done, and in many cases will be more experienced in their particular area than a solicitor. However, clients are usually unaware that, when they pay for a solicitor, they may be receiving the services of a legal executive.

Following the Courts and Legal Services Act 1990 and the Access to Justice Act 1999, the Institute of Legal Executives is now able to grant its members the rights to conduct litigation on the completion of suitable training. The first six legal executives qualified as advocates in the year 2000 and now have extended rights of audience in civil and matrimonial proceedings in the county court and magistrates' courts. In 2006, suitably qualified legal executives were granted rights of audience in criminal proceedings in the magistrates' courts, and on bail applications in the Crown Court. They are not able, at the moment, to become judges.

Legal executives are generally less well paid than solicitors. A survey carried out by the Institute of Legal Executives in 2001 found that a third of legal executives earned between £15,000 and £21,000, while 11 per cent earned over £27,000. If alternative business structures are introduced, legal executives may be able to own one of these. As part of the Government's efforts to increase judicial diversity, legal executives are likely to be given the right to apply for junior judicial appointments with relevant provisions contained in the Tribunals, Courts and Enforcement Act 2007.

Qualifications and training

To qualify as a legal executive, a person works full time and studies part time. Studying will either be undertaken at a local college or through distance learning with ILEX Tutorial College. It takes on average six years to qualify fully as a legal executive, though students with a law degree benefit from exemptions from some of the examinations. Only about 600 people qualify each year as legal executives, with many people failing to complete their education. Once qualified as a legal executive, a person can undertake further part-time study to become a solicitor, unless they had unsuccessfully attempted the Legal Practice Course before becoming a legal executive.

Licensed conveyancers

The Courts and Legal Services Act 1990 abolished the solicitor's monopoly of conveyancing and paved the way for a new profession, licensed conveyancers. As their name suggests, these professionals are purely involved in conveyancing and are increasingly being used by people buying and selling a home.

Do we need legal professionals?

In many areas, non-legally qualified people do the work of lawyers as well as professionals could, and sometimes more effectively – an obvious example is the large number of volunteer and employed lay advisers in the Citizens' Advice Bureaux who provide an accessible, economic and uncomplicated service to deal with legal and other queries. Legal executives often become so well experienced in particular areas that they need no supervision from their legally qualified colleagues, and take on much of the work that the general public assumes only solicitors can do. Some work may even be better done by clients themselves. So why should we need a profession (or two), and why should that profession be allowed sole access to certain types of work?

Where litigants choose to represent themselves in court, they may take along someone (who may not be a lawyer) to advise them. They are called a 'McKenzie friend' after the case in which the court made it clear that the attendance of a lay adviser was permissible: **McKenzie v McKenzie** (1970). Workers from Citizens' Advice Bureaux, Law Centres and law student groups are among those who commonly act as McKenzie friends, though anyone (including friends and relatives) requested by the litigant could do so. Heather Mills used a McKenzie friend when she represented herself during her divorce from Paul McCartney. If a person acting for themselves in legal proceedings (known as a 'litigant in person') wishes to use a McKenzie friend they need to make this request to the judge. The judge will give permission for this provided the assistance is not contrary to the interests of justice and a fair trial. For example, Dr Pelling was a campaigner for fathers' rights, and on a number of occasions he has been refused permission to act as a McKenzie friend on the basis that his campaigning agenda had a tendency to take over and his experience led to him, rather than the litigant, running the case (**R v Bow County Court, ex parte Pelling (No. 1)** (1999). McKenzie friends may assist a litigant by providing quiet advice and support in court and, in exceptional circumstances with the court's permission, they can act as the litigant's advocate by directly addressing the court. With increasing numbers of litigants in person because of the reduced availability of legal aid, the use of McKenzie friends is likely to increase.

There are many reasons why a legal profession might be considered desirable, but two broad theories shed some interesting light on the reasons why we maintain it. The first, functionalism, emphasises the importance of keeping society together, and it sees one important way of doing this as maintaining the status quo, keeping the structure of society the same.

Functionalists believe professions in general contribute to this process. They say those within a profession will share certain values, put public service before profit, and use expert knowledge for the good of society – the implication is that professionals have higher moral standards than ordinary people. They are supposed to believe in 'public service' and 'shared professional ethics', while plumbers, car manufacturers and shopkeepers, for example, are only interested in money. This is used to justify the fact that they are the only people to have access to certain types of work. It is difficult to reconcile this view with the fact that many lawyers compete to work for the big legal firms, working for the most powerful members of society – not because the work is interesting or socially useful, but because it pays so well.

A second theory, that of market control, has a very different view of the role played by professionals. It takes as its starting point the marketplace, where different suppliers compete with each other to get consumers to buy their goods and services. Economic theory reasons that at any given level of quality, consumers will choose the cheapest goods or services, so those offering good quality services cheaply will sell a lot, and the rest will go bust.

This may be good news for consumers, but tough for producers, who must be constantly striving to provide a better product for less money, while looking over their shoulder to make sure that someone else is not providing it cheaper or better than they can. Consequently, producers try to get round this competitive situation, and they can do so in a number of different ways – by forming monopolies and cartels, or by controlling the raw materials or the patents to a manufacturing process, for example.

Market control theory suggests that having professions is just one of those ways of escaping uncontrolled competition. Professions restrict access to their market by controlling who enters the profession, saying that only those with complicated qualifications can offer services in this area; they control the way in which professionals offer their services, for example by stopping members of the profession using aggressive advertising to compete with each other; and they keep their own special area of expertise as complex and as obscure as they can.

One of the leading proponents of this point of view is Richard Abel, Professor of Law at the University of California. His book on the legal profession in England and Wales (1988) describes in great detail how solicitors and barristers have controlled who become lawyers, how they operate and what they sell. He suggests that they have done this in their own interests, to keep the price of legal services high. A recent example of this process is that during the difficult economic situation at the end of the 1980s, when there was increased competition for jobs, the Bar Council raised its entry requirement for initial training from a second class to an upper second class degree. Similarly, Abel has shown that the pass rate in Law Society exams goes up when there is a shortage of jobs, and down when there is a shortage of recruits.

Answering questions

1 Do you consider that the current system of legal education and training can provide the lawyers that this country needs?

The first thing to note about this question is that it is not asking what the present system of legal education and training is; it wants to know how well that system performs. You do need to show that you are aware of the system, but a detailed description of it will waste time and gain few marks.

Your introduction should point out what you understand by the term lawyers – we suggest that you concentrate on barristers and solicitors in your answer, even though technically judges are also lawyers. Then you need to state what you think are the qualities this country needs in its lawyers – you might mention legal knowledge and practical skills, efficiency, cost-effectiveness, and an ability to use its skills for the benefit of all the members of society, for example.

You can then go on to outline the system of legal education and training but *keep it brief*! There is no point in writing pages of detailed description, because that is not what the question asks for. You need to point out that training for barristers and solicitors is different, and then just mention the stages for each.

The main part of your essay should be concerned with assessing whether the system provides the qualities you have mentioned in your introduction, and we suggest you consider them in turn. The following are points you might like to make:

● the need for legal knowledge and practical skills. You could mention the various criticisms of lawyers' performances, and point out that both professions are moving towards a more practical approach.
● the need for a cost-effective, efficient service. Here you might mention some of the disadvantages of the fact that we train two different types of lawyers to play two different roles – the criticisms of the divided profession in terms of cost and inefficiency are relevant here. You could also put forward the argument that a divided profession is wasteful of talent, especially as it divides so early on.
● the need for lawyers to be accessible to all members of the community. Here you will need to use some of the material on unmet legal need from Chapter 17, pointing out that the middle-class image of solicitors puts many people off using them, especially for problems such as social security and employment. You can then point out that the system of training contributes directly to this problem, because it is so difficult for a student without well-off parents to survive financially during training, and so the profession continues its middle-class base.

You might want to bring in the issue of whether we need professional lawyers at all, mentioning the work done by unqualified legal advisers in agencies such as the Citizens' Advice Bureaux. You could also discuss here the market control theory which suggests that professions exist not to provide the best services, but as a way of controlling competition – so the emphasis on high academic qualifications can be seen as a way of limiting entry to the market.

It would be a good idea to point out that one of the reasons why this question is so important is that legal education and training provides not only lawyers, but eventually the judiciary – point out, for example, that only when the legal profession becomes more mixed in terms of race, class and sex will the judiciary follow suit. You could discuss the reforms that the Law Society is currently considering introducing to the process of qualifying as a solicitor. These reforms aim to increase the diversity of people joining the profession.

Your conclusion should sum up whether you feel legal education does provide the lawyers we need.

2 Critically evaluate the recent reforms to the governance of the legal professions.

Changes have been made against a background of restrictive practices and criticism over the handling of complaints against barristers and solicitors. The OFT Report *Competition in the Professions* looked at restrictive practices, but, according to Professor Zander, ignored the issue of standards, integrity and concern for the client. Both professions made some amendments to their regulations, such as allowing employed barristers to undertake litigation work for their employers and permitting some lay clients direct access to a barrister.

In his subsequent report, Sir David Clementi addressed the self-regulation of the professions by suggesting a separation of the representative function from the regulatory function through the establishment of a Legal Services Board. The Bar is particularly unhappy about losing its self-governance. The key reforms are now contained in the Legal Services Act 2007.

In evaluating these reforms, you could note that the new Board is supposed to exercise 'light touch' supervision, partly to keep costs down, but may risk giving excessive control to the Government, whose decisions lawyers may seek to challenge.

3 **It is arguable that the once separate professions of barrister and solicitor have been covertly and gradually fused over recent years. Use your knowledge of the different roles that barristers and solicitors serve in the legal system to either support or oppose the above statement.**

A possible starting point for your answer is to set out the roles of barristers and solicitors. Even if you eventually disagree with the statement, there are a number of developments which suggest that it may be true (see especially pp. 219–21). For example:

- The Courts and Legal Services Act 1990 and the Access to Justice Act 1999 give solicitors the same rights of audience as barristers (subject to training), and the fact that solicitors can now wear wigs reinforces their equality. Certainly solicitors do as much – if not more – advocacy work than barristers (see the examples on pp. 191 and 210).
- Solicitors can become judges in higher courts where they could previously only become circuit judges.
- The rule whereby members of the public could only access a barrister through a solicitor was abolished in 2004 (p. 198).
- Legal disciplinary practices, as provided for in the Legal Services Act 2007, enable the formation of partnerships between barristers and solicitors (p. 215).

You could conclude your essay by commenting on whether or not you think complete fusion would improve the present system (arguments for and against can be found at p. 220).

Summary of Chapter 11: The legal professions

The three main professions in the legal field are:

- solicitors;
- barristers; and
- legal executives.

Solicitors
- *Work*: traditionally solicitors focused primarily on paperwork but they are now doing more advocacy.
- *Qualifications and training*: usually a university degree, followed by a conversion course if this was not in law. Then they take the one-year Legal Practice Course and a two-year training contract.
- *Complaints*: can be made to the Legal Complaints Service, the Legal Services Ombudsman and the courts.

Barristers
- *Work*: traditionally advocacy, but they also do some paperwork.
- *Qualifications and training*: usually a university degree, followed by a conversion course if this is not in law. Then the one-year Bar Vocational Course and one-year pupillage.

- *Complaints*: can be made to the Complaints Commissioner, the Legal Services Ombudsman and the courts.

Background of barristers and solicitors

Barristers and solicitors have traditionally come from a very narrow social background, in terms of class, race and sex, and disabled people are under-represented. They now come from a wider range of backgrounds, but there is a problem with promotion and retention of women and people from minority groups.

Increasing diversity through educational reforms

The Law Society is considering reforming the way people qualify as solicitors.

The future of the profession

A number of Government reports have been published in recent years pushing for changes in the professions. In July 2003, the Government established an independent review into the regulation of legal services, chaired by Sir David Clementi. A range of reforms have subsequently been introduced in the Legal Services Act 2007.

Regulation of the legal professions

The Legal Services Act 2007 contains provisions for the establishment of a Legal Services Board to oversee the way the existing professional bodies regulate the professions.

Regulation of claims management companies

There has been concern that some claims management companies have behaved unscrupulously. Legislation has been introduced to improve the regulation of these companies.

Legal disciplinary practices

Legal disciplinary practices (LDPs) consist of solicitors, barristers and other professionals being able to work together in the same organisation to provide legal services directly to the public.

Multi-disciplinary partnerships

Multi-disciplinary partnerships would bring together lawyers with other professionals, such as accountants, surveyors and estate agents. These organisations would be able to provide legal and non-legal services, so that they could be described as a 'one-stop shop', providing a range of services to their clients. Sir David Clementi did not recommend that these should be allowed for the time being.

Alternative business structures

The Government is proposing that legal services could be provided to the public through a wide range of alternative business structures where the owners and investors would not be limited to lawyers. Provisions for this are contained in the Legal Services Act 2007.

Office for Legal Complaints

Sir David Clementi recommended that an Office for Legal Complaints should be created to hear complaints against all legal professions and the Legal Services Act 2007 contains statutory provision for this body.

Moves towards fusion?

Since the late 1960s there has been a series of moves towards breaking down the division between barristers and solicitors.

Reading list

Abel, R. (1988) *The Legal Profession in England and Wales*, Oxford: Basil Blackwell.

Boon, A. and Levin, J. (2008) *Ethics and Conduct of Lawyers in the UK*, Oxford: Hart.

Cruickshank, E. (2007) 'Sisters in the Law', *Solicitors Journal* 1510.

Grout, P.A. (2005) *The Clementi Report: Potential Risks of External Ownership and Regulatory Responses – A Report to the Department for Constitutional Affairs*, London: Department for Constitutional Affairs.

Johnson, N. (2005) 'The training framework review – what's all the fuss about?', 155 *New Law Journal* 357.

Joseph, M. (1985) *Lawyers Can Seriously Damage Your Health*, London: Michael Joseph.

Ryan, E. (2007) 'The unmet need: focus on the future', 157 *New Law Journal* 134.

Susskind, R. (1996) *The Future of Law*, Oxford: Oxford University Press.

Susskind, R. (2008) *The End of Lawyers? Rethinking the Nature of Legal Services*, Oxford: Oxford University Press.

Young, S. (2005) 'Clementi: in practice', 155 *New Law Journal* 45.

Reading on the Internet

www

The research carried out by Paul Grout (2005), *The Clementi Report: Potential Risks of External Ownership and Regulatory Responses – A Report to the Department for Constitutional Affairs*, is available on the website of the Department for Constitutional Affairs at:

http://www.dca.gov.uk/legalsys/grout.pdf

The research carried out by James Dow and Carlos Lapuerta (2005), *The Benefits of Multiple Ownership Models in Law Services*, is available on the website of the Department for Constitutional Affairs at:

http://www.dca.gov.uk/legalsys/dow-lapuerta.pdf

The Law Society's consultation paper (2006), *A new framework for work based learning*, is available on its website at:

http://www.lawsociety.org.uk/newsandevents/news/view=newsarticle.law?NEWSID=296854

Sir David Clementi's report, *Review of the Regulatory Framework for Legal Services in England and Wales* (2004), is available at:

http://www.legal-services-review.org.uk

The report of the Office of Fair Trading, *Competition in the Professions* (2001), is available on their website:

http://www.oft.gov.uk/shared_oft/reports/professional_bodies/oft328.pdf

The Bar Council website can be found at:

http://www.barcouncil.org.uk/

The website of the Bar Standards Board is available at:

http://www.barstandardsboard.org.uk

The report *Entry to the Bar* (2007) reviewing access to the barrister profession is published by the Bar Council at:

http://www.barcouncil.org.uk/news/TheEntrytotheBarWorkingPartyFinalReport/

The Law Society's website can be found at:
   http://www.lawsociety.org.uk/home.law

The website of the Solicitors Regulation Authority is available at:
   http://www.sra.org.uk/about/strategy.page

The consultation paper issued by the Government in 2003 on the future of QCs is available on the Department for Constitutional Affairs' website:
   http://www.dca.gov.uk/consult/qcfuture/index.htm

Visit www.mylawchamber.co.uk/ElliottELS to access multiple-choice questions, flashcards and practice exam questions to test yourself on this chapter.

11

The legal professions

12

The jury system

This chapter discusses:

- the role of the jury in civil and criminal cases;
- who can serve as a juror;
- the jury selection process;
- how the jury works in secret and reaches its verdict;
- the advantages and disadvantages of jury service; and
- some possible ways that the jury system could be reformed.

History

The jury system was imported to Britain after the Norman Conquest, though its early functions were quite different from those it fulfils today. The first jurors acted as witnesses, providing information about local matters, and were largely used for administrative business – gathering information for the Domesday Book for example. Later, under Henry II, the jury began to take on an important judicial function, moving from reporting on events they knew about, to deliberating on evidence produced by the parties involved in a dispute. Gradually it became accepted that a juror should know as little as possible about the facts of the case before the trial, and this is the case today.

KEY CASE

A major milestone in the history of the jury was in **Bushell's Case** (1670). Before this, judges would try to bully juries into convicting the defendant, particularly where the crime had political overtones, but in **Bushell's Case** it was established that the jury were the sole judges of fact, with the right to give a verdict according to their conscience, and could not be penalised for taking a view of the facts opposed to that of the judge.

> Jurors can give a verdict according to their conscience.

The importance of the juror's right to give a verdict according to their conscience is that juries may acquit a defendant, even when the law demands a guilty verdict. This right was recently reinforced by the House of Lords' decision of **R v Wang** (2005). The House confirmed that a judge can never tell a jury to convict. Mr Wang's bag had been stolen from a train station. When it was retrieved, it was found to contain a large martial arts sword and knife. Mr Wang was prosecuted for having 'an article with a blade . . . in a public place'. At his trial he argued in his defence that he was a Buddhist practising Shaolin – an ancient martial art which requires the mastery of nearly 20 weapons. He stated that he had taken the weapons with him because he did not like to leave them unsupervised in his flat. The trial judge rejected this defence and told the jury: 'As a matter of law, the offences themselves are proved and I direct that you return guilty verdicts.' The House of Lords allowed Mr Wang's appeal. The trial judge had been wrong to direct the jury that they had to convict. The judge should have told the jury that they alone were to decide what the evidence was and how to apply the law. It is for the jury and not the judge to decide whether the defendant was guilty. In answer to the Court of Appeal's question: 'In what circumstances, if any, is a judge entitled to direct a jury to return a verdict of guilty?', the House of Lords replied, 'none'.

Today the jury is considered a fundamental part of the English legal system, though, as we shall see, only a minority of cases are tried by jury. It is considered to play a vital role in making sure that the criminal justice system works for the benefit of the public rather than for the benefit of unjust leaders. This has implications not just

12

The jury system

for a healthy criminal justice system but also for a healthy society because the criminal justice system can potentially be abused by political leaders to silence their opponents. The French philosopher Alexis de Tocqueville (1835) wrote in his book *Democracy in America*:

> . . . to regard the jury simply as a judicial institution would be taking a very narrow view of the matter, for great though its influence on the outcome of lawsuits, its influence on the fate of society is much greater still. The jury is above all a political institution, and it is from that point of view that it must always be judged.

It has attained symbolic importance, so that Lord Devlin wrote in 1956:

> Trial by jury is more than an instrument of justice and more than one wheel of the constitution; it is the lamp that shows that freedom lives.

This statement led to a classic rebuttal by the academic Penny Darbyshire (1991), who wrote an article entitled 'The Lamp that Shows that Freedom Lives – Is it Worth the Candle?' She argued in that article that:

> . . . juries are not random, not representative, but anti-democratic, irrational and haphazard legislators, whose erratic and secret decisions run counter to the rule of law.

The main Act that now governs jury trial is the Juries Act 1974.

The function of the jury

The jury have to weigh up the evidence and decide what are the true facts of the case – in other words, what actually happened. The judge directs them as to what is the relevant law, and the jury then have to apply the law to the facts that they have found and thereby reach a verdict. If it is a criminal case and the jury have given a verdict of guilty, the judge will then decide on the appropriate sentence. In civil cases the jury decide on how much money should be awarded in damages.

In reaching their verdict, the jury are only entitled to consider evidence that arose in court; they cannot consider in the jury room evidence that has not been introduced in court. This issue arose in **R v Marshall and Crump** (2007). Two defendants had been convicted of offences including robbery and manslaughter. After their conviction material printed off the Internet was found in the jury room. The defendants appealed on the basis that their convictions were unsafe as they had not had any opportunity to discuss this material in open court. While it was accepted that in principle a jury should not consider material that had not been considered in court, on the facts of the case the evidence had been printed off legitimate websites to which the public had general access and only concerned issues as to sentencing. Therefore, on the facts of the particular case, the convictions were found to have been safe.

When are juries used?

Criminal cases

Though juries are symbolically important in the criminal justice system, they actually operate only in a minority of cases and their role is constantly being reduced to save money. Criminal offences are classified into three groups: summary only offences, which are tried in the magistrates' courts; indictable offences, which are tried in the Crown Court; and either way offences, which, as the name suggests, may be tried in either the magistrates' courts or the Crown Court. The majority of criminal offences are summary only, and because these are, in general, the least serious offences, they are also the ones most commonly committed (most road traffic offences, for example, are summary only). As a result, 95 per cent of criminal cases are heard in the magistrates' courts, where juries have no role (this proportion also includes cases involving either way offences where the defendant chooses to be tried by magistrates). Juries only decide cases heard in the Crown Court. Even among the 5 per cent of cases heard there, in a high proportion of these the defendant will plead guilty, which means there is no need for a jury and, on top of that, there are cases where the judge directs the jury that the law demands that they acquit the defendant, so that the jury effectively makes no decision here either. The result is that juries actually decide only around 1 per cent of criminal cases.

Photo 12.1 The Old Bailey, the Central Criminal Court in London
Source: Jupiter Unlimited

On the other hand, it is important to realise that even this 1 per cent amounts to 30,000 trials, and that these are usually the most serious ones to come before the courts – though here too the picture can be misleading, since some serious offences, such as assaulting a police officer or drink-driving, are dealt with only by magistrates, while even the most trivial theft can be tried in the Crown Court if the defendant wishes.

Despite its historical role in the English legal system, and the almost sacred place it occupies in the public imagination, the jury has come under increasing attack in recent years. Successive governments have attempted to reduce the use of juries in criminal cases in order to save money. The Criminal Law Act 1977 removed the right to jury trial in a significant number of offences, by making most driving offences and relatively minor criminal damage cases summary only. Since 1977, more and more offences have been removed from the realm of jury trial by being made summary only. The sentencing powers of magistrates have been increased by the Criminal Justice Act 2003. Prior to that Act, magistrates could only sentence a person to six months' imprisonment for a single offence. Following the passing of the 2003 Act, magistrates can sentence offenders to up to 12 months' imprisonment for a single offence, and this could be increased further to 18 months by delegated legislation. The Government hopes that by increasing the magistrates' sentencing powers, more cases will be tried in the magistrates' court rather than being referred up to the Crown Court to be tried by an expensive jury.

TOPICAL ISSUE

Legislating to reduce the role of the jury

Ess. Cases
p. 178 →

The Criminal Justice Act 2003 provides for trial by judge alone in the Crown Court in two situations:

- where a serious risk of jury tampering exists (s. 44); or
- where the case involves complex or lengthy financial and commercial arrangements (s. 43).

In this second scenario, trial by judge alone would be possible where the trial would be so burdensome upon a jury that it is necessary in the interests of justice for the case to be heard without a jury. Alternatively, it would be possible where the trial would be likely to place an excessive burden on the life of a typical juror. While s. 44 has been brought into force, the Government agreed with the opposition not to implement s. 43 while alternative proposals for specialist juries and judges sitting in panels were investigated. The legislative provision can only be brought into force by a parliamentary order approving its implementation, which will require debates and a vote in both Houses of Parliament. This process was initiated at the end of 2005, but following strong opposition the provision was not brought into force. Instead, the Government introduced in 2006 a single issue Bill, the Fraud (Trials without Jury) Bill, aimed solely at abolishing the jury in a limited range of serious and complex fraud trials. This Bill did not complete its progress through Parliament before Parliament closed for the summer of 2007. It may be that the Government will not try to push through this piece of legislation as no mention was made of it in the Queen's Speech when Parliament reopened in November 2007 and it has not been reintroduced to Parliament.

The first Crown Court trial to be ordered without a jury in England and Wales under s. 44 occurred in the case of **R v Twomey** in 2009. The trial was concerned with an attempted robbery that occurred in Heathrow in 2004. The defendants had originally been put on trial in 2008, but the trial had been stopped after six months when two jurors had been approached. The cost of that first, unsuccessful trial had been £22 million. The cost of giving a new jury adequate protection would be £1.5 million. The Court of Appeal concluded that in those circumstances s. 44 applied and the trial was ordered to proceed without a jury.

12

The jury system

Civil cases

In the past most civil cases were tried by juries, but trial by jury in the civil system is now almost obsolete. The erosion of the use of juries in civil cases was very gradual and appears to have started in the middle of the nineteenth century, when judges were given the right, in certain situations, to refuse to let a case be heard before a jury and insist that it be heard in front of a sole judge instead. Now less than 1 per cent of civil cases are tried by a jury. Today the Senior Courts Act 1981 gives a qualified right to jury trial of civil cases in four types of case:

- libel and slander;
- malicious prosecution;
- false imprisonment; and
- fraud.

In these cases jury trial is to be granted, unless the court is of the opinion that the trial requires any prolonged examination of documents or accounts, or any scientific or local investigation which cannot conveniently be made with a jury. This right is exercised most frequently in defamation actions, although its use may be more limited now that the Defamation Act 1996 has introduced a new summary procedure for claims of less than £10,000, which can be heard by a judge alone.

In all other cases the right to jury trial is at the discretion of the court. In **Ward v James** (1966) the Court of Appeal stated that in personal injury cases (which constitute the majority of civil actions), trial should be by judge alone unless there were special considerations. In **Singh v London Underground** (1990) an application for trial by jury of a personal injury claim arising from the King's Cross underground fire of November 1987 was refused on the ground that a case involving such wide issues and technical topics was unsuitable for a jury.

There has been criticism of the distinction drawn between the four types of case which carry a qualified right to trial by jury and other civil cases. The Faulks Committee on Defamation 1975 rejected arguments for the complete abolition of juries

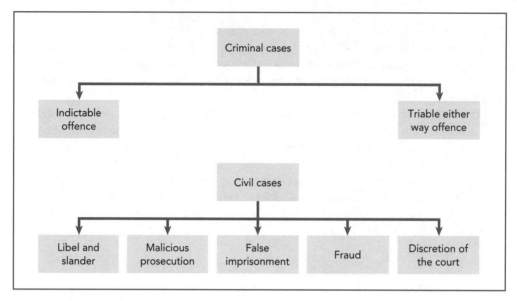

Figure 12.1 Role of the jury

in defamation cases, but recommended that in such cases the court should have the same discretion to order jury trial as it does in other civil cases, and that the function of the jury should be limited to deciding issues of liability, leaving the assessment of damages to the judge.

Qualifications for jury service

Before 1972, only those who owned a home which was over a prescribed rateable value were eligible for jury service. The Morris Committee in 1965 estimated that 78 per cent of the names on the electoral register did not qualify for jury service under this criterion, and 95 per cent of women were ineligible. This was either because they lived in rented accommodation or because they were wives or other relatives of the person in whose name the property was held. The Committee recommended that the right to do jury service should correspond with the right to vote. This reform was introduced in 1972. Despite this reform, there continued to be the problem that, in practice, juries were not truly representative of the society which they served. While it was under-standable that some people with criminal convictions were disqualified from jury service, a wide range of other people were either excluded or excused from jury service.

Ineligibility

Five categories of people were ineligible for jury service:

1 the judiciary;
2 those concerned with the administration of justice, such as barristers, solicitors, prison officers, police officers and even secretaries working for the Crown Prosecution Service;

3 the clergy (the Runciman Commission (1993) saw no logical reason for the existence of this exception and recommended its abolition);

4 people with mental ill-health;

5 people on bail in criminal proceedings. This disqualification was introduced by s. 40 of the Criminal Justice and Public Order Act 1994 following a recommendation made by the Runciman Commission.

Excusal as of right

People who had duties that were considered more important than jury service could choose whether or not they wished to serve. These included MPs, members of the House of Lords, members of the armed forces and doctors and nurses. People over 65 could also be excused as of right.

Discretionary excusal

Others could be excused at the discretion of the judge if they could show good reason, such as childcare problems, holidays booked which would clash with the jury service, personal involvement with the facts of the case, or conscientious objection. Where appropriate, jury service could be deferred rather than excused completely.

Reform of qualification rules

The basis of the use of juries in serious criminal cases is that the 12 people are randomly selected, and should therefore comprise a representative sample of the population as a whole. This ideal came closer with the abolition of the property qualification and

Table 12.1 How jury service was avoided before 2003

Disqualification	People who had been sentenced to prison or a young offenders' institute or its equivalent could be disqualified from jury service.
Ineligibility	Five categories of people were ineligible for jury service, including the judiciary and the mentally ill.
Excusal as of right	Certain professionals and those over 65 could choose whether or not to do jury service.
Discretionary excusal	People could be excused from doing jury service if they showed good reason.
Discharge	People could be discharged from jury service if there was doubt over their capacity to do jury service. Jurors could also be discharged to prevent scandal or the perversion of justice.
Challenge for cause	A potential juror could be prevented from sitting on a jury on the grounds of privilege of peerage, disqualification, ineligibility or assumed bias.
Stand by	The prosecution could request that a potential juror was not allowed to sit on the jury, without having to give reasons for this.

12

The jury system

with the use of computers for the random selection process. Despite this, research carried out for the Home Office (*Jury Excusal and Deferral* (2000)) found that only two-thirds of the people summoned for jury service made themselves available to do it each year. About 15 per cent of summoned jurors failed to attend court on the day or had their summonses returned as 'undelivered'. Because enforcement has been poor, it became widely known that a jury summons could be ignored with impunity.

In his *Review of the Criminal Courts* (2001), Sir Robin Auld argued that the many exclusions and excusals from jury service deprived juries of the experience and skills of a wide range of professional and successful people. Their absence created the impression that jury service was only for those not important or clever enough to get out of it. He was keen to make juries more representative of the general population. He wanted jury service to become a compulsory public duty for all, to stop middle-class professionals opting out. He proposed that everyone should be eligible for jury service, save for the mentally ill.

The Government accepted these recommendations. The Criminal Justice Act 2003, s. 321 and Sched. 33 amended the Juries Act 1974. This Act now provides that potential jury members must be:

- aged 18 to 70; and
- on the electoral register; and
- resident in the UK, Channel Islands or Isle of Man for at least five years since the age of 13; and
- not a mentally disordered person; and
- not disqualified from jury service.

Most of the grounds for ineligibility and excusal have been removed. People can now be disqualified or excused from jury service due to age, residency, mental disability, criminal record, language, medical or other reasons. While these reforms have made juries more representative, the inclusive nature of the reforms has created new problems. Cases have been brought arguing that having police officers or prosecutors sitting as jurors creates the risk of bias. Before 2003 the police, prosecutors, barristers, solicitors and prison officers were ineligible to sit as jurors so this problem was avoided. Sir Robin Auld, who recommended this reform, considered that the danger of a police officer or prosecutor being biased was no greater than for any other member of the public, such as home owners who had been burgled in the past, or people with controversial views on drugs.

KEY CASE

Ess. Cases
p. 158 →

Membership of the jury of people who ordinarily work within the criminal justice system was considered by the House of Lords in R v Abdroikof (2007). The majority of the judges applied the basic principle that justice must not only be done, but manifestly be seen to be done. Legislation cannot override that principle. The House of Lords stated that the issue in each case was not actual bias but whether a fair-minded and informed observer

People will not be allowed to sit as a juror if their ordinary employment would lead a fair-minded and informed observer to conclude that there was a real possibility that they would be biased.

would conclude that there was a real possibility the jury was biased. The question was the appearance of bias. It would be for the trial judge to decide whether there was any special danger of apprehension of bias that distinguished the individual from other members of the jury. The House of Lords observed that most adults harboured prejudices, both conscious and unconscious. The assumption is that the 12 jurors will be able to neutralise any bias on the part of one or more members and so reach an impartial verdict.

The case involved three separate appeals which were heard together as they raised the same legal issues. The first appellant had been convicted of attempted murder. A minor issue in the six-day trial concerned one aspect of the evidence of a police witness. While the jury were considering their verdict, the foreman sent a note to the judge revealing that he was a serving police officer. He was supposed to report for duty at the Notting Hill Carnival on the following bank holiday Monday when the court would not be sitting. His concern was the possibility that he might meet officers who had given evidence in the case. The defence did not object to the case going forward. The first appellant's appeal was not allowed. The House noted:

> It is difficult to see what argument defence counsel could have urged other than the general undesirability of police officers serving on juries, a difficult argument to advance in face of the parliamentary enactment. It was not a case which turned on a contest between the evidence of the police and that of the appellant, and it would have been hard to suggest that the case was one in which unconscious prejudice, even if present, would have been likely to operate to the disadvantage of the appellant, and it makes no difference that the officer was the foreman of the jury.

The second appellant appealed against their conviction for assault occasioning actual bodily harm committed against a police officer. The officer had pricked himself against a syringe during a search of the person. There was a crucial dispute on the evidence between the appellant and the officer about the way in which he was searched and what had been said. After the trial, his solicitor discovered by chance that a policeman had sat on the jury. This policeman had not known the victim, but had previously served in the same police station at the same time. The House of Lords noted that, unlike the first appellant, there was a link between the case and the police officer serving on the jury and an important issue turned on a conflict between police and defence evidence:

> In this context the instinct (however unconscious) of a police officer on the jury to prefer the evidence of a brother officer to that of a drug-addicted defendant would be judged by the fair-minded and informed observer to be a real and possible source of unfairness, beyond the reach of standard judicial warnings and directions. The second appellant was not tried by a tribunal which was and appeared to be impartial.

The third appellant had been convicted of rape. The jury included a solicitor employed by the Crown Prosecution Service. Before the trial began he wrote informing the court of this fact. The defence counsel challenged the juror on the ground of potential bias, but the judge rejected this challenge and the third appellant was selected to be the foreman of the jury. The conviction was quashed and the House of Lords commented:

▶

> It must, perhaps, be doubted whether Lord Justice Auld or Parliament contemplated that employed Crown prosecutors would sit as jurors in prosecutions brought by their own authority. It is in my opinion clear that justice is not seen to be done if one discharging the very important neutral role of juror is a full-time, salaried, long-serving employee of the prosecutor.
>
> Thus, unfortunately, following this case, there is no hard and fast rule regarding whether CPS lawyers and police officers can sit on juries. Instead, the issue will be decided on a case-by-case basis. It is easy to identify jurors whose employment may compromise their impartiality; the problem is establishing whether or not that employment history does, in fact, lead to apparent bias. In deciding whether to allow a juror to hear a case, the judge will have to consider the proximity of the relevant juror to the police and prosecution in each case. Where there is a close connection there is apparent bias and the juror should not sit. Where there is no personal or service connection then the juror can hear the case. As in practice most prosecutions are brought by the CPS, most CPS lawyers will be unable to sit on a jury. Where a personal connection between a juror and witness has been identified the judge should be satisfied that the evidence of the witness will play no contested part in the trial. If this cannot be established with certainty, the juror should stand down.

The implications of **R v Abdroikof** were considered by the Court of Appeal in **R v Khan** (2008). Sadly, it concluded:

> We have not found it easy to deduce on the part of the majority of the committee clear principles that apply where a juror is a police officer.

To try to clarify the legal position, it stated that a two-stage test should be applied:

- would the fair-minded observer consider that the partiality of a juror to the witness may have caused the jury to accept the evidence of that witness; and, if so
- would the fair-minded observer consider that this may have affected the outcome of the trial?

Only if the answer to both questions is 'yes' will a trial be rendered unfair by appearance. Trial judges should identify any risk of juror partiality before the start of a trial. People summoned for jury service must write to inform the court if they are employed in the criminal justice system so that the trial judge can consider whether there would be apparent bias before the trial begins. Unfortunately, in practice, it will not always be possible for a trial judge to evaluate the significance of evidence before it is called.

Research carried out by Thomas and Balmer (2007) into jury service has found that juries are today representative of the communities they serve. The most significant factors predicting whether a summoned juror will serve or not are income and employment status. Among all people summoned, those with the lowest household income and those who were economically inactive were the least likely to serve. The highest income earners and those in higher status professions were fully represented among serving jurors. The employed in general are over-represented among serving jurors, while it is the retired and unemployed that are under-represented. The proportion of men and women serving as jurors was exactly the same (50 per cent), and gender had no significant impact on whether those summoned served or not.

Summoning the jury

Every year almost half a million people are summoned to do jury service. In 2001 a Central Juror Summoning Bureau was established to administer the juror summoning process for the whole of the country. Computers are used to produce a random list of potential jurors from the electoral register. Summons are sent out (with a form to return confirming that the person does not fall into any of the disqualified or ineligible groups), and from the resulting list the jury panel is produced. This is made public for both sides in forthcoming cases to inspect, though only names and addresses are shown (before 1977 the occupation of the juror was also stated). It is at this stage that jury vetting may take place (see below). Jurors also receive a set of notes which explain a little of the procedure of the jury service and the functions of the juror.

Jury service is compulsory and failure to attend on the specified date, or unfitness for service through drink or drugs, is contempt of court and can result in a fine.

The jury for a particular case is chosen by random ballot in open court – the clerk has each panel member's name on a card, the cards are shuffled and the first 12 names called out. Unless there are any challenges (see p. 245), these 12 people will be sworn in. In a criminal case there are usually 12 jurors and there must never be fewer than nine. In civil cases in the county court there are eight jurors.

Sir Robin Auld also recommended that potential jurors should no longer only be selected from the electoral register. Many people are not registered to vote in elections, even though they are entitled to do so. To reach as many people as possible he therefore proposed that a range of publicly maintained lists and directories should be used. The Government has not adopted this recommendation.

Jury vetting

Jury vetting consists of checking that the potential juror does not hold 'extremist' views which some feel would make them unsuitable for hearing a case. It is done by checking police, Special Branch and security service records.

This controversial practice first came to light in the 1978 'ABC Trial' (**R v Aubrey, Berry and Campbell** (1978)), in which two journalists and a soldier were accused of collecting secret information, in breach of the Official Secrets Act. During the trial it became known that the jury had been vetted to check their 'loyalty', under guidelines laid down by the Attorney General, and a new trial was ordered.

The ensuing publicity eventually led to the publication of the Attorney General's guidelines, which it was admitted had been in use since 1974. These guidelines were revised in 1988. They confirm that, as a rule, juries should be chosen at random, with people being excluded only under the statutory exceptions, and that the proper way for the prosecution to exclude a juror was challenge for cause in open court (see below). But it was also stated that vetting might be necessary in certain special cases: those involving terrorism, where it was felt a juror's political beliefs might prevent him or her being impartial or lead to undue pressure on other jurors; and those concerning national security, where in addition to the problem of strong political beliefs there was the danger that some jurors might reveal evidence given *in camera* (i.e. heard in private and not in open court). Jurors could only be 'stood by' (see below) if the vetting revealed a very strong reason for doing so. In order to vet a jury in these cases authorisation from the Attorney General is required, who will be acting on the advice of the Director of Public Prosecutions. Checking whether a person has a criminal record is permissible in a much wider range of cases without special permission.

The legality of vetting was considered by the Court of Appeal in two cases during 1980. In **R v Sheffield Crown Court, ex parte Brownlow**, the defendants were police officers, and the defence wanted the jury vetted for previous convictions. The prosecution opposed it, but the Crown Court judge ordered that vetting should take place, and this decision was upheld by the Court of Appeal. Lords Denning and Shaw, *obiter dicta*, vigorously condemned vetting in security and terrorist cases as unconstitutional (because it was not provided for in the Juries Act 1974), and an invasion of privacy.

In **R v Mason** (1980), a convicted burglar appealed on the ground that the jury had been vetted for previous convictions, a common practice in the particular court at the time. The Court of Appeal decreed that vetting for previous convictions was necessary in order to ensure that disqualified persons could not serve. In such situations Lord Lawton described vetting as 'just common sense', though it should not be used to gain tactical advantage in minor cases.

The limits on vetting for previous convictions were, however, stressed again in **R v Obellim** (1996). The case concerned a criminal trial in which the judge had received a written question from the jury, which displayed a lot of knowledge about police powers and led him to suspect that one of the jurors might have such previous convictions as should have disqualified him or her. The judge ordered a security check on the jury, without telling the defence counsel, who only discovered the check had taken place when the jury complained about it after delivering their verdict.

The defendant, who was convicted, appealed on the grounds that the check on jury members might have prejudiced them. The Court of Appeal agreed, and quashed the conviction, stating that it was questionable whether the check should have been ordered at all on such grounds, and it certainly should not have been without informing defence counsel.

Vetting for any purpose remains controversial. Supporters claim that it can promote impartiality by excluding those whose views might bias the other members of the jury, and make them put pressure on others, as well as protecting national security and preventing disqualified persons from serving. Opponents say it infringes the individual's right to privacy, and gives the prosecution an unfair advantage, since it is too expensive for most defendants to undertake, and they do not have access to the same sources of information as the prosecution. Only on very rare occasions has the defence been granted legal aid to make its inquiries into the panel.

The whole process is still not sanctioned by legislation and, despite the publication of the Attorney General's guidelines, it is impossible to know whether they are being followed – 60 potential jurors were vetted by MI5 for the Clive Ponting case (see p. 252), despite the fact that there was no apparent threat to national security.

Challenges

As members of the jury panel are called, and before they are sworn in, they may be challenged in one of two ways.

Challenge for cause

Either side may challenge for cause, on the grounds of privilege of peerage, disqualification, ineligibility or assumed bias. Jurors cannot be questioned before being challenged to ascertain whether there are grounds for a challenge. A successful challenge for cause is therefore only likely to succeed if the juror is personally known, or if jury vetting has been undertaken. If a challenge for cause is made it is tried by the trial judge.

Stand by

Only the prosecution may ask jurors to stand by for the Crown. Although there are specified grounds for this, in practice no reason need be given, and this is generally how the information supplied by jury vetting is used. The use of the power to stand by has been limited by guidelines issued by the Attorney General which specifically state that the abolition of the peremptory challenge (see below) means that the power to stand by should only be used in connection with jury vetting or where the juror is manifestly unsuitable and the defence agrees with the exercise of the power.

Until 1988 there was a third type of challenge, peremptory challenge, available only to the defence. This meant that the defence could challenge up to three jurors without showing cause, which was equivalent to the prosecution's power to 'stand by' a juror. This was abolished, amid much opposition, on the recommendation of the Roskill Committee (1986) on fraud trials, on the grounds that it interfered with the random selection process and allowed defence lawyers to 'pack' the jury with those they thought were likely to be sympathetic. This was felt to be a particular problem when there were several defendants as (theoretically) they could combine their rights to peremptory challenge.

This limited process of challenging the jury should be contrasted with the system in the US where it can take days to empanel a jury, particularly where the case has received a lot of pre-trial media coverage. Potential jury members can be asked a wide range of questions about their attitudes to the issues raised by a case, and a great deal of money may be spent employing special consultants who claim to be able to judge which way people are likely to vote, based on their age, sex, politics, religion and other personal information.

In a high-profile 1998 case, **R** *v* **Andrews**, the defence wanted to use the American approach to establish whether members of the jury panel were likely to be biased against the defendant. She was accused of murdering her boyfriend, and the case had received an enormous amount of publicity since Ms Andrews had initially told police that her boyfriend was killed by an unknown assailant in a 'road rage' incident, sparking off a media hunt for the killer. Her lawyers wanted to issue questionnaires to the jury panel to check whether any of them showed a prejudice against her. The trial judge refused the request and when Ms Andrews was convicted, she appealed, arguing that the failure to allow questioning of the jury meant her conviction was unsafe. The argument was rejected by the Court of Appeal, which stated that questioning of the jury panel, whether orally or by written questionnaire, should be avoided in all but the most exceptional cases, such as where potential jurors might have a direct or indirect connection to the facts of the trial (for example, if they were related to someone involved in the trial, or had lost money as a result of the defendant's actions).

Discharging the jury

The judge may discharge any juror, or even the whole jury, to prevent scandal or the perversion of justice. The courts have had to consider whether a jury needs to be discharged where there is a risk of racism. In **Gregory** *v* **United Kingdom** (1997), Gregory was a black defendant accused of robbery. During his trial the jury had handed the judge a note asking that one juror be excused because of racial bias. The judge did not excuse the juror, but instead issued a strong direction to the jury to decide the case on the evidence alone. Gregory was convicted on a majority verdict and brought a case before the European Court of Human Rights, claiming that the judge should have discharged the whole jury, and that failure to do so infringed his right to a fair trial under the European Convention on Human Rights. The European Court of Human Rights however, held that, in the circumstances, issuing a clear and carefully worded warning to the jury was sufficient to ensure a fair trial.

This case was distinguished in **Sander** *v* **United Kingdom** (2001). The applicant was an Asian man, who had been tried in the Crown Court with another Asian man on a charge of conspiracy to defraud. During the trial, a juror passed a note to the judge alleging that certain of his fellow jurors had made racist remarks and jokes. The juror who made the complaint was initially segregated from the rest of the jury while the court considered representations made by the lawyers. The judge then asked the complainant to rejoin the other jurors and instructed them to consider whether they were able to put aside any prejudices which they had and to try the case solely on the evidence. All of the jurors signed a letter to the judge stating:

> We utterly refute the allegation of possible racial bias. We are deeply offended by the allegation. We assure the Court that we intend to reach a verdict solely according to the evidence and without racial bias.

One juror, who believed that the allegations were directed at him, wrote a separate letter to confirm that he was not racially biased. The judge concluded that there was no real risk of bias and allowed the trial to continue with the same jury, and rejected the defence request to discharge the jury. At first instance, the applicant was convicted and his co-accused was acquitted.

The applicant appealed against his conviction up to the European Court of Human Rights. He complained that he had been denied the right to a fair trial before an impartial court, guaranteed by Art. 6(1) of the European Convention on Human Rights. The European Court held that it was not possible to state whether some of the jurors were actually biased as the matter had not been investigated. The fact that at least one juror had made comments that could be construed as jokes about Asians was not evidence of actual bias. But it was also important for the jurors to be viewed as objectively impartial, in other words that they were not just as a matter of fact impartial, but also that they would appear to an observer to be impartial. There was doubt as to the credibility of the letter which denied the allegations because the juror who had made the allegations also signed the letter. The identity of the juror who had made the allegations was revealed by his separation from the other jurors and this must have compromised his position with his fellow jurors, and inhibited him in the further discussion of the case. An admonition by a judge 'however clear, detailed and forceful would not change racist views overnight'. Even though it was not established that the jurors had such views, the judge's direction could not dispel the reasonable impression and fear of a lack of impartiality based on the original note. The fact that the jury had acquitted one Asian defendant was irrelevant since the case against him was much weaker. The judge should have discharged the jury. Thus, the court concluded that the appellant had not received a fair trial and Art. 6(1) had been breached.

The court distinguished its earlier decision of **Gregory v United Kingdom** (1997), mainly on the ground that in that case there was no admission by a juror that he had made racist comments, nor an indication as to which juror had made the complaint and the complaint was vague and imprecise.

Professor Zander (2000) has criticised the decision in **Sander v United Kingdom**. He controversially argues that:

> The decision in **Sander** is disturbing since it suggests that the Strasbourg court does not sufficiently understand or value the jury system. The great strength of the system is that generally the verdict of twelve ordinary citizens is felt to be understandable in terms either of the evidence or of the jury's sense of equity. This is despite the fact that most jurors probably have prejudices, which will often include racial prejudice. To pretend otherwise is naïve. But the process of deliberation in the jury room tends to neutralise individual prejudices. The possibility of a majority verdict provides an additional safeguard against the effect of prejudice but in fact in the great majority of cases the verdict is unanimous.

The secrecy of the jury

Once they retire to consider their verdict, jurors are not allowed to communicate with anyone other than the judge and an assigned court official, until after the verdict is delivered. Afterwards they are forbidden by s. 8 of the Contempt of Court Act 1981 from revealing anything that was said or done during their deliberations. Breach of this section amounts to a criminal offence.

The arguments in favour of secrecy are that:

- it ensures freedom of discussion in the jury room;
- it protects jurors from outside influences, and from harassment;
- if the public knew how juries reached their verdict they might respect the decision less;
- without secrecy citizens would be reluctant to serve as jurors;
- it ensures the finality of the verdict;
- it enables jurors to bring in unpopular verdicts;
- it prevents unreliable disclosures by jurors and misunderstanding of verdicts.

The arguments against secrecy and in favour of disclosure are that this reform would:

- make juries more accountable;
- make it easier to inquire into the reliability of convictions and rectify injustices;
- show where reform is required;
- educate the public;
- ensure each juror's freedom of expression.

Research into the work of juries has always been made difficult by the requirement for secrecy. The Runciman Commission has recommended that the 1981 Act should be amended so that valid research can be carried out into the way juries reach their verdicts.

The House of Lords' case of **R v Mirza** (2004) drew attention to the problem of jury secrecy where, after the trial, a juror writes to the court expressing their concern with how the verdict was reached. Now that a majority verdict is possible, a letter after verdict is often the only option open to a juror where a verdict has been reached which they did not agree with. There was a suggestion in one of the cases being considered in **R v Mirza** that some of the jurors were racist. The House of Lords took the view that, due to the secrecy of the jury, it could not investigate what had happened in the jury room. However, the trial court could make such an inquiry before a verdict was reached and, if an appeal was launched, the Court of Appeal could ask a judge to provide a report about the trial. A Practice Direction has now been issued stating that trial judges should ensure that the jury is alerted to the need to bring any concerns about fellow jurors to the attention of the judge immediately, and not to wait until the case is concluded. The point should be made that, unless that is done while the case is continuing, it may be impossible to put matters right.

In **Attorney General v Scotcher** (2005), Scotcher had been a juror on a trial of two brothers. After the brothers were convicted, he wrote to the mother suggesting that he was unhappy with the way the jury had reached its verdict and that there might have been a miscarriage of justice. He was subsequently successfully prosecuted for the offence under s. 8 of the Contempt of Court Act 1981. His defence that this offence breached his right to freedom of expression under Art. 10 of the European Convention of Human Rights was rejected by the House of Lords.

The Government issued a consultation paper, *Jury research and impropriety* (2005), considering when it was appropriate to allow the secrecy of the jury room to be breached, particularly for the purposes of research into juries. About 75 per cent of respondents opposed allowing researchers any form of access to the jury room itself. The majority of respondents were happy, however, to allow more research into jurors to take place provided it did not involve access to the jury room.

The Government's conclusions are that initially more research should be carried out into the jury within the confines of the present law, for example, by using shadow juries and mock trials. This initial research could generate questions which subsequently need to be answered by allowing researchers access to the jury room by amending the Contempt of Court Act 1981, s. 8. The academic, Michael Zander (2000), had expressed concern that if jury rooms could be 'bugged' for research purposes, it risked undermining the public's confidence in the jury system and therefore could ultimately lead to its abolition.

As well as looking at where jury research should be allowed, the consultation paper considered what approach should be taken if jurors themselves decide to break the jury secrecy, for example, to report jury malpractice. The most recent House of Lords' case on this issue is **R** *v* **Mirza** (2004) (see above). Following consultation, the Government has decided to allow the courts to develop the common law on a case-by-case basis rather than to legislate.

The verdict

Ideally, juries should produce a unanimous verdict, but in 1967 majority verdicts were introduced of ten to two (or nine to one if the jury has been reduced during the trial). This is now provided for in the Juries Act 1974. When the jury withdraw to consider their verdict they must be told by the judge to reach a unanimous verdict. If, however, the jury have failed to reach a unanimous verdict after what the judge considers a reasonable period of deliberation, given the complexity of the case (not less than two hours), the judge can direct them that they may reach a majority verdict. The foreman of the jury must state in open court the numbers of the jurors agreeing and disagreeing with the verdict. Majority verdicts were intended to help prevent jury 'nobbling' (where someone involved in the trial puts pressure on jurors to vote in a particular way, by bribes or threats). It also avoids the problem of one juror with extreme or intractable views holding out against the rest, and should lessen the need for expensive and time-consuming retrials. However, Brown and Neal's 1988 research found that the introduction of majority verdicts has not substantially affected the number of hung juries and consequent retrials. Freeman (1981) has suggested that majority verdicts dilute the concept of proof beyond reasonable doubt – on the grounds that if one juror is not satisfied, a doubt must exist – and give less protection against the risk of convicting the innocent. This in turn weakens public confidence in the system.

In Scotland the jury consists of 15 people and a conviction can be based on a simple majority verdict.

Strengths of the jury system

Public participation

Juries allow the ordinary citizen to take part in the administration of justice, so that verdicts are seen to be those of society rather than of the judicial system, and satisfy the constitutional tradition of judgment by one's peers. Lord Denning described jury service as giving 'ordinary folk their finest lesson in citizenship'. This has particular importance when one considers the background of magistrates, which continues to be largely white and middle class. A defendant who does not come from this sector of society may well prefer to be judged by a jury, which is more likely to include members of his or her own race and/or class: a 1990 study by the Runnymede Trust found that black defendants charged with either way offences were more likely to opt for jury trial than white defendants in the same position. This is not to say that magistrates are biased against those from outside their race and/or class, and so unable to give them a fair trial, merely that if defendants believe this to be the case, trust in the legal system is reduced, and reduced even more if the option to choose a mode of trial which looks fairer is taken away.

Ess. Cases
p. 161
The Home Office has carried out research into the experience of being a juror: Matthews, Hancock and Briggs, *Jurors' perceptions, understanding, confidence and satisfaction in the jury system: a study in six courts* (2004). The research questioned 361 jurors about their jury service. More than half (55 per cent) said they would be happy to do it again, 19 per cent said they would not mind doing jury service again, but 25 per cent said they would never want to be a juror again. About two-thirds felt that their experience had boosted their opinion of the jury system and they were impressed by the professionalism and helpfulness of the court staff and the performance of the judge. A minority were unhappy with the delays in the system, the trivial nature of some cases and the standard of facilities. Thirty-six per cent of jurors felt intimidated or very uncomfortable in the courtroom, primarily because they were worried about meeting defendants or their family members coming out of court or in the street.

When questioned by Professor Lloyd-Bostock (2007) about their experience, the jurors in the collapsed Jubilee Line case (see p. 254) were found to be enthusiastic about their role, committed to it, and furious when the trial was aborted. They were a remarkably co-operative and mutually supportive group. Two compared being on the jury with being on *Big Brother*. However, as the trial progressed the jurors felt increasingly like 'jury fodder', on tap but not informed. They would be telephoned at short notice and told not to turn up for several days but no explanation would be given. Even more frustrating was when they turned up for jury service and then, after a lengthy delay, were sent home again. The main difficulties suffered by the jurors were in relation to their employment. All seven jurors who were employed said their employers were very unhappy about the long trial. Most felt that the court should have more responsibility for communicating directly with their employers rather than placing the onus on the jurors. Uncooperative employers could cause problems over claims for allowances. One juror had been made redundant, one was in an employment dispute, one had missed a definite and much-desired promotion and was required to undertake extensive retraining, and one had been signed off by his doctor as suffering from stress as a result of his work situation. Most of the jurors had suffered financially as a result of the trial. One suggestion is that a juror liaison person could be appointed for long jury trials whose remit is to look after jurors' needs and alleviate the burden of jury service as much as possible.

It is important to realise that despite the symbolic importance of juries, the system remains dominated by judges and magistrates. Only a small proportion of cases are tried by juries and, even in these, judges can exert considerable influence.

Certainty

The jury adds certainty to the law, since it gives a general verdict which cannot give rise to misinterpretation. In a criminal case the jury simply states that the accused is guilty or not guilty, and gives no reasons. Consequently, the decision is not open to dispute.

Ability to judge according to conscience

Because juries have the ultimate right to find defendants innocent or guilty, they have been seen as a vital protection against oppressive or politically motivated prosecutions, and as a kind of safety valve for those cases where the law demands a guilty verdict, but it can be argued that genuine justice does not. For example, in the early nineteenth century, all felonies (a classification of crimes used at the time, marking out those considered most serious) were in theory punishable by death. Theft of goods or money above the value of a shilling was a felony, but juries were frequently reluctant to allow the death penalty to be imposed in what seemed to them trivial cases, so they would often find that the defendant was guilty, but the property stolen was worth less than a shilling.

There are several well-known cases of juries using their right to find according to their consciences, often concerning issues of political and moral controversy, such as **R v Kronlid** (1996). The defendants here were three women who broke into a British Aerospace factory and caused damage costing over £1.5 million to a Hawk fighter plane. The women admitted doing this – they had left a video explaining their actions in the plane's cockpit – but claimed that they had a defence under s. 3 of the Criminal Law Act 1967, which provides that it is lawful to commit a crime in order to prevent another (usually more serious) crime being committed, and that this may involve using 'such force as is reasonable in all the circumstances'.

The defendants pointed out that the plane was part of a consignment due to be sold to the Government of Indonesia, which was involved in oppressive measures against the population of East Timor, a region forcibly annexed by Indonesia in 1975. They further explained that Amnesty International had estimated that the Indonesians have killed at least a third of the population of East Timor, and that the jet was likely to be used in a genocidal attack against the survivors. Genocide is a crime and therefore, they argued, their criminal damage was done in order to prevent a crime. However, the prosecution gave evidence that the Indonesian Government had given assurances that the planes would not be used against the East Timorese, and the British Government had accepted this and granted an export licence. Acquitting the women was therefore a criticism of the British Government's position on the issue, as well as the actions of the Indonesian Government and, in the face of the clear evidence that they had caused the damage, they were widely expected to be convicted. The jury found them all not guilty.

Other cases have involved what were seen to be oppressive prosecutions in matters involving the Government, such as **R v Ponting** (1985), where the defendant, a civil servant, was prosecuted for breaking the Official Secrets Act after passing confidential information to a journalist – even though doing so exposed a matter of public interest, namely the fact that the then Government had lied to Parliament about the circumstances in which an Argentinian warship, the *General Belgrano*, was sunk by a British submarine during the Falklands war. At his trial, Ponting admitted that he had leaked the confidential information, but said in his defence that he was acting in the public interest. The trial judge directed the jury to convict, dismissing Ponting's public interest defence with the words: 'the public interest is what the government of the day says it is'. Ponting had apparently brought his toothbrush with him to court on the day the verdict was due, expecting to be convicted, but the jury acquitted. As juries do not give reasons for their decisions we do not know why the jury acquitted in the case, but it may have been because it considered Ponting had done the right thing and thereby it protected a private citizen against the oppressive use of power by the state.

Not all cases in which juries exercise this right are overtly political. In **R v Owen** (1991), the defendant was a man whose son had been knocked down and killed by a lorry driver who had never taken a driving test, and had a long criminal record for drink-driving and violence. The driver, who apparently showed no remorse for killing the boy, was convicted of a driving offence, sentenced to 18 months in prison and released after a year. He then resumed driving his lorry unlawfully. After contacting a number of different authorities to try to secure what he considered to be some sort of justice for his son's death, Mr Owen eventually took a shotgun and injured the lorry driver. He was charged with a number of offences, including attempted murder but, despite a great deal of evidence against him, the jury acquitted.

The importance of this aspect of the jury's involvement in criminal justice is very difficult to assess. In high-profile cases such as **Ponting** and **Kronlid**, it can be a valuable statement of public feeling to those in authority, but, even in this kind of case, it cannot be relied on. Shortly after Ponting's acquittal, a similar case, **R v Tisdall** (1984) came to trial. As in **Ponting**, the information Ms Tisdall leaked exposed Government wrongdoing, and it was admitted that the leak was no threat to national security, yet she was convicted.

Juries are never actually told that they can acquit if their consciences suggest they should: their instructions are quite the opposite and, before the case begins, they must swear to try the case according to the evidence. Nor do they give reasons for their decisions, so there is no way of knowing how often juries acquit defendants out of a sense of justice, even though they know that the law demands a guilty verdict. Where the verdict does clearly seem perverse in the face of the evidence, there may be other reasons for an acquittal, such as not understanding the evidence or the law.

However, there is one modern example of law reform being brought about at least partly in response to the actions of juries. This is the creation of the offence of causing death by dangerous driving, which was introduced after juries proved reluctant to convict of manslaughter those who had killed people by dangerous driving. It can be argued, however, that this example shows that allowing the jury such freedom is not always a good thing, since the reason for the reluctance was thought to be that many jurors who were motorists could see how easily they could have found themselves in the dock: Sir Robin Auld (2001) appears to consider perverse verdicts by juries an affront to the criminal justice system, and has recommended reforms which would seek to prevent juries handing down such verdicts.

Criticisms of the jury system

Lack of competence

Lord Denning argued in *What Next in the Law?* (1982) that the selection of jurors is too wide, resulting in jurors that are not competent to perform their task. Praising the 'Golden Age' of jury service when only 'responsible heads of household from a select band of the middle classes' were eligible to serve, he claimed that the 1972 changes have led to jurors being summoned who are not sufficiently intelligent or educated to perform their task properly. In one unfortunate case a jury hearing a murder trial had apparently set up an Ouija board in an attempt to make contact with the spirit of the deceased: **R *v* Young** (1995). Denning suggested that jurors should be selected in much the same way as magistrates are, with interviews and references required. This throws up several obvious problems: a more complicated selection process would be more time-consuming and costly; finding sufficient people willing to take part might prove difficult; and a jury that is intelligent and educated can still be biased, and may be more likely to be so if drawn from a narrow social group.

Particular concern has been expressed about the average jury's understanding of complex fraud cases. The Roskill Committee concluded that trial by random jury was not a satisfactory way of achieving justice in such cases, with many jurors 'out of their depth'. However, the Roskill Committee was unable to find accurate evidence of a higher proportion of acquittals in complex fraud cases than in any other kind of case – many of their conclusions were based on research by Baldwin and McConville (1979), yet none of the questionable acquittals reported there was in a complex fraud case. Smith and Bailey (2002) point out that the research on the decision-making abilities of juries suggests that they are capable of coming to reasoned and fair verdicts in even complex cases. Evidence of the police to the Runciman Commission stated that the conviction rates for serious fraud, when compared with the overall conviction rate for cases that are considered by a jury, show that in serious fraud trials the jury are actually convicting a slightly higher percentage. The academic, Terry Honess, conducted an extended simulation study of jurors' comprehension of some of the evidence in the

Maxwell fraud trial (Honess, Charman and Levi, 2003). He estimated that four out of five of the participants could be regarded as competent to serve on a major fraud trial, and concluded that abolition of the jury system for complex fraud trials was not justified on the grounds of 'cognitive unfitness'.

Following the collapse of the trial of six men prosecuted for alleged fraud in the awarding of contracts for the construction of the extension to the Jubilee underground line, **R v Rayment and others** (2005), the jurors were questioned about their experience of the trial as part of a Government review of the case. This review found that 'when the case collapsed this jury, taken as a group, had a good understanding of the case, the issues and the evidence so far, as presented to them'. The jurors said they had no problem with technical language or documents. They displayed quite impressive familiarity with the charges, issues and evidence, and were able to engage in detailed discussion of the prosecution case nearly a year after it had closed. The chief difficulty expressed by the jurors was not in finding evidence too technical or complex, but in finding the pace of the trial extremely slow and parts of the defence evidence tedious. It is questionable whether the trial needed to be unmanageably long. In the preface to his report on the case, Stephen Wooler (2006) describes it as 'probably one of the best examples' of cases 'which are neither sufficiently complex to be beyond the comprehension of juries, nor necessarily lengthy'. Discussion was evidently facilitated by the provision of a jury deliberating room for much of the trial, where the jury went while at court but not in court. The jurors said they found discussion much more difficult, if not impossible, when they did not have use of this room. The jurors were not allowed to take their notes from the courtroom and several said it would have been helpful to do so. The academic, Professor Findlay (2001) has noted that juror comprehension and memory for complex evidence can be assisted through, for example, the use of visual aids. Discussion among jurors, taking notes and asking questions can enhance juror comprehension (Horowitz and Fosterlee (2001)). Professor Lloyd-Bostock (2007) has concluded:

> ... where the jury is concerned, the 'problem' with the Jubilee Line case was not the jury's ability to cope, but the unnecessarily excessive length of the case with its consequences for the jurors' lives, together with some aspects of their treatment at court.
> ... Taken in context, the jurors' perspective on the ill-fated Jubilee Line trial does not indicate that the solution is to abandon jury trial for such cases. Rather, it confirms that jury trial is valued, and that improvements through trial preparation, and trial and jury management, should be fully explored before the jury itself is threatened.

Ess. Cases p. 179 → An American lawyer, Robert Julian (2007), interviewed all the judges who had tried a fraud case prosecuted by the Serious Fraud Office over a one-year period. They were unanimously in favour of jury trials of serious fraud cases and did not want them to be replaced by judge-alone trials. They were not convinced that judge-alone trials would automatically be shorter, as the prosecution would not have the same pressure to prune the case to make it manageable for a jury. As one judge observed:

> I have no reason to doubt that juries understand the issues in serious fraud cases ... Fundamentally we are talking about honesty and dishonesty. That's very well suited to the jury trial process.

Many of the judges gave objective bases for their favourable opinions about the juries' understanding of the issues, pointing to the pertinent questions asked by jurors and the fact that they discriminated between different defendants, convicting some, while acquitting others.

The 'perverse verdicts' problem

It is a matter of fact that juries acquit proportionately more defendants than magistrates do; research from the Home Office Planning Unit suggests that an acquittal is approximately twice as likely in a jury trial. Many critics of the jury system argue that this is a major failing on the part of juries, arising either from their inability to perform their role properly, as discussed above, or from their sympathy with defendants, or both. Others would argue that apparently 'perverse' judgments are frequently just the juries deciding the case according to their conscience (see p. 251).

This is a difficult area to research, as the Contempt of Court Act 1981 prohibits asking jurors about the basis on which they reached their decision. What research there is generally involves comparing actual jury decisions with those reached by legal professionals, or by shadow juries, who sit in on the case and reach their own decision just as the official jurors are asked to do.

A piece of research commissioned by the Roskill Committee on fraud trials concluded that jurors who found difficulty in comprehending the complex issues involved in fraud prosecution were more likely to acquit. They suggested that the jurors characterised their own confusions as a form of 'reasonable doubt' leading them to a decision to acquit.

A study by McCabe and Purves, *The Jury at Work* (1972), looked at 173 acquittals, and concluded that 15 (9 per cent) defied the evidence, the rest being attributable to weakness of the prosecution case or failure of their witnesses, or the credibility of the accused's explanation. McCabe and Purves viewed the proportion of apparently perverse verdicts as quite small and, from their observations of shadow juries, concluded that jurors did work methodically and rationally through the evidence, and try to put aside their own prejudices.

However, Baldwin and McConville's 1979 study (*Jury Trials*) examined 500 cases, both convictions and acquittals, and found up to 25 per cent of acquittals were questionable (as well as 5 per cent of convictions), and concluded that, given the serious nature of the cases concerned, this was a problem. They describe trial by jury as 'an arbitrary and unpredictable business'.

Zander (1988) points out that the high rate of acquittals must be seen in the light of the high number of guilty pleas in the Crown Court. It must also be noted that many acquittals are directed or ordered by the judge: according to evidence from the Lord Chancellor's Department to the Runciman Commission, 40 per cent of all acquittals in 1990–91 were ordered by the judge because the prosecution offered no evidence at the start of the trial. A further 16 per cent of the acquittals were directed by the judge after the prosecution had made their case as there was insufficient evidence to leave to the jury. Thus the jury were only responsible for 41 per cent of the acquittals, which was merely 7 per cent of all cases in the Crown Court. Bearing in mind the pressures on defendants to plead guilty, it is not surprising that those who resist tend to be those with the strongest cases – and of course the standard of proof required is very high. Nor is it beyond the bounds of possibility that part of the difference in conviction rates between magistrates and juries is due to magistrates convicting the innocent rather than juries acquitting the guilty.

In a high-profile case the Court of Appeal overturned a jury decision in civil proceedings on the basis that the jury decision had been perverse. In **Grobbelaar v News Group Newspapers Ltd** (2001) a jury had awarded the former goalkeeper for Liverpool FC, Bruce Grobbelaar, £85,000 on the basis that he had been defamed in *The Sun* newspaper. *The Sun* had published a story claiming that Bruce Grobbelaar had received cash to fix football matches. They had obtained secretly taped videos of Grobbelaar where he apparently admitted receiving money in the past to lose matches, and appeared to accept cash following a proposal to fix matches in the future. A criminal prosecution of Grobbelaar had failed and he had sued in the civil courts for defamation. Grobbelaar accepted that he had made the confessions and accepted cash, but claimed that he had done so as a trick in order to bring the other person to justice. The jury accepted his claim and awarded damages. *The Sun*'s appeal was allowed on the basis that the jury's decision had been perverse. The Court of Appeal found Grobbelaar's story 'incredible'. The House of Lords allowed a further appeal. It considered it wrong to overturn the jury's verdict as perverse, as the verdict could have been given an alternative explanation.

Bias

Ingman (2008) suggests that jurors may be biased for or against certain groups – for example, they may favour attractive members of the opposite sex, or be prejudiced against the police in cases of malicious prosecution or false imprisonment (and, of course, some jurors may also be biased towards the police, and other figures of authority such as customs officers).

Bias appears to be a particular problem in libel cases, where juries prejudiced against newspapers award huge damages, apparently using them punitively rather than as compensation for the victim. Examples include the £500,000 awarded to Jeffrey Archer in 1987, and the £300,000 to Koo Stark a year later, as well as **Sutcliffe v Pressdram Ltd** (1990), in which *Private Eye* was ordered to pay £600,000 to the wife of the Yorkshire Ripper. In the latter case Lord Donaldson described the award as irrational, and suggested that judges should give more guidance on the amounts to be awarded – not by referring to previous cases or specific amounts, but by asking juries to think about the real value of money (such as what income the capital would produce, or what could be bought with it). The Courts and Legal Services Act 1990 now allows the Court of Appeal to reduce damages considered excessive.

For a discussion of cases concerned with potentially racist jurors see p. 246.

Representation of ethnic minorities

Black defendants have no right to have black people sitting on the jury. In **R v Bansal** (1985) the case involved an Anti-National Front demonstration and the trial judge ordered that the jury should be drawn from an area with a large Asian population. However, this approach was rejected as wrong in **R v Ford** (1989). The Court of Appeal held that race could not be taken into account when selecting jurors, and that a judge could not discharge jurors in order to achieve a racially representative jury as this would undermine the principle that juries should be randomly selected.

Research carried out by Professor Cheryl Thomas (2007) found that there is today no significant under-representation of black and minority ethnic groups (BME) among those summoned for jury service. The process of computerised random summoning from the electoral lists provided by local authorities is successfully reaching an ethnically representative group of potential jurors in almost every court. In most courts there is no significant difference between the proportion of BME jurors serving and the BME population levels in the juror catchment area for each court. Ethnicity was only relevant as to whether a summoned juror serves or not where English was not a first language because those without a sufficient command of English are excused from jury service. However, the research found that the ethnicity of summoned jurors may be more problematic for some Crown Courts where ethnic minorities make up less than 10 per cent of the entire juror catchment area. Unfortunately, only 21 per cent of Crown Courts in England and Wales (mainly in London) have juror catchment areas where ethnic minorities comprise more than 10 per cent of the population. This is a particular problem where the catchment has large pockets of ethnic minorities within a catchment area but which represents less than 10 per cent of the total population in that area. The people living in that 'pocket' might have an expectation that they will be tried by some of their ethnic peers but find that they are faced by an all-white jury.

In this context it is significant that Professor Thomas's research found that the defendant's race had a significant impact on the individual votes of some jurors. In certain cases BME jurors were significantly less likely to vote to convict a BME defendant than a white defendant, though this did not affect the outcome of the trial because the BME jurors were in the minority and the defendant was convicted regardless.

Manipulation by defendants

The Government's consultation paper, *Determining Mode of Trial in Either Way Cases* (1998), suggests that manipulation of the right to jury trial by defendants is a major problem. It claims that many guilty defendants choose jury trial in a bid to make use of the delay such a choice provides. The report puts forward three reasons why guilty defendants want to do this. First, delay may put pressure on the Crown Prosecution Service to reduce the charge in exchange for the defendant pleading guilty and so speeding up the process. Secondly, it may make it more likely that prosecution witnesses will fail to attend the eventual trial, or at least weaken their recollections if they do attend, so making an acquittal more likely. Thirdly, if a defendant is being held on remand, they are kept at a local prison, and allowed additional visits and other privileges not given to convicted prisoners; time spent on remand is deducted from any eventual prison sentence, so for a defendant on remand who calculates that he or she is likely to be found guilty and sentenced to imprisonment, putting off the trial for as long as possible will maximise the amount of the sentence that can be spent under

12

The jury system

the more favourable conditions. Such manipulation is obviously undesirable from the point of view of justice, and it also wastes a great deal of time and money, since many defendants who manipulate the system in this way end up pleading guilty at the last minute (resulting in what is known as a 'cracked trial'), so that the time and money spent preparing the prosecution's case is wasted; in most cases, state funding will also have been spent on the defence case.

However, those who support jury trials argue that this is a declining problem, as a result of the decision in **R v Hollington** and **R v Emmens** (1986). Where a defendant has pleaded guilty to an offence, the courts generally impose a lesser sentence than they otherwise would, but in this case, the Court of Appeal stated that a defendant charged with an either way offence who opts for Crown Court trial in an attempt to benefit by the subsequent delay cannot expect to receive the same reduction in sentence as someone who pleads guilty in the magistrates' court (this decision has now been incorporated into s. 48 of the Criminal Justice and Public Order Act 1994, which allows courts to take account of the stage at which a guilty plea was made when deciding how far to reduce the sentence). Lawyers were obviously bound to warn their clients that if they chose Crown Court trial and then pleaded guilty, they would receive heavier sentences than if they simply pleaded guilty in the magistrates' court. The Government's own consultation paper points out that, since 1986, there has been a steady decline in the number of defendants in either way cases choosing jury trial. In 1987, defendants choosing jury trial accounted for 53 per cent of either way cases sent to the Crown Court, but by 1997, the proportion had fallen to 28 per cent.

Jury nobbling

This problem led to the suspension of jury trials for terrorist offences in Northern Ireland, and has caused problems in some English trials. In 1982 several Old Bailey trials had to be stopped because of attempted 'nobbling', one after seven months, and the problem became so serious that juries had to sit out of sight of the public gallery, brown paper was stuck over the windows in court doors, and jurors were warned to avoid local pubs and cafés and eat only in their own canteen. In 1984, jurors in the Brinks-Mat trial had to have police protection to and from the court, and their telephone calls intercepted, while in August 1994 a four-month fraud trial at Southwark Crown Court had to be abandoned after the jury had already delivered their verdict on one of the charges.

A new criminal offence was created under the Criminal Justice and Public Order Act 1994 to try to give additional protection to the jury. This provides under s. 51 that it is an offence to intimidate or threaten to harm, either physically or financially, certain people involved in a trial including jurors.

A more radical reform was introduced in the Criminal Procedure and Investigations Act 1996. Section 54 of the Act provides that where a person has been acquitted of an offence and someone is subsequently convicted of interfering with or intimidating jurors or witnesses in the case, then the High Court can quash the acquittal and the person can be retried. This is a wholly exceptional development in the law since traditionally acquittals were considered final, and subsequent retrial a breach of fundamental human rights. Following the Criminal Justice Act 2003, where there is a real risk of jury nobbling a case can be heard by a single judge.

Absence of reasons

When judges sit alone their judgment consists of a detailed and explicit finding of fact. When there is a jury it returns an unexplained verdict which simply finds in favour of one party or another. The former is more easily reviewed by appellate courts because the findings and the inferences of the trial judge can be examined. But when the appellate court is faced with a jury's verdict, it must support that verdict if there is any reasonable view of the evidence which leads to it.

Article 6 of the European Convention on Human Rights requires courts to give reasons for their judgments. In his review of the criminal courts Sir Robin Auld considered this matter in relation to the unreasoned jury verdicts. However, he concluded that the European Court of Human Rights would take into account the way the British jury trial works as a whole, and not find a violation of Art. 6.

Problems with compulsory jury service

Jury service is often unpopular but a refusal to act as a juror amounts to a contempt of court. Resentful jurors might make unsatisfactory decisions: in particular, jurors keen to get away as soon as possible are likely simply to go along with what the majority say, whether they agree or not.

Excessive damages

In the past juries in civil cases have awarded very high damages. The Court of Appeal now has the power either to order a new trial on the ground that damages awarded by a jury are excessive or, without the agreement of the parties, to substitute for the sum awarded by the jury such sum as appears to the court to be proper.

Cost and time

A Crown Court trial currently costs the taxpayer around £7,400 per day, as opposed to £1,000 per day for trial by magistrates. The jury process is time-consuming for all involved, with juries spending much of their time waiting around to be summoned into court.

Distress to jury members

Juries trying cases involving serious crimes of violence, particularly rape, murder or child abuse may have to listen to deeply distressing evidence and, in some cases, to inspect photographs of injuries. One juror in a particularly gruesome murder case told a newspaper how he felt on hearing a tape of the last words of the victim as, fatally injured, she struggled to make herself understood on the phone to the emergency services:

> It was your worst nightmare. I've watched American police programmes where you have a murder every 15 seconds, pools of blood, chalk lines where the bodies were . . . that's nothing compared to the sound of this tape. You cannot believe the shock that runs through you, the fear when you know this is what happened. (*Sunday Times*, 13 April 1997)

At the end of the case, most members of the jury were in tears and, after delivering their verdict, it was over an hour before they could compose themselves sufficiently to leave the jury room. The problem is made worse by the fact that jurors are told not to discuss the case with anyone else.

The potential for distress to jurors was recognised in the trials of Rosemary West and the killers of James Bulger, where the jurors were offered counselling afterwards, and since these cases the Ministry of Justice has provided that court-appointed welfare officers should be made available. However, these are provided only in cases judges deem to be exceptional, and only if jurors request their help.

Other criticisms

See also the notes on jury vetting, the non-representative nature of juries, and the termination of peremptory challenges. The material on mode of trial discussed at p. 436 is also relevant.

Reform of the jury

A wide range of proposals have been put forward for the reform of the jury system.

Serious fraud trials

The Government would have liked to remove jury trials from most serious fraud cases (see p. 236), a reform that has been heavily criticised. There has been an ongoing debate as to whether juries are suitable for such cases and the issue was considered in the Roskill Fraud Trials Committee Report of 1986. Public attention was drawn to this issue by the collapse of the trial of six men accused of fraud relating to the awarding of contracts for the construction of the Jubilee Line extension on the London Underground system (**R v Rayment and others** (2005)). The trial lasted two years – the longest ever jury trial – before it collapsed, having cost the taxpayer £60 million. It had suffered from a range of delays due to illness, scheduled holidays and paternity leave among the jury and lawyers, since it began in February 2000. Legal arguments also involved substantial periods where the jury was not required to hear evidence. In the last seven months before the case was dropped, the jury heard evidence on only

13 days of the 140 available. The prosecution eventually dropped the case after deciding there had been so many interruptions that a fair trial had become impossible.

ss. Cases
p. 165 ➤ To try to prevent such a waste of time and money occurring again, the Lord Chief Justice issued a Protocol requiring judges to exercise strong case management over cases likely to last more than eight weeks, including strict deadlines. The aim is to reduce the length of such trials to a maximum of three months. Trials will only be allowed to go on longer than six months in 'exceptional circumstances'. In addition, since April 2005 large criminal cases are monitored by a case management panel chaired by the Director of Public Prosecutions. Research carried out by Robert Julian (2008) has found that the judges involved in hearing fraud trials consider that the Protocol and judicial case management have been successful in reducing the length of complex fraud trials and have brought about a cultural change in the approach to this type of case.

The Government had not wanted to wait to see whether this new Protocol would lead to shorter fraud trials and instead tried to remove juries from such cases by introducing the Fraud (Trials Without Jury) Bill into Parliament. However, it faced strong opposition to this Bill and it looks unlikely that this Bill will be passed.

The use of a single judge has the advantages of making trials quicker, reducing the likelihood of 'perverse' verdicts, and defeating the problem of 'jury nobbling' (in Northern Ireland single judges have long been used in some cases because of the problem of jury nobbling). However, the benefits of public participation in the legal system would be lost, and all the problems associated with judicial bias and the restricted social background of judges (described in Chapter 10) would be let loose on cases which involve vital questions for both the individuals concerned and society as a whole. The Bar Council believes that juries should be retained in all cases where the defendant faces serious loss of liberty or reputation. It considers that fraud cases can appear complex but, if they are properly managed, juries are capable of deciding the case, which usually comes down to determining whether the defendant has been dishonest.

Using a bench of perhaps three or five judges would give a little more protection against individual bias, but would still not give the benefit of community participation that the jury offers (and would also require massive investment to train the increased number of judges that would be required).

Abolishing juries

It can be argued that since juries have already been abolished in all but a handful of civil cases with no apparent ill effects, and that they decide only 1 per cent of criminal cases anyway, the system really no longer needs them at all and they should be abolished. The pros and cons of this argument naturally depend on what would be put in their place.

Lay participation and increased speed (and lower costs) could be achieved by allowing magistrates to decide all criminal cases, but it is highly unlikely that society would ever wish to trust decisions on the most serious crimes to non-legally qualified judges. Of course, it could be argued that that is exactly what the jury system does, but in that case the number of jurors, and the advantages of random selection in terms of representing society as a whole, is thought by supporters to outweigh the amateur status of jurors – and in jury trials, the judge is always there to offer guidance on matters of law, and to decide the sentence in criminal cases.

The Government's 1998 consultation paper on the criminal justice system considered four possible options for serious fraud trials:

- abolishing the use of juries in fraud trials completely and replacing them with a specially trained single judge and two lay people with expertise in commercial affairs;
- replacing juries with a specially trained single judge or panel of judges, possibly with access to advisers on commercial matters;
- retaining jury trial but restricting the jury's role to deciding questions of dishonesty, with the judge deciding other matters; or
- replacing the traditional, randomly selected jury with a special jury, selected on the basis of qualifications or tests, or drawn from those who can demonstrate specialist knowledge of business and finance.

Ess. Cases p. 172 → In his review of the criminal justice system in 2001, Sir Robin Auld favoured the first option of a specially trained single judge and two lay people with expertise on the subject. Under his recommendations, a panel of experts would be set up and the trial judge would select the lay members after giving the parties the opportunity to make written representations as to their suitability. The judge would be the sole judge of law, procedure, admissibility of evidence and sentence. All three would be judges of fact and they would therefore decide the verdict together. A majority of any two would suffice for a conviction. The defendant would always have the option of choosing, with the consent of the court, a trial by judge alone.

There are weaknesses in this proposal. The selection process and limited powers of the lay members would risk undermining their stature in the eyes of the public. The power to convict on a majority of two to one could be seen as undermining the usual requirement in criminal law that, in order to convict, a defendant should be found guilty beyond reasonable doubt.

The Government is currently considering allowing trials without a jury for some terrorist cases where sensitive evidence cannot be made public.

Improving the performance of the jury

Ess. Cases p. 172 → As well as favouring a reduction in the role of the jury (discussed above), Sir Robin Auld made a range of specific recommendations to improve the performance of the jury.

Help the jury to work effectively

The Auld Review (2001) recommended that in order to assist a jury in their work, the prosecution and defence advocates should prepare a written summary of the case and the issues that needed to be decided. This 'case and issues' summary would be agreed by the judge and distributed to the jurors at the start of the trial.

The judge would sum up the case at the end of the trial by forming questions which needed to be considered by the jurors. Juries would reach verdicts by answering these questions during their deliberations. Where the judge thought it appropriate he or she would be able to require the jury publicly to answer each of the questions and to declare a verdict in accordance with those answers. Sir Robin Auld argues that this would strengthen the jury as a tribunal of fact, provide a reasoned basis for jury verdicts and reduce the risk of perverse verdicts. While there can only be benefits from presenting the case more clearly to the jury, the use of questions which the jury may be forced to answer publicly seems to be an unnecessary restriction on the jury's freedom to reach a decision in accordance with their conscience as well as in accordance with the law.

Research was carried out for the Law Commission in New Zealand. This research included watching juries deliberate their verdict, a process that would be illegal in the UK. In the light of this research the New Zealand Law Commission has recommended in its *Report on the Jury in Criminal Trials* (2001) that reforms should be introduced to assist the work of a criminal jury. These reforms include changing the ways in which evidence is put before the jury. Evidence should be put before a jury in the same way that other information is given to them in their everyday lives. For example, clear explanations of legal terms ought to be given in writing. The court should make notes of the evidence and give these to the jury. If appropriate, visual aids should be supplied. Where possible, the court should set out briefly in writing what decisions the jury need to make, and in what order – a 'decision tree'. The court should tell the jury what the key issues are between the parties. Sir Robin Auld seems to have been attracted to this approach.

Professor Zander (2001b) has criticised Sir Robin Auld's recommendations on the subject. He argues persuasively that Sir Robin Auld demonstrates

> . . . an authoritarian attitude that disregards history and reveals a grievously misjudged sense of the proper balance of the criminal justice system. For centuries the role of the jury has included the power to stand between the citizen and unjust law . . . [G]etting it right does not necessarily mean giving the verdict a judge would have given . . . To want to inquire whether they reached their decision in the 'right' way, is foolish because it ignores the nature of the institution.

Prevent perverse verdicts

ss. Cases
p. 172

The Auld Review was concerned by the risk of juries reaching perverse verdicts. Rather than seeing these as a potential safeguard of civil liberties the Review seems to consider these as an insult to the law. It has therefore recommended that legislation should declare that juries have no right to acquit defendants in defiance of the law or in disregard of the evidence. The prosecution would be given a right to appeal against what it considered to be a perverse acquittal by a jury.

Sir Robin Auld recommended that, where appropriate, the trial judge and the Court of Appeal should be allowed to investigate any alleged impropriety or failure in the way the jury reached their verdict, even where this is supposed to have happened during the traditionally secret deliberations of the jury. Such an investigation might look at accusations that some jurors ignored or slept through the deliberation or that the jury reached their verdict because of an irrational prejudice or whim, deliberately ignoring the evidence.

These recommendations show insufficient respect for the jurors and have been rejected by the Government.

Reserve jurors

One recommendation of the *Review of the Criminal Courts* was that, where appropriate, for long cases judges should be able to swear in extra jurors. These reserve jurors would be able to replace jurors who are unable to continue to hear a case, for example, because of illness.

Black jurors

It has been argued by the Commission for Racial Equality that consideration needs to be given to the racial balance in particular cases. They suggest that where a case has a racial dimension and the defendant reasonably believes that he or she cannot receive a fair trial from an all white jury, then the judge should have the power to order that three of the jurors come from the same ethnic minority as the defendant or the victim. Both the Runciman Commission (1993) and the *Review of the Criminal Courts* (2001) have given their endorsement to this proposal but it has never been implemented.

The Society of Black Lawyers had, in addition, submitted to the Runciman Commission that there should always be a right to a multi-racial trial, that peremptory challenges should be reinstated and that certain cases with a black defendant should be tried by courts in areas with high black populations, and panels of black jurors who would be available at short notice should be set up. These proposals have not been implemented either.

The problems caused by lack of racial representation on juries can be seen in the high-profile Rodney King case in Los Angeles, where a policeman was found not guilty of assaulting a black motorist despite a videotape of the incident showing brutal conduct. The case was tried in an area with a very high white population, while the incident itself had occurred in an area with a high black population. However, the decision in **R** *v* **Ford** (1989), that there is no principle that a jury should be racially balanced, still holds.

Peremptory challenge was abolished because it was said to have interfered with the principle of random selection, especially in multi-defendant trials. However, Vennard and Riley's study (1988a) found that the peremptory challenge was only used in 22 per cent of cases, with no evidence of widespread pooling of challenges, and research for the Crown Prosecution Service in 1987 showed that the use of peremptory challenge had no significant effect on the rate of acquittals.

Peremptory challenge could in fact be used to make juries more balanced in terms of race and sex, and it seems rather unjust that, while the defence have had their right to a peremptory challenge removed, the prosecution is still allowed to stand by for the Crown.

Answering questions

1 **'Those who argued for restricting the right to jury trial misunderstood the symbolic role of the jury – this symbolic role is as important as the need for just decision-making.' Discuss.** *London External LLB*

An answer to this essay might be divided into three parts:

- The symbolic importance of the jury.
- Moves to restrict the use of the jury.
- Just decision-making.

You could use these three subjects as subheadings so that the reader can clearly see the structure of your essay.

The symbolic importance of the jury
The symbolic role of juries is founded on the fact that jury trial represents judgment by one's peers. It is important because it is currently used for the most serious criminal trials following which people can be imprisoned for life. The jury is therefore seen as a major control over abuse of state power. It is in this context that Lord Devlin's support of the jury system can be understood (see p. 234). It is also part of our historical heritage.

Moves to restrict the use of the jury
You could point out that the jury's role has already been significantly reduced in the English legal system. They sit in less than 1 per cent of civil cases each year, and 95 per cent of criminal cases are heard in the magistrates' court without a jury. You could then look at the most recent attempts to further restrict the use of a jury (see p. 236) and consider whether the main motivation for these reforms is to save costs rather than to achieve 'just decision-making'.

Just decision-making
In this context you could look at the issue of perverse judgments (see p. 255) and Lord Auld's suggestions on how the procedures could be tightened to reduce the chance of a perverse judgment (see p. 263).

2 **'The jury is often described as "the jewel in the Crown" or "the corner-stone" of the British criminal justice system. It is a hallowed institution which, because of its ancient origin and involvement of 12 randomly selected lay people in the criminal process, commands much public confidence.' (Lord Justice Auld (1999)** *Review of the Criminal Courts of England and Wales*, **chapter 5, para. 1)**

Is this confidence in the jury misplaced? *LLB*

This question requires a critical analysis of the jury system. Issues that could have been discussed included:

- The jury selection process, and the recent reforms that have been made to this process, following Lord Justice Auld's recommendations.
- Moves to restrict the use of juries.
- The cost of a jury trial.
- The risk of bias entering into a jury verdict.
- The issue of perverse verdicts, and the role of juries in protecting civil liberties.

12

The jury system

3 'We believe that twelve persons selected at random are likely to be a cross-selection of the people as a whole and thus represent the views of the common man.' (Lord Denning MR in R v Sheffield Crown Court, ex parte Brownlow (1980))

Do you consider that this statement justifies the use of juries in criminal cases? Is there any other satisfactory justification?

Here you first need to discuss to what extent juries are representative, mentioning the limitations on random selection imposed by the rules on eligibility, disqualification and jury vetting. Having outlined this you should say whether in your opinion this alone justifies trial by jury in criminal cases, and why, using the material on public participation as an advantage of the jury system (p. 250).

Then move on to the other justifications for jury trials in criminal cases, which are of course the advantages listed on pp. 250–3. You should make it clear whether you feel these are alternative justifications to the principle of representing society, or complementary ones. You can then point out that, despite these justifications, there are problems with the jury system, and work through the disadvantages we have listed (remember that this question deals with juries in criminal trials only, and leave out irrelevant material such as the problems with damages for libel). Go through the alternatives to the jury system as well if you have time.

Your conclusion should sum up whether you think that the principles of random selection and being representative of society (or any of the other advantages you have discussed) outweigh the disadvantages strongly enough to justify the use of juries in criminal trials. If you conclude that the justifications are not sufficient, you should say what you feel should replace the jury system and why.

4 Critically discuss the impact of the jury composition provisions, contained in the Criminal Justice Act 2003, on the efficacy of criminal jury trials.

This requires an examination of the old and new qualification rules for jury service. You must therefore be familiar with the old provisions of the Juries Act 1974 and the reforming provisions, especially s. 321 and Schedule 33, of the Criminal Justice Act 2003. The new provisions ensure a much more representative jury in that they allow a range of people to sit as jurors who were previously prohibited. For example, members of the legal profession are now entitled to sit as jurors and you could consider whether their presence might help a jury work more efficiently. You could argue that allegations of bias are more likely with legally trained jury members or those who have been involved in the administration of justice. Specific cases to mention would be **R v Abdroikof** (2007) and **R v Khan** (2008) (pp. 240–2). In contrast, you could note that black jurors cannot be selected simply to provide an ethnically representative jury (you should discuss **R v Ford** (1989) (see p. 257 and p. 264). Do you think that selection on this basis would make the jury more efficient?

5 What is the role of the jury in a criminal trial and to what extent may it ignore the law?

A strong response would start with **Bushell's Case** (1670) which established that jurors are the sole judge of fact and they can give a verdict according to their conscience – principles recently reiterated in **R v Wang** (2005). Thus it is wrong for a trial judge to direct the jury to convict.

The jury's duty is to listen to, and weigh up, the evidence in order to decide what are the true facts. The judge directs them as to the relevant law and the jury then applies it to the facts to reach a verdict.

These rules also allow juries to decide according to their conscience and whilst this can allow them to reflect modern values, it can lead to some 'perverse' verdicts, such as those in **R** v **Kronlid**, **R** v **Ponting**, and **R** v **Owen**. One difficulty is that because the jury deliberations are secret, it is not possible to establish how a jury has reached its verdict. Sir Robin Auld suggested ways in which the use of juries could be reformed to reduce the opportunity for them to ignore the law, but others feel that the jury discretion provides an important safety net to protect citizens from an unjust law.

Summary of Chapter 12: The jury system

When are juries used?
Juries decide only about 1 per cent of criminal cases and a very small number of civil cases.

Qualifications for jury service
Potential jury members must be:

- aged 18 to 70;
- on the electoral register; and
- resident in the UK, Channel Islands or Isle of Man for at least five years since the age of 13.

Jury vetting
Jury vetting consists of checking that the potential juror does not hold 'extremist' views which some feel would make them unsuitable for hearing a case. It is done by checking police, Special Branch and security service records.

The secrecy of the jury
Once they retire to consider their verdict, jurors are not allowed to communicate with anyone other than the judge and an assigned court official, until after the verdict is delivered.

Arguments in favour of the jury system
Juries allow ordinary citizens to participate in the administration of justice and decide cases according to their conscience.

Criticisms of the jury system
In practice, juries are not representative of the general population. Some of their judgments are perverse; they can be biased and susceptible to manipulation.

Reform of the jury
Proposals have been put forward for restricting the role of juries or abolishing juries altogether. Significant reform proposals were drawn up by Sir Robin Auld but many of these have been rejected by the Government. The Government introduced the Fraud (Trials Without Jury) Bill which aimed to abolish the use of juries for many fraud trials. After facing strong opposition, it looks unlikely this Bill will be passed.

Reading list

Baldwin, J. and McConville, M. (1979) *Jury Trials*, Oxford: Clarendon Press.

Brown, D. and Neal, D. (1988) 'Show Trials: The Media and the Gang of Twelve' in Findlay, M. and Duff, P. (eds) *The Jury under Attack*, London: Butterworths.

Darbyshire, P. (1991) 'The lamp that shows that freedom lives – is it worth the candle?' *Criminal Law Review* 740.

Devlin, P. (1956) *Trial by Jury*, London: Stevens.

Findlay, M. (2001) 'Juror comprehension and complexity: strategies to enhance understanding' (2001) 41 *British Journal of Criminology* 56.

Freeman, M.D.A. (1981) 'The Jury on Trial', 34 *Current Legal Problems* 65.

Home Office Research Development and Statistics Directorate (2000) *Jury Excusal and Deferral* (Research Findings No. 102).

Horowitz, I. and Fosterlee, L. (2001) 'The effects of note-taking and trial transcript access on mock jury decisions in a complex civil trial' (2001) 25 *Law and Human Behaviour* 373.

Julian, R. (2007) 'Judicial Perspectives on the Conduct of Serious Fraud Trials', *Criminal Law Review* 751.

Julian, R. (2008) 'Judicial perspectives in serious fraud cases – the present status of and problems posed by case management practices, jury selection rules, juror expertise, plea bargaining and choice of mode of trial', [2008] *Criminal Law Review* 764.

Levi, M. (1988) 'The Role of the Jury in Complex Cases' in Findlay, M. and Duff, P. (eds) *The Jury under Attack*, London: Butterworths.

Levi, M. (1992) *The Investigation, Prosecution and Trial of Serious Fraud*, London: HMSO.

Lloyd-Bostock, S. (2007) 'The Jubilee Line jurors: does their experience strengthen the argument for judge-only trial in long and complex fraud cases?' [2007] *Criminal Law Review* 255.

Matthews, R., Hancock, L. and Briggs, D. (2004) *Jurors' Perceptions, Understanding, Confidence and Satisfaction in the Jury Systems: A Study in Six Courts*, London: Home Office.

McCabe, S. and Purves, R. (1972) *The Jury at Work: A Study of a Series of Jury Trials in which the Defendant was Acquitted*, Oxford: Blackwell.

Roskill Committee (1986) *Report of the Committee on Fraud Trials*, London: HMSO.

Thomas, C. (2008) 'Exposing the Myths of Jury Service', [2008] *Criminal Law Review* 415.

Thomas, C. and Balmer, N.J. (2007) *Diversity and Fairness in the Jury System*, London: Ministry of Justice.

Zander, M. (2000) '*The complaining juror*', 150 *New Law Journal* 723.

Reading on the Internet

www   The report of Professor Cheryl Thomas, *Diversity and Fairness in the Jury System*, Ministry of Justice Research Series 02/07 (2007) is available on the internet at:
http://www.justice.gov.uk/publications/research130607.htm

The *Report on Interviews with Jurors in the Jubilee Line Case* (2006) by Professor Sally Lloyd-Bostock is available on the website of Her Majesty's Crown Prosecution Service Inspectorate at:
www.hmcpsi.gov.uk/reports/JLJury-IntsRep.pdf

The *Review of the Investigation and Criminal Proceedings Relating to the Jubilee Line Case* (2006) by Stephen Wooler is available on the website of Her Majesty's Crown Prosecution Service Inspectorate at:
www.hmcpsi.gov.uk/reports/JubileeLineReponly.pdf

The consultation document *Jury Research and Impropriety* (2005), considering when the law should allow the secrecy of jury deliberations to be broken, can be found on the Department for Constitutional Affairs' website at:

http://www.dca.gov.uk/consult/juryresearch/juryresearch_cp0405.htm

Leaflets on jury service are published on the Court Service website at:

http://www.hmcourts-service.gov.uk

Visit www.mylawchamber.co.uk/ElliottELS to access multiple-choice questions, flashcards and practice exam questions to test yourself on this chapter.

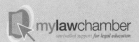

13

Magistrates

This chapter discusses:

- the organisation of the magistrates' courts;

- the selection and appointment of lay magistrates;

- their social background;

- the training provided;

- their role in criminal and civil cases;

- the work of justices' clerks and legal advisers;

- whether lay magistrates or professional judges should work in the magistrates' court; and

- possible reforms to the magistrates' system.

The magistrates' courts

The magistrates' courts are managed by the Ministry of Justice. The legislative provisions concerning the organisation of these courts are contained in the Courts Act 2003, which introduced significant reforms. These reforms are broadly in line with recommendations on the subject made by Sir Robin Auld in his *Review of the Criminal Courts* in 2001.

The Act introduces a central administration for all the courts (except the Supreme Court), so that they will be managed at a national rather than a local level. The Lord Chancellor has a general duty to maintain an efficient and effective court system. The country is divided into about 600 local justice areas (previously known as commission and petty sessional areas – the name 'local justice area' is considered to be a more modern and more appropriate title for these administrative areas). Each local justice area has its own courthouse and justices' clerk.

In the past, the courthouses were essentially run by local committees consisting of up to 35 magistrates. But this approach was criticised by a Scrutiny Report carried out for the Home Office in 1989. The study concluded that at the time there was no coherent management structure; the system was inefficient and not giving value for money. These local committees were therefore replaced in 1994 by Magistrates' Courts Committees, which had a smaller membership and a wider range of members. A justices' chief executive carried out the day-to-day administration of the local justice area.

The Magistrates' Court Committees and the position of justices' chief executives have now been abolished by the Courts Act 2003. They have been replaced by Her Majesty's Court Service, which is a single national executive agency which administers all the courts (excluding the Supreme Court). A limited local input is provided by local 'courts' boards'. These are made up of local community representatives and the judiciary, but their power is limited to offering recommendations to the Lord Chancellor as to the local needs of the courts. The magistrates themselves no longer play a significant role in the administration of the courts.

The reforms have incited considerable debate. The Government is hoping that the changes will create a cohesive, national court system within which personnel, buildings and facilities can be interchanged to make the most of resources. Professor Zander (2004) has commented:

> If sensitively implemented over the coming years this piece of legislation could provide a good basis for a courts system that combines the advantages of a centrally managed national system with the right amount of recognition of local concerns and interests.

Critics have argued that courts should be managed locally so that they reflect the local needs of the community, and that the courts' boards will have insufficient powers compared to the central court agency to achieve this. The Magistrates' Association has described the courts' boards as 'impotent and insufficiently representative of the lay magistracy'.

As regards the financial arrangements for the magistrates' courts, 60 per cent of their funding is now allocated on the basis of their workload, 25 per cent according to their efficiency in fine enforcement, 10 per cent depends on the time taken to deal with cases and the remaining 5 per cent for 'quality of service'. Performance targets have also been introduced. These arrangements have led to fears that the independence of the courts is threatened. Magistrates' courts' accounts can be reviewed by the Audit Commission.

TOPICAL ISSUE

Closing local courts

Concern has been expressed at the closure of small local courts which have been rehoused in large new complexes. The justification for these closures is that the smaller courthouses had poor facilities and the new multi-jurisdictional centres were modern with separate waiting areas for victims, witnesses and defendants and better access for the disabled. They also offer a pleasant environment for court staff to work in. The downside is that the smaller courts were local courts offering local justice to the local community, while the larger multi-jurisdictional centres can be inconvenient for users to travel to and be perceived as remote.

Magistrates

History

Like juries, lay magistrates have a long history in the English legal system, dating back to the Justices of the Peace Act 1361, which, probably in response to a crime wave, gave judicial powers to appointed lay people. Their main role then, as now, was dealing with criminals, but they also exercised certain administrative functions, and until the nineteenth century the business of local government was largely entrusted to them. A few of these administrative powers remain today.

There are over 28,000 lay magistrates (also called justices of the peace, or JPs), hearing over 1 million criminal cases a year – 95 per cent of all criminal trials, with the remaining being heard in the Crown Court. They are therefore often described as the backbone of the English criminal justice system. Lay magistrates do not receive a salary, but they receive travel, subsistence and financial loss allowances.

There are also 129 professional judges who sit in the magistrates' courts. These are now called 'district judges (magistrates' courts)' following a reform introduced by the Access to Justice Act 1999. They had previously been known as stipendiary magistrates. They receive a salary of over £90,000. On top of the permanent district judges (magistrates' courts) there are also deputy district judges who work part time, usually with a view to establishing their competence in order to get a full-time position in the future. These professional judges are appointed by the Queen on the recommendation of the Lord Chancellor. Following the passing of the Constitutional Reform Act 2005, the new Judicial Appointments Commission is involved in the appointment process of these professional judges. Applicants must have a relevant qualification and at least five years' post qualification experience. Under the Access to Justice Act 1999, they are appointed to a single bench with national jurisdiction. They act as sole judge in their particular court, mostly in the large cities and London in particular, where 46 are based. They are part of the professional judiciary, and most of the comments about magistrates in this chapter do not apply to them.

Upon appointment magistrates are required to take an oath that they will apply the law of the land. They are therefore not allowed to refuse to hear cases because of their

ss. Cases p. 184 ➜ personal beliefs. Thus, in 2008, a Christian magistrate could not require cases to be filtered so that he did not have to hear cases involving adoptions by same-sex couples.

Selection and appointment

Lay magistrates are appointed by the Lord Chancellor in the name of the Crown, on the advice of local Advisory Committees. For historical reasons, magistrates in Lancashire, Greater Manchester and Merseyside are appointed by the Chancellor of the Duchy of Lancaster in the name of the Crown. Candidates are interviewed by the Committee, who then make a recommendation to the Minister, who usually follows the recommendation.

Members of the local Advisory Committees are appointed by the Minister of Justice. Two-thirds of them are magistrates, and the Minister is supposed to ensure that they have good local knowledge, and represent a balance of political opinion. Their identity was at one time kept secret, but names are now available to the public.

Candidates are usually put forward to the Committee by local political parties, voluntary groups, trade unions and other organisations, though individuals may apply in person. The only qualifications laid down for appointment to the magistracy are that the applicants must be under 65 and live within 15 miles of the commission area in which they will work. These qualifications may be dispensed with if it is considered to be in the public interest to do so. In practice they must also be able to devote an average of half a day a week to the task, for which usually only expenses and a small loss of earnings allowance are paid. Legal knowledge or experience is not required; nor is any level of academic qualification.

Certain people are excluded from appointment, including: police officers, traffic wardens and members of the armed forces; anyone whose work is considered incompatible with the duties of a magistrate; anyone who due to a disability could not carry out all the duties of a magistrate; people with certain criminal convictions; undischarged bankrupts; and those who have a close relative who is already a magistrate on the same bench.

In 1998 the procedures for appointing lay magistrates were revised. The reforms aimed to make the appointment criteria open and clear. Thus a job description for magistrates was introduced which declares that the six key qualities defining the personal suitability of candidates are: having good character, understanding and communication, social awareness, maturity and sound temperament, sound judgement and commitment and reliability. Positions are now advertised widely, including in publications such as 'Inside Soaps' to attract a wider range of people.

Following the Courts Act 2003, magistrates are appointed nationally rather than locally. The new Judicial Appointments Commission established by the Constitutional Reform Act 2005 is not currently involved in the appointment of lay magistrates, though it is responsible for the appointment of district judges (magistrates' court).

Removal and retirement

Magistrates usually have to retire at 70. Under the Criminal Justice Act 2003, the Lord Chancellor can remove a lay magistrate from office:

- on the ground of incapacity or misbehaviour;
- on the ground of a persistent failure to meet the prescribed standards of competence; and
- if the Minister is satisfied that the lay justice is declining or neglecting to take a proper part in the exercise of his or her functions as a magistrate.

In addition, magistrates are prevented from exercising their functions if they suffer from an incapacity.

In 2009 a magistrate resigned after he inappropriately used the networking website Twitter. One message he posted stated: 'Called into court today to deal with those arrested last night and held in custody. I guess they will be mostly drunks but you never know.' Ironically, he announced his resignation on Twitter.

Background

Class

The 1948 Report of the Royal Commission on Justices of the Peace showed that approximately three-quarters of all magistrates came from professional or middle-class occupations. Little seems to have changed since: research carried out by Rod Morgan and Neil Russell (2000) found that more than two-thirds of lay magistrates were, or had been until retirement, employed in a professional or managerial position. Their social backgrounds were not representative of the community in which they served. For example, in a deprived metropolitan area, 79 per cent of the bench members were professionals or managers compared with only 20 per cent of the local population.

One of the reasons for this may be financial; while employers are required to give an employee who is appointed as a magistrate reasonable time off work, not all employers are able or willing to pay wages during their absence. To meet this difficulty, lay magistrates receive a loss of earnings allowance, but this is not overly generous and will usually be less than the employee would have earned.

A further problem is that employees who take up the appointment against the wishes of their employer may find their promotion prospects jeopardised. This means that only those who are self-employed, or sufficiently far up the career ladder to have some power of their own, can serve as magistrates without risking damage to their own employment prospects. The outcome is that those outside the professional and managerial classes are proportionately under-represented on the bench which is still predominantly drawn from the more middle-class occupations. The minimum age for appointment has been raised to 65 in the hope that working-class people, who were prevented from serving during their working lives, will do so in retirement, though so far the change has had little impact.

In the past the Government sought to achieve a social balance on the bench by taking into account a person's political affiliation when making appointments. This stemmed from the time when people tended to vote along class lines, with people from the working class voting predominantly for the Labour Party. Political opinion is no longer a reliable gauge of a person's social background and the Government has therefore replaced the question about 'political associations' on the application form for magistrates. It has been replaced by a question about the applicant's employment. The Ministry of Justice believes that this will provide a better means of achieving a socially balanced bench.

The Government has issued a White Paper, *Supporting Magistrates' Courts to Provide Justice* (2005). This includes proposals to encourage the recruitment of more young magistrates to make them representative of the communities they serve. Legislation will be introduced to clarify the process of magistrates taking time off work to attend court, including a requirement for employers to explain a refusal to allow a person to take time off.

Age

There are few young magistrates – most are middle-aged or older. The average age of a magistrate is 57, only 4 per cent of magistrates are under the age of 40, and almost a third are in their 60s. The problems concerning employment are likely to have an effect on the age as well as the social class of magistrates; people at the beginning of their careers are most dependent on the goodwill of employers for promotion, and least likely to be able to take regular time off without damaging their career prospects. They are also more likely to be busy bringing up families.

While a certain maturity is obviously a necessity for magistrates, younger justices would bring some understanding of the lifestyles of a younger generation. The Government is concerned that 11,000 magistrates are due to retire within the next ten years.

Politics

Government figures released in 1995 showed that a high proportion of magistrates were Conservative supporters, and few voted Labour. A sample survey of 218 new appointments as magistrates in England and Wales showed that 91 were Conservative voters, 56 Labour, 41 Liberal Democrat, 24 had no political affiliation, and four voted for the Welsh party, Plaid Cymru. A report analysing the figures for 1992 compared the proportion of Conservative voters among magistrates to the proportion in their local area: in two Oldham constituencies, 52 per cent of the local people voted Labour, but only 27 per cent of magistrates, and slightly more magistrates than constituents in general voted Conservative. In Bristol, Labour had won 40 per cent of the votes, slightly more than the Tories; of the magistrates, 142 said they were Tory, and only 85 described themselves as Labour supporters.

Race

The Government reported in 1987 that the proportion of black magistrates was only 2 per cent. The figures for 2003 show that lay magistrates increasingly reflect the ethnic diversity of contemporary Britain. Just over 6 per cent of magistrates come from ethnic

Table 13.1 Ethnicity: lay magistrates and population generally

	White	Black Caribbean, Black African, Black other	Indian, Pakistani, Bangladeshi, Chinese	Other	Not known	Total
Magistrates England and Wales						
Number	21,950	430	541	186	2,825	25,932
Percentage	85%	2%	2%	1%	10%	100%
General population for England and Wales (1991 census)	94%	2%	3%	1%	–	100%

The data exclude magistrate in the Duchy of Lancaster

Source: Morgan and Russell (2000) *The Judiciary in the Magistrates' Courts*, Home Office RDS Occasional Paper No. 66

minority communities, who make up 7.9 per cent of the general population. But there is a considerable variation locally and the fit between the local benches and the local communities they serve is, in several instances, very wide.

Sex

The sexes are fairly evenly balanced among lay magistrates with 51 per cent men and 49 per cent women. However, district judges (magistrates' courts) are primarily male, with only 13 women holding this position.

Training

The Magistrates' Commission Committees are responsible for providing training under the supervision of the Judicial Studies Board. Magistrates are not expected to be experts on the law, and the aim of their training is mainly to familiarise them with court procedure, the techniques of chairing, and the theory and practice of sentencing. They undergo a short induction course on appointment, and have to undergo basic continuous training comprising 12 hours every three years. Magistrates who sit in juvenile courts or on domestic court panels receive additional training. In order to chair a court hearing a magistrate must, since 1996, take a Chairmanship Course the syllabus of which is set by the Judicial Studies Board. Since 1998 the training has included more 'hands on' practical experience, sessions in equality awareness, and experienced magistrates act as monitors of more junior members of the bench.

Criminal jurisdiction

Magistrates have three main functions in criminal cases:

- Hearing applications for bail.
- Trial. Magistrates mainly try the least serious criminal cases. They are advised on matters of law by a justices' clerk, but they alone decide the facts, the law and the sentence.

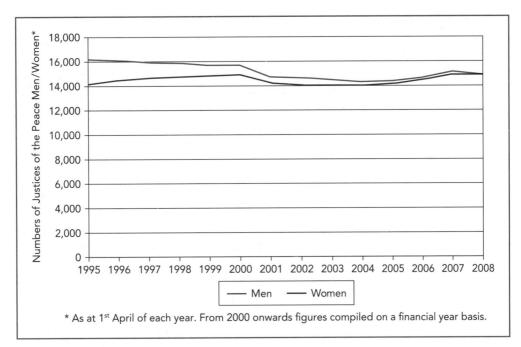

Figure 13.1 Justices of the Peace, 1995–2008

Source: Judicial and Court Statistics 2007, p. 175

- Appeals. In ordinary appeals from the magistrates' court to the Crown Court, magistrates sit with a judge. But, following a reform by the Access to Justice Act 1999, they no longer have this role in relation to appeals against sentence.

Magistrates also exercise some control over the investigation of crime, since they deal with applications for bail and requests by the police for arrest and search warrants.

Lay magistrates generally sit in groups of three. However, s. 49 of the Crime and Disorder Act 1998 provides that certain pre-trial judicial powers may be exercised by a single justice of the peace sitting alone. These include decisions to extend or vary the conditions of bail, to remit an offender to another court for sentence and to give directions as to the timetable for proceedings, the attendance of the parties, the service of documents and the manner in which evidence is to be given. These powers of single justices were tested in six pilot studies and, having proved to be successful, were applied nationally in November 1999.

The role of magistrates in the criminal justice system has been effectively increased in recent years. Some offences which were previously triable either way have been made summary only, notably in the Criminal Law Act 1977, where most motoring offences, and criminal damage worth less than £2,000, were made summary only (since raised to £5,000 in the Criminal Justice and Public Order Act 1994). The Government proposed at the time that thefts involving small amounts of money should also be made summary offences, but there was great opposition to the idea of removing the right to jury trial for offences which reflected on the accused's honesty. The proposal was dropped, but is still suggested from time to time.

The vast majority of new offences are summary only – there was controversy over the fact that the first offence created to deal with so-called 'joyriding' was summary, given that the problem appeared to be a serious one, and critics assume that it was made a summary offence in the interests of keeping costs down. Since then, the more serious joyriding offence, known as aggravated vehicle-taking, which occurs when joyriding causes serious personal injury or death, has been reduced to a summary offence by the Criminal Justice and Public Order Act 1994. Other serious offences which are summary only include assaulting a police officer, and many of the offences under the Public Order Act 1986.

The Courts Act 2003 has given district judges (magistrates' court) for the first time limited powers to sit in the Crown Court. This is in order to deal with some preliminary administrative matters.

The Government is considering dramatically halving the workload of magistrates. It would achieve this by not requiring a court hearing for certain relatively minor cases where the defendant pleads guilty, such as cases concerned with TV licence and council tax evasion, the less serious motoring offences, petty theft (such as shoplifting) and criminal damage cases (mainly involving graffiti). Currently, 50 per cent of the magistrates' time is taken up with summary motor offences, while 4 million cases were commenced in 2004 for unpaid council tax. In these cases, if the reforms were introduced, the sentence would be determined by the prosecutor in consultation with the police. The stated aim would be to reduce the workload of the magistrates' court and help them to work more efficiently.

The Government is also pushing to speed up the trial process in the magistrates' court, in particular by reducing the number of hearings each case requires. The reform proposals are contained in its report *Delivering simple, speedy, summary justice – an evaluation of the magistrates' courts tests* (2006).

Civil jurisdiction

Magistrates' courts are responsible for granting licences to betting shops and casinos, and hearing appeals from local authority decisions regarding the issuing of pub and

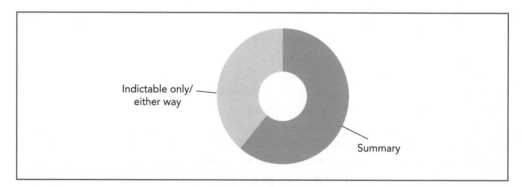

Figure 13.2 Magistrates' courts: type of offence

Source: Crown Prosecution Service Annual Report 2005–2006, p. 80

restaurant licences. They also have jurisdiction over domestic matters, such as adoption. When hearing such cases they are known as family proceedings courts. The Child Support Agency has taken over most of their work in relation to fixing child maintenance payments.

The courts' domestic functions overlap considerably with the jurisdiction of the county court and the High Court, though some uniformity of approach is encouraged by the fact that appeals arising from these cases are all heard by the Family Division of the High Court.

The fact that for domestic matters different procedures and law are applied in the different courts, and cases are generally assigned to the magistrates' court because they fall within certain financial limits, has led to the criticism that there is a second class system of domestic courts for the poor, with the better off using the High Court and county courts where cases are heard by professional and highly qualified judges. Because of this, magistrates sitting in domestic cases must receive special training and the bench must contain both male and female magistrates.

The justices' clerk and legal advisers

There are about 250 justices' clerks in the country. Most must have a five-year magistrates' court qualification, that is to say they must be qualified as barristers or solicitors with a right of audience in relation to all proceedings in the magistrates' courts for at least five years, though some hold office by reason of their length of service. In the past there have been problems with recruiting suitably qualified people, partly because the local organisation of the courts meant there was no clear career structure. This led many clerks to leave for the Crown Prosecution Service where pay and promotion prospects were better.

The justices' clerks delegate many of their powers in practice to legal advisers (previously known as court clerks). This wide delegation has caused concerns about the qualifications of the people to whom these powers are being delegated. In an effort to raise standards, since 1 January 1999 all newly appointed legal advisers must be qualified solicitors or barristers. Those in post prior to this date who have a specialist diploma in magisterial law have ten years in which to requalify. There is an exemption for legal advisers aged 40 or over on 1 January 1999. Not surprisingly, this reform was angrily received by legal advisers who did not have the requisite qualification.

A Practice Direction was issued by the High Court in 2000 clarifying the powers of the justices' clerk – Practice Direction (Justices: Clerk to Court) (2000). This was issued to make it clear that their powers conform with the European Convention on Human Rights following the passing of the Human Rights Act 1998.

The primary function of the justices' clerk and legal adviser is to advise the lay magistrates on law and procedure. They are not supposed to take any part in the actual decision of the bench; legal and procedural advice should be given in open court, and the justices' clerk and legal adviser should not accompany the magistrates if they retire to consider their decision. Section 49(2) of the Crime and Disorder Act 1998 provides that many of the pre-trial judicial powers that are exercisable by a single justice of the peace can be delegated to a justices' clerk. Their independence is guaranteed by s. 29

Table 13.2 The cost of appearing before lay and professional magistrates (per appearance)

	Lay magistrates	Professional magistrates
	£	£
Direct costs (salary, expenses, training)	3.59	20.96
Indirect costs (premises, administration staff etc.)	48.51	40.82
Direct & indirect costs	52.10	61.78

Source: Morgan and Russell (2000) The Judiciary in the Magistrates' Courts, Home Office RDS Occasional Paper No. 66

of the Courts Act 2003. In the past the justices' clerk also had considerable administrative functions, but these are increasingly being passed to other staff.

Lay magistrates versus professional judges

In recent years there has been some discussion as to whether lay magistrates should be replaced by professional judges. There have been suspicions that this may be on the Government's political agenda. These suspicions have been fuelled by the increasing role of justices' clerks and the commission of research in the field by Rod Morgan and Neil Russell. Their report The Judiciary in the Magistrates' Courts (2000) has provided some useful up-to-date information to support the debate on the future role of lay magistrates in the criminal justice system. That research concluded:

> At no stage during the study was it suggested that . . . the magistrates' courts do not work well or fail to command general confidence. It is our view, therefore, that eliminating or greatly diminishing the role of lay magistrates would not be widely understood or supported.

Advantages of lay magistrates

Cost

It has traditionally been assumed that because lay magistrates are unpaid volunteers, they are necessarily cheaper than their stipendiary colleagues. However, it is not clear that this is the case. The research by Rod Morgan and Neil Russell (2000) found that a simple analysis of the direct costs for the Magistrates' Courts Service of using the two types of magistrates shows that lay magistrates are extraordinarily cheap compared with professional judges. The direct average cost of a lay justice is £495 per annum, that of a district judge £90,000. However, lay magistrates incur more indirect costs than professional judges. They are much slower than professional judges in hearing cases, as one professional judge handles as much work as 30 lay magistrates. Lay magistrates therefore make greater proportionate use of the court buildings. They need the support of legally qualified legal advisers. Administrative support is required for their recruitment, training and rota arrangements. When all the overheads are brought into the equation the cost per appearance for lay and professional magistrates becomes £52.10 and £61.78 respectively. These figures have to be seen in the context that professional judges are currently more likely to send someone to prison which is more expensive than the alternative sentences frequently imposed by lay magistrates. They are almost twice as likely to remand defendants in custody and they are also twice as likely to sentence defendants to immediate custody, a finding that may be partly attributable to their hearing the most serious cases.

Switching to Crown Court trials would be extremely expensive. The Home Office Research and Planning Unit has estimated that the average cost of a contested trial in the Crown Court is around £13,500, with guilty pleas costing about £2,500. By contrast, the costs of trial by lay magistrates are £1,500 and £500 respectively. This is partly a reflection of the more serious nature of cases tried in the Crown Court, but clearly Crown Court trials are a great deal more expensive overall.

Lay involvement

This is the same point as that cited in favour of the jury (see p. 250). Lay magistrates are an ancient and important tradition of voluntary public service. They can also be seen as an example of participatory democracy. Lay involvement in judicial decision-making ensures that the courts are aware of community concerns. However, given the restricted social background of magistrates, and their alleged bias towards the police, the true value of this may be doubtful. Magistrates do not have the option, as juries do, of delivering a verdict according to their conscience.

Weight of numbers

The simple fact that magistrates must usually sit in threes may make a balanced view more likely.

Local knowledge

Magistrates must live within a reasonable distance of the court in which they sit, and therefore may have a more informed picture of local life than professional judges.

Disadvantages of lay magistrates

Inconsistent

Historically there has been concern that magistrates' courts around the country were not treating like cases alike. To achieve the fundamental goal of a fair trial, similar crimes committed in similar circumstance by offenders with similar backgrounds should receive a similar punishment. In 1985, the Home Office noted in *Managing Criminal Justice* (edited by David Moxon), that though benches tried to ensure their own decisions were consistent, they did not strive to achieve consistency with other benches. The researchers Flood-Page and Mackie found in 1998 that district judges (magistrates' courts) sentenced a higher proportion of offenders to custody than lay magistrates after allowing for other factors. There are also marked variations in the granting of bail applications: in 1985, magistrates' courts in Hampshire granted 89 per cent of bail applications, while in Dorset only 63 per cent were allowed.

The Government has tried to put an end to the differences in sentencing patterns in different areas, a situation which was described as 'postcode sentencing'. In order to do this, the Sentencing Guidelines Council was established, to ensure greater consistency in sentencing across England and Wales. This is not intended to be a threat to the independence of the magistracy who need to be able to take into account individual circumstances. But where circumstances are similar, the aim is to reduce the regional disparity in sentencing. The Sentencing Guidelines Council has now issued legally binding sentencing guidelines for magistrates. Magistrates have to take into account any relevant guideline, and if a decision is reached that the particular facts of a case justify a sentence outside the range indicated, they must state their reasons for doing so.

Inefficient

Most of the public sampled in the research by Rod Morgan and Neil Russell (2000) was largely unaware that there were two types of magistrate. When enlightened and questioned, a majority considered that magistrates' court work should be divided equally between the two types of magistrate or that the type of magistrate did not matter. However, professional court users have significantly greater levels of confidence in the district judges (magistrates' courts). They regard these judges as quicker than lay justices, more efficient and consistent in their decision-making, better able to control unruly defendants and better at questioning CPS and defence lawyers appropriately. In practice, straightforward guilty pleas to minor matters are normally dealt with by panels of lay magistrates whereas serious contested matters are increasingly dealt with by a single, professional judge who decides questions of both guilt and sentence. Rod Morgan and Neil Russell question whether the work should be distributed in the opposite way.

Bias towards the police

Police officers are frequent witnesses, and become well known to members of the bench, and it is alleged that this results in an almost automatic tendency to believe police evidence. One magistrate was incautious enough to admit this: in **R v Bingham Justices, ex parte Jowitt** (1974), a speeding case where the only evidence was that of the motorist and a police constable, the chairman of the bench said 'Quite the most unpleasant cases that we have to decide are those where the evidence is a direct conflict between a police officer and a member of the public. My principle in such cases has always been to believe the evidence of the police officer, and therefore we find the case proved.' The conviction was quashed on appeal because of this remark.

Magistrates were particularly criticised in this respect during the 1984 miners' strike for imposing wide bail conditions which prevented attendance on picket lines, and dispensing what appeared to be conveyor-belt justice.

Background

Despite the recommendations of two Royal Commissions (1910 and 1948) and the *Review of the Criminal Courts* (2001), that magistrates should come from varied social backgrounds, magistrates still appear to be predominantly middle class and middle-aged, with a strong Conservative bias.

The selection process has been blamed for the general narrowness of magistrates' backgrounds: Elizabeth Burney's 1979 study into selection methods concluded that the process was almost entirely dominated by existing magistrates who over and over again simply appointed people with similar backgrounds to their own.

The effect of their narrow background on the quality and fairness of magistrates' decisions is unclear. A survey of 160 magistrates by Bond and Lemon (1979) found no real evidence of significant differences in approach between those of different classes, but they did conclude that political affiliation had a noticeable effect on magistrates' attitudes to sentencing, with Conservatives tending to take a harder line. The research did not reveal whether these differences actually influenced the way magistrates carried out their duties in practice, but there is obviously a risk that they would do so.

In 1997, there was a slight controversy when, on winning the general election, the Labour Lord Chancellor called for more Labour voting candidates to be recommended for appointment as magistrates by Advisory Committees. His reasoning was that the political make-up of the magistrates needed to reflect that of the general population which had shifted towards Labour. The Labour Government has now reversed its position, having concluded that it is no longer necessary to seek a political balance among magistrates because people no longer vote along class lines.

Some feel that the background of the bench is not a particular problem: in *The Machinery of Justice in England* (1989) Jackson points out that 'Benches do tend to be largely middle to upper class, but that is a characteristic of those set in authority over us, whether in the town hall, Whitehall, hospitals and all manner of institutions.'

However, a predominantly old and middle-class bench is unrepresentative of the general public and may weaken confidence in its decisions, on the part of society in general as well as the defendants before them. Jackson's argument that those 'set in authority over us' always tend to be middle to upper class is not a good reason for not trying to change things.

Suggested reforms

Professional judges

Professional judges could either replace lay magistrates, or sit together with them. In no other jurisdiction do lay judges alone or in panels deal with offences of the seriousness dealt with in the English and Welsh magistrates' courts by lay magistrates. But putting a professional judge in all magistrates' courts would be very expensive, and is unlikely to happen, though the Royal Commission on Criminal Justice did recommend in 1993 that more use should be made of professional judges. Rod Morgan and Neil Russell (2000) calculated that if the work of lay magistrates was transferred to professional judges, one professional judge would be needed for every 30 magistrates replaced.

The role of the justices' clerk

The current Government seems to be moving in the direction of allowing justices' clerks to have increased powers to manage cases, while limiting their administrative functions. These reforms could be taken further by appointing them to the bench, making them legally qualified chairpersons, or giving them formal powers to rule on all points of law, while leaving the determination of the facts to the lay justices. The academic Penny Darbyshire has, however, sounded a note of caution to such developments. In an article in 1999 she argues that case management is not an administrative activity but a judicial one. She considers that such powers should not be delegated to justices' clerks unless they are selected and screened in the same way as judges and given the same protection as judges to ensure their independence.

In its submission to the Auld Review of the Criminal Courts in 2001, the Association of Magisterial Officers, which represents staff in magistrates' courts, called for a major transfer of powers from lay magistrates to justices' clerks. The union argued that the role of lay magistrates should be restricted to arbiters of fact. Justices' clerks would take on full responsibility for all pre-trial issues apart from the grant or removal of bail. Where lay magistrates were involved, they would act as 'wingers' in three-person tribunals chaired by justices' clerks. The clerks' decision on points of law would be final, but any decision on the facts would be by simple majority. Sir Robin Auld rejected this submission and essentially recommended that the role of justices' clerks should remain unchanged.

The selection process

The *Review of the Criminal Courts* (Auld 2001) recommended that steps should be taken to make magistrates reflect more broadly than at present the communities they serve. Increased loss of earnings allowances and crèche facilities at courts (to help young parents) are all ways of attracting a more varied range of candidates. Legislation preventing employers from discriminating against magistrates would be difficult to enforce, but might at least make employers more wary about being seen to discriminate, and thus encourage more working class and younger applicants.

Membership of local Advisory Committees could be broadened to include members of the ethnic minorities and the working class, perhaps drawn from community organisations and trade unions.

The Auld Review (2001) recommended that local Advisory Committees should be equipped with the information they need to enable them to submit for consideration for appointment candidates that will produce and maintain benches broadly reflective of the communities they serve. This would include the establishment and maintenance of national and local databases of information on the make-up of the local community and on the composition of the local magistracy.

Improvements in consistency

Achieving precise uniformity in sentencing and the granting of bail throughout the country is probably impossible, given the number of cases handled by magistrates' courts; but more detailed guidelines, regularly updated, more training, and some supervision by the higher courts could at least curb the more significant variations.

A District Division

The Government commissioned a major review of the criminal courts by Sir Robin Auld. The Review was primarily focused on the practices and procedures of the criminal courts and a wide range of recommendations were made. The central recommendation of the report was essentially that a new criminal court should be created (though it would for administrative purposes be a division of a court), which would be called the District Division.

Instead of having a separate Crown Court and magistrates' court, there would be a single unified criminal court containing three divisions. The three divisions would be the Crown Division (currently the Crown Court), the Magistrates' Division (currently the magistrates' court) and a new intermediate District Division.

Cases before the District Division would be heard by a judge and two lay magistrates. The District Division would deal with a middle range of either way cases which were unlikely to attract a sentence of more than two years' imprisonment. This would include most burglaries and thefts as well as some assault cases.

Only the judge would be able to determine questions of law, but the judge and lay magistrates would together be judges of fact. The order of proceedings would be broadly the same as in the Crown Division. The judge would rule on matters of law, procedure and inadmissibility of evidence, in the absence of the magistrates where it would be potentially unfair to the defendant to do so in their presence. The judge would not sum up the case to the magistrates, but would retire with them to consider the court's decision. They would reach their verdicts together, each having an equal vote. The judge would give a reasoned judgment and he or she would have sole responsibility for determining the sentence.

Defendants would lose their right to insist on a jury trial. Instead, cases would be allocated by magistrates to the relevant Division according to their seriousness.

These recommendations of Sir Robin Auld would have significantly increased the role of magistrates in the criminal justice system, but also represented a major attack on jury trials, since they would have significantly reduced the number of cases being heard by a jury. The proposals were heavily criticised by supporters of the jury system. It is questionable whether they would have produced any financial savings. The Law Society expressed its concern that an intermediate court 'would add an unnecessary level of bureaucracy'. After reflection, the Government rejected these recommendations.

Community justice centres

The Government has set up some pilot community justice centres which are modelled on similar centres that have been established in the US. These centres seek to bring together the courts and a range of relevant agencies, such as the social services and drug charities, to tackle the underlying problems in a community that lead to crime and anti-social behaviour. As well as bringing offenders to justice, the centres aim to develop crime prevention and to solve community problems. The centres also offer mediation for minor disputes.

13

Magistrates

Answering questions

As well as the following examples, the role of magistrates may also be considered as part of a question on lay involvement in the criminal justice system generally, and in questions on the criminal justice system itself.

1 **While magistrates may be cheap, is it right that matters of vital concern to the citizen are being decided by amateurs?**

You need to address the four key points raised by this question in turn:

- Are magistrates cheap?
- Are they amateurs?
- What matters of vital concern do they deal with?
- Should magistrates deal with important cases?

Looking first at whether magistrates are cheap, this issue is covered in the first point under 'Advantages of lay magistrates' on p. 280.

Secondly, can they be fairly described as amateurs? You could mention here that lay magistrates do not have legal qualifications, but do have some training – you might refer to the extra training given to magistrates dealing with family and juvenile cases and to those acting as the chairperson. You should also mention the role of the justices' clerk, who can guide them on the law.

You then need to point out what matters of vital concern they decide – these will mainly be criminal, and you should note that some summary and either way offences can be serious, and even those which appear minor, such as driving offences, can have serious consequences for individuals. You could also draw attention to the fact that the criminal jurisdiction of the magistrates' court has been increased with more offences being made summary only. In civil cases, the magistrates' family jurisdiction can be seen as being of vital importance for the citizen.

The main emphasis in your essay should be on the next part: do you think it is right that amateur magistrates should decide such important cases? Do not be tempted simply to list the advantages and disadvantages of magistrates – although that is the information you will use, you must relate it to the idea of magistrates as amateurs. Obvious points to make would be those about inconsistency, and possibly about bias towards the police.

You might then go on to state any advantages of magistrates which could outweigh, or balance out, the problems of being amateurs – their local knowledge, and the fact that they involve the community, for example. You could make a brief comparison between trial by magistrates and trial by jury, drawing attention to the fact that juries too are lay people who have also been accused of providing amateur justice. You could also compare trial by magistrates with the other alternatives – those listed as alternatives to juries (pp. 260–2) are also alternatives to magistrates. You might point out that one of the allegations made against magistrates – that they come from a narrow social background – is even more true of professional judges. If you have time, run through some of the suggested reforms to magistrates, such as better training.

Your conclusion should state your opinion – you might say that magistrates are amateur and should not be given such vital matters to deal with, or that their advantages outweigh their amateur status. You could conclude that if reforms were made the position would be improved, or even suggest that amateur status is a positive advantage – it all depends what the rest of your answer has argued – but you should give some opinion.

2 Recent reforms have increased the powers of magistrates in the criminal justice system. Are their powers now too great – or too small?

You need to start by outlining the criminal powers of magistrates, and particularly those powers which have come about as a result of recent changes – these are described in the section on criminal jurisdiction in this chapter. You could point out that there are also areas where magistrates have lost powers – the abolition of committal proceedings, and the decreased use of magistrates' warrants (see Chapter 18). You could point to the recent reforms discussed at p. 277 allowing magistrates to exercise certain case management powers on their own. The main part of your essay should concentrate on whether their powers should be increased or decreased.

You need to go through any reasons why it might be seen as a good idea to increase the powers of magistrates – cost is obviously one, and you might also consider some of the other advantages of magistrates, such as local knowledge or community involvement, which also justify increased powers.

Then consider any reasons why magistrates' powers should not be increased, or should even be decreased. The problems of bias towards the police and inconsistency are clearly relevant here.

If you have time, you could run through any of the relevant reforms mentioned in this chapter, and, if you have been arguing that magistrates' powers are too great, say whether you think those powers would be acceptable, or could be increased, if these reforms were carried out.

3 To what extent do lay magistrates provide justice 'on the cheap'?

This question prompts discussion of two key issues:

- the cost-effectiveness of the magistrates courts; and
- the quality of justice delivered.

Although lay magistrates are unpaid, they do receive allowances and incur incidental indirect costs (for example, requiring the attendance of legally qualified advisers), and usually sit in benches of three. Moreover, they tend to work more slowly than a professional magistrate who, being a qualified lawyer, sits alone and without the attendance of a legally qualified adviser. Thus the net cost per appearance before lay magistrates is only approximately 20 per cent cheaper than before a professional judge.

It is difficult to compare the quality of justice delivered by lay magistrates and that by district judges, but lay magistrates often look to use community and other non-custodial sentences. Lay magistrates may be less consistent in their decision-making and favour prosecution cases.

One conclusion might be that the cost-savings achieved by using lay magistrates risks being outweighed by less robust decisions. An alternative conclusion could be that lay magistrates might not be particularly cheap, but they provide a justice that is close to the community in which they serve.

4 Discuss the extent to which lay magistrates are representative of society.

Lay magistrates deal with 95 per cent of all criminal trials and are appointed by the Lord Chancellor in the name of the Queen, on the advice of local Advisory Committees (comprised mostly of existing magistrates). The only formal requirement is that an applicant should be under 65 and live within 15 miles of the commission area to which they will be appointed (although appointments are now made on a national basis). There is an expectation that they will be able to devote one half day per week to acting as a magistrate. There is no minimum educational qualification or requirement of legal knowledge, but they receive only expenses and a small allowance.

Research by Morgan and Russell (2000) found that whilst the percentage of magistrates from the ethnic minorities was increasing, magistrates remained predominantly professional or managerial, middle-aged (or older) and so increasingly unrepresentative of the community they served. One explanation might be the employers' reluctance to give paid time off work, thus effectively facilitating the appointment of the self-employed and those in senior positions.

Summary of Chapter 13: Magistrates

Introduction
There are over 28,000 lay magistrates and 129 professional judges who sit in the magistrates' courts.

Selection and appointment
Lay magistrates are appointed by the Lord Chancellor in the name of the Crown, on the advice of local Advisory Committees.

Background
More than two-thirds of lay magistrates are employed in a professional or managerial position, or were until they retired. Almost a third of magistrates are in their sixties. A high proportion are Conservative voters. Lay magistrates do, however, increasingly reflect the ethnic diversity of contemporary Britain and the sexes are fairly evenly balanced.

Training
The Magistrates' Commission Committees are responsible for providing training under the supervision of the Judicial Studies Board.

Jurisdiction
Magistrates are primarily concerned with criminal matters but they exercise a limited jurisdiction over some civil matters.

The justices' clerk and legal adviser
The primary function of the justices' clerk and legal adviser is to advise the lay magistrates on law and procedure. They are not supposed to take any part in the actual decision of the bench.

Lay magistrates versus professional judges
In recent years there has been some discussion as to whether lay magistrates should be replaced by professional judges.

Reading list

Bond, R.A. and Lemon, N.F. (1979) 'Changes in Magistrates: Attitudes During the First Year on the Bench' in Farrington, D.P. *et al.* (eds) *Psychology, Law and Legal Processes*, London: Macmillan.

Burney, E. (1979) *Magistrates, Court and Community*, London: Hutchinson.

Darbyshire, P. (1999) 'A comment on the powers of magistrates' clerks', *Criminal Law Review* 377.

Hedderman, C. and Moxon, D. (1992) *Magistrates' Court or Crown Court? Mode of Trial Decisions and Sentencing*, London: HMSO.

Herbert, A. (2003) 'Mode of trial and magistrates' sentencing powers: will increased powers inevitably lead to a reduction in the committal rate?' *Criminal Law Review* 314.

King, M. and May, C. (1985) *Black Magistrates: A Study of Selection and Appointment*, London: Cobden Trust.

Lidstone, K. (1984) *Magisterial Review of the Pre-Trial Criminal Process: A Research Report*, Sheffield: University of Sheffield Centre for Criminological and Socio-Legal Studies.

Morgan, R. and Russell, N. (2000) *The Judiciary in the Magistrates' Courts* (Home Office RDS Occasional Paper No. 66), London: Home Office.

Reading on the Internet

www

The research of Rod Morgan and Neil Russell, *The Judiciary in the Magistrates' Courts* (2000), is available on the Home Office's website in the section dedicated to the Research Development and Statistics Directorate:

    http://www.homeoffice.gov.uk/rds/pdfs/occ-judiciary.pdf

The website of the Magistrates Association, which represents the interests of magistrates, is available at:

    http://www.magistrates-association.org.uk

General information about magistrates is available on the following website:

    http://www.dca.gov.uk/magistrates

The report *Delivering simple, speedy, summary justice – an evaluation of the magistrates' courts tests* (2006) is available on the Internet at:

    http://www.dca.gov.uk/publications/reports_reviews/mag_courts_evaluation.pdf

Visit **www.mylawchamber.co.uk/ElliottELS** to access multiple-choice questions, flashcards and practice exam questions to test yourself on this chapter.

13

Magistrates

14

Administration of justice

This chapter discusses:

- national changes to the arrangements for the administration of justice;
- the separate roles of the Home Office and the Ministry of Justice;
- the Lord Chancellor; and
- the Attorney General.

Introduction

In recent years the Government has made radical reforms to the administration of the English legal system. Historically, this system was administered by both the Lord Chancellor's Department and the Home Office. In 2003, the Lord Chancellor's Department was abolished and replaced by a Department for Constitutional Affairs.

The position of the Lord Chancellor has been particularly problematic (discussed at p. 156). He (no woman has ever been appointed) did not sit in the House of Commons but was speaker of the House of Lords. This meant that MPs were not able to ask direct questions in the House of Commons about the work of the Lord Chancellor's Department, so that the Department's democratic accountability was limited. The Lord Chancellor's Department was not subject to the select committee system, which is another way in which MPs can question the running of departments. Instead, the Attorney General took parliamentary questions about every four weeks, which could include questions about the Lord Chancellor's Department. However, in most cases such questions were merely referred back to the Lord Chancellor, rather than being answered by the Attorney General, and replies were not always forthcoming after such referrals.

It was sometimes claimed that the Lord Chancellor was accountable through the House of Lords but, while such accountability may have been possible in theory, in practice it was ineffective. For example, during Lord Hailsham's Chancellorship there were incidents, such as the removal of a circuit judge in 1983, and refusals to renew temporary judicial posts, which would certainly have provoked challenges to a Minister sitting in the House of Commons. Yet, despite many opportunities for peers to inquire into such matters relating to the judiciary, there were no questions or debate in the Lords on the subject.

This overall lack of accountability was problematic, not only because of the importance of the issues with which the Lord Chancellor's Department dealt, but also because it was responsible for spending a great deal of public money.

In 2003 the Government announced that it intended to abolish the office of Lord Chancellor, and replace the position with a Minister for Constitutional Affairs. Following debate over this reform, the Government agreed to retain the position of Lord Chancellor, but his or her role has been significantly reduced (see p. 156) so that he or she has become a more conventional Cabinet Minister and head of department.

The Department for Constitutional Affairs had similar responsibilities to its predecessor. It was responsible for the appointment of judges, judicial salaries and the disciplining of the lower judiciary. It administered the courts, oversaw the state funding of legal services and contributed to the work on law reform. The Home Office was responsible for the police, national security, reform of the criminal law, prisons, immigration, elections and civil rights. The division of most of the important legal work between the Home Office and the Ministry for Constitutional Affairs was subsequently criticised as illogical. Why should two different departments each play a leading role in the same area? It appears that at the time of this reform the Prime Minister might have been interested in making some changes to the remit of the Home Office, but the then Home Office Minister was not prepared to see any of his powers removed.

Under these arrangements legal matters could be easily ignored when the Government was unenthusiastic about them, since there was no single Minister who could

14

Administration of justice

be pressurised in Parliament. An example is the issue of funding for Law Centres: while the Department of the Environment had given grants to set up centres, their continued funding appeared not to be the responsibility of any department, and so they were forced to rely on local authorities – themselves under severe financial restraints – and any other sources of funding they could drum up themselves.

Ess. Cases
p. 192 → In 2006, following a number of scandals relating to the prison service and immigration, the Home Secretary announced that the Home Office was 'not fit for purpose'. In 2007 the Department for Constitutional Affairs was abolished and replaced by a larger Ministry of Justice. There had long been a debate as to whether the UK should have a Ministry of Justice and the Government appears to have accepted the arguments in favour of this. The new Ministry is responsible for all the matters that fell within the remit of the Department for Constitutional Affairs, but in addition it has taken over responsibility for prisons and the probation service from the Home Office. Following the Courts Act 2003, the courts (apart from the Supreme Court) are administered by Her Majesty's Courts Service. This executive body falls within the responsibilities of the Ministry of Justice.

In summary, the Ministry of Justice has responsibility for three core policy areas:

● the court service (including the judges),
● the penal system (both prisons and community punishments), and
● legal aid.

The Home Office is now responsible for:

● terrorism,
● security,
● policing,
● immigration, and
● asylum.

The hope is that the new Ministry of Justice will focus on reducing crime and run an effective penal system. Thus a key focus of the Home Office will be on the detection of crime, while the Ministry of Justice will concentrate on the task of delivering a fair trial and sentence.

Members of the senior judiciary expressed concern that these new administrative arrangements could pose a threat to the independence of the judiciary. They were particularly anxious to avoid any pressure to impose sentences that the judges considered inappropriate now that the courts were being administered by the same department as the prisons. They demanded that the structures be put in place to prevent any threat to their independence arising. They have failed to get any guarantees for the funding of the court service, but a new board has been established to provide leadership for Her Majesty's Court Service whose members include three judges and a representative of the Ministry of Justice. The aims of the Court Service will be agreed by the Lord Chancellor and the Lord Chief Justice.

A Lord Chancellor can now sit either in the House of Commons or the House of Lords. Opponents of a Ministry of Justice argued that the political pressure a Minister in the House of Commons would be under could endanger the independence of the

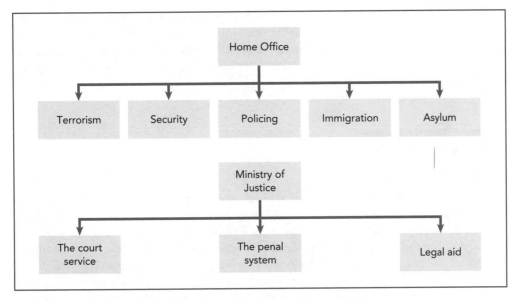

Figure 14.1 Home Office and Ministry of Justice responsibilities

Ess. Cases
p. 193

judiciary, which should be completely free of political involvement. This fear seems to be somewhat over-cautious, given that the vast majority of the work performed by a Ministry of Justice (like that carried out by the Ministry for Constitutional Affairs before) has nothing to do with matters of judicial service. As Professor Brazier (1998) points out, the earlier arrangements, with a powerful Lord Chancellor, did not avoid the danger of political decisions being made in relation to judges, since the Lord Chancellor was both head of the judiciary and a member of the Government. If there is a choice to be made between political decisions based on pressure from Government, or political decisions based on pressure from Parliament, the latter would seem to be the more attractive option. In any case, the risks have been reduced with the creation of an independent Judicial Appointments Commission responsible for the selection, promotion and disciplining of judges (see pp. 162–4).

There is also a small Law Officers' Department. The Law Officers are the Attorney General and the Solicitor General, who are both Ministers, though not members of the Cabinet. The Attorney General is the Government's main legal adviser and advised the Government on the legality of going to war against Iraq, which the Government initially refused to publish. He or she is responsible for major domestic and international litigation involving the Government. Other functions of the post include appealing against lenient sentences and bringing contempt proceedings when media coverage risks jeopardising a fair trial. As regards the prosecution process, the consent of the Attorney General is required for certain categories of prosecution (see p. 432), he or she grants immunities from prosecution and terminates prosecutions where appropriate, through a process known as *nolle prosequi*. The Director of Public Prosecutions answers to the Attorney General in relation to the running of the Crown Prosecution Service.

The Solicitor General used to carry out such functions as the Attorney General delegated to that office. Following the Law Officers Act 1997, the Law Officers can agree a general division of labour between them, as the Act specifically empowers the Solicitor General to perform all the functions of the Attorney General. Thus, formal authorisation for any delegation is no longer required.

TOPICAL ISSUE

The Attorney General

At the moment the Attorney General is chief government legal adviser, government minister and superintendent of the prosecuting authorities. Due to the breadth of the Attorney General's role and the fundamental violations of the principle of the separation of powers (discussed on p. 3), there has been suspicion of political interference in his or her decisions, even where there has not actually been any. The Attorney General's powers in relation to prosecutions have proved particularly controversial. At the time of the police investigation as to whether politicians had put forward individuals for peerages in return for financial payments (known as the 'cash-for-peerages' investigation), the Attorney General was under statute the person who would make the final decision as to whether to prosecute the politicians. This looked very uncomfortable when he was himself closely linked to those politicians. Although the Attorney General of the day, Lord Goldsmith, stated that as he could not delegate his statutory responsibility to make this decision to someone else he would take and publish independent legal advice on the subject, there remained the risk that the decision looked political rather than legal. In 2007, the Attorney General made a controversial decision that no prosecution should be brought against BAE Systems following a police investigation over the possible payment of huge bribes to a member of the Saudi Royal family, in order to be awarded a valuable contract for the supply of weapons.

Ess. Cases
p. 194 → The Government issued a Green Paper, *The Governance of Britain: A Consultation on the Role of the Attorney General* (2007). This was followed in 2008 by a White Paper looking at ways to improve the current constitution: *The Governance of Britain: Constitutional Renewal (2008)* along with a Draft Constitutional Renewal Bill. The White Paper considered possible reforms to the role of the Attorney General in order to enhance public trust and confidence. It suggested that the person holding this office could remain the Government's chief legal adviser, but changes could be made to their role with regard to prosecutions. The Attorney General would lose the power to give directions on the prosecution of individual criminal cases, including the power to prevent cases going ahead (the *nolle prosequi* power). These powers would be handed over to the directors of the different prosecuting authorities – the Crown Prosecution Service, Serious Fraud Office and Revenue and Customs Prosecution Office. The Attorney General would only retain a power to give directions in individual cases where they involved national security. The consent of the Attorney General to begin prosecutions would only be required where there was a particularly powerful public interest argument involved, such as in official secrets or war crimes cases.

The consultation paper suggested that 'both in perception and reality, it would improve the independence and public confidence in the impartial nature and authority of the provision of legal advice if it were not the responsibility of someone in political life'. However, the White Paper concluded that the Attorney General should continue to operate as the Government's legal adviser and remain as a Government Minister within Parliament.

Ultimately, the Government has decided to pursue more limited reforms, with the Attorney General simply required to issue a protocol making it clear that he or she will not be consulted in criminal cases concerning an MP or peer or where there is a personal or professional conflict of interest.

14

Answering questions

1 **To what extent has the creation of a Ministry of Justice improved the administration of justice?**

Your answer could start by briefly describing what a Ministry of Justice is, and pointing out that most other countries have one. You could discuss some of the criticisms of the previous arrangements, with legal responsibilities being divided first between the Home Office and the Lord Chancellor's Department and then the Home Office and the Department for Constitutional Affairs. The new Ministry of Justice includes a large number of agencies including Her Majesty's Prison Service and the Probation Service, the Youth Justice Board, the Parole Board, Her Majesty's Inspectorates of Prison and Probation, the Sentencing Guidelines Council, the Sentencing Advisory Panel, the Law Commission, Her Majesty's Courts Service, the Tribunals Service, the Legal Services Commission and the Judicial Appointments Commission. You could consider the criticism of the existing arrangements, in particular the potential threat to the independence of the judiciary.

It is too early to evaluate the improvements to the administration of justice flowing from the creation of this Ministry, but its creation has brought together various aspects of the administration of justice and provides a single minister to report to Parliament. Your conclusion should state, drawing on the points you have made, whether you think this reform was justified.

2 **Has the creation of the Ministry of Justice facilitated or – as alleged by some members of the judiciary – threatened the independence of the judiciary?**

You would need to start by setting out what the Ministry of Justice is and explaining the previous administrative arrangements and bodies. The alleged threat to judicial independence has been raised because the Ministry of Justice administers both the courts *and* the prisons and there is therefore a perceived pressure to impose inappropriate sentences (p. 292). You could argue that judicial independence is protected by:

- the reduced role of the Lord Chancellor (refer back to Chapter 10);
- the creation of the Judicial Appointments Commission (see p. 162); and
- s. 3 of the Constitutional Reform Act 2005, which 'guarantees' judicial independence (discussed in Chapter 10).

Summary of Chapter 14: Administration of justice

In 2003 the Government commenced a radical reform of the administration of the English legal system. The Lord Chancellor's Department was abolished and replaced by a Ministry for Constitutional Affairs. The office of Lord Chancellor was reformed so that it respects the principle of the separation of powers. In 2006 the Home Secretary stated that the Home Office was 'not fit for purpose' and in 2007 the Ministry of Justice was established, with legal work redistributed between that department and the Home Office. There is also a small Law Officers' Department. The Law Officers are the Attorney General and the Solicitor General, who are both Ministers, though not members of the Cabinet.

Reading list

Brazier, R. (1998) *Constitutional Reform*, Oxford: Oxford University Press.

Drewry, G. (1987) 'The debate about a Ministry of Justice – A Joad's Eye View', *Public Law* 502.

Jackson, R.M. (1989) *The Machinery of Justice in England*, Cambridge: Cambridge University Press.

Reading on the Internet

www   The consultation paper *The Governance of Britain: A Consultation on the Role of the Attorney General* (2007) is available at:

> http://www.attorneygeneral.gov.uk/attachments/Consultation%20on%20the%20Role%20of%20the%20AGO.pdf

The website for the Ministry of Justice is at:

> http://www.justice.gov.uk

The website of the Department for Constitutional Affairs has been retained for archive purposes and can be found at:

> http://www.dca.gov.uk

The Home Office website is at:

> http://www.homeoffice.gov.uk

Visit www.mylawchamber.co.uk/ElliottELS to access multiple-choice questions, flashcards and practice exam questions to test yourself on this chapter.

HUMAN RIGHTS

In democratic societies, it is usually felt that there are certain basic rights – often called civil liberties, civil rights or human rights – which should be available to everyone. Exactly what these rights are varies in different legal systems, but they generally include such freedoms as the right to say, think and believe what you like (freedom of expression, thought and conscience); to form groups with others, such as trade unions and pressure groups (freedom of assembly); to protest peacefully; and to be imprisoned or otherwise punished only for breaking the law and after a fair trial. Part of the reason why these freedoms are considered important is the nature of democracy: citizens can only make the kind of free choice of government required by a democratic system if there is open discussion and debate.

In this Part we consider the place of human rights in England and Wales.

15

Introduction to human rights

This chapter discusses:

- the European Convention on Human Rights;
- the Human Rights Act 1998;
- recent developments in human rights law; and
- whether the UK needs a Bill of Rights.

Introduction

Most democratic countries have a written Bill of Rights, which lays down the rights which, by law, can be enjoyed by citizens of that country. These rights have to be respected by the courts, Parliament, the police and private citizens, unless the Bill of Rights allows otherwise (for example, some rights may be suspended in times of war or when it is necessary in the interests of national security). Such a Bill may form part of a written constitution or sit alongside such a constitution: either way, it will usually have a status which is superior to that of ordinary law, in that it can only be changed by a special procedure. This will vary from country to country, but might involve holding a referendum, or securing a larger than usual majority in Parliament. Legislation which is protected in this way is said to be entrenched.

Britain is unusual among democratic countries in having, to date, neither a Bill of Rights nor a written constitution. In this country, our rights and freedoms are traditionally considered to be protected by a presumption that we are free to do whatever is not specifically forbidden by either legislation or the common law. Anyone prevented by the state from doing something which they are legally entitled to do should have a remedy against the state – an example is that a person wrongly detained in a police station can sue for false imprisonment. Citizens' rights in the UK were described as residual, in that they consisted of what was left after taking into account the lawful limitations.

The system of residual freedoms had shown itself to be seriously flawed over the past couple of decades. The idea that a person is free to do anything not specifically prohibited by law also applies to the state, so that the Government may violate individual freedom even though it is not formally empowered to do so, on the ground that it is doing nothing which is prohibited. An example of this is **Malone v Metropolitan Police Commissioner** (1979). Mr Malone's telephone had been tapped, and he was able to prove that this was done without any lawful authority – that is, there was no law which allowed the Government or its agencies to tap his phone. But equally, there was no law which forbade them to do so as English law gives no general right to privacy. Therefore, Mr Malone's action failed.

Ess. Cases p. 202 → A significant change in the British position was made by the Human Rights Act 1998. This came into force in October 2000. The Act makes the European Convention on Human Rights (ECHR) part of the law of the UK. While the Convention had been part of the international law that is recognised by the UK, it had never been integrated as part of our domestic law. While the Human Rights Act represents a major shift in approach to civil liberties it still fails to give the UK a Bill of Rights, because the Act is not entrenched and can be repealed by a future Act of Parliament. How it could be repealed by an Act is open to debate. Lord Justice Laws stated in **Thoburn v Sunderland City Council** (2002) that the Human Rights Act was a constitutional Act which could only be repealed by express provisions of an Act of Parliament (and not by implication). This could be described as a 'soft' form of entrenchment.

The European Convention on Human Rights

The ECHR was drawn up by the Council of Europe, which was established after the Second World War when countries tried to unite to prevent such horrors ever happening again. The Council now has 47 members, including the 27 members of the EU. Signed in Rome in 1950, the Convention was ratified by the UK in 1951 and became binding on those states which had ratified it in 1953.

A special court, known as the European Court of Human Rights, was set up to deal with claims concerning breaches of the ECHR. The Court sits in Strasbourg, and handles claims made by one state against another and by individuals against a state. It only hears individual claims where the relevant state has accepted the right of individuals to bring such cases; not all states accept this right of individual petition, though the UK Government agreed to this in 1966.

The fact that a state has ratified the Convention does not mean it has to incorporate Convention provisions into its domestic law: each state can choose whether or not to do this, and about half have done so. In these cases, citizens can claim their rights under the Convention through domestic courts and the national parliaments cannot usually legislate in conflict with the Convention.

The UK refused for many years to incorporate the Convention and so it was not recognised by the national courts as part of English law. UK citizens who believed that their rights under the Convention had been breached could not bring their claim through the normal domestic courts, but had to take their case to the European Court of Human Rights; if they succeeded there, the UK Government was expected to amend whatever aspect of domestic law caused the problem. But such litigation is slow and expensive and the eventual remedies often inadequate. As with any other international treaty, British courts could take the Convention into account when interpreting UK legislation, and presume that Parliament did not intend to legislate inconsistently with it. Where a statute was ambiguous, they could use the Convention as a guide to its correct interpretation; an example of this is provided by **Waddington** *v* **Miah** (1974), where the House of Lords referred to Art. 7 of the Convention to support its view that s. 34 of the Immigration Act 1971 could not be interpreted as having retrospective effect. Where the words of a statute were clear, domestic courts have to apply them, even if they obviously conflict with the Convention. This position has changed radically with the passing of the Human Rights Act 1998 incorporating the Convention into domestic law.

The scope of the Convention

The rights protected by the ECHR include the right to life (Art. 2); freedom from torture, inhuman or degrading treatment (Art. 3); freedom from slavery or forced labour (Art. 4); the right to liberty and security of the person (Art. 5); the right to a fair trial (Art. 6); the prohibition of retrospective criminal laws (Art. 7); the right to respect

15

Introduction to human rights

for a person's private and family life, home and correspondence (Art. 8); freedom of thought, conscience and religion (Art. 9); freedom of expression (Art. 10); freedom of peaceful assembly and association, including the right to join a trade union (Art. 11); and the right to marry and have a family (Art. 12).

The Convention provides that people should be able to enjoy these rights without discrimination (Art. 14). Some additions, known as Protocols, have been made to the ECHR since it was first drawn up. The First Protocol was written in 1952 and provides three new rights: the right to peaceful enjoyment of one's possessions (Art. 1); the right to education (Art. 2); and the right to take part in free elections by secret ballot (Art. 3). The other important Protocol is the fourth, concluded in 1963, which guarantees freedom of movement within a state and freedom to leave any country; it precludes a country from expelling or refusing to admit its own nationals. This Protocol has not been ratified by the UK and, in the past, some citizens from Northern Ireland have been excluded from mainland Britain.

Many of the rights provided under the Convention contain specific restrictions and exemptions. For example, Art. 10 allows restrictions on freedom of expression where they are:

> necessary in a democratic society, in the interests of national security, territorial integrity or public safety, for the prevention of disorder or crime, for the protection of health or morals, for the protection of the reputation or rights of others, for preventing the disclosure of information received in confidence, or for maintaining the authority and impartiality of the judiciary.

Member states may decline to carry out most of their obligations under the Convention in time of war or some other national emergency if this is strictly required by the situation. The UK has done so in respect of Northern Ireland. In such cases a state must inform the Secretary-General of the Council of Europe with its reasons (Art. 15). There are some rights, most importantly freedom from torture, inhuman or degrading treatment, from which states are never permitted to derogate. The Convention does not cover the whole field of human rights. It omits general economic and social rights, such as a right to housing, a minimum income and free health care, which some would argue should be guaranteed in a civilised society. This is because there is less agreement between different countries on such issues than there is on the traditional freedoms currently protected by the ECHR.

The Human Rights Act 1998

The Human Rights Act 1998 incorporated the ECHR (and its first protocol) into domestic law. The effect of this is to strengthen the protection of individual rights by UK courts and provide improved remedies where these are violated. The Convention is now applicable directly in the UK courts (s. 7), so that it is no longer necessary to go all the way to Strasbourg, though it is still possible. Under s. 2 of the Human Rights Act, the domestic judiciary 'must take into account' any relevant Strasbourg jurisprudence,

Table 15.1 The European Convention on Human Rights

Article	Rights and freedoms
2	The right to life
3	Freedom from torture or inhuman or degrading treatment
4	Freedom from slavery and forced labour
5	The right to liberty and security of the person
6	The right to a fair trial
7	Protection from the criminal law having retrospective effect
8	The right to respect of one's private and family life
9	Freedom of thought, conscience and religion
10	Freedom of expression
11	Freedom of assembly and association
12	The right to marry
14	The right to enjoy Convention rights without discrimination on the grounds of sex, race, colour, language, religion, political or other opinion, national or social origin, association with a national minority, property, birth or other status.
The First Protocol	
1	The right to peaceful enjoyment of one's possessions
2	The right to education
3	The right to free elections

15

Introduction to human rights

although they are not bound by it. This is quite a weak obligation, since it is open to the judiciary to consider but disapply a particular decision.

The UK courts are required to interpret all legislation in a way which is compatible with Convention rights 'so far as it is possible to do so' (s. 3). This goes much further than the previous position of allowing ambiguities to be interpreted in favour of the Convention.

It is unlawful for public authorities to act in a way which is incompatible with Convention rights (s. 6). A public authority includes central and local government, the police and the NHS. In addition, a private body can be regarded as a public authority for the purposes of the Human Rights Act if, under s. 6(3)(b), it performs 'functions of a public nature'. Such a body is described as a hybrid public authority. The obligation on such hybrid bodies to observe Convention rights attaches only to functions which are of a public nature; other work that it carries out will not be affected.

There has been some debate as to whether the Act allows individual citizens to enforce Convention rights in proceedings against other individuals (known as 'horizontal effect'). Section 6 states that public authorities cannot breach Convention rights. It is therefore clear from s. 6 that citizens can rely on their Convention rights against the state (known as 'vertical effect'). The reference primarily to 'public authorities' would suggest that individual citizens can breach the Convention with impunity. But the courts are public authorities. It is therefore arguable that if a civil court failed to apply a Convention right in legal proceedings between private parties it would be in breach of the Human Rights Act. Academic opinion on this issue has been sharply divided.

The application of s. 6(3)(b) of the Human Rights Act was considered by the House of Lords in **YL v Birmingham City Council** (2007). It did not lay down a single test to be applied to determine this issue, but said that the question had to be decided on a case-by-case basis, though it identified the sort of factors that would be taken into account. The case involved an appeal of an 84-year-old lady suffering from dementia. Under the National Assistance Act 1948, Birmingham City Council had a statutory obligation to make residential arrangements for old people in need of care. She had been placed by the council in a private care home operated by a company called Southern Cross Healthcare Ltd. Unfortunately, the relationship between some of the old lady's family and the care home's management deteriorated, and Southern Cross gave notice that she would have to leave the home. The House of Lords had to decide whether Southern Cross was required to respect Convention rights when exercising its powers in relation to the old lady. The majority of the Law Lords concluded that it was not. It noted that in determining the scope of s. 6 it should reflect the extent of the UK Government's liabilities before the European Court of Human Rights, as the section aimed to allow UK citizens remedies in the UK to avoid the need for them to go to Strasbourg to get a remedy. Section 6 is therefore designed to mirror the scope of state responsibility at Strasbourg. The fact that public funding was used to pay Southern Cross was not decisive, as on the facts this was equivalent to a payment for services. The greater the powers given to the private body the more likely that it is exercising a public function. For example, a private prison has the power to detain individuals and is therefore exercising a public function, whereas Southern Cross had no such power. The House concluded that Southern Cross was not carrying out a public function and their state-funded residents could not therefore benefit from Convention rights. The House of Lords observed that a finding to the contrary would have created rights which sat uneasily with the ordinary private law freedom of contract enjoyed in the private sector.

> A private body can be regarded as a public authority for the purposes of the Human Rights Act 1998 under s. 6(3)(b), if it performs functions of a public nature and this will be determined on a case-by-case basis.

The courts appear to have accepted that the Convention has a limited form of horizontal effect. Thus, in **Douglas v Hello!** (2001) photographs of the marriage of the Hollywood celebrities Michael Douglas and Catherine Zeta-Jones had been published without their authority by the popular magazine *Hello!* The legal proceedings were between private parties, but all the judges treated the Convention as relevant to the case because of the Human Rights Act 1998.

In **R (on the application of Al-Skeini) v Secretary of State for Defence** (2007) the House of Lords considered whether Iraqi civilians arrested and detained by British soldiers had the protection of the 1998 Act. It concluded that the Act has a potentially wide geographical application, beyond the physical boundaries of the United Kingdom itself, to places where the UK has effective control.

Under s. 19 Government Ministers have to publish a written statement as to whether or not a Bill is compatible with the Convention. The House of Lords Parliamentary Committee has issued a report *Relations Between the Executive, the Judiciary and Parliament* (2007) in which it has suggested that there have been cases where Ministers had adopted a 'far too optimistic view' about the compatibility of provisions in Bills with the European Convention. It recommended that in cases of doubt about compatibility, Ministers should seek the involvement of the Law Officers (discussed on p. 293) to ensure that the Bill is compatible.

While the Human Rights Act represents an important advance for civil liberties in the UK, there are still significant limitations on the impact that the Act will have. In particular, legislation which is incompatible with the Convention is still valid; judges do not have the power to strike down offending statutes as unconstitutional. Thus, the principle of parliamentary sovereignty remains intact. If a higher court does find that legislation is incompatible with the Convention, then it can choose to make a declaration to this effect (Art. 4) and a Minister can subsequently amend the offending legislation by a fast-track procedure which avoids the full parliamentary process. An early example of a declaration of incompatibility is provided by the case of **Wilson** *v* **First County Trust** (2003) where the House of Lords declared that a provision of the Consumer Credit Act 1974 violated the Convention.

The judiciary has a lot of power in determining the impact and success of the Human Rights Act 1998. The Convention rights are very loosely drafted and through their interpretation the judges could easily dilute them and render them ineffective. The Government is clearly aware of the central role of the judges in the success or failure of the Act. It spent £4.5 million training the judges, magistrates and tribunal chairpersons ready for the implementation of the Act. The Lord Chancellor wrote directly to all the judges pointing out their vital role. The letter stated:

> With proper training and planning, I am confident that all courts and tribunals will be able to give full effect to the rights recognised by the Convention and to make their distinctive contribution to fostering a culture of awareness of, and respect for, human rights throughout the whole of society. I hope you look forward to playing your part in making those rights real, as do I.

The Human Rights Act 1998 appears to have been successfully implemented and has engendered a stronger human rights culture in the courts. Research has been carried out by Raine and Walker (2002) into the impact of the Act in its first 18 months. Their research points to 'the comparative success with which the courts managed the implementation process and the ways in which they have adapted their practices'. Prior to the Act's implementation, there had been fears that the courts would be overrun with speculative human rights claims. This has not in fact happened. The report states that:

> . . . the general picture from the research was one of relatively limited impact of the Human Rights Act in terms of challenges and additional workload for the courts, although it had invoked a number of significant and specific policy and practice changes.

The Government has issued a statistical analysis of the first effects of the Human Rights Act 1998 on the work of the civil courts. In the last three months of the year 2000, 76

15

Introduction to human rights

claims for damages were issued in the civil courts relying wholly on the Human Rights Act 1998, out of a total of 467,000 claims.

One of the first cases to seek to rely on the Human Rights Act 1998 was **Procurator Fiscal *v* Brown** (2000), which started in the Scottish courts. Under the road traffic legislation, Ms Brown had been required to inform the police of the identity of the person driving her car on the evening she was questioned. It would have been a criminal offence for her not to have answered the question. She admitted that she had been driving her car and was prosecuted for drink-driving. She claimed at her trial that her confession should not be admissible as evidence as she had been forced to incriminate herself in breach of her right to a fair trial in Art. 6 of the European Convention. The High Court in Scotland accepted this argument. This decision was highly controversial as it threatened the credibility of the Human Rights Act. It appeared to justify fears that the Act would create a large amount of litigation and give people rights that went against the general interests of society. However, on appeal the Privy Council ruled that the road traffic legislation did not breach the European Convention and the evidence was admissible at her trial. Reviewing the case law of the European Court of Human Rights, Lord Bingham concluded:

> The jurisprudence of the European Court very clearly established that while the overall fairness of a criminal trial cannot be compromised, the constituent rights comprised, whether expressly or implicitly, within Art. 6 [such as freedom from self-incrimination] are not themselves absolute.

The privilege against self-incrimination was not absolute, but had to be balanced against the wider interests of the community, in particular public safety. The Privy Council found that the obligation to state who was driving the vehicle represented a proportionate response to the serious social problem of death and injury on the roads. The case was distinguished from **Saunders *v* UK** (1997) (discussed at p. 308) where the UK legislation had allowed prolonged questioning, as opposed to the answering of a single question in this case. The decision shows that the courts will not tolerate attempts to misuse provisions of the Convention in ways which are contrary to the public interest.

Retrospective effect?

The Human Rights Act 1998 was brought into force in October 2000. In **R *v* Lambert** (2001) the House of Lords ruled that the Act did not have retrospective effect.

KEY CASE

In **Wilson *v* Secretary of State for Trade and Industry** (2003) the House of Lords took a slightly more flexible view as to whether the Human Rights Act could have retrospective effect. It cited with approval a statement of Staughton LJ in **Secretary of State for Social Security *v* Tunnicliffe** (1991) on the presumption that Acts of Parliament will not have retrospective effect:

Provisions of the Human Rights Act 1998 can have retrospective effect if it would not be unfair to the parties in a particular case.

> [T]he true principle is that Parliament is presumed not to have intended to alter the law applicable to past events and transactions in a manner which is unfair to those concerned in them, unless a contrary intention appears. It is not simply a question of classifying an enactment as retrospective or not retrospective. Rather it may well be a matter of degree – the greater the unfairness, the more it is to be expected that Parliament will make it clear if that is intended.

> Thus, some of the provisions of the Human Rights Act 1998 could have retrospective effect if that would not be unfair to the parties in a particular case.

Commission for Equality and Human Rights

When preparing the Human Rights Act, the Labour Government considered establishing a Human Rights Commission, but then rejected this idea. However, in 2004, the Government announced that it intended to establish a Commission for Equality and Human Rights. A consultation paper, *Fairness for All: a New Commission for Equality and Human Rights*, was published in 2004 by the Department for Trade and Industry. Following this consultation process, the Equality Act 2006 was passed by Parliament which contained provisions for the creation of the new Commission. It has replaced the Commission for Racial Equality, the Disability Rights Commission and the Equal Opportunities Commission, which had fought against racism, disability discrimination and sexism. The Commission is responsible for promoting both human rights and equality of opportunity. It seeks to prevent a wider range of discriminatory behaviour, including discrimination on the grounds of religion, age and sexual orientation. The new body was launched in October 2007 and will be fully operative in 2009. Its functions include:

- providing advice and guidance to people wishing to assert their rights;
- conducting inquiries;
- bringing legal proceedings;
- monitoring the operation of the ECHR in domestic law;
- scrutinising new legislation; and
- publishing regular reports on the state of the nation.

Advantages of incorporation

Improved access

Bringing a case to Strasbourg can take up to six years and can be very expensive. Through incorporation, UK citizens are now able to enforce their rights under the Convention directly before the domestic courts (though applications to Strasbourg are still possible as a last resort).

Remedies

The remedies available from the European Court of Human Rights are inadequate. Also, the long delays mean that the remedies awarded can be too late to be effective. The national courts are able to provide quicker and more effective remedies.

Tried and tested

The ECHR has already been tried and tested over the last 30 years. The UK courts have developed some knowledge of its provisions as their decisions have been challenged in Strasbourg. The Privy Council has also developed case law in relation to similar provisions to be found in the written constitutions of Commonwealth countries, which were often drafted with the Convention in mind. It is therefore likely to prove easier to incorporate the Convention into domestic law than a completely new Bill of Rights.

Avoid conflict between domestic and international law

Problems with the current arrangements were highlighted by recent litigation. In **R v Saunders** (1996) evidence obtained by Government inspectors under s. 177 of the Financial Services Act 1986 was used against Saunders in criminal proceedings for insider dealing. The English courts ruled that in English law this evidence was admissible at a criminal trial. The court in Strasbourg ruled that this evidence had been obtained by an unfair procedure and should have been excluded from the trial – **Saunders v UK** (1997). Evidence obtained in the same way was accepted by the trial court in **R v Morrissey** and **R v Staines** (1997). The Court of Appeal stated that it was 'an unsatisfactory position' that it was obliged to follow the domestic decision, which had held Saunders's evidence was admissible, despite the fact that the European Court had subsequently ruled that this breached the Convention. Now, under ss. 2 and 3 of the Human Rights Act 1998 a court would be able to take into account the Strasbourg jurisprudence and interpret relevant legislation in a way which is compatible with Convention rights 'so far as it is possible to do so'.

Encouraging conformity

While there are many instances of UK Governments changing the law as a result of losing cases in the European Court of Human Rights, they are not always keen to do so. In **Brogan v United Kingdom** (1988) the provisions of the Prevention of Terrorism (Temporary Provisions) Act 1984, allowing detention of suspects for up to seven days without judicial authority, were found to violate Art. 5, protecting freedom of the person. The Government responded by declaring that the power was necessary on security grounds and by depositing at Strasbourg a limited derogation under Art. 15 from the Convention to the extent that the legislation violated Art. 5.

In **Abdulaziz v United Kingdom** (1985) the Government technically complied with the European Court of Human Rights' decision, but in such a way as to decrease rather than increase rights. The case alleged that British immigration rules discriminated against women, because men permanently settled in the UK were allowed to bring their wives and fiancées to live with them here, but women in the same position could not bring their husbands and fiancés into the country. The European Court agreed, but the Government was determined not to increase immigration rights. Instead of allowing husbands and fiancés to settle here, they removed the right of wives and fiancées to do so, thereby ending the sexual discrimination but making the immigration laws even more restrictive.

Incorporation has reduced the problem of bringing domestic law into line with the ECHR. The courts are contributing to this process in every case where a conflict arises between the Convention and domestic law. But tensions can still arise between the European Court of Human Rights and the British Government, and on occasion the British Government is still prepared to ignore a decision of the European Court. In 2008 two men, Faisal Al-Saadoon and Khalaf Mufdhi were being held prisoner by UK soldiers in Iraq accused of being responsible for the deaths of two British soldiers. The UK Government wished to transfer these men to the Iraqi Government as part of the process of handing back power in Iraq in accordance with a United Nations' mandate. The two prisoners objected to the handover, claiming that the Iraqi Government tortured prisoners and if they were convicted they faced the death penalty. They took their case to the European Court of Human Rights and before the Court had time to give a final judgment it issued an injunction ordering the UK Government not to hand over the men until the Court had heard the case. The UK Government was concerned that if it continued to detain the men after 1 January 2009 it would be in breach of the UN mandate. It therefore went ahead and handed over the men to the Iraqi Government in breach of the European Court's injunction.

International image

It is not good for the UK's image abroad frequently to be found in error by a 'foreign' court, as it has been many times.

Clarity and accessibility

The law on civil rights has been complex and disorderly. For example, there has been no clear definition of the right to freedom of expression, only a collection of statutes and cases which state when and how such a freedom can be restricted. The ECHR provides a comprehensive and easily accessible statement of rights and freedoms enforceable in the UK.

Education

The ECHR sets out for citizens, Government and the judiciary the basic rights and freedoms we are all entitled to expect. This should lead to better awareness by citizens of their legal rights, and to legislation and judicial decisions which take those rights as their starting point, rather than just one of many things to be considered.

Disadvantages of incorporation

Judicial power

The Government has been unhappy with some of the decisions handed down by the judges relying on the Human Rights Act, which undermine its national policies. For example, the High Court ruled that the Government had breached the human rights of some Afghan nationals who had hijacked an aircraft in order to escape to the UK. The High Court held that the Home Secretary had behaved unlawfully when he had denied the applicants leave to enter the UK after they had already successfully claimed before the courts that it would be in breach of their human rights to return them to Afghanistan. Instead, the Home Secretary had sought to delay granting the men leave to enter so that the rules could be changed and the men refused leave to enter. The High Court considered this to amount to an abuse of power. Following this case, the Prime Minister described the judgment as an 'abuse of common sense' and announced that he would consider restricting the rights granted in the Human Rights Act. The Prime Minister wrote to the Home Secretary stating: 'we will need to look again at whether primary legislation is needed to address the issue of court rulings which overrule the government in a way that is inconsistent with other EU countries' interpretation of the European Convention on Human Rights.' English judges would be required to balance individual rights with the security of the country. However, such a change would actually increase the powers of the European Court of Human Rights over the English courts. The Lord Chancellor has clarified that the UK will not repeal the Human Rights Act.

Legal status

Incorporation of the ECHR would have had more impact if it had been entrenched. Any legislation which did not comply with it would have been struck down by the courts, and the ECHR itself could only have been changed in domestic law by special procedures, such as a referendum or an increased parliamentary majority. The Human Rights Act 1998 does not give UK citizens a Bill of Rights.

Many experts believe it would be constitutionally impossible to make the ECHR an entrenched Bill of Rights. This is because the doctrine of parliamentary sovereignty provides that no sitting Parliament can bind a future one: in other words, every Parliament is free to unmake laws made by their predecessors. This means that a future Parliament could simply abolish a Bill of Rights and any arrangements for entrenchment could be legislated away.

Not everybody agrees that such entrenchment would be impossible. Many Commonwealth countries which have inherited ideas of parliamentary sovereignty from the UK have enacted entrenched Bills of Rights without any constitutional problems arising. Alternatively, the ECHR could have been partially entrenched so that it was treated in the same way as EU law is today.

As the Labour Government has decided not to entrench or partly entrench the ECHR into domestic law, so the legal protections provided by it are limited. Real weight would be given to the Convention both if it was entrenched and if a constitutional court were created.

Because the Convention is not entrenched into domestic law, the UK Government can derogate from it (which means they can obtain permission to breach a provision of the Convention with impunity). It has chosen to do this in order to be able to detain terrorist suspects without trial for indefinite periods under the Anti-Terrorism, Crime and Security Act 2001. To enable the above legislation to be passed, the Government obtained a derogation from Art. 5 of the European Convention which guarantees the right to liberty of the person. This piece of legislation followed the attacks on the US on 11 September 2001 and constitutes a significant violation of an individual's human rights. By January 2002, 11 individuals had been detained under these powers. Investigators from the European Committee for the Prevention of Torture and Degrading Treatment or Punishment visited the UK amid concerns over the treatment of these suspects. The Committee raised a number of concerns, including the fact that the detainees were being denied access to their family and lawyers for long periods of time.

Limited scope

The Convention is probably only enforceable against the state and not against private individuals. This is not the case, for example, in relation to the rights provided under the new Constitution in South Africa.

The ECHR is over 30 years old and, since its creation, new rights have become important – for example, the Convention makes limited provision for preventing racial discrimination and none at all for preventing discrimination on the basis of disability or sexual orientation. Some people feel that a UK Bill of Rights should be broader, including environmental, economic and social rights.

There is also the question of whether the same protection is appropriate for all parts of the UK. Northern Ireland may require special treatment given the intensity of religious and political animosity.

The Convention is proving to be totally ineffective in the face of international violations of human rights. UK citizens being held by the US in Camp X-ray on Guantanamo Bay in Cuba appear to have no effective human rights.

Drafting style

The ECHR follows the more general, looser European style of legislative drafting, in contrast to the more tightly worded legislation our courts are used to applying – though, as EU law has grown in importance, British courts are gaining more experience of this approach.

The administration

The European Court of Human Rights has the same number of judges as contracting states, which is currently 45. The court is divided into four Sections, there are Committees of three judges and Chambers of seven judges. There is also a Grand Chamber

Photo 15.1 European Court of Human Rights in Strasbourg
Source: Jupiter Unlimited

of 17 judges. Any contracting state or individual claiming to be a victim of a violation of the Convention by a contracting state may lodge an application directly with the court in Strasbourg. Each individual application is assigned to a Section and a judge, called a rapporteur, makes a preliminary examination of the case and decides whether it should be dealt with by a three-member Committee or by a Chamber. A Committee may decide, by unanimous vote, to declare an application inadmissible or strike it out. Cases are admissible only after the applicant has exhausted all available domestic remedies and makes the application no more than six months after the final national decision (Art. 26). The Committee will also reject as inadmissible any petition which is outside the scope of the Convention or manifestly ill-founded (Art. 27). Apart from those cases that are struck out by a Committee, all the other cases are heard by a Chamber. Chambers may at any time relinquish jurisdiction in favour of a Grand Chamber where a case raises a serious question of interpretation of the Convention or where there is a risk of departing from existing case law, unless one of the parties objects to this transfer.

Within three months of delivery of the judgment of a Chamber, any party may request that a case be referred to the Grand Chamber if it raises a serious question of interpretation or application or a serious issue of general importance. Such requests are examined by a Grand Chamber panel of five judges. If the panel accepts the request the decision of the Grand Chamber is final. As well as deciding whether a state is in breach of the Convention, the court can award compensation or other 'just satisfaction' of the complaint (Art. 50). Responsibility for supervising the execution of judgments lies with the Committee of Ministers of the Council of Europe.

Unfortunately, the European Court of Human Rights has become a victim of its own success – in 2008 it had a backlog of 100,000 cases. Russia has refused to sign a protocol which would have reformed some of its court procedures to speed up the way it handles the majority of its cases.

The European Court of Human Rights and the ECJ

The European Court of Human Rights in Strasbourg is often confused with the European Court of Justice (ECJ) in Luxembourg, but these are quite separate institutions, as are the Commission of Human Rights and the Commission of the European Community. The phrase 'taking your case to Europe' tends to be used broadly, but the process and grounds for bringing an action to the ECJ are quite distinct from those for the European Court of Human Rights.

There are, however, growing links between the ECHR and European Union law. Article 164 of the Treaty of Rome provides that one of the functions of the ECJ is to ensure observance of the general principles of law contained in that treaty. In recent cases the ECJ has suggested that respect for human rights is one of these principles, and that for guidance in understanding the scope of this principle they can look to the Convention. For example in **P v S and Cornwall CC** (1996) P was dismissed from her employment because she was a transsexual. Her application to the UK courts for sex discrimination was rejected. When the case was heard by the ECJ the Court referred to the European Court of Human Rights' judgment in **Re Rees** (1986). It concluded that the European Equal Treatment Directive had been breached, as this directive encapsulated the fundamental principle of equality.

In addition, the preamble to the Single European Act 1986 pledges members to 'work together to promote democracy on the basis of the fundamental rights recognised in the Convention'. Similar commitments to respect for fundamental human rights are included in the Maastricht Treaty.

There have been moves recently towards the European Union acceding to the ECHR which would effectively make its provisions part of European law. With this in mind, the Council of Ministers requested an opinion from the ECJ to confirm whether or not the EU, as it now stands, could accede to the Convention. The ECJ concluded (**Re Accession of the Community to the European Human Rights Convention** (1996)) that the EU currently had no competence to accede to the ECHR and that therefore the EC Treaty would have to be amended in order for this to happen.

Today's debates

If one person extends their rights, it tends to be at the expense of another person's rights. For example, when a newspaper exercises its right to freedom of expression, this

Photo 15.2 Bus bombed in London on 7 July 2005
Source: Eddie Mulholland/Rex Features

will frequently be to the detriment of another person's right to privacy. Thus careful controls need to be in place to make sure that one person or organisation does not extend their rights too far at the expense of another. This is particularly the case where a Government is seeking to extend its rights over its citizens. In recent years there has been particular concern that in its fight against terrorism the Government has not been respecting human rights. After the bombing of the public transport system in London in July 2005, Tony Blair stated that the 'rules of the game had changed' and outlined some of his ideas for amending the law in the UK to tackle this threat to our society. At the same time, civil liberties organisations are concerned that the Government might respond to these attacks in a way that amounted to a significant attack on an individual's human rights, while at the same time proving to be counter-productive in the fight against terrorism. In 2008, the Government was forced to drop its provision in the Counter-Terrorism Bill to allow the detention of suspected terrorists for 42 days without charge, but the judges will still be placed in a very sensitive position when interpreting this piece of legislation.

Immediately after the terrorist attacks a consultation paper was published, *Exclusion or Deportation from the UK on Non-conducive Grounds* (Home Office, 2005). The Government currently plans to broaden its powers to exclude and deport people who have 'fostered hatred' or 'advocated violence'. These orders could breach Art. 3 of the European Convention where a person is sent to a country which carries out torture. The Government hopes to avoid this problem by gaining assurances from the relevant countries that the deportees will not be subjected to torture on their return. However, civil liberties organisations have stated that these guarantees are worthless, as the relevant countries always lie by claiming that they do not carry out torture when in fact there is clear evidence that they do. The former Prime Minister, Tony Blair, said that if legal obstacles arose, he would, if necessary, legislate to amend the Human Rights Act.

Following the 11 September 2001 attacks on the United States, there was international concern about terrorism. This led the UK Government to pass the Anti-Terrorism, Crime and Security Act 2001, which allowed it to detain in prison suspected terrorists without trial. This was in breach of their right to freedom of movement which is guaranteed under Art. 5 of the European Convention. The UK Government therefore gained permission from the European Council to not comply with this article on the basis that there was a national emergency under Art. 15 (see p. 302).

ss. Cases p. 208

Under this legislation, nine foreign nationals were certified as suspected terrorists and detained without trial. The legality of the detention was challenged through the courts in **A and X and others v Secretary of State for the Home Department** (2004). Some of the applicants had been detained in a high security prison for three years, with no prospect of release or a trial. Because the case was so important, nine judges in the House of Lords heard the case instead of the usual five. The House held that the detentions were unlawful. It accepted that there was a national emergency justifying derogation under Art. 15, but the measures taken were not strictly required. Indefinite detention without trial was not strictly required because it was being imposed only on foreign nationals unable to leave Britain and not on foreign nationals who could leave for another country or on British nationals. The legislation also therefore discriminated against foreign nationals and so breached Art. 14 of the Convention.

As a result, the legislation was repealed and replaced by the Prevention of Terrorism Act 2005. This established control orders, which can potentially amount to house arrest – the first time we have seen this measure in the UK. The people who had been detained without trial were released and were allowed to return home, but they were placed under control orders (not amounting to house arrest). Up to 16 different restrictions can be placed on an individual who is subjected to a control order, such as the use of electronic tagging, surveillance, permission to search their premises, and a curfew. The order is usually made by the High Court following an application by the Home Secretary. It will be imposed where the individual is suspected of having been involved in terrorism-related activity. Breach of a control order without reasonable excuse is a criminal offence punishable by up to five years' imprisonment.

In **Secretary of State for the Home Department v JJ** (2007) control orders had been imposed on six suspects, under which they were electronically tagged, required to remain at home for 18 hours a day and have all visitors vetted by the Home Office. The House of Lords concluded that these orders amounted to a deprivation of liberty in breach of Art. 5 of the Convention. As a result of this decision, the Home Office has amended the restrictions imposed on the complainants under the control orders and they are currently subjected to a 16-hour curfew.

ss. Cases p. 214

In **Re MB** (2006), the High Court described control orders as an 'affront to justice'. MB is a British Muslim who was arrested when trying to leave the country in March 2005. The judge concluded that he could not quash the order due to the 'one-sided information' available to the court. However, he criticised the control orders for allowing a suspect's rights to be determined by 'executive decision-making, untrammelled by any prospect of effective judicial supervision'.

> To say that the [Prevention of Terrorism] Act does not give the respondent in the case . . . a 'fair hearing'. . . would be an understatement. The court would be failing in its duty under the Human Rights Act, a duty imposed upon the court by Parliament, if it did not say, loud and clear that the procedure under the Act whereby the court merely reviews the lawfulness of the Secretary of State's decision to make the order upon the basis of the material available to him at the early stage is conspicuously unfair.

An appeal against the High Court decision was subsequently successful before the Court of Appeal, which held that the control order procedures did not breach a right to a fair trial under Art. 6 of the Convention. MB appealed to the House of Lords, which held that a control order review hearing would only be fair if the Home Office disclosed the allegation against the individual along with enough information for the person to have sufficient knowledge of the case against them to be able to contest the allegation. The House sent the case back to the High Court to consider whether the control order was fair in the light of this ruling.

Eighteen control orders had been issued by 2006. In that year, Lord Carlile, the Government's independent terrorism watchdog, issued his first annual review of the Prevention of Terrorism Act 2005. He has access to secret security service papers and makes clear that current activities are 'sufficiently alarming for me to re-emphasise . . . the real and present danger of shocking terrorism acts involving suicide bombers'. He considers that further suicide bombings in the UK must be expected and that in his view such an ongoing threat means that 'as a last resort (only), in my view the control order system as operated currently in its non-derogating form is a justifiable and proportionate safety valve for the proper protection of civil society'.

Another very different area that has given rise to considerable debate is whether the European Convention protects the right to privacy of celebrities. While the courts are recognising that the Convention does provide a right to privacy they are anxious to balance this against the right to freedom of expression. In April 2005, the celebrities Victoria and David Beckham tried to prevent the publication by the *News of the World* of revelations by their former nanny about their private lives. The court allowed the newspaper to publish, pointing to the public interest in the publication of the stories, despite the fact that the story was merely trivial information primarily about the state of their marriage and Victoria's cosmetic surgery.

Article 9 of the Convention protects the right to freedom of religion and Protocol 1, Art. 2 protects the right to education. In **R (on the application of Shabina Begum) v Head Teacher and Governors of Denbigh School** (2006) a Muslim schoolgirl, Shabina Begum, wanted to wear a jilbab (a full-length gown) to school instead of the agreed school uniform, because of her religious beliefs. In 2002 she had arrived at school wearing a jilbab, but she was told to go home and change. Because of her continued refusal to wear a school uniform, she was excluded from school for two years. Pupils at the school were allowed to wear a shalwar kameez (trousers and tunic) but not a jilbab. The House of Lords concluded that the school's conduct did not amount to a breach of her right to freedom of religion or right to education. She had not attended school for two years, but her school was entitled to exclude her while she refused to comply with the uniform and she could have attended another local school where the jilbab was allowed.

Article 2 of the First Protocol to the Convention provides for a right to education. In **Ali _v_ Head Teacher and Governors of Lord Grey School** (2006) the House of Lords held a pupil's exclusion from school for eight months did not amount to a breach of his right to education. Following the exclusion, the 13-year-old pupil had access to educational facilities outside the school (including homework and tuition in a pupil referral unit) and failed to attend a meeting to re-integrate him back into the school. Schools can insist on compliance with rules: as long as alternative educational facilities are made available to excluded pupils, their Convention rights have not been breached. The House of Lords said that the right to education would only be breached in extreme cases, where virtually no education had been provided.

The Government is currently planning to introduce compulsory identity cards into the UK and the Identity Cards Act 2006 has been passed by Parliament. The justification for ID cards is that they would help to fight terrorism, organised crime, illegal immigration, identity fraud and benefit fraud. On the other hand, ID cards can be a dangerous tool for controlling a population and their absence in this country has to date been seen as a sign of our freedom.

A Bill of Rights for the UK?

It has been observed that the ECHR does not constitute a Bill of Rights for the UK because it has not been entrenched. Many people feel that while the Human Rights Act 1998 is a first step in the right direction, ultimately the UK needs a properly entrenched Bill of Rights to protect its citizens. Among developed Western countries, Israel and the UK are the only ones without such a Bill.

Arguments in favour of a Bill of Rights

Curbs on the executive

A Bill of Rights provides an important check on the enormous powers of the executive (the Government of the day and its agencies, such as the police, the army and Government departments). Constitutional writers of the nineteenth century, such as Dicey, made much of the role of Parliament as a watchdog over the executive, ensuring that oppressive legislation could not be passed. Since Dicey's time, the growth of a strong party system has fundamentally altered the nature of Parliament; in the vast majority of cases, a Government can expect its own members to obey party discipline, so that Government proposals will almost invariably be passed – during the 1980s, for example, only one Government Bill was defeated. Not only do those in opposition lack the numbers to prevent this, but the pressures of parliamentary time may even curtail a detailed scrutiny of proposed legislation. This can result in Governments being able to legislate against individual rights and freedoms almost at will.

The movement in favour of a Bill of Rights gained considerable support during the later years of the Thatcher regime, when the Government showed itself willing to compromise many important civil liberties. Many commentators were alarmed as they watched the banning of trade unions at Government Communications Headquarters (GCHQ), the attempts to ban the publication of *Spycatcher* (the memoirs of a retired security service agent) and the use of the Official Secrets Act 1911 to prosecute civil servants Sarah Tisdall and Clive Ponting who leaked official information the Government had wished to keep secret.

The fact that, given a decent majority in Parliament, Governments can make whatever law they like, means that they can simply legislate freedoms away, secure in the knowledge that the courts cannot refuse to apply their legislation, as they can in countries which have a Bill of Rights or written constitution. The Public Order Act 1986 and the Criminal Justice and Public Order Act 1994, for example, severely restrict rights of peaceful protest, of assembly and of movement, but English courts must apply this legislation nevertheless.

Supporters of a Bill of Rights claim it would curb executive powers, since the courts could simply refuse to apply laws which conflicted with it. This in turn would be a powerful incentive for a Government to avoid introducing such legislative provisions in the first place.

While the provision in s. 19 of the Human Rights Act 1998, requiring Ministers to state whether a Bill conforms with the 1998 Act, will discourage the executive in some circumstances from introducing legislation that breaches the ECHR, they are still able to do so.

Attitude of the judiciary

Even where the constitution does allow for judicial protection of civil rights, British judges have frequently proved themselves unequal to the task. As Griffith (1997) has famously pointed out, they show a tendency to view the public interest as the maintenance of established authority and traditional values. Though exceptions can always be found, the overall result has been that the maintenance of 'order' and the suppression of challenges to established authority – whether of trade unions or terrorists – have taken precedence over the kind of liberties a Bill of Rights might seek to protect. For example, in **R** v **Secretary of State for the Home Department, ex parte Brind** (1989), the judiciary upheld a broadcasting ban on members of a legitimate political party in Northern Ireland; in **Council of Civil Service Unions** v **Minister for the Civil Service** (1984), the ban on trade unions at GCHQ was accepted; and in **Kent** v **Metropolitan Police Commissioner** (1981) a blanket ban on protest marches through an area of London was allowed.

The numerous miscarriages of justice suggest there is little protection of the right to a fair trial, nor, given the treatment of some of those involved while in police custody, to freedom from torture and inhuman treatment. The wide powers of surveillance permitted under statute to the police and security services prove the right to privacy a fallacy.

The Human Rights Act 1998 only requires the UK courts to interpret legislation in a way which is compatible with Convention rights 'so far as it is possible to do so' (s. 3). If a judge decides that the Act breaches a Convention right, the Act prevails.

Conservative Party policy

The leader of the Conservative Party, David Cameron, has suggested that, if in power, the Conservative Party would consider repealing the Human Rights Act and replacing it with a British Bill of Rights. Mr Cameron has argued that the Human Rights Act is hindering the fight against crime and terrorism (for example, by preventing certain deportations). The Conservatives also oppose the influence of European human rights law over UK law, through the incorporation of the European Convention on Human Rights. The UK would return to its previous position of being a signatory to the Convention, giving individuals merely a right to take cases to the European Court of Human Rights. But individuals in UK courts would have to rely on the new Bill of Rights, rather than being able to rely on the European Convention. The new Bill of Rights would contain 'human rights with common sense'. The Lord Chancellor has criticised these proposals, arguing:

> If we remain in the Convention and have our own separate Bill of Rights, as David Cameron suggests, we will have to comply with the Convention's rights and Cameron's new rights. It's a recipe for confusion, not clarity.

It should be remembered that the Human Rights Act did not create any new rights, it simply enabled people in this country to access their basic rights and liberties in their own courts instead of having to go to Strasbourg.

Arguments against a Bill of Rights

Unnecessary

The previous Conservative Government was among those who asserted that civil liberties were already adequately protected in this country.

Increased power for the judiciary

Among those who oppose a Bill of Rights, mistrust of the judiciary, and constitutional objections to taking power from Parliament and giving it to judges, are perhaps the most frequent reasons given. There is no doubt that such a Bill would considerably increase judicial power. Unlike British statutes, the language of a Bill of Rights is typically open and imprecise, setting out broad principles rather than detailed provisions. This gives judges a wide discretion in interpretation – so wide that in the US, for example, the provisions against racial discrimination in the American Bill of Rights were once held to allow a form of apartheid, yet since 1954 such a system has been held to violate the Bill. Even within the last decade, the US Bill of Rights has been interpreted to allow discrimination against minorities. Thus, in the Supreme Court's decision in **Bowers v Hardwick** (1986), the constitutional right of privacy was effectively denied to homosexuals.

A Bill of Rights also calls upon judges to decide the relative importance of protected rights where two of them clash. Should, for example, the right to free expression of members of the British National Party override or give way to that of ethnic minorities to be free of racial harassment? Does a foetus have a right to life which overrides its mother's right to liberty and security of the person? There are no obvious right or wrong answers to questions like these and nor are there always obvious legal answers, even where there is a Bill of Rights. In many such cases the real problem is not what the law is, but what the law should be. Many people believe that is not a question which should be answered by judges who are not elected, but appointed from a narrow social elite by a secretive procedure. As Griffith (1997) has pointed out, these questions are political and political questions should, as far as possible, be answered by politicians elected to do so.

Supporters of such a Bill argue that the problems associated with greater judicial power could be dealt with by reforming judicial selection and drawing judges from a wider spread of the population. While this is clearly desirable in itself, it would not remove the fundamental objection that judges are not elected and nor, whatever the reforms, is it likely to avoid the fact that, by virtue of their education and their lifestyle, judges would be unrepresentative of the mass of the population. Those like Griffith, who oppose a Bill of Rights, argue that what is needed is not so much reform of the judiciary, but political reforms that would allow a democratically elected legislature genuinely to supervise the acts of the executive and to fetter the exercise of executive discretion. The protection of fundamental freedoms and rights should not be for the individual to establish in court, but for the legislature to safeguard as part of their job.

Inflexibility

Supporters of our current constitutional arrangements argue that, without a written constitution, our system can adapt over time, meeting new needs as they arise. They contend that a Bill of Rights would lack this flexibility. Two responses to this are that first, the open and imprecise language of a Bill of Rights allows flexibility, and secondly, the Bills can be changed when necessary: the arrangements for entrenchment will usually set down a special procedure that can be used to make amendments. The fact that these procedures may be long and difficult simply protects those rights originally laid down from rash or unpopular change; it does not set them in stone.

Too much flexibility

Ironically, it is also argued that the imprecise language typical of a Bill of Rights would lead to uncertainty about the law, leading to increased litigation with no clear objectives as to how general principles might emerge and policies be interpreted. This is clearly linked to the problem of mistrust of the judiciary.

Rights are not powers

A more fundamental problem is the idea that merely granting rights is not enough to secure individual freedom and empowerment. It is all very well to grant rights but, unless they are underpinned by economic and social provision, they may prove to be useless. Freedom of labour is effectively useless in times of high unemployment, when it becomes nothing more than the freedom to live in poverty. Freedom of movement fails to help disabled people who cannot use public transport or afford their own. Freedom of association offers little advantage if employers refuse to recognise trade unions, and liberty of the person means nothing for the battered wife or abused child who has neither the personal nor the practical resources to escape.

Where there are huge imbalances in power in society, giving equal rights to all may be of limited use because those who have the most power can use it to find a way round the rights of those who are less powerful. For example, recent compensation payments made to women sacked for being pregnant have led to speculation that as a result employers may simply become even less keen than before to employ women; cases on racial discrimination may have had similar effects on the employment prospects of members of ethnic minorities. While it should not be denied that this kind of provision helps people, it can be argued that in focusing on individual rights, rather than social duties, a Bill of Rights might detract attention from any real commitment to a just society. The point is not that a Bill of Rights is undesirable but that, on its own, it cannot make the kind of changes sought by its supporters.

There is also the question of whether the same Bill of Rights would be appropriate for all parts of the UK. Northern Ireland may require special treatment given the intensity of religious and political animosity.

Drafting style

The ECHR follows the more general, looser European style of legislative drafting, in contrast to the more tightly worded legislation our courts are used to applying – though, as European law has grown in importance, British courts are gaining more experience of this approach.

Ess. Cases
p. 218

TOPICAL ISSUE

The European Union and Human Rights

The European Union looks set to become more involved in the protection of human rights within Europe. Article 6 of the Lisbon Treaty came into force in 2009 and recognises the rights and freedoms set out in the European Charter of Fundamental Rights. Thus the treaty provides for the incorporation of the Charter into EU law. It also states that the fundamental rights guaranteed by the European Convention on Human Rights 'constitute general principles of the Union's law'.

The Charter lays down more extensive rights than those contained in the European Convention because, as well as containing civil and political rights, it lays down social and economic rights, such as freedom of information, freedom of the arts and sciences, and rights for children and the elderly. The Charter also extends some of the existing Convention rights to a more modern context. Thus it includes the established right to life and prohibition of torture, but also prohibits more modern problems of human trafficking, forced labour, human cloning and the sale of body parts. The rights in the Charter are divided into six sections:

- Dignity
- Freedoms
- Equality
- Solidarity
- Citizens' rights, and
- Justice.

In the section on 'justice' it explicitly requires criminal sentences to be proportionate to the offence and lays down a right not to be tried twice for the same offence (known as the double jeopardy rule). The section entitled 'solidarity' deals with workers' rights, including a right to consultation, protection from unjustified dismissals, fair and just working conditions, parental leave and, most importantly, the right to strike (a right which has never been recognised in this country).

The UK has obtained a legally binding protocol, which states that no court can rule that UK laws or practices are inconsistent with the principles laid down in the Charter and the Charter will not therefore create new legal rights in the UK.

The European Union is also considering establishing a Fundamental Rights Agency. There has been some criticism of this suggestion on the basis that the new agency might simply duplicate much of the work being done by existing bodies, particularly the European Court of Human Rights. However, with the current backlash to terrorist activity, greater involvement of the EU in the protection of human rights might be desirable.

Answering questions

1 **Critically evaluate the impact of the Human Rights Act 1998 upon the English legal system.**

A strong answer would explain the position prior to the introduction of the Convention into UK law by the Human Rights Act 1998, emphasising the lack of directly enforceable rights in the UK and the need to proceed to the ECtHR to enforce Convention rights. Changes in domestic law following a successful application to the ECtHR were not inevitable and there are several cases where such a change was not effected – see, for example, **Brogan** v **UK** and **Abdulaziz** v **UK**.

This historical discussion could be followed by a description of the principal rights contained in the European Convention. It should be mentioned that the Convention itself contains some restrictions on the rights it protects.

You could discuss how the Convention has been implemented into the UK by the Human Rights Act 1998, and in particular the requirement of a statement of compatibility when legislation is introduced and the means by which an individual can assert rights under the Convention in the national courts.

Finally, you could point out that the 1998 Act has increased the power of the judiciary to protect human rights, but the Act does not enjoy an enhanced status and so could, at least in theory, be repealed by Parliament.

2 **What has been the effect of s. 2 of the Human Rights Act 1998 on the exercise of precedent by UK judges?**

You need to begin by explaining what precedent is and what it means (refer back to Chapter 1). Then briefly explain the relevant background to the Human Rights Act 1998, in particular that although the European Convention on Human Rights was ratified by the UK in 1951, it did not become part of UK law until it was incorporated therein by the 1998 Act. The Act does, however, have the status of any other piece of domestic legislation in the sense that it is not entrenched.

You should set out the provisions of s. 2 and its effect. Sections 3 and 4 are also relevant (p. 303). You could also compare the obligation under s. 2 to s. 3 of the European Communities Act 1972, noting that the latter gives the judges less power. As judges are building up a familiarity with loosely drafted European legislation, it can be argued that they are adopting a more purposive approach to interpretation in general (see Chapter 3).

To conclude, you could say that, contrary to fears, the Human Rights Act has not led to an excess of speculative human rights claims and that it has succeeded in creating a stronger human rights culture in the courts (p. 305). However, judges are likely to encounter problems in deciding how to implement, for example, new terrorist legislation which restricts human rights (see the section entitled 'Today's debates' on p. 313).

3 **To what extent would a Bill of Rights provide additional protection of human rights in the United Kingdom?**

Whilst the Human Rights Act 1998 applies the European Convention on Human Rights in the UK, those provisions are not entrenched. A Bill of Rights would entrench human rights into national law and empower the courts to refuse to apply legislation inconsistent with the entrenched rights. It would thereby provide some additional protection against a strong executive with a large parliamentary majority. However, such a step would affect a significant shift of power from an elected Parliament to an unelected judiciary. Moreover, a Bill of Rights is usually expressed in wide terms that may not provide sufficient certainty, and give the judges too much discretion as to how to interpret it. Rights are meaningless without an effective means of enforcement, and a Bill of Rights without a pro-liberty judiciary would offer only nominal protection.

15

Introduction to human rights

Summary of Chapter 15: Introduction to human rights

Introduction
Most democratic countries have a written Bill of Rights. Britain is unusual among democratic countries in having, to date, neither a Bill of Rights nor a written constitution. In this country, our rights and freedoms are traditionally considered to be protected by a presumption that we are free to do whatever is not specifically forbidden either by legislation or by the common law. A significant change in the British position was made by the Human Rights Act 1998, which makes the European Convention on Human Rights (ECHR) part of the law of the UK.

The European Convention on Human Rights
The ECHR was drawn up by the Council of Europe, which was established after the Second World War. A special court, known as the European Court of Human Rights, was set up to deal with claims concerning breaches of the ECHR.

The Human Rights Act 1998
The Convention is now applicable directly in the UK courts under s. 7 of the Human Rights Act. Under s. 2 of the Act, the domestic judiciary 'must take into account' any relevant Strasbourg jurisprudence, although they are not bound by it. The UK courts are required to interpret all legislation in a way which is compatible with Convention rights 'so far as

it is possible to do so' (s. 3). It is unlawful for public authorities to act in a way which is incompatible with Convention rights (s. 6).

Retrospective effect?

Following the case of **Wilson** v **Secretary of State for Trade and Industry** (2003) some provisions of the Human Rights Act 1998 could have retrospective effect if that would not be unfair to the parties in a particular case.

The scope of the Convention

The rights protected by the ECHR include the right to life (Art. 2); freedom from torture, inhuman or degrading treatment (Art. 3); freedom from slavery or forced labour (Art. 4); the right to liberty and security of the person (Art. 5); the right to a fair trial (Art. 6); the prohibition of retrospective criminal laws (Art. 7); the right to respect for a person's private and family life, home and correspondence (Art. 8); freedom of thought, conscience and religion (Art. 9); freedom of expression (Art. 10); freedom of peaceful assembly and association, including the right to join a trade union (Art. 11); and the right to marry and have a family (Art. 12).

A Bill of Rights for the UK?

It has been observed that the ECHR does not constitute a Bill of Rights for the UK because it has not been entrenched. Many people feel that while the Human Rights Act 1998 is a first step in the right direction, ultimately the UK needs a properly entrenched Bill of Rights to protect its citizens. Among developed Western countries, Israel and the UK are the only ones without such a Bill.

Reform

The European Union looks set to become more involved in the protection of human rights within Europe.

Reading list

Laws, J. (1998) 'The limitations of human rights', *Public Law* 254.

Raine, J. and Walker, C. (2002) *The Impact of the Courts and the Administration of Justice of the Human Rights Act 1998*, London: Lord Chancellor's Department, Research Secretariat.

Reading on the Internet

www   The Human Rights Act 1998 is available on the Office of Public Sector Information website at:
http://www.opsi.gov.uk/acts/acts1998/19980042.htm

The website of the European Court of Human Rights is:
http://www.echr.coe.int/echr

Visit **www.mylawchamber.co.uk/ElliottELS** to access multiple-choice questions, flashcards and practice exam questions to test yourself on this chapter.

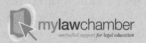

16 Remedies for infringement of human rights

This chapter discusses the different remedies available when a person's human rights have been breached, including:

- judicial review;
- *habeas corpus*;
- civil proceedings;
- compensation paid by the state;
- criminal proceedings;
- the Criminal Injuries Compensation Scheme;
- the European Court of Human Rights;
- disciplinary proceedings against the police;
- the exclusion of evidence from the criminal courts;
- the right to use force in self-defence; and
- parliamentary controls.

Introduction

Rights are only worthwhile if there are adequate remedies for their enforcement. The fact that we do not yet have a Bill of Rights, but only a collection of laws detailing what we may not do, has inevitably meant that remedies are similarly scattered. Some of the main remedies available in English law for unlawful infringement of basic rights are the subject of this section.

Judicial review

Where a public body – such as a local authority, the police, or a Government department – acts illegally, the result will often be an infringement of an individual's rights, and in some cases the remedy for this is a procedure known as judicial review. This is discussed in Chapter 24.

Habeas corpus

Personal liberty is regarded as the most fundamental of all freedoms, and where individuals are wrongfully deprived of their liberty, the fact that, on release, they can sue their captor for damages under the ordinary civil law is not regarded as sufficient. *Habeas corpus* is an ancient remedy which allows a person detained to challenge the legality of detention and, if successful, get themselves quickly released. It does not punish the person responsible for the detention, but once the detainee is set free, they can still pursue any other available remedies for compensation or punishment.

Habeas corpus may be sought by, among others, convicted prisoners; those detained in custody pending trial or held by the police during criminal investigations; those awaiting extradition; psychiatric patients; and those with excessive bail conditions imposed on them. Application is made to the Divisional Court, and takes priority over all other court business.

Civil action

Where a public body breaches a person's rights in such a way as to amount to a tort, that body may be sued in the same way as a private citizen would be; since the Crown Proceedings Act 1947, this includes the Crown.

As far as civil rights are concerned, this remedy is of particular importance in relation to illegal behaviour by the police: possible actions include assault, malicious prosecution, false imprisonment, wrongful arrest and trespass to property or goods. Exemplary damages may be awarded against the police even where there has been no oppressive behaviour or other aggravating circumstances. These cases are usually heard by a jury.

In the past the police have benefited from an effective immunity from liability for negligence in their investigations. This immunity stems from the case of **Hill** *v* **Chief Constable of West Yorkshire** (1989). The case looked at whether the police owed a duty of care to a victim of Peter Sutcliffe, known as the Yorkshire Ripper. The House of Lords ruled that public policy prevented any action for negligence lying in respect of police strategies for the investigation and prevention of crime.

In **Osman** *v* **UK** (1999) the European Court of Human Rights threw into doubt the future of this immunity. In that case, a teacher had developed a fixation with a 14-year-old boy at his school. He gave him money, took photographs of him and sometimes followed him home. Graffiti of a sexual nature appeared in the neighbourhood and the parents' house and car suffered criminal damage but the teacher denied any involvement. The teacher changed his name by deed poll to include the boy's name. He was suspended from his position as a teacher and he indicated that he was thinking of 'doing a Hungerford' by which it was assumed he meant he might use firearms to kill the deputy headmaster and other victims at random. In December 1987 the police sought to interview the man in connection with allegations of criminal damage but he had disappeared. Two months later he went to the boy's home, shot and wounded him and killed his father. He also went to the home of the deputy headmaster and shot and wounded him and killed his son. He was convicted of manslaughter and placed in a psychiatric hospital.

The pupil with whom he had had an obsession and the mother brought a civil action against the Metropolitan Police for negligence. They claimed that the police had been negligent in not apprehending the man before the incident that led to the killing. Relying on **Hill** *v* **Chief Constable of West Yorkshire** the Court of Appeal upheld a ruling to strike out the case as disclosing no cause of action. The Court of Appeal treated that case as laying down a watertight defence. It was contended before the European Court of Human Rights that the rule of public policy preventing the action for negligence breached the European Convention on Human Rights. The European Court ruled that Art. 6 of the Convention, which guarantees the right to a fair trial, had been violated. It considered that the exclusionary rule formulated in the **Hill** case should not be used as a blanket immunity, but that the existence of competing public policy issues had to be considered. The approach of the Court of Appeal had amounted to an unjustifiable restriction on the right of access to a court to have a claim determined on its merits.

This interference by the European Court into the substantive law of tort has not been well received by some academics and judges in the UK. It has been argued that the right to a fair trial under Art. 6 should be restricted to looking at procedural matters rather than examining the substantive law of the country. There are some signs that the European Court may be reconsidering its approach. In **Z** *v* **UK** (2001) the European Court of Human Rights acknowledged that it had not fully understood the English law as laid down in the **Hill** case. It stated:

> The Court considers that its reasoning in the **Osman** judgment was based on an understanding of the law of negligence ... which has to be reviewed in the light of the clarifications subsequently made by the domestic courts and notably the House of Lords

16

Remedies for infringement of human rights

... In the present case, the Court is led to the conclusion that the inability of the applicants to sue the local authority flowed not from an immunity but from the applicable principles governing the substantive right of action in domestic law. There was no restriction on access to the court of the kind contemplated in the **Ashingdane v United Kingdom** (1985) judgment.

The European Court appears at least to be restricting the impact of **Osman**. In **TP v UK** (2001) the European Court distinguished the **Osman** case and ruled that there had been no breach of Art. 6 when a case had been struck out by the UK courts because the case was doomed to fail.

The number of actions against the Metropolitan Police has risen considerably in recent years from 182 in 1982 to 495 in 1995/96 with £2,014,000 being paid out in damages and settlements; 1996 saw a number of very high awards of damages in civil actions by the courts of first instance. For example, in **Goswell v Commissioner of Metropolitan Police** (1998) Mr Goswell was waiting in his car for his girlfriend when PC Trigg approached. Mr Goswell complained about the police failure to investigate an arson attack on his home. He was handcuffed to another officer, struck by PC Trigg (causing injuries which required stitches and left a permanent scar) and then arrested for assault and threatening behaviour. His prosecution for these charges failed and when he brought a civil action he was awarded £120,000 damages for assault, £12,000 for false imprisonment and £170,000 exemplary damages for arbitrary and oppressive behaviour.

Appeals were lodged against the more substantial payments in damages and they were reduced by the Court of Appeal to £47,600. Strict guidelines were laid down for future allocations of damages by a jury, including figures as a starting-point in their deliberations for different types of cases. For example, basic damages for false imprisonment should be between £500 for one hour and £3,000 for 24 hours with an upper limit of £50,000 on exemplary damages. Their Lordships claimed to be at pains to establish a proper balance between the need to add teeth to the damages paid by the defendant and the fact that this money has to be drawn from public funds. Lawyers have taken issue with the likely impact of a £50,000 award on an institution with an annual budget close to £2 billion.

Compensation

Where there has been a failure in the trial process leading to a miscarriage of justice an award of compensation can be made by the state under s. 133 of the Criminal Justice Act 1988, though the sums awarded were reduced in 2006 and the maximum payable is now £1 million. Controversially, when calculating the award, the House of Lords confirmed in **R (O'Brien) v Independent Assessor** (2007) that deductions can be made to take into account the fact that the claimant did not have to pay for food and lodging while in prison, and previous criminal convictions and conduct leading to their wrongful imprisonment. Under the Criminal Justice and Immigration Act 2008, deductions can be made from an award of compensation to take into account the claimant's conduct that contributed to their wrongful conviction and any previous convictions.

In the past, discretionary payments could also be awarded by the Home Secretary where there had been gross misconduct that fell outside the statutory scheme. This discretionary scheme was abolished in 2006, on the pretext that the money should be spent on the victims of crime, ignoring the fact that people who have been wrongly held in prison are themselves victims.

Criminal proceedings

Criminal proceedings may be brought for false imprisonment or assault, if necessary by means of a private prosecution. In 2003, 195 police officers were convicted of a criminal offence; of these, 61 were for non-traffic offences. Sadly, not one police officer accused of malpractice arising from the many high-profile miscarriages of justice put right by the Court of Appeal since 1989 has been convicted of a criminal offence.

> **TOPICAL ISSUE**
>
> ### The shooting of Jean Charles de Menezes
>
> Following the fatal shooting by a police officer of Jean Charles de Menezes, who was mistaken for a suicide bomber, the Metropolitan Police was found guilty of breaching Health and Safety Rules and fined £175,000. Section 3 of the Health and Safety at Work etc. Act 1974 provides that it is:
>
> > the duty of every employer to conduct his undertaking in such a way as to ensure, so far as reasonably practicable, that persons not in his employment who may be affected are not thereby exposed to risks to their health and safety.
>
> Members of the de Menezes family would have preferred to have seen a prosecution for a homicide offence, but this would have been unlikely to succeed. No individuals were prosecuted for the death and no disciplinary proceedings were brought against those involved in the surveillance and shooting. At the inquest into Jean Charles's death, the coroner controversially instructed the jury that they could not find that the death was an unlawful killing.

Criminal Injuries Compensation Scheme

The Criminal Injuries Compensation Scheme (CICS) aims to compensate innocent victims of violent crime. Compensation is awarded by the Criminal Injuries Compensation Authority according to a tariff system. The CICS currently pays £170 million each year in compensation to about 40,000 victims, which is more than all the other equivalent schemes in Europe put together. Two-thirds of the awards are for less than £3,000. The maximum that can be awarded is £500,000. The award seeks to provide financial assistance while at the same time showing solidarity for the victim from the community.

These arrangements for compensation were subject to some criticism following the 7 July 2005 bombing in Central London. Many of the victims of the bombing had to wait a considerable amount of time before receiving any compensation and when they did receive compensation this was considered inadequate for those who had been more seriously injured. Where a person was killed, their families were only eligible for £11,000 compared to the £1.13 million paid to the victims of the 9/11 bombing in America.

The Government has published proposals for reforming the scheme in a consultation paper, *Rebuilding Lives, Supporting Victims of Crime* (2005). One of the proposals in the consultation paper is that if an employee is assaulted while at work, and sustains injury, it should be the employer rather than the state that compensates the victim. The paper considers removing the maximum limit for compensation awards to allow very serious cases to receive adequate financial support, while giving no financial compensation for minor injuries, about two-thirds of cases. Instead, such victims would receive more practical and emotional help (such as professional counselling and help with insurance claims). But for victims the crime is always serious and a denial of compensation on the basis that the injury was not serious will be adding insult to injury. One benefit of the proposed arrangements is that those people with more serious injuries should receive compensation more swiftly.

The European Court of Human Rights

A person whose rights have been breached may find that they have an eventual remedy in the European Court of Human Rights (see p. 301).

Disciplinary proceedings

Ess. Cases
p. 225
Misconduct by the police can be punished by internal disciplinary procedures. The Home Office report, *Police Complaints and Discipline* (Cotton and Povey (2004)) found that, in 2003, disciplinary misconduct charges were brought against 1,529 police officers and these led to 115 police officers being dismissed or required to resign.

In the past, complaints against the police could be made to the Police Complaints Authority. Following persistent criticism of this organisation both by the public and the police, the Police Reform Act 2002 abolished this body and replaced it with the
Ess. Cases
p. 230
Independent Police Complaints Commission (IPCC). The Government hopes that the new complaints procedure will be more accessible, open and independent than its predecessor.

The primary responsibility for recording complaints against the police and civilian staff remains with the police. Certain complaints can be handled informally (called 'local resolution'). There are three situations in which a complaint must be referred to the Commission. These are where:

- the conduct complained of is alleged to have resulted in death or serious injury;
- the complainant falls into a specified category of people;
- the Commission requires the complaint to be referred to it.

There is a discretion to refer a complaint to the Commission due to the gravity of the subject matter, or exceptional circumstances. These provisions have been criticised as too narrow, as, for example, complaints of assault, corruption and racism will not automatically be referred to the Commission.

The Commission has the power to determine, according to the seriousness of the case and the public interest, the form the investigation should take. There are four options:

- a police investigation on behalf of the appropriate authority;
- a police investigation supervised by the Commission;
- a police investigation managed by the Commission; or
- an investigation by the Commission, independent of the police.

Investigations by the Commission are carried out for the most serious complaints. The investigators have the same powers as the police. The most high-profile case to be the subject of such an investigation is the fatal shooting in 2005 by a police officer of Jean Charles de Menezes, who was mistaken for a suicide bomber at Stockwell tube station. Initially, the Metropolitan Police were reluctant to allow an independent investigation to take place and there were clear tensions between the police and the Commission during the course of the investigation.

Complainants have a right to appeal against a decision taken concerning the handling of a complaint.

The IPCC has itself been the subject of some criticism, as being ineffective and too close to the police. The Legal Action Group produced a damaging report on the subject in 2007. In 2008 a hundred lawyers refused to continue to work with the organisation because they were concerned the IPCC was not handling complaints effectively.

The admissibility of evidence

Where police officers commit serious infringements of a suspect's rights during the investigation of an offence, the courts may hold that evidence obtained as a result of such misbehaviour is inadmissible in court, the idea being to remove any incentive for the police to break the rules.

Under s. 76(2) of PACE, confession evidence is inadmissible where it was obtained by oppression or in circumstances likely to render it unreliable and, if the defence alleges that this is the case, the onus is on the prosecution to establish otherwise (s. 76(1)). Oppression is defined as including 'torture, inhuman or degrading treatment, and the use or threat of violence (whether or not amounting to torture)' (s. 76(8)). The definition of 'oppression' was considered in **R v Fulling** (1987). In that case, the police had persuaded a woman to make a confession by telling her that her lover was being

16

Remedies for infringement of human rights

unfaithful. The court held that this did not amount to oppression, and stated that the term should carry its ordinary meaning, that of unjust treatment or cruelty, or the wrongful use of power. Excluding evidence is potentially a powerful safeguard against oppressive treatment by the police, since there is little point in pressurising a suspect to confess if that confession cannot be used to obtain a conviction. However, the extent of this protection is diluted by s. 76(4), which states that, even if a confession is excluded, any facts discovered as a result of it may still be admissible. Parts of an excluded confession may also be allowed if relevant to show that the defendant speaks or writes in a particular way. This means that the police can use oppressive treatment to secure a confession which will help them find other evidence.

Section 78 provides that in any proceedings the court may refuse to admit evidence 'if it appears to the court that, having regard to all the circumstances, including the circumstances in which the evidence was obtained, the admission of the evidence would have such an adverse effect on the fairness of the proceedings that the court ought not to admit it'. This provision covers all types of evidence, not just confessions. It is generally invoked only if the police have committed serious breaches of PACE, such as refusing a suspect access to legal advice over a long period.

The right to exercise self-defence

Any citizen may use reasonable force to prevent unlawful interference with their person or property, or to protect others from such interference. This can affect both civil and criminal liability.

Parliamentary controls

One of the basic functions of Parliament is to act as a watchdog over the rights of citizens, protecting them from undue interference by Government. A number of methods are available, from questions directed to Ministers in Parliament, to committees designed to scrutinise legislation. However, this function has suffered as a result of the strength of party discipline, which means that many MPs appear to put loyalty to their party above loyalty to the citizens they represent. The result is that even measures which clearly restrict fundamental rights can be voted through if the Government has a clear majority.

The Ombudsman

The Parliamentary Commissioner for Administration, known as the Ombudsman, has a role in protecting individual rights.

Answering questions

1 Critically discuss the effectiveness of remedies available to individuals for infringement of human rights by the police.

Note the question is limited to discussing police infringements only. There are a variety of remedies available to individuals whose rights are breached:

- the police force is a public body, so s. 6 of the Human Rights Act 1998 applies and judicial review may be available;
- *habeus corpus* (p. 326);
- civil proceedings (you could discuss **Hill** (1989); **Osman** (1999); and **Z v UK** (2001) here (p. 327);
- criminal proceedings (p. 329);
- disciplinary procedures against the police (p. 330); and
- prevention of disclosure of previous evidence (p. 331).

2 Mary had been convicted in the past of theft and burglary, but had no convictions for violence. One Friday afternoon the police received an urgent telephone call telling them that someone had been stabbed in a car park. Two young women had been seen running away from the car park and the description of one of the women bore similarities to Mary's appearance. Police officer Percy saw Mary walking down the street with her friend Kelly two miles away from the car park. He grabbed hold of Mary's arm and said that she had to empty her pockets so that he could check whether she was carrying a knife. Mary refused to do so and Kelly kicked Percy to help her friend run away, but was unsuccessful and ran off herself. Percy then pushed Mary against a wall and carried out a thorough search of her person. He found that she was carrying nothing suspicious, but told Mary that she had to give her friend's name and address or she would have to go down to the police station. Mary gave him the details and together they went round to Kelly's house. Percy told Mary to pretend she was alone so that Kelly would open the door. When Kelly opened the door, Percy rushed inside and searched the house. He found a number of televisions with their serial numbers rubbed out and seized them all, despite Kelly's claims that she was just a lodger and the televisions were in the homeowner's bedroom and she had no knowledge of them. Mary and Kelly were then taken down to the police station where they were detained for 28 hours. They were only allowed to see a duty solicitor briefly on one occasion and were subjected to lengthy questioning about the stabbing and the televisions. They were finally released without charge when two other women were arrested for the stabbing and Kelly's landlady provided a satisfactory explanation for the presence of the televisions in her bedroom.

Consider whether the police were legally entitled to act as they did and whether Mary and Kelly have any remedies for their ordeal.

Your answer should be divided into two halves, first looking at the police powers (see p. 384 onwards) and secondly the remedies available. On the first issue of the police powers, Percy may have had reasonable grounds to suspect that he would find offensive weapons or blades on Mary because of the information he had received. Thus, stop and search under s. 1 of PACE may have been justified. However, the search was carried out in breach of Code provisions.

It is unclear whether Mary was placed under arrest at any point before the discovery of the televisions. If she was, the grounds are unclear and it would almost certainly be unlawful. The entry into Kelly's house is unlawful as it was not carried out with Kelly's genuine consent and there are no other grounds to make it lawful (such as to arrest, consequent on arrest, or to

16

Remedies for infringement of human rights

prevent breach of the peace). Thus, seizure of the televisions is also unlawful. However, the presence of the televisions did give rise to a reasonable suspicion that an offence had been or was being committed (either theft or handling stolen goods) with the involvement of Kelly, and possibly Mary. As a result, Percy could reasonably believe that an arrest at this stage was necessary.

The detention and questioning of Mary and Kelly may have contravened the time limits imposed by the Code of Practice requirements about breaks and refreshments, and the restricted access to the solicitor may contravene the requirements of s. 58.

On the second half of the essay concerning the remedies available, breach of the Code provisions in the carrying out of the search and questioning do not give rise to any rights under civil or criminal law, but can be the subject of a complaint to the Independent Police Complaints Commission. The violations of PACE could give rise to civil actions for unlawful arrest, trespass to premises and false imprisonment. Criminal proceedings in relation to the unlawful detention and excessive use of force could be brought and disciplinary proceedings would be possible.

3 Explain how people can obtain a remedy when they consider that the state has breached one of their human rights.

Civil proceedings can be brought for breach of the Human Rights Act 1998 either independently or as part of more traditional civil or administrative court proceedings. The High Court has a number of inherent powers to control abusive state conduct. It can hear judicial review applications and may quash executive decisions that have been wrongly taken. The High Court can also examine the legality of any detention (and order release) through an application of *habeas corpus*.

Civil actions are possible for assault, false imprisonment and trespass. In **Hill** v **Chief Constable of West Yorkshire** the House of Lords suggested that a police authority effectively enjoyed an immunity from liability for negligence, although **Osman** *v* **UK** has now questioned this immunity. Criminal proceedings could be brought against the police, an application could be made to the Criminal Injuries Compensation Scheme, a complaint could be issued to the Independent Police Complaints Commission and disciplinary proceedings could be taken against individual police officers. In addition, a court has the power to hold as inadmissible in criminal proceedings evidence obtained contrary to PACE.

Summary of Chapter 16: Remedies for infringement of human rights

Introduction
Rights are only worthwhile if there are adequate remedies for their enforcement. Some of the main remedies available in English law for unlawful infringement of basic rights are the subject of this chapter:

Judicial review
Where a public body acts illegally a remedy may be available through the procedure of judicial review.

Habeas corpus

Habeas corpus is an ancient remedy which allows people detained to challenge the legality of their detention and, if successful, get themselves quickly released.

Civil action

Where a public body breaches a person's rights it may be sued in the civil courts.

Compensation

If there has been a miscarriage of justice an award of compensation can be made by the state under s. 133 of the Criminal Justice Act 1988.

Criminal proceedings

Criminal proceedings may be brought for false imprisonment or assault, if necessary by means of a private prosecution.

The European Court of Human Rights

A person whose rights have been breached may find that they have an eventual remedy in the European Court of Human Rights.

Disciplinary proceedings

Misconduct by the police can be punished by internal disciplinary procedures. Complaints against the police can be made to the Independent Police Complaints Commission (IPCC).

The admissibility of evidence

Where police officers commit serious infringements of a suspect's rights during the investigation of an offence, the courts may hold that evidence obtained as a result of such misbehaviour is inadmissible in court.

The right to exercise self-defence

Any citizen may use reasonable force to prevent unlawful interference with their person or property, or to protect others from such interference. This can affect both civil and criminal liability.

Parliamentary controls

One of the basic functions of Parliament is to act as a watchdog over the rights of citizens, protecting them from undue interference by Government.

The Ombudsman

The Parliamentary Commissioner for Administration, known as the Ombudsman, has a role in protecting individual rights.

Reading list

Department for Trade and Industry (2004) *Fairness for All: A New Commission for Equality and Human Rights*, Cm 6185, London: Stationery Office.

Ormerod, D. (2003) 'ECHR and the Exclusion of Evidence: Trial Remedies for Article 8 Breaches?', *Criminal Law Review* 61.

Reading on the Internet

www   The consultation paper, *Rebuilding Lives, Supporting Victims of Crime* (2005), looking at the future of the Criminal Injuries Compensation Scheme, is available at:

    http://www.cjsonline.gov.uk/downloads/application/pdf/Rebuilding%20Lives%20-%20supporting%20victims%20of%20crime.pdf

The website address of the Independent Police Complaints Commission is:

    http://www.ipcc.gov.uk

Visit www.mylawchamber.co.uk/ElliottELS to access multiple-choice questions, flashcards and practice exam questions to test yourself on this chapter.

DISPUTE RESOLUTION

This Part looks at the formal and informal methods available in England and Wales to solve disputes. The formal methods pass through either the criminal justice system or the civil justice system and include a structured appeal process. Less formal methods fall within the concept of alternative methods of dispute resolution and include references to ombudsmen. All of these methods of resolving disputes require funding, and we look first at the different sources of funding available in Chapter 17: Paying for legal services.

17 Paying for legal services

This chapter discusses:

- the unmet need for legal services;
- legal aid before the Access to Justice Act 1999;
- private funding of legal services;
- the Community Legal Service providing state funding for civil cases;
- the Criminal Defence Service providing state funding for criminal cases;
- the Public Defender Service;
- conditional fee agreements as an alternative method of funding legal proceedings;
- alternative sources of legal advice;
- criticisms and reform of the current funding arrangements.

Introduction

Since society requires that all its members keep the law, it follows that all members of society should be not only equally bound by, but also equally served by, the legal system. Legal rights are after all worthless unless they can be enforced. Yet justice may be open to all, but only in the same way as the Ritz Hotel. In other words, anyone can go there, but only if they can afford it – and just like the Ritz Hotel, legal advice and help can be very expensive. As a result, many people simply cannot afford to enforce their legal rights and are therefore denied access to justice.

What is more, cost is not the only thing which stops many ordinary people from using the legal system. Other issues such as awareness of legal rights, the elitist image of the legal profession and even its geographical situation all contribute to the problem which legal writers call 'unmet legal need'. In the following section, we look at what unmet legal need really means, and the causes of it; later in the chapter we consider the various attempts which have been made to resolve the problem, including the provision of state funding, which, as we will see, is currently in the process of radical change.

Unmet need for legal services

Unmet legal need essentially describes the situation where a person has a problem that could potentially be solved through the law, but the person is unable to get whatever help he or she needs to use the legal system. Research carried out by Pascoe Pleasence and others for the Legal Services Commission in 2004 has found that over a three and a half year period, more than one in three adults experienced a civil law problem; one in five took no action to solve their problem; and around 1 million problems went unsolved because people did not understand their basic rights or know how to seek help. About 15 per cent of people who sought advice did not succeed in obtaining any. The research revealed that civil law problems are not evenly distributed. Groups vulnerable to social exclusion suffer more problems more often. The survey showed civil justice problems were experienced by:

- four in five people living in temporary accommodation;
- two in three lone parents; and
- more than half of unemployed people.

Many civil justice problems trigger other problems and increase the risk of social exclusion. For example, an accident could lead to personal injury, which could lead to loss of income and then the loss of a person's home.

Research by Richard White in 1973 suggested four situations where someone would fail to get the legal help they needed:

1 The person fails to recognise a problem as having legal implications and so does not seek out legal advice.
2 The problem is recognised as being a legal one, but the person involved does not know of the existence of a legal service that could help, or their own eligibility to use it.

3 The person knows the problem is a legal one, and knows of the service that could help with it, but chooses not to make use of it because of some barrier, such as cost, ignorance of state funding or the unapproachable image of solicitors.

4 The person knows there is a legal problem and wants legal help, but fails to get it because they cannot find a service to deal with it.

Of these reasons, the barrier of cost has traditionally received most attention, and it is an important one; a 1991 *Which?* report found one in ten people were put off seeking legal advice by cost. With court costs going up and eligibility for legal aid decreasing, access to justice risks becoming more of an aspiration than a reality. Simply obtaining legal advice from a private solicitor is expensive, and taking a case to court much more so – and in English law, the loser in a civil case must usually pay the costs of the winner as well as their own costs. This gives the rich three major advantages: they can hire good lawyers and pay for the time needed to do the job properly; they can afford to take the risk of losing litigation; and they can use their wealth to bully a less well-off opponent, by dragging out the case or making it more complex (and therefore more expensive). Bear in mind that 'the rich' does not just mean the millionaire in the Rolls-Royce, but also the employer you might want to sue for unfair dismissal, the company whose products could make you ill or the builder who left you with a leaky roof, and you can see the problem.

However, as White's research shows, cost is not the only reason why people fail to secure help with their legal problems. This is backed up by the 1973 research of Abel-Smith *et al.*, which compared people's own perception of their need for legal help and the action they took to get it. Almost all the respondents consulted a solicitor when they felt they needed advice on buying a house (though, of course, this only includes those with sufficient means to buy their own home). For employment problems though, only 4 per cent consulted a solicitor; 34 per cent took advice from some other source and 62 per cent took no advice at all. For Social Security problems, solicitors were consulted by even fewer people: just 3 per cent saw a solicitor, while 16 per cent took other advice and 81 per cent took none at all. Yet, in all these cases, the people surveyed realised that they did need some legal advice.

Similarly, Zander (1988) has pointed out that even the poorest members of society consult solicitors about divorce, while the middle classes seem no more likely than working class people to consult solicitors about employment or consumer problems.

American sociologists Mayhew and Reiss (1969) put forward a 'social organization' theory to explain why solicitors are consulted in some cases and not others. This theory suggests that certain types of work are related to social contact – most people know people who have used solicitors for conveyancing and divorce, and it becomes an obvious step to take. As Zander points out, lawyers adjust the services they offer to demand and so it becomes a self-fulfilling prophecy.

Research carried out by Professor Hazel Genn in 1982 categorised the different types of people who are confronted by a legal problem. Five per cent were labelled as 'lumpers'. This group had low incomes, low education levels and were frequently unemployed. They were unable to see any way out of their money and employment problems and therefore did absolutely nothing. This could lead to a 'cluster' of problems where the person was increasingly incapable of helping him or herself. The next group were described as 'self-helpers' and only had a 50 per cent chance of resolving their legal problems. They often believed until the last minute that nothing could be done to help them and when they tried to take action they found they had gone, or been sent, to the wrong place; or were confronted by queues, unanswered telephones and restricted opening times. Professor Genn found that social distress could be caused where legal problems were left unresolved. By contrast, if people got good quality early advice they could help themselves.

Another problem, identified by the Royal Commission on Legal Services, is the uneven geographical distribution of solicitors throughout the country. A third of all solicitors practise in London. The Commission highlighted research showing that while there was one solicitor's office for every 4,700 people in England and Wales, their distribution varied enormously, from one office for every 2,000 people in prosperous owner-occupier areas such as Bournemouth and Guildford, to one for every 66,000 in working class areas such as Huyton in Liverpool. The Commission concluded that the low rates for state-funded work had much to do with this; most private firms need to subsidise such work with privately funded work, and the poorer areas may not provide enough of this to keep more than a few solicitors in each area in business. Other advice agencies, such as law centres and Citizens' Advice Bureaux, may also be thin on the ground in some, particularly rural, areas. The image of lawyers as predominantly white, male and from privileged backgrounds may also contribute to the problem, making them unapproachable to many people.

In its 1999 report, *A Balancing Act: Surviving the Risk Society*, the National Association of Citizens' Advice Bureaux (NACAB) suggested that the problem of unmet legal need may still be growing. It pointed out that changes in society are forcing more and more people to take on responsibility for their own welfare in areas where the state would once have made provision, while insecurity in work, housing and family relationships is increasing. This means more and more people are placed in situations where they need to assert their legal rights – divorce, homelessness, debt or employment problems, for example – but are unable to do so because there is too little access to free, independent legal advice.

In the following sections, we look at the attempts that successive governments have made to ease the problem of unmet legal need by providing state-funded legal help, and then at a range of other approaches to the problem.

State-funded legal services

The system of state-funded legal help in this country goes back more than half a century. After the Second World War, the Labour Government introduced a range of measures designed to address the huge inequalities between rich and poor. These included the National Health Service, the beginnings of today's Social Security system and, in 1949, the first state-funded legal aid scheme. The legal aid scheme was designed to allow poorer people access to legal advice and representation in court: this would be provided by solicitors in private practice, but the state, rather than the client, would pay all or part of the fees. By the 1980s, the system had developed into six different schemes, covering most kinds of legal case, and administered by the Legal Aid Board. But the growing cost of these schemes was causing concern. In the 1990s the Conservative Government sought to keep the escalating costs down by reducing financial eligibility for the schemes, which in turn led to criticisms that they were also reducing access to justice. As a result of all this, the Labour Government passed the Access to Justice Act 1999.

With the passing of the Access to Justice Act 1999 the Labour Government introduced some major reforms to the provision of state-funded legal services. Through these reforms the Government hoped to improve the quality and accessibility of the legal services on offer, while keeping a tighter control on their budget. On 1 April 2001 the Legal Aid Board was abolished and replaced by the Legal Services Commission. It currently has a budget of £2 billion a year to spend on state-funded legal services – effectively each taxpayer is contributing annually £100 to legal aid work. The Commission is guided in its work by the Minister for Justice (who must make any such guidance public) but the Minister is not allowed to give guidance about the handling of any individual case.

The Community Legal Service

Funding

Whereas previously legal aid in civil cases was available on a demand-led basis (meaning that all cases which met the merits and means tests would be funded), there is now a Community Legal Service Fund, containing a fixed amount of money, set each year as part of the normal round of Government spending plans.

The detailed way in which the Fund is to be spent is decided by a Funding Code, drawn up by the Legal Services Commission and approved by the Lord Chancellor. This sets out the criteria and procedures to be used when deciding whether a particular case should be funded. The Commission has a duty to obtain the best value for money, which the explanatory notes to the Access to Justice Act 1999 defines as taking into account 'a combination of price and quality'. In other words, the Commission is not obliged to choose the cheapest possible service, but it is not obliged to choose the best quality one either; it has to find the best balance between the two.

Community Legal Service

Figure 17.1 The logo of the Community Legal Service

Source: Legal Services Commission

Levels of funded legal services

Only solicitors or advice agencies holding a contract with the Legal Services Commission are able to provide advice or representation directly funded by the Commission. For specialist areas of law such as family law, immigration, mental health and clinical negligence only specialist firms are funded to do the work. The merits test for civil legal aid has been replaced by the new Funding Code discussed above. This Code lays down the rules as to which cases should receive funding. Direct funding is provided for different categories of legal service, as follows:

- **Legal Help**. Legal Help provides initial advice and assistance with any legal problem. A means test is applied.
- **Legal Representation**. Funding is available for a person to be represented in court proceedings. Both a means and a merits test are applied. This scheme replaces civil legal aid.
- **Help at Court**. Help at Court allows somebody (a solicitor or adviser) to speak on another's behalf at certain court hearings, without formally acting for them in the whole proceedings. A means test is applied.
- **Approved Family Help**. Approved Family Help provides help in relation to a family dispute, including assistance in resolving that dispute through negotiation or otherwise. This overlaps with the services covered by Legal Help, but also includes issuing proceedings and representation where necessary to obtain disclosure of information from another party, or to obtain a consent order where the parties have reached an agreement.
- **Family Mediation**. This level of service covers mediation for a family dispute, including finding out whether mediation appears suitable or not.

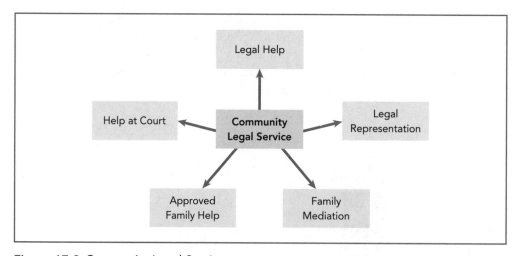

Figure 17.2 Community Legal Service

Coverage

Certain types of case have been removed from the state-funded system altogether. These are:

- **Personal injury cases** (with the exception of clinical negligence cases). Instead these are funded by conditional fee agreements which are discussed later in this chapter.
- **Cases of defamation and malicious falsehood**. Legal aid was never available for defamation. When the legal aid system was first established in 1949, defamation was excluded because the Attorney General of the day was concerned that it would produce frivolous and unnecessary claims. While he accepted that the reputation of a poor person is just as deserving of legal protection as that of a wealthy person, he was worried that the legal aid scheme would be seriously overloaded if every slander uttered across the back garden wall could be pursued at the expense of the state. In some cases, behaviour which would normally be classed as defamation could be categorised as the related tort of malicious falsehood, for which legal aid was available. Now, neither is eligible for state funding. Under the Access to Justice Act 1999, legal aid can exceptionally be made available for such cases, but this has only happened once. Proceedings for defamation and malicious falsehood can, instead, be brought under a conditional fee agreement, discussed at p. 359.
- **Disputes arising in the course of a business**. Business traders can insure against the cost of having to bring or defend a legal action, and the Government believes that taxpayers should not be required to meet the legal costs of those who fail to do so.
- **Matters concerning the law relating to companies, partnerships, trusts or boundary disputes**. Trusts are a way of holding property and, as such, tend mainly to affect wealthier people. Boundary disputes include, for example, disputes between neighbours as to where each party's garden begins and ends.

The Government considers that none of these types of case is sufficiently important to justify public funding. Approximately 80,000 people are injured each year at work, on the road or during a leisure activity. It has been estimated that personal injury cases accounted for around 60 per cent of cases previously funded by legal aid. However, the Access to Justice Act 1999 provides that the Lord Chancellor can direct the Commission to provide services for excluded categories in exceptional circumstances.

Eligibility

There continue to be both merits and means tests for some forms of state funding of civil legal services. A single means test applies. State funding is not available if a person earns more than £2,288 per month and, if a person has £8,000 savings, availability depends on the service required. In practice the proportion of the population entitled to legal aid has been reducing, from 52 per cent in 1998 to 29 per cent in 2007. Of those entitled to legal aid, most are on income support and where they are in low paid employment they are often required to pay part of their legal costs.

The Funding Code lays down which types of cases should be given priority. It is intended to be flexible, in that different criteria can be applied to different types of case, depending on their priority. For example, the chances of success might be relevant in many types of case, but might not be in cases about whether a child should be taken into local authority care.

Suppliers

In the past, a person who wanted help with a problem covered by legal aid could go to any lawyer and, providing the client met the relevant means and merits tests, that lawyer would be paid by the Government for the help given in that particular case. This situation was beginning to change even before the 1999 Act was passed. In 1994 the Legal Aid Board began a quality assurance scheme called franchising. Law firms could apply for a franchise in particular areas of work, and would have to pass quality control tests in order to get one, but would then be able to attract more work in that area. Similar agreements were made, on a pilot basis, with advice agencies, so that they could provide advice and assistance in specific areas. The Act takes this idea further, so that only solicitors and advice agencies holding contracts with the Legal Services Commission are able to get state funding. Once they hold a contract, they are paid by the hour for their work.

The 1999 Act also gives the Commission power to make grants to service providers, such as advice centres, and to employ staff directly to deliver legal services to the public. This latter point means that the Commission could, if it wished, create a system of lawyers employed by the state to provide legal help to the public, though there appear to be no plans to do so with regard to civil cases at the moment.

Future changes

The Act allows for a new way of funding legal help for individuals, which at present the Government has no plans to use. It provides for a scheme in which people could be given state funding, but required to agree that if they win their case, they will pay back the state funding (which they would presumably claim from the losing party), plus a further sum. This would make it possible to fund certain types of case on a self-financing basis, with the extra sums paid by winning litigants funding the costs of those who lose their cases.

Community Legal Advice

In 2004, Community Legal Advice was established. This is a national telephone and website service providing free legal advice on civil law matters. Members of the public can telephone the helpline on 0845 345 4345 for advice on such matters as housing, social security benefits and debt. Alternatively, they can visit the website at www.clsdirect.org.uk. This website is visited over 50,000 times each month. Community Legal Advice is intended to provide an alternative to face-to-face advice, which will be particularly attractive to those with mobility problems, caring responsibilities or accommodation in a remote area. In addition, some people may feel more comfortable talking about their problems with the relative anonymity of a telephone line, rather than in a face-to-face meeting.

The Criminal Defence Service

In April 2001 a Criminal Defence Service was introduced, replacing the old system of criminal legal aid. This Criminal Defence Service is administered by the Legal Services Commission.

Funding

Unlike legal aid in civil cases, state-funded criminal defence work is still given on a demand-led basis; there is no set budget and all cases which fit the merits criteria and the means test are funded.

Levels of funded legal services

As part of this service the Commission directly funds the provision of criminal legal services, employs public defenders and pays for duty solicitor schemes. Thus under the Criminal Defence Service, legal services are provided by both lawyers in private practice and employed lawyers. The Government believes that a mixed system of public and private lawyers will provide the best value for money for the taxpayer. The salaried service is intended to provide a benchmark to assess whether prices charged by private practice lawyers are reasonable, as well as filling in gaps in the system.

Direct funding

Only solicitor firms having a contract with the Legal Services Commission are able to offer state-funded criminal defence work. Unlike the contracts for civil matters, the contracts for criminal defence matters do not limit the number of cases that can be taken on, nor the total value of the payments that may be made. Contracted solicitors will be paid for all work actually undertaken in accordance with the contract. Solicitors with a contract should be able to provide the full range of criminal defence services, from the time of arrest until the end of the case (unlike with the previous system, where defendants could receive assistance relating to the same alleged offence under several different schemes, each resulting in a separate payment for the lawyers involved). In certain cases – such as serious fraud trials – there are panels of firms or individual lawyers who specialise in the relevant type of case, and defendants will be required to choose from that panel. State funding can support three types of service.

- **Advice and assistance**. Funding is available for the provision of advice and assistance from a solicitor, including giving general advice, writing letters, negotiating, getting a barrister's opinion and preparing a written case. A means test is applied but people who are eligible do not have to make any contribution to the legal costs. It does not cover representation in court. When a person is questioned by the police they have a right to free legal advice from a contracted solicitor and no means test is applied.

- **Advocacy assistance**. Advocacy assistance covers the costs of a solicitor preparing a client's case and their initial representation in certain proceedings in both the magistrates' court and the Crown Court and in certain other circumstances. There is no means test but there is a merits test.
- **Representation**. When a person has been charged with a criminal offence, representation covers the cost of a solicitor to prepare their defence and to represent them in court. It may also be available for a bail application. It will sometimes pay for a barrister, particularly for the Crown Court and for the cost of an appeal.

Decisions to grant representation in individual cases are made by the magistrates' courts. Representation will be granted when it is in the 'interests of justice'. The court may decide that it is in the interests of justice to grant representation where, for example, the case is so serious that on conviction a person is likely to be sent to prison or to lose their job, where there are substantial questions of law to be argued, or where the defendant is unable to follow the proceedings and explain their case because they do not speak English well enough or are suffering from a psychiatric illness.

Means test

Before the Access to Justice Act 1999, criminal legal aid was means tested. The means test was criticised because most defendants were too poor to pay for their defence lawyers – only 1 per cent of applicants were refused criminal legal aid. As a result, the cost of administering the means test was more than the sum that was collected by defendants and the process also caused delays in the criminal system. The 1999 Act therefore abolished the means test for criminal cases. Instead, for cases heard in the Crown Court, orders could be issued at the end of a trial to recover the defence costs against wealthy people who had been convicted of an offence. Abolition of the means test led to concern in the media that some wealthy defendants were receiving legal aid when they could have comfortably afforded to pay themselves. Following such criticisms, the Criminal Defence Service Act 2006 reintroduced a means test for criminal cases in the magistrates' courts (apart from the first hearing, to avoid court delays). A means test will be reintroduced for Crown Court cases from January 2010. If the defendant is acquitted their contributions will be refunded with interest. There remains a risk that these reforms will cause delays in the criminal system, both because evidence of means will need to be obtained and because the number of unrepresented defendants is likely to increase.

Public defenders

Since May 2001 the Legal Services Commission directly employs a number of criminal defence lawyers, known as public defenders. Eight regional offices were piloted. The public defenders can provide the same services as lawyers in private practice and have to compete for work.

There was strong opposition to the introduction of public defenders. The explanatory notes to the Access to Justice Act 1999 state that the idea is to provide flexibility, so that employed lawyers could be used if, for example, there is a shortage of suitable private lawyers in remoter areas. The notes point out that using salaried lawyers will also give the Commission better information about the real costs of providing the services. Public defenders will provide an element of competition with solicitors in private practice. They are required to follow a code of conduct guaranteeing certain standards of professional behaviour, including duties to avoid discrimination, to protect the interests of those whom they are defending, to avoid conflicts of interest and to maintain confidentiality.

The Government had planned to eventually set up a national network of public defender offices. People suspected of crime would then have had a choice only between these public defenders and lawyers who had a contract with the Legal Services Commission, though within that limited range it was intended that there would be some choice in all but the most exceptional circumstances. However, following research carried out by Lee Bridges and others entitled *Evaluation of the Public Defender Service in England and Wales* (2007) the Government concluded that four of the public defender offices were not delivering value for money and decided to close these down. It noted that all of the offices that were earmarked to be closed operated in areas with alternative criminal defence services, which was probably why they did not capture enough work to be cost-effective. There are therefore four offices remaining and no plans at the moment to expand the scheme.

Duty solicitor schemes

The duty solicitor schemes have remained unchanged by the reforms. Duty solicitors are available at police stations and magistrates' courts and offer free legal advice.

Criminal Defence Service Direct

A telephone service, known as Criminal Defence Service Direct (CDSD), was established in 2005 to provide free telephone advice primarily to people detained by police for non-imprisonable offences. If a person requests to see their own solicitor, they will have to pay for this themselves. The Legal Services Commission considers that telephone advice is a modern and appropriate way to assist people detained at police stations who are accused of less serious offences. It is also much cheaper than face-to-face advice. CDSD attempts to contact the client within 15 minutes of being informed of the case. Unfortunately, in over half of cases the police fail to pick up the telephone, which causes delay.

The academics Lee Bridges and Ed Cape have published research into this telephone service: *CDS Direct: Flying in the face of the evidence* (2008). They have argued that the telephone service is of 'questionable legality' as it could breach the European Convention on Human Rights and does not satisfy the requirements of PACE. While s. 58 of PACE states that suspects in a police station are entitled to consult a solicitor, the telephone service is not manned by solicitors, but instead by paralegals. Bridges and Cape argue that the right to consult a solicitor has been 'undermined' by the introduction of the telephone service. They conclude that, while the Government has paid lip service to quality, its main aims are to reduce costs, secure convictions and limit access to legal services.

17

Paying for legal services

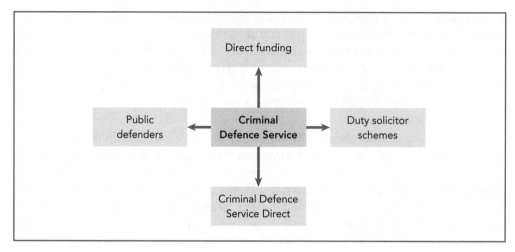

Figure 17.3 Criminal Defence Service

Even before the telephone service was introduced, it was increasingly only a para-legal from the solicitor's office who was attending the police station, not solicitors themselves. The Legal Services Commission has stated that the telephone service is saving the taxpayer £8 million a year. As increasing numbers of cases are being handled by the police instead of going to court because of the use of cautions, fixed-penalty notices and police bail, the legal controls over what happens in the police station are increasingly important.

Other participants in the Community Legal Service

There are a number of non-profit-making agencies which give legal advice and some-times representation, and initiatives by the legal profession and other commercial organisations also address the issue of access to justice.

Law centres

Law centres offer a free, non-means-tested service to people who live or work in their area. They aim to be accessible to anyone who needs legal help, and in order to achieve this they usually operate from ground floor, high street premises, stay open beyond office hours, employ a high proportion of lay people as well as lawyers and generally encourage a more relaxed atmosphere than that found in most private solicitors' offices. Most law centres are run by a management committee drawn from the local area, so that they have direct links with the community.

The first law centres were established in 1969 and today there are 54 of them in England and Wales. The Law Society allowed them to advertise (before the restriction on advertising was lifted for solicitors in general) in exchange for the centres not undertaking certain areas of work which were the mainstay of the average high street solicitor – small personal injury cases, wills and conveyancing. Their main areas of work are housing, welfare, immigration and employment.

Law centres are largely funded by grants from central and local government, though a few have also managed to secure some financial support from large local private firms. This method of funding means that they do not have to work on a case-by-case basis but can allocate funding according to community priorities.

Because they do not depend on case-by-case funding, law centres have developed innovative ways of solving legal problems. As well as dealing with individual cases, they run campaigns designed to make local people aware of their legal rights, act as a pressure group on local issues such as bad housing, and take action where appropriate on behalf of groups as well as individuals. The reasoning behind this approach is that resources and time are better used tackling problems as a whole, rather than aspects of those problems as they appear case by case. For example, if a council has failed to replace lead piping or asbestos in its council houses, it would seem more efficient to approach the council about all the properties rather than take out individual cases for each tenant as they become aware that they have a problem.

Law centres also provide valuable services in areas not covered by the statutory schemes, such as inquests, and several have set up duty solicitor schemes to deal with housing cases in the county court and help prevent evictions. They may offer a 24 hour general emergency service.

Most law centres face long-term problems with funding; some have been forced to close due to a lack of funding and others go through periodic struggles for survival.

Citizens' Advice Bureaux

There are around 700 Citizens' Advice Bureaux across the country, offering free advice and help with a whole range of problems, though the most common areas at the moment are social security and debt. They are largely staffed by trained volunteers, who can become expert in the areas they most frequently deal with. Where professional legal help is required, some Bureaux employ solicitors, some have regular help from solicitor volunteers and others refer individuals to local solicitors who undertake state-funded work. The Bureaux are overseen by the National Association of Citizens' Advice Bureaux and must conform to its standards and codes of practice.

One of their major advantages is a very high level of public awareness – because they are frequently mentioned in the press and have easily recognisable high street offices, most people know where they are and what they do.

Like law centres, they have come under considerable financial pressure in recent years, with the result that many can only open for a very limited number of hours a week. The Access to Justice Act may mean better funding in future.

Alternative sources of legal help

Some local authorities run money, welfare, consumer and housing advice centres to provide both advice and a mechanism for dealing with complaints, while charities such as Shelter, the Child Poverty Action Group and MIND often offer legal help in their specialist areas. Other organisations, such as trade unions, motoring organisations, such as the AA and RAC, and the Consumers' Association give free or inexpensive legal help to their members. Some university law faculties run 'law clinics', where students, supervised by their tutors, give free help and advice to members of the public.

There are a number of Internet sites giving basic legal advice for free, and some magazines publish legal advice lines, which charge a premium rate for readers to phone and get one-to-one legal advice from qualified solicitors. It is also possible to insure against legal expenses, either as a stand-alone policy, or more usually, as part of household, credit card or motor insurance.

As we saw earlier, cost is not the only cause of unmet legal need; a reluctance among many ordinary people to bring problems to lawyers is also recognised. In recent years the profession has taken steps to address the issue, including the use of advertising and public relations campaigns. Many high street firms now advertise their services locally, while some of the firms currently involved in suing cigarette manufacturers for illnesses caused by smoking attracted potential clients by advertising specifically for people with smoking-related diseases.

The Access to Justice Act: an assessment

The Access to Justice Act 1999 was the subject of much opposition during the legislative process, and though some of the criticisms were addressed during the passing of the Act, some of this opposition remains. Below we detail the main criticisms, but first we look at some of the advantages claimed for the new system.

Advantages of the Access to Justice Act reforms

Control of costs

Spending on legal aid has increased from £536 million in 1982 to around £2 billion today – an average annual growth of 5.7 per cent in real terms. As we have seen, the cost of the previous legal aid system was a major problem. The Government claims that the issuing of contracts, the fixed budget for state funding in civil cases and the fact that the Funding Code sets out clear criteria which reflect agreed priorities, will help keep costs under control.

A report from the National Audit Office (2003) identified significant improvements that have taken place in the administration of state funding of legal services, with the creation of the Community Legal Service. The new funding arrangements have led to greater control and targeting of resources and better scrutiny of suppliers. Despite this, England and Wales is spending at least four times more on legal aid than any other European country according to a survey carried out by the European Commission for the Efficiency of Justice (2008).

Better allocation of resources

The Funding Code for civil matters is designed to reflect agreed priorities, so money can be channelled into those areas which the Government considers to reflect best the needs of society, whereas the demand-led approach of the past could not do this.

Higher standards of work

By limiting state funding to contracted lawyers and firms who have passed quality control standards, the Government claims that standards of work should be consistently high. In addition, the Lord Chancellor has suggested (*The Times*, 7 September 1999) that the creation of defence lawyers employed by the Commission would create a 'healthy rivalry' with private criminal lawyers and so stimulate them to give a better service.

◼ Disadvantages of the reforms

Access to justice

The reforms were intended to improve access to justice, but they seem to have achieved the opposite. Because many state-funded legal services can only be obtained from lawyers who have a contract with the Legal Services Commission, members of the public are finding it increasingly difficult to find a state-funded lawyer with the relevant expertise close to their home.

Part of the problem is that many law firms have in the past done a small amount of legal aid work alongside their privately-funded work. Such firms have not wanted to bid for block contracts because they have not wanted to increase the amount of comparatively poorly paid state-funded work they take on. There are now only 5,000 solicitor firms offering state-funded legal services, compared with 11,000 under the old legal aid system. Between January 2000 and June 2003 the number of civil contracts offered for housing law fell by a third from 743 to 489. In the same period, contracts for debt law fell by more than half, from 462 to 206. One result, many fear, will be the creation of a two-tier legal profession, with one set of firms doing poorly paid state-funded work and another doing exclusively private work.

The National Audit Office (2003) has identified a problem of lawyers opting out of contracting in family work. It also points to a need for more lawyers to undertake work in community care, housing and mental health. A study undertaken by the Citizens' Advice Bureau (2004) has reinforced this picture of growing gaps in the supply of state-funded legal services, what it calls 'advice deserts'. Their survey found that people were often having to travel up to 50 miles to find a lawyer. Over two-thirds of Citizens' Advice Bureaux said they had difficulty finding a legal aid immigration lawyer for clients, and 60 per cent reported problems finding solicitors to deal with housing and family law problems. The Legal Services Commission has, however, rejected the suggestion that there are legal aid 'advice deserts'. It has pointed out that almost 95 per cent of the population live within five miles of a civil legal aid provider. It has also stated that the number of people who received civil legal help in 2005–06 was at a six-year high. The Minister for Justice has commented in 2009:

I think access is at risk of being confused with physical proximity. People have grown used to a far wider range of telephone and internet-based services – and demand more rapid and convenient access to services, but not necessarily an office on the street corner.

State funding is not available for legal representation at most tribunals.

Community Legal Service Partnerships

A review of the Community Legal Service Partnerships (CLSPs) has been carried out by consultancy firm Matrix and Sheffield University. This found that CLSPs had failed to achieve their goals and were proving ineffective. More than half the advisers working for the CLSPs 'did not believe their CLSPs had been effective in improving access to justice for the public'. A study by the Advice Services Alliance (2004) found that many CLSPs were 'dying on their feet'. It found that the lawyers involved felt they were wasting their time.

Problems with conditional fee agreements

The Access to Justice Act 1999 removed personal injury cases from the state funding system, so that these can only be funded privately or by a conditional fee agreement. Much of the criticism of the current funding arrangements is concerned with the use of these conditional fee agreements which are discussed on pp. 359–65.

Cost-cutting

Critics, including the legal professions and some MPs, have accused the Government of putting cost-cutting before access to justice. The Legal Aid Practitioners Group chairman, Richard Miller, told *The Lawyer* newspaper in December 1998 that he believed the fixed budget for civil matters was designed to make it easy for the Government to cut the amount spent in later years: 'The Legal Services Commission will simply be able to say, this is the budget and if there are any more cases, tough luck.'

There are particular concerns that civil cases will suffer from the priority given to criminal defence work. In order to meet its obligations to guarantee a fair trial under human rights legislation, the Government has had to continue to allow the funding for criminal defence to be demand-led. It has admitted, however, that there is a fixed overall budget for legal services, which means that the budget for civil cases is effectively whatever is left over once criminal defence work is paid for.

Public defenders

The legal profession has fiercely opposed the idea of the Commission employing its own lawyers to do criminal defence work. Both the Bar Council and the Criminal Law Solicitors Association have expressed concern that lawyers who are wholly dependent on the state for their income cannot be sufficiently independent to defend properly people suspected of crime – people who, by definition, are on the opposite side to the state. Interviewed by *The Lawyer* newspaper in December 1998, Bar Council chairperson, Heather Hallett QC, pointed to the example of the US, where public defenders have been used for some years, arguing that, as a result, the justice system there has become geared towards administrative convenience and cost-cutting, leading to an emphasis on plea bargaining and uncontested cases.

The experience of foreign jurisdictions such as the US and Canada shows that any system of public defenders must be properly funded and staffed if it is to retain the confidence of providers, users and the courts. Unfortunately they are frequently underfunded in practice, relying as a result on inexperienced lawyers with excessive caseloads and who are not respected by their clients, opponents or the court.

ss. Cases
p. 247 ➤
Research carried out by Cyrus Tata and others (2004) has evaluated the success of the Public Defence Solicitors Office in Scotland in its first three years. The research compared the performance of the public defenders with that of solicitors in private practice receiving state funding. The conclusions of this research were mixed. It found that public defender clients pleaded guilty earlier than clients of solicitors in private practice. But it found no evidence to suggest that public defenders put explicit pressure on clients to plead guilty. Instead, the clients criticised the public defenders for being too neutral and too willing to go along with whatever the client decided. The change in economic incentives involved in receiving a salary rather than a legal aid payment appeared to produce a change in behaviour, because solicitors in private practice earn very little if a client immediately pleads guilty, so ending the case, compared to where there is a late guilty plea. Public defender clients were more likely to be convicted. Representation by a public defender increased the chances of a client being convicted from around 83 per cent to 88 per cent. This was primarily because clients of private solicitors were more likely to plead late, allowing for a greater chance in the meantime for the case against them to be dropped by the prosecution, for example because a witness fails to attend the trial. There was no difference between the sentences handed down.

The levels of trust and satisfaction expressed by public defender clients who had not volunteered to use the service, but been obliged to do so, were consistently lower than those expressed by clients using private practitioners. They were less likely to say that their solicitor had done 'a very good job' in listening to what they had to say; telling them what was happening; being there when they wanted them; or having enough time for them. They were also less likely to agree strongly that the solicitor had told the court their side of the story or treated them as though they mattered. Part of the problem appears to have been that clients resented not being able to choose their solicitor and this choice has now been reinstated. Those who had chosen to use the public defender service were more positive about the service. However, they were still significantly less likely than private clients to agree strongly that their lawyer had told the court their side of the story or had treated them as if they mattered, rather than as 'a job to be done'. Public defenders tended to be seen as more 'business-like' and less personally committed than private solicitors. Public defender clients were less likely to say that they would use the service again compared to clients of private solicitors.

The research concluded:

From a managerial perspective, the fact that public defenders resolved cases at an earlier stage has advantages. It has the potential to save legal aid costs and also reduce court and prosecution costs, inconveniencing fewer witnesses. Clients were spared the wait and worry of repeated court [hearings] and were less likely to be held in detention pending the resolution of their case.

At the moment, surprisingly, the public defender service is proving more expensive than private solicitors. The average cost of a case handled by the public defender service is over £800, compared with £506 for private practice. The Legal Aid Practitioners Group has suggested that this is because the taxpayer has to pay the salary of public defenders even if they have failed to attract clients, while private solicitors are only paid for the work they do.

Small businesses

Research has been carried out at the Institute of Advanced Legal Studies into the impact of the Access to Justice Act 1999 funding reforms (*Breaking the Code: the impact of legal aid reforms on general civil litigation* (Goriely and Gysta, 2001)). It highlights problems resulting from the removal of state funding for legal services relating to business disputes. The removal of state funding in this area has attracted little attention, which has led the researchers to comment:

The problem with any discussion of 'businessmen' is that the phrase is laden with overtones. It conjures up an image of a man in a 'business suit', possibly flying 'business class' to a 'business meeting'.

While this is an accurate picture of some business people, it is far from accurate for many others. The Government justified excluding business disputes from state funding on the basis that such cases did not lead to social exclusion and, according to the Government, 'it is not thought justified to spend public money helping businessmen, who fail to insure against the risk of facing legal costs'.

In fact, the research has found that the withdrawal of state funding for business disputes is leaving low-paid workers, such as self-employed cleaners and taxi drivers, with no means of redress if their businesses run into legal difficulties. The researchers found that '[b]usiness failure is a fast track to social exclusion'. When small businesses fail, the impact on a person's life can be enormous. People often end up losing 'their homes, their savings, their marriages, their health and their self-esteem'. Legal expenses insurance is often too expensive and specifically excludes the kinds of difficulties that failing small businesses face. Many policies have clearly been developed for businesses with million-pound turnovers, not for self-employed builders and taxi drivers.

Lack of independence from Government

State-funded work is likely to become the most important source of income for those firms which hold contracts – in some cases, even the only source of income. There are therefore concerns that the threat of losing their contract if they make themselves unpopular with the Government might lead firms to shy away from taking on cases that challenge Government action, or might in any other way embarrass or annoy the Government.

Poorer standards of work

A survey carried out in 1999 for the Legal Aid Practitioners Group found that 84 per cent of legal aid firms believed the Act's reliance on exclusive contracts would reduce the quality of legal services.

The Consumers' Association undertook in 2001 research into the experiences of people seeking help from the Community Legal Service. The research consisted of in-depth interviews of people who had sought help from the service, particularly those from vulnerable groups in society. It found that community centres and law centres provided the best help and advice, but many people felt that the legal system gave them a second-rate service. The research criticised the apparent lack of commitment and poor communication of some solicitors. There were still not enough solicitors and advisers specialising in areas like Social Security, housing, disability discrimination, employment and immigration law. People with disabilities complained of poor physical access to buildings.

The Legal Services Commission has paid for some research into the impact of different funding arrangements on the quality of the provision of legal services (*Quality and Cost: Final report on the contracting of civil, non-family advice and assistance pilot* (2001)). A study was undertaken over two years of 80,000 cases handled by 43 not-for-profit agencies and 100 solicitors' firms. The solicitors' firms were randomly allocated to one of three payment groups: those who continued to be paid as under the old legal aid system; those paid a fixed sum and left to determine how many cases it was reasonable for them to do for the money; and those paid a fixed sum and given a specific number of cases which had to be undertaken. The research concluded that where the payment system gave firms an incentive to do work cheaply, the quality of work suffered. Thus firms in the third group performed worst on most indicators, with 20 per cent of the contracted advisers doing poor quality work. Group 2, in general, performed better than Group 1.

In his *Review of the Criminal Courts* (2001) Sir Robin Auld recommended that changes should be made to the arrangements for the payment of defence lawyers so that they are rewarded for carrying out adequate case preparation.

Over-billing

Lawyers may be charging the Government too much for their work. Audits conducted by the Legal Services Commission of case files kept by suppliers suggest that 35 per cent of suppliers were claiming 20 per cent more than they should have been, although some suppliers have complained about the basis of some of these decisions.

The cost of criminal cases

Criminal legal aid is becoming increasingly expensive. Research on the subject has been carried out by Professors Richard Moorhead and Ed Cape, *Demand Induced Supply?*

Identifying Cost Drivers in Criminal Defence Work (2005). The study concluded that much of the increase in the cost of criminal legal aid was the result of endless changes to the system made by Government.

It seems that currently 1 per cent of criminal cases consume 49 per cent of the budget for the Criminal Defence Service. Following the publication of a consultation paper, *Delivering Value for Money in the Criminal Defence Service* (Lord Chancellor's Department, 2003), the Government has tried to reduce the cost of these cases. Lawyers working on cases lasting more than five weeks, or costing more than £150,000, have to negotiate contracts for payment at each stage of the case.

Criminal barristers consider that they are underpaid for their work and in 2005 they effectively took strike action (they could not officially strike because they were self-employed and not members of a trade union). Fixed fees for Crown Court trials lasting up to ten days were introduced in 1997. The remuneration for these cases has been frozen since it came into force and this represents a 22.5 per cent pay cut in real terms. It has been estimated that junior criminal barristers relying on legal aid work, with up to five years' experience, are earning only between £15,000 and £30,000 a year. They are paid just £46.50 to attend a Crown Court hearing which is not a trial, even though this can take up a whole day due to court delays.

Currently, the Government allocates a single budget to both civil and criminal state funding of legal services. Within this budget criminal defence work takes priority. So while the cost of criminal legal aid is expanding, this leaves less and less for civil legal aid. In 2004 the national legal aid budget was £2 billion, and 60 per cent of this was spent on criminal legal aid. Spending on civil legal aid fell by 22 per cent between 1997 and 2006.

Reliance on private practice

When the legal aid system was first set up, the Government had a choice between using the existing private practice structures or setting up a totally separate system of lawyers, who would be paid salaries from public funds (as doctors are in the NHS), rather than being paid on a case-by-case basis. They chose to give legal aid work to lawyers in private practice. This continues to be the case for state funding under the Community Legal Service, with the sole exception of the criminal defenders. Kate Markus, writing in *The Critical Lawyer's Handbook* (1992), argues that this causes five main problems. First, rather than responding to need, state-funded practitioners in private practice are ruled by the requirements of running a business in a highly competitive marketplace. Private practitioners have to make a profit, even where they are paid by the state, and therefore often feel that they must limit the time they spend on state-funded cases. This problem severely limits the services they can offer to the clients. It is also the reason why so many lawyers have refused to do state-funded work which, given the funding problems, has never been able to compete with privately paid work in terms of the salaries paid.

Secondly, private solicitors' practices are very much geared towards legal problems concerning money and property, which means that, as far as general high street so-licitors are concerned, their expertise is often not developed in those areas affecting the poorer client.

The third problem, which we have mentioned before, is that solicitors in private practice may be seen as intimidating by the majority of poorer clients. They are then put off bringing their problems to them, especially in areas where they are not sure whether it is appropriate to involve a lawyer.

The fourth issue Markus highlights is that private practice is geared largely to litigation (bringing cases to court), which is not always the best solution to the kind of problems facing the poorer members of society. Let us say, for example, that a local council is failing to fulfil its obligations to tenants, with the result that many of them are living in unacceptable housing. Each affected family could take the council to court, but that would be expensive and time-consuming, and only solve the problem for those families who actually did so. But with access to good legal advice on their rights, the tenants could get together and put pressure on the council themselves, potentially solving a problem affecting lots of people in one action, and much more cheaply. Law centres (see pp. 350–1) often work this way, but the working practices of private practitioners, and the case-by-case way in which legal aid was funded, made it impossible for them to do much, if any, of this kind of work.

Finally, Markus makes the point that any system which seeks to make justice truly accessible has to address the problem of widespread ignorance of legal rights and how to assert them; after all, if a person with a legal problem is unaware that there might be a legal right which could solve it, he or she will not even think of getting legal help in the first place. That means educating people about their rights, and private practice, where every task a lawyer does has to be paid for, is simply not set up to do that kind of work.

Conditional fee agreements

In the US, a great many cases brought by ordinary individuals are funded by what are called contingency fees, or 'no win, no fee' agreements. Lawyers can agree with clients that no fee will be charged if they lose the case but, if they win, the fee will be an agreed percentage of the damages won. This obviously gives the lawyer a direct personal interest in the level of damages, and there have been suggestions that this is partly responsible for the soaring levels of damages seen in the US courts.

In the English legal system, contingency fees are banned, but in 1990 the Courts and Legal Services Act (CLSA) made provision for the introduction of conditional fee agreements. Under a conditional fee agreement, solicitors can agree to take no fee or a reduced fee if they lose, and raise their fee by an agreed percentage if they win, up to a maximum of double the usual fee. The solicitor calculates the extra fee (usually called the 'uplift' or 'success fee') on the basis of the size of the risk involved – if the client seems very likely to win, the uplift will generally be lower than in a case where the outcome is more difficult to predict. The rule that the losing party must pay the winner's costs remains, so a party using a conditional fee agreement will usually take out insurance to cover this if he or she should lose.

The Access to Justice Act 1999 makes some changes to the arrangements for conditional fee agreements in order to promote their use. Where a person who has made a conditional fee agreement wins his or her case, it will be possible for the court to order the losing party to pay the success fee, as well as the normal legal costs. Thus the success fee is now only ever payable by the losing party, which is a complete reversal of the previous situation. This provision is designed to meet the criticism that damages are calculated to compensate the litigant for the harm caused to him or her, so if the 'uplift' has to come out of the client's damages, the amount left will be less than the court calculated as necessary for the purpose of full compensation.

Similarly, where a winning litigant has taken out insurance to provide for payment of the other side's costs if he or she loses, the court can order that the other side also pays the cost of the insurance premium. As a result, people who are bringing actions for remedies other than the payment of money can use a conditional fee arrangement. These changes have caused problems in practice. The cost of after-the-event insurance has increased considerably, and some clients are finding it difficult to get such insurance. There has been a lot of litigation over paying these extra costs by the losing party. To try to reduce this problem, new rules of court have been written which fix the success fee for particular types of litigation, such as road traffic accidents, depending on the circumstances of the case. For example, where litigation involves an accident at work and the employee brings a claim on the basis of a conditional fee agreement; if that action is successful, the employer's insurer will pay the employee's solicitor their normal costs, plus a success fee of 25 per cent of these costs if the case settled before trial, and a 100 per cent success fee for a riskier case that went to trial. It might be better if the sums were simply covered by judges increasing the award of damages to take into account these extra expenses.

There is no means test to determine whether a person is entitled to bring litigation on the basis of a conditional fee agreement. Naomi Campbell had brought legal proceedings against the publishers of the *Daily Mirror*. The case claimed that the newspaper had breached her right to privacy because it had published pictures of her leaving a support group for recovering drug users. Her claim was rejected by the Court of Appeal and she proceeded to appeal to the House of Lords. To pay for this appeal she reached a conditional fee agreement with her solicitors and her barrister. Her appeal to the House of Lords was successful and the publishing company was ordered to pay her £3,500 in damages and her costs. Her costs were £1,086,295.47 in total. The size of the bill for the appeal to the House of Lords was particularly high because the conditional fee agreement allowed for a success fee of 95 per cent for her solicitor and 100 per cent for her barrister. The publishers contested these costs, arguing that the success fee was so disproportionate that it infringed their rights to free speech under Art. 10 of the European Convention on Human Rights. It argued that as Naomi Campbell was a rich celebrity she could have afforded to fund her litigation without a conditional fee agreement, while the conditional fee agreement scheme was intended to help people who could not otherwise afford to sue. The House of Lords rejected this argument – conditional fee agreements were not means tested, and the publishers had to pay all the costs.

The Access to Justice Act 1999 made conditional fee agreements available for all cases apart from medical negligence. The Government is now considering stopping state funding for medical negligence actions, so that these too would fall within the remit of conditional fee agreements. The Government's consultation paper, *A new focus for civil legal aid: encouraging early resolution; discouraging unnecessary litigation* (2005), suggests that medical negligence cases could be transferred to the conditional fee agreement system after research into the possible impact of this change has been completed. It is questionable whether conditional fees are appropriate for such cases. They are generally very difficult for claimants to win – the success rate is around 17 per cent, compared with 85 per cent for other personal injury claims (often caused by road accidents). While the outcome of litigation arising from a road accident is often reasonably easy to predict, medical negligence cases require detailed reports before anyone can hazard a guess about whether any party is to blame. The evidence is that solicitors will only take on a case under a conditional fee agreement if they estimate there is at least a 70 per cent chance of being successful. It can cost between £2,000 and £5,000 simply to do the initial investigations necessary to assess accurately whether the case is worth pursuing. As a result, solicitors would be very unlikely to want to take on such cases on a conditional fee basis and, even if they did, the uncertainty of outcome means that insurance against losing would be extremely expensive, possibly amounting to thousands of pounds. On the other hand, removing state funding could be an effective way of reducing the National Health Service's legal costs. In 2003 the NHS was facing a record £4.4 billion bill in outstanding negligence claims.

The Government is currently considering introducing collective conditional fee agreements. These are designed for bulk users of legal services such as trade unions and insurers.

Advantages of conditional fee agreements

Cost to the state

Conditional fee agreements cost the state nothing – the costs are entirely borne by the solicitor or the losing party, depending on the outcome. By removing the huge number of personal injury cases from state funding and promoting conditional fee agreements for them instead, the Government claims it can devote more resources to those cases which still need state funding, such as tenants' claims against landlords, and direct more money towards suppliers of free legal advice, such as Citizens' Advice Bureaux.

Wider access to justice

The Government believes that conditional fee agreements will allow many people to bring or defend cases who would not have been eligible for state funding and who could not previously have afforded to bring cases at their own expense. As long as they can afford to insure against losing, and can persuade a solicitor that the case is worth the risk, anyone will be able to bring or defend a case for damages. Critics point out that there are a number of problems with this argument (see below).

Performance incentives

Supporters claim conditional fees encourage solicitors to perform better, since they have a financial interest in winning cases funded this way.

Wider coverage

Conditional fee agreements are allowed for defamation actions, and cases brought before tribunals, two major gaps in the provision of state funding.

Public acceptance

The Law Society suggests that clients have readily accepted conditional fee agreements in those areas where they have been permitted in the past. Within two years of the agreements being introduced, almost 30,000 conditional fee agreements had been signed, and by 1999 around 25,000 were in operation.

Fairness to opponents

There are restrictions on the costs state-funded clients can be made to pay to the other side, which can give them an unfair advantage, particularly in cases where both sides are ordinary individuals but only one has qualified for state funding. The requirement for insurance in conditional fee cases solves this problem.

Disadvantages of conditional fee agreements

Uncertain cases

Most of those who have criticised the legislation on conditional fee agreements accept that they are a good addition to the state-funded system, but are concerned that they may not be adequate as a substitute. In particular, critics – including the Bar, the Law Society, the Legal Action Group and the Vice-Chancellor of the Supreme Court, Sir Richard Scott – have expressed strong concerns that certain types of case will lose out under the new rules. They suggest that solicitors will only want to take on cases under conditional fee agreements where there is a very high chance of winning. It was for this reason that medical negligence cases have been kept within the state-funded system.

Another area which could be hit is that of cases which have enormous public importance, but which need large amounts of work, are difficult to win, and may attract relatively low levels of damages even if successful. These include some types of action against the police and Government, such as complaints by prisoners about their treatment. The Act does address these issues in that it provides for cases in excluded categories to be funded in exceptional circumstances; it remains to be seen whether this will be sufficiently flexible in practice.

Unfair trials

Where legal aid is refused, a subsequent trial may prove to be unfair if one party is unrepresented by a lawyer as a result, and the other party benefited from legal representation. This can amount to a breach of Art. 6 of the European Convention, which guarantees the right to a fair trial.

Ess. Cases
p. 243 →

KEY CASE

The problem of unrepresented defendants was highlighted by the case which has come to be known as the McLibel Two (**Steel v United Kingdom** (2005)). The defendants were two environmental campaigners who had distributed leaflets outside McDonald's restaurants. These leaflets criticised the nutritional content of the food sold in the restaurants. McDonald's sued the two defendants for defamation. The defendants were refused legal aid because it is not generally available for defamation cases (see p. 345). They therefore represented themselves throughout the proceedings, with only limited help from some sympathetic lawyers who provided a small amount of assistance for free. McDonald's were represented by a team of specialist lawyers. The libel trial lasted for 313 days and was the longest civil action in English legal history. The defendants lost the case and were ordered to pay £60,000 in damages (later reduced to £40,000 on appeal). They challenged the fairness of the UK proceedings in the European Court of Human Rights. That challenge was successful. The European Court held that the McLibel Two had not had a fair trial in breach of Art. 6 of the European Convention on Human Rights and there had been a breach of their right to freedom of expression under Art. 10 of the Convention.

> Where state-funded legal representation is unavailable to a private individual in legal proceedings, there may sometimes be a breach of the European Convention guaranteeing the right to a fair trial and freedom of expression.

17

Paying for legal services

Claimants misled

Ess. Cases
p. 240 →

The Citizens' Advice Bureau has issued a report entitled *No win, no fee, no chance* (2005). This expresses concern that consumers are being misled by the term 'no win, no fee'. Often consumers find that the system costs them more than they gain. Consumers are subjected to aggressive and high-pressured sales tactics from unqualified employees of claims management companies. These companies receive a fee from solicitors for passing them a case. Consumers can be subjected to inappropriate marketing tactics; for example, accident victims have been approached in hospital. Consumers are not informed clearly of the financial risks that the legal proceedings will involve, and are misled into believing that the system will genuinely be 'no win, no fee'. In fact, consumers may need to take out an insurance policy to offset any legal expenses incurred if they lose the case and are required to pay the other side's costs. If the claim is, for example, against the council for failure to repair a council flat, a building surveyor may need to be paid as well as the lawyers. These legal expenses can be artificially inflated by unscrupulous claims management companies. The consumer can be encouraged to take out a loan to pay the monthly instalments of the insurance policy. The consumer frequently discovers that these expenses have wiped out any compensation they win. The injured person does not as a result benefit from the compensation they are entitled to. In some cases, the consumer even ends up owing money. In one case handled by the Citizens' Advice Bureau a woman was left with just £15 from a £2,150 compensation payout, and in another case a man received compensation of £1,250 for an accident at work, but owed nearly £2,400 for insurance relating to the litigation.

In **Bowne and ten others** *v* **Bridgend County Borough Council** (2004) the litigation had arisen when employees of a claims management company had knocked on council tenants' doors suggesting that claims could be made. An action was brought against the council for failing to carry out housing repairs. The claimants had taken out loans to pay for insurance policies to cover any legal expenses they incurred. The average compensation paid to claimants was £1,631, but the claimants' solicitors sought an average of £8,000 in costs against the local authority. In fact the court only ordered £250 to be paid, holding that many of the legal fees were unjustified and not payable.

The Government is hoping to improve the conduct of claims management companies through provisions contained in the Compensation Act 2006 to regulate these companies.

Insurance costs

There are concerns that insurance against losing can be expensive. In the area of personal injury, the Law Society provides an affordable insurance scheme, but in other areas the only suppliers are private insurance companies, who charge according to risk, so that clients with cases where the outcome is uncertain may be faced with very high premiums.

Both the Law Society and the Bar have suggested that a better idea would be the establishment of a self-financing Contingency Fund, which would pay for cases on the understanding that successful litigants would pay a proportion of their damages back to the fund. As we said earlier, this is allowed by the Act, but the Government has said it has no plans to use the power at the moment.

Financial involvement of lawyers

The evidence on solicitors' approach to the uplift on fees is currently rather inconclusive. A 1998 report by the Policy Studies Institute on the effects of the changes made under the Courts and Legal Services Act 1990 found that the average uplift was 43 per cent, less than half the 100 per cent maximum allowed – but, within that average, one in ten solicitors was charging between 90 and 100 per cent. The author of the study, Stella Yarrow, commented that the number of cases assessed as having a low chance of success was surprisingly large, suggesting that solicitors might be under-estimating the chances of winning, in order to increase the uplift. The Minister for Justice has threatened to impose tighter limits on the success fees that can be charged by lawyers because he claims lawyers are abusing the system to increase their earnings.

In 1999, the Forum of Insurance Lawyers (Foil) suggested that the chance to make extra money was encouraging solicitors to push clients into conditional fee agreements, even where the clients did not need such an agreement. Around 17 million people in Britain have some form of legal expenses insurance attached to their home, car or credit card insurance, and in many cases this will pay their legal costs for them. However, Foil points out, many people have this insurance without realising it, and it claims that, instead of suggesting that clients check whether they have it, solicitors are persuading them to enter into unnecessary conditional fee agreements.

A further problem was highlighted by members of the Bar in an article on the subject in *The Lawyer* newspaper in 1999. The piece gave as an example one barrister who had lost three conditional fee cases in a row, thus earning nothing at all for his work on them. This is clearly a risk that lawyers choose to face, but human nature being what it is, the article points out, the temptation for that barrister next time would be to settle the case early, even if that means accepting compensation lower than the client might get in court, with the guarantee of some financial reward, rather than going to court and risking the fee again. The result is that there will be cases where the lawyer's financial interest is in direct opposition to the client's.

A large amount of satellite litigation has also arisen involving disputes over the legal costs of the case. In other words, once the main case has finished the parties sometimes start arguing over how much legal costs the losing party should have to pay and this argument ends up back in court.

Insurance pressures

There may also be pressure to settle from insurance companies, some of whom have been known to threaten to withdraw their cover if a client refuses to accept an offer of settlement that the insurance company considers reasonable. Clearly the insurance company's primary interest will be to avoid having to pay out, so it is not difficult to see that their idea of a reasonable settlement might be very different from the client's – or from what the client could expect to get if the case continued.

Abuse in defamation proceedings

There is concern that conditional fee agreements are being used inappropriately in defamation proceedings, and thereby threatening the right to freedom of expression. Bringing a case to court using a conditional fee agreement is equivalent to bringing litigation on credit. Following a critical newspaper article, it is easy for a person to bring proceedings for defamation at no expense to themselves, but the newspaper is forced to incur considerable expense to defend such a claim. Claimants will not be worried by the costs being incurred on their behalf and will have no incentive to settle. While it may be clear that a newspaper article damages the reputation of the claimant, the burden of proof will pass to the defendant to show, for example, that the article was true or fair comment. As a result, there needs to be strong case management by judges in defamation cases and the capping of costs where appropriate.

Are lawyers always necessary?

As we have seen, many of the non-statutory advice schemes use advisers who are not legally qualified. Some of these lay advisers appear as advocates in tribunals and in some cases have been granted discretionary rights of audience in the county courts, as well as giving legal advice. In particular, advisers for charities such as MIND have shown themselves to be more than a match for most solicitors in their knowledge of the law in their fields. Many solicitor firms also employ non-qualified workers to do legal work.

The skills of a good adviser are not always the same as those of a good lawyer; what the client needs is someone who can interview sympathetically, ascertain the pertinent facts from what may be a long, rambling and in some cases emotional story, analyse the problem and suggest a course of action. The preliminary skills are just as likely to be possessed by a lay person as by a lawyer, even if a lawyer may be needed to advise on the course of action.

Nor are lawyers considered to be the best advocates in every situation. The National Consumer Council advised against allowing them to represent clients in the Small Claims Court, on the grounds that they could make the procedure unnecessarily long-winded and legalistic.

However, critics identify two possible problems in the growing use of lay advisers. First, although most organisations are scrupulous in training their advisers, some may be more casual, and there is no obligatory check on advisers before they are allowed to deal with cases. The general public may not always be in a position to assess the quality of the advice they are given. Secondly, the large number of overlapping agencies means it can be difficult for consumers of legal advice to find the best provider for them and can be wasteful of scarce resources. The Government hopes that the development of Community Legal Service Partnerships will help to tackle this problem.

Proposals for further reform

With the Access to Justice Act 1999 the Government introduced major reforms to the provision of state funding of legal services and further reforms are already in the pipeline.

TOPICAL ISSUE

Best value tendering

In 2005, the Lord Chancellor asked Lord Carter to carry out a review of the legal aid system. Major reforms have now been recommended by Lord Carter in his report, *Legal aid: a market-based approach to reform* (2006). Immediately after the publication of this report, the Government issued a consultation paper, *Legal Aid: a sustainable future* (2006). It published a second consultation paper in 2007 entitled *Best Value Tendering for Criminal Defence Services*. These papers consider many of Lord Carter's recommendations.

Ess. Cases
p. 254 →

Lord Carter has recommended the introduction of a new procurement process for state-funded legal aid, known as best value tendering. This would involve asking legal service providers to make bids for contracts to deliver categories of state-funded legal services in a particular geographical area. The reforms are likely to be introduced for criminal defence work in 2013 and for civil work in 2015 at the earliest. To prepare for this procurement process two pilot schemes are to be established in 2010 and a national system of peer review is currently being undertaken. Peer review means that law firms are assessed for the quality of their service by their peers; in other words, by other experienced and independent solicitors. The peer review system identifies firms that have attained the requisite quality thresholds, known as preferred suppliers, and they will be invited to apply for a contract with the Legal Services Commission. The tendering competition will be decided according to which firm bids to do the most work for the lowest price. A pilot scheme of a preferred supplier system, involving 25 firms through-out 2004–05, was shown to reduce bureaucracy and raise standards of service, as well as improve the relationship between the Legal Services Commission and legal aid firms. Legal aid lawyers have been strongly opposed to the introduction of competitive tendering and have pointed to hospital cleaning, school dinners and prison transport as examples of why tendering should not be used as a procurement mechanism.

Lord Carter criticised the current criminal legal aid system for spending money on 'unproductive time and anomalies in the system'. Payment is calculated on the basis of the number of hours spent on a case, and does not therefore reward efficiency. He recommends that criminal legal aid lawyers should no longer be paid by the hour, but by the case. Fixed fees will be introduced across the board for criminal cases, calculated according to the type of case. Fees will be front-loaded to encourage early preparation and discourage trials. It is argued that a fixed fee regime allows efficient firms to be more profitable, since they expend less input to produce the same quality service and get the same fee as a less efficient firm:

> Fixed pricing rewards efficiency and suppliers who can deliver increased volumes of work. However pricing should be graduated for more complex work so that cases genuinely requiring more expertise and effort are priced fairly.

Also, under the planned reforms, efficient firms will be able to win new contracts in the best value tendering process.

Lord Carter is also of the view that large law firms are more efficient than small ones. He predicts that his recommendations for procurement contracts, combined with the implementation of Sir David Clementi's recommendations (see p. 210), will lead to 'an increase in the average size of firms through growth and mergers, ration-alization and harmonization of the way separate services are delivered'. To encourage this move towards larger law firms, the Legal Services Commission is proposing to grant legal aid contracts worth at least £25,000. Contracts could be awarded to either individual firms or a collection of firms formed to deliver the benefits of scale. Thus, there will be a move towards granting fewer and larger contracts. The number of people involved might not change dramatically but they would work for fewer employers.

Lord Carter considers that it is uneconomic for both the Legal Services Commission and solicitors to deliver small amounts of legal aid work. He suggests that grants should be made available to support this transition, including money for investment in com-puter technology and modernisation. However, while the Government is prepared to provide some practical support to law firms during this period of transition, it will not provide financial grants. Lord Carter argues that this reorganisation will be in the inter-ests of legal aid lawyers, saying that sole practitioners (lawyers working in an office on their own) are likely to earn between £36,000 and £55,000, while equity partners in a legal aid firm with 40 fee earners could expect to earn between £120,000 and £150,000.

17

Paying for legal services

The aim of these reforms is to control the cost and quality of legal aid and to promote efficiency of service in the public interest. Lord Carter predicts that implementation of his proposals could lead to a saving of £100 million a year, with criminal legal aid costing 20 per cent less than in 2005. He suggests that, without these new procurement reforms, the same sort of price inflation as seen in the past decade would more than likely be repeated in the future.

The reform plans have been the subject of considerable criticism from legal aid lawyers. A consultation paper on price-competitive tendering issued by the Legal Services Commission in 2005 found that 85 per cent of respondents were opposed to this system. Sixty per cent said the proposals would have a negative effect on the quality of legal advice. Lord Carter's strategy has been dismissed by critics as 'pile them high, sell them cheap'. Black and minority ethnic solicitors frequently work as sole practitioners or in small legal aid firms, and this has led to concern that such firms may suffer if these reforms are introduced. The reforms are likely to lead to a legal aid client having a narrower choice of lawyer. The contracts will only last for one or two years. Initially, there will be intense competition to obtain one of these contracts. Once the contracts have been allocated, a monopoly will have been created in each geographical area for the contract period – economically, an extremely unhealthy market structure and quite the opposite of the 'diverse and competitive market' intended. A criminal law firm which fails to get a contract is unlikely to survive six months and it will be difficult for any new solicitor to enter the market given the emphasis on larger firms being preferred suppliers.

America already has some experience of contracting out criminal defence services through competitive bidding. Research into their experience was carried out by Roger Smith (1998), who is now the director of the pressure group JUSTICE. This concluded that the process led to reductions in quality, the compromising of professional ethics and the creation of cartels leading to an increase in costs. The US Department of Justice produced a special report on the subject in 2000 and found that such schemes lead to an increase of complaints by defendants, partly because the contracting process encouraged lawyers to take on too many cases. It also led to an increase in costs as some legal service providers submitted a low bid to win a contract and then raised the bid in the second and subsequent bidding rounds, once the local competition had been destroyed. Roger Smith (2007) has commented on the Government reforms:

> The future is now pretty clear. By the end of the period of this spending round, we will be well on the way to a new pattern of provision. A small group of large firms will control legal aid – maybe eventually as low as 100. Given the Legal Services Bill, they may be owned by external corporate interests and milked – like gas, water and football clubs – as steady cash cows for foreign corporate interests. The firms will operate as a cartel: prices will stabilise at a low but predictable level; contractors will covertly reduce the number of clients and the quality of their services; clients will be allocated lawyers without choice. Here and there, a few angry, passionate souls will deliver excellence: the norm will be mediocrity.

A national legal service?

Perhaps the most radical reform would be to take the statutory scheme entirely out of the hands of private practice and establish a nationwide network of salaried lawyers on the law centre model. All funding could be given on a block rather than case-by-case basis, for centres to use in whatever ways best met the needs of their own locality, in consultation with management committees representing the community. The nationalisation of criminal defence work was considered briefly in the Government's consultation paper *Best Value Tendering for Criminal Defence Services* (2007).

The nationalisation of state-funded legal services would deal with some of the criticisms of the current schemes made by Kate Markus and discussed above (pp. 358–9). In particular the advantages of this idea include:

- state-funded work would no longer have to compete with private work for lawyers' time;
- state funding would no longer have to include an element of profit for the lawyer;
- resources could be more flexibly employed, on a combination of individual casework and litigation, education and campaigning, or any other approach that suited particular problems;
- this more flexible approach to dealing with problems would get away from the over-emphasis on litigation of solicitors in private practice;
- the ability to run educative campaigns would help deal with public ignorance of legal rights;
- law centres appear not to suffer from the unapproachable image of the legal profession in general;
- law centres have been successful in attracting problems not previously brought to lawyers, especially welfare and employment cases;
- a nationwide network of such centres would help overcome the uneven distribution of solicitors' firms.

The 1979 Royal Commission on Legal Services did suggest the establishment of a nationwide network of centrally financed Citizens' Law Centres, but felt that these should be restricted to individual casework only and not get involved in general work for the community. This idea would fail to take advantage of one of the real strengths of the law centre movement, and the fact that solicitors in private practice would still be allowed to undertake state-funded work would limit the improvements to be made in cost-efficiency. The Law Centres Federation rejected the idea.

In a 1995 article for *The Guardian* newspaper barrister Daniel Stilitz argued for a similar scheme, though not necessarily based on law centres. Under his National Justice Service, anyone seeking to bring a legal action would need to show a reasonable cause. If the case had a reasonable prospect of success, the National Justice Service would decide what services were needed, fix a budget and allocate a lawyer on the basis of suitability and availability. Stilitz points out that for such a scheme to equalise access to justice, it would have to be compulsory – if one side was allowed to 'go private', the scales might be tipped unfairly in their favour. So, both sides would be obliged to use National Justice Service lawyers. The service would be means-tested, with contributions of up to 100 per cent, ensuring that those who could afford to pay the whole cost did so, but could not use that wealth to secure an advantage in the justice system. Those who could not afford to pay would receive free or subsidised help. The result, says Stilitz, would be a level playing field, with cases decided on merits and wasteful tactics designed to drive up costs eliminated.

Stilitz acknowledges that the plan would remove client choice, but argues that improving access to justice is more important. He also points out that while many might object to the loss of independence involved in tying lawyers so closely to the state, this cannot have a worse effect on individual rights than the current system, under which financial pressures mean that for many citizens their rights are useless because they cannot afford to enforce them.

No-fault compensation

Instead of looking to conditional fee agreements to secure justice for those injured in accidents, such cases could be removed from the litigation arena by the establishment of a system of no-fault compensation for personal injury cases, as was done in New Zealand.

Class actions

Some people would like to see the American approach to class actions introduced to the UK (see, for example, Howard Epstein (2003)). In America, a single claimant can bring an action for damages on behalf of a whole class of claimants, who may be assumed to have suffered the same harm. After an award of damages has been made the lawyer can then locate those who are entitled to share it.

Encouraging ADR

The Government issued a consultation paper, *A new focus for civil legal aid: encouraging early resolution; discouraging unnecessary litigation* (2005). This paper suggests that state funding of legal services should be shifted from supporting litigation to supporting pre-trial settlements. This change would be achieved by introducing new pay structures which would provide incentives to settle disputes before going to court.

Contingency fees

The Law Society has issued a consultation paper (2009) considering whether conditional fee agreements have proved too costly and should be replaced by contingency fees. While a conditional fee agreement allows the lawyer to be paid an increased fee if the action is successful, under a contingency fee agreement lawyers receive a share of the successful claimant's award of damages. Research carried out for the Civil Justice Council by Professor Moorhead and Senior Costs Judge Peter Hurst (2008) has found that contingency fees could operate effectively in England and Wales, particularly if each party was responsible for their own costs, rather than the traditional rule that the loser pays the winner's costs (known as cost shifting). The introduction of contingency fees would eliminate much of the satellite litigation over costs in conditional fee cases.

Contingency fees would provide a 'cleaner and less complicated model' of litigation than conditional fee agreements and there was a 'surprising absence of evidence' of consumer disquiet. There was also no evidence that in the US they discouraged the parties from reaching an out of court settlement or that they led to high rates of litigation, frivolous claims or a litigation culture. There was no evidence that the use of contingency fees had led to excessive awards of damages to take into account the lawyers' fees that will need to be deducted. However, there is a risk that contingency fees could narrow access to justice, particularly for low-value cases, risky cases and cases that are not seeking a financial remedy, as these are less likely to be brought under a contingency fee. The final conclusion of the report was that there was no urgent need to introduce contingency fees to the UK.

Contingency fees are already allowed in employment tribunals and they do not appear to have given rise to major problems. Research by Professor Moorhead (Moorhead and Cumming, 2008) on contingency fees in tribunals found that they provide a very slight improvement in access to justice. There was no evidence that contingency fees led to an increase in weak tribunal claims, or that the percentage fees charged were excessive. Moorhead found that there needed to be greater openness in the way lawyers' fees were calculated and there was some evidence that the contingency fee arrangements increased the pressure to settle, leading to cases being compromised inappropriately.

17

Paying for legal services

TOPICAL ISSUE

Class actions

Sometimes one unlawful act does not only harm a single individual but a large group of individuals. In these circumstances it can be much more efficient for a single group action to be brought to the courts, rather than lots of individual cases. However, at the moment there are many obstacles in the way of bringing successful group actions in England, unlike in America. In particular, the Legal Services Commission imposes tight controls on the award of public funds for multi-party actions and only £3 million is allocated each year for such cases. At the moment class actions can only be brought in the UK on behalf of a clearly identified claimant group. This is known as the opt-in system as you will only be entitled to damages if you first commence your own litigation against the defence, and your case is then managed collectively under a Group Litigation Order or representative action provided for by the Civil Procedure Rules. The damages awarded are calculated on an individual basis looking at the entitlement of each of the individual claimants. In America an opt-out system is used, where the court can make an award taking into account any potential claimant and then, once the award is made, relevant claimants can come forward to receive their share of the damages (otherwise they opt out if they do not want to be involved). In practice this is much easier to administer than the UK opt-in system. Under the American system aggregate damages can be awarded by which the amount of damages are calculated to take into account the loss suffered by the whole class of claimant, rather than just that of the individual claimants before the court. Class members are then notified after the judgment of their entitlement to a share of the settlement.

▶

The Civil Justice Council has issued a report on this subject – *Improving Access to Justice Through Collective Actions* (2008) – calling for legislation enabling class actions for groups of consumers or businesses to be possible on an opt-out basis. Cases would only be allowed to proceed with the permission of a court. Class actions would be subject to an enhanced form of case management by specialist judges and any settlement agreed should be approved by the court by means of a 'fairness hearing'. The Civil Justice Council has found that there is overwhelming evidence that valid consumer claims are not being pursued at the moment and it has recommended that class actions should be possible for consumer cases. To try to avoid one of the weaknesses in the American class action system, the opt-out system would maintain the loser pays costs principle, and the court would only allow the case to proceed if the claimant had sufficient funds in place to cover any adverse costs orders.

The European Union issued a consultation paper in 2005 in which it recommended the use of collective actions for damages in competition cases. Consumer groups and trade associations would be able to bring cases against companies illegally fixing prices. There is a practical problem of how to fund these cases and most European countries do not want to see the introduction of American-style contingency fees.

While group litigation has been successful in America against cigarette manufacturers it has not been successful in the United Kingdom. In November 2007 the drugs manufacturer Merck announced plans to pay more than $4.85 billion to Americans who claim to have suffered heart attacks and strokes after taking a drug for arthritis. The pharmaceutical company has refused to make any payments to the UK claimants (and claimants elsewhere) who took their legal action in the United Kingdom where they had been refused legal aid. When the Italian company Parmalat collapsed in 2003, group litigation was brought in America because this was considered more effective than the litigation options in Europe. The risk therefore is that if Europe does not make appropriate arrangements for group litigation, then forum shopping will lead to the American system being introduced through the back door.

Answering questions

1 **Recent reforms in legal aid are motivated by financial concerns rather than the desire to ensure access to justice for all.** *London External LLB*

An answer to this question might be divided into four main parts:

- Reforms in the Access to Justice Act 1999.
- Financial concerns.
- Problems with access to justice.
- Ensuring access to justice.

You could use these as subheadings so that the reader can see the clear structure of your answer.

Reforms in the Access to Justice Act 1999

You could provide a brief explanation of the reforms that were introduced (discussed at pp. 343–52). Keep this part of your answer quite short, as it is only one aspect of an answer to the question.

Financial concerns

Clearly, financial concerns were a key reason for the introduction of these reforms. We mentioned that there were problems in the 1990s with the escalating costs of the legal aid scheme, and unsuccessful attempts were made to keep the costs down. A key aim of the reforms was to put in place tighter controls on the budget, though the scheme is still not cheap, costing £2 billion a year (see pp. 352–4 under the subheadings 'Control of costs' and 'Cost-cutting').

Problems with access to justice

These problems are discussed at p. 340.

Ensuring access to justice

You could look at what aspects of the reforms specifically target improving access to justice. For example, the creation of a website for the Legal Services Commission, the establishment of Community Legal Service Partnerships which try to match legal services to the local needs, the improved means test for civil cases, and the abolition of the means test for criminal cases.

On the other hand, you can point to ways in which access has been reduced. At p. 345 there is a list of cases for which state funding has been removed altogether. The number of legal suppliers has also been reduced (see p. 353). The material under the subheading 'Small businesses' on p. 356 is relevant here.

2 **The financial reform provisions on state-funded legal help contained in the Access to Justice Act 1999 were intended to enhance access to justice. In your view, have these reforms achieved their intended purpose?**

The obvious starting point is to set out what the main financial reform provisions were, what the Legal Services Commission is and what it does. It is arguable that the reforms have lessened access to justice and not improved it. Problems with access include that:

● certain types of case fall outside the scheme;
● delays result from the application of the merits and means tests;
● only a limited amount of firms have contracts with the Legal Services Commission;
● there are tight financial constraints; and
● individuals are unwilling to pursue their legal rights.

The strengths and weaknesses of the reforms are discussed on pp. 352–9. You could conclude by discussing future reforms and any suggestions as to how access to justice could be improved (see the 'Topical issue' on p. 366).

3 **Should all state funding for legal services be replaced by conditional fee agreements?** *LLB*

You could look at the impact of increasing the role of conditional fee agreements in the English legal system since the relevant provisions of the Courts and Legal Services Act 1990 were brought into force in 1995. Conditional fee agreements have already replaced state funding for all personal injury cases (except medical negligence cases), and the Government is currently considering whether state funding could be removed for medical negligence cases. You could examine the arguments for and against such a move. It could be noted that conditional fee agreements cost the state nothing and allow for access to justice, encourage performance by

17

Paying for legal services

legal professionals and are in common use. However, conditional fee agreements encourage lawyers to take only those cases with a strong prospect of success and give lawyers a financial interest in the outcome of a case.

Summary of Chapter 17: Paying for legal services

Unmet need for legal services

Unmet legal need essentially describes the situation where a person has a problem that could potentially be solved through the law, but the person is unable to get whatever help he or she needs to use the legal system.

Legal aid before the Access to Justice Act 1999

The six schemes which made up the legal aid scheme until the 1999 Access to Justice Act was brought into force were:

- the legal advice and assistance scheme (known as the 'green form' scheme because of the paperwork used);
- assistance by way of representation (ABWOR);
- civil legal aid;
- criminal legal aid;
- duty solicitor schemes in police stations; and
- duty solicitor schemes for criminal cases in magistrates' courts.

State funding of legal services today

With the passing of the Access to Justice Act 1999 the Labour Government introduced some major reforms to the provision of state-funded legal services. On 1 April 2000 the Legal Aid Board was replaced by the Legal Services Commission.

The Legal Services Commission administers two schemes: the Community Legal Service which is concerned with civil matters and the Criminal Defence Service which is concerned with criminal matters.

The Community Legal Service

Direct funding is provided for different categories of legal service as follows:

- legal help;
- legal representation;
- help at court;
- approved family help; and
- family mediation.

The Criminal Defence Service

State funding can provide direct funding for three types of service in the criminal field:

- advice and assistance;
- advocacy assistance; and
- representation.

In addition, the Legal Services Commission employs public defenders and pays for duty solicitor schemes.

Conditional fee agreements

In 1990 the Courts and Legal Services Act made provision for the introduction of conditional fee agreements. The scope for their use was increased by the Access to Justice Act 1999.

Reform

In his report, *Legal aid: a market-based approach to reform* (2006), Lord Carter has recommended the introduction of some important, money-saving reforms to the system of state-funded legal services and the Government is in the process of introducing these reforms.

Reading list

Abel-Smith, B., Zander, M. and Brooke, R. (1973) *Legal Problems and the Citizen*, London: Heinemann-Educational.

Citizens' Advice Bureau (2004) *Geography of Advice*, London: Citizens' Advice Bureau.

Citizens' Advice Bureau (2005) *No win, no fee, no chance*, London: Citizens' Advice Bureau.

Epstein, H. (2003) 'The liberalisation of claim financing', 153 *New Law Journal* 153.

Genn, H. (1982) *Meeting Legal Needs? An Evaluation of a Scheme for Personal Injury Victims*, Oxford: SSRC Centre for Socio-Legal Studies.

Goriely, T. and Gysta, P. (2001) *Breaking the Code: The Impact of Legal Aid Reforms on General Civil Litigation*, London: Institute of Advanced Legal Studies.

Hynes, S. and Robins, J. (2009) *The Justice Gap: Whatever Happened to Legal Aid?* London: Legal Action Group.

Law Society (2008) *Conditional Fees: A Guide to CFAs and Other Funding Options*, London: Law Society.

Lord Chancellor's Department (2003) *Delivering Value for Money in the Criminal Defence Service*, Consultation Paper, London: Lord Chancellor's Department.

Making Simple CFAs a Reality (2004) London: Department for Constitutional Affairs.

Markus, K. (1992) 'The Politics of Legal Aid' in *The Critical Lawyer's Handbook*, London: Pluto Press.

National Audit Office (2003) *Community Legal Service: The Introduction of Contracting*, HC 89, 2002–03, London: HMSO.

Sanders, A. and Bridges, L. (1993) 'Access to Legal Advice' in Walker, C. and Starmer, K. (eds) *Justice in Error*, London: Blackstone Press.

Smith, R. (1998) *Legal Aid Contracting: Lessons from North America*, London: Legal Action Group.

Smith, R. (2007) 'Ever decreasing circles', 157 *New Law Journal* 1437.

Tata, C. *et al.* (2004) 'Does mode of delivery make a difference to criminal case outcomes and clients' satisfaction? The public defence solicitor experiment', *Criminal Law Review* 120.

White, R. (1973) 'Lawyers and the Enforcement of Rights' in Morris, P., White, R. and Lewis, P. (eds) *Social Needs and Legal Action*, London: Martin Robertson.

Yarrow, S. (1997) *The Price of Success: Lawyers, Clients and Conditional Fees*, London: Policy Studies Institute.

Zander, M. (2007a) 'Carter's wake (1)', 157 *New Law Journal* 872.

Zander, M. (2007b) 'Carter's wake (2)', 157 *New Law Journal* 912.

Zander, M. (2007c) 'Full speed ahead?', 157 *New Law Journal* 992.

17

Paying for legal services

Reading on the Internet

www   The consultation paper published by the Legal Services Commission, *Best Value Tendering for Criminal Defence Services* (2007), is available at:

> https://consult.legalservices.gov.uk/inovem/consult.ti/bestvaluetendering/consultationHome

The special report, *Contracting for Indigent Defense Services* (2000), is available at:

> http://www.ncjrs.gov/pdffiles1/bja/181160.pdf

The report of the Constitutional Affairs Committee criticising the government's plans to implement Lord Carter's legal aid reforms, *Implementation of the Carter Review of Legal Aid* (2007) is available on Parliament's website at:

> http://www.publications.parliament.uk/pa/cm200607/cmselect/cmconst/223/223i.pdf

The report by Lee Bridges and others (2007), *Evaluation of the Public Defender Service in England and Wales* is available on the website of the Legal Services Commission at:

> http://www.legalservices.gov.uk/docs/pds/Public_Defenders_Report_PDFVersion6.pdf

Lord Carter's report, *Legal aid: a market-based approach to reform* (2006), is available at:

> http://www.legalaidprocurementreview.gov.uk/publications.htm

The consultation paper, *Legal Aid: a sustainable future* (2006), is available at:

> http://www.dca.gov.uk/consult/legal-aidsf/sustainable-future.htm

The judgment of the European Court of Human Rights in the McLibel Two case was application number 6841/01 and can be found on the Court's website at:

> http://www.echr.coe.int/echr

The research carried out by Professors Cape and Moorhead, *Demand Induced Supply? Identifying Cost Drivers in Criminal Defence Work* (2005) is available at:

> http://www.lsrc.org.uk/publications.htm

The website of the Legal Services Commission is:

> http://www.legalservices.gov.uk

The website of the Community Legal Service is:

> http://www.legalservices.gov.uk/civil.asp

The website of Community Legal advice is:

> http://www.communitylegaladvice.org.uk

Visit www.mylawchamber.co.uk/ElliottELS to access multiple-choice questions, flashcards and practice exam questions to test yourself on this chapter.

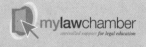

18

The police

This chapter discusses:

- miscarriages of justice, where an appropriate balance has not been achieved between an individual's rights and police powers, so that innocent people have been convicted of a criminal offence they did not commit;

- the police powers of stop and search, arrest and detention;

- the treatment of suspects at the police station;

- the safeguards of the suspect; and

- problems with the police.

Introduction

The criminal justice system is one of the most important tools available to society for the control of anti-social behaviour. It is also the area of the English legal system which has most potential for controversy given that, through the criminal justice system, the state has the means to interfere with individual freedom in the strongest way: by sending people to prison.

An effective criminal justice system needs to strike a balance between punishing the guilty and protecting the innocent; our systems of investigating crime need safeguards which prevent the innocent being found guilty, but those safeguards must not make it impossible to convict those who are guilty. This balance has been the subject of much debate in recent years: a large number of miscarriages of justice, where innocent people were sent to prison, suggested the system was weighted too heavily towards proving guilt, yet, shortly after these cases had been uncovered, there were claims, particularly from the police, that the balance had tipped too far in the other direction. It may be that the incorporation of the European Convention on Human Rights into British law will lead to a further shift in the balance, as the British courts interpret such rights as the right to a 'fair trial' contained in Art. 6 of the Convention.

Miscarriages of justice

In recent years, confidence in the criminal justice system has been seriously dented by the revelation that innocent people had been wrongly convicted and sentenced to long periods in prison. High-profile cases have included the Guildford Four, the Birmingham Six and the Tottenham Three. We will look closely at just two of these cases, to see where the system went wrong, before examining in detail the rules that govern the criminal justice system.

The Guildford Four

In October 1974, the IRA bombed a pub in Guildford. A year later, Patrick Armstrong, Paul Hill, Carole Richardson, Gerard Conlon and two others were convicted of the five murders arising from the bombing. Mr Armstrong and Mr Hill were also convicted of two murders arising from an explosion in November 1974 at a pub in Woolwich. All were sentenced to life imprisonment.

The prosecution case was based almost entirely on confessions which were alleged to have been made while the four were in police custody. There was no other evidence that any of the four were members of the IRA, and they were certainly not the type of people that an effective terrorist organisation would choose to carry out such an important part of its campaign – Patrick Armstrong and Carole Richardson, for example, took drugs, lived in a squat and were involved in petty crime.

Like the other victims of miscarriages of justice, they tried to get their convictions referred to the Court of Appeal under s. 17 of the Criminal Appeal Act 1968 (since repealed), but were initially unsuccessful. In 1987, a Home Office memorandum recognised that the Four were unlikely terrorists, but the Home Office concluded that this could not be considered to be new evidence justifying referral to the Court of Appeal.

Then, in 1989, a police detective looking into the case found a set of typed notes of interviews with Patrick Armstrong, which contained deletions and additions, both typed and handwritten, as well as some rearrangements of material. At their original trial the police evidence had consisted of a set of handwritten notes which they said were made at the time of the interview, and a typed version of these notes; both incorporated the corrections made on the newly discovered typewritten set, suggesting that the handwritten version was actually made after the interviews had been conducted. The implication was that the notes had been constructed so as to fit in with the case the police wished to present.

Patrick Armstrong's confession was central to the prosecution case. Anything which cast doubt on it would undermine all four convictions. The Director of Public Prosecutions, Alan Green, decided that he should not oppose a further appeal, and this took place in 1989. Giving judgment, the Lord Chief Justice said there were two possible explanations. The first was that the typescripts were a complete fabrication, amended to make them more effective and then written out by hand to appear as if they were contemporaneous. Alternatively, the police had started with a contemporaneous note, typed it up to improve legibility, amended it to make it read better and then converted it back to a manuscript note. Either way, the police officers had not told the truth. The Lord Chief Justice concluded: 'If they were prepared to tell this sort of lie then the whole of their evidence became suspect.' As a result, the Guildford Four were released, after having spent 15 years in prison for crimes which they did not commit.

The Birmingham Six

In November 1974, 21 people died and 162 were injured when IRA bombs exploded in two crowded pubs in the centre of Birmingham. The bombs caused outrage in Britain, and led to a wave of anti-Irish feeling.

The six Irishmen who became known as the Birmingham Six were arrested after police kept a watch on ports immediately after the bombings. The police asked them to undergo forensic tests in order to eliminate them from their inquiries. The men had told the police that they were travelling to Northern Ireland to see relatives; this was partly true, but their main reason for travelling was to attend the funeral of James McDade, an IRA man. Although some of the Six may well have had Republican sympathies, none was actually a member of the IRA. They were unaware, until McDade was killed, that he was involved in terrorism. Nevertheless, they all knew his family, and intended to go to the funeral as a mark of respect, a normal practice in Northern Ireland which would not necessarily suggest support for the dead person's political views.

Perhaps not surprisingly given the situation at the time, the men did not mention the funeral when the police asked why they were travelling and, equally unsurprisingly, when the police searched their luggage and found evidence of the real reason for their journey, they became extremely suspicious. When the forensic tests, conducted by a Dr Skuse, indicated that the men had been handling explosives, the police were convinced their suspicions were right.

18

The police

Photo 18.1 The Birmingham Six outside the Old Bailey after their convictions were quashed
Source: PA Photos

At their trial, the case rested on two main pieces of evidence: the forensic tests and confessions which the men had made to the police. The Six claimed that, while at the police station, they had been beaten, kicked and threatened with death; they were also told that their families were in danger and would only be protected if the men confessed. There was clear evidence that the Six were beaten up; photos taken three days after their admission on remand to Winston Green prison show serious scars. However, the men were also beaten up by prison officers once they were remanded in custody, and the prosecution used this beating to explain the photographic evidence, stating that there had been no physical abuse by the police and that, therefore, the confessions were valid. Yet a close examination of the confessions would have made it obvious that they were made by people who knew nothing about the bombings: they contradicted each other, none of them revealed anything about the way the terrorist attacks were carried out that the police did not know already, and some of the 'revelations' proved to be untrue – for example, three of the men said the bombs were left in carrier bags, when forensic evidence later showed them to have been in holdalls. The men were never put on identity parades, even though at least one person who had been present in one of the bombed pubs felt he could have identified the bombers. Nevertheless, the Six were convicted and sentenced to life imprisonment, the judge commenting: 'You have been convicted on the clearest and most overwhelming evidence I have ever heard in a case of murder.' On appeal, the judges reprimanded the trial judge for aspects of his summing up and a character attack on a defence witness; they acknowledged the weaknesses in the forensic evidence, yet concluded that this evidence would have played a small part in the jury's decision; and as far as the confession evidence was concerned, a judge mentioned the black eye on one of the defendants, 'the origin of which I have forgotten', but said 'I do not think it matters much anyway'. The appeal was dismissed.

Fourteen prison officers were subsequently tried for assaulting the Six; their victims were not allowed to appear as witnesses, and they were all acquitted. Evidence given suggested that the men had already been injured when they arrived at the prison. The Six then brought a civil action for assault against the police force. This claim was struck out. Lord Denning's judgment summed up the legal system's attitude to the case, pointing out that if the Six won, and proved they had been assaulted in order to secure their confessions, this would mean the police had lied, used violence and threats, and that the convictions were false; the Home Secretary would have to recommend a pardon or send the case back to the Court of Appeal. The general feeling seemed to be that such serious miscarriages were simply unthinkable, and so the system for a long time turned its back on the growing claims that the unthinkable had actually happened.

In January 1987, the Home Secretary referred the case back to the Court of Appeal. The appeal took a year; the convictions were upheld. The Lord Chief Justice Lord Lane ended the court's judgment with remarks which were to become notorious: 'The longer this hearing has gone on, the more convinced this court has become that the verdict of the jury was correct. We have no doubt that these convictions were both safe and satisfactory.'

In the end, it took 16 years for the Six to get their convictions quashed. In 1990, another Home Secretary referred the case back to the Court of Appeal. A new technique had been developed, known as Electrostatic Document Analysis (ESDA), which could examine the indentations made on paper by writing on the sheets above. The test suggested that notes of a police interview with one of the Six had not been recorded contemporaneously, as West Midlands detectives had claimed in court. The prosecution decided not to seek to sustain the convictions and the Six were finally freed in 1991.

The response to the miscarriages of justice

The miscarriages of justice described above, and others, showed that there was something seriously wrong with the criminal justice system. On 14 March 1991, when the Court of Appeal quashed the convictions of the Birmingham Six, the Home Secretary announced that a Royal Commission on Criminal Justice (RCCJ) would be set up to examine the penal process from start to finish – from the time the police first investigate to the final appeal. The RCCJ (sometimes called the Runciman Commission, after its chairperson) considered these issues for two years, during which they received evidence from over 600 organisations and asked academics to carry out 22 research studies on how the system works in practice. In July 1993 they published their final report. In examining the criminal justice system, some of the research presented to the RCCJ,

18

The police

its recommendations and some changes that have subsequently been made, will be considered.

Human Rights Act 1998

The passing of the Human Rights Act 1998, incorporating the European Convention on Human Rights into domestic law (see p. 302) will have a significant impact on all stages of the criminal justice system. The provisions of the European Convention could potentially provide an important safeguard against abuses and excesses within the system. Of particular relevance in this field are Art. 3 prohibiting torture and inhuman or degrading treatment; Art. 5 protecting the right to liberty including the right not to be arrested or detained by the police without lawful authority; Art. 6 guaranteeing a fair trial; and Art. 8 which recognises the right to respect of an individual's right to private and family life. The powers of arrest, stop and search and the refusal of bail are all likely to be the subject of legal challenges on the basis that their exercise has breached the Convention. For example, in **Caballero** v **UK** (2000) the UK Government accepted that the law on bail breached Art. 5 of the Convention and the domestic law was reformed as a result.

The organisation of the police

In the UK the tradition is to have local police forces, rather than one single national police force. This decentralisation was considered to help build the links between the police and the local community that is being policed, and to reduce the risk of the police behaving oppressively. However, a step towards centralisation was taken when the Police and Magistrates' Courts Act 1994 provided that the Home Secretary was allowed to 'determine objectives for the policing of the areas of all police authorities'. The Police Reform Act 2002 has continued to increase the power of central Government over the police. The Home Secretary is now required to produce an annual National Policing Plan. This will set out strategic policing priorities generally for police forces in England and Wales. He or she is given additional supervisory powers over the police, with increased powers to issue codes of practice and regulations relating to the discharge of police functions. In an inquiry into police failures leading up to the murder of Soham schoolgirls, Holly Wells and Jessica Chapman, the police force of Humberside was heavily criticised. The chief constable of Humberside refused to resign, and the Home Secretary ordered his suspension. He challenged in the courts the Home Secretary's power to do this, and the courts accepted that the Home Secretary held this power under legislation. The Police and Justice Act 2006 further increased the Home Secretary's powers over the police.

Following the publication of a consultation paper, *One Step Ahead: A 21st Century Strategy to Defeat Organised Criminals* (2004), Parliament passed the Serious Organised

Crime and Police Act 2005. This Act contained provisions for the establishment in April 2006 of the Serious Organised Crime Agency (SOCA). It is chaired by a former head of MI5, Stephen Lander, and consists of a national team of about 4,000 specialist investigators who are not formally police officers and who have more powers than ordinary police constables. They can issue disclosure notices to compel witnesses to answer questions, or be the subject of a criminal conviction themselves, and can strike deals with informants to give evidence against other offenders (known as 'Queen's evidence'). Their role is to tackle the people at the head of criminal gangs, whose illegal enterprises range from drug-trafficking, paedophile rings and people smuggling, to fraud and money-laundering. A specialist team of prosecutors helps the organisation secure convictions. SOCA has been compared with the FBI in America. The Police Federation is unhappy with the creation of SOCA, commenting:

> There is a huge difference between an officer of the Crown who bears personal responsibility to the law, and a civilian employee. The blurring of these boundaries sets a dangerous precedent for the future and will further erode the status of police.

The academics Ben Bowling and James Ross (2006) have suggested that SOCA may have too much power, commenting that it has 'unprecedented powers for surveillance, intrusion and coercion'. Particularly controversial sections of the Act were those which extended to SOCA the use of 'compulsory powers', which are investigatory powers to require an individual to answer questions, provide information or produce documents. A refusal to comply with one of these compulsory powers amounts to a criminal offence. They also point out that SOCA may take advantage of the absence of a definition of what constitutes 'serious organised crime' in the Act, by deciding its own mandate and functions and not restricting itself to combatting classic mafia-style activities such as drugs and violence.

TOPICAL ISSUE

Civilian support staff

Ess. Cases
p. 269 →

The Police Reform Act 2002 allows a range of civilians to exercise police powers. The most significant in practice are likely to be the community support officers. These are civilians who are employed by a police authority. The only qualifications required for the post are that the chief officer is satisfied the person is suitable, capable and has been adequately trained. They are paid two-thirds of a regular police officer's salary. Their powers, extended by the Police and Justice Act 2006, include the right to issue fixed penalty notices for such anti-social behaviour as dropping litter, cycling on footpaths, dog fouling and drinking in public. They are able to carry out searches and road checks and to stop and detain school truants. Where a suspect fails to provide his name and address, or if the community support officer reasonably suspects the details to be inaccurate, the community support officer may deprive the individual of their liberty (using reasonable force if necessary) for up to 30 minutes until a police officer arrives.

The Police Federation is unhappy that community support officers were given this power to detain suspects, commenting:

Community Support Officers are supposed to just be the eyes and ears of the police service and therefore should not be placed in potentially confrontational situations, which detaining someone clearly is. They do not have the appropriate experience, the right training or adequate safety equipment to deal with this, which places the wellbeing of the public, police officers and themselves in jeopardy. By giving them more powers, we are effectively taking them away from the communities they serve and creating even greater confusion as to the differences between CSOs and police officers.

Chief officers can also establish accreditation schemes to support community safety and to combat nuisance. Under these schemes private employees are given some police powers. The employer must have adequate training facilities and mechanisms for handling complaints. Shops and shopping centres are likely to seek accreditation for their security guards. They will then have broader powers to deal with low level criminal behaviour. Accredited individuals can issue fixed penalty notices for trivial offences, prevent alcohol consumption in designated places and confiscate alcohol and tobacco from children. They are allowed to require provision of the name and address of those reasonably suspected of committing one of a limited range of offences or of behaving in an anti-social manner. Failure to comply with this request is an offence.

These reforms have been highly controversial. The Government's view is that the use of civilians for matters that are essentially administrative and routine will allow more police time for investigative work. In addition, the police role in the establishment of community safety accreditation schemes may lead to a greater degree of police influence over the activities of private security guards and store detectives. But some have criticised this development as a step towards privatising policing. The Home Affairs Committee (2002) saw a danger of

civilians with insufficient training, working in poor conditions, for less money while doing jobs that until recently were undertaken by police officers.

The shops and shopping centres which are likely to seek accreditation are, ironically, areas in which there is arguably adequate policing and private security. This reform may result in over policing of safe areas without increasing the protection in areas in real need of extra reassurance policing.

Police powers

Most people's first contact with the criminal justice system involves the police and, because they have responsibility for investigating crimes, gathering evidence and deciding whether to charge a suspect, they play an important part in its overall operation. They also have wide powers over suspects, which may be used to help convict the guilty or, as the miscarriages of justice have shown, abused to convict the innocent.

Photo 18.2 Community Support Officer and Police Officer in their respective uniforms
Source: Jan Brayley/Hampshire Constabulary

The main piece of legislation regulating police powers is the Police and Criminal Evidence Act 1984 (PACE). The Act was the product of a Royal Commission set up following an earlier miscarriage of justice, concerning the murder in 1977 of a man called Maxwell Confait. Confait was found strangled with electric flex in a burning house, and three boys, aged 14, 15 and 18, one of whom was educationally subnormal, were arrested, interrogated and, as a result of their confessions, charged with murder. Three years later, they were all released after an official report into the case (the Fisher Report) concluded that they had nothing to do with the killing.

In the light of concern over the police conduct of this case, and in particular the interrogation process, the then Labour Government set up the Royal Commission on Criminal Procedure (RCCP), sometimes known as the Philips Commission, to examine police procedures. It concluded in its report of 1981 that a balance needed to be reached between 'the interests of the community in bringing offenders to justice and the rights and liberties of persons suspected or accused of crime'. A criminal justice system that achieved this balance would reach the required standards of fairness, openness and accountability. However, the Commission, and the subsequent Act (PACE), were criticised by some as unjustifiably extending police powers, especially in the areas of stop and search, arrest and detention at the police station.

PACE was intended to replace a confusing mixture of common law, legislation and local bye-laws on pre-trial procedure with a single coherent statute. The Act provides a comprehensive code of police powers to stop, search, arrest, detain and interrogate members of the public. It also lays down the suspects' rights. The Criminal Justice and Public Order Act 1994 (CJPOA) extended police powers significantly. It introduced some of the recommendations of the RCCJ, and other changes that the RCCJ was opposed to: for example, the abolition of the right to silence. Police powers have been further increased by the Serious Organised Crime and Police Act 2005.

As well as the statutory rules on police powers, contained in PACE and the CJPOA, there are Codes of Practice, drawn up by the Home Office under s. 66 of PACE and revised in 2006, which do not form part of the law, but which provide extra detail on the provisions of the legislation. Breach of these Codes cannot be the ground for a legal action, but can give rise to disciplinary procedures and, if they are breached in very serious ways, evidence obtained as a result of such a breach may be excluded in a criminal trial. It has been argued that some of the Code provisions should be legally enforceable and form part of PACE itself.

Pre-arrest powers

Police officers are always free to ask members of the public questions in order to prevent and detect crime, but members of the public are not obliged to answer such questions, nor to go to a police station unless they are lawfully arrested.

KEY CASE

In **Rice v Connolly** (1966), the appellant was spotted by police officers in the early hours of the morning, behaving suspiciously in an area where burglaries had taken place that night. The officers asked where he was going and where he had come from; he refused to answer, or to give his full name and address, though he did give a name and the name of a road, which were not untrue. The officers asked him to go with them to a police box for identification purposes, but he refused, saying, 'If you want me, you will have to arrest me.' He was arrested and eventually convicted of obstructing a police officer in the execution of his duty. His conviction was quashed on appeal on the basis that nobody is obliged in common law to answer police questions.

> Nobody is obliged in common law to answer police questions.

The line between maintaining the freedom not to answer questions and actually obstructing the police would appear to be a thin one. In **Ricketts v Cox** (1982), two police officers, who were looking for youths responsible for a serious assault, approached the defendant and another man in the early hours of the morning. The defendant was said to have been abusive, uncooperative and hostile to the officers, using obscene language which was designed to provoke and antagonise the officers and eventually trying to walk away from them. The magistrates found that the police acted in a proper manner and were entitled to put questions to the two men; the defendant's behaviour and attitude amounted to an obstruction of the police officers in the execution of their duty. An appeal was dismissed, and the implication appears to be that, while merely refusing to answer questions is lawful, rudely refusing to do so may amount to the offence of obstruction.

An even more problematic area is the question of how far the police are allowed to detain a person without arresting them. The courts appear to have concluded that under common law the police cannot actually prevent a person from moving away, though they can touch them to attract their attention (they also have some statutory powers in this area, discussed below). Two schoolboys, in **Kenlin v Gardiner** (1967), were going from house to house to remind members of their rugby team about a game. Two plain-clothed police officers became suspicious and, producing a warrant card, asked what they were doing. The boys did not believe the men were police officers, and one of them appeared to try to run away. A police officer caught hold of his arm, and the boy responded by struggling violently, punching and kicking the officer, at which point the second boy got involved and struck the other officer. Both boys were convicted of assaulting a police constable in the execution of his duty in the magistrates' court, but an appeal was allowed, on the ground that the police did not have the power to detain the boys prior to arrest, and so the boys were merely acting in self-defence.

In **Donnelly v Jackman** (1970), the appellant was walking along a road one Saturday evening at about 11.15 pm, when a uniformed police officer came up to him, intending to make inquiries about an offence which the officer had reason to believe the appellant might have committed. The officer asked the appellant if he could have a word with him, but the appellant ignored him and walked on. The officer followed close behind him, repeated the request and, on being ignored, tapped him on the shoulder. The appellant turned round and tapped the officer on the chest saying 'Now we are even, copper.' When the officer tapped him on the shoulder a second time, the appellant turned round again, and this time hit him with force. He was convicted of assaulting an officer in the execution of his duty, and argued in his defence that in tapping him on the shoulder the officer had acted outside his duty. The Court of Appeal held that what the officer had done was not unlawful detention but merely 'a trivial interference with liberty', and the conviction was upheld.

Under the Police Reform Act 2002, s. 50 a uniformed police officer can require a person who has behaved in an anti-social manner to give their name and address. Failure to comply is an offence and may form the basis for an arrest under s. 25 of PACE. This is a significant extension of police powers which could be abused to harass young people.

ss. Cases p. 290 → ## Stop and search under PACE

PACE repealed a variety of often obscure and unsatisfactory statutory provisions on stop and search; the main powers in this area are now contained in s. 1 of PACE. Under s. 1 a constable may search a person or vehicle in public for stolen or prohibited articles (defined as offensive weapons, articles used for the purpose of burglary or related crimes and professional display fireworks). This power can only be used where the police have 'reasonable grounds for suspecting that they will find stolen or prohibited articles' (s. 1(3)). The Criminal Justice Act 2003 extended the power to stop and search to cover searches for articles intended to cause criminal damage. This reform is aimed at people suspected of causing graffiti and who might be carrying cans of spray paint in their pockets.

The exercise of the power to stop and search is also governed by Code of Practice A. This Code starts by stating:

> 1.1 Powers to stop and search must be used fairly, responsibly, with respect for people being searched and without unlawful discrimination. The Race Relations (Amendment) Act 2000 makes it unlawful for police officers to discriminate on the grounds of race, colour, ethnic origin, nationality or national origins when using their powers.

The requirement of reasonable suspicion is intended to protect individuals from being subject to stop and search on a random basis, or on grounds that the law rightly finds unacceptable, such as age or racial background. Code of Practice A provides guidance on the meaning of 'reasonable grounds for suspecting':

> 2.2 Reasonable grounds for suspicion depend on the circumstances in each case. There must be an objective basis for that suspicion based on facts, information, and/or intelligence which are relevant to the likelihood of finding an article of a certain kind or, in the case of searches under section 43 of the Terrorism Act 2000, to the likelihood that the person is a terrorist. Reasonable suspicion can never be supported on the basis of personal factors alone without reliable supporting intelligence or information or some specific behaviour by the person concerned. For example, a person's race, age, appearance, or the fact that the person is known to have a previous conviction, cannot be used alone or in combination with each other as the reason for searching that person. Reasonable suspicion cannot be based on generalisations or stereotypical images of certain groups or categories of people as more likely to be involved in criminal activity. A person's religion cannot be considered as reasonable grounds for suspicion and should never be considered as a reason to stop or stop and search an individual.

> 2.3 Reasonable suspicion can sometimes exist without specific information or intelligence and on the basis of some level of generalisation stemming from the behaviour of a person. For example, if an officer encounters someone on the street at night who is obviously trying to hide something, the officer may (depending on the other surrounding circumstances) base such suspicion on the fact that this kind of behaviour is often linked to stolen or prohibited articles being carried. Similarly, for the purposes of s. 43 of the Terrorism Act 2000, suspicion that a person is a terrorist may arise from the person's behaviour at or near a location which has been identified as a potential target for terrorists.

Before searching under these powers, police officers must, among other things, identify themselves and the station where they are based, and tell the person to be searched the grounds for the search (s. 2). If not in uniform, police officers must provide documentary identification (s. 2(3)). In **R** v **Bristol** (2007) the Court of Appeal confirmed that a failure to provide the necessary information would render a stop and search unlawful. The appellant was in a street where there was a problem with drug dealing. A police officer saw him and thought that he was carrying drugs in his mouth, ready to supply to a customer. The policeman asked the appellant what he had in his mouth

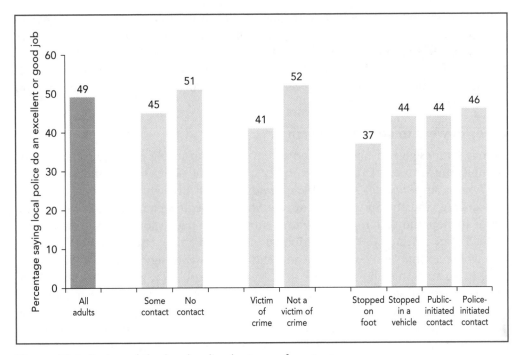

Figure 18.1 Rating of the local police by type of contact

Source: 'Policing and the criminal justice system – public confidence and perceptions': findings from the 2004/05 British Crime Survey, p. 16

and he replied it was chewing gum. Not satisfied with this response, the officer immediately applied pressure to his throat to stop him swallowing and said 'Drugs search, spit it out.' A struggle ensued and the appellant was arrested. He was subsequently convicted of intentionally obstructing a police officer in carrying out a search for drugs and sentenced to 12 months' imprisonment. The appellant appealed. The appeal was allowed because the search was unlawful as the police officer had failed to give his name and station. The Court of Appeal pointed out that the police officer could have satisfied the statutory requirements by simply adding three words – 'Mason, Charing Cross' – before commencing the search.

Reasonable force may be used during a stop and search (s. 117), but the suspect cannot be required to remove any clothing in public, except for an outer coat, jacket or gloves (s. 2(9)). Police officers must ask anyone stopped to give their name, address and define their ethnicity.

Any stolen or prohibited articles discovered by the police during the search may be seized (s. 1(6)). A written record of the search must be made at the time of the search, unless there are exceptional circumstances which would make this wholly impracticable. The record should state why the person was stopped and what the outcome was. The person searched must be given a copy of this immediately. If a person is stopped but not searched then the police do not need to make a full record of the encounter. Instead they simply need to make a note of the person's ethnicity and provide the person with a receipt.

In the past the police could, and frequently did, carry out a search where there was no statutory power to search but with the member of the public's consent. These searches could then take place without any of the legislative safeguards. In practice, some people would 'consent' to a search in that they would offer no resistance to it, because they did not know their legal rights. Since 2003, voluntary searches are no longer allowed.

Other powers to stop and search

Various statutes give specific stop and search powers regarding particular offences. For example, the Misuse of Drugs Act 1971, s. 23, allows the police to stop and search anyone who is suspected on reasonable grounds to be in unlawful possession of a controlled drug; and the Sporting Events (Control of Alcohol etc.) Act 1985 contains a power to stop and search people before entry into certain sporting events such as a football match. Section 60 of the Criminal Justice and Public Order Act 1994 provides that where a senior police officer reasonably believes that serious violence may take place in an area, they may, in order to prevent its occurrence, give written authorisation for officers to stop and search persons and vehicles in that area for up to 24 hours. This can be extended by a further 30 hours. When such authorisation is in place, police officers can stop and search any pedestrian or vehicle for offensive weapons or dangerous instruments. Offensive weapon bears the same meaning as in s. 1 of PACE; a dangerous instrument refers to an object which has a blade or is sharply pointed (s. 60(11)). Unlike s. 1 of PACE, these powers do not require reasonable grounds for suspicion. The police can also be authorised to stop and search randomly any pedestrian or vehicle in an area where it is suspected that knives or offensive weapons are being carried without good reason.

Under s. 65 of the Criminal Justice and Public Order Act 1994, an officer can stop anyone on their way to a 'rave' and direct them not to proceed. Similar powers exist under s. 71, in relation to trespassory assemblies. These rather draconian powers can be exercised within five miles of the rave or assembly.

Under s. 44 of the Terrorism Act 2000 the Home Secretary can secretly authorise the police to carry out random stop and searches in the fight against terrorism. There is no requirement that the police have reasonable suspicion against the person being searched. These powers have, in practice, been used extensively and controversially by the police.

The legality of the exercise of this power to stop and search was challenged before the House of Lords in **R (on the application of Gillan) v Commissioner of Police for the Metropolis** (2006). Kevin Gillan and Pennie Quinton were students who attended a peaceful demonstration against an arms fair in East London. The police stopped and searched them, relying on the terrorist legislation. Authorisation had repeatedly been given to carry out stop and searches across London since the 2001 Act was passed. With the support of the civil rights group Liberty, the students challenged the legality of the stop and search. They argued that Parliament only intended these powers to be used exceptionally and for short periods, but they were in fact being used as 'an everyday tool of public order'. The House of Lords rejected this application and concluded that the stop and search powers were lawful.

Lord Carlile, the Government's terrorist watchdog, concluded in his annual report for 2005 that the s. 44 powers to stop and search are unnecessary. There is no evidence that the use of s. 44 has a greater potential to prevent an act of terrorism than the existing powers to stop and search founded on a police officer having reasonable suspicion.

There are clearly potential dangers in granting wide stop and search powers to the police if there is a possibility that the powers will be abused, with harassment of ethnic minority groups being a particular concern. This problem is discussed in detail at pp. 413–14.

Powers of arrest

Powers of arrest allow people to be detained against their will. Such detention is only lawful if the arrest is carried out in accordance with the law. An arrest can take place either with or without a warrant. As well as the relevant legislative provisions, guidance for the police on the use of their power of arrest is provided in Code of Practice G.

Arrest with a warrant

Under s. 1 of the Magistrates' Courts Act 1980, criminal proceedings may be initiated either by the issue of a summons requiring the accused to attend court on a particular day or, in more serious cases, by a warrant of arrest issued by the magistrates' court. The police obtain a warrant by applying in writing to a magistrate, and backing up the application with an oral statement made on oath. The warrant issued must specify the name of the person to be arrested and general particulars of the offence. When an arrest warrant has been granted, a constable may enter and search premises to make the arrest, using such reasonable force as is necessary (PACE, s. 117).

Arrest without a warrant

The powers of the police to arrest without a warrant were increased by the Serious Organised Crime and Police Act 2005. The extension of police arrest powers were considered in the consultation paper, *Modernising Police Powers to Meet Community Needs* (Home Office, 2004). The reforms have simplified the police powers of arrest, but at the same time they have given the police more powers than they need, and are open to abuse.

In the past s. 24 of PACE allowed a person to be arrested only for quite serious offences, known as arrestable offences, unless certain additional requirements were satisfied when an arrest would also be possible for a minor offence. The 2005 Act amended PACE so that now a police officer can arrest a person for committing any offence if this is necessary. Police officers must reasonably suspect that a person has committed, is committing, or is about to commit an offence and have reasonable grounds for believing that it is necessary to arrest that person. It will be necessary to carry out an arrest if:

- the person will not give their name and address, or the police officer reasonably suspects that the name or address given is false; or
- the arrest will prevent the person from causing physical injury to him or herself or another person; suffering physical injury; causing loss or damage to property; committing an offence against public decency; or obstructing the highway;
- to protect a child or other vulnerable person;
- to allow the prompt and effective investigation of the offence or of the conduct of the person in question;
- to prevent the person disappearing.

These last two reasons are likely to justify an arrest in most cases. Further guidance on the issue is contained in paragraph 2.9 of Code of Practice G. In **G v DPP** (1989) it was held that a belief of the police officer concerned that suspects generally give false names was not sufficient to satisfy the general arrest conditions.

The same rules apply to the concept of reasonable suspicion for arrest as were discussed for stop and search powers. Its meaning in the context of an arrest was considered by the House of Lords in **O'Hara v Chief Constable of the Royal Ulster Constabulary** (1996). A two-stage test was identified. First, there must be actual suspicion on the part of the arresting officer (the subjective test) and, secondly, there must be reasonable grounds for that suspicion (the objective test). This approach was upheld by the European Court of Human Rights in **O'Hara v UK** (2002).

Citizen's arrest

A member of the public is entitled to arrest a person in certain circumstances. This power to carry out a citizen's arrest is contained in s. 24A of PACE. The exercise of the citizen's power of arrest is limited to indictable offences. The person must have reasonable grounds for believing that an arrest is necessary and that it is not reasonably practicable for a police officer to carry out the arrest instead. If the citizen has made a mistake, and an offence has not actually been committed by anyone, the citizen may be liable for damages (**Walters v WH Smith & Son Ltd** (1914)). For example, if a man hears somebody shout 'Stop thief' and seeing a woman running away with a handbag wrongly assumes she is the thief, he can be sued for damages by that woman if he tries to grab her.

Manner of arrest

PACE requires that at the time of, or as soon as practicable after, the arrest the person arrested must be informed that they are under arrest, and given the grounds for that arrest, even if it is perfectly obvious that they are being arrested and why (s. 28). This is in line with the pre-existing case law, where in **Christie v Leachinsky** (1947) Viscount Simon said: 'No one, I think, would approve a situation in which when the person arrested asked for the reason, the policeman replied "that has nothing to do with you: come along with me" . . .'

There is no set form of words that must be used, and colloquial language such as 'You're nicked for mugging' may be acceptable.

In carrying out the arrest, the police are entitled to use reasonable force under s. 117 of PACE and s. 3 of the Criminal Law Act 1967. In assessing the reasonableness of the force used, the courts will consider two issues:

- Was it necessary to use force?
- Was the force used reasonable or excessive in the circumstances?

Section 76 of the Criminal Justice and Immigration Act 2008 seeks to clarify when force has been used reasonably. It provides that the courts can take into account any genuine mistakes as to the circumstances made by the defendant unless the mistake was made under the influence of drink or drugs. The force will not be viewed as reasonable if it is 'disproportionate'. In determining whether reasonable force has been used, the courts will remember:

(a) that a person acting for a legitimate purpose may not be able to weigh to a nicety the exact measure of any necessary action; and

(b) that evidence of a person's having only done what the person honestly and instinctively thought was necessary for a legitimate purpose constitutes strong evidence that only reasonable action was taken by that person for that purpose.

Police detention

Apart from powers given by anti-terrorist legislation, before 1984 the police in England and Wales had no express power to detain suspects for further investigations to be carried out, nor did they have a general power to detain individuals for questioning, whether as suspects or potential witnesses. In practice, the police often acted as if they had these powers.

The 1981 Royal Commission on Criminal Procedure (Philips, 1981) recommended that the police should be given express powers to detain suspects for questioning, with safeguards to ensure that those powers were not abused. These express powers were granted by PACE. Before PACE, it was generally thought that the police were obliged to bring a suspect before a court within 24 hours, or release them; the Act allows suspects to be detained without charge for up to four days, although there are some safeguards designed to prevent abuse of this power. PACE provides that an arrested person must be brought to a police station as soon as practicable after the arrest, though this may be delayed if their presence elsewhere is necessary for an immediate investigation (s. 30). Alternatively, the police can put the person on bail to attend a police station at a future date. Conditions can be attached to the granting of bail (PACE, ss. 30A–30D). On arrival at the police station, they should usually be taken to the custody officer, who has to decide whether sufficient evidence exists to charge the person. If, on arrest, there is already sufficient evidence to charge the suspect, they must be charged and then released on bail unless there are reasons why this is not appropriate. Such reasons include the fact that the defendant's name and address are not known, there are reasonable grounds for believing that the address given is false, or that the suspect may commit an offence while on bail (s. 38(1)). A person who has been charged and is being held in custody must be brought before magistrates as soon as practicable, and in any event not later than the first sitting after being charged with the offence (s. 46).

If there is not sufficient evidence to charge the suspect, then the person can be detained for the purpose of securing or obtaining such evidence – often through questioning (s. 37). Where a person is being detained and has not been charged, a review officer should assess whether there are grounds for continued detention after the first six hours and then at intervals of not more than nine hours (s. 40). These reviews can sometimes be carried out by telephone. As a basic rule, the police can detain a person for up to 36 hours from the time of arrival at the police station (this was increased from 24 hours by the Criminal Justice Act 2003). After this time the suspect should generally be either released or charged (s. 41). However, there are major exceptions to this.

Continued detention for a further 12 hours can be authorised by the police themselves, if the detention is necessary to secure or preserve evidence and the offence is an indictable offence (meaning an offence which can be tried in the Crown Court rather than the magistrates' court).

Further periods of continued detention, up to 96 hours, are possible with approval from the magistrates' court. After 96 hours the suspect must be charged or released. In fact prolonged detention is rare, with only 5 per cent of suspects detained for more than 18 hours, and 1 per cent for more than 24 hours.

In terrorist cases, under the Terrorism Act 2006, a person can be detained for up to 28 days and some politicians have been pushing unsuccessfully for this to be increased to 42 days.

The custody officer is responsible for keeping the custody record (which records the various stages of detention) and checks that the provisions of PACE in relation to the detention are complied with. These theoretical safeguards for the suspect have proved weak in practice. PACE seems to contemplate that custody officers will be quasi-judicial figures, who can distance themselves from the needs of the investigation and put the rights of the suspect first. In practice this has never been realistic; custody officers are ordinary members of the station staff, and likely to share their view of the investigation. In addition, they will often be of a more junior rank than the investigating officer. They are therefore highly unlikely to refuse to allow the detention of a suspect, or to prevent breaches of PACE and its codes during the detention.

Once a person has been charged, they cannot normally be subject to further questioning by the police. Post-charge questioning is only currently allowed if an interview is necessary to prevent or minimise harm or loss, to clear up an ambiguity in a previous statement, or where it is in the interests of justice for a person to be given the opportunity to comment on information that has come to light following charge. If suspects are interviewed in these circumstances, inferences cannot be drawn under ss. 34, 36 or 37 of CJPOA 1994 so they have a genuine right to silence.

The current ban on post-charge questioning aims to reduce the risk of false confessions, which become increasingly likely the longer a person is detained or questioned.

Ess. Cases
p. 263 In a consultation paper, *Modernising Police Powers: Review of the Police and Criminal Evidence Act 1984* (2007), the Home Office is considering whether this ban on further questioning should be lifted in the future, combined with the possibility of inferring guilt when a person refuses to answer questions (see p. 401). Several pilot studies have been set up where post-charge questioning is being allowed. The aim of this reform is to increase police powers to question suspects about new evidence as it emerges. But after charge the suspect should be under the authority of the courts not the police. There is also a risk that the questioning could be oppressive as the suspect might have been held on remand in custody for a long time between the time of charge and the trial hearing.

Police interrogation

The usual reason for detaining a suspect is so that the police can question them, in the hope of securing a confession. This has come to be a very important investigative tool, since it is cheap (compared, for example, with scientific evidence) and the end result, a confession, is seen as reliable and convincing evidence by judges and juries alike. Research by Mitchell (1983) suggests that a high proportion of suspects do make either partial or complete confessions.

Unfortunately, as the miscarriages of justice show, relying too much on confession evidence can have severe drawbacks. Instances of police completely falsifying confessions, or threatening or beating suspects so that they confess even when they are innocent, may be rare but the miscarriages show that police have been willing to use these techniques where they think they can get away with it. In addition, there are less dramatic, but probably more widespread problems. The 1993 Royal Commission raised questions about the poor standard of police interviewing; research by John Baldwin (*Video Taping Police Interviews with Suspects: an Evaluation* (1992b) suggested that police officers went into the interview situation not with the aim of finding out whether the person was guilty, but on the assumption that they were and with the intention of securing a confession to that effect. Interviews were often rambling and repetitious; police officers dismissed the suspect's explanations and asked the same questions over and over again until they were given the answer they wanted. In some cases the researchers felt this treatment amounted to bullying or harassment and in several cases the 'admissions' were one-word answers given in response to leading questions. Suspects were also offered inducements to confess, such as lighter sentences.

Obviously, the implication here is that, under this kind of pressure, suspects might confess to crimes they did not commit – as many of the miscarriage of justice victims did. But such false confessions do not only occur where the suspects are physically threatened. A study by psychologist G.H. Gudjonsson (*The Psychology of Interrogations, Confessions and Testimony*, 1992) found that there were four situations in which people were likely to confess to crimes they did not commit. First, a minority may make confessions quite voluntarily, out of a disturbed desire for publicity, to relieve general feelings of guilt or because they cannot distinguish between reality and fantasy. Secondly, they may want to protect someone else, perhaps a friend or relative, from interrogation and prosecution. Thirdly, they may be unable to see further than a desire to put the questioning to an end and get away from the police station, which can, after all, be a frightening place for those who are not accustomed to it. A psychologist giving evidence to the 1993 Royal Commission commented that: 'Some children are brought up in such a way that confession always seems to produce forgiveness, in which case a false confession may be one way of bringing an unpleasant situation [the interrogation] to an end.' Among this group there may also be a feeling that, once they get out of the police station, they will be able to make everyone see sense, and realise their innocence: unfortunately this does not always happen.

Finally, the pressure of questioning, and the fact that the police seem convinced of their case, may temporarily persuade the suspect that they must have done the act in question. Obviously the young and the mentally ill are likely to be particularly vulnerable to this last situation, but Gudjonsson's research found that its effects were not confined to those who might be considered abnormally suggestible. Their subjects included people of reasonable intelligence who scored highly in tests on suggestibility, showing that they were particularly prepared to go along with what someone in authority was saying. Under hostile interrogation in the psychologically intimidating environment of a police station, even non-vulnerable people are likely to make admissions which are not true, failing to realise that once a statement has been made it will be extremely difficult to retract.

Safeguards for the suspect

Certain safeguards are contained in PACE to try to protect the suspect in the police station. Some of these – the custody officer, the custody record, and the time limits for detention – have already been mentioned, and we will now look at the rest. It has been claimed that these safeguards would prevent miscarriages of justice in the future, yet the police station where Winston Silcott was questioned was meant to be following the PACE guidelines on a pilot basis. PACE officially came into force in January 1986 and Mark Braithwaite was arrested in February of that year, yet he was denied access to the legal advice guaranteed by the Act.

The caution

Under Code C, a person must normally be cautioned on arrest, and a person whom there are grounds to suspect of an offence must be cautioned before being asked any questions regarding involvement, or suspected involvement, in that offence. Until recently, the caution was: 'You do not have to say anything unless you wish to do so but what you say may be given in evidence.' Since the abolition of the right to silence (see p. 401), the correct wording is: 'You do not have to say anything, but it may harm your defence if you do not mention when questioned anything which you later rely on in court. Anything that you do say may be given in evidence.'

Tape-recording

Section 60 of PACE states that interviews must be tape-recorded. This measure was designed to ensure that oppressive treatment and threats could not be used, nor confessions made up by the police. Sadly, it has proved a weaker safeguard than it might seem. In the first place, research presented to the RCCJ showed that police routinely got round the provision by beginning their questioning outside the interview room – in the car on the way to the police station, for example. In addition, they appeared quite willing to use oppressive questioning methods even once the tape-recorder was running – the RCCJ listened to tapes of interviews with the Cardiff Three, victims of another miscarriage of justice whose convictions were quashed in December 1992, and expressed concern at the continuous repetitive questioning that the tapes revealed. The Home Office is carrying out pilot schemes for the use of video recordings in interviews. However, video recording is unlikely to be introduced at a national level in the near future as the the cost of establishing such a scheme would be about £100 million.

The right to inform someone of the detention

Section 56 of PACE provides that, on arrival at a police station, a suspect is entitled to have someone, such as a relative, informed of their arrest. The person who the suspect chooses must be told of the arrest, and where the suspect is being held, without delay.

This right may be suspended for up to 36 hours if the detention is in connection with an indictable offence, and the authorising officer reasonably believes that informing the person chosen by the suspect would lead to: interference with, or harm to, evidence connected with a serious arrestable offence; the alerting of other suspects; interference with or injury to others; hindrance in recovering any property gained as a result of a serious arrestable offence; or in drug-trafficking offences, hindrance in recovering the profits of that offence.

The right to consult a legal adviser

Under s. 58 of PACE, a person held in custody is entitled to consult a legal adviser, privately and free of charge. About 1.5 million people are arrested every year, of which about a half choose to receive free legal advice. Since 2004, for non-imprisonable offences, this advice is usually given over the telephone by the Criminal Defence Service Direct (see p. 349). Those accused of an imprisonable offence are entitled to see a lawyer in person. In addition, those accused of a non-imprisonable offence continue to have the right to see a legal adviser in person where:

- a police interview or ID procedure is to take place;
- they are entitled to the assistance of an appropriate adult (see p. 399);
- they need an interpreter or cannot communicate on the telephone;
- they complain that they have been maltreated by the police; or
- their preferred solicitor is already at the police station.

The House of Lords ruled in **R v Chief Constable of the RUC, ex parte Begley** (1997) that there was no equivalent right to consult a lawyer under common law. The legal adviser will be either a solicitor or, since 1995, an 'accredited representative'. To become an accredited representative a person must register with the Legal Services Commission with a signed undertaking from a solicitor that they are 'suitable' for this work. Once registered they can attend police stations on behalf of their solicitor and deal with summary or either way offences, but not indictable only offences. Within six months the representative must complete and submit a portfolio of work undertaken. This will include two police station visits where they observed their instructing solicitor, two visits where the solicitor observed them and five visits which they completed on their own. If they pass the portfolio stage they then have to take a written and an oral examination, at which point they are fully qualified to represent clients in the police station for any criminal matters.

Where the legal advice is to be given over the telephone by a Criminal Defence Service Direct adviser, the adviser will start the telephone conversation with the following statement:

My name is [first name and surname]. I am an accredited representative [or solicitor] working for CDS Direct. My job is to give you free and independent legal advice on the telephone. I have nothing to do with the police. You may have asked to speak to a particular solicitor. Your call has been put through to CDS Direct because the type of offence you have been arrested for is one where the necessary advice is provided by telephone. If the police decide to interview you then we will arrange for the solicitor of your choice to attend free of charge at the police station to advise you in person. If you wish to speak to your own solicitor at this stage then it is possible you may have to pay as the call will not be covered by legal aid. Do you wish to continue with free advice from me?

If the suspect answers yes to the question, then the accredited representative will proceed to advise the individual. If, during the conversation, it becomes apparent that the person is entitled to see a legal adviser in person at the police station (for example, because they are about to be interviewed by the police) then the case will either be referred to the particular solicitor requested by the suspect, or to a duty solicitor (including where the requested solicitor could not be contacted within two hours).

The right to speak to a legal adviser may be suspended for up to 36 hours on the same grounds as the right to have another person informed.

KEY CASE

In **R v Samuel** (1988) the appellant was detained for six hours on suspicion of armed robbery and then refused access to a lawyer because the police claimed there was a danger that other suspects might be warned. He was interviewed on two further occasions, and denied the suspected offence but admitted carrying out two burglaries. After 48 hours, a lawyer sent by Samuel's mother arrived at the police station, but was refused access to Samuel for a further three hours, during which time he confessed to the armed robbery. The Court of Appeal said that the denial of access to legal advice was unjustified and the confession obtained as a result was inadmissible. They stated that a police officer who sought to justify refusal of legal advice had to do so by reference to the specific circumstances of the case. It was not enough to believe that giving access to a solicitor might generally lead to the alerting of accomplices; there had to be a belief that in the specific case it probably would, and such cases would be very rare – especially where the lawyer called was the duty solicitor.

> Under the Police and Criminal Evidence Act 1984, access to a legal adviser can only be refused where this is justified by the specific facts of the case.

On the other hand, in **R v Alladice** (1988), a suspect was refused access to a lawyer. Despite this clear breach of PACE, the court held that the interview was in fact conducted with propriety, and that legal advice would have added nothing to the defendant's knowledge of his rights, so the suspect's confession was allowed in evidence.

In the past there had been concern as to the quality of the legal advice given in the police station. Research by Baldwin (1992a) found that in 66 per cent of interviews the legal representative said nothing at all, and in only 9 per cent of cases did they actively intervene on behalf of the suspect or object to police questions. Baldwin comments:

> The interview takes place on police territory and it is police officers who are in charge of it . . . Passivity and compliance on the part of lawyers are therefore the normal, the expected, almost the required responses at the police station. Solicitors are conditioned by their history, their experience, even their professional training and guidance, to be passive in the police interview room, and the existing rules reinforce this by giving police officers the upper hand. The junior staff who mainly turn up to police stations are more inclined to facilitate police questioning than they are to challenge it.

Research by McConville and Hodgson (1993) noted that legal advisers sometimes appeared to identify more with the police than with the suspect. They were usually told very little about the case by the police, and had only minimal discussions with their client beforehand (around half spent less than ten minutes alone with the client). They were therefore rarely in a position to give useful advice.

In the light of concerns about the quality of advice given by solicitors' representatives, the accreditation scheme was introduced in 1995 to raise the standard of legal advice offered at this vital stage in the criminal system. This scheme seems to have led to significant improvements in the advice given. Research carried out by Lee Bridges and Satnam Choongh (*Improving Police Station Legal Advice* (1998)) found that accredited representatives performed as well as duty solicitors and other solicitors, though there were still high rates of non-compliance with the Law Society's standards of performance. In particular, they observed failures to ask suspects about their treatment by the police, to inform them of their right to break interviews for further advice and to intervene where police questioning was inappropriate.

There remains a danger that the police may have questioned the suspect before the official interview, and may continue to do so after a lawyer has visited. In some situations, legal advisers have proved reluctant to visit the police station at all, preferring to speak to suspects on the telephone instead (Sanders *et al.* (1989)).

Taking into account these problems, the RCCJ recommended that the police should ask suspects for reasons if they chose to waive their rights; and these communications should be videoed (along with the interview itself). Police training should include formal instruction in the role that solicitors are properly expected to play in the criminal justice system. The Law Society should take appropriate action to ensure that its advice becomes more widely known, better understood, and more consistently acted upon.

An 'appropriate adult'

PACE and Code C provide that young people and adults with a mental disorder or mental disability must have an 'appropriate adult' with them during a police interview, as well as having the usual right to legal advice. This may be a parent, but is often a social worker. Surprisingly, Evans's 1993 research for the RCCJ found that parents were not necessarily a protection for the suspect, since they often took the side of the police and helped them to produce a confession.

With more and more patients of psychiatric institutions being released into so-called 'community care', higher numbers of mentally vulnerable adults are finding themselves in police stations. Unlike children, they may be difficult to identify, making it likely that the required safeguards will not be in place when they are interviewed. Research by the psychologist Gudjonsson (1992) calculated that between 15 and 20 per cent of suspects may need an appropriate adult present – considerably more than the 4 per cent whom the police currently identify. The RCCJ recommended that the police ought to be given clearer guidelines and special training in identifying vulnerable individuals, and that there should be a full review of who should be considered an 'appropriate adult', and what their role in the police station should be.

They also raised the possibility of establishing duty psychiatrist schemes at busy police stations in city centres, and felt that, in any event, all police stations should have arrangements for calling in psychiatric help where necessary.

Treatment of suspects

PACE codes stipulate that interview rooms must be adequately lit, heated and ventilated, that suspects must be allowed to sit during questioning, and that adequate breaks for meals, refreshments and sleep must be given.

Record of the interview

After the interview is over, the police must make a record of it, which is kept on file. Baldwin's 1992(b) research checked a sample of such records against the taped recordings, and concluded that even those police forces considered to be more progressive were often failing to produce good quality records of interviews. Half the records were faulty or misleading, and the longer the interview, the more likely the record was to be inaccurate. These findings were backed up by a separate study carried out by Roger Evans (1993). He found that, in some summaries, the police stated that suspects had confessed during the interview, but, on listening to the tape recordings the researchers could find no evidence of this, and felt that the suspects were in fact denying the offence.

Baldwin points out that the job of police officers is to catch criminals, and their temperament, aptitude and training are focused on this; the skills required for making careful summaries of complex material are not among those generally thought to be required in the job. Since police officers would inevitably summarise interviews from the point of view of a prosecution, defence lawyers should be prepared to take this into account and, rather than taking the summaries on trust, needed to listen to the interview tapes themselves. In practice, solicitors request interview tapes in only 10 per cent of cases.

Exclusion of evidence

One of the most important safeguards in PACE is the possibility for the courts to refuse to admit evidence which has been improperly obtained. Given that the reason why police officers bend or break the rules is to secure a conviction, preventing them from using the evidence obtained in this way is likely to constitute an effective deterrent.

PACE contains two provisions on the admissibility of evidence. Section 76(2) requires the prosecution to prove beyond reasonable doubt that a confession was not obtained by oppression (which is defined in s. 76(8) as torture, inhuman or degrading treatment or the use or threat of violence), or otherwise in circumstances likely to render the confession unreliable. Section 78 allows the court to refuse evidence (of any kind) if it appears to the court that the admission of such evidence would have such an adverse effect on the fairness of the proceedings that the court ought not to admit it.

These provisions have been used to render evidence inadmissible when the police have breached PACE or its Codes, although breaches of the Codes alone must be 'serious and substantial' in order to make evidence inadmissible. Such breaches were found in **R v Canale** (1990), where the court refused to accept evidence of interviews which were not contemporaneously written up, describing this breach of a Code as 'flagrant, deliberate and cynical'. In **R v Latif and Shahzad** (1996) the House of Lords took a very narrow approach to s. 78. The appellants had been convicted of being knowingly concerned in the importation of heroin into the UK from Pakistan. An undercover police officer had assisted in the importation in order to trick Shahzad into entering the UK so that he could be prosecuted here, there being no extradition treaty with Pakistan. Despite the fact that the court found that the police officer's conduct had been criminal and had involved trickery and deception, the House of Lords refused to exclude his evidence under s. 78.

The House of Lords in **A v Secretary of State for the Home Department** (2005) held that, if it was established that evidence had been obtained by torture abroad, such as from detainees of Guantanamo Bay, this evidence would not be admissible in proceedings in English courts.

Article 8 of the European Convention on Human Rights protects the right to privacy. Article 8(2) adds that interference with that right is permitted if it is in accordance with the law and necessary in a democratic society for the prevention of crime. A careful balance has to be drawn by the law where surveillance techniques are used: for example, by bugging a private home. Breach of Art. 8 can give rise to a right to damages, but there is no guarantee that the evidence will be excluded at trial as the ordinary rules in s. 76 and s. 78 of PACE apply.

The right to silence

Until 1994, the law provided a further safeguard for those suspected of criminal conduct, in the form of the traditional 'right to silence'. This essentially meant that suspects were free to say nothing at all in response to police questioning, and the prosecution could not suggest in court that this silence implied guilt (with some very limited exceptions).

Once PACE was introduced, the police argued that its safeguards, especially the right of access to legal advice, had tipped the balance too far in favour of suspects, so that the right to silence was no longer needed. Despite the fact that the Royal Commission on Criminal Justice (1993) opposed this view, the Government agreed with the police, and the right to silence was abolished by the Criminal Justice and Public Order Act 1994. This does not mean that suspects can be forced to speak, but it provides four situations in which, if the suspect chooses not to speak, the court will be entitled to draw such inferences from that silence as appear proper. The four situations are where suspects:

- when questioned under caution or charge, fail to mention facts which they later rely on as part of their defence and which it is reasonable to expect them to have mentioned (s. 34);
- are silent during the trial, including choosing not to give evidence or to answer any question without good cause (s. 35);
- following arrest, fail to account for objects, substances or marks on clothing when requested to do so (s. 36);
- following arrest, fail to account for their presence at a particular place when requested to do so (s. 37).

No inferences from silence can be drawn where a suspect was at a police station and has been denied access to legal advice (s. 34(2A)).

The European Court of Human Rights stated in **Murray v United Kingdom** (1996) that, in the context of the anti-terrorist legislation, the abolition of the right to silence was not in breach of the European Convention, because of the existence of a range of other safeguards ensuring that the defendant had a fair trial.

The abolition of the right to silence by the Criminal Justice and Public Order Act 1994 did not amount to a breach of the European Convention on Human Rights.

Adverse inferences cannot always be drawn from silence. Where the statute does not apply, the judge should explicitly direct the jury that they should not draw adverse inferences from the defendant's silence, as the old common law applies. In **R v McGarry** (1998) the defendant, on leaving a club, had punched a man in the face. When questioned by the police about the incident after being cautioned, he had provided a short written statement that he had acted in self-defence and then had answered 'no comment' to all subsequent questions. At his trial he relied on the defence of self-defence and the jury heard the tape of his interview when he had refused to answer questions. The Court of Appeal ruled that he fell outside s. 34 as he had not failed to mention facts that he later relied on at his trial in his defence. The judge should therefore have directed the jury not to draw adverse inferences from his refusal to answer questions.

In **R v N** (1998) the defendant was prosecuted for indecent assault. At his trial the judge informed the jury that they could draw an adverse inference from the appellant's failure in the police interview to provide the explanation for the presence of semen on the victim's nightdress that he had given at his trial. The appellant was convicted and appealed. The Court of Appeal ruled that the trial judge had made a mistake since, at the time of the interview, it was not known that there were semen stains on the nightdress, and so the appellant was not asked to explain them. Section 34 of the CJPOA had to be limited to its express terms: an adverse inference could only be drawn from a failure to mention a fact when being questioned in relation to it. Merely failing to mention a fact during the police interview was not sufficient.

The courts have had some difficulty determining when adverse inferences can be drawn from a suspect's silence, if he or she remained silent following advice from their solicitor. In **Condron v UK** (2000) the applicants were heroin addicts accused of being involved in the supply and possession of heroin. The prosecution case was that the applicants kept the wholesale heroin in their flat, and passed retail packets to the adjacent flat, where another person made the actual sales. Modest support was given to this theory by surveillance videos which showed small objects (such as a cigarette packet) being passed from the balcony of the applicants' flat to the window of the adjacent flat.

To avoid adverse inferences being drawn under the Criminal Justice and Public Order Act 1994 when remaining silent during questioning, suspects must reveal good reasons why their solicitor advised them to remain silent.

In the police station their solicitor had concluded that they were unfit to be interviewed because they were suffering from withdrawal symptoms, and therefore advised them not to answer questions. At their trial the applicants gave various innocent explanations for the transactions on the balcony. The trial judge directed the jury that they could draw adverse inferences of guilt from the applicants' silence in the police station.

The applicants took their case to the European Court of Human Rights, claiming that their right to a fair trial guaranteed under Art. 6(1) of the European Convention on Human Rights had been violated by the judge's direction to the jury. Their application was successful. If suspects are told to remain silent by their solicitor, they are likely to see this as a good reason to remain silent. But that reason will not be sufficient to prevent adverse inferences being drawn. To avoid these adverse inferences the suspects have to reveal good reasons why the solicitor advised them to remain silent.

18

In **Beckles** *v* **United Kingdom** (2002) the European Court merely emphasised the requirement that the defendant should have genuinely relied on the solicitor's advice. But when the case was subsequently reconsidered by the Court of Appeal (**R** *v* **Beckles** (2004)) that Court emphasised that there needed to be both a genuine and a reasonable reliance on the advice of the solicitor.

In **R** *v* **Bresa** (2005) the Court of Appeal recommended that a jury should be directed in the following terms:

You have no explanation for the advice in this case. It is the defendant's right not to reveal the contents of any advice from his solicitor or what transpired between himself and his solicitor. The question for you is whether the defendant could reasonably have been expected to mention the facts on which he now relies and saying that he had legal advice without more cannot automatically make it reasonable. If, for example, you consider that he had or may have had an answer to give, i.e. that he was acting in self-defence, but genuinely and reasonably relied on the legal advice to remain silent, you should not draw any conclusion against him. But if, for example, you were sure that the defendant remained silent not because of the legal advice but because he had not acted in self-defence and that was a matter which he fabricated later, and merely latched on to the legal advice as a convenient shield behind which to hide, you would be entitled to draw a conclusion against him.

Interviews outside the police station

PACE states that, where practicable, interviews with arrested suspects should always take place at a police station. However, evidence obtained by questioning or voluntary statements outside the police station may still be admissible. Since such interviews are not subject to most of the safeguards explained above, the obvious danger is that police may evade PACE requirements by conducting 'unofficial' interviews – such as the practice known as taking the 'scenic route' to the station, in which suspects are questioned in the police car. The RCCJ found that about 30 per cent of suspects report being questioned prior to arrest.

Even at the police station, research by McConville ('Videotaping Interrogations: Police Behaviour On and Off Camera' (1992)) shows that illegal, informal and

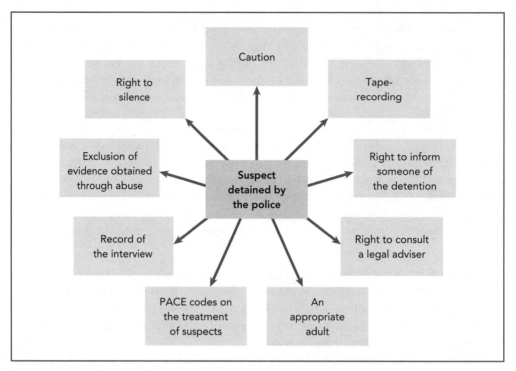

Figure 18.2 Safeguards for the suspect

unrecorded visits were made to suspects in cells to prepare the ground for an interview and to persuade them not to raise a defence. Sometimes suspects themselves ask to see police officers informally, in the hope of doing some kind of deal. In some cases the formal interview that followed was little more than a set piece, scripted by the police. Yet defence lawyers often accepted the police version of these events as the truth. Despite the obvious dangers of these practices, the RCCJ did not recommend excluding evidence obtained in this way, but merely discussed the possibility of requiring tape-recording of all contact between a suspect and the police.

Non-intimate samples

Urine and other non-intimate samples can be taken after arrest for a trigger offence, such as theft and burglary, to test for the presence of Class A drugs.

Search of the person after arrest

Section 32 of PACE provides that the police may search an arrested person at a place other than a police station if there are reasonable grounds for believing they are in possession of evidence, or anything that might assist escape or present a danger.

The police have the power to search arrested persons on arrival at the police station, and to seize anything which they reasonably believe the suspect might use to injure anyone, or use to make an escape, or that is evidence of an offence or has been obtained as the result of an offence (s. 54).

Searches in school

Under the Violent Crime Reduction Act 2006 school staff, with the permission of the head teacher, are able to carry out a search of school pupils for knives and other offensive weapons. If an offensive weapon is found, or any other evidence of an offence, the police must be immediately informed. Thus, the school does not have the option of merely dealing with this as an internal disciplinary matter.

Intimate searches

Section 55 of PACE gives police the power to conduct intimate searches of a suspect, which means searches of the body's orifices. Such a search must be authorised by a superintendent, who must have reasonable grounds for believing that a weapon or drug is concealed, and must be carried out by a registered health care professional.

The safeguards on the use of this power caused problems for the police when confronted with drug dealers. The dealers frequently stored drugs in their mouths, knowing that search of the mouth was regarded as an intimate search needing to be carried out by a member of the medical profession with special authorisation. To address this problem, s. 65 of PACE, as amended by the CJPOA 1994, now provides that a search of the mouth is not an intimate search.

The Criminal Justice and Court Services Act 2000 allows the compulsory drug testing of alleged offenders.

TOPICAL ISSUE

Fingerprints, biological samples and DNA profiles

The police are permitted to take fingerprints from a suspect under ss. 27 and 61 of PACE. Section 62 of PACE states that intimate samples, including blood, saliva or semen, can be taken from a suspect. Non-intimate samples, such as hair or nail clippings, can be authorised by an officer at the level of inspector or above. The authorisation must be in writing and recorded on the custody record.

DNA information can be extracted from these samples and under s. 64 of PACE it can be stored and the information placed on a national DNA database indefinitely. DNA is an invaluable investigative tool, allowing the police to check for a match on the database with DNA taken from the scene of a crime. Even where there is no match, the DNA profile enables the police to determine the gender, ethnicity and certain medical conditions of a suspect.

The police can currently store DNA samples from all individuals convicted in England or Wales for an imprisonable offence with the sample remaining indefinitely on the database. The retention of DNA samples where there is no conviction was found to breach the European Convention in **S and Michael Marper** v UK (2008).

The DNA database is proportionately the largest in the world, holding over 4 million samples (about 6 per cent of the population). There is concern that at the moment the database risks adding to the problem of race discrimination in the criminal justice

▶

system. Over a quarter of the black population is on the database, compared to only 6 per cent of white people and 9 per cent of Asians. In London, over half the people on the database are black or Asian, whereas they constitute only 29 per cent of the London population. This imbalance may be the result of discriminatory police practices. Some of the people on the database will have to be removed following **S and Michael Marper** where they have not been convicted of a criminal offence. The Home Office has issued a consultation paper *Keeping the Right People on the DNA Database: Science and Public Protection* (2009). It is considering limiting the time for which DNA information can be kept on a database to 12 years where a person was arrested but not convicted of a violent, sexual or terrorist offence, or 6 years for other offences.

Photo 18.3 Taking a DNA sample
Source: © iStockphoto/Leah-Anne Thompson

Powers to search premises

The police can always search premises if the occupier consents to this. In addition, Part II of PACE (ss. 8–18) provides the police with statutory powers to enter and search premises for evidence. These powers can be executed either with or without a warrant.

Search with a warrant

A number of statutes allow the granting of search warrants, but the main provisions are to be found in s. 8 of PACE. The police apply for the warrant to a magistrate, who must be satisfied that the police reasonably believe an indictable offence has been committed, and that the premises concerned contain relevant evidence or material likely to be of substantial use to the investigation. In addition, it must be impractical to make the search without a warrant (which means with the consent of the person entitled to grant entry or access to evidence), because:

- it is not practicable to communicate with that person;
- entry would not be granted without a warrant; or
- the purpose of the search would be frustrated or seriously prejudiced if immediate entry could not be obtained on arrival.

The search warrant may allow entry to:

- specific premises;
- any premises occupied or controlled by the person specified on the application;
- premises on more than one occasion. The number of entries may be specified or unlimited.

The latter two search powers were created by the Serious Organised Crime and Police Act 2005 and are known colloquially as 'super-warrants'.

In practice, research by Lidstone (1984) indicates that magistrates rarely refuse to grant a warrant; if certain magistrates were known to refuse applications, the police would simply stop applying to them and go to another magistrate instead. About 12 per cent of searches are made with a warrant.

There are certain classes of material for which these basic powers cannot be used:

- privileged material (communications between lawyers and their clients);
- excluded material (medical records and journalistic material held in confidence); and
- special procedure material (other journalistic material and material acquired through business and held in confidence).

Once the warrant is issued, entry and search must take place within three months, and must be undertaken at a reasonable hour, unless that would frustrate the search. Reasonable force may be used (PACE, s. 117). The officers concerned should provide documentary evidence of their status, plus a copy of the warrant, unless it is impracticable to do so. The Codes also require that police hand out a notice giving information about the grounds for and powers of search, and the rights of the occupier, including rights to compensation for any damage done.

Search without a warrant

PACE provides a range of powers of search which can be exercised without a warrant. Section 17 allows the police to enter and search to execute a warrant of arrest; to make an arrest without warrant; to capture a person unlawfully at large; or to protect people from serious injury or prevent serious damage to property.

18

The police

Under s. 18, after an arrest for an indictable offence, the police can search premises occupied or controlled by the suspect if they reasonably suspect that there is evidence of the immediate offence or other offences on the premises.

Section 32 provides that, after an arrest for an indictable offence, an officer can lawfully enter and search premises where the person was when arrested or immediately before they were arrested, if the constable reasonably suspects that there is evidence relating to the offence in question on the premises.

There is also a common law power to enter and remain on premises 'to deal with or prevent a breach of the peace'. This is based on **Thomas** *v* **Sawkins** (1935), where it was held to be lawful for police to enter and insist on remaining in a hall where a political meeting was taking place, because their past experience of such meetings gave them reasonable grounds to apprehend a breach of the peace.

In **McLeod** *v* **UK** (1998), Mrs McLeod was ordered by the county court to deliver certain property to her ex-husband. Mr McLeod mistakenly believed he had the right to collect the property from her home. His solicitors asked two police officers to escort him to prevent a breach of the peace. Mrs McLeod was not actually at home when he arrived and he entered her house escorted by two police officers. The Court of Appeal found that the police entry was lawful. Lord Neill commented:

> I am satisfied that Parliament in s. 17(6) has now recognised that there is a power to enter premises to prevent a breach of the peace as a form of preventive justice. I can see no satisfactory basis for restricting that power to particular classes of premises such as those where public meetings are held. If the police reasonably believe that a breach of the peace is likely to take place on private premises, they have power to enter those premises to prevent it. The apprehension must, of course, be genuine and it must relate to the near future.

Mrs McLeod took her case to the European Court of Human Rights. That court ruled that Art. 8 of the European Convention on Human Rights, which protects the right to privacy, had been violated. While the breach of the peace doctrine could in certain circumstances justify an interference with a person's privacy, on the facts of the case there were almost no grounds to apprehend that a breach of the peace would occur, and so it provided no justification for the interference with Mrs McLeod's privacy. As soon as it became apparent that she was away from home, the officers should not have entered her house since it should have been clear that there was no risk of a breach of the peace.

Searches of premises are governed by Code B, which states that searches should be made at a reasonable time, that only reasonable force should be used and that the police should show due consideration and courtesy towards the property and privacy of the occupier. How far this is observed in practice might be doubted by anyone who watched television news coverage of the anti-burglary campaign Operation Bumblebee, in which police broke down suspects' doors with sledgehammers at 6 am. The fact that in high-profile cases such searches are often accompanied by TV cameras suggests that the media may be tipped off by the police, which, whether such tip-offs are official or not, suggests little regard for the suspects' privacy.

Once the police are lawfully on premises, then under s. 19 of PACE they may seize and retain any item that is evidence of a crime.

TOPICAL ISSUE

Surveillance operations

In recent years a combination of developing technology, concern about confession evidence and the changing nature of financial and drug-related crime has led the police to adopt increasingly sophisticated and intrusive methods of investigation. Surveillance operations can include the placing of bugging devices on private property, the interception of communications, including mobile phones and e-mails, and the use of undercover police officers. Such surveillance activities were in the past unregulated, which may have been in breach of the European Convention on Human Rights which protects the right to privacy (Art. 8). Legislation was therefore required. The relevant legislative provisions are now contained in the Police Act 1997 and the Regulation of Investigatory Powers Act 2000. Except in the case of an emergency, the police have to obtain the authorisation of an independent Commissioner before they can use intrusive surveillance techniques.

Cautions

In appropriate cases an offender can be issued with a caution rather than being subjected to a full criminal prosecution. This is a formal warning to offenders about what they have done, and their conduct in the future. Home Office guidelines lay down the criteria on which the decision to caution should be made. A caution can only be given where the offender admits guilt, and there would be a realistic prospect of a successful prosecution. In the case of a juvenile, the parents or guardian must consent to a caution being given. If these criteria are met, other factors to be taken into account are the seriousness of the offence and the extent of the damage done; the interests and desires of the victim; the previous conduct of the offender; the family background of the offender; and the offender's conduct after the offence, such as a willingness to make reparation to the victim.

Formal cautions are recorded and, if the person is convicted of another offence afterwards, can be cited as part of their criminal record. The 1980s saw a substantial increase in the use of cautioning with the number of cautions given doubling between 1983 and 1993, peaking at 311,300 cautions for that year, primarily to juveniles. There has subsequently been a slight decline in their use with the figures for 1995 showing a 6 per cent reduction in the use of cautions.

The Criminal Justice Act 2003 introduced conditional cautions. Conditions can seek either to facilitate rehabilitation or ensure that reparation is made. Failure to comply with the conditions can trigger a criminal trial for the offence. This is a dangerous reform, as cautions will take on the form of a punishment administered outside the court system. As such, they might well breach the European Convention on Human Rights.

Cautioning appears to be effective in terms of preventing reoffending: 87 per cent of those cautioned in 1985 were not convicted of a standard list offence within two years of the caution. However, this may reflect the kind of individuals and offences that are seen as suitable for a caution: for example, 80 per cent of those cautioned had no previous

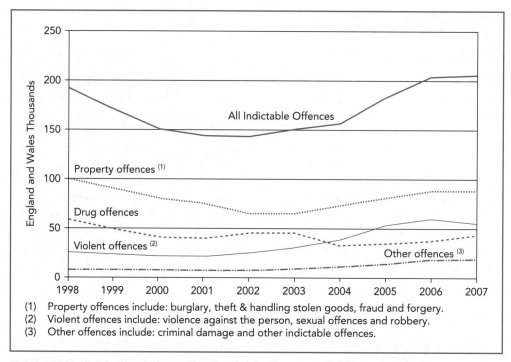

Figure 18.3 Offenders cautioned for indictable offences by offence group, 1998–2007

Source: Criminal Statistics 2007 England and Wales, p. 51 [Figure 3.7]

cautions or convictions, but for those who had been previously convicted there was a much greater likelihood that they would reoffend. Prosecution is the most expensive method of dealing with offenders. The RCCJ recognised the value of diversionary schemes, stating that there could safely be more cautioning of petty offenders. They were concerned, though, that rates of cautioning varied widely across the country, and recommended the introduction of statutory guidelines. The initial decision on whether to caution should remain with the police, but the Crown Prosecution Service (CPS) should be able to require the police to caution instead of bringing a prosecution.

Despite the RCCJ's recommendations for more cautioning, the national guidelines that were subsequently introduced are more restrictive than previous practice, removing any presumption that juveniles should be cautioned, and discouraging repeat cautions and cautions for serious offences. Problems with variations in the use of cautioning continue – the Criminal Statistics 1995 showed that there were big differences in police caution rates between different police forces, with Gloucestershire, Suffolk and Warwickshire having a rate of over 54 per cent, while Merseyside, Durham, Dorset, South Wales and Cumbria had a rate of 30 per cent or less.

Bail

A person accused, convicted or under arrest for an offence may be granted bail, which means they are released under a duty to attend court or the police station at a given time. The right to bail has been reduced in recent years amid concern that individuals on bail reoffend and fail to turn up at court for their trial. Fourteen per cent of those bailed to appear at court fail to do so (*Criminal Justice Statistics 2003*) and nearly 25 per cent of defendants commit at least one offence while on bail (Brown (1998) *Offending While on Bail*, Home Office, Report No. 72). The criteria for granting or refusing bail are contained in the Bail Act 1976. There is a general presumption in favour of bail for unconvicted defendants, but there are some important exceptions. Bail need not be granted where there are substantial grounds for believing that, unless kept in custody, the accused would fail to surrender to bail, or would commit an offence, interfere with witnesses or otherwise obstruct the course of justice. In assessing these risks, the court may take account of the nature and seriousness of the offence and the probable sentence, along with the character, antecedents, associations and community ties of the defendant. A court considering the question of bail must take into account any drug misuse by the defendant. The Criminal Justice Act 2003 has created a presumption against bail for a person charged with an imprisonable offence, who tests positive for a specified Class A drug and refuses treatment, unless there are exceptional circumstances. This provision may breach Art. 5 of the European Convention on Human Rights, which guarantees the right to freedom of the person.

The courts need not grant bail when the accused should be kept in custody for their own protection, where the accused is already serving a prison sentence or where there has been insufficient time to obtain information as to the criteria for bail. If the court does choose to grant bail in such cases, its reasons for doing so must be included in the bail record. The presumption in favour of bail is reversed where someone is charged with a further indictable offence which appears to have been committed while on bail.

The Criminal Justice and Public Order Act 1994, following concern at offences being committed by accused while on bail, provided that a person charged or convicted of murder, manslaughter, rape, attempted murder or attempted rape could never be granted bail if they had a previous conviction for such an offence. This complete ban breached the European Convention on Human Rights. The law has now been reformed by the Crime and Disorder Act 1998, under which such a person may only be granted bail where there are exceptional circumstances which justify doing so. Thus Sion Jenkins, who was put on trial for the murder of his foster-daughter Billy-Jo, was on bail throughout most of the proceedings.

When bail is refused for any of the stated reasons, other than insufficient information, the accused will usually be allowed only one further bail application; the court does not have to hear further applications unless there has been a change in circumstances. Where the remand in custody is on the basis of insufficient information, this is not technically a refusal of bail, so the accused may still make two applications.

Bail can be granted subject to conditions, such as that the accused obtain legal advice before their next court appearance or that the accused or a third party give a security (which is a payment into court that will be forfeited if the accused fails to attend a court hearing). The Police and Justice Act 2006 significantly increased the range of conditions that can be imposed when granting bail. When a defendant fails to attend court any money held by the court is immediately forfeited and it is up to the person who paid that money to show why it should not be forfeited. A defendant

18

The police

refused bail, or who objects to the conditions under which it is offered, must be told the reasons for the decision, and informed of their right to appeal. The prosecution also has increasing rights to appeal against a decision to grant bail.

The Criminal Justice Act 2003 has given the police the power to grant bail at the place of arrest. This is called 'street bail'. It means that the police do not have to take suspects to the police station and undertake lengthy paperwork. A form is completed on the street and later entered in police records. The power has not been used much by the police and is unlikely to be used much until compulsory ID cards have been introduced.

To try to reduce the prison population, Lord Carter (2007) recommended that pre-trial custody be used primarily for individuals being prosecuted for dangerous and serious offences and only as a last resort for women. Under the Criminal Justice and Immigration Act 2008, half the time spent on bail with an electronically tagged curfew of at least eight hours a day can be deducted from any subsequent custodial sentence.

Criticism and reform

Criticisms and suggestions for reform have been made throughout this chapter, but the following have been the subject of particular debate.

A graduate profession

The work of a police officer requires a wide range of skills, both intellectual and personal. At the moment, a candidate does not need any formal qualifications to join the police force. Now that increasing numbers of young people are going to university, it is time to transform the police force into a graduate profession. Only then would the United Kingdom have an efficient police force with the skills to combat crime effectively. The police force currently struggles with the paperwork that their job requires because they have an inadequate education. Without better preparation for their career, the police will continue to be perceived by many in the public as slow, lazy and inefficient. With the creation of community support officers, the higher pay and status of the police can only be justified if they actually have better qualifications and skills.

Review of PACE

Ess. Cases
p. 263
The Home Office issued a consultation paper in 2007, *Modernising Police Powers: Review of the Police and Criminal Evidence Act 1984*. The paper covers a wide variety of topics and seems to be looking at ways to reduce unnecessary paperwork to help the police to work more efficiently and effectively, to spend more time on front-line duty. It considers whether the codes could be simplified and shortened to make them more accessible. To save police time, short-term holding facilities could be established in shopping centres. People arrested for minor crimes, such as shoplifting, could be taken there instead of the police station. The cells could hold suspects for up to four hours to

enable fingerprinting, photographing and DNA sampling. Suspects would be transferred to a police station where an investigation was required. The rules relating to the taking and storing of identification samples could be relaxed so that DNA samples and fingerprints could be taken from those suspected of minor crimes. The pressure group, Liberty, has commented that 'Six years ago, DNA sampling was about combatting serious crime. Today, dropping litter is proposed as a lame excuse for an ever-growing national DNA database.'

TOPICAL ISSUE

Racism and the police

Ess. Cases
p. 270

Britain is a multicultural and ethnically diverse community. Three per cent of the population aged ten and over is of black ethnic origin, 5 per cent of Asian origin. Successful policing requires that all members of British society must have confidence in the police force. Following the fatal stabbing of Stephen Lawrence, a black teenager who was an A-level student from south London, by a group of racist youths in 1993, defects in several aspects of the English legal system failed to bring his killers to justice. Following concern at the handling of the police investigation into the killing, a judicial inquiry headed by a former High Court judge, Sir William Macpherson, was set up by the Government in 1997 and its report was published in February 1999. It found that the Metropolitan Police suffered from 'institutional racism'. This is defined as existing where there is a 'collective failure of an organisation to provide an appropriate and professional service to people because of their colour, culture and ethnic origin. It can be seen or detected in processes, attitudes and behaviour which amount to discrimination through unwitting prejudice, ignorance, thoughtlessness and racist stereotypical behaviour.'

The presence of institutional racism was reflected in the fact that the first senior officer at the scene of the crime assumed that what had occurred had been a fight; it was also expressed in the absence of adequate family liaison and the 'patronising and thoughtless approach' of some officers to Mr and Mrs Lawrence; and it could be seen in the side-lining of Stephen Lawrence's friend, the surviving victim of the attack. There was, furthermore, a refusal to accept, by at least five officers involved in the case, that this was a racist murder. Finally, there was the use of inappropriate and offensive language by police officers, including, on occasion, during their appearance before the inquiry itself. It found that racism awareness training was 'almost non-existent at every level', and concluded that institutional racism could only be tackled effectively if there was an 'unequivocal acceptance that the problem actually exists'.

The inquiry, however, concluded that institutional racism was not 'universally the cause of the failure of this investigation'. The investigation by the Metropolitan Police was 'marred by a combination of professional incompetence, institutional racism and a failure of leadership by senior officers'.

The report contained 20 recommendations for reform. In March 1999, the Government issued its Action Plan in response to the Macpherson Report. A steering group, chaired by the Home Secretary, was established to oversee the programme of reform. In the past the Race Relations Act 1976 did not apply to the police, so that there was no legal remedy if a black person thought they had been stopped by the police because of racial prejudice. Now the Race Relations (Amendment) Act 2000 has been passed. This Act amends the 1976 Act, making it unlawful for a public authority, including the police, to discriminate in carrying out any of their functions. Police forces have reviewed their provision of racism awareness training. Targets have been set for the recruitment and retention of ethnic minority police officers. Currently 2.6 per cent of police officers are from an ethnic minority. The recommendation that the use of racist language in private should be criminalised has been rejected.

While the Macpherson Report is one step towards tackling institutional racism in the police, it is worrying that Lord Scarman's report into the Brixton riots of 1981 had already identified this problem, and though some progress was subsequently made, this had clearly not been sufficient. In 1999/2000 the British Crime Survey suggested that there were 143,000 racially motivated crimes committed and yet only 1,832 defendants were prosecuted for such offences.

A particularly sensitive area of policing is the power to stop and search. A police operation against street robberies in Lambeth (south London) in 1981, codenamed SWAMP 81, involved 943 stops, mostly of young black men, over a period of two weeks. Of these, only 118 led to arrests and 75 to charges, one of which was for robbery. The operation, which had no noticeable effect on the crime figures, shattered relations between the police and the ethnic community, and was one of the triggers of the Brixton riots that occurred soon afterwards. Nevertheless, in his report on the Brixton disorders, Lord Scarman thought such powers necessary to combat street crime, provided that the safeguard of 'reasonable suspicion' was properly and objectively applied. But in 1999 the Macpherson Report concluded that the 'perception and experience of the minority communities that discrimination is a major element in the stop and search problem is correct'.

In accordance with recommendations made by Macpherson, the police are now required to monitor the use of stop and search powers, and 'consider in particular whether there is any evidence that they are being exercised on the basis of stereotyped images or inappropriate generalisations'. Regrettably, these statistics show that an increasing proportion of those stopped and searched by the police are black. Home Office statistics (*Statistics on Race and the Criminal Justice System 2003*) show that while black people make up only 3 per cent of the population, 14 per cent of stop and searches were carried out on black people, an increase of more than a third on the previous year. The Commission for Racial Equality (2004) has concluded that stop and search has been used disproportionately against black and Asian people. This has:

> led to the perception among some communities that stop and search is being used in a discriminatory way – affecting confidence levels in the police and in some cases reducing the willingness of people to assist with the investigation of crime.

An increasing worry is the number of black murder victims and the failure of the police to bring the offenders to court. Between 2000 and 2003, 10 per cent of homicide victims were black. The police were statistically less likely to identify suspects for homicides involving black and Asian victims than for white victims, though this can partly be explained by the method of killing used.

Police corruption

The police exercise an extremely delicate role in society and, as criminals are able to generate large sums of money from their criminal conduct, the danger of corruption is real. High risk areas include the handling of informers and positions within drug, vice and crime squads where constant vigilance is required. Where corruption is rife, one can no longer fall back on the idea of a few rotten apples and must accept that the system itself must be corrupting its members.

Sir Paul Condon made anti-corruption a touchstone of his tenure as Commissioner of the Metropolitan Police. He has estimated that there may be as many as 250 corrupt officers in his force, some of whom are directly involved in very serious criminal activity, and has dedicated resources to their detection. A more proactive approach can be expected at a national level, as New Scotland Yard has established a special squad concentrating on corruption in the police and the Association of Chief Police Officers established in 1998 a Taskforce on Corruption. During the course of that year, 28 police officers were convicted of corruption-related offences and, at the end of the year, 153 police officers were suspended for alleged corruption and similar matters.

Armed officers

There is an ongoing debate as to whether our police officers should carry guns. The majority of police in other countries do carry guns. In the UK the tradition is that police do not carry guns, and only 5 per cent have carried out special training to be authorised to carry them. They work, for example, in armed response vehicles, so that they can provide swift support to their colleagues where necessary. Following the fatal shooting in Bradford of a 28-year-old police officer, Sharon Beshenivsky, who was investigating a robbery at a travel agent, the Police Federation and the Association of Chief Police Officers called for more police to be armed in the UK. On the other hand, the fatal shooting of Jean Charles de Menezes at Stockwell tube station in the summer of 2005 highlighted the risks of police officers being armed, as the police are only human and can make mistakes.

'Bobbies on the beat'

Four billion pounds is spent each year on police patrols, but the reality is that at any one time only 5 per cent of police officers are out on patrol. The Audit Commission report, *Streetwise – Effective Police Patrol* (1996), notes that the public are keen to see more 'bobbies on the beat' and that this provides the public with a feeling of security. A review of research in 1998 found that random patrols are ineffective in reducing crime but that targeted patrols on crime hot spots can be effective (Nuttall, Goldblatt and Lewis, *Reducing Offending: An Assessment of Research Evidence on Ways of Dealing with Offending Behaviour* (1998)).

Police conduct

During 1997, well over 6,000 complaints of alleged rudeness and incivility by police officers were recorded. Her Majesty's Inspectorate of Constabulary undertook a wide-ranging exploration of the level of integrity in the police because it was recognised that 'public confidence was becoming seriously affected by the bad behaviour of a small minority of police'. In *Police Integrity: Securing and Maintaining Public Confidence* (1999) Her Majesty's Inspectorate reported that: 'Numerous examples were found in all forces visited of poor behaviour towards members of the public and colleagues alike, including rudeness, arrogance and discriminatory comment.' In the Inspectorate's view, one consequence of tolerating bullying, rudeness and racist or sexist behaviour is that 'corruption and other wrongdoing will flourish'.

TOPICAL ISSUE

Policing demonstrations

The death of Ian Tomlinson at the G20 summit demonstrations in 2009 highlighted concerns about the current policing arrangements for demonstrations. The right to demonstrate forms an important part of a democratic system. When Ian Tomlinson died the public were originally told that he had suffered a heart attack. It was only after video footage was published in the media showing that Ian Tomlinson had been pushed violently from behind by a police officer that a second autopsy was ordered and it was revealed he had died as a result of internal injuries. Ian Tomlinson himself was not part of the G20 demonstration but just looking for a route to get back from work to the hostel where he was living.

The controversy surrounding his death has also drawn attention to the police practice of 'kettling' demonstrators, whereby demonstrators are cordoned off and not allowed to leave for a number of hours until they are released in small groups. This method of policing has proved effective at reducing the risk of demonstrations becoming violent riots, but also constitutes a significant restriction on a person's freedom of movement and right to demonstrate. It was held to be lawful by the House of Lords in **Austin v Metropolitan Police Commissioner** (2009). Austin had attended a demonstration in Oxford Street when the police had cordoned off the demonstrators and refused to allow them to leave for seven hours, with no access to toilet facilities. The House of Lords held that there was no breach of the right to liberty in Art. 5 of the European Convention on Human Rights. The police are entitled to restrict the movement of demonstrators provided their actions are proportionate and reasonable and any confinement is restricted to the minimum necessary to prevent serious public disorder and violence. If a cordon was maintained beyond the time necessary for crowd control, in order to punish the demonstrators, then there would be a breach of Art. 5.

Police as witnesses

In **R v Momodou and Limani** (2005) the principle was confirmed that discussions between witnesses should not take place before a trial and statements of one witness should not be disclosed to any other witness, to prevent them tailoring their evidence in the light of what others are saying. But when the police are to act as witnesses in court they are allowed to confer together. This occurred following the shooting of Jean Charles de Menezes and led the jury at his inquest to be unhappy with the police evidence. It also occurred following the shooting dead of a barrister at his home in Chelsea by the police, after the barrister had started shooting at random from the window of his home. The barrister was naked at the time and appears to have had a mental breakdown. His family brought legal proceedings questioning the legality of the police conferring together when they were preparing their notes of the incident. The High Court held that the police had acted legally: **R (on the application of Saunders)** *v* **IPCC** (2008).

The right to silence

The abolition of the right to silence has been one of the most severely criticised changes to the criminal justice system in recent years. As the academic John Fitzpatrick has written, the basis of the right to silence is the presumption of innocence, which places the burden of proof on the prosecution: 'this burden begins to shift, and the presumption of innocence to dwindle, as soon as we are obliged to explain or justify our actions in any way' (*Legal Action*, May 1994).

Those who objected to the right to silence claimed that only the guilty would have anything to hide and that the innocent should therefore have no objection to answering questions. It was suggested that the calculated use of this right by professional criminals was leading to serious cases being dropped for lack of evidence, and that 'ambush' defences (in which defendants remain silent till the last moment and then produce an unexpected defence) were leading to acquittals because the prosecution had no time to prepare for the defence.

These arguments were put to the RCCJ, by a Home Office Working Group among others, but after commissioning its own research into the subject the RCCJ rejected the idea of abolishing the right to silence. This research, by Leng (1993), and McConville and Hodgson (1993), showed that in fact only 5 per cent of suspects exercised their right to silence, and there was no evidence of an unacceptable acquittal rate for these defendants. Nor was there any serious problem with ambush defences.

As we have seen, the Conservative Government decided to ignore the RCCJ's recommendations and abolish the right to silence – a somewhat strange decision considering that it was the same Government which set up the Commission in the first place. The law reform body, JUSTICE, has claimed that this decision will lead to increased pressure on suspects and, in turn, to more miscarriages of justice. It studied the effects of removing the right to silence in Northern Ireland (which took place five years before removal of the right in England and Wales). Apparently, suspects frequently failed to understand the new caution and were put under unfair pressure to speak, while lawyers found it difficult to advise suspects when they did not know the full case against them. Most importantly, JUSTICE claims that while at first trial judges were cautious about drawing inferences of guilt from a suspect's silence, five years on, they were giving such silence considerable weight, and in some cases treating it almost as a presumption of guilt.

18

The police

Deaths in police custody

Almost 700 people have died in police custody or in contact with the police since 1990. The majority of those who die in police custody have been arrested for drink- or drug-related offences or minor thefts (Leigh *et al.*, 1998). Very few police officers have been prosecuted following a death in custody, and none has been convicted. A report on the subject by Vogt and Wadham (2003), *Deaths in custody: redress and remedies*, for the pressure group Liberty, concluded that these deaths were not being adequately investigated. The police, the Police Complaints Authority (now the Independent Police Complaints Commission) and the coroner could all be involved. These investigations were ineffective, secretive, slow and insufficiently independent. Deaths in custody can now be the subject of a criminal prosecution under the Corporate Manslaughter and Corporate Homicide Act 2007 and this may help to combat this problem.

Answering questions

1 Simon is 15 years old. He is walking home at 3 am after playing computer games at a friend's house when a police officer stops him in the street and asks to see what he is carrying in his pockets. Simon is fed up with the police in his neighbourhood and ignores the police officer and keeps walking. The police officer takes Simon by the arm, pushes him into the police car and drives him to the police station.

(a) Explain when the police have the power to stop and search, and when they have the right to arrest someone.

(b) Advise Simon on whether the police officer acted lawfully.

(a) You need to divide your answer into two parts, looking first at the power to stop and search and secondly the power to arrest. The power to stop and search is contained in s. 1 of PACE, accompanied by the Code of Practice A (discussed at p. 387). The power of the police to arrest without a warrant is contained in s. 24 of PACE (discussed at pp. 391–2). There is also a power to arrest with a warrant (discussed at p. 391).

(b) This part of the question requires you to apply the law outlined in your answer to part (a) to the facts of the case. Looking first at the power to stop and search, the only apparent reason that the police had for stopping Simon was that it was 3 in the morning and Simon was young. These are not sufficient grounds to give rise to reasonable suspicion for the purposes of a s. 1 stop and search. The police officer was required to tell Simon the reason for the search and as he failed to do so the subsequent search is likely to be considered unlawful.

As regards the power to arrest, again, the police officer does not appear to have grounds for reasonable suspicion that Simon has committed, is committing or will commit an offence giving him reasonable grounds to believe that an arrest under s. 24 was necessary. Reasons had to be given for the arrest which have not been given. It is not clear whether the amount of force used by the police officer in grabbing Simon by the shoulder and pushing him into the car would fall within the legal limit of 'reasonable force'. It is therefore likely that the police officer's actions were unlawful.

2 **Sir William Macpherson's inquiry into the investigation of Stephen Lawrence's murder concluded that the Metropolitan Police was institutionally racist. On a national level, is the police force racist?** *LLB*

This is a controversial subject which you would need to handle sensitively. You could point to provisions of the Codes of Practice which are intended to prevent police decisions being made on the basis of racist stereotypes. However, the Commission for Racial Equality in 2004 expressed concern with the use of stop and search powers by the police force. Relevant material to answer this question can be found at pp. 413–14.

3 **How successful, in reality, are the PACE safeguards in protecting suspects held at police stations?**

Say what the safeguards are (and there are a number of these, ranging from time limits for detention, to the exclusion of evidence, discussed from p. 396 onwards). These safeguards are weak in practice (p. 395) because each individual safeguard can potentially be avoided – for example:

- the exceptions to the right to inform a third person when detained;
- the police taking the 'scenic route' before official tape-recorded interviews start;
- limits to the right to a legal adviser (mention here **R** *v* **Samuel** (1988) and **R** *v* **Alladice** (1988) and Baldwin's 1992 research, discussed on p. 398);
- restrictions to the right to silence; and
- misleading records of interviews.

4 **Critically contrast the powers of arrest exercisable by a police officer and a citizen.**

The exercise of the power of arrest leads to the detention of the person and that detention will be lawful only if the arrest is executed in accordance with the law. The arrest can be carried out either with or without a warrant, though a warrant to arrest a member of the public would only be issued to a police officer. Under s. 1 Magistrates' Courts Act 1980, a police officer may apply to the magistrates' court for an arrest warrant specifying the name of the person to be arrested and the alleged offence. In the past section 24 of the Police and Criminal Evidence Act 1984 (PACE) only allowed an officer to effect an arrest without a warrant if it was an 'arrestable' offence. This power of arrest without a warrant was extended by the Serious Organised Crime and Police Act 2005 to any offence where the police officer considered that it was necessary.

In contrast, under s. 24A PACE, a citizen may effect an arrest for indictable offences where the person exercising the power believes that an arrest is necessary and that it is not reasonably practical for an officer to carry out the arrest. If no offence has taken place, the arrest will be unlawful and the citizen liable for damages. Thus, while a police officer must merely hold a reasonable belief regarding the commission of an offence, a citizen's arrest requires that an offence has actually taken place.

It is acceptable that the citizen's powers of arrest are more restricted than a police officer's because a police officer has received special training on how to undertake an arrest and has to follow procedures which prevent the abusive use of these powers. The power of a citizen to carry out an arrest is primarily retained to deal with emergency situations where a police officer is not on hand.

Summary of Chapter 18: The police

Introduction
The criminal justice system needs to strike a balance between punishing the guilty and protecting the innocent. Recent miscarriages of justice have raised concerns as to whether this balance is being achieved.

The organisation of the police
The organisation of the police is becoming increasingly centralised.

Civilian support staff
The Police Reform Act 2002 allows a range of civilians to exercise police powers.

Pre-arrest powers of the police
Even without carrying out an arrest, the police enjoy a range of powers to stop and search a member of the public, in particular under s. 1 of PACE.

Powers of arrest
An arrest can take place either with or without a warrant. The powers of the police to arrest without a warrant were increased by the Serious Organised Crime and Police Act 2005.

Citizen's arrest
A member of the public is entitled to arrest a person in certain circumstances. This power to carry out a citizen's arrest is contained in s. 24A of PACE.

Police detention
Under PACE the police can detain a suspect for up to four days without charge.

Police interrogation
The usual reason for detaining suspects is so that the police can question them, in the hope of securing a confession. Certain safeguards exist to protect people while they are being detained and questioned. These include the tape-recording of police interviews in the police station and the right to inform someone of the detention. Since 1994 the right to silence has been effectively abolished.

Bail
A person accused, convicted or under arrest for an offence may be granted bail, which means the person is released under a duty to attend court or the police station at a given time.

Criticism and reform
A range of criticisms and reform proposals have been put forward relating to the police.

A graduate profession
Now that increasing numbers of young people are going to university, it is time to transform the police force into a graduate profession. Only then would the United Kingdom have an efficient police force with the skills to combat crime effectively.

Review of PACE

The Home Office issued a consultation paper in 2007, *Modernising Police Powers: Review of the Police and Criminal Evidence Act 1984*. The paper covers a wide variety of topics and seems to be looking at ways to reduce unnecessary paperwork to help the police to work more efficiently.

Racism and the police

Following the unsuccessful police investigation into the murder of the black teenager Stephen Lawrence, Sir William Macpherson found that the Metropolitan Police suffered from 'institutional racism'. A particularly sensitive area of policing is the power to stop and search and the targeting of black people can have a detrimental effect on the relationship of the police with black people generally.

Police corruption

The police exercise an extremely delicate role in society and, as criminals are able to generate large sums of money from their criminal conduct, the danger of corruption is real.

The right to silence

The abolition of the right to silence has been one of the most severely criticised changes to the criminal justice system in recent years.

Deaths in police custody

Almost 700 people have died in police custody or in contact with the police since 1990. Very few police officers have been prosecuted following a death in custody, and none has been convicted.

Reading list

Audit Commission (1996) *Streetwise: Effective Police Patrol*, London: HMSO.

Austin, R. (2007) 'The New Powers of Arrest: *Plus ça Change*: More of the Same or Major Change?', [2007] *Criminal Law Review* 459.

Baldwin, J. (1992a) *The Role of Legal Representatives at the Police Station* (Royal Commission on Criminal Justice Research Study No. 2), London: HMSO.

Baldwin, J. (1992b) *Video Taping Police Interviews with Suspects: an Evaluation*, London: Home Office.

Baldwin, J. and Moloney, T. (1992) *Supervision of police investigations in serious criminal cases* (Royal Commission on Criminal Justice Research Study No. 4), London: HMSO.

Bowling, B. and Ross, J. (2006) 'The serious organised crime agency – should we be afraid?' [2006] *Criminal Law Review* 1019.

Bridges, L. and Cape, E. (2008) *CDS Direct: Flying in the Face of the Evidence*, London: Centre for Crime and Justice Studies at King's College London.

Bridges, L. and Choongh, S. (1998) *Improving Police Station Legal Advice: The Impact of the Accreditation Scheme for Police Station Legal Advisers*, London: Law Society's Research and Planning Unit: Legal Aid Board.

Brown, D. (1998) *Offending While on Bail* (Home Office, Report No. 72), London: Home Office.

Brownlee, I. (2004) 'The statutory charging scheme in England and Wales: towards a unified prosecution system', *Criminal Law Review* 896.

18

The police

Cape, E. (2007) 'Modernising Police Powers – Again?', [2007] *Criminal Law Review* 934.

Cape, E. and Young, R. (2008) *Regulation Policing: The Police and Criminal Evidence Act 1984 Past, Present and Future*, Oxford: Hart Publishing.

Cotton, J. and Povey, D. (2004) *Police Complaints and Discipline, April 2002–March 2003*, London: Home Office.

Doak, J. (2008) *Victims' Rights, Human Rights and Criminal Justice: Reconceiving the Role of Third Parties*, Oxford: Hart Publishing.

Gudjonsson, G.H. (1992) *The Psychology of Interrogations, Confessions and Testimony*, Chichester: Wiley.

Hamer, D. (2009) 'The Expectation of Incorrect Acquittals and the "New and Compelling Evidence" Exception to Double Jeopardy', [2009] *Criminal Law Review* 63.

HM Inspectorate (1999) *Police Integrity: Securing and Maintaining Public Confidence*, London: Home Office Communication Directorate.

Home Office (2006) *Rebalancing the Criminal Justice System in Favour of the Law-Abiding Majority*, London: Home Office.

Hucklesby, A. (2004) 'Not necessarily a trip to the police station: the introduction of street bail', *Criminal Law Review* 803.

Idriss, M. (2004) 'Police perceptions of race relations in the West Midlands', *Criminal Law Review* 814.

Jackson, J. (2003) 'Justice for All: Putting Victims at the Heart of Criminal Justice?', 30 *J. Law and Society* 309.

Law Commission (1999) *Bail and the Human Rights Act 1998* (Report No. 157), London: HMSO.

Leigh, A. *et al.* (1998) *Deaths in Police Custody: Learning the Lessons*, London: Home Office.

Leigh, L. and Zedner, L. (1992) *A Report on the Administration of Criminal Justice in the Pretrial Phase in London, France and Germany*, London: HMSO.

Leng, R. (1993) *The Right to Silence in Police Interrogation* (Royal Commission on Criminal Justice Research Study No. 10), London: HMSO.

McConville, M. (1992) 'Videotaping Interrogations: Police Behaviour On and Off Camera', *Criminal Law Review* 532.

McConville, M. and Hodgson, J. (1993) *Custodial Legal Advice and the Right to Silence* (Royal Commission on Criminal Justice Research Study No. 16), London: HMSO.

McConville, M., Sanders, A. and Leng, P. (1993) *The Case for the Prosecution: Police Suspects and the Construction of Criminality*, London: Routledge.

Millar, J. (2000) *Upping the PACE? An Evaluation of the Recommendations of the Stephen Lawrence Inquiry on Stop and Search* (Police Research Series Paper 128), London: Home Office.

Millar, J., Bland, N. and Quinton, P. (2000) *The Impact of Stop and Search on Crime and the Community* (Police Research Series Paper 127), London: Home Office.

Mullins, C. (1990) *Error of Judgement: The Truth About the Birmingham Bombings*, Dublin: Poolbeg Press.

Ormerod, D. and Roberts, A. (2003) 'The Police Reform Act 2002 – Increasing Centralisation, Maintaining Confidence and Contracting Out Crime Control', *Criminal Law Review* 141.

Quinton, P., Bland, N. and Miller, J. (2000) *Police Stops, Decision-making and Practice* (Police Research Series Paper 130), London: Home Office.

Roberts, P. and Saunders, C. (2008) 'Introducing Pre-Trial Witness Interviews: A Flexible New Fixture in the Crown Prosecutor's Toolkit', [2008] *Criminal Law Review* 831.

Rock, P. (2004) *Constructing Victims' Rights*, Oxford: Oxford University Press.

Royal Commission on Criminal Justice Report (1993), Cm 2263, London: HMSO.

Sanders, A. (1993) 'Controlling the Discretion of the Individual Officer' in Reiner, R. and Spencer, S. (eds) *Accountable Policing*, London: Institute for Public Policy Research.

Sanders, A. *et al.* (1989) *Advice and Assistance at Police Stations and the 24 hour Duty Solicitor Scheme*, London: Lord Chancellor's Department.

Walker, C. (2008) 'Post-Charge Questioning of Suspects', [2008] *Criminal Law Review* 509.

Zander, M. (2007d) 'Change of PACE', 157 *New Law Journal* 504.

Reading on the Internet

www   The revised Code A for PACE can be found on the Home Office website at:
   http://www.police.homeoffice.gov.uk/news-and-publications/publication/operational-policing/PACE_Chapter_A.pdf

Information on the criminal justice system is available at:
   http://www.cjsonline.org/index.html

Visit **www.mylawchamber.co.uk/ElliottELS** to access multiple-choice questions, flashcards and practice exam questions to test yourself on this chapter.

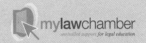

18

The police

19 The criminal trial process

This chapter discusses:

- the adversarial process followed in the criminal justice system;

- the Crown Prosecution Service;

- the classification of offences as summary, indictable or either way offences;

- the pre-trial hearings – mode of trial hearings, case management hearings and sending for trial and plea;

- disclosure of evidence between the prosecution and the defence;

- plea bargaining;

- the criminal trial;

- criticisms and possible reforms of the criminal trial process.

The adversarial process

The English system of criminal justice can be described as adversarial. This means each side is responsible for putting their own case: collecting evidence, interviewing witnesses and retaining experts. In court they will present their own evidence and attack their opponent's evidence by cross-examining their adversary's witnesses. Both parties call only those witnesses likely to advance their cause and both parties are permitted to attack the credibility and reliability of the witnesses testifying for the other side. The role of the judge is limited to that of a referee ensuring fair play, and making sure that the rules on procedure and evidence are followed. It is often compared with a battle, with each side fighting their own corner. The adversarial system is typical of common law countries. The alternative is an inquisitorial system, which exists in most of the rest of Europe. Under that system, a judge (known in France as the *juge d'instruction*) plays the dominant role in collecting evidence before the trial. During the course of a lengthy investigation, the judge will interview witnesses and inspect documents, and the final trial is often just to 'rubber stamp' the investigating judge's findings.

In the light of the recent miscarriages of justice, some people suggested that we should introduce an inquisitorial system into England. Arguments were put forward that the inquisitorial system provides a properly organised and regulated pre-trial phase, with an independent figure supervising the whole investigation. The Royal Commission on Criminal Justice ordered research into the French and German criminal justice system (Leigh and Zedner, 1992). The researchers rejected the idea of introducing the inquisitorial system into England. They did not think that the *juge d'instruction* was a real protection against overbearing police practices, except in rare cases where physical brutality was involved. Furthermore, despite the fact that only 10 per cent of cases go before the *juge d'instruction* in France, the system is overburdened and works slowly. In Germany and Italy the powers of the investigating judge have been transferred to the public prosecutor, to avoid potential conflict between the functions of investigator and judge.

In recent years the English system has shifted slightly towards an inquisitorial system in an effort to achieve greater efficiency. Thus, the role of the judge has been increased, through, for example, an emphasis on judicial case management.

Criminal Procedure Rules

In 2005, the main rules on criminal procedure that apply to the trial and pre-trial process were brought together in new Criminal Procedure Rules. These rules did not introduce any radical changes to the law and practice, but they aim to make the relevant rules more accessible as they are all now brought together in one place. They emphasise that the judges need to take an active role in case management. Rule 3 states that active case management includes:

19

The criminal trial process

(a) the early identification of the real issues;

(b) the early identification of the needs of witnesses;

(c) achieving certainty as to what must be done, by whom, and when, in particular by the early setting of a timetable for the progress of the case;

(d) monitoring the progress of the case and compliance with directions;

(e) ensuring that evidence, whether disputed or not, is presented in the shortest and clearest way;

(f) discouraging delay, dealing with as many aspects of the case as possible on the same occasion, and avoiding unnecessary hearings;

(g) encouraging the participants to cooperate in the progression of the case; and

(h) making use of technology.

The emphasis on case management in criminal proceedings is clearly influenced by its relative success in the civil system. It is hoped that through the use of active case management, cases will progress more rapidly through the criminal system and fewer cases will collapse.

The Courts Act 2003 established a Rules Committee which updates the Criminal Procedure Rules twice a year. The Committee hopes eventually to develop a criminal procedure code.

The rules of criminal procedure must be respected, but the courts are trying to achieve a balance between the importance of following these rules and the requirements of justice. Cases can be thrown out for breach of a technicality where that breach undermines justice or where there is at least a real possibility of the defendant suffering prejudice as a consequence of a procedural failure. But if no damage is done then the procedural irregularity can be corrected after the event and the case can proceed.

KEY CASE

In the case of **R v Clarke and McDaid** (2008) an appeal against conviction was allowed when an indictment had not been signed because this procedural requirement was not viewed by the court as a meaningless formality, but as a requirement that made sure the prosecution had given careful consideration to the case. The House of Lords noted:

> An appeal against conviction will be allowed where there has been a breach of a technical procedural rule which does not amount to a meaningless formality.

> technicality is always distasteful when it appears to contradict the merits of a case. But the duty of the court is to apply the law, which is sometimes technical, and it may be thought that if the state exercises its coercive power to put a citizen on trial for serious crime a certain degree of formality is not out of place.

At the same time, the House of Lords acknowledged that their decision:

> will produce from time to time unsatisfactory results. Guilty men may go free or, if not free, have to be retried . . . A retrial will involve delay, expense and inconvenience and may cause particular witnesses . . . considerable distress.

The Crown Prosecution Service

Until 1986, criminal prosecutions were officially brought by private citizens rather than by the state; in practice most prosecutions were brought by the police (though technically they were prosecuting as private citizens). Although the police obviously employed solicitors to help them in this task, their relationship with those solicitors was a normal client relationship, and so the police were not obliged to act on the solicitors' advice.

In 1970, a report by the law reform pressure group, JUSTICE, criticised the role of the police in the prosecution process (*The Prosecution in England and Wales*, 1970). It argued that it was not in the interests of justice for the same body to be responsible for the two very different functions of investigation and prosecution. This dual role prevented the prosecution from being independent and impartial: the police had become concerned with winning or losing, when the aim of the prosecution should be the discovery of the truth. As a result, there was a danger of the police withholding from the defence information that might make a conviction less likely.

The prosecution process was reviewed by the Royal Commission on Criminal Procedure (RCCP) in 1981. Their report highlighted a range of problems. There was a lack of uniformity, with differing procedures and standards applied across the country on such matters as whether to prosecute or caution, and the system prevented a consistent national prosecution policy. The process was inefficient, with inadequate preparation of cases. The RCCP agreed with JUSTICE that, in principle, investigation and prosecution should be separate processes, conducted by different people. As a result of these findings, the RCCP recommended the establishment of a Crown Prosecution Service, divided into separate local services for each police force area.

The Government followed the main recommendations, though it opposed the establishment of separate local services. The Crown Prosecution Service (CPS) was set up under the Prosecution of Offences Act 1985, as a national prosecution service for England and Wales. The service as a whole is headed by the Director of Public Prosecutions (DPP). The DPP reports on the running of the service to the Attorney General. The only formal mechanism for accountability of the CPS is the requirement that an annual report must be presented to the Attorney General, who is obliged to lay it before Parliament. The Attorney General is responsible in Parliament for general policy, but not for individual cases.

The establishment of the CPS means that the prosecution of offences is now separated from their detection and investigation, which is undertaken by the police.

Administration of the CPS

When the CPS first started to operate in 1986, it was organised into 31 areas, each with a Chief Crown Prosecutor. These were subsequently increased to 38, but in 1993, in an effort to improve efficiency, the areas were enlarged into just 13 across the country. The administration was centralised around headquarters in London, with the DPP playing an increased role in the direct administration of the CPS. In the light of continuing concern over the functioning of the CPS, a review was carried out by a body chaired by Sir Ian Glidewell which reported in 1998. The *Review of the Crown Prosecution Service* (also known as the Glidewell Report) heavily criticised the CPS. It concluded that the 1993 reform had been a mistake, as it made the organisation too centralised and excessively bureaucratic. It found that there was a problem with judge-ordered acquittals (where the case is too weak to be left to the jury), which constituted over 20 per cent of acquittals in 1996. Not all of these were due to poor case preparation by the CPS, as some involved errors in witness warnings by the police. But many were due to inadequate compilation of case papers between committal and trial by non-qualified staff who lacked supervision; the drafting of inadequate or erroneous indictments; and counsel being briefed too late to put things right.

Glidewell concluded that the CPS 'has the potential to become a lively, successful and esteemed part of the criminal justice system, but . . . sadly none of these adjectives applies to the service as a whole at present'.

The key recommendation of the Report was that there should be a devolution of powers from the centre to the regions, with the London headquarters playing a more limited role. This would involve replacing the 13 CPS areas with 42 areas corresponding to police force areas.

The Glidewell Report proposed that teams of CPS lawyers, police and administrative caseworkers (together known as a Criminal Justice Unit), should be established to prepare and deal with many straightforward cases in their entirety (in other words, both the case preparation and the court advocacy); the section which dealt with the most serious cases, called Central Casework, needed more staff, with more training and closer monitoring; there should be at least one full-time CPS lawyer in each Crown Court; CPS lawyers should be allowed to concentrate more on court work rather than paperwork; and that the DPP ought to play less of a role in the administration of the CPS and concentrate largely on the prosecution and legal process.

The Government accepted the main recommendations of the Glidewell Report and the new 42 areas of the CPS came into effect on 22 April 1999.

Powers of CPS employees

In the past, barristers from the independent Bar had to be paid by the CPS to carry out the advocacy required for prosecutions in the Crown Court, because lawyers employed in the CPS, including qualified barristers, did not have rights of audience in the Crown Court. The Access to Justice Act 1999 allows CPS lawyers to carry out this work themselves, with the aim of achieving greater efficiency while saving money. This was heavily criticised, particularly by the Bar Council and Professor Michael Zander, on the basis that, as full-time salaried employees with performance targets, CPS lawyers would sometimes be tempted to get convictions using dubious tactics because their jobs and prospects of promotion would depend on conviction success rates. To reduce this risk, s. 37 of the Act states that every advocate 'has a duty to the court to act in the interests of justice', which overrides any inconsistent duty, for example, to an employer.

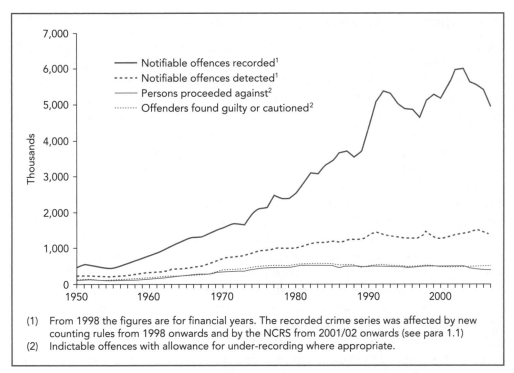

(1) From 1998 the figures are for financial years. The recorded crime series was affected by new counting rules from 1998 onwards and by the NCRS from 2001/02 onwards (see para 1.1)
(2) Indictable offences with allowance for under-recording where appropriate.

Figure 19.1 Recorded crime, prosecutions and 'known' offenders, 1950–2007

Source: *Criminal Statistics 2007 England and Wales*, p. 12 [Figure 1.2]

Professor Michael Zander dismissed these as 'mere words', writing in a letter to *The Times* (29 December 1998), that:

> The CPS as an organisation is constantly under pressure in regard to proportion of discontinuances, acquittal and conviction rates. These are factors in the day to day work of any CPS lawyer. It is disingenuous to imagine they will not have a powerful effect on decision making.

Despite these criticisms, CPS employees are increasingly carrying out the advocacy themselves in the Crown Court and less work is being passed on to the Bar. In the magistrates' court, s. 55 of the Criminal Justice and Immigration Act 2008 allows associate prosecutors (employees of the CPS who are not qualified lawyers) to undertake advocacy work in the magistrates' court, including contested trials of summary, non-imprisonable offences. Trials of triable either way offences will continue to be prosecuted by qualified lawyers. These associate prosecutors currently handle 20 per cent of the prosecution advocacy work in the magistrates' courts. A key reason why the CPS chooses to use associate prosecutors is that they are considerably cheaper than qualified lawyers. The Law Society has pointed out that as a result of these reforms a large proportion of criminal cases could be prosecuted and decided by unqualified individuals – lay magistrates hearing a case prosecuted by an associate prosecutor against an unrepresented defendant.

Charging and prosecuting defendants

The normal practice has been for the police to decide whether to charge a defendant and then after charge send the file to the CPS to proceed with the prosecution. The Criminal Justice Act 2003 has amended s. 37 of the Police and Criminal Evidence Act 1984, moving the decision to charge from the police to the CPS. The police only retain the right to charge for certain minor offences. Lord Auld recommended this reform in his *Review of the Criminal Courts*. The hope is to improve the relationship between the CPS and the police so that they work efficiently together in the preparation of cases for trial. The police have in the past felt very unhappy about the number of prosecutions that have been discontinued after they had decided to charge a suspect. Six pilot schemes were established around the country where the decision to charge was moved from the police to the CPS, and these proved to be very successful. Convictions rose by 15 per cent. The instances of charges being reduced or dropped fell from 51 per cent to 18 per cent. The Attorney General concluded that: 'Getting cases right from the start means less abandoned prosecution, less of the frustrating delays and more criminals brought to justice.'

Ess. Cases
p. 295 →

When the CPS receives the file, it reviews whether a prosecution should be brought on the basis of criteria set out in the Code for Crown Prosecutors. This Code is issued by the CPS under s. 10 of the Prosecution of Offences Act 1985. The latest edition of the Code explains that this decision is taken in two stages. First, prosecutors must ask whether there is enough evidence to provide a 'realistic prospect of conviction', that is to say that a court is more likely than not to convict. If the case does not pass this evidential test, the prosecution must not go ahead, no matter how important or serious the case may be. If the case does pass the evidential test, the CPS must then consider whether the public interest requires a prosecution. For example, a prosecution is more likely to be in the public interest if a conviction is likely to result in a significant sentence, if the offence was committed against a person serving the public (such as a police officer) or if the offence is widespread in the area where it was committed. On the other hand, a prosecution is less likely to be in the public interest where the defendant is elderly, or suffering from significant mental or physical ill-health.

At the end of this two-stage test, the CPS may decide to go ahead with the prosecution, send the case back to the police for a caution instead of a prosecution, or take no further action. The decision is theirs, and the police need not be consulted.

The CPS continues to have no involvement in cases where the police decide not to charge, including those where the offender is given a caution.

The clear distinction that was initially drawn between the police and the CPS has been weakened by subsequent reforms. Following the Glidewell Report and the Narey Report (*Review of Delay in the Criminal Justice System* (1997)), some CPS staff now work alongside police officers in Criminal Justice Units to prepare cases for court.

KEY CASE

A decision not to prosecute can be as sensitive as a decision to prosecute. The case of **R (on the application of Corner House Research and others) v Director of the Serious Fraud Office** (2008) concerned a decision

A prosecutor is entitled to decide to discontinue a prosecution, to avoid a threat to national security.

not to prosecute following allegations of corruption. The Serious Fraud Office had carried out an investigation into an allegation that a bribe was paid by the company BAE in order to secure a contract worth £43 billion to sell military aircraft to Saudi Arabia. In July 2006, a Saudi representative made a specific threat to the Prime Minister's chief of staff – that if the police investigation was not stopped the UK would lose a valuable contract for military aircraft and the previous close intelligence and diplomatic relationship would cease, putting the UK at an increased risk of suffering terrorist attacks. As a result, the director of the Serious Fraud Office decided to stop the investigation on the grounds of national security. The claimants applied to challenge that decision by way of judicial review.

The High Court had held that any decision as to whether the investigation and prosecution should continue in these circumstances should have been taken by the court and not by the executive, as the threat amounted to a threat to the court system, as well as a threat to the UK's commercial, diplomatic and security interests:

> No one, whether within the country or outside, is entitled to interfere with the course of our justice.

Under the rule of law, the decision to discontinue the case should have been reached as an exercise of independent judgment of the court. The director of the Serious Fraud Office had submitted too readily to the threat because he had not focused on the need to fight corruption. The House of Lords allowed an appeal against the High Court's decision, finding that in the circumstances the director of the Serious Fraud Office was entitled to take the decision to discontinue the investigation.

Private prosecutions

Private prosecutions can still be brought and, although statistically these are few, they can play an important role, particularly in highlighting or encouraging public concern over relevant issues.

In 1974, a PC Joy stopped a motorist and reported him for a motoring offence. The motorist was a Member of Parliament and PC Joy's superiors refused to pursue the case; PC Joy thought this unjust and successfully brought a private prosecution. Mary Whitehouse also brought important private prosecutions in the past. More recently, the family of Stephen Lawrence, the teenager murdered in south London, took out a private prosecution against three men suspected of the killing, after the CPS dropped the case because it said there was insufficient evidence. Unfortunately, the private prosecution was unsuccessful for lack of evidence. The case primarily relied on the identification evidence of Duwayne Brooks. This was weak because the attack had lasted for only a matter of seconds. He was unable to be specific about the number of attackers, saying that it was a 'group of 4 to 6'. In his initial statement to the police, he said that, 'Of the group of 6 youths, I can only really describe one of them.' At one identification parade, he identified a member of the public. At another he identified no one although there was a suspect present. He had originally said Stephen had been hit on the head with an iron bar although he was later found to have sustained no head injuries. The judge summed up by saying: 'Where recognition or identification is concerned, [Brooks] simply does not know whether he is on his head or his heels . . .

Adding one injustice to another does not cure the first injustice done to the Lawrence family.' The judge withdrew the case from the jury and ordered an acquittal. The decision to bring the private prosecution has been criticised as their acquittal prevented the suspects from being prosecuted for the same offence in the future when stronger evidence might have been available (see pp. 594–5 for a discussion of the double jeopardy rule).

Historical powers of the Attorney General and Director of Public Prosecutions

We have noted that, with the creation of the CPS, the Director of Public Prosecutions (DPP) was placed at its head. However, before the creation of this body, the DPP and the Attorney General had certain powers to control the bringing of prosecutions and both have kept these powers despite the existence of the CPS.

For certain offences prosecutions can be brought only if the Attorney General or the DPP has given their consent. The sensitivity of the decision whether or not to consent to a prosecution has been highlighted in the context of prosecutions against family members who have assisted a seriously ill relative to die. Under the Suicide Act 1961 prosecutions can only be brought for the offence of assisting a person to commit suicide with the consent of the DPP. In **R (on the application of Debbie Purdy)** *v* **DPP** (2009) Debbie Purdy suffered from multiple sclerosis. When her condition became unbearable for her she wanted her husband to go with her to Switzerland where there are facilities for a person to be assisted to commit suicide. She was concerned that her husband might be prosecuted under the Suicide Act on his return to the UK. She brought legal proceedings arguing that the DPP should be required to issue guidelines which explained when he would give consent to such a prosecution so that she and her husband would know the legal consequences of their conduct. The House of Lords declared that the DPP was required to issue guidelines on this subject which the DPP has now done.

The Attorney General has the power to stop proceedings that would be brought before the Crown Court. This is known as granting a *nolle prosequi* and is not actually an acquittal, so a prosecution can be brought in the future on the same charge. Controversy was caused in 1998 when the Attorney General entered a *nolle prosequi* in the trial of Justice Richard Gee who had been accused of a £1 million fraud.

The position of the Attorney General attracted attention during the 'cash for honours' scandal. The police carried out an investigation into whether cash had been paid by wealthy individuals in return for the promise that they would receive the prestigious title of 'Sir' or 'Lord'. The Prime Minister of the day, Tony Blair, himself was questioned as part of this investigation. If the police had decided that there was sufficient evidence to show that a crime had been committed then they would have passed the papers for the case to the Crown Prosecution Service. But the final decision as to whether a prosecution should be brought in such a case would normally be taken by the Attorney General. Unfortunately, as the Attorney General is effectively a political appointment, it would be difficult for the public to have confidence that this was an impartial decision, particularly if he had decided that it was not appropriate to proceed. In fact, the police themselves decided that there was insufficient evidence to take the case further. The role of the Attorney General is likely to be reformed and these proposed reforms are discussed on p. 294.

When a private prosecution is brought, the DPP may choose to take over the case. Those powers are exercised in practice on his or her behalf by the CPS. Although the CPS has so far been reluctant to interfere in the individual's right to prosecute, it could take over such a case only to discontinue it, on either evidential or public interest grounds.

Following the Hillsborough football disaster, a private prosecution was brought by the Hillsborough Family Support Group against two of the senior police officers on duty at the stadium. The DPP refused to intervene to terminate this prosecution and his decision was challenged by the police officers in **R v DPP, ex parte Duckenfield** and **R v South Yorkshire Police Authority, ex parte Chief Constable of South Yorkshire** (1999). This challenge was only partially successful.

Public defenders

The Access to Justice Act 1999 provides for the appointment of public defenders. For a discussion of public defenders see pp. 354–5.

Appearance in court

Persons charged with an offence can be called to court by means of a summons, or by a charge following arrest without a warrant. Arrest under a warrant signed by a magistrate under s. 1(1) of the Magistrates' Courts Act 1980 is not common today, and its main use is to arrest those who, having been granted bail, do not turn up for trial.

In order to have a summons served, the prosecutor must give a short account of the alleged offence, usually in writing, to the magistrates or their clerk (a process called laying an information). The information may be substantiated by an oral statement from the police, given on oath before a magistrate; such a statement must be given if the information is to be used as the basis for a warrant for arrest. A summons setting out the offence is then issued and served, either in person or, for minor offences, through Recorded Delivery or Registered post.

The defendant is entitled to plead guilty by post for any summary offence for which the maximum penalty does not exceed three months' imprisonment (s. 12 of the Magistrates' Courts Act 1980). In this situation the defendant does not need to attend court, and the procedure is frequently used for traffic offences. In the past, delays were caused when people failed to respond to the summons in which they were given the opportunity to plead guilty by post: neither pleading guilty by post nor turning up for the court hearing. This led to the case being adjourned while witness statements were prepared or arrangements made for witnesses to attend. To avoid such adjournments in future, the Magistrates' Courts (Procedure) Act 1998 was passed which allows witness statements to be served with the original correspondence, so that if the defendant fails to respond the case can be tried at the first hearing.

Under s. 57 of the Crime and Disorder Act 1998, if an accused is being held in custody, all pre-trial hearings can take place using a live TV link between the court and the prison. The accused will be treated as if he or she is present at the court.

Classification of offences

There are three different categories of criminal offence.

Summary offences

These are the most minor crimes, and are only triable summarily in the magistrates' court. 'Summary' refers to the process of ordering the defendant to attend the court by summons, a written order usually delivered by post which is the most frequent procedure adopted in the magistrates' courts. There has been some criticism of the fact that more and more offences have been made summary only, reducing the right to trial by jury.

Indictable offences

These are the more serious offences, such as rape and murder. They can only be heard by the Crown Court. The indictment is a formal document containing the alleged offences against the accused, supported by brief facts.

Offences triable either way

These offences may be tried in either the magistrates' court or the Crown Court. Common examples are theft and burglary.

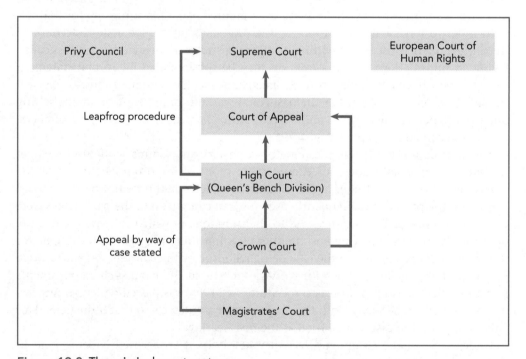

Figure 19.2 The criminal court system

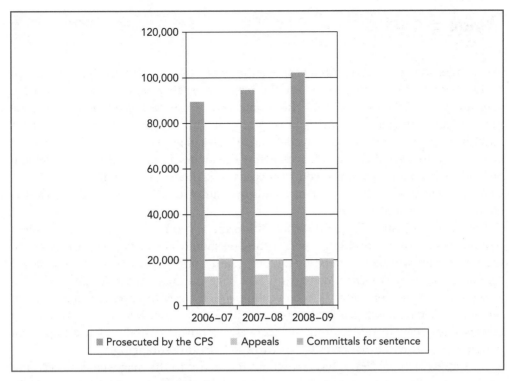

Figure 19.3 Crown Court caseload

Source: *Crown Prosecution Service Annual Report 2008, Annex B-Casework Statistics*

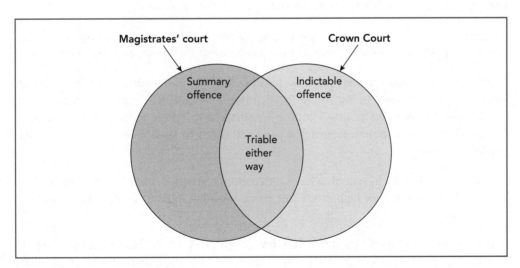

Figure 19.4 Trial courts

19

The criminal trial process

Mode of trial

Where a person is charged with a triable either way offence, they can insist on a trial by jury, otherwise the decision is for the magistrates. In reaching this decision the magistrates will take into account the seriousness of the case and whether they are likely to have sufficient sentencing powers to deal with it. Since 1996 the magistrates are also able to take into account the defendant's plea of guilty or not guilty, which will be given, for triable either way offences, before the mode of trial decision. If the defendant indicates a guilty plea, the court proceeds to sentence or commit to the Crown Court for sentence. If the defendant pleads not guilty, or fails to indicate a plea, the court decides the mode of trial.

The Criminal Justice Act 2003, Sched. 3 has made certain changes to the mode of trial procedures. When deciding whether the case should stay in the magistrates' court, the magistrates will be informed of the defendant's prior convictions. If they decide summary trial is appropriate, defendants will have the right to ask for an indication of sentence on plea of guilty before deciding which court to choose. Committal for sentence has been abolished for less serious either way cases. Magistrates' sentencing powers have been increased from six to twelve months' custody, in the hope that magistrates will send fewer cases to the Crown Court for sentencing.

Dr Andrew Herbert (2003) has carried out research into the magistrates' decision to send cases to the Crown Court. He has concluded that the reforms in the Criminal Justice Act 2003 are doomed to fail to reduce the number of cases referred to the Crown Court. The main Home Office reason for the recent reform attempts has been to reduce costs and increase efficiency. The chief finding of the research is that the magistrates overwhelmingly reject this reason for changing the court venue:

> There was a virtual consensus among those interviewed that there was no need for any significant change in the division of business between the higher and the lower courts.

Magistrates felt that the existing law produced a fair and realistic choice of court. They resented reforms being made for economic or political reasons. Some of the magistrates interviewed pointed to the importance of their judicial independence, so that Government policy would not persuade them to keep more cases. One of the magistrates said:

> I would never agree to retaining cases on economic grounds. I am fed up with political speak. There should not be pressure put on us. We are trained to do a job and should be left to do it.

The lawyers interviewed thought that lay magistrates were already being asked to handle cases at the extreme of their ability and were not capable of dealing with more serious cases. This is significant in practice because lay magistrates usually follow the agreed recommendation of the CPS and defence lawyers. Lay magistrates reached a decision contrary to the agreed recommendations in only one case out of 123 cases observed.

It was hoped that the early plea procedure would increase the number of cases retained in the magistrates' courts with predicted savings for the CPS alone of up to £7.5 million. In fact, the new system of plea before venue has meant that there are many more people being sent to the Crown Court for sentencing, though fewer are being sent to the Crown Court for trial.

Research undertaken prior to the 1996 amendment (Hedderman and Moxon, 1992) showed that most offences tried in the Crown Court were 'either way' offences. Just 18 per cent were indictable only. There are three main reasons why defendants may choose to be dealt with by the Crown Court. First, it automatically puts off the day of trial. This has particular benefits to those who are remanded in custody and believe they will be found guilty and sent back to prison, because remand prisoners are entitled to privileges which are not available to sentenced prisoners (and time spent on remand is included in the time the prisoner eventually serves).

Secondly, many defendants believe they stand a better chance of acquittal in the Crown Court. A study by Vennard in 1985 ('The Outcome of Contested Trials') suggests that they may be right: acquittal rates were significantly higher in the Crown Court (57 per cent) than in magistrates' courts (30 per cent). However, most of those who choose to be tried in the Crown Court then proceed to plead guilty. Hedderman and Moxon's 1992 study found that 27 per cent of defendants who elected Crown Court trial intended from the outset to plead guilty and, on the day of trial, many more did so, with 70 per cent pleading guilty to all charges and a further 13 per cent pleading guilty to some of them.

Thirdly, around a half of defendants are under the mistaken impression that they will get lighter sentences in the Crown Court. The RCCJ noted that, in fact, judges were three times more likely to impose prison sentences, and their sentences were, on average, two-and-a-half times longer than those imposed by magistrates. Perhaps not surprisingly, a third of the defendants who chose Crown Court trial thought that they had made a mistake, and would have been better off being dealt with by magistrates.

There are now serious moves to reduce the use of jury trials. These developments are discussed in Chapter 12 at p. 235.

Sending for trial

The 'sending for trial' hearing is a new procedure created by s. 51 of the Crime and Disorder Act 1998, and is intended to be quicker than the old committal procedures which were finally abolished by the Criminal Justice Act 2003. Until this reform was introduced, a case might have given rise to half a dozen hearings in a magistrates' court before being sent up to the Crown Court for trial. Under the new system, every adult charged with an indictable offence has to appear only once in a magistrates' court to determine issues concerning funding from the Legal Services Commission, bail, and the use of statements and exhibits. The magistrates' court then provides defendants with a statement of the evidence against them as well as a notice setting out the offence(s) for which they are to be sent for trial and the place where they are to be tried.

They are then sent immediately for trial in the Crown Court. The Crown Court has taken over from the magistrates' court all remaining case management duties.

Plea and case management hearings

The plea and case management hearings were introduced by the new Criminal Procedure Rules in 2005 and replace the old plea and directions hearings. They aim to encourage early preparation of cases before trial, with a view to reducing the number of 'cracked' trials. These hearings are normally held in open court with the defendants present, who are required to plead guilty or not guilty to the charges against them. This process is known as the 'arraignment'. If the defendants plead guilty, the judge will proceed to sentence the defendants wherever possible. Where they plead not guilty the prosecution and defence will have to identify the key issues, and provide any additional information required to organise the actual trial, such as which witnesses will have to attend, facts that are admitted by both sides and issues of law that are likely to arise.

Disclosure

The issue of disclosure is concerned with the responsibility of the prosecution and defence to reveal information related to the case prior to the trial. Under the Criminal Justice Act 2003 the defence has an obligation to disclose all its evidence to the prosecution. They have to identify any defences they intend to rely on and any points of law they intend to raise. They must give the prosecution the names and addresses of all the witnesses they intend to call and the name of any expert witness they have consulted. There seems to be nothing to stop the police going to see these witnesses, though this would be a highly undesirable practice. The prosecution is under a continuing duty to disclose material that might reasonably be considered capable of undermining its case or assisting the defence case.

Research carried out by Dr Hannah Quirk (2006) has shown that there have been difficulties with the implementation of the disclosure legislation. The police do not have sufficient training to perform this duty satisfactorily and the CPS lawyers often do not have sufficient time to check this process. A Protocol for the Control and Management of Unused Material in the Crown Court has been produced, but Professor Zander (2006) has argued that this is unlikely to be successful in improving the disclosure system.

Plea bargaining

Plea bargaining is the name given to negotiations between the prosecution and defence lawyers over the outcome of a case; for example, where a defendant is choosing to plead not guilty, the prosecution may offer to reduce the charge to a similar offence with a smaller maximum sentence, in return for the defendant pleading guilty. Although plea bargaining is well known in the US criminal justice system, for many years the official view was that it did not happen here, although those involved in the system knew quite well that in fact it happened all the time. Its existence in the English penal system was confirmed in a 1977 study by McConville and Baldwin, and it is now recognised to be a widespread phenomenon.

Effective plea bargaining requires the active cooperation of the judge, but following the Court of Appeal case of **R** *v* **Turner** (1970) judges were not allowed to get involved in plea bargaining in the UK. That case effectively banned judges from indicating what sentence they would give if a defendant pleaded guilty. The case was not always followed in practice. In the 1993 Crown Court Study carried out by Zander and Henderson, 86 per cent of prosecution barristers, 88 per cent of defence barristers and 67 per cent of judges thought that **Turner** should be reformed so as to permit realistic discussion of plea, and especially sentence between the defence and prosecution lawyers and the judge.

ss. Cases
p. 301 ➡

KEY CASE

The ban against plea bargaining was dramatically removed by the Court of Appeal case of R *v* Goodyear (2005). Defendants can now request in writing an indication from the judge of their likely sentence if they plead guilty. Following such a request, trial judges are allowed to indicate in public the maximum sentence they would give on the agreed facts of the case. This indication binds the judge, so that a higher sentence cannot subsequently be given. Judges cannot state what sentence they would give if the case went to trial, as this risks placing undue pressure on defendants to plead guilty.

> Defendants can request in writing an indication from the judge of their likely sentence if they plead guilty.

Should plea bargaining be allowed?

It can be argued that plea bargaining offers benefits on all sides: for the defendant, there is obviously a shorter sentence; for the courts, the police, and ultimately the taxpayers, there are the financial savings made by drastically shortening trials. In fact, without a high proportion of guilty pleas, the courts would be seriously overloaded, causing severe delays which in turn would raise costs still further, especially given the number of prisoners remanded in custody awaiting trial.

Despite this, plea bargaining has been widely criticised as being against the interests of justice. Several studies have shown that the practice may place undue pressure on the accused and persuade innocent people to plead guilty: Zander and Henderson (1993) concluded that each year there were some 1,400 possibly innocent persons whose counsel felt they had pleaded guilty in order to achieve a reduction in the charges faced or in the sentence. Critics also point out that the judge should be, and be seen to be, an impartial referee, acting in accordance with the law rather than the dictates of cost-efficiency. In addition, plea bargaining goes against the principle that offenders should be punished for what they have actually done. As well as leading to cases where people are punished more leniently than their conduct would seem to demand, it may lead to quite inappropriate punishments. For example, the high rate of acquittals in rape trials frequently leads to the prosecution reducing the charge to an ordinary offence against the person, in exchange for a guilty plea; this means that offenders who might usefully be given psychiatric help never receive it.

These criticisms are backed up by the fact that, in practice, plea bargaining does not necessarily save time or money because, in many cases, it occurs at the last moment, so there is no time to arrange for another case to slot into the court timetable. Such cases are often known as 'cracked trials', and Zander and Henderson's study found that 43 per cent of those cases listed as not guilty pleas 'cracked', which represented 26 per cent of listed cases overall.

The trial

Apart from the role played by the jury in the Crown Court, the law and procedure in the Crown Court and magistrates' court are essentially the same. The burden of proof is on the prosecution, which means that they must prove, beyond reasonable doubt, that the accused is guilty; the defendant is not required to prove his or her innocence.

Defendants should normally be present at the trial, though the trial can proceed without them if they have chosen to abscond. A lawyer should usually represent them in their absence (**R v Jones** (2002)).

The trial begins with the prosecution outlining the case against the accused, and then producing evidence to prove its case. The prosecution calls its witnesses, who will give their evidence in response to questions from the prosecution (called examination-in-chief). These witnesses can then be questioned by the defence (called cross-examination), and then if required, re-examined by the prosecution to address any points brought up in cross-examination.

When the prosecution has presented all its evidence, the defence can submit that there is no case to answer, which means that on the prosecution evidence, no reasonable jury (or bench of magistrates) could convict. If the submission is successful, a verdict of not guilty will be given straight away. If no such submission is made, or if the submission is unsuccessful, the defence then puts forward its case, using the same procedure for examining witnesses as the prosecution did. The accused is the only witness who cannot be forced to give evidence.

The Youth Justice and Criminal Evidence Act 1999 contains a range of measures to make it easier for disabled and vulnerable witnesses to give evidence, including children under 17 and victims of sexual offences. The special arrangements that can be made for such witnesses include the use of screens, the giving of evidence by live television link, the abandoning of formal court dress and the use of pre-recorded video evidence.

Once the defence has presented all its evidence, each side makes a closing speech, outlining their case and seeking to persuade the magistrates or jury of it. In the Crown Court, this is followed by the judge's summing up to the jury. The judge should review the evidence, draw the jury's attention to the important points of the case, and direct them on the law if necessary, but must not trespass on the jury's function of deciding the true facts of the case. At the end of the summing up the judge reminds the jury that the prosecution must prove its case beyond reasonable doubt, and tries to explain in simple terms what this means.

Evidence of bad character and previous convictions

In the past, previous convictions have only been exceptionally available to the court when determining guilt. Following the passing of ss. 101–103 of the Criminal Justice Act 2003, this evidence will be more widely available. The Court of Appeal stated in **R v Hanson** (2005) that the legislation required the consideration of three questions, namely:

1 Did the defendant's history of offending show a propensity to commit offences?
2 Did that propensity make it more likely the defendant committed the current offence? and
3 Is it just to rely on convictions of the same description or category having in mind the overriding principle that proceedings must be fair?

About 70 per cent of defendants have past convictions, so this reform will be important in practice. Critics argue that admitting this evidence undermines the presumption of innocence. It increases the risk of miscarriages of justice, with the courts being distracted by the defendant's past convictions, rather than focusing on the actual evidence about whether the defendant committed the particular offence before the court.

TOPICAL ISSUE

Simple, speedy, summary justice

The Government is concerned to speed up the criminal justice system, particularly in the magistrates' court. In a paper entitled *Delivering simple, speedy, summary justice* (2006) the Government laid down various practical ways in which it would try to speed up the criminal justice system. When charged at the police station, defendants are provided with advance information and an information sheet informing them that the court expects a plea to be entered on first appearance and that legal advice should therefore be sought without delay. Courts will not be sympathetic to a defendant who was unrepresented at the police station and on this basis seeks an adjournment at the first hearing. The aim is to ensure that the first court hearing is always an effective hearing. Pre-sentence reports are increasingly available on the day of the conviction, so cases can be disposed of at the first hearing where a guilty plea is entered. If the defendant pleads not guilty, then the trial should normally take place within six to ten weeks. Under four pilot schemes of these arrangements the average time taken between charge and conclusion was more than halved to 23 days; there was a 30 per cent increase in guilty pleas at the first hearing and 59 per cent of guilty pleas were dealt with at the initial court appearance. Following the success of the pilot schemes, these arrangements were launched nationally in 2008.

Models of criminal justice systems

In order to judge the effectiveness of a criminal justice system (or anything else for that matter), you need first to know what that system sets out to do. The academic Herbert Packer (1968) identified two quite different potential aims for criminal justice systems: the 'due process' model; and the 'crime control' model. The former gives priority to fairness of procedure and to protecting the innocent from wrongful conviction, accepting that a high level of protection for suspects makes it more difficult to convict the guilty, and that some guilty people will therefore go free. The latter places most importance on convicting the guilty, taking the risk that occasionally some innocent people will be convicted. Obviously, criminal justice systems tend not to fall completely within one model or the other: most seek to strike a balance between the two. This is not always easy: imagine for a moment that you are put in charge of our criminal justice system, and you have to decide the balance at which it should aim. How many innocent people do you believe it is acceptable to convict? Bear in mind that if you answer 'none', the chances are that protections against this may have to be so strong that very few guilty people will be convicted either. Would it be acceptable for 10 per cent of innocent people to be convicted if that means 50 per cent of the guilty were also convicted? If that 10 per cent seems totally unacceptable, does it become more reasonable if it means that 90 per cent of the guilty are convicted? It is not an easy choice to make.

Looking at the balance which a criminal justice system seeks to strike, and how well that balance is in fact struck, is a useful way to assess the system's effectiveness. As mentioned at the beginning of Chapter 18, in recent years this balance has been the subject of much debate and disagreement as regards our criminal justice system, with the police, magistrates and the Government claiming that the balance has been tipped too far in favour of suspects' rights, at the expense of convicting the guilty. On the other hand, civil liberties organisations, many academics and the lawyers involved in the well-known miscarriages of justice feel that the system has not learned from those miscarriages, and that the protections for suspects are still inadequate.

The latter group have particularly criticised the findings of the RCCJ. Sean Enright (1993) has written: 'One would not guess from a reading of the Commission's proposals that this Royal Commission was set up in response to some astonishing miscarriages of justice. Rather, the abiding impression is that this Commission was primarily concerned with a ruthlessly efficient and cost effective disposal of criminal business.' The barrister Michael Mansfield, who represented some of the Birmingham Six, among others, agrees, pointing out that the RCCJ proposals and the subsequent changes made to the criminal justice system are 'a complete denial of the basic principle of the presumption of innocence . . . the position has deteriorated to such an extent that further wrongful convictions are guaranteed' (*Presumed Guilty* (1993)).

Criticism and reform

The following criticisms and suggestions for reform have been the subject of particular debate.

Racism and the CPS

A report prepared by the Crown Prosecution Inspectorate in 2003 has criticised the CPS for failing to weed out weak cases against ethnic minorities. The report says acquittal rates for black and Asian defendants stand at 42 per cent, compared to 30 per cent for white defendants. The CPS is therefore failing in its duty to eliminate differential treatment. The Inspectorate is of the view that, as members of minority groups are more likely to be stopped by the police, the CPS should consider whether the behaviour of the arresting officer 'might have been inappropriate or provocative'. It concludes:

> The CPS would appear to be discriminating against ethnic minority defendants by failing to correct the bias [of police] and allowing a disproportionate number of weak cases against ethnic minority defendants to go to trial.

Racism and the courts

Research was undertaken in 2003 by Roger Hood *et al.*, which was published in a paper called *Ethnic Minorities in the Criminal Courts: perceptions of fairness and equality of treatment*. The research found that, over recent years, members of the ethnic minorities were increasingly satisfied that the criminal courts were racially impartial. Several judges said that attitudes had changed a lot and many lawyers also reported that racial bias or inappropriate language was becoming a thing of the past. This improvement was partly due to the fact that judges and magistrates are increasingly receiving training in racial awareness, and partly due to improvements in society as a whole.

While there has been this improvement in the courts, there still remains a significant minority of defendants who consider that they have been treated unfairly because of their race. One in five black defendants in the Crown Court, one in ten in the magistrates' courts, and one in eight Asian defendants in both types of court, considered they had been treated unfairly because of their race. Most complaints were about sentencing, which were perceived to be higher than for white defendants. Very few perceived racial bias in the conduct or attitude of judges or magistrates – only 3 per cent in the Crown Court and 1 per cent in the magistrates' courts. There were no complaints about racist remarks from the bench. Of some concern is the fact that black lawyers had a more negative view of proceedings. A third of black lawyers said they had personally witnessed incidents in court that they regarded as 'racist'.

Black defendants and lawyers felt that the authority and legitimacy of the courts would be strengthened if more ethnic minorities were employed in the criminal justice system. Many judges agreed that more could be done to avoid the impression that the courts were 'white dominated institutions'.

19

The criminal trial process

The Crown Prosecution Service

The CPS ran into problems from the very beginning. Because the Home Office had apparently underestimated the cost of the new service, the salaries offered were low, making it impossible to find sufficient numbers of good lawyers. As a result, the CPS gained a reputation for incompetence and delay. In 1996 a MORI poll found that 70 per cent of CPS lawyers responding to a questionnaire considered that the CPS was either below average or one of the worst places to work. In 1990 the House of Commons Public Accounts Committee noted that the CPS appeared to be costing almost twice as much as the previous prosecution arrangements, and the number of staff required was practically double that originally envisaged.

Relations between the police and the CPS have not been good: the police resented the new service and its demands for a higher standard of case preparation from police. While the CPS saw a high rate of discontinued cases as a success story, the police saw this as letting offenders off the hook. Reforms introduced following the Glidewell Report aim to improve police/CPS relations, with police and CPS staff working in integrated teams and the creation of 42 prosecuting authorities which correlate with the 42 police forces. Following the 1997 Narey Report into delay in the criminal justice system, CPS staff now work alongside police officers in police stations to prepare cases for court. However, it may be that these reforms could go to the opposite extreme. The CPS was created to put an end to the close and often cosy relations between police officers and the lawyers who used to prosecute their cases, as this could lead to malpractice.

Some of the teething problems have now been ironed out, but problems still remain. There is doubt as to how far the CPS provides an independent perspective on deciding whether or not to prosecute. The CPS has no control over the police decision to caution rather than to prosecute.

In 1990 the Home Affairs Committee expressed concern at the large proportion of discontinued cases which were not dropped until the court hearing, and was surprised that the CPS undertook no systematic analysis of the reasons for discontinuance. In 1993 the RCCJ found that the CPS did exercise the power to discontinue appropriately, citing one study (Moxon and Crisp, 1994) which suggested that nearly a third of discontinuances were dropped on public interest grounds. Of these, nearly half were discontinued because the offence was trivial and/or the likely penalty was nominal. Only 5 per cent of the cases were discontinued before any court appearance and, where cases were terminated at the court, the decision to discontinue was often taken before the hearing but not communicated to the defendant in time to save a court appearance – either because the decision had been taken too late in the day or because the CPS did not know where the defendant was.

In assessing the incidence of weak cases in the Crown Court (which may be cases that should have been discontinued), the numbers of ordered and directed acquittals are relevant. According to the 1996 Judicial Statistics, in one in every five cases a judge ordered an acquittal.

Improvements in decision-making are expected following the Criminal Justice Act 2003, which has moved the power to charge from the police to the Crown Prosecution Service, with the exception of some very minor offences.

New arrangements are being piloted in which the CPS will offer to meet victims of certain crimes, including racially aggravated crimes, to explain its decisions not to prosecute or to substantially alter charges. This is part of a much wider plan to improve victim and witness care across the whole of the criminal justice system.

Disclosure

The intention of the Criminal Procedure and Investigations Act 1996 was to redress the balance between the prosecution and defence, but there is a danger that it has gone too far in favour of the prosecution. The new rules allow considerable discretion to the prosecution to decide what should be disclosed to the defence solicitor. There is a risk that they will not disclose information highlighting weaknesses in the prosecution case. Such a failure was one of the main causes of the high-profile miscarriages of justice. For example, Judith Ward's conviction was quashed after 18 years of incarceration for a terrorist attack she did not commit when medical evidence came to light which ought to have been disclosed by the prosecution at the time of her original trial. The Law Society fears that the changes in prosecution disclosure may leave future miscarriages of justice undetected.

Prosecution disclosure does not have to take place until after the defendant has pleaded not guilty, and many have argued that the defendant needs to see this information before they can sensibly decide their plea.

The new rules for defence disclosure have given rise to considerable controversy, as many feel that they further undermine the right to silence. According to the Consultation Paper that preceded the Act, the reforms are intended to prevent defendants 'ambushing' the trial by producing an unexpected defence at the last moment which the prosecution is unprepared for, and therefore enabling the defendant to be wrongly acquitted. In fact, research prepared for the RCCJ suggested that there was little evidence of this happening in practice. Sir Robin Auld has recommended some limited changes to the existing system of disclosure. These include that prosecutors should be made responsible for identifying all potentially disclosable material and automatic prosecution disclosure of certain documents.

Cracked and ineffective trials

The Government has been concerned by the problem of 'cracked and ineffective trials'. Cracked trials occur when a case is concluded without a trial, usually because the defendant has pleaded guilty at a very late stage. An ineffective trial happens when a hearing is cancelled on the day it was due to go ahead. The Crown Prosecution Service is responsible for 20 per cent of all ineffective trials in the magistrates' courts (National Audit Office (2006)). This was due to insufficient oversight of cases, urgent cases not being prioritised, incomplete evidence and mislaid files. Over a quarter of Crown Court hearings are cancelled on the day of the trial. Of these, a quarter are due to a witness not attending (*Criminal Justice: Working Together*, National Audit Office, 1999). This is sometimes because they are too frightened to give evidence. It is frequently too late to

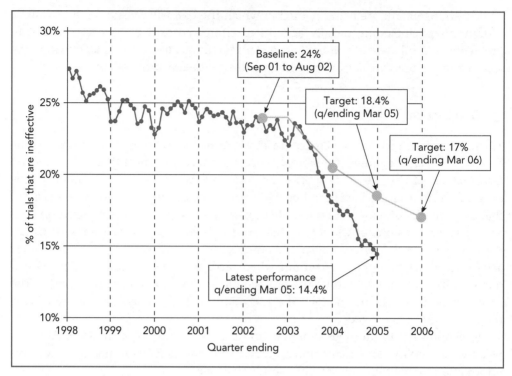

Figure 19.5 Ineffective trials in Crown Court cases

Source: Crown Prosecution Service Annual Report 2004–2005, p. 9

arrange for another case to slot into the court timetable. Cracked and ineffective trials are a waste of public money and resources and can cause unnecessary stress for victims and witnesses keen for justice to be done without delay. Statistics published by the Office for Criminal Justice Reform suggest that in 2003 as many as 20 per cent of Crown Court trials were ineffective.

The report of Her Majesty's Inspectors of the Magistrates' Court Service (1995–96) has observed that the problem of cracked trials is not limited to the Crown Court but also occurs in the magistrates' court. The report observes: 'Where monitoring data is available, the incidence of cracked trials is commonly found to be at least 50 per cent of all trials listed, with even higher rates in some areas.' About £41 million a year is wasted on cracked and ineffective trials in the magistrates' courts, according to a December 1999 National Audit Office report.

Figures contained in the report *Facing Justice: Tackling Defendants: Non-attendance at Court* (2005) prepared by the Committee of Public Accounts, show that a defendant failing to attend court was the second highest cause of ineffective trials. Unfortunately, of the 15 per cent of defendants that fail to attend court hearings, only 45 per cent had bail warrants executed against them within three months.

Following the introduction of the plea before venue procedure, and the reduction in sentence for early pleas, the number of cracked trials was halved but remains a problem.

To try to deal with the problem of cracked trials, the Courts Act 2003 has given the criminal courts a power to award costs against third parties who cause a case to collapse or be delayed.

A corroboration rule?

The major role played by confession evidence in the miscarriages of justice has led to suggestions that confession evidence alone should be regarded as insufficient to secure a conviction; in other words, the prosecution would be required to produce other evidence (such as witnesses, or forensic evidence) to support the confession.

Research by McConville for the RCCJ (1992) suggests that in 95 per cent of cases where confession evidence played a part, supporting evidence was available, indicating that a requirement for such extra evidence would lead to automatic acquittals in only a handful of cases. He calculated that, even without changes in police investigative practices, only 8 per cent of prosecutions would be affected, and these would mostly be less serious cases: a reasonable price to pay for avoiding more miscarriages of justice.

Three members of the RCCJ agreed that there should be a requirement for corroborating evidence of confessions. However, the majority merely recommended that judges should warn juries that care was needed in convicting on the basis of the confession alone, and explain the reasons why people might confess to crimes that they did not commit.

Confession evidence usually consists of confessions given to the police, but the case of Michael Stone also highlighted the danger of courts relying on uncorroborated evidence of confessions given to other prisoners. Michael Stone was convicted in 1998 of the murder of Lin Russell and her daughter Megan. They had been walking home from school through a cornfield with the other daughter Josie, when they were brutally attacked. Josie had been left for dead but had survived. While Josie had regained some memory of the incident, she was not able to pick out Stone from the identity parade. Apart from circumstantial evidence, the main evidence against Michael Stone were statements that Stone had allegedly made to three other prisoners while in prison on remand. One of these prisoners subsequently told *The Mirror* newspaper that he had lied to the court. Confessions made to fellow prisoners have none of the protections surrounding confessions made to the police that are laid down in PACE. As the defence lawyer pointed out to the jury in Michael Stone's trial: 'In an unconscious way you may think that everyone desperately wants Michael Stone to be guilty. If he's guilty the police guessed right and if he's guilty then the killer's caught and if he's guilty then all of us can sleep a little sounder in our beds tonight.' Confession evidence may be attractive but it does not necessarily do justice.

Conviction rates

Recent years have seen a large rise in reported crime but falling conviction rates. For example, for sexual offences there were 21,107 cases reported in 1980 and 31,284 by 1993. By contrast, the convictions in those years were 8,000 in 1980 and only 4,300 in 1993. In 2002 the Audit Commission reported that criminals only have a one in 16 chance of being caught and convicted.

Victims and witnesses

Victims and other witnesses play a vital role in getting convictions and thereby achieving justice. In 2003, more than 5 per cent of Crown Court cases did not go ahead on the first day because a witness failed to turn up. Twenty-two per cent of Crown Court cases and more than a quarter of magistrates' court cases that collapsed did so because prosecution witnesses failed to come to court.

There is now a growing awareness that the criminal justice system has paid insufficient attention to the needs of victims and witnesses of crime, with lawyers taking the centre stage in legal proceedings instead. For many years, victims of crime had virtually no rights. In English legal theory and practice, victims are not parties to the prosecution, but are only witnesses. Traditionally, victims have had no legal right to participation, consultation, or even information about their cases. By comparison, suspects and defendants do have rights, even if not all of them are enforceable in practice.

Victims have repeatedly complained about the lack of information they received from the criminal justice system about the progress of their case. The Witness Satisfaction Survey in 2000 showed that more than half of prosecution witnesses were not kept informed about the progress of the case and over 40 per cent were not told the verdict but had to find out for themselves.

Organisations such as Victim Support campaigned for many years to persuade the Government to recognise that victims should have distinct rights. The Government has accepted these arguments, and the rights of victims are gradually being increased.

Ess. Cases p. 306 → These rights have been put together in a Code of Practice for Victims of Crime produced by the Home Office in 2006 with enabling powers from the Domestic Violence, Crime and Victims Act 2004. The Code replaces the Victims' Charter, which had been created in 1990 but which lacked teeth. The new Code sets out the services victims should expect to receive in future from the criminal justice system, including the right to be notified of any arrests and court hearings related to their case, the right to be told if charges are being dropped, and the right to be informed about whether or not they are eligible to compensation.

The Criminal Injuries Compensation Scheme provides limited financial compensation to the victims of some forms of crime (see p. 329). Dedicated witness care units have been set up to improve the experience of victims and witnesses of crime. Their needs should be assessed at the start of the criminal process, to identify their specific requirements, such as childcare needs and the risk of intimidation. Witness care officers should then help to guide individuals through the criminal justice system.

The Audit Commission (2003) found that the majority of victims and witnesses felt they had been treated with respect by the police, but were less complimentary about their treatment by the courts. Many witnesses were unaware they could reclaim travel and other expenses incurred, and said their expenses were increased by delays in the court system. Once at court, witnesses reported intimidation, such as name-calling by the defendant's family and friends who were around in the corridors. Non-smoking policies meant people (including defendants and victims) gathered around the entrance to the court, causing stress not only to those wanting to smoke, but also to witnesses arriving at the building. The report concludes:

There is a tension between supporting victims and witnesses through a court case and the adversarial nature of a trial. Many witnesses have no idea what to expect in court, and perceptions are often based on media and dramatic portrayals. Many also perceive that the current culture of the court is not one that responds to witness needs and demands as readily as it does to those of court professionals and the defence.

In response to these concerns, Her Majesty's Courts Service is striving to provide separate facilities for victims and prosecution witnesses at court. A victim can now make a Victim Personal Statement, which is a written statement presented to the trial court. This should be considered by the court prior to passing sentence. The court can take into account the effect of the offence on the victim when passing sentence, but not the victim's opinions on what the sentence should be. According to research carried out by the National Centre for Social Research in 2004, the Victim's Personal Statement Scheme has revealed that take-up and understanding of the scheme is patchy. Many people involved in the criminal justice system simply view the scheme as a political gimmick, and some police are either not inclined to take such a statement from the victim, or unaware that they could collect this statement from the victim. The research concludes that the purpose of the scheme is unclear and that if this was clarified then it might prove more successful.

The Government has introduced family impact statements for murder and manslaughter cases. This allows a member of the victim's family to be appointed as the 'victim's advocate' and provide an oral or written statement to the court explaining the impact of the crime on the family. The statement can either be made personally or through a lawyer representing the victim. Victim support groups have backed this innovation. Lawyers (including judges) have, however, opposed it because they are concerned that evidence excluded for legal reasons from the trial may be mentioned by the family, offenders may receive an unduly harsh sentence and the process may prove very stressful to the family.

In 2008 public protection advocates were introduced. These will communicate victims' views at oral hearings of the Parole Board in cases where a prisoner serving an open-ended sentence (called an indeterminate sentence) is applying for release or transfer to open conditions. Victims will be able to attend and speak in person at an oral hearing, but they will also be subject to cross-examination by the prisoner's advocate and to questioning by the panel.

As victims have been allowed a greater say in criminal proceedings, the question has been raised as to whether the right balance has been achieved between the defendant's and victim's interests. In his response to the Home Office consultation paper, *Modernising Police Powers: Review of the Police and Criminal Evidence Act 1984*, Professor Zander (2007d) has commented:

> I do not accept that the interests of victims should be a central concern of the criminal justice system. Where relevant they should of course be taken into account. But in regard to the investigation and evidence gathering processes of the criminal justice system the interests of victims as victims (as opposed to potential witnesses), have little, if any, relevance. The victim is of course likely to have an entirely legitimate concern that the person responsible for the crime be apprehended and convicted. But it is as wrong to make that personal interest the basis for altering the balance of the criminal justice system as it would be to do so because of the personal interest of the victim's mother.

TOPICAL ISSUE

Anonymous witnesses

The Youth Justice and Criminal Evidence Act 1999 allows courts to issue special measures directions. These directions seek to reduce the stress and problems experienced by vulnerable and intimidated witnesses giving evidence to courts. The directions can allow the courts to put up a screen between the witness and the defendant, their evidence can be video-recorded in advance and submitted as a video to the court, or it can be given by a live TV link, the public can be asked to leave the court and the lawyers can remove their wigs and gowns.

One special arrangement to prevent the intimidation of witnesses which has caused problems in the criminal courts is where witnesses have been granted complete anonymity when giving evidence. Anonymity can be secured by, for example, putting up a screen and electronically disguising the voice of the witness. The House of Lords concluded in **R v Davis** (2008) that this arrangement was unlawful because the defendant had not been given a fair trial. The Law Lords were concerned that without knowing the identity of the person giving evidence against them, defendants were unable to effectively reply to the accusations. If they knew who their accuser was, they might, for example, be able to show that the individual had a personal vendetta against them which provided the motive to tell lies to the court. The facts of the actual case were that two men had been shot and killed at a party. Davis had been prosecuted, but argued that his ex-girlfriend had told lies about him to the police and had arranged for others also to tell lies about him. Three witnesses gave evidence against Davis anonymously and, as a result, he was not allowed to ask them questions which might reveal their identity. He was therefore unable to find out whether they were acquaintances of his ex-girlfriend, which had hindered the presentation of his defence.

The Government considered that this ruling went too far in protecting the rights of defendants at the expense of the rights of witnesses. Following the House of Lords' judgment, it quickly pushed through Parliament emergency legislation, the Criminal Evidence (Witness Anonymity) Act 2008, which allowed witnesses in sensitive criminal trials to give evidence anonymously. This Act has now been replaced by more detailed provisions for the protection of anonymous witnesses in the Coroners and Justice Act 2009.

The Home Office has undertaken research into the use of special measures by the courts: *Are Special Measures Working? Evidence from surveys of vulnerable and intimidated witnesses* (2004). This found that a large number of witnesses are getting the benefit of these special measures. The vast majority of people who used these arrangements to give evidence found them helpful, particularly live link TV and video-recorded evidence. One-third of witnesses using special measures said that they would not have been willing and able to give evidence without them.

The role of the media and public opinion

It is noticeable that all the serious miscarriages of justice occurred in cases where a particular crime had outraged public opinion, and led to enormous pressure on the police to find the culprits. In the case of the Birmingham Six, feelings ran so high that the trial judge consented to the case being heard away from Birmingham, on the ground that a Birmingham jury might be 'unable to bring to the trial that degree of detachment that is necessary to reach a dispassionate and objective verdict'. Given the graphic media descriptions of the carnage the real bombers had left behind them, it was in fact debatable whether any jury, anywhere, would have found it easy to summon up such detachment. The chances of a fair trial must have decreased even further when, halfway through the trial, the *Daily Mirror* devoted an entire front page to photographs of the Six, boasting that they were the 'first pictures' (implying that they were the first pictures of the bombers).

The miscarriages of justice were characterised by a reluctance to refer cases back to appeal. While campaigning by some newspapers and television programmes was eventually to help bring about the successful appeals, other sections of the media, and in particular the tabloid newspapers, were keen to dismiss the idea that miscarriages of justice might have occurred. Nor was there a great amount of public interest in the alleged plight of the Birmingham Six or the other victims – in stark contrast to the petitioning on behalf of Private Lee Clegg during 1995. There was a common feeling of satisfaction that someone had been punished for such terrible crimes, and the public did not want to hear that the system had punished the wrong people.

Even when the miscarriages of justice were finally uncovered, a lingering 'whispering campaign' suggested that the victims of those miscarriages had been let off on some kind of technicality – that there had been police misbehaviour, but that those accused of the bombings and so on were really guilty. Again, tabloid newspapers were only too pleased to contribute to this view. On the day that the report of the Royal Commission on Criminal Justice was published, the *Daily Mail* printed an article entitled 'The true victims of injustice'. In it, victims of the bombings expressed anger that the Guildford Four and the Birmingham Six had been released – as though justice for those wrongly convicted of a crime somehow meant less justice for the victims of that crime – and raised doubts as to their innocence. The newspaper commented that 'the decent majority' were more concerned to see measures designed to convict criminals than to prevent further miscarriages of justice.

On the other hand, in the case of Stephen Lawrence, the young black student murdered at a bus stop in south London in an apparently racially motivated attack, one branch of the media saw itself as a vital tool in fighting for justice. The refusal of five youths, whom many suspected to be the murderers, to give evidence at the coroner's court led to the *Daily Mail* labelling them as the killers on its front pages, despite the fact that they had already been acquitted by a criminal court.

The implications of all this for the criminal justice system are important. Clearly such a system does not operate in a vacuum and, in jury trials in particular, public opinion can never really be kept out of the courtroom. That does not mean that juries should not be used in emotive cases, nor that the media should be gagged. What it

Table 19.1 Public confidence in the criminal justice system, 2001/02 to 2006/07 (British Crime Survey)

Percentage very/fairly confident	2001/02 ints	2002/03 ints	2003/04 ints	2004/05 ints	2005/06 ints	2006/07 ints
Respects the rights of people accused of committing a crime and treats them fairly	76	77	77	78	80	79
Treats people who come forward as witnesses well*	n/a	n/a	n/a	65	68	67
Effective in bringing people who commit crimes to justice	44	39	41	43	44	41
Deals with cases promptly and efficiently	39	36	38	39	41	40
Effective at reducing crime	36	31	35	39	38	36
Meets the needs of victims of crime	34	30	32	34	36	33
Dealing with young people accused of crime	25	21	24	27	26	25
Unweighted base	32,782	36,007	37,393	45,069	47,729	47,138

Source: Adapted from Crime in England and Wales 2006–07, p. 105 [Table 19.5d]

does mean is that, in those cases which arouse strong public opinion, the police, the prosecution, judges and defence lawyers must all be extra vigilant to ensure that the natural desire to find a culprit does not take the place of the need to find the truth – and to make clear to juries that they must do the same. In addition, measures must be taken to prevent 'trial by newspaper' – the Contempt of Court Act 1981 already provides powers in this respect but, in using these powers, the courts must be able to take into account the profits to be made from crime 'scoops' by newspapers, and punish breaches of the law accordingly. Rather than impose fines, which can be paid from the increased profits, preventing newspapers from publishing for a day or more might be a greater deterrent.

Fears that the media are prejudicing the course of justice led the Government to issue a consultation document on proposals to ban payments by the media to potential witnesses in criminal trials. The issue was highlighted by breaches of the Press Complaints Commission's Code of Practice during the trial of Rosemary West. The Code of Practice has been tightened up to ban any payments to potential witnesses.

Under the Courts Act 2003, newspapers which publish material that causes trials to collapse can now be punished with a heavy fine.

ss. Cases
p. 310 →

TOPICAL ISSUE

Television in court

The Government published a consultation paper, *Broadcasting Courts* (2004). This paper considered whether television cameras should be allowed into courts so that the public can gain an insight into the workings of the law. The Government was considering whether to allow cameras into the Court of Appeal. The Lord Chancellor commented:

> Most people's knowledge and perception of what goes on in court comes from court reporting and from fictionalized accounts of trials. But the medium that gives most access to most people, television, is not allowed in court. Is there a public interest in allowing people, through television, to see what actually happens in our courts in their name?

For the first time ever, cameras were permitted into an English courtroom when a pilot study was carried out in the Court of Appeal. Criminal and civil cases were filmed and edited for mock news pieces and documentaries. These pictures were not broadcast to the public, but circulated to Ministers, senior judges and representatives from legal professional bodies so that they could consider their impact. In America, cameras are frequently allowed into a courtroom, but the Lord Chancellor has commented:

> We don't want our courts turned into US-style media circuses. We will not have OJ Simpson-style trials in Britain. Justice should be seen to be done. But our priority must be that justice is done.

The response to the consultation paper was mixed, with the views of respondents very much split over the issue. The Government has therefore not yet reached a decision on the future of television in the courts.

Recommendations of Sir Robin Auld

In his *Review of the Criminal Courts* (2001) Sir Robin Auld made a wide range of recommendations, some of which have already been considered at relevant points in this book. Other interesting recommendations have included codification, increased use of information technology and the introduction of standard timetables.

Codification

Sir Robin Auld recommended that the law covering offences, court procedures, evidence and sentencing should be codified. This would make the law simpler and more accessible for the legal professions and members of the public to whom these rules can be applied. The Government seems committed to doing this at some point in the future.

Information technology

Sir Robin Auld has emphasised the need for much greater use to be made of information technology in the criminal justice system. He is particularly keen to see the introduction of single electronic case files, managed by a new criminal Case Management Agency. The Government is currently investing in information technology for the criminal justice system.

Standard timetables

The Review proposes that there should be a move away from all forms of pre-trial hearings. Instead, standard timetables would be issued and the parties would be required to cooperate with each other in order to comply with these timetables. There would then be a written or electronic 'pre-trial assessment' by the court (discretionary for the magistrates' court) of the parties' readiness for trial. Only if the court or the parties are unable to resolve all matters in this way would there be a pre-trial hearing.

Expert witnesses

The case of Sally Clark has highlighted potential problems with the use of expert witnesses. Sally Clark was a solicitor who was convicted of killing her two young sons. In 2003, the Court of Appeal found her conviction to be unsafe (**R v Clark** (2003)). An expert witness gave very misleading evidence about the chances of a woman having two of her children die naturally from unexplained causes. He stated that the chances of a second child dying from natural causes in the same family were one in 73 million. This evidence probably heavily influenced the jury's decision to convict, but the figure was subsequently criticised by statisticians as not having a genuine scientific foundation. In addition, a Home Office pathologist failed to inform the court that one of the dead children had been suffering from an illness that could have accounted for his death. In its annual report for 2004, the Criminal Cases Review Commission has criticised expert witnesses. It considers that high fees are tempting experts to give strong evidence to please their client, to ensure that they will be asked to give expert evidence in the future. Some experts earn more than £1,500 a day and are keen to keep this source of income. They are frequently doctors who are employed by the NHS and earn some extra money by working privately as expert witnesses at the same time. The Criminal Cases Review Commission is concerned that unless expert witnesses are more tightly regulated there will be a risk of more miscarriages of justice.

Community Justice Centres

The Government is considering establishing Community Justice Centres, which have apparently operated successfully in New York. These would deal with low level crime and anti-social behaviour. They would seek to tackle the public's perception of the

Photo 19.1 Sally Clark
Source: © Trinity Mirror/Mirrorpix

courts as distant and unapproachable. Before sentence, representatives of the community, such as a tenants' association, would have the opportunity to tell the court what impact the offence had on the local community. Court sentences would combine punishment with support to deal with the cause of the offending behaviour, such as alcoholism. Eleven pilot centres have been set up around the country.

Rethinking the criminal justice system

In 2006 the Prime Minister announced that there needed to be a radical rethink of the criminal justice system. Launching a consultation process on the subject, he stated:

> Despite our attempts to toughen the law and reform the criminal justice system – reform that has often uncovered problems long untouched – the criminal justice system is still the public service most distant from what reasonable people want.

However, the move towards further legislation and reform has been criticised by a Professor of Criminology from Oxford University, Ian Loader. He had been invited by the Prime Minister to contribute to the debate on law and order. Professor Loader has commented to the BBC that:

We have had 25 years of government that have taken law and order very seriously. We have had 40 pieces of law and order legislation from this government. We have had countless new criminal offences, we've got a prison population that is bursting at the seams and we have got sentences in aggregate terms going up not going down. And yet he [Mr Blair] is expecting us to believe that the criminal justice system has become unbalanced and therefore we need a further round of reform in order to protect the rights of the victim.

He considered that the Government's 'legislative hyperactivity' was in fact making it more difficult for those working in the criminal justice system to deliver results.

Answering questions

1 **Why was the Crown Prosecution Service created and how successful has the CPS proved to be?**

Your answer could be divided between the two parts of the question:

- why the CPS was created; and
- has the CPS been successful?

The material for the first part of your answer is contained in pp. 427–8. Prior to the Prosecution of Offences Act 1985, prosecutions were effected by individuals (usually police officers) with the assistance of solicitors and the independent Bar; but this prompted criticism that the police both investigated and prosecuted so the prosecution was not independent and impartial. The 1985 Act established the Crown Prosecution Service headed by the Director of Public Prosecutions which separated the police investigation from the prosecution.

The material for the second part of your answer is contained at pp. 427–31, with pp. 444–5 providing some particularly useful critical material for you to evaluate how successful the organisation has been. The Glidewell Report criticised the CPS as too centralised and excessively bureaucratic with poor compilation of case papers. The Access to Justice Act 1999 allowed CPS lawyers (who are not always legally professionally qualified) to appear in the courts and this has led to criticism about the standard of some prosecutors. In recent years there has been a move back towards bringing the police and CPS closer together, both physically and in their decision-making process, to improve relations between the two groups and encourage efficiency. This drive, however, undermines much of the reasoning for creating the CPS in the first place.

2 **Who, in the UK, has the authority to decide whether or not a defendant should be prosecuted?**

This is a relatively easy and factually orientated question, but extra marks can be gained by including some critical comment on the present discretion to prosecute exercised by the PPP and the Attorney General. You could start with a discussion of the Crown Prosecution Service, explaining the reasons for its creation and how it decides whether to prosecute by reference to the Code for Crown Prosecutors.

You could then look at the role of the Director of Public Prosecutions (DPP). Although head of the CPS, he or she enjoys separate powers to consent to or control the bringing of certain prosecutions (a good current example here would be in relation to the offence of assisting a suicide as seen in the case of Debbie Purdy).

You could also explain the DPP's role in taking over private prosecutions, but the question implicitly excludes any other reference to private prosecutions. The whole point of creating the CPS was in order to provide a clear division between the police and the prosecuting authority, but that division is not as clear-cut as originally intended (see, for example, the implications of the House of Lords' decision in **R v Director of the Serious Fraud Office** (2008) discussed on p. 430).

3 **How far can miscarriages of justice be avoided in the future?**

There are a range of approaches that could be taken to answering this question. You could start by discussing the information contained under the subheading 'Models of criminal justice systems' at p. 442 and the material in the introduction to Chapter 18. This highlights the fact that the law has to draw a balance between the desire to convict the guilty and the need to prevent innocent people being wrongly convicted.

You could then move on to mention briefly some of the high-profile miscarriage of justice cases, such as the Birmingham Six and the Stephen Lawrence investigation. You could point to ways these miscarriages of justice could have been avoided by, for example, the introduction of a corroboration rule for confession evidence, stricter controls of the activities of the police in the police station and more money for the defence to challenge forensic evidence. The material contained in the section headed 'Safeguards for the suspect' at p. 396 could be considered, which are all means of preventing miscarriages of justice.

In your conclusion, you could return to the concept of a balance and discuss the fact that a miscarriage of justice occurs not only when an innocent person is convicted but also when a guilty person is not convicted. It is impossible to create a system where no miscarriages of justice could ever occur, but the aim should be to minimise them. You could question how far such developments as the abolition of the right to silence are likely to achieve this.

4 **Peter has been charged with murder.**

(a) **Explain the role of his solicitor and barrister as his case progresses through the courts;**

(b) **Describe the work of the Crown Prosecution Service in relation to his case; and**

(c) **What criticisms have been made of the Crown Prosecution Service?**

(a) Your answer to this part of the question would draw from material both in this chapter and the chapter on the legal professions. Looking first at the role of the solicitor, the solicitor would be able to give individual advice during and after police questioning. He or she could interview witnesses about the case and put together a file for the defence. This would be used to give instructions to Peter's barrister about the case. The solicitor would be able to represent Peter at a magistrates' court during the preliminary proceedings. He or she would even be able to represent Peter in the Crown Court if he or she had completed the necessary training (see p. 192). Otherwise, the solicitor would sit behind the barrister during the plea and case management hearing and the actual trial.

As regards Peter's barrister, because this is a serious case a QC (discussed at p. 201) is likely to be employed as well as a junior barrister. The QC would do most of the advocacy work and the junior barrister would provide support. The barrister(s) would see Peter after the solicitor had done some initial work on the case. He or she would normally receive a file containing the instructions from the solicitor and then interview Peter prior to the trial. The barrister would, in particular, give Peter some initial advice as to his plea. He or she could represent Peter in the magistrates' court and Crown Court instead of the solicitor. This would include cross-examining witnesses and examining defence witnesses.

At the end of your answer to this part of the question you could take a critical approach to the subject, looking at the advantages and disadvantages of using both a barrister and solicitor. In particular, you could highlight that the two professionals can provide expertise in their different areas: the barrister can offer independent advice on the case and the solicitor can offer an accessible contact for Peter. The disadvantages of using both professions are that problems can arise if communications are poor between the barrister and solicitor and the barrister is dependent on the solicitor preparing the case properly. While Peter is unlikely to have to pay for his legal representation, use of two professionals will be expensive for the taxpayer.

(b) The Crown Prosecution Service would receive the file from the police to decide whether to charge and bring a prosecution. It would decide whether there was sufficient evidence to give rise to a reasonable chance of conviction and whether it was in the public interest to proceed with the prosecution. An employee of the Crown Prosecution Service (who need not be a lawyer) can present the prosecution case in the magistrates' court. The Crown Prosecution Service will then usually instruct an independent barrister to take the case to the Crown Court, though it does have the right now to use one of its own employees.

(c) The material you need to answer this question is contained at pp. 444–5.

5 Can plea-bargaining ever be justified?

Plea-bargaining is the process of negotiation between the parties over the outcome of a case. Generally the prosecution offers to proceed on a reduced charge (with a lower maximum sentence) in return for the defendant's guilty plea. The practice is widespread but requires active participation by the judge. Following **R** v **Goodyear** a judge can give a binding advance indication of the likely sentence so that the final sentence cannot exceed that indicated.

Whilst there are financial benefits to the criminal justice system in securing convictions, in applying shorter sentences and in shortened trials, there has been criticism that the process risks imposing excessive pressure on the defendant even when innocent to enter into a plea bargain. Thus some innocent people may 'play safe' with a guilty plea and the guilty are punished more leniently. Moreover, where the bargain is effected at the last moment, there is only a limited saving in trial costs.

Summary of Chapter 19: The criminal trial process

The adversarial process
The English system of criminal justice can be described as adversarial. This means each side is responsible for putting their own case. The role of the judge is limited to that of a referee ensuring fair play. The adversarial system is typical of common law countries. The alternative is an inquisitorial system, which exists in most of the rest of Europe.

Criminal Procedure Rules
In 2005, the main rules on criminal procedure that apply to the trial and pre-trial process were brought together in new Criminal Procedure Rules.

The Crown Prosecution Service

Most prosecutions are now brought by the Crown Prosecution Service. Significant reforms of this body were introduced following the Glidewell Report, which was published in 1998.

Appearance in court

Persons charged with an offence can be called to court by means of a summons, or by a charge following arrest without a warrant.

Classification of offences

There are three different categories of offence: summary offences, indictable offences and offences triable either way.

Mode of trial

Where a person is charged with a triable either way offence, they can insist on a trial by jury, otherwise the decision is for the magistrates.

Disclosure

The issue of disclosure is concerned with the responsibility of the prosecution and defence to reveal information related to the case prior to the trial.

Plea bargaining

Plea bargaining is the name given to negotiations between the prosecution and defence lawyers over the outcome of a case.

The trial

Apart from the role played by the jury in the Crown Court, the law and procedure in the Crown Court and magistrates' court are essentially the same. The burden of proof is on the prosecution.

Models of criminal justice systems

The academic, Herbert Packer (1968) has identified two quite different potential aims for criminal justice systems: the 'due process' model; and the 'crime control' model.

Criticism and reform

The following issues have been the subject of particular debate:

Racism and the CPS

The CPS is failing to weed out weak cases against ethnic minorities.

Racism and the courts

Over recent years members of the ethnic minorities are increasingly satisfied that the criminal courts are racially impartial.

The Crown Prosecution Service

The CPS ran into problems from the very beginning and has continued to be the subject of much controversy.

Cracked and ineffective trials

The Government has been concerned by the problem of 'cracked and ineffective trials'.

Conviction rates

Recent years have seen a large rise in reported crime but falling conviction rates.

Victims and witnesses

There is now a growing awareness that the criminal justice system has paid insufficient attention to the needs of victims and witnesses of crime.

Reading list

Audit Commission (2003) *Victims and Witnesses*, London: Audit Commission Publications.

Criminal Justice: The Way Ahead (2001) Cm 5074, London: Home Office.

Cutting Crime – Delivering Justice: Strategic Plan for Criminal Justice 2004–08 (2004) Cm 6288, London: Home Office.

Duff, A., Farmer, L., Marshall, S. and Tadros, V. (2007) *The Trial on Trial (Volume 3): Towards a Normative Theory of the Criminal Trial*, Oxford: Hart Publishing.

Enright, S. (1993) 'Cost effective criminal justice', 143 *New Law Journal* 1023.

Hedderman, C. and Hough, M. (1994) *Does the Criminal Justice System Treat Men and Women Differently?* London: Home Office Research and Planning Unit.

Home Office (2003) *Statistics on Women and the Criminal Justice System*, London: Home Office.

Home Office (2004) *Are Special Measures Working? Evidence from surveys of vulnerable and intimidated witnesses* (Home Office Research Study 283), London: Home Office.

Home Office (2004) *One Step Ahead: A 21st Century Strategy to Defeat Organised Crime*, London: Stationery Office.

Hood, R., Shute, S. and Seemungal, F. (2003) *Ethnic Minorities in the Criminal Courts: perceptions of fairness and equality of treatment*, London: Lord Chancellor's Department.

Jeremy, D. (2008) 'The Prosecutor's Rock and Hard Place', [2008] *Criminal Law Review* 925.

Mansfield, M. (1993) *Presumed Guilty: The British Legal System Exposed*, London: Heinemann.

McConville, M. and Baldwin, J. (1977) *Negotiated Justice: Pressures to Plead Guilty*, Oxford: Martin Robertson.

McConville, M. and Baldwin, J. (1981) *Courts, Prosecution and Conviction*, Oxford: Oxford University Press.

Moxon, D. and Crisp, D. (1994) *Case Screening by the Crown Prosecution Service: How and Why Cases are Terminated*, London: HMSO.

Narey, M. (1997) *Review of Delay in the Criminal Justice System*, London: Home Office.

National Audit Office (1999) *Criminal Justice Working Together*, London: Stationery Office.

National Audit Office (2006) *CPS: effective use of magistrates' court hearings*, London: Stationery Office.

Packer, H. (1968) *The Limits of the Criminal Sanction*, Stanford, California: Stanford University Press.

Quirk, H. (2006) 'The significance of culture in criminal procedure reform: why the revised disclosure scheme cannot work', 10 *International Journal of Evidence and Proof* 42.

Race and the Criminal Justice System: an overview to the complete statistics 2003–2004 (2005) London: Criminal Justice System Race Unit.

Zander, M. and Henderson, P. (1993) *Crown Court Study*, London: HMSO.

Reading on the Internet

www   The *Code of Practice for Victims of Crime* (2006) has been published on the Home Office website:
http://www.homeoffice.gov.uk/documents/victims-code-of-practice

The revised Code A for PACE can be found on the Home Office website at:
http://www.police.homeoffice.gov.uk/news-and-publications/publication/operational-policing/PACE_Chapter_A.pdf

The Code for Crown Prosecutors is available on the Crown Prosecution Service's website:
http://www.cps.gov.uk

The Auld Report is available on:
http://www.criminal-courts-review.org.uk

The Home Office Report *Crime in England and Wales 2002/2003* is published at:
http://www.homeoffice.gov.uk/rds/pdfs2/hosb703.pdf

Information on the criminal justice system is available at:
http://www.cjsonline.org

Visit www.mylawchamber.co.uk/ElliottELS to access multiple-choice questions, flashcards and practice exam questions to test yourself on this chapter.

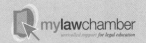

19

The criminal trial process

20

Sentencing

This chapter discusses:

- the Criminal Justice Act 2003 introducing important changes to the sentencing process;

- the purposes of sentencing laid out in the 2003 Act;

- sentencing practice in the courts;

- fines;

- custodial sentences;

- community sentences; and

- problems with sentencing.

The Criminal Justice Act 2003

The Home Office undertook a review of sentencing that was carried out by John Halliday and published in 2001. A wide range of recommendations were contained in his report, *Making Punishment Work, Report of the Review of the Sentencing Framework for England and Wales*. Central to the approach of the Halliday Review is that the courts should have a greater role in the implementation of sentences and that offenders should spend more time under supervision after their release from custody. He also wanted to see a greater predictability in sentencing so that the sentencing practice would have a stronger deterrent effect on potential offenders. He was particularly concerned by the approach of the courts to persistent offenders, who he thought committed a disproportionate amount of crime.

The Government accepted many of the Report's recommendations and introduced significant reforms to the sentencing system in the Criminal Justice Act 2003. Politicians are continually tinkering with the sentencing system and the process of consultation and reform is ongoing.

Purposes of sentencing

This chapter is concerned with the sentencing of those convicted of crimes, including the types of punishment available, and how the choice between them is made by the sentencer. But, first, we need to consider why people are punished at all – what is the punishment supposed to achieve? Section 142 of the Criminal Justice Act 2003 states that:

> Any court dealing with an [adult] offender in respect of his offence must have regard to the following purposes of sentencing –
> (a) the punishment of offenders,
> (b) the reduction of crime (including its reduction by deterrence),
> (c) the reform and rehabilitation of offenders,
> (d) the protection of the public, and
> (e) the making of reparation by offenders to persons affected by their offences.

Each of these purposes of sentencing will be examined in turn.

Punishment of offenders

Punishment is concerned with recognising that the criminal has done something wrong and taking revenge on behalf of both the victim and society as a whole. This can also be described as retribution. Making punishments achieve retribution was a high priority during the last years of the Conservative Government with Michael Howard as the Home Secretary. In the White Paper of 1990, *Crime, Justice and Protecting the Public*, reference was made to the need for sentences to achieve 'just deserts',

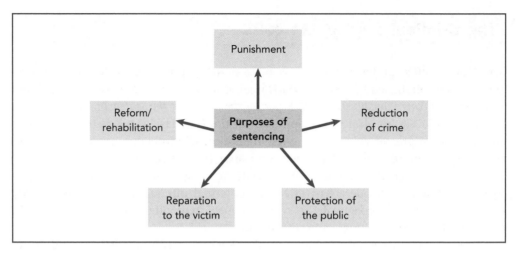

Figure 20.1 Purposes of sentencing

stating that punishments should match the harm done, and show society's disapproval of that harm. The problem with this is that other factors all too often intervene: for example, those from stable homes, with jobs, are more likely to get non-custodial sentences than those without, who may be sent to prison even though their crime more properly fits a non-custodial sentence.

The reduction of crime

Crime is a harm which society wishes to eradicate. One way of reducing crime is through using a sentence as a deterrent. Deterrence is concerned with preventing the commission of future crimes; the idea is that the prospect of an unpleasant punishment will put people who might otherwise commit crime off the idea. Punishments may aim at individual deterrence (dissuading the offender in question from committing crime again), or general deterrence (showing other people what is likely to happen to them if they commit crime).

One problem with the use of punishment as a deterrent is that its effectiveness depends on the chances of detection: a serious punishment for a particular crime will not deter people from committing that offence if there is very little chance of being caught and prosecuted for it. This was shown when Denmark was occupied during the Second World War. All the Danish police were interned, drastically cutting the risk for ordinary criminals of being arrested. Despite increases in punishment, the number of property offences soared.

Linked with this problem is the fact that a deterrent effect requires the offender to stop and think about the consequences of what they are about to do, and, as the previous Government's 1990 White Paper pointed out, this is often unrealistic:

> Deterrence is a principle with much immediate appeal . . . But much crime is committed on impulse, given the opportunity presented by an open window or unlocked door, and it is committed by offenders who live from moment to moment; their crimes are as

impulsive as the rest of their feckless, sad or pathetic lives. It is unrealistic to construct sentencing arrangements on the assumption that most offenders will weigh up the possibilities in advance and base their conduct on rational calculation. Often they do not.

The deterrent effect of punishment on individuals becomes weaker each time they are punished. The more deeply a person becomes involved with a criminal way of life, the harder it is to reform and, at the same time, the fear of punishment becomes less because they have been through it all before.

It has been argued that, to deal with this problem, offenders should be given a severe sentence at an early stage – which politicians like to call a 'short, sharp shock' – rather than having gradually increased sentences which are counterbalanced by the progressive hardening of the offender to the effects of punishment. Successive attempts at the 'short, sharp shock' treatment have, however, shown themselves to have no meaningful effect on reconviction rates. The approach was introduced under the Detention Centre Order, created by the Criminal Justice Act 1982; it was abolished in the Criminal Justice Act 1988.

Where a specific crime is thought to be on the increase, the courts will sometimes try to stem this increase by passing what is called an exemplary sentence. This is a sentence higher than that which would normally be imposed to show people that the problem is being treated seriously, and to make potential offenders aware that they may be severely punished. There is some debate as to whether exemplary sentences actually work; their effectiveness depends on publicity, yet British newspapers tend to highlight only those sentences which seem too low for an offence which concerns society, or which seem too high for a trivial offence. In addition, even where there is publicity, the results may be negligible – Smith and Hogan (2002) point to an exemplary sentence passed for street robbery at a time when mugging was the subject of great social concern. The sentence was publicised by newspapers and television, yet there was no apparent effect on rates of street robbery even in the area where the case in question took place. We should also question whether exemplary sentences are in the interests of justice, which demands that like cases be treated alike; the person who mugs someone in the street when there has not been a public outcry about that offence is no better than one who mugs when there has.

Reform and rehabilitation

The aim of rehabilitation is to reform offenders, so that they are less likely to commit offences in the future – either because they learn to see the harm they are causing, or because, through education, training and other help, they find other ways to make a living or spend their leisure time. During the 1960s, a great deal of emphasis was placed on the need for rehabilitation, but the results were felt by many to be disappointing. By 1974 the American researcher Robert Martinson was denouncing rehabilitation programmes for prisoners in his paper *What Works?*, in which he came to the conclusion that 'nothing works'.

Although rehabilitation sounds like a sensible aim, Bottoms and Preston argue in *The Coming Penal Crisis* (1980) that rehabilitative sentences are fundamentally flawed. First, such sentences assume that all crime is the result of some deficiency or fault in the individual offender; Marxist academics argue that crime is actually a result of the way society is organised. Secondly, they discriminate against the less advantaged in society, who are seen as in need of reform, whereas when an offender comes from a more privileged background, their offence tends to be seen as a one-off, temporary slip. This means that punishment is dictated not by the harm caused, but by the background of the offender. Thirdly, in some cases the pursuit of reform can encourage inexcusable interference with the dignity and privacy of individuals. This has included, in some countries, implanting electrodes in the brain, and in the UK in the 1970s experiments were carried out involving hormone drug treatment for sex offenders.

Faced with a growing prison population, there seems to be a renewed interest in the idea of rehabilitation. Over the past five years, offending behaviour programmes have been developed in many of the prisons of England and Wales. From an initial fragmented range of courses on such matters as anger management, alcohol and drug abuse, domestic violence and victim awareness, the emphasis is now on programmes aimed at changing the way the prisoners think, such as 'Reasoning and Rehabilitation' and 'Enhanced Thinking Skills'. Reasoning and Rehabilitation courses do not look directly at the prisoners' offending; instead, over a 35-session course run by prison probation officers and psychologists, they focus on six key areas – impulse control, flexible thinking (learning from experience), means-end testing (predicting probable outcomes of behaviour), perspective taking (seeing other people's points of view), problem solving and social skills. Enhanced Thinking Skills courses follow a similar pattern, but over 20 sessions. Attendance on the courses is voluntary – but a long-term prisoner is unlikely to be released early without having completed one.

In 1998–99, 3,000 prisoners successfully completed one of these programmes, but this still represents only a very small proportion of the prison population. Whether a prisoner has the opportunity to undertake a course depends on the establishment in which he or she is being held. Not all prisons run these courses and, in most of the ones that do, priority is given to prisoners serving four years or more; in other words, those who have to apply for early release. Yet many persistent offenders are in prison for less than four years. It is common to find people who have had a series of successive two- and three-year sentences, separated by mere weeks and often only days of freedom before they have reoffended and returned to prison. The senior judge, Lord Bingham, would like to see offending behaviour programmes made a legal requirement for all prisoners.

But how far will efforts to change the way a prisoner thinks reduce reoffending? One of the main problems faced by prisoners on release is a lack of work and consequent lack of an honest income or legitimate ways to spend their time. Many prisoners come out with the best of intentions but, faced with empty days and even emptier pockets, they soon succumb to their old temptations. There is a danger that prisoners released into their old environment without having acquired any practical or vocational skills to help them on their way will fall back into a life of crime.

A report of the Parliamentary Penal Affairs Group, *Changing Offending Behaviour – Some Things Work* (1999), found that 'cognitive behavioural' programmes did work. But in addition, they argued that there is increasing evidence that programmes focused directly on the needs of the offender in relation to the offending behaviour are successful in reducing the risk of reoffending. The types of needs that can be tackled include the need for employment, education, improved social skills and a break from negative peer groups. The need to tackle alcohol and drug problems was also highlighted.

Protection of the public

By placing an offender in custody, they are prevented from committing further offences and the public are thereby protected. While this has its merits where highly dangerous offenders are concerned, it is an extremely expensive way of dealing with crime prevention and, since prison is often the place where criminals pick up new ideas and techniques, may be ultimately counter-productive.

Reparation

The Government has been developing ways in which offenders can provide remedies to their victims or the community at large. This is sometimes known as 'restorative justice', and has been pioneered for young offenders. So far it seems to have been surprisingly successful in reducing reoffending and increasing victim satisfaction with the criminal justice system. Restorative justice gives the victim the opportunity to tell offenders how they have been affected by crime, to get an apology and to have a say in what offenders will do to put right the harm they have inflicted. It also provides the victim with an explanation of why the crime was committed. Offenders can be required, for example, to write letters of apology to their victims, help to repair damage they have caused or undertake other community work.

The Office for Criminal Justice Reform has published a guide entitled *Restorative justice: helping to meet local need* (2004). This advises criminal justice agencies on how restorative justice can be achieved at a local level. Following the publication of the guide, the Criminal Justice Minister said:

> Restorative Justice is about helping every victim get over the crime they've suffered. When a victim chooses to meet the offender it often helps them feel safer and more satisfied that justice has been done. It can also be part of the rehabilitation process for offenders themselves.

Research has been carried out into the effectiveness of restorative justice which was published in a report *Restorative Justice: the Evidence* (Sherman and Strang, 2007). This concluded that many violent criminals are less likely to commit further offences after participating in a restorative justice programme. The victim's symptoms of post traumatic stress disorder are reduced, partly because meeting their offender demystifies the offence. Restorative justice was also cheaper than traditional criminal sentences. Research carried out by Professor Shapland (2008) found that offenders who participated in restorative justice were reconvicted for significantly fewer offences in the subsequent two years than those who had not. The research concluded that restorative justice provides an opportunity for offenders who want to put a stop to their criminal lifestyle to use the process to gain support for that decision, particularly where the outcome of the process is an agreement targeting problems relating to their reoffending.

20

Sentencing

As regards the question of value for money, the conclusions of the research are mixed with one scheme saving a significant amount of money but two others not leading to any savings, though there were high levels of victim and offender satisfaction.

Sentencing practice

On conviction in the Crown Court, it is the trial judge alone (without the help of the jury) who determines the appropriate sentence. On conviction in the magistrates' court, the magistrates can determine the sentence themselves or, under s. 3 of the Powers of Criminal Courts (Sentencing) Act 2000, the defendant can be committed to the Crown Court for sentence. If sentenced by the magistrates' court, the maximum sentence that can be imposed for a summary offence has been increased from six months to 12 months by the Criminal Justice Act 2003, s. 154. The minimum is five days (Magistrates' Courts Act 1980, s. 132).

Once the defendant has been found guilty, it must be decided first what category of sentence is appropriate and then the amount, duration and form of that sentence.

In recent years there has been a considerable amount of legislation trying to control and regulate the sentencing practices of the judges. The legislature has increasingly sought to reduce the discretion available to the judiciary in selecting the sentence. We will look first at the legislative provisions and then at the common law practice known as the tariff system.

Legislation

Parliamentary legislation has, for a minority of offences, fixed the sentence that must be imposed. Since 1997 it has applied minimum sentences to some offenders. Some rules have also been laid down restricting the judiciary's choice of sentence.

Mandatory sentences

Certain offences have a mandatory sentence when committed for the first time. The most notable example of this is murder, which has a mandatory sentence of life imprisonment.

Minimum sentences

There are also now minimum sentences for certain firearms offences under the Criminal Justice Act 2003, s. 287. These minimum sentences were introduced in an attempt to tackle the growing problem of criminals using guns.

General restrictions on sentences

The legislator has divided sentences into four categories: custodial sentences, community sentences, fines and certain miscellaneous sentences. A custodial or community sentence can only be ordered where certain statutory conditions are satisfied. The judges must give reasons for their sentence and explain the effect of the sentence to the offender (Criminal Justice Act 2003, s. 174).

Custodial sentences

A custodial sentence is defined by s. 76 of the PCC(S)A 2000. For a person aged 18 or over it is a sentence of imprisonment or a suspended sentence. For a person under 18 a custodial sentence includes detention in a young offenders' institution or a sentence of custody for life.

A court should not pass a custodial sentence unless it considers that the crime was so serious that only a custodial sentence is justified (CJA 2003, s. 152). Section 153 of the Criminal Justice Act 2003 directs the court to impose the shortest custodial term that is commensurate with the seriousness of the offence(s), subject to certain exceptions. Section 143 of the 2003 Act states that:

> In considering the seriousness of any offence, the court must consider the offender's culpability in committing the offence and any harm which the offence caused, was intended to cause or might foreseeably have caused.

The court also has to take into account previous convictions, failure to respond to previous sentences and the commission of an offence while on bail (CJA 2003, s. 143).

Where a judge intends to impose a custodial sentence (unless the sentence is fixed by law), a pre-sentence report must normally be prepared by the probation service, containing background information about the defendant. This will assist the judge in selecting the appropriate sentence.

Community sentences

Section 148 of the Criminal Justice Act 2003 states that a community sentence can only be imposed if the offence was 'serious enough to warrant such a sentence'. Where a court passes a community sentence, the particular requirements of the sentence must be the most suitable for the offender. The restrictions on liberty imposed by the order must be 'commensurate with the seriousness of the offence, or the combination of the offence and one or more offences associated with it'.

TOPICAL ISSUE

Dangerous offenders

Section 225 of the Criminal Justice Act 2003 provides that violent dangerous offenders must receive either a life sentence or an indeterminate sentence for public protection (IPP). An IPP allows the state to hold offenders in prison for longer than is required by the gravity of their offence in order to protect the public. The court can impose an IPP where an offender has committed a specified sexual or violent offence (153 offences are listed) and has been assessed as dangerous because they continue to pose a substantial risk to the public. In addition, the judge can hand down, where the gravity of the offence justifies it, a life sentence or, where the maximum sentence is for less than 10 years, an extended sentence. If an extended sentence is imposed prisoners will automatically be released after they have served half that sentence.

The heavy use of IPPs has significantly increased the size of the prison population and led to prison overcrowding. In setting the IPP the judge states the minimum time that the offender should remain in prison, but not the maximum. When the minimum period is completed, the offender is not released until the probation board has concluded the offender is no longer dangerous. In practice, offenders will need to show the board that they have undertaken rehabilitation courses aimed at changing their offending behaviour (such as anger management and alcohol awareness courses – see p. 466). Unfortunately, there have not been enough of these courses provided in the prisons, so some individuals have not had the opportunity to undertake the courses. As a result, a test case was brought by two prisoners sentenced to IPPs, whose minimum tariff had been served but who had not been released: **R v James and Lee** (2009). While the Court of Appeal had held that their continued detention was unlawful because there had been 'a general and systematic legal failure', the House of Lords ruled that their detention was lawful.

The Government has tried to reduce the use of IPPs by passing provisions in the Criminal Justice and Immigration Act 2008 to restrict their use to where a minimum tariff of two years' imprisonment has been imposed.

The tariff system

The legislation regulates the type of sentence imposed and, in its focus on seriousness, clearly has implications for the length of a custodial or community sentence or the amount of a fine. In deciding the latter issues, judges also rely on what has been called the tariff principle, first recognised by Dr David Thomas in his book *Principles of Sentencing* (1970).

The tariff system is based on treating like cases alike: people with similar backgrounds who commit similar offences in similar circumstances should receive similar sentences. That does not mean that judges apply a rigid scale of penalties, but that for most types of criminal offence it is possible to identify a range within which the sentence for different factual situations will fall.

The system works in two stages: calculation of the initial tariff sentence, and then the application of secondary tariff principles. To begin with, the judge will take the tariff sentence that is generally thought appropriate for the offence. This may then be lowered by taking into account secondary tariff principles such as mitigating factors – reasons why the defendant should be punished less severely than the facts of the case might suggest (Criminal Justice Act 2003, s. 166). These include youth or old age; previous good character; the 'jump effect' (a requirement that sentences for repeat offenders should increase steadily rather than by large jumps); provocation; domestic or financial problems; drink, drugs or ill-health; and any special hardship offenders may have to undergo in prison, such as the fact that sex offenders and police informers may have to be held in solitary confinement for their own protection. In some cases, where an offender has already been held on remand, the courts may reduce the tariff sentence on the basis that the shock of being locked up has already constituted a severe punishment. The offender's behaviour after committing the offence may also be a factor, including efforts to help the police and/or compensate the victim. A plea of guilty is usually taken as a sign of remorse and an offender's sentence can now be reduced by up to a third in the light of the stage at which they indicate an intention to plead guilty and the circumstances in which that indication was given (Criminal Justice Act 2003, s. 144). The recommended level of reduction is set by the Sentencing Guidelines Council on a sliding scale at one-third for a plea at the first reasonable opportunity, to one-quarter where a trial date has been set, to one-tenth when the plea is entered just before or during the trial. The application of s. 144 has proved politically sensitive as the reduction in sentence is available even where the offender has been caught red-handed. As far as the offence itself is concerned, the fact that it was committed on impulse and not premeditated may be a mitigating factor.

There may also be aggravating factors, as a result of which the court may want to pass an exemplary sentence. The Court of Appeal has stated that the correct way to deal with this is to ignore mitigating factors and not to increase the initial tariff. Under the Criminal Justice Act 2003, a court must treat the fact that an offence was racially or religiously motivated as an aggravating factor which increased the seriousness of the offence. Any previous convictions, which are recent and relevant, should be regarded as an aggravating factor which will also increase the severity of the sentence.

20

Sentencing

TOPICAL ISSUE

Giving 'Queen's evidence'

The US law enforcement agencies have traditionally favoured the practice of using those who admit offences to provide evidence against others, in exchange for a substantially reduced sentence or immunity from prosecution. This has enabled them to prosecute corporate crime successfully, particularly in relation to cartel offences (where businesses in the same sector reach secret agreements to artificially inflate prices). Historically, the UK law enforcement agencies were reluctant to do the same because of the risk that such evidence against a purported accomplice might be lies to protect themselves. However, influenced by successes in America, the Serious Organised Crime and Police Act 2005 provides that an offender can benefit from a reduced sentence, or even immunity from sentence, if they give evidence against other criminals (sometimes called 'Queen's evidence').

Sentencing Guidelines Council and Sentencing Advisory Panel

The Court of Appeal plays a central role in developing the tariff system by providing guidance to the judges of first instance as to the appropriate sentence for certain types of offence and offender. The Crime and Disorder Act 1998 created a Sentencing Advisory Panel to assist in the development of a fair sentencing practice. The Court of Appeal was required to consider the views of this Panel in framing its sentencing guidelines, and it has taken account of a range of guidelines produced by the Sentencing Advisory Panel.

The Criminal Justice Act 2003, ss. 167–173 has established a new Sentencing Guidelines Council. This will produce a set of sentencing guidelines for all criminal courts (and guidelines on allocation of cases between courts). The courts are obliged to take these guidelines into account when determining what sentence to impose, and have to give reasons if they depart from a recommended sentence in a guideline. The aim of these guidelines is to help the courts to approach sentencing from a common starting point. They also enable practitioners and the general public to know the starting point for each offence. The Council has seven judicial members and five non-judicial members, and is chaired by the Lord Chief Justice.

The Sentencing Advisory Panel now tenders its advice to the Sentencing Guidelines Council, instead of the Court of Appeal. There is a risk that the Council will simply duplicate the work of the Panel, and it is questionable whether we need both of these bodies.

Individualised sentences

In some cases, the courts prefer not to use the tariff system, but to impose a sentence aimed at dealing with the individual needs of the offender. There are four main types of offender for whom individualised sentencing is used: young offenders; intermediate recidivists; inadequate recidivists; and those who need psychiatric treatment. Individualised sentences are often given to young offenders in the hope of steering them away from a life of crime. Intermediate recidivists are offenders in their late twenties or early thirties, with a criminal record dating back to their childhood; rather than simply ordering steadily increased tariff sentences for them, the courts may give an individualised sentence if there is evidence that a new approach may work. Inadequate recidivists are middle-aged or elderly offenders who have a long history of committing relatively minor crimes, which have resulted in imprisonment and most other types of sentence; individualised sentences may be ordered for them on the simple basis that their record shows increasing tariff sentences to have been ineffective in stopping their offending. Finally, offenders who need psychiatric treatment are given individualised sentences within which such treatment can be undertaken.

Types of sentence

It was mentioned above (p. 468) that there are four main categories of sentence: custodial sentences; community sentences; fines; and other miscellaneous sentences. The death penalty has been abolished. We will now look at the particular forms that the four existing sentences can take.

Fines

A fine may be imposed for almost any offence other than murder. Offences tried in the magistrates' court carry a set maximum, depending on the offence; the highest is

£5,000. There is no maximum in the Crown Court. The courts must ensure that the amount of the fine reflects the seriousness of the offence, and also takes account of the offender's means, reducing or increasing it as a result (Criminal Justice Act 2003, s. 167). Magistrates' courts can arrange for the automatic deduction of a fine from the offender's earnings, known as an 'attachment of earnings order', when imposing the fine or following a failure to pay. Under ss. 300 and 301 of the Criminal Justice Act 2003 the court has the power to impose unpaid work or curfew requirements on a fine defaulter or to disqualify them from driving, rather than sending them to prison.

The Courts Act 2003 seeks to improve the information available to magistrates on offenders' means prior to sentence, and to ensure that enforcement action is taken promptly. The Act has introduced a new framework for fine enforcement. When a collection order is issued by the court, fine officers manage and collect fines instead of the court. Discounts of up to 50 per cent are given to those who pay promptly. If the offender fails to pay promptly the fine can be increased by the fines officer by up to 50 per cent without the case being referred back to the courts. The fines officer may also issue a further steps notice. This can, for example, require payments to be deducted automatically from an offender's pay, for their property to be seized and sold, or their car clamped. Once clamped, the car can be removed for sale or other disposal and any proceeds are used to discharge or reduce the offender's outstanding fine.

The fine is the most common sentence issued by the court, with three-quarters of all offenders sentenced at magistrates' courts in 2000 being issued with a fine. The number of fines issued has decreased in recent years and the researchers Flood-Page and Mackie (1998) concluded that 'there seems to have been a general disenchantment with financial penalties'. Lord Carter (2007) has noted that the courts are imposing community sentences whereas before they imposed fines. He suggests removing that option from low level offences to reduce the strain on the probation service.

Since 2007, alongside every fine issued by the magistrates, the defendant also has to pay an additional £15 towards services for victims and witnesses. Some magistrates have been unhappy with this requirement as they feel like unofficial tax collectors and the amount collected cannot be adapted to reflect the financial means of the convicted person.

Advantages of fines

Evidence suggests that people are less likely to reoffend after being sentenced to a fine than following other sentences, though this can be partly explained by the type of offenders that are given fines in the first place. Fines also bring income into the system, and they do not have the long-term disruptive effects of imprisonment.

Disadvantages of fines

There have been high rates of non-payment – a problem which the Courts Act 2003 is intended to tackle. A third of fines are never paid, so that in the years 2000–01 £74 million of fines were written off (mainly because the offender could not be traced), according to the National Audit Office. This not only makes the sentence ineffective, but repeated non-payment of a fine can lead to a custodial sentence, with the result that some inmates of English prisons are there for very minor offences, such as failure to pay for a television licence.

20

Sentencing

Research carried out for the Home Office, *Enforcing Financial Penalties* (Whittaker and Mackie, 1997), found that the majority of fine defaulters were out of work (only 22 per cent of the men and 11 per cent of the women had any paid employment, even part time). Predominant among reasons for non-payment were changes in circumstances through illness or job loss, and financial difficulties brought on by other debts.

A wide range of enforcement methods is available to the courts, including attachment of earnings orders and the automatic deduction of fines from social security benefits. In practice, these enforcement methods are only rarely used. The 1997 Home Office study highlighted practical difficulties in trying to arrange the deduction of fines from social security benefits. Some magistrates felt that attachment of earnings orders removed the responsibility from the defaulter for ensuring that the fine was paid, which was seen as part of the punishment. The Government announced in 2005 that it was going to establish a National Enforcement Service which would employ 4,000 uniformed officers with responsibility for ensuring that fines are paid and other court orders obeyed. However, this reform plan seems to have been dropped for the time being as the Service has not been created.

Fines can be unfair, since the same fine may be a very severe punishment to a poor defendant, but make little impact on one who is well-off. In an attempt to address this problem, the Criminal Justice Act 1991 originally laid down a system of unit fines for the magistrates' courts. A maximum number of units was allocated to each offence, up to a total of 50. Within that maximum, the court had to determine the number of units which was commensurate with the seriousness of the case. The value of the unit depended on the offender's disposable weekly income (their income after having deducted any regular household expenses), with the minimum value of a unit being £4, and the maximum £100. The unit fines system aimed to even out the effects of fines so that, although the sums to be paid were different, the impact on the offender would be similar. The pilot schemes for the unit fines suggested that fines were paid more quickly and there was a drop in debtors ending up in prison, because of the more realistic assessment of the fines.

Unfortunately, the idea aroused huge public opposition after press coverage of what seemed to be high fines for relatively minor offences and very low fines for the unemployed – despite the fact that even if some of these were unfair, they were less unfair than the previous system. There was public uproar when a man received a £1,200 fine for dropping a crisp packet. As a result, unit fines were abolished, and the courts reverted to their previous practice, except that they are now required to take into account ability to pay when setting fines.

The Government has been considering the reintroduction of the unit fine scheme. The relevant legislative provisions were contained in the Management of Offenders and Sentencing Bill, but were removed during the legislative process.

Fixed penalty fines

In order to clamp down on loutish behaviour, the Criminal Justice and Police Act 2001 has given the police the power to impose fixed penalty fines. These fines can be imposed for such offences as being drunk in a public place and being drunk and disorderly. A police officer may give a person aged 16 and over a penalty notice if there is reason to believe that the person has committed a penalty offence (s. 2). The fine for each offence is fixed by the Home Secretary and can be for up to a quarter of the maximum fine applicable to the offence. Recipients must either pay the fine within 21 days or opt for trial (they will not be marched off to the cashpoint by the police officer, as was originally suggested). If they fail to do either, then a sum which is one and a half times the penalty will be registered against them for enforcement as a fine. If the person pays the fixed penalty fine there is no criminal conviction or admission of guilt associated with the payment of the penalty.

Under s. 237A of the Local Government Act 1972 the Secretary of State can make regulations allowing classes of bye-laws to be enforced by means of fixed penalty notices. In the past, bye-laws have been enforced by going to the magistrates' courts, but few proceedings were being brought in practice, so it is hoped that fixed penalty notices will be quicker and more effective.

The system of fixed penalty fines was tested in a number of pilot schemes before being rolled out nationally. Analysis of the pilot schemes showed that 50 per cent of the fines had not been paid, and there was a problem with people giving false names and addresses.

Advantages of fixed penalty fines

In the past much minor offending escaped sanction because of the need to focus police and court resources on more important matters. It is hoped that fixed penalty fines will provide a quick and efficient way of dealing with low-level, but disruptive, criminal behaviour.

Disadvantages of fixed penalty fines

Fixed penalty fines take place outside the protective framework of the court system, and there is therefore a danger of abuse and corruption.

Custodial sentences

For adult defendants, a custodial sentence means prison. Most of those given custodial sentences do not serve the full sentence in custody, but are released early on licence. If they breach the terms of that licence, then they can be recalled to prison.

Custody plus

John Halliday's report on sentencing (discussed at p. 463) argued that prison sentences of less than 12 months had little meaningful impact on criminal behaviour, because only half of the sentence time was actually served in prison, and the person was then released without conditions. The Prison Service had little opportunity to tackle criminal behaviour as the period served in custody was so short. In addition, such sentences could have long-term adverse effects on family cohesion, employment and training prospects – all of which are key to the rehabilitation of offenders. This was particularly regrettable, as these sentences are used for large numbers of persistent offenders who are likely to reoffend.

Photo 20.1 Wormwood Scrubs, an example of a Victorian prison
Source: © David Hawgood

Halliday recommended that to tackle this weakness in short prison sentences, there should be a new sentence which he described as 'custody plus'. The Government has adopted this reform in the Criminal Justice Act 2003. Under s. 181, all sentences for less than 12 months' custody are replaced by custody plus (or intermittent custody). After spending a maximum of three months in custody, the offender will be released and subjected to at least six months' post-release supervision in the community. The court can attach specific requirements to the sentence, based upon those available under a community sentence. If an offender fails to comply with the terms of the community part of the sentence, he will be returned to custody for 28 days.

Sentences for more than 12 months require the offender to spend half their time in custody (unless they obtain early release on home detention curfew); they are then automatically released and the remainder of their sentence is served under supervision in the community. It is hoped that these reforms will provide a more effective framework within which to address the needs of offenders.

Suspended sentence

Under ss. 189–194 of the Criminal Justice Act 2003 a custodial sentence can be suspended. A court is able to suspend a short custodial sentence for between six months and two years. The offender can be required to undertake certain activities in the community. If the offender breaches the terms of the suspension, the suspended sentence will be activated. Committal of a further offence during the entire length of suspension will also count as breach, and the offender's existing suspended sentence will be dealt with at the time the court sentences him or her for the new offence. Courts have a discretion to review an offender's progress under a suspended sentence.

Suspended sentences were created in 1967 and were intended to be used as an alternative to a custodial sentence. In practice, they have sometimes been used where a community sentence would have been adequate. If the offender then commits another offence the suspended sentence is activated, so that the offender ends up in prison. The Criminal Justice and Immigration Act 2008 abolishes suspended sentences for summary only offences to reduce this problem.

Home detention curfew

Home detention curfews were introduced by the Crime and Disorder Act 1998. Prisoners sentenced to between three months' and four years' imprisonment can be released early (usually 60 days early) on a licence that includes a curfew condition. This requires the released prisoners to remain at a certain address at set times, during which period they will be subjected to electronic monitoring. Most curfews are set for 12 hours between 7 pm and 7 am. The person can be recalled to prison if there is a failure to comply with the conditions of the curfew condition or in order to protect the public from serious harm. Private contractors fit the tag to a person's ankle, install monitoring equipment which plugs into the telephone system in their home and connects with a central computer system, and notify breaches of curfew to the Prison Service.

Research has been carried out by Dodgson *et al.* (2001) into the first 16 months' experience of home detention curfew. It found that only 5 per cent were recalled to prison. The main reasons for recall were breach of the curfew conditions (68 per cent) or a change of circumstances (25 per cent). The use of home detention curfew appeared to have eased the transition from prison to the community. Offenders were very positive about the scheme, with only 2 per cent saying that they would have preferred to have spent their time in prison. Prior to release, over a third of prisoners said that the prospect of being granted home detention curfew influenced their behaviour in prison. Other household members were also very positive about the scheme.

20

Sentencing

TOPICAL ISSUE

Sentences for murder

An area that has caused considerable controversy and litigation in recent years is the question of the release of prisoners sentenced to life imprisonment, and in particular the Home Secretary's involvement in this decision. In the recent past, the final decision as to when murderers should be released on licence lay with a politician, the

▶

Home Secretary. This was found to be in breach of the European Convention in the case of **R (on the application of Anderson)** v **Secretary of State for the Home Department** (2002). The danger was that Home Secretaries might be influenced by issues of political popularity rather than the justice in the particular case. The matter was highlighted in the case of Myra Hindley, who was convicted for life in 1966 for the murder of two children and for her involvement in the killing of a third.

The Home Secretary, however, seems anxious to retain some control in this area. Provisions were added to the Criminal Justice Act 2003 which aim to promote consistency in the sentencing of murderers. Under these provisions, judges are required to slot offenders into one of three categories according to the severity of their crime. For the first category, actual life will be served by those convicted of the most serious and heinous crimes: multiple murderers, child killers and terrorist murderers. For the second category, there is a starting point of 30 years. This category includes murders of police and prison officers and murders with sexual, racial or religious motives. For the third category, the starting point is 15 years. In addition, there are 14 mitigating and aggravating factors which will affect the sentence imposed. Judges are able to ignore these guidelines, provided they explain why. Once the minimum term has expired, the Parole Board will consider the person's suitability for release. If the Parole Board considers that the person no longer poses a significant risk of reoffending it can order their release. They are released on licence for the rest of their lives, and are supervised by the probation service until they are assessed as being fully reintegrated into the community. If they reoffend while under supervision, or if they fail to cooperate, or to keep in contact with the probation service, the licence is revoked by the Lifer Review and Recall Section at the Home Office; a warrant of arrest is issued by Scotland Yard, and they are classed as unlawfully at large until arrested and returned to prison.

There are currently over 12,000 people serving life sentences in England and Wales, which is more than in all 46 other Council of Europe member states combined. Twenty-two people are serving whole-life tariffs in England and Wales (in other words, they are expected to spend the rest of their lives in prison), none in Europe and 25,000 in America (along with 3,500 individuals under sentence of death).

Advantages of custodial sentences

The previous Conservative Government claimed that prison 'works', in the sense that offenders cannot commit crime while they are in prison, and so the public is protected. The current Government claims that prison can be made to work both by protecting the public and by making use of the opportunity for rehabilitation.

Disadvantages of custodial sentences

Fifty-nine per cent of prisoners are reconvicted within two years of being released. In her book, *Bricks of Shame* (1987), Vivienne Stern highlights several reasons why imprisonment lacks any great reformative power, and may even make people more, rather than less, likely to reoffend. Prisoners spend time with other criminals, from whom they frequently acquire new ideas for criminal enterprises; budget cuts have meant there

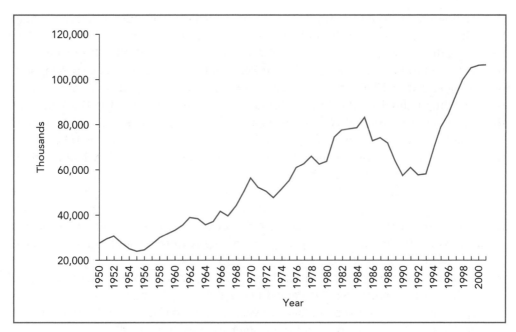

Figure 20.2 Persons sentenced to immediate custody, 1950–2001
Source: Criminal Statistics England and Wales 2001, p. 18 [Figure 1.3]

20

Sentencing

is now little effective training and education in prisons, while the stigma of having been in prison means their opportunities for employment are fewer when they are released; and families often break down, so that the ex-prisoner may become homeless. The result, says Stern, is that 'going straight can present the quite unattractive option of a boring, lonely existence in a hostel or rented room, eking out the Income Support'. All this can also mean that prison punishes the innocent as well as the guilty, with the prisoner's family suffering stigma, financial difficulties, the misery of being parted from the prisoner, and often family breakdown in the end. The research, *Poverty and Disadvantage Among Prisoners' Families* (Smith *et al.,* 2007) noted that about 4 per cent of children experience the imprisonment of their father during their school years. It found that this frequently caused them to suffer emotional and economic hardship, with a negative effect on their personal development.

Stern rejects the idea that prison works because it protects the public. She points out that, although it may prevent the individual offending for a while, the percentage of crime that is actually detected and prosecuted is so small that imprisonment has little effect on the crime rate.

Prisons are also extremely expensive – at £37,500 a year per prisoner, three weeks in prison costs as much as a lengthy community sentence. The Lord Chief Justice pointed out in a public lecture in 2008 that by locking up a person in prison for 30 years, the state is investing a million pounds in punishing that individual. Prisons cost the taxpayer £1.9 billion every year. To this must be added the costs associated with the family breakdown and unemployment that imprisonment frequently causes. As well as those who find themselves in prison through non-payment of fines, many of those actually sentenced to prison have committed relatively minor offences and could be dealt with just as effectively, and far more cheaply, in the community.

The conditions within prisons continue to cause concern. While all prisoners are now supposed to have 24-hour access to toilet facilities, with the practice of 'slopping out' being ended in 1996, other problems remain. A continuing area of concern that has been highlighted in the Prison Ombudsman's report for 1998 is the failure of the Prison Service's internal complaints system to investigate complaints adequately. Lord Woolf, in his inquiry into the prison disturbances that took place in 1990, found that one of the root causes of the riots was that prisoners believed they had no other effective method of airing their grievances.

Where prison conditions are poor, there is an increased risk of suicide. Between 1999 and 2003 a total of 434 people committed suicide in prison. There were over 16,000 incidents of self-harm recorded in 2003. A report of the Joint Committee on deaths in custody in 2004 found that the young, the mentally unstable and women are most at risk.

The number of people in prison has been growing at an alarming rate over recent years. There are currently 82,000 people being held in prison, which is more than double the number that was being held 15 years ago. Lord Carter (2007) has identified five reasons why the prison population has increased so dramatically:

● changes to legislation and sentencing;
● more offenders brought to justice (though the conviction rate has only increased by 5 per cent since 1995);
● increased sentence rates and longer terms;
● greater focus on enforcement of sentences (which means more licence recalls); and
● greater awareness of risk and increased political prominence of public protection.

The growing prison population cannot be explained by an increase in criminal activity because recent years have actually seen an overall drop in crime, including a 41 per cent drop in violent crime and a 59 per cent drop in domestic burglary since 1995.

A Council of Europe study revealed that defendants in English courts get longer sentences for assault, robbery or theft than they do elsewhere in Europe. Average prison populations in Europe are approximately a third lower as a proportion of the population to that of the UK. In 2006 America had a prison population of 737 per 100,000 of the population, the United Kingdom 148, Germany 94, Sweden 82 and Japan 62.

The inevitable result of a growing prison population is prison overcrowding. In 2007 there was such a shortage of prison places that the Government decided to put some prisoners in police cells. This was an unsatisfactory solution to prison overcrowding because it is more expensive than prisons while providing no facilities for education and rehabilitation. Following a recommendation made by Lord Carter (see p. 496), the Government has now decided to build three new, large prisons able to hold 2,500 prisoners. Upon completion in 2014, the UK prisons will have places for 96,000 people. This building programme ignores the advantages of having smaller prisons located near to prisoners' homes.

The benefits of locking more people up in prison are not clear. A report carried out by the businessman Patrick Carter in 2003 estimated that the increased use of custody

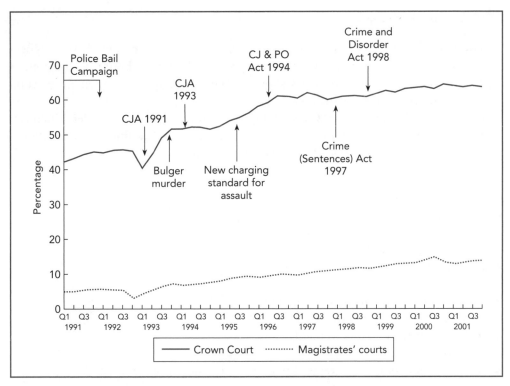

Figure 20.3 Proportion of persons sentenced to immediate custody for indictable offences by type of court, 1991–2001

Source: Criminal Statistics England and Wales 2001, p. 81 [Figure 7.4]

20

Sentencing

had only reduced crime by 5 per cent at the most. The Chief Inspector of Prisons claimed in an interview for *The Guardian* in 2001 that the prison population could be cut to 40,000 if 'the kids, the elderly, the mentally ill, the asylum seekers, those inside for trivial shoplifting or drug offences' were taken away.

In 2004 the Home Office issued a five-year strategic plan (*Cutting Crime – Delivering Justice: Strategic Plan for Criminal Justice 2004–08*). This stated that the Government wished to stop the drift towards longer custodial sentences. In fact, during that period the prison population continued to rise rapidly.

In recent years there has been concern that dangerous offenders have been released on licence, and have subsequently reoffended. There have been suggestions that the Parole Board has been wrong to agree the release of certain individuals and, when they have been released, they have not been adequately supervised by the probation service. Such concerns were expressed in the media following the murder of the wealthy banker, John Monckton, at his home in Chelsea by Damien Hanson when he was on probation. The Parole Board may be giving undue weight to the human rights of the offender rather than the rights of potential victims, but they may also not have sufficient information to make a fully informed decision. Some of the criticism of the probation service may reflect an unrealistic expectation of the level of supervision that can be provided with the level of funding available.

Community sentence

Recent governments have been anxious to emphasise that community sentences impose substantial restrictions on the offender's freedom and should not be seen as 'soft options'. Home Office statistics show that 56 per cent of offenders given community sentences reoffend within two years.

The Criminal Justice Act 2003 has established a single community order which can be applied to an offender aged 16 or over who has committed an imprisonable offence. This order can contain a range of possible requirements. These are:

- an unpaid work requirement;
- an activity requirement;
- a programme requirement;
- a prohibited activity requirement;
- a curfew requirement;
- an exclusion requirement;
- a residence requirement;
- a mental health treatment requirement;
- a drug rehabilitation requirement;
- an alcohol treatment requirement;
- a supervision requirement;
- an attendance centre requirement (where the offender is aged under 25).

Each of these requirements will now be considered in turn.

Unpaid work requirement

The offender can be required to perform, over a period of 12 months, a specified number of hours of unpaid work for the benefit of the community. The number of hours must be between 40 and 300. The kind of work done includes tasks on conservation projects, archaeological sites and canal clearance. This requirement allows useful community work to be done, and may give offenders a sense of achievement which helps them stay out of trouble afterwards.

Controversially, people carrying out unpaid work as part of a community sentence are now required to wear high-visibility jackets branded with the 'community payback' logo. The Minister for Justice has stated that: 'The taxpayer has an absolute right to know what unpaid work is being done to pay back to them for the wrongs the offender has committed.' On the other hand the human rights organisation, Liberty, has described this practice as medieval, unnecessarily humiliating and dangerous, as people wearing these jackets could themselves be the victim of an attack by angry members of the public.

Activity requirement

Under an activity requirement offenders must either present themselves to a specified person, at a specified place, for a maximum of 60 days, and/or take part in specified activities for a certain number of days. An activity requirement may include such tasks as receiving help with employment, group work on social problems and providing reparation to the victim.

Programme requirement

A programme requirement obliges the offender to participate in an accredited programme on a certain number of days. Programmes are courses which address offending behaviour, such as anger management, sex offending and drug abuse.

Prohibited activity requirement

The court can instruct an offender to refrain from participating in certain activities. For example, it might forbid an offender from contacting a certain person, or from participating in specified activities during a period of time. The court can make a prohibited activity requirement which prohibits a defendant from possessing, using or carrying a firearm.

Curfew requirement

An offender can be ordered to remain in a specified place or places for periods of not less than two hours or more than 12 hours in any one day for up to six months. The court should avoid imposing conditions which would interfere with the offender's work or education, or cause conflict with their religious beliefs. A specified person must be made responsible for monitoring the offender's whereabouts. Courts can require offenders to wear electronic tags, in order to monitor that they are conforming to their curfew order.

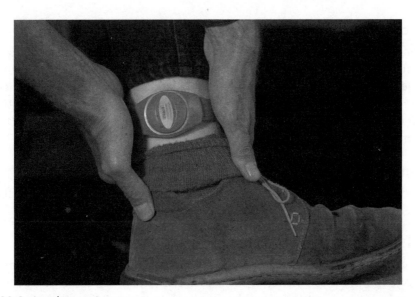

Photo 20.2 An electronic tag
Source: © 67Photo/Alamy

Advantages of curfew orders

Tagging costs about £4,000 a year compared with £37,500 for a prison place. Curfew orders have the potential to keep offenders out of trouble and protect the public, without the disruptive effects of imprisonment. In the US city of Atlanta, a night curfew has been imposed on anyone under 16. This was introduced to protect children, but has also had the effect of considerably reducing juvenile crime. While such use of curfew orders on those who have not been convicted of crimes intrudes on the right to freedom of movement, the results show that, as a sentence, it could prove very useful.

At the moment the electronic tags set off an alarm if a curfew is breached, but cannot identify where the criminal has then gone. The Government is now considering a more technologically advanced system which can track the precise movements of the offender. This could have the advantage, for example, of making sure that a convicted paedophile does not enter a school building.

Disadvantages of curfew orders

The Penal Affairs Consortium have argued that the money spent on electronic tagging would be better spent on constructive options, such as supervision requirements, which work to change offenders' long-term attitudes towards offending. Opponents to electronic tagging claim they are degrading to the person concerned, but their supporters – including one or two well-known former prisoners – point out that it is far less degrading than imprisonment. This argument applies only where tagging is used as an alternative to imprisonment: its opponents claim that it is likely to be used in practice to replace other non-custodial measures. Existing research suggests, however, that curfew orders with tagging are being seen as a genuine alternative to custody (Nuttall, Goldblatt and Lewis (1998)).

Exclusion requirement

An offender can be required to stay away from a certain place or places at set times. Electronic tags can be used to monitor compliance with this requirement. It is aimed at people, such as stalkers, who present a particular danger or nuisance to a victim. An exclusion requirement is similar in many respects to a curfew requirement. However, whereas under a curfew requirement an offender has to remain at a specified place, an exclusion requirement prohibits an offender from entering a specific place.

Residence requirement

A residence requirement obliges the offender to reside at a place specified in the order for a specified period.

Mental health treatment requirement

A court can direct an offender to undergo mental health treatment for certain periods as part of a community sentence or suspended sentence order, under the treatment of a registered medical practitioner or chartered psychologist. Before including a mental health treatment requirement, the court must be satisfied that the mental condition of the offender requires treatment and may be helped by treatment, but is not such that it warrants making a hospital or guardianship order (within the meaning of the Mental Health Act 1983). The offender's consent must be obtained before imposing the requirement.

Drug rehabilitation requirement

As part of a community sentence or suspended sentence the court may impose a drug rehabilitation requirement, which includes drug treatment and testing. In order to impose such a requirement, the court must be satisfied that the offender is dependent on, or has a propensity to misuse, any controlled drug and as such requires and would benefit from treatment. In addition, the court must be satisfied that the necessary arrangements are or can be made for the treatment and that the offender has expressed a willingness to comply with the drug rehabilitation requirement. The treatment provided must be for a minimum of six months.

A court may provide for the review of this requirement, and such reviews must take place if the order is for more than 12 months. Review hearings provide the court with information about the offender's progress, including the results of any drug tests.

Alcohol treatment requirement

A court can require an offender to undergo alcohol treatment to reduce or eliminate the offender's dependency on alcohol. The offender's consent is required. This requirement must last at least six months.

Supervision requirement

The offender can be placed under the supervision of a probation officer for a fixed period of between six months and three years. Home Office research into the probation service (Mair and May, *Offenders on Probation* (1997)) found that 90 per cent of the people supervised thought that their supervision had been useful. The most common reason given for this view was that it offered them someone independent to talk to about their problems. A third mentioned getting practical help or advice with specific problems and about 20 per cent mentioned being helped to keep out of trouble and avoid offending. The research concluded:

> The message contained in this report is a good one for the probation service; it is viewed favourably by most of those it supervises, and seems to work hard at trying to achieve its formal aims and objectives as stated in the National Standards. However this should not lead to any sense of complacency. It is arguable that any agency which provided similar help to that provided by the probation service to the poor and unemployed would be seen in an equally positive light.

Due to staff shortages, particularly in London, some offenders who are subject to a supervision requirement are merely being required to turn up and have their names ticked off.

20

Sentencing

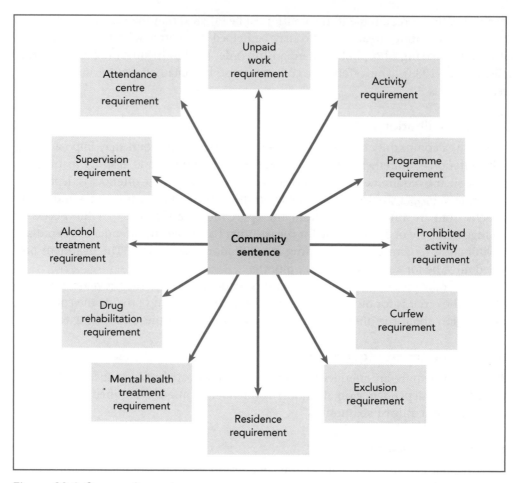

Figure 20.4 Community sentence

Attendance centre requirement

Attendance centres are discussed at p. 518.

Miscellaneous sentences

A range of other sentences are also available to the court. These include the following.

Compensation orders

Where an offence causes personal injury, loss or damage (unless it arises from a road accident), the courts may order the offender to pay compensation. This may be up to £1,000 in a magistrates' court and is unlimited in the Crown Court. Orders can also be made for the return of stolen property to its owner, or, where stolen property has been

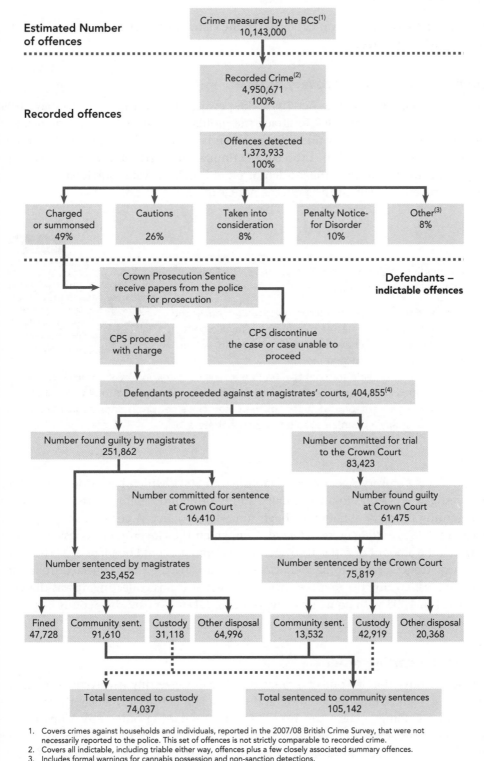

Figure 20.5 Flows through the criminal justice system

Source: Adapted from *Criminal Statistics in England and Wales 2007*, p. 10 [Figure 1.1]

disposed of, for compensation to be paid to the victim from any money taken from the offender when arrested.

Confiscation and civil recovery orders

Under the Proceeds of Crime Act 2002, the powers to confiscate property have been increased. The Act is intended to attack the profits of organised crime. The recovery rates had been disappointing under the previous law. For the first time, the Act permits the use of civil recovery of the proceeds of criminal conduct, even where a person has not been convicted. It puts the burden of proof on the private individual to account for any property for which the source is not clear.

KEY CASE

In the leading case on confiscation orders, **R v May** (2008), the House of Lords said:

> Confiscation orders should deprive defendants of the benefit they have gained from their criminal conduct within the limits of their available means.

> The legislation is intended to deprive defendants of the benefit they have gained from relevant criminal conduct, whether or not they have retained such benefit, within the limits of their available means.
>
> It does not provide for confiscation in the sense understood by schoolchildren . . . but nor does it operate by way of a fine. The benefit gained is the total value of the operation or advantage obtained, not the defendant's net profit after deduction of expenses or any amounts payable to co-conspirators.

The Assets Recovery Agency was established in 2003, which had wide powers both to investigate a person's financial affairs, and to bring proceedings to recover property representing property obtained through unlawful conduct. A consultation paper was issued in 2007, *Asset Recovery Action Plan*, in which the Government considered ways in which the amount of assets recovered from criminals could be increased. The Assets Recovery Agency proved to be ineffective in increasing the sums collected from criminals and was costing the taxpayer twice as much as it was collecting. It was therefore abolished in 2008 with some of its work being taken over by the Serious Organised Crime Agency.

Financial reporting order

Following conviction for one of a range of offences suggesting involvement in organised crime, such as drug importation and money laundering and where there is a risk of repeat offending, a court can issue a financial reporting order. Provisions for this order are contained in the Serious Organised Crime and Police Act 2005. It requires offenders to give the authorities regular information about their financial affairs for up to 20 years, to try to prevent the individual from profiting from any criminal enterprise.

TOPICAL ISSUE

Serious crime prevention orders

Part one of the Serious Crime Act 2007 creates serious crime prevention orders (SCPOs). These are a new type of civil order aiming to prevent the commission of serious crime. The orders mandate or restrict the activities of individuals or organisations for up to five years. Section 5 lists the type of conduct that might be the subject of an order, including the compulsory provision of financial information and the imposition of travel restrictions, but the list is not definitive so the courts can add to this. The order can be made where the court is satisfied that a person over 18 years of age has been involved in serious crime (which includes facilitating another person to commit a serious crime, regardless of whether it was actually committed) and it has reasonable grounds to believe that the order would protect the public by preventing, restricting or disrupting involvement in such criminal activities. Whether a crime is 'serious' is left for the court to decide.

An order can be issued by the Crown Court following a criminal conviction. Where there is no criminal conviction, the prosecution may apply to the High Court for an order in cases where there is insufficient evidence to meet the required standard of proof for a criminal prosecution or, in respect of individuals suspected of being on the fringes of criminal activity, where the prospect of a criminal trial is unattractive for reasons of cost or public interest.

A failure to comply with the terms of an SCPO without reasonable excuse is a criminal offence punishable by up to five years' imprisonment. The media has described these sentences as 'super ASBOs' and there have been suggestions that they could amount to an unjustified invasion of a person's liberty, with insufficient safeguards to prevent injustice.

Mental health orders

Under the Mental Health Act 1983, the Crown Court can order the detention of offenders in hospital on conviction for an imprisonable offence if they are suffering from a mental disorder, the nature or degree of which makes detention in hospital for medical treatment appropriate; and, if psychopathic disorder or mental impairment is present, the court is satisfied that the treatment is likely to help the condition or stop it getting worse. The order can only be made if the court considers such an order to be the most suitable way of dealing with the case. Alternatively, the court may place the offender under the guardianship of a local authority.

Where detention in hospital is ordered by the Crown Court, and it believes the public needs to be protected from the offender, it can make an order restricting their discharge either for a specified period or without limit. A magistrates' court can make an order for detention in a hospital when an offender has been convicted of an imprisonable offence, or even if the offender has not been convicted, if the court is satisfied as to guilt.

There has been growing concern about offences committed by persons benefiting from care in the community. The case of Michael Stone was particularly distressing. He was accused of killing Lin and Megan Russell in a brutal attack in the countryside. It appears that he suffers from a severe personality disorder but could not be detained under the current legislation because his condition was not treatable. The Home Secretary therefore announced plans in 1999 to introduce new powers to detain individuals. These would allow indefinite detention without trial of dangerous persons with severe and untreatable personality disorders. A court could make a care and treatment order where a person posed a significant risk of serious harm to others as a result of their severe personality disorder.

Binding over to be of good behaviour

This order dates back to the thirteenth century and the relevant legislative provisions can be found in the Justices of the Peace Act 1361 and the Magistrates' Courts Act 1980. It can be made against any person who is before a court and has 'breached the peace' – not just the defendant, but also any witness or victim. People who are bound over have to put up a sum of money and/or find someone else to do so, which will be forfeited if the undertaking is broken. A person who refuses to be bound over can be imprisoned, despite the fact that they may not have been convicted of any offence. The order usually lasts for a year.

KEY CASE

The power of the courts to bind people over to be of good behaviour was considered by the European Court of Human Rights in **Steel** v **UK** (1998). The first applicant, Ms Steel, was arrested in 1992 when she walked in front of an armed member of a grouse shoot, preventing him from shooting. She was charged with causing a breach of the peace and was detained for 44 hours. At her trial the complaint of breach of the peace was proved true and she was bound over to keep the peace for 12 months. Her appeal to the Crown Court was dismissed and when she refused to be bound over she was imprisoned for 28 days.

> The English courts' power to bind people over to be of good behaviour does not breach the European Convention on Human Rights.

The second applicant was arrested while demonstrating against the building of a motorway. She had stood in front of a digging machine to stop it being used, and was charged with conduct likely to cause a breach of the peace. She was found to have committed a breach of the peace and was bound over for 12 months. She refused, and was sent to prison for seven days.

The other three applicants were all arrested for handing out leaflets and displaying banners against the sale of weapons at the 'Fighter Helicopter II Conference' in London in 1994.

The applicants claimed that their arrests and detention had not been 'prescribed by law' as required by Art. 5 of the Convention and had amounted to a disproportionate interference with their freedom of expression in breach of Art. 10. The European Court of Human Rights found that the powers to bind over were compatible with the European Convention on Human Rights. It was satisfied that the concept of breach of the peace was clear and that it had been established in English law that it was committed only when a person caused harm to persons or property, or acted in a manner the natural consequence of which was to provoke others to violence.

The court accepted that in the case of the first and second applicants the police had been justified in fearing that their behaviour might provoke others to violence. Bearing in mind the aim of deterrence, and also the importance in a democratic society of maintaining the rule of law and the authority of the judiciary, the court did not find it disproportionate that they were sent to prison.

However, concerning the three protesters at the arms fair, the court found that their behaviour had been entirely peaceful and could not have justified the police in fearing that a breach of the peace was likely to occur. For that reason, it found that their arrest and detention had been unlawful, under both the English law on breach of the peace and under Arts. 5 and 10 of the Convention. The arrest and detention of these protesters had been disproportionate to the aim of preventing disorder or of protecting the rights of others.

Absolute and conditional discharges

If the court finds an offender guilty of any offence (except one for which the penalty is fixed by law), but believes that in the circumstances it is unnecessary to punish the person and a community rehabilitation order is inappropriate, it may discharge the defendant either absolutely or conditionally.

An absolute discharge effectively means that no action is taken at all, and is generally made where the defendant's conduct is wrong in law, but no reasonable person would blame them for doing what they did. A conditional discharge means that no further action will be taken unless the offender commits another offence within a specified period of up to three years. This order is commonly made where the court accepts that the offender's conduct was wrong as well as illegal but the mitigating circumstances are very strong. If an offender who has received a conditional discharge is convicted of another offence during the specified period, they may, in addition to any other punishment imposed, be sentenced for the original offence. A discharge does not count as a conviction unless it is conditional and the offender reoffends within the specified period.

Deferred sentences

Section 1 of the PCC(S)A 2000 allows the courts to defer passing sentence for a period of up to six months after conviction. The Act contains few guidelines on the use of this power, but does state that it can be exercised only with the consent of the offender, and where deferring sentence is in the interests of justice. The Criminal Justice Act 2003 has added that the power to defer passing sentence is exercisable only if offenders undertake to comply with any requirements as to their conduct that the court considers appropriate. Failure to comply with a requirement will result in the offender being brought back to court early for sentence. If the offender commits another offence during the deferment period, the court will deal with both sentences at once.

Deferred sentences are intended for situations where the sentencer has reason to believe that, within the deferral period, the offender's circumstances will materially change, with the result that no punishment will be necessary, or that the punishment imposed should be less than it would have been if imposed at the time of conviction. For example, offenders may make reparation to the victim, settle down to employment or otherwise demonstrate that they have changed for the better.

Disqualification

This is most common as a punishment for motoring offences when offenders can be disqualified from driving. Under ss. 146–147 of the PCC(S)A 2000, a court may disqualify a person from driving as a punishment for a non-motoring offence. A conviction for offences concerning cruelty to animals may also lead to disqualification from keeping pets or livestock.

TOPICAL ISSUE

Anti-social behaviour orders

Anti-social behaviour orders are civil orders issued by a court to protect the public from behaviour that causes harassment, alarm or distress. Section 1 of the Crime and Disorder Act 1998 provides that bodies such as local authorities or the police may apply under civil procedures to a court for an anti-social behaviour order (ASBO). An ASBO can also be ordered as part of a criminal sentence. The order will be made against a person aged ten or over who has acted in an anti-social manner, that is, a manner which is likely to cause harassment, alarm or distress to someone not in the same household as the person described in the order, and who is likely to do so again. Guidance on the legislation provided by the Home Office suggests that typical behaviour which might fall within this provision includes 'serious vandalism or persistent intimidation of elderly people'. The court has power to prohibit that person from doing anything described in the order for a period of not less than two years. For example, a person could be prohibited from entering a certain geographical area. Thus, in 2002, a woman was banned from going near her local police station for three years, as she had been harassing police officers. While the ASBO is obtained using civil procedures, breach of the ASBO can give rise to the criminal sanctions of a fine or five years' imprisonment.

There has been much controversy over the way ASBOs have been used in practice. The pressure groups Liberty, the National Association of Probation Officers (Napo) and the Howard League for Penal Reform have together formed a campaign group, ASBO Concern, calling for a public review of the way anti-social behaviour orders are used. Initially, ASBOs were intended to deal primarily with anti-social behaviour by neighbours and young people, but they are increasingly being used for a wider range of problems. For example, an anti-social behaviour order was issued in 2004 against Sony Music Entertainment (UK) Ltd, to stop flyposting around the country.

A survey published by the probation officers' union, Napo, has revealed that ASBOs are being inappropriately used against the mentally ill (*Anti-Social Behaviour Orders –*

Analysis of the first six years (2004)). As a result, people who are unable to control their behaviour due to mental ill health are being sanctioned, when treatment would actually be more effective and humane. Napo give an example of a man who had been standing on a windowsill and moaning while pretending to dance with a Christmas tree. An ASBO was issued against him banning him from shouting, swearing and banging windows. He breached the order in August 2004, and was imprisoned for two months for continuing to moan in public. He breached the order again and was imprisoned for four months.

By the end of 2003, 42 per cent of all ASBOs were breached and 55 per cent of the breaches resulted in custody. In 2005, 41 per cent of all ASBOs were issued against children aged under 18. Nearly half of children subject to such an order have breached it, with ten young people each week being placed in custody for breaching an ASBO. Custodial sentences are being handed down for breach of an ASBO where the triggering anti-social conduct was not actually criminal.

The local authorities and police feel that it is necessary for photographs of people sanctioned with an ASBO to be made public in order for the ASBO to be effectively enforced. Photographs have been posted on council websites, leaflets distributed and local newspapers informed. There is concern that such publicity simply stigmatises families, could lead to a surge in vigilantism and does nothing to tackle the underlying causes of a person's anti-social behaviour. In **R (on the application of Stanley, Marshall and Kelly)** v **Metropolitan Police Commissioner** (2004) the High Court held that the authorities were entitled to 'name and shame' people who have been subjected to an ASBO, and it did not amount to a breach of their right to a private and family life which is guaranteed by Art. 8 of the European Convention.

Appeals against sentence

The defence may appeal against a sentence considered too harsh, while the prosecution can appeal if they feel the sentence was too low. In addition, ss. 35 and 36 of the Criminal Justice Act 1988 give the Attorney General the power to refer a case to the Court of Appeal where the sentence is believed to have been too lenient.

Problems with sentencing

The role of the judge

We have seen that the sentence in England is traditionally a decision for the judge, which can lead to inconsistent punishments, especially among magistrates' courts. This situation clearly offends against the principle of justice that requires like cases to be treated alike.

The Government has tried to restrict judicial discretion through legislative guidelines and has also set up a Sentencing Advisory Panel, a Sentencing Guidelines Council and a Judicial Studies Board. Overseen by the Ministry of Justice, the functions of the Judicial Studies Board include running seminars on sentencing, which seek to reduce inconsistencies; courses for newly appointed judges; and refresher courses for more experienced members of the judiciary. The Board also publishes a regular bulletin summarising recent legislation, sentencing decisions, research findings and developments in other countries, while the Magistrates' Association issues a *Sentencing Guide for Criminal Offences* to its members.

Other jurisdictions generally allow judges less discretion in sentencing. In the US, for example, many states use 'indeterminate' sentencing by which a conviction automatically means a punishment of, say, one to five years' imprisonment, and the exact length of the sentence is decided by the prison authorities. However, in this country, control of sentencing is seen as an important aspect of judicial independence, and the introduction of more legislative controls has been criticised as interfering with the judiciary's constitutional position.

Racism

Critics of sentencing practice in England have frequently alleged that members of ethnic minorities are treated more harshly than white defendants. For example, in 2001, 21 per cent of the prison population was from an ethnic minority, which is significantly higher than their representation in the general population. This difference becomes much less if only UK nationals are considered, because one in four black people in prison is a foreign national, often imprisoned for illegally importing drugs. Whether these figures actually point to racial discrimination in sentencing is the subject of much debate.

What is clear from recent research is that some members of the ethnic minorities perceive the sentencing process as racist. Research undertaken in 2003 by Roger Hood *et al.* (*Ethnic Minorities in the Criminal Courts: perceptions of fairness and equality of treatment*) investigated how far black and Asian defendants considered that they had been treated unfairly by the courts because of their race. Most complaints about racial bias concerned sentences perceived to be more severe than those imposed on a similar white defendant.

In addition to any racism in the system, the legal and procedural factors which affect sentencing may account for some of the differences in the punishment of black and white offenders. More black offenders elect for Crown Court trial and plead not guilty, which means that if convicted they would probably receive harsher sentences, because the sentences in the Crown Court are higher than those in the magistrates' court and they would not benefit from a discount for a guilty plea. Research by Flood-Page and Mackie in 1998 found that there was no evidence that black or Asian offenders were more likely than white offenders to receive a custodial sentence when all relevant factors were taken into account.

The experience of black people when in the prison system has also given rise to concern. An internal report commissioned by the Prison Service in 2000 found a blatantly racist regime at Brixton prison, where black staff as well as inmates suffered from bullying and harassment. The head of the Prison Service acknowledged that the service is 'institutionally racist' and that 'pockets of malicious racism exist'. He promised to sack all prison officers found to be members of extreme right-wing groups such as the British National Party. Prison officers' training now includes classes on race relations.

s. Cases
). 321

Sexism

There is enormous controversy over the treatment of women by sentencers. On the one hand, many claim that women are treated more leniently than men. In 2001, 19 per cent of known offenders were women. In 2003, women made up only 6 per cent of the prison population, but their numbers are growing. A Home Office study carried out by Hedderman and Hough in 1994 reported that, regardless of their previous records, women were far less likely than men to receive a custodial sentence for virtually all indictable offences except those concerning drugs, and that when they do receive prison sentences these tend to be shorter than those imposed on men. Flood-Page and Mackie also found in 1998 that women were less likely to receive a prison sentence or be fined when all relevant factors were taken into account. This has been variously attributed to the fact that women are less likely to be tried in the Crown Court; chivalry on the part of sentencers; assumptions that women are not really bad, but offend only as a result of mental illness or medical problems; and reluctance to harm children by sending their mothers to prison.

On the other hand, some surveys have suggested that women are actually treated less leniently than men. A 1990 study by the National Association for the Care and Resettlement of Offenders found that one-third of sentenced female prisoners had no previous convictions, compared with 11 per cent of men, and most of them were in prison for minor, non-violent offences. Because they are usually on lower incomes than men, women are thought more likely to end up in prison for non-payment of fines.

Several critics have suggested that women who step outside traditional female roles are treated more harshly than both men and other women. Sociologist Pat Carlen (1983) studied the sentencing of a large group of women, and found that judges were more likely to imprison those who were seen as failing in their female role as wife and mother – those who were single or divorced, or had children in care. This was reflected in the comments made by sentencers, including 'It may not be necessary to send her to prison if she has a husband. He may tell her to stop it', and 'If she's a good mother we don't want to take her away. If she's not, it doesn't really matter.'

Today women represent the fastest growing sector of the prison population, their numbers having more than trebled in the space of ten years, from 1,300 in 1992 to 4,300 in 2002. About one-fifth of the total female prison population have been sentenced as drugs couriers and, of these, some seven out of every ten are foreign nationals (Penny Green, *Drug Couriers: A New Perspective* (1996)). A former HM Chief Inspector of Prisons, Sir David Ramsbotham, has commented: 'There is considerable doubt whether all the women in custody [at Holloway] really needed to be there in order for the public to be protected' (*Report on Holloway Prison* (unpublished, 1997)). The vast majority of women in prison do not commit violent offences and much of their offending relates to addiction and poverty. Prison is not an appropriate, necessary or cost-effective way of dealing with these problems.

The needs of women prisoners have wrongly been assumed to be the same as men. The Chief Inspector of Prisons has emphasised that female prisoners have different social and criminal profiles, as well as different health care, dietary and other needs. The Home Office published a study of women in prison: *Women in Prison: A Thematic Review* (Ramsbotham, 1997). Their survey revealed that the great majority of women in prison come from deprived backgrounds. Over half had spent time in local authority care, had attended a special school or had been in an institution as a child. A third had had a period of being homeless, half had run away from home, half reported having suffered violence at home (from a parent or a partner) and a third had been sexually abused. Forty per cent of sentenced women prisoners had a drug dependency, and alcohol problems were also found to be very common. Almost 20 per cent had spent time in a psychiatric hospital prior to being imprisoned and 40 per cent reported receiving help or treatment for a psychiatric, nervous or emotional problem in the year before coming into prison. Nearly two in five reported having attempted suicide.

The Government has established a three-year plan, called 'The Women's Offending Reduction Programme'. This aims to increase the opportunities for tackling women's offending in the community. Each year about 17,000 children are separated from their mothers when they are put into prison.

Privatisation

Criminal justice has, historically, been regarded as a matter for the state. Recently, however, first under the Conservative Government in the early 1990s, and now under Labour, various parts of the system have been privatised, including 11 prisons. The Home Secretary said in 1998 that all new prisons would be privately built and run. Such moves have not generally been seen as runaway successes. Privatised prison escort services have come in for severe criticism, with prisoners managing to escape or not being brought to the court on time.

TOPICAL ISSUE

A structured sentencing framework

Ess. Cases p. 312 → The Government asked Lord Carter to review the law on sentencing and, in particular, to consider options for improving the balance between the supply and demand for prison places. His report was published in December 2007, entitled *Securing the Future – Proposals for the efficient and sustainable use of custody in England and Wales*. He recommended that a working group should be set up to consider the advantages and disadvantages of replacing our current sentencing arrangements with a structured sentencing system similar to that found in some American states, such as Minnesota and North Carolina. This system involves a permanent Sentencing Commission drawing up a single comprehensive set of sentencing guidelines that are approved by parliament and then rigidly applied by the judges. In Minnesota these guidelines are mandatory, they can only be departed from in exceptional circumstances, and where they are departed from the prosecution and defence have an automatic right of appeal. The system, therefore, significantly restricts the scope for judicial discretion in sentencing. The aim of this approach is to maximise consistency, transparency and predictability and thereby help match the number of prison places to the number of prisoners. In Minnesota and North Carolina, the sentencing system allows accurate forecasting of prison numbers. In Minnesota in 2006 the state was able to predict the prison population to within 0.7 per cent and in North Carolina the over-all prison population of 38,500 was predicted within 11 places. But unexpected social or political changes can render these predictions unsafe.

ss. Cases p. 318 → Following Lord Carter's recommendation, the Government established a working group chaired by Lord Justice Gage. It published its final report in 2008 rejecting the idea of a structured sentencing framework and recommending instead improvements to the existing system of issuing guidelines. The Government looks set to push ahead with reforms. The Coroners and Justice Act 2009 contains relevant provisions which are expected to be bought into force in 2010. These provide for the abolition of the Sentencing Advisory Panel and the Sentencing Guidelines Council. Instead, a Sentencing Council for England and Wales will be established. This will have the power to lay down new sentencing guidelines. Every court will have to follow the relevant guide-lines unless it is satisfied that it would be contrary to the interests of justice to do so.

This reform direction has been criticised by Professor Zander (2008). He has pointed out that the New Zealand Law Commission rejected such reforms on the basis that they were 'too crude and blunt to ensure justice in the individual case' (*Sentencing Guidelines and Parole Reform* (2006)). Meantime, some American states have actually abolished their sentencing commissions because they were considered to have failed.

20

Sentencing

Answering questions

1 (a) **What are the purposes of sentencing and how effective are they?**

and

(b) **How much sentencing discretion does a judge have?**

(a) To answer this part of the question you simply need to state what the purposes of sentenc-ing are and point out the problems with each (pp. 463–8).

(b) Judicial discretion in sentencing has been gradually reduced because:

- Some offences have minimum sentences.
- Some offences have mandatory sentences (for example, murder).
- The Criminal Justice Act 2003 lays down three categories of sentencing for murderers ('Topical issue' on p. 477) and judges have to give reasons if they do not follow these guidelines.
- A judge must, in order to pass a custodial sentence, comply with ss. 43, 152 and 153 of the Criminal Justice Act 2003.
- The tariff system and the Sentencing Guidelines Council potentially restrict the judges' discretion.

- Section 144 of the Criminal Justice Act 2003 requires the judge to take into account a guilty plea when sentencing – see p. 471.

Some sentencing discretion remains, however, for example when the judge imposes an individualised sentence or an exemplary sentence. In writing your conclusion you could draw on the material in the section entitled 'Problems with sentencing: the role of the judge' (p. 493).

You could achieve extra marks by expressing an opinion as to whether or not you think judges should be given more discretion. Certainly it is good that like offences are treated alike. You could also mention Lord Carter's review of sentencing (p. 496) – and the idea of introducing a structured sentencing system that would be rigidly applied by judges.

2 **To what extent is there consistency in sentencing?**

Except where a conviction attracts a mandatory sentence, sentencing is a matter for the trial judge who may exercise significant discretion, notwithstanding sentencing guidelines and tariffs. The Judicial Studies Board conducts seminars on sentencing, publishes bulletins on sentencing decisions and research findings. The overriding principle is that like offences should receive like punishments. In practice there has been concern that judges tend to be white males and are harsher on members of the ethnic minorities, but any discrepancy in sentencing might be explained by other factors (such as not guilty pleas, election for Crown Court jury trial). Research looking at sentences given to females have concluded both that they are treated more leniently and that they are treated more harshly than men – so the picture is unclear. Your conclusion could note that while consistency seems highly desirable, in practice every person is different and their circumstances are different and the sentencing needs to reflect these personal differences in order to achieve justice.

3 **John, aged 40, is charged with manslaughter and has appeared before Claydon magistrates.**

(a) **What are the powers of the magistrates' court to deal with John?**

(b) **How may John obtain funding from the Legal Services Commission?**

(c) **If John is convicted, what sentences might be passed upon him?**

(a) The information needed for this part is covered fully in Chapters 18 and 19 but essentially the powers of the magistrates concern bail and sending the case to the Crown Court for trial, since manslaughter is a crime triable only on indictment.

(b) These issues are covered in Chapter 17 at pp. 347–8.

(c) As we are given no details about the form of manslaughter or the circumstances, and as John is an adult offender, in theory any of the sentencing options described above could be relevant. You need to outline what these options are and the criteria that would be used to decide which of these is imposed on John. He is most likely to receive a custodial sentence.

4 **After conviction, how do judges choose the defendant's sentence?**

You could start your answer to this question by pointing out the important role that judges have traditionally played in sentencing in our system, highlighting the fact that, although there are some mandatory sentences and now greater statutory guidance for judges, they still maintain a wide discretion in sentencing. You could then mention that there are a number of principles which are officially accepted as guiding such judicial decisions but that it is alleged that these decisions may also be affected by certain unadmitted factors, such as racism and sexism.

You can proceed to look at the official factors that determine how judges choose a sentence first. Thus you could discuss the five purposes of sentencing that a judge must have regard to when deciding a sentence under s. 142 of the Criminal Justice Act 2003. You could then move on to looking at the process of sentencing, including a discussion of the statutory guidance, the tariff system and individualised sentences. After this you could examine some of the allegations that racism and sexism also influence judges in arriving at sentencing decisions, mentioning the research studies detailed in the relevant sections above.

Summary of Chapter 20: Sentencing

The Home Office undertook a review of sentencing that was carried out by John Halliday and published in 2001. The Government accepted many of Halliday's recommendations and introduced significant reforms to the sentencing system in the Criminal Justice Act 2003.

Purposes of sentencing

Section 142 of the Criminal Justice Act 2003 states that:

> . . . any court dealing with an [adult] offender in respect of his offence must have regard to the following purposes of sentencing –
>
> (a) the punishment of offenders,
> (b) the reduction of crime (including its reduction by deterrence),
> (c) the reform and rehabilitation of offenders,
> (d) the protection of the public, and
> (e) the making of reparation by offenders to persons affected by their offences.

Sentencing practice

In recent years there has been a considerable amount of legislation trying to control and regulate the sentencing practices of the judges.

Legislation

The legislation applies rules relating to:

- mandatory sentences;
- minimum sentences;
- general restrictions on sentencing;
- dangerous offenders.

The tariff system

In selecting a sentence, judges rely on the tariff system. This system is based on treating like cases alike.

Types of sentence

The judge has the power to impose a wide range of sentences.

Fines
The fine is the most common sentence issued by the court, but there is a major problem with fines not being paid.

Custodial sentences
Adult offenders can be sent to prison. Some offenders will be released early on home detention curfew. The Criminal Justice Act 2003 has introduced custody plus.

Community sentence
The Criminal Justice Act 2003 has established a single community order that can be applied to an offender aged 16 or over. This order can contain a range of possible require-ments. These are:

- an unpaid work requirement;
- an activity requirement;
- a programme requirement;
- a prohibited activity requirement;
- a curfew requirement;
- an exclusion requirement;
- a residence requirement;
- a mental health treatment requirement;
- a drug rehabilitation requirement;
- an alcohol treatment requirement;
- a supervision requirement; and
- an attendance centre requirement (where the offender is aged under 25).

Miscellaneous sentences
A range of other sentences is also available to the court. These include:

- compensation orders;
- confiscation and civil recovery orders;
- serious crime prevention orders;
- financial reporting order;
- mental health orders;
- binding over to be of good behaviour;
- absolute and conditional discharges;
- deferred sentences;
- disqualification;
- anti-social behaviour orders.

Appeals against sentence
The defence may appeal against a sentence considered too harsh, while the prosecution can appeal if they feel the sentence was too low.

Problems with sentencing
The role of the judge
There has been concern that there is inconsistency in sentencing.

Racism

Critics of sentencing practice in England have frequently alleged that members of ethnic minorities are treated more harshly than white defendants.

Sexism

There is enormous controversy over the treatment of women by sentencers.

Privatisation

Criminal justice has, historically, been regarded as a matter for the state. Recently, however, various parts of the system have been privatised, including ten prisons.

Reading list

Anti-Social Behaviour Orders – Analysis of the first six years (2004), London: National Association of Probation Officers.

Campbell, S. (2002) *A review of anti-social behaviour orders* (Home Office Research Study No. 236), London: Home Office.

Carlen, P. (1983) *Women's Imprisonment: A Study in Social Control*, London: Routledge.

Carter, P. (2003) *Managing Offenders, Reducing Crime*, London: Strategy Unit, Home Office.

Chalmers, J., Duff, P. and Leverick, F. (2007) 'Victim impact statements: can work, do work (for those who bother to make them)', *Criminal Law Review* 360.

Dodgson, K. *et al.* (2001) *Electronic monitoring of released prisoners: an Evaluation of the Home Detention Curfew Scheme*, London: Home Office.

Edwards, I. (2002) 'The Place of Victims' Preferences in the Sentencing of "Their" Offenders', *Criminal Law Review* 689.

Ellis, T. and Hedderman, C. (1996) *Enforcing Community Sentences: Supervisors' Perspectives on Ensuring Compliance and Dealing with Breach*, London: Home Office.

Flood-Page, C. and Mackie, A. (1998) *Sentencing During the Nineties*, London: Home Office Research and Statistics Directorate.

Jacobson, J. and Hough, M. (2007) *Mitigation: the role of personal factors in sentencing*, London: Prison Reform Trust.

Mair, G. and May, C. (1997) *Offenders on Probation* (Home Office Research Study No. 167), London: HMSO.

Moore, R. (2003) 'The use of financial penalties and the amounts imposed: The need for a new approach', *Criminal Law Review* 13.

Moore, R. (2004) 'The methods for enforcing financial penalties: the need for a multidimensional approach', *Criminal Law Review* 728.

Nuttall, C., Goldblatt, P. and Lewis, C. (1998) *Reducing Offending: An Assessment of Research Evidence on Ways of Dealing with Offending Behaviour* (Home Office Research Study No. 187), London: Home Office.

Ramsbotham, Sir D. (1997) *Women in Prison: A Thematic Review*, London: Home Office.

Restorative justice: helping to meet local need (2004) London: Office for Criminal Justice Reform.

Review of the Crown Prosecution Service (The Glidewell Report) (1998) Cm 3960, London: HMSO.

Roberts, J. (2008) 'Aggravating and Mitigating Factors at Sentencing: Towards Greater Consistency of Application', [2008] *Criminal Law Review* 264.

Sanders, A., Hoyle C., Morgan, R. and Cape, E. (2001) 'Victim Impact Statements: Don't Work, Can't Work', *Criminal Law Review* 447.

Shapland, J. (2008) *Does Restorative Justice Affect Reconviction?*, Ministry of Justice Research Series 10/08, London: Ministry of Justice.

Thomas, D. (2004) 'The Criminal Justice Act 2003: Custodial sentences', *Criminal Law Review* 702.

Vogt, G. and Wadham, J. (2003) *Deaths in custody: redress and remedies*, London: Liberty.

Wasik, M. (2008) 'Sentencing guidelines in England and Wales – state of the art?' *Criminal Law Review* 253.

White, P. and Power, I. (1998) *Revised Projections of Long Term Trends in the Prison Population to 2005*, London: Home Office.

White, P. and Woodbridge, J. (1998) *The Prison Population in 1997*, London: Home Office.

Whittaker, C. and Mackie, A. (1997) *Enforcing Financial Penalties*, London: Home Office.

Young, W. and Browning, C. (2008) 'New Zealand's Sentencing Council', *Criminal Law Review* 287.

Reading on the Internet

www

The report of John Halliday on sentencing is available at:
http://www.homeoffice.gov.uk/documents/halliday-report-sppu/?version=1

The guide entitled *Restorative justice: helping to meet local needs* (2004), published by the Office for Criminal Justice Reform, is available on the Home Office website at:
http://www.crimereduction.gov.uk/criminaljusticesystem12.htm

The report of the National Association of Probation Officers entitled *Anti-Social Behaviour Orders – Analysis of the First Six Years*, is available on their website:
http://www.napo.org.uk

The consultation paper *Making Sentencing Clearer* (2006) is available on the website of the National Offender Management Service:
http://www.noms.homeoffice.gov.uk

The report by L. Sherman and H. Strang, *Restorative Justice: the Evidence* (2007), is available on the website of the Esmée Fairbairn Foundation at:
http://www.esmeefairbairn.org.uk/docs/RJ_full_report.pdf

The report by R. Smith and others, *Poverty and Disadvantage Among Prisoners' Families* (2007) is available on the website of the Joseph Rowntree Foundation at:
http://www.jrf.org.uk/bookshop/eBooks/2003-poverty-prisoners-families.pdf

The Sentencing Guidelines Council and the Sentencing Advisory Panel share a website which is available at:
http://www.sentencing-guidelines.gov.uk/

The report *Sentencing Guidelines and Parole Reform* (2006) is available on the website of the New Zealand Law Commission at:
http://www.lawcom.govt.nz/UploadFiles/Publications/Publication_126_338_R94.pdf

Lord Carter's report, *Securing the Future – Proposals for the efficient and sustainable use of custody in England and Wales* (2007), is available on the website of the Ministry of Justice at:
http://www.justice.gov.uk/publications/securing-the-future.htm

The consultation paper of the Sentencing Commission Working Group, *A Structured Sentencing Framework and Sentencing Commission* (2008), is available on the website of the Ministry of Justice at:

   http://www.justice.gov.uk/publications/sentencing-commission.htm

A website which gives students the opportunity to choose how they would sentence different offenders can be found at:

   http://www.ezstream.co.uk/coi/

Visit www.mylawchamber.co.uk/ElliottELS to access multiple-choice questions, flashcards and practice exam questions to test yourself on this chapter.

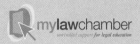

20

Sentencing

21

Young offenders

This chapter discusses:

- when criminal liability can be imposed on young people;
- young offenders and the police;
- the imposition of bail on young people;
- reprimands and warnings;
- the criminal trial; and
- sentencing young offenders.

Introduction

Offenders who are under 18 years old are dealt with differently from adults by the criminal justice system. There have in the past been a number of reasons for this, including a belief that children are less responsible for their actions than adults, a wish to steer children away from any further involvement in crime, and the feeling that sentencing can be used to reform as well as, or instead of, punishing them. However, in recent years the mood towards young offenders has become more severe due to a widespread public perception of mounting youth crime and the killing of the toddler James Bulger by two 10-year-old boys. The Audit Commission found that in some neighbourhoods 26 per cent of known offenders were aged under 18 (*Misspent Youth: Young People and Crime* (1997)). At present one in three young men is found guilty of a criminal offence by the age of 22 and nine out of ten under-17s are reconvicted within two years of release from a custodial sentence. Youth crime costs the public services £1 billion a year. In fact, some of the public's fears are exaggerated. The Home Office British Crime Survey for 1998 found that two-thirds of the people questioned for the survey believed young people were becoming increasingly involved in crime between 1995 and 1997, while official statistics showed the numbers remaining constant, or declining. Only 17 per cent of known offenders are aged between 10 and 17.

21

Young offenders

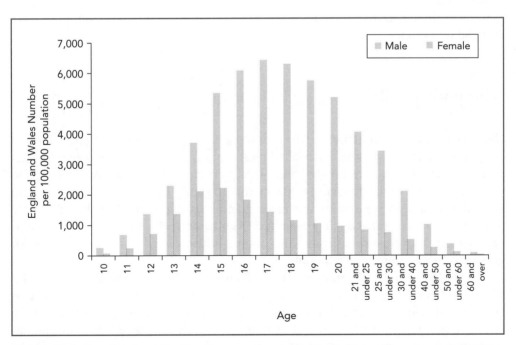

Figure 21.1 Persons found guilty of, or cautioned for, indictable offences per 100,000 population by age group, 2007

Source: Criminal Statistics in England and Wales 2007, p. 45 [Figure 3.3]

The Government stated in its 1998 White Paper, *No More Excuses – A New Approach to Tackling Youth Crime in England and Wales* (1998) that it wanted to reverse the 'excuse culture' that had developed within the youth justice system. A change in approach was signalled by the passing of the Crime and Disorder Act 1998. This piece of legislation was central to the current Government's approach to youth crime. The Act sought to reduce offending by young people in two ways. First, by promoting strategies for the prevention of youth crime and, secondly, by creating a range of extended powers available to the police and the courts to deal with young offenders and their parents. Many of its key provisions are now contained in the Powers of Criminal Courts (Sentencing) Act 2000.

Section 37 of the 1998 Act specifies that the aim of the youth justice system is to prevent offending by young people. A Youth Justice Board for England and Wales has been established under s. 41 of the 1998 Act. Its principal functions are to monitor, set standards and promote good practice for the youth justice system. Its main focus to date has been to try to speed up the youth justice system, encourage the creation of programmes aimed at preventing youth crime and assist in the implementation of the provisions in the 1998 Act concerning young offenders.

Local authorities must formulate and implement a youth justice plan setting out how youth justice services are to be provided and funded (s. 40). They must, acting in cooperation with police authorities, probation committees and health authorities, establish one or more youth offending teams whose duty it is to coordinate the provision of youth justice services and to carry out their functions under the youth justice plan (s. 39).

Some of these reforms appear to have been successful as youth reoffending in 2002 dropped by a quarter.

Criminal liability

Under criminal law children under 10 cannot be liable for a criminal offence at all. In the past there was also a well-established presumption that children between the ages of 10 and 14 were not criminally liable. This presumption could be rebutted by the prosecution successfully adducing evidence that the child knew right from wrong and knew that what they were doing was more than just naughty. In 1998 this rebuttable presumption was repealed by the Crime and Disorder Act 1998. In this respect children aged 10 and above are now treated like adults. British children are almost alone in Europe in being regarded as criminals at the age of 10.

The United Nations Committee on the Rights of the Child has condemned the United Kingdom for imposing criminal liability on young children. In a report in 2002, it criticised the 'high and increasing numbers of children being held in custody at earlier ages for lesser offences and for longer custodial sentences'. It has called on the Government to raise the age of criminal responsibility to 14 or above, which would bring it into line with most other European countries.

Young people and the police

Most of the police powers concerning adults also apply to young suspects but, because they are thought to be more vulnerable, some extra rules apply. For example, Code C of the Police and Criminal Evidence Act 1984 (PACE) states that young suspects should not be arrested or interviewed at school and, when brought to a police station, they should not be held in a cell. The police must find out who is responsible for the young person's welfare as quickly as possible and then inform that person of the arrest, stating where and why the suspect is being held. If the person responsible for their welfare chooses not to come to the police station, the police must find another 'appropriate adult', who should be present during the various stages of cautioning, identification, intimate searches and questioning. Where the suspect's parent is not present the appropriate adult will often be a social worker, though it may be anyone defined as a responsible adult, except someone involved in the offence, a person of low intelligence, someone hostile to the young person or a solicitor acting in a professional capacity.

The role of the adult is to ensure that the young person is aware of their rights, particularly to legal advice. The adult should be told that their function is not just that of observer, but also of adviser to the young person, ensuring that the interview is conducted properly and facilitating communication between suspect and interviewer. Unfortunately, research by Brown *et al.* (1992) suggests that some adults are so over-awed by the whole process that they are of little use as advisers; they may even side with the interviewer.

Remand and bail

A young person charged with an offence has the right to bail under the Bail Act 1976 (see Chapter 18). Where the police refuse bail, children under 17 are usually remanded to local authority accommodation, which can range from remand fostering schemes to accommodation with high levels of supervision. Secure accommodation can, however, be used if children persistently offend while on bail. Those under 17 should not usually be held in police custody before being brought to court; instead they should be held in local authority accommodation.

Reprimands and warnings

People involved in administering the criminal justice system have, in the past, been concerned to try to stop a young offender from a cycle of court appearances, punishments and further offending, often aggravated by contact with other offenders during the process. The police therefore tried to divert the young offenders from the criminal justice system by issuing them with a caution rather than bringing a prosecution. A caution is an official warning about what the person has done, designed to make them see that they have done wrong and deter them from further offending (it is quite separate from the caution administered before questioning, concerning the right to silence).

However, there was growing concern that the caution procedure was being overused in practice, so that young repeat offenders were acting with a sense of impunity. Section 65 of the Crime and Disorder Act 1998 therefore abolished the system of cautions for young offenders aged between 10 and 17, and replaced them with a new system of reprimands and warnings.

Section 65 of the Crime and Disorder Act 1998 provides that a first offence can be met with a reprimand, a final warning or a criminal charge, depending on its serious-ness. The usual sequence will be a reprimand for a first offence, followed by a warning for a subsequent offence, followed by a charge on a third occasion (or a warning where the offender has not received a warning for at least two years and the offence is not serious enough for a charge).

Before the police can issue a reprimand or warning, four conditions must be satisfied:

1 there must be sufficient evidence;
2 the young person must admit the crime;
3 they must have no previous convictions; and
4 it is not in the public interest to bring a prosecution.

The consent of the young offender is not required (**R (on the application of R)** *v* **Durham Constabulary** (2005)). The reprimand or warning will be given in the presence of an 'appropriate' adult. Where a warning has been given, the officer must refer the offender to a youth offending team as soon as practicable. The youth offending team will assess the offender to determine whether a rehabilitation scheme aimed at preventing the person from reoffending is appropriate. Where it is appropriate, a scheme should be established for the offender.

Youth conditional caution

Youth conditional cautions were introduced by the Criminal Justice and Immigration Act 2008. They aim to reduce the number of young people being taken to court for a low-level offence. These cautions are available for children aged between 10 and 17 (though they are initially being piloted on 16 to 17 year olds). This type of caution can be issued where the offender has not previously been convicted of an offence, admits guilt and consents to the caution. The conditions must be approved by the Crown Prosecution Service. They may include a fine or an attendance requirement. If the offender does not satisfy the conditions, the prosecution has the right to bring a pros-ecution for the original offence.

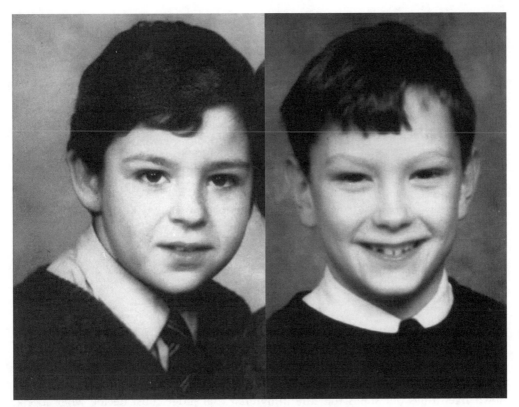

Photo 21.1 Jon Venables and Robert Thompson as children
Source: Mercury Press

Trial

Young offenders are usually tried in youth courts (formerly called juvenile courts), which are a branch of the magistrates' court. Other than those involved in the proceedings, the parents and the press, nobody may be present unless authorised by the court. Parents or guardians of children under 16 must attend court at all stages of the proceedings, and the court has the power to order parents of older children to attend.

Young persons can, in limited circumstances, be tried in a Crown Court: for example, if the offence charged is murder, manslaughter or causing death by dangerous driving. They may sometimes be tried in an adult magistrates' court or the Crown Court if there is a co-defendant in the case who is an adult. Following a Practice Direction, discussed below, a separate trial should be ordered unless it is in the interests of justice to do otherwise. If a joint trial is ordered, the ordinary procedures apply 'subject to such modifications (if any) as the court might see fit to order'.

The trial procedures for young offenders have been reformed in the light of a ruling of the European Court of Human Rights in **T** v **UK and V** v **UK** (2000). This found that Jon Venables and Robert Thompson, who were convicted by a Crown Court of murdering the 2-year-old James Bulger in 1993, did not have a fair trial in accordance with Art. 6 of the European Convention on Human Rights. It concluded that the criminal procedures adopted in the trial prevented their participation:

Young defendants will not receive a fair trial in accordance with the European Convention unless the criminal court procedures are adapted to allow them to participate in a meaningful manner.

> The public trial process in an adult court with attendant publicity was a severely intimidating procedure for eleven year old children . . . The way in which the trial placed the accused in a raised dock as the focus of intense public attention over a period of three weeks, had impinged on their ability to participate in the proceedings in any meaningful manner.

Following the decision in the Thompson and Venables case, a Practice Direction was issued by the Lord Chief Justice laying down guidance on how young offenders should be tried when their case is to be heard in the Crown Court. The language used by the Practice Direction follows closely that used in the European decision. It does not lay down fixed rules but states that the individual trial judge must decide what special measures are required by the particular case taking into account 'the age, maturity and development (intellectual and emotional) of the young defendant on trial'. The trial process should not expose that defendant to avoidable intimidation, humiliation or distress. All possible steps should be taken to assist the defendant to understand and participate in the proceedings. It recommends that young defendants should be brought into the court out of hours in order to become accustomed to its layout. Jon Venables and Robert Thompson had both benefited from these familiarisation visits. The police should make every effort to avoid exposure of the defendant to intimidation, vilification or abuse.

As regards the trial, it is recommended that wigs and gowns should not be worn and public access should be limited. The courtroom should be adapted so that, ordinarily, everyone sits on the same level. In the Bulger trial, the two defendants sat in a specially raised dock. The decision to raise the dock had been taken so that the defendants could view the proceedings, but the European Court of Human Rights noted that, while it did accomplish this, it also made the defendants aware that everyone was looking at them. Placing everyone on the same level should alleviate this problem. In addition, the Practice Direction states that young defendants should sit next to their families or an appropriate adult and near their lawyers.

The Practice Direction suggests that only those with a direct interest in the outcome of the trial should be permitted inside the courtroom. Where the press are restricted, provision should be made for the trial to be viewed through a CCTV link to another court area.

It seems that in most other European countries, children aged under 14 who commit offences do not appear before criminal courts, but are dealt with by civil family courts as children in need of compulsory measures of care.

Sentencing

Sentencing for young offenders has always posed a dilemma: should such offenders be seen as a product of their upbringing and have their problems treated, or are they to be regarded as bad, and have their actions punished? Over the past couple of decades, sentencing policy has swung between these two views. In 1969, the Labour Government took the approach that delinquency was a result of deprivation, which could be 'treated', and one of the aims of the Children and Young Persons Act of that year was to decriminalise the offending of young people. Instead of going through criminal proceedings, they would be handed over to the social services, under either a supervision order or a care order, the latter giving the social services the power to take the young person into some form of custody. The magistracy constantly fought against this approach and, when a Conservative Government was elected in 1970, they declined to bring much of the Act into force and the care order provisions have now been repealed.

The opposite approach introduced by the Conservatives led to the UK having a higher number of young people locked up than any other west European country, but reconviction rates of 75–80 per cent suggested that this was benefiting neither the young offenders themselves, nor the country as a whole.

Since 1982, the philosophy behind the legislation has been that the sentencing of young people should be based on the offence committed and not on the offender's personal or social circumstances, or the consequent chances of reform. Following the passing of the Criminal Justice and Immigration Act 2008, when sentencing a young offender the courts must have regard to:

- the principal aim of the youth justice system to prevent offending;
- the welfare of the offender; and
- the purposes of sentencing.

Section 9 of the 2008 Act lays down the purposes of sentencing young offenders. These are:

- punishment;
- reform and rehabilitation;
- the protection of the public;
- the making of reparation by offenders to persons affected by their offences.

Custodial sentences

Currently, the courts may not pass a sentence of imprisonment on an offender under the age of 18. Such offenders may be detained in other places, such as a young offenders' institution or local authority accommodation but, in order to pass a sentence of this

21

Young offenders

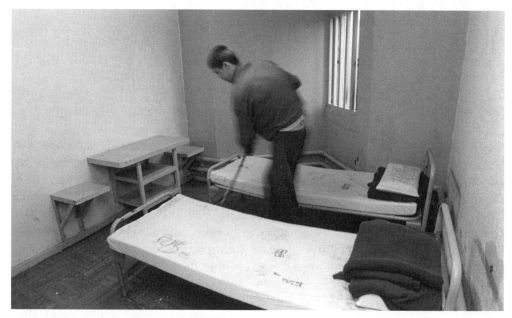

Photo 21.2 Feltham young offenders' institution
Source: © Photofusion Picture Library/Alamy

kind, the court must satisfy the same conditions as for adults (discussed in Chapter 20) and in some cases additional criteria as well.

There has been a rapid increase in the number of people under the age of 18 being placed in custody. Between 1993 and 2005 this number increased from 1,300 to 3,400.

TOPICAL ISSUE

Young people in custody

Placing young people in custody is hugely controversial as any criminal conduct is likely to be a reflection of an unsatisfactory childhood for which they themselves are not to blame. In addition, young people are, by definition, vulnerable and when they are placed in custody the conditions of their detention are very important, or they risk being inhumane. The quality of the custodial accommodation has on occasion given rise to concern. For example, large sums of money have been spent developing the Feltham young offenders' institution near Heathrow Airport. It is now the largest such institution in the UK, with places for 900 young offenders. In 1999 Sir David Ramsbotham was Her Majesty's Chief Inspector of Prisons. He reported that the conditions in Feltham were 'unacceptable in a civilised society'. As the inspector makes clear in a blistering report, the problem was not one of lack of resources, but of staff attitudes and management. This is exemplified by the Inspectorate finding two cases of appalling bedding conditions while there were new and unused mattresses being held in storage. Cell and common areas were dilapidated, dirty and cold. Despite ample stocks of available clothing in the central stores, the personal clothing provision was pitifully inadequate. All meals had to be taken not in dining rooms but in dirty cells with filthy toilets. Most of the youngsters were locked up for 22 hours a day. A 16-year-old boy who had been on the unit for three months told the inspector: 'I have nothing to do. I get hungry and there's nothing to distract me. If I get depressed, I talk to the chaplain and ask him to pray for me. Most of the time I sleep. My mum's not home during the day and I'm not allowed to phone her in the evening.' The report concluded that 'there were too many examples of distant and disinterested staff throughout the institution who were palpably failing to meet the health and welfare needs of the young people in their charge'. Sir David Ramsbotham has gone as far as describing the conditions in some institutions as 'institutionalised child abuse'.

Twenty-nine children died in custody between 1990 and 2005. Of the children who died, 27 took their own lives, one boy died while being restrained by staff, and one young Asian boy, Zahid Mubarke, was killed by his cell mate. An inquiry was established to look at the death of Zahid Mubarke and a report was published in 2006. This concluded that Mubarke's death could have been prevented and that improper attitudes to ethnic minority prisoners, particularly Muslims, contributed to the death. It recommended that a new concept of 'institutional religious intolerance' should be recognised by the Home Office, adapting the concept of institutional racism that had been developed by the Stephen Lawrence Inquiry, as institutional prejudice can be on the basis of religion as well as race. This recommendation has been adopted in the Equality Act 2006. The Act prohibits discrimination by public authorities on the grounds of religion or belief.

The Audit Commission (2004) has concluded that placing young offenders in custody is the most expensive and least effective way of tackling crime. Eighty-four per cent of young offenders are reconvicted within two years after their release from custody.

Detention 'during Her Majesty's pleasure'

Under the Powers of Criminal Courts (Sentencing) Act 2000, s. 90 an offender convicted of murder who was under 18 when the offence was committed must be sentenced to be detained indefinitely, known as 'during Her Majesty's pleasure'.

This form of sentence was considered by the House of Lords in **R** *v* **Secretary of State for the Home Department, ex parte Venables and Thompson** (1997). The two applicants had been convicted of the murder of James Bulger. They had been 10 years old at the time of the offence and were given a sentence of detention during Her Majesty's pleasure. The Home Secretary received several petitions signed by thousands of people demanding that the boys serve at least 25 years in custody. In 1994 the Home Secretary, applying the same procedures to children detained at Her Majesty's pleasure as to adults given a mandatory life sentence, decided that the minimum sentence that they should serve was 15 years. The case was taken to the European Court of Human Rights. In **T** *v* **UK** and **V** *v* **UK** (2000) the court held that it was not compatible with the Convention for the Home Secretary to set tariffs in the case of detention during Her

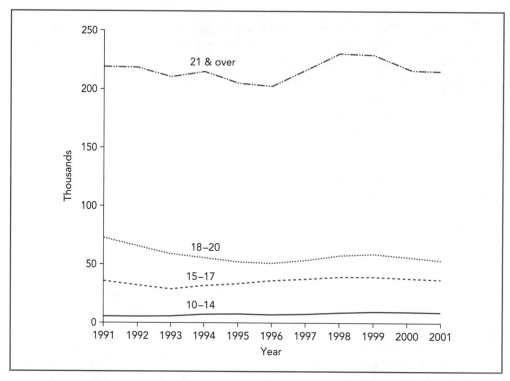

Figure 21.2 Persons sentenced for indictable offences, by age, 1991–2001
Source: Criminal Statistics England and Wales 2001, p. 78 [Figure 7.1]

Majesty's pleasure. In response to this finding the Criminal Justice and Court Services Act 2000 makes provision for the sentencing court to set the tariff in these cases.

Detention under PCC(S)A 2000, s. 91

The Powers of Criminal Courts (Sentencing) Act 2000, s. 91 provides that where a person aged 10 or over has been convicted in the Crown Court of an offence with a maximum sentence of 14 years' imprisonment or more, the court may pass a sentence not exceeding that maximum.

Under the Crime (Sentences) Act 1997, s. 28 the Home Secretary must release on licence a life prisoner who was under 18 at the time of the offence when directed to do so by the Parole Board. If a young person on licence is recalled to prison, then the recall will only be for 28 days and then they will be released again.

Detention and training orders

The only custodial sentence available in the youth court is a detention and training order of up to two years. The use of custody against young children is particularly controversial as, by definition, this involves their removal from their family. Under s. 100 of the PCC(S)A 2000 the courts can make a detention and training order. Such an order must be for a term of between four and 24 months. Half this period will be spent in detention and the other half under supervision. The detention period can be served in any secure accommodation deemed suitable by the Home Secretary: for example, a Young Offenders' Institution, Secure Training Centre, Youth Treatment Centre or local authority secure unit. The order will be available initially for offenders aged at least 12 years, but the Home Secretary has power to extend it to 10 and 11 year olds. The sentence of detention in a Young Offenders' Institution will remain available for offenders aged 18 to 20 years.

The privately run Medway Secure Training Centre in Kent was completed in 1998 in order to detain 12 to 14 year olds. This has places for 40 trainees. As the children detained are very young, it is important that they can maintain links with their families during their detention. Many will be detained far away from home and there will be an assisted visits scheme financed by the Home Office for visits on a weekly basis and arrangements for contact through letters and telephone calls. The training and education programmes will include education for 25 hours a week based on the national curriculum, one hour daily for tackling offending behaviour and crime avoidance, regular practical tuition in social skills and domestic training. There will also be the opportunity to acquire and develop interests to occupy leisure time while in custody and after release.

It is debatable whether it is necessary to impose custodial sentences on children by means of a detention and training order. The vast majority of crimes committed by this age group are minor property offences, and for more serious cases s. 91 of the PCC(S)A 2000 applies. Given the problems associated with custodial sentences, putting young persons at risk of custody for more minor offences may not be effective in crime reduction in the long term.

The tariff

Because the maximum custodial sentences for young offenders are usually quite short, the tariff approach described in the chapter on sentencing is of limited application to the sentencing of young offenders, except in the sense that young offenders can usually rely on their youth as strong mitigation.

ss. Cases p. 331 → ## Referral orders

Most young offenders appearing before a youth court for the first time are given a mandatory referral to a youth offender panel if they plead guilty. Following a change made by the Criminal Justice and Immigration Act 2008, a referral order can also be made on a second conviction if the offender did not receive a referral order for the first conviction but was bound over to keep the peace or received a conditional discharge. Exceptionally, the courts can make a second referral order. This order was created by the Youth Justice and Criminal Evidence Act 1999, and the relevant legislative provisions are now contained in PCC(S)A 2000, s. 16. Referral orders are automatically made for first-time convictions where the offence is imprisonable, the sentence is not fixed by law and where a custodial sentence is not appropriate. The court has a discretion to make a referral order if the defendant has pleaded guilty to a single non-imprisonable offence and this is their first conviction. The youth offender panel agrees a 'programme of behaviour' with the young offender, the primary aims of which are the prevention of reoffending and restorative justice (in other words, that the offender pays back the victim or society in some way). Once agreed the terms of the programme of behaviour are written in a youth offender contract. This may require the offender, among other things, to compensate financially or otherwise victims or other people whom the panel consider to have been affected by the offence; to attend mediation sessions with victims; to carry out unpaid work in the community or to observe prescribed curfews. The order is administered by the local youth offending team (mentioned at p. 506). Subsequent meetings will be arranged with the panel to review compliance with the contract and a final meeting will determine whether the contract has been satisfactorily completed. The courts have a discretion to discharge referral orders early for good behaviour or extend the term of the order for up to three months at the recommendation of the youth offender panel, for example, when dealing with cases of breach.

It is hoped that this procedure will prove more effective than the traditional court sentencing process, which the Home Secretary has criticised in Parliament, saying:

> [T]he young offender is, at best, a spectator in a theatre where other people are the actors. At worst, the young offender is wholly detached and contemptuous of what is going on . . . never asked to engage his brain as to what he has done, or why he hurt the victim.

In many ways the sentence provides the young offender with a second chance. They can admit their guilt knowing what sentence they will receive. Their future employment prospects are not unduly damaged as the offence is deemed spent on the completion of the sentence so that they do not have a criminal record.

Reparation orders

Under s. 73 of the PCC(S)A 2000 a court can hand down a reparation order requiring an offender under the age of 18 to make reparation commensurate with the seriousness of the offence, to the victim or to the community at large. Before making such an order, the court must obtain a report as to what type of work is suitable for the offender and the attitude of the victim or victims to the proposed requirements (PCC(S)A 2000, s. 74). Guidance from the Home Office indicates that the order may require the writing of a letter of apology to the victim, help to be given in repairing damage caused by the offending conduct, the cleaning of graffiti, weeding a garden, collecting litter or doing other work to help the community. The work required must not exceed 24 hours over a period of three months. Most importantly, the order may require a meeting with the victim in an attempt to make them understand the emotional and physical damage their actions have caused. For example, a burglar frequently thinks that a burglary will merely require the victim to make an insurance claim. They do not realise the fear and pain it actually causes, partly because traditionally the criminal justice system has been very impersonal. Reparation orders try to personalise the system, by putting offenders face to face with victims, forcing them to see the pain they have caused. The order may be combined with a compensation order if the court considers

.ss. Cases
p. 333 → that financial compensation would also be appropriate. These orders are part of a system of restorative justice, and are becoming increasingly important in the youth justice system.

In the 1998 British Crime Survey, 60 per cent of respondents approved of the concept of reparation orders, though only 40 per cent would be prepared to meet the offender. The orders not only help to rehabilitate criminals, but also help victims and their families come to terms with their feelings of fear and anger caused by the crime and give them positive input into the process of getting the offender to make amends. A small pilot study carried out in the Thames Valley area found that the young offenders who met the victims in controlled mediation sessions were half as likely to reoffend as those who were given police cautions. In Australia, where restorative justice is practised more widely, there has been a 38 per cent reduction in reoffending after violent criminals met their victims.

Community sentences

A range of youth community orders have been developed to tackle the problem of young offenders.

Supervision orders

These are applied to offenders aged between 10 and 16, and require a probation officer or social services department to supervise the offender for up to three years. The order is basically a junior version of probation, except that a stronger emphasis is placed on assisting the personal development of the young person; it was introduced by the

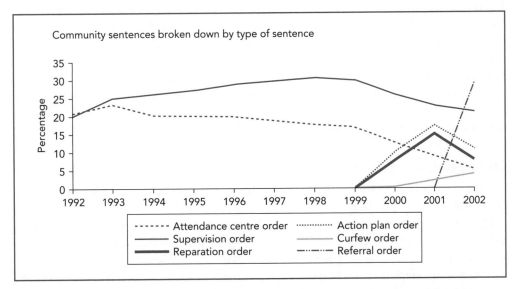

Figure 21.3 Percentage of male offenders aged 10 to 14 sentenced for indictable offences who received community sentences, broken down by sentence, 1992–2002

Source: Criminal Statistics England and Wales 2002, p. 90 [Figure 4.10]

Children and Young Persons Act 1969 to replace community rehabilitation orders for young offenders. The consent of a young person to a basic supervision order is not required.

As with community rehabilitation orders, the supervisor must assist, advise and befriend the offender. Schedule 6 to the PCC(S)A 2000 lays down certain requirements that can be included as part of a supervision order. The young offender can be ordered to live in specified accommodation, attend a particular place, take part in set activities, or any combination of the three, for up to 180 days. The purpose of such requirements is to remove the young person from their home environment and make them take part in challenging activities – these might include rock climbing, pot-holing or even simply attending a local youth club. Youth court magistrates, after consultation with the supervisors, can also specify activities which the offender should not participate in; for this, consent must be obtained from the young person and a parent or guardian. A young offender of compulsory school age can be ordered to comply with arrangements for their education.

If an offender breaches a requirement in a supervision order and the supervisor brings this to the court's attention, the court may change the order, fine the offender up to £100, or make an attendance centre order. If they have reached the age of 17, the court may discharge the order and pass a new sentence for the original offence.

Young offenders over 16 may be made subject to a community rehabilitation order.

Attendance centre orders

An offender under 25 convicted of an imprisonable offence may be ordered to go to an attendance centre for a specified number of hours spread over a certain period of time. The number of hours of attendance that may be ordered is not less than 12 (unless the offender is under 14 and 12 hours seems excessive), and not more than 24 in the case of those under 16, and 36 for those aged 16 to 25. Breach of an attendance centre order may result in the offender being sentenced again for the original offence. The centres are normally run by the police, and tend to involve attendance on Saturday afternoons for physical education classes or practical courses. Unless there are special circumstances, such an order should not be made if the offender has previously been sentenced to detention in a young offenders' institution.

Curfew orders

A court can impose a curfew order with electronic monitoring of up to six months on an offender under the age of 16 years.

Compliance with the curfew order can be monitored through the use of an electronic tag. The use of electronic tagging on young offenders was piloted in two schemes, the results of which were not particularly promising. In Manchester 39 per cent of young offenders breached the curfew order. The majority of the offenders spent their time at home watching more television or sleeping. There is also a danger that some children will wear their tags with pride, seeing them as trophies to be shown off to their peers.

Under the Anti-social Behaviour Act 2003 curfews can be imposed on whole neighbourhoods. The curfew can ban for a specified period children under 16 from being in a public place between 9 pm and 6 am unless they are accompanied by an adult. A police officer who has reasonable cause to believe a child to be in contravention of the ban may inform the local authority of the contravention. To date, the police have imposed 150 local curfews, which cover large parts of the country including much of central London. These are the first curfews we have seen in Britain since the Second World War. No other European country imposes curfews on young people. The legality of a curfew order imposed in Richmond, Surrey, was challenged by a teenage boy in **R (on the application of W) v Commissioners of Police of the Metropolis** (2005). The Court of Appeal held that the Act allowed police to use reasonable force to remove children from a public place.

Exclusion orders

These are discussed at p. 484.

Action plan orders

Action plan orders were introduced in 1998 and are now contained in s. 69 of the PCC(S)A 2000. They are tailored to address the cause of the young person's offending behaviour with the aim of securing the rehabilitation of the offender or the prevention of further offending. Under such an order, a young offender under the age of 18 who is convicted of an offence will be placed under supervision for a maximum of three months and obliged to comply with a series of requirements with respect to their actions and whereabouts for a specified period. The Home Office guidance lists examples of requirements to include attendance at anger management classes, motor education projects, drug or alcohol misuse programmes or specified remedial educational classes. The action plan order cannot be combined with a custodial sentence or any other community sentence.

Parents of young offenders

Where a young offender is under 16, a parent or guardian must be required to attend the court hearing, unless the court considers that this would be unreasonable. If the offender is convicted, the court is required to bind over the parents to take proper care and exercise proper control over their child; the courts also have discretion to do this in the case of 16 or 17 year olds. Although the consent of the parents is required, an unreasonable refusal can attract a fine of up to £1,000. Parents or guardians can also be bound over to ensure that the young offender complies with a community order (PCC(S)A 2000, s. 150).

Where an offender under 16 is sentenced to a fine, the parents are required to pay it. The court may also order parents to pay in the case of 16 and 17 year old children. The fine will be assessed taking into account the financial situation of the parent, rather than the young offender. Where a local authority has parental responsibility for a young person who is in their care, or has provided accommodation for them, it is to be treated as the young person's parent for these purposes. Where a fine has not been paid, the courts can impose a youth default order, which requires a 16 or 17 year old child to carry out unpaid work, or imposes a curfew or attendance centre requirement.

In 1997 the Home Office published a study, *Women in Prison: A Thematic Review*. It noted that when fines for juvenile offences are imposed on the parent or guardian, this is usually in practice the mother, often alone, and coping in difficult circumstances. If she does not (or cannot) pay the fine, she runs the risk of imprisonment. The report gives the example of Margaret, aged 46 and on income support. She had to pay fines imposed as a result of her son's criminal offences (he was then 16). Magistrates sentenced her to 27 days' imprisonment for a remaining debt of £170.50, despite the fact that she had not personally committed any crime.

Individual support order

Sections 322 and 323 of the Criminal Justice Act 2003 create an individual support order. This order can be made after an anti-social behaviour order (see p. 492) has been issued against a person under 18. The individual support order may require the young person to undertake activities to tackle the underlying causes of their anti-social behaviour.

Child safety orders

A local authority can commence civil proceedings for a child safety order to be made by a magistrates' court under ss. 11–13 of the Crime and Disorder Act 1998. It can require a child under the age of 10 to be at home at specified times or to avoid certain people or places to limit the risk of their involvement in crime. The order can be made if the child has committed or risks committing an act which would have constituted an offence if they had been older, they have breached a curfew notice, or have behaved in an anti-social manner. The aim of this order is to divert children below the age of 10 from behaviour that would bring them into conflict with the criminal law. The child will be placed under the supervision of a social worker or member of a youth offending team for up to three months (and exceptionally 12 months), and the child will be required to comply with the requirements in the order. These requirements are not specified in the Act and are whatever the court considers desirable in the interests of securing that the child receives appropriate care, protection and support and is subject to proper control, and to prevent the repetition of the offending behaviour. It is targeting those children who are 'running wild' but are too young to be the subject of criminal proceedings. Where longer-term intervention is required, care proceedings will be brought by the local authority instead, with a care order continuing until the child becomes an adult. If the child safety order is breached care proceedings may also be brought.

Parenting orders

Under s. 8 of the Crime and Disorder Act 1998, a court may make a parenting order. The order is designed to help and support parents (or guardians) in addressing their child's anti-social behaviour. It is available in seven situations:

1 a court makes a referral order;
2 a court makes a child safety order;

3 a court makes a sex-offender order against a young person;

4 a court makes an anti-social behaviour order against a young person;

5 a young person has been convicted of an offence;

6 a parent has been convicted for failing to secure their child's attendance at school;

7 a young person has been excluded from school.

The order can be for a maximum of 12 months and consists of two elements. First, the parent will have to attend counselling or guidance sessions for up to three months. Secondly, the parent must comply with certain specific requirements aimed at ensuring that they exercise control over their child. Following the Anti-social Behaviour Act 2003, this may take the form of a residential course if this is likely to be more effective than a non-residential course and the interference with family life is proportionate. Parents convicted of failing to comply with a parenting order are liable to a fine.

Nearly 3,000 parents participated in 34 parenting programmes across England and Wales between 1999 and 2001. The Youth Justice Board has found that parenting programmes, aimed at giving parents support and advice in child rearing, reduced reoffending by the children by one-third. They have concluded that while the introduction of these programmes was controversial, they actually provide a powerful way to reach parents who need help and who might otherwise never attend a parenting support service.

In its 'Respect Action Plan', published in 2006, the Government proposed the creation of a National Parenting Academy, to train social workers and other professionals to help families with anti-social children.

Parenting contracts

Under the Anti-social Behaviour Act 2003, s. 25 parenting contracts can be made with Youth Offending Teams or local education authorities. These are designed to provide support for parents when their children are beginning to display anti-social or criminal behaviour, and are intended to prevent the young person from engaging in criminal conduct. This is a voluntary agreement and there is no penalty for its breach.

Time limits

In 1998 the criminal justice system took, on average, four-and-a-half months to process a young offender from the time of arrest to sentence. The Audit Commission found that in 1997 cases were generally adjourned on four occasions before completion. The Crime and Disorder Act 1998 aimed to reduce this period as there is concern that delays in the system are undermining the impact of the sentence on the offender. In cases involving persons under the age of 18, s. 44 provides that time limits may be applied from arrest to the commencement of proceedings and from conviction to sentence. The Home Secretary commented:

> Young people must be made to recognise and accept responsibility for their crimes – at the time, not many months later. Only when this happens will there be serious pressure on young offenders to change their behaviour rather than settle into a life of crime.

21

Young offenders

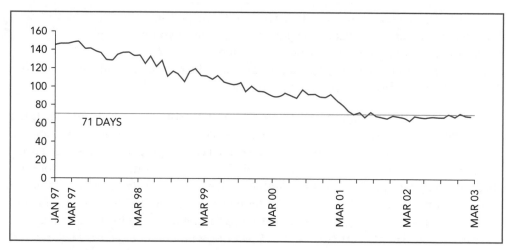

Figure 21.4 Average time between arrest and sentence for persistent young offenders England and Wales, January 1997 to March 2003

Source: Crown Prosecution Service Annual Report 2002–2003, p. 14

In order to assist practitioners in delivering the current target, the Government has provided guidelines on the length of time each stage of the youth justice process should take in a straightforward case involving a persistent young offender. These are as follows:

- arrest to charge: 2 days
- charge to first appearance at court: 7 days
- first appearance to start of trial: 28 days
- verdict to sentence: 14 days.

By 2004 the Government had succeeded in cutting the time taken to deal with most persistent young offenders in the magistrates' courts from 142 days to 56 days, though this had risen to 68 days in 2005.

TOPICAL ISSUE

Zero tolerance

The Labour Party has described its approach to young offenders as being one of 'zero tolerance'. This is a concept that was developed by academics during the 1980s and was adopted by President Ronald Reagan as part of his war against drugs. The principle behind zero tolerance is the 'broken windows theory'. Under this theory, when a neighbourhood shows such signs of decay as graffiti, litter and broken windows, decent people leave, disorder takes over and the area slides into crime. The theory demands that even the most minor offences be pursued with the same vigilance as serious ones, to create a deterrent effect.

Zero Tolerance policing was used in New York under the leadership of Mayor Giuliani. The results in New York were impressive, with falls of 50 per cent in overall crime and nearly two-thirds in the murder rate. But some of the police methods were criticised as aggressive by the pressure group Human Rights Watch. Critics also suggested that problematic people were simply shifted from rich to poor neighbourhoods – by putting thousands of homeless people onto buses and sending them to remote hostels. There may be other reasons for the drop in crime, such as a reduction in the number of young people in the general population, as this group is statistically more likely to offend. Thus, for example, San Diego saw a significant reduction in crime over a similar period without using zero tolerance policing, but by building partnerships between the police and the public. A recent use of 'zero tolerance' policy has been by the police in Los Angeles in an attempt to curtail the activities of gang members. Concern had developed that gangs in Los Angeles were disrupting neighbourhoods by dealing in drugs, painting graffiti on walls, urinating on private property, having all-night parties, and committing violence and murder. The Los Angeles police, in conjunction with local prosecutors, strictly applied existing law by issuing civil court injunctions against gang members which prevented them from, for example, 'standing, sitting, walking, driving, gathering or appearing anywhere in public view' in a four-block area where their activities were disruptive. Since the imposition of the zero tolerance policy some local residents say that the injunctions have returned their neighbourhoods to normal, allowing their children once again to play outside. Opponents to the policy claim that it breaches individuals' rights to freedom of association and speech.

One of the main forms of implementation of the zero tolerance policy by the Labour Government is through the introduction of anti-social behaviour orders discussed at p. 492. Zero tolerance policing was spearheaded in the UK in Cleveland. Home Office statistics suggest that the policing method was successful in reducing offences targeted by the policy. Between January and December 1997 reported burglary in Cleveland dropped by 26 per cent, robbery by 25 per cent and overall reported crime by 18 per cent. This was the highest reported reduction in England and Wales. At the same time, the area saw a threefold increase in the incidence of stop and searches. Its clear-up rate had also declined from 27 per cent in 1993 to 25 per cent in 1997, a figure that was 3 per cent below the British average.

Youth rehabilitation orders

Ess. Cases
p. 339
In 2003 the Government published a consultation paper, *Youth Justice – the Next Steps*. This paper set out possible reforms to the youth justice system. Some of these reform proposals can now be found in the Criminal Justice and Immigration Act 2008. The provisions relating to the sentencing of young offenders are expected to be brought into force in 2010.

The Act provides for the creation of youth rehabilitation orders. These will combine the existing community sentences into one generic community sentence for young people.

When imposing a youth rehabilitation order a court will be able to choose from the following 'menu' of requirements that the offender must comply with:

- an activity requirement;
- a supervision requirement;
- an unpaid work requirement (if the offender is aged 16 or 17);
- a programme requirement (a new requirement for juveniles designed to allow them to engage in programmes that will address their offending behaviour or teach life skills);
- an attendance centre requirement;
- a prohibited activity requirement (including a prohibition on carrying a gun);
- a curfew requirement;
- an exclusion requirement;
- a residence requirement (16 to 17 year olds);
- a local authority residence requirement;
- a mental health treatment requirement;
- a drug treatment requirement;
- a drug testing requirement;
- an intoxicating substance requirement;
- an education requirement;
- an electronic monitoring requirement;
- intensive supervision and surveillance (for a minimum of six months);
- intensive fostering.

A youth rehabilitation order will be the standard community sentence for the majority of young offenders. It will be imposed if the court considers that:

- the offending was serious enough to warrant it;
- the requirements forming part of the order are the most suitable for the offender; and
- the restrictions on liberty imposed by the order are commensurate with the seriousness of the offence.

A youth rehabilitation order with intensive supervision and surveillance or intensive fostering can only be made if the offence committed was imprisonable and so serious that if that sentence was not available a sentence of custody would be appropriate; and, in addition, for under-15 year olds the young person must be a persistent offender.

The order can be issued for a maximum of three years. The Act will abolish all the main community sentences discussed earlier in this chapter (such as supervision orders, curfew orders and attendance centre orders). Referral orders will continue to exist. The aim of this reform is both to simplify the law and to make the sentencing interventions more flexible.

If the youth rehabilitation order is breached then the young person will be issued with a warning. After the third warning (or earlier if appropriate), a young person can be returned to court. At court the offender can be given a custodial sentence if the original offence was imprisonable. If there is 'wilful and persistent' non-compliance with an order and the original offence was non-imprisonable, then the young offender should be given intensive supervision and surveillance or placed in intensive fostering. If there is still wilful and persistent non-compliance, then the young person can be placed in custody.

Answering questions

1 How effectively does the criminal justice system deal with offenders under the age of 18 before trial?

The criminal law applies to everybody equally and as the Crime and Disorder Act 1998 abolished the rebuttable presumption that children aged 10–14 were not criminally liable, only children under 10 years of age have a complete defence against criminal liability. There are specific legislative provisions applicable to young people. Code C of PACE requires that young suspects should not be arrested or interviewed at school, and should not normally be held in a police cell. The person responsible for the young person should be present during the interview to ensure awareness of rights, particularly to legal advice. A young offender refused bail will be remanded to local authority accommodation rather than prison.

Section 65 the Crime and Disorder Act 1998 replaced cautions with a progressive system of a reprimand for a first offence, a warning for a second offence and usually a charge for a third offence, but this requires that there must be sufficient evidence, admission, no previous convictions and a prosecution not being in the public interest. Historically there had been problems with delays in the youth justice system but the government has made considerable efforts to speed up the time between arrest and trial for young offenders. The youth justice system is trying to achieve a balance between the desire to avoid criminalising young people by moving them away from the criminal system into the social services and the need to punish serious offending behaviour by young people to reduce social distress.

2 Critically discuss the legislative provisions which have been put in place to protect child/youth offenders.

Essentially, what you need to do is set out what the protective provisions are, and then identify the criticisms. The protective provisions include:

- the Crime and Disorder Act 1998;
- Code C, PACE 1984;
- the Bail Act 1976;
- Article 6 ECHR (see the key case on p. 510);
- the Criminal Justice and Immigration Act 2008;
- restrictions on detention;
- parents and guardians are required to attend court hearings; and
- recent reforms aim to make sentencing interventions more flexible (see p. 523).

Critics of the legislative provisions point out that:

- children under 10 can be criminally liable;
- the legal proceedings can be intimidating; and
- the conditions for detention and the attitudes of staff can be unacceptable (see 'Topical issue' on p. 512).

3 To what extent is a parent liable for the actions of an offender aged under 16?

Parents are liable for the actions of a child under the age of 16 in a number of ways. They are required to attend the court hearing unless the court considers this unreasonable. Upon the offender's conviction, the parents (or local authority if exercising parental responsibility) can be

21

Young offenders

bound over to take proper care and control and ensure compliance with a community order (s. 150 Powers of Criminal Courts (Sentencing) Act 2000). Under threat of imprisonment, parents can be required to pay any fine imposed. In addition, in certain circumstances, under s. 8 Crime and Disorder Act 1998, the court may make a parenting order under which the parents have to attend guidance or counselling sessions and comply with specific requirements relating to the exercise of control over the child. Evidence indicates that parenting orders have had some success. Under s. 25 Anti-Social Behaviour Act 2003, parents of children exhibiting anti-social or criminal behaviour may voluntarily enter into a parenting contract with a Youth Offending Team to secure support for the parents.

4 Deborah, aged 15, has been seen by a police officer attacking an old man. He arrests her and takes her to the police station.

(a) Explain the rules concerning the police powers to question Deborah about the offence.

(b) If Deborah is charged and prosecuted, which courts are likely to deal with her case (excluding possible appeals)?

(c) What sentencing powers do the courts have in respect of her offence?

(a) Note that because of Deborah's age, you are talking about a young offender and not an adult. The general rules concerning a suspect in the police station are explained in Chapter 18, but you also need to include the particular rules that apply to Deborah because of her age, which are detailed at p. 507.

(b) Special rules apply to the trial of young offenders, which are discussed in this chapter at p. 509.

(c) If it is Deborah's first conviction then she will automatically get a referral order (discussed at p. 515). If she is a repeat offender the other sentencing powers will be important. The material in Chapter 20 covering the statutory guidance on sentencing is relevant here. As to the specific sentences that could be passed, starting with the most serious, custodial sentences, note that Deborah cannot be sent to prison – if custody is felt to be appropriate she would be given a detention and training order. As regards a community sentence, supervision orders and attendance centre orders are specific to young offenders, but the other forms of community sentences discussed in Chapter 20 are also relevant here. She might be given a reparation order, action plan order or be referred to a youth offender panel. The maximum length of sentences is often shorter for young offenders. A fine is a possibility and, if imposed, will have to be paid by Deborah's parents. You might also want to mention the fact that her parents may themselves be subject to sanctions, such as being bound over or receiving a parenting order.

5 Louise, aged 16, has been seen by a police officer stabbing an old lady and snatching her handbag. He arrests her and takes her to the police station.

(a) Explain the rules concerning the police powers to question Louise about the offence.

(b) If Louise is charged and prosecuted, which court(s) are likely to deal with her case at first instance?

(a) Note that because of Louise's age, you are talking about a young offender and not an adult. The general rules concerning a suspect in the police station are explained in Chapter 18, but you also need to include the particular rules that apply to Louise because of her age, which are detailed at p. 507.

(b) Special rules apply to the trial of young offenders, which are discussed in this chapter at p. 509. Because of the gravity of this case, you would need to discuss the fact that, while most cases involving young offenders are heard by the youth courts, this case might be heard by the Crown Court.

Summary of Chapter 21: Young offenders

Introduction
Offenders under 18 are in some respects dealt with differently by the criminal justice system from adult offenders. In 1998 a Youth Justice Board was established to monitor, set standards and promote good practice.

Criminal liability
Children under the age of 10 cannot be liable for a criminal offence.

Young people and the police
An adult responsible for a young person's welfare or an appropriate adult should normally be present in the police station with the young person.

Remand and bail
Young offenders should usually be granted bail, and when bail is refused they should not be held in adult prisons or remand centres.

Reprimands and warnings
In 1998 the system of cautions for young offenders was abolished and replaced by a new system of reprimands and warnings.

Youth conditional cautions
These cautions are combined with conditions, such as the payment of a fine, and were introduced in 2008.

Trial
Young offenders are usually tried in youth courts, and only occasionally can they be tried in the Crown Court. The European Court of Human Rights found that Jon Venables and Robert Thompson, who were convicted by a Crown Court of murdering the two-year-old James Bulger in 1993, did not receive a fair trial in accordance with Art. 6 of the European Convention on Human Rights. As a result, a Practice Direction was issued by the Lord Chief Justice which lays down guidance on how young offenders should be tried when their case is heard in the Crown Court.

Custodial sentences
The courts may not pass a sentence of imprisonment on an offender under the age of 18. Such offenders may be detained in other places, such as a young offenders' institution or local authority accommodation.

Detention 'during Her Majesty's pleasure'

Under s. 90, PCC(S)A 2000, an offender convicted of murder who was under 18 when the offence was committed must be sentenced to be detained indefinitely, known as 'during Her Majesty's pleasure'.

Detention under s. 91, PCC(S)A 2000

Where a person aged 10 or over has been convicted in the Crown Court of an offence with a maximum sentence of 14 years' imprisonment or more, the court may pass a sentence not exceeding that maximum.

Detention and training orders

Under s. 100, PCC(S)A 2000 the courts can make a detention and training order against offenders aged between 12 and 17. Half the sentence will be spent in detention and the other half under supervision.

Referral orders

Most young offenders appearing before a youth court for the first time are given a mandatory referral to a youth offender panel if they plead guilty.

Reparation order

A reparation order requires an offender under the age of 18 to make reparation commensurate with the seriousness of the offence to the victim or to the community at large.

Community sentences

Community sentences that have been developed to tackle the problem of young offenders include:

- supervision orders;
- attendance centre orders;
- curfew orders;
- exclusion orders; and
- action plan orders.

Parents of young offenders

Certain powers exist to coerce parents to take responsibility for the offending conduct of their children.

Time limits

The Government has set targets for the handling of cases involving young offenders to try to speed up the youth justice system.

Zero tolerance

The Labour Party has described its approach to young offenders as being one of 'zero tolerance', which means that the law will be strictly enforced in order to reduce crime.

Youth rehabilitation orders

In 2003 the Government published a consultation paper, Youth Justice – the Next Steps. This paper set out possible reforms to the youth justice system. Provisions for the introduction of youth rehabilitation orders are contained in the Criminal Justice and Immigration Act 2008.

Reading list

Audit Commission (1997) *Misspent Youth: Young People and Crime*, London: Audit Commission Publications.

Audit Commission (2004) *Youth Justice*, London: Audit Commission Publications.

Evans, R. (1993) *The Conduct of Police Interviews with Juveniles*, London: HMSO.

Field, S. (2008) 'Early Intervention and the "New" Youth Justice: A Study of Initial Decision-Making', [2008] *Criminal Law Review* 177.

Fionda, J. (2006) *Devils and Angels*, Oxford: Hart Publishing.

No More Excuses – A New Approach to Tackling Youth Crime in England and Wales (1998), London: Home Office.

Reading on the Internet

www

Research carried out for the Home Office on referral orders (*Youth Justice: the Introduction of Referral Orders into the Youth Justice System* (2001), RDS Occasional Paper No. 70) is available on the Home Office website:

http://www.homeoffice.gov.uk/rds/pdfs/occ70-youth.pdf

The Youth Justice Board has a website that can be found at:

http://www.yjb.gov.uk/en-gb

The consultation paper *Youth Justice – the Next Steps* (2003) is available on the Home Office website at:

http://www.homeoffice.gov.uk/documents/cons-youth-justice-next-steps/

A summary of the responses to the consultation paper *Youth Justice – the Next Steps* (2003) is published on the Home Office website at:

http://www.homeoffice.gov.uk/documents/cons-youth-jus-next-steps-summ/

A report into young black people in the criminal justice system is available on the Ministry of Justice website at:

www.justice.gov.uk/publications/young-black-people-cjs-dec-08.htm

Visit www.mylawchamber.co.uk/ElliottELS to access multiple-choice questions, flashcards and practice exam questions to test yourself on this chapter.

21

Young offenders

22

The civil justice system

This chapter discusses:

- the evolution of the civil justice system;

- the civil procedure rules, including pre-action protocols, case management and sanctions for breach;

- Money Claim Online – a debt recovery service provided over the internet; and

- problems with the civil court system, along with possible reforms.

Introduction

The civil justice system is designed to sort out disputes between individuals or organisations. One party, known as the claimant, sues the other, called the defendant, usually for money they claim is owed or for compensation for a harm to their interests. Typical examples might be the victim of a car accident suing the driver of the car for compensation, or one business suing another for payment due on goods supplied. The burden of proof is usually on the claimant, who must prove their case on a balance of probabilities – that it is more likely than not. This is a lower standard of proof than the 'beyond reasonable doubt' test used by the criminal courts and, for this reason, it is possible to be acquitted of a criminal charge yet still be found to have breached the civil law. This happened to the celebrity O.J. Simpson in the US who, having been acquitted of murdering his ex-wife and her friend by the criminal courts, was successfully sued in the civil courts for damages by the victim's family.

ss. Cases p. 342 → Major changes have been made to the civil justice system in recent years. After the Civil Justice Review of 1988, reforms were made by the Courts and Legal Services Act 1990. Following continued criticism of the civil justice system, Lord Woolf was appointed to carry out a far-reaching review of the civil justice system. Lord Woolf's inquiry is the 63rd such review in 100 years. Lord Woolf made far-reaching recommendations in his report, *Access to Justice*, which was published in 1996. As with the Civil Justice Review, his aim was to reduce the cost, delay and complexity of the system and increase access to justice. Most of his recommendations were implemented in April 1999.

History

The legal process for civil cases developed in a rather piecemeal fashion, responding to different needs at different times with the result that, at the end of the eighteenth century, civil matters were being dealt with by several different series of courts. Three common law courts, supplemented by the Court of Chancery, did most of the work, but there was also a Court of Admiralty and the ecclesiastical (church) courts. They had separate, but often overlapping, jurisdictions and between them administered three different 'systems' of law: civilian law (based on Roman law), common law and equity. The courts were also largely centralised in London, making access difficult for those in the provinces.

With no coordination of the increasingly complex court system, inefficiency, incompetence and delays were common and the courts acquired a reputation for binding themselves up in cumbersome procedural rules. Until well into the nineteenth century, litigation in the higher courts was an extravagance which could be afforded only by the very rich and, in many respects, the system benefited the judges and the legal professions far more than litigants. Reform began in 1846, with the creation of a nationwide system of county courts, designed to provide cheaper, quicker justice at a local level for businessmen. This was followed, in the early 1870s, by the creation of one Supreme Court consisting of the High Court, the Court of Appeal and the Crown Court, although the High Court was still divided into five divisions. In 1881, these

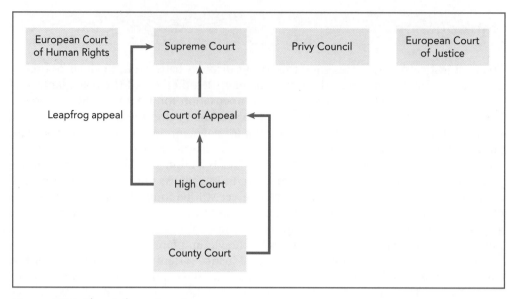

Figure 22.1 The civil court system

were reduced to three: Queen's Bench, Chancery, and what is now known as the Family Division.

The civil courts

There are currently around 300 county courts concerned exclusively with civil work. About 170 of them are designated as divorce county courts and, thereby, have jurisdiction to hear undefended divorces and cases concerning adoption and guardianship.

In the High Court, the three divisions mentioned above remain today – they act as separate courts, with judges usually working within one division only. Lord Woolf recommended that these divisions should remain. The Family Division hears cases concerning marriage, children and the family, such as divorce, adoption and wills. The Chancery Division deals with matters of finance and property, such as tax and bankruptcy. The Queen's Bench Division is the biggest of the three, with the most varied jurisdiction. The major part of its work is handling those contract and tort cases which are unsuitable for the county courts (see below). Sitting as the Divisional Court of the Queen's Bench, its judges also hear certain criminal appeals (originating primarily from the magistrates' courts) and applications for judicial review – for details see Chapter 1. High Court judges usually sit alone, but the Divisional Court is so important that two or three judges sit together.

Trials in the High Court are heard either in London or in one of the 26 provincial trial centres. In theory, they are all presided over by High Court judges, but in fact there are not enough High Court judges to cope with the case load. Some cases, therefore, have to be dealt with by circuit judges and others by barristers sitting as part-time, temporary, deputy judges.

Photo 22.1 Lord Woolf
Source: © Alex Segre/Alamy

Following the Woolf reforms, trial centres have been identified, headed by a Designated Civil Justice. They report to the Head of Civil Justice, a position currently held by Lord Phillips.

Although most civil cases are dealt with by either the county courts or the High Court, magistrates' courts have a limited civil jurisdiction, and some types of cases are tried by tribunals.

The civil justice system before April 1999

Before the implementation of the Woolf reforms, there were two separate sets of civil procedure rules: the Rules of the Supreme Court in the 'White Book' for the High Court and the Court of Appeal, and the County Court Rules in the 'Green Book' for the county courts. High Court actions were started with a writ, county court ones by a summons, but there were also specialised procedures which required specific documents and formalities to be used. These documents were served on the defendant to a case, and informed the person that an action was being brought against them. The rules on serving documents were fairly restrictive and ignored modern modes of communication. Defendants had to acknowledge service. The claimant served a statement of claim if bringing an action in the High Court, or the particulars of a claim in the county court. Both were formal pleadings which outlined the facts and legal basis of the action and the remedy sought. The defendant responded with a defence.

The Civil Justice Review was set up in 1985 by the Lord Chancellor in response to public criticism of the delay, cost and complexity of the civil court system. Unusually, it was chaired by a non-lawyer, Maurice Hodgson, the Chairman of Bhs, and only a minority of its members were lawyers. They therefore tended to be less pro-lawyer than previous committees that had been dominated by judges and barristers, which may explain why many of the Review's more innovative suggestions were ignored or only partially implemented. Some important changes were made to the division of work between the county courts and High Court by the Courts and Legal Services Act 1990 in response to some of the proposals of the 1985 Review.

One of the Review's main findings was that too many cases were being heard in the High Court rather than the cheaper and quicker county courts, often for relatively small amounts of money. Consequently, the Review aimed to increase the number of cases heard in the county courts.

As a result, following the Courts and Legal Services Act 1990, claims worth under £3,000 were automatically dealt with by the Small Claims procedure of the county court, the amount having been increased at the beginning of 1996 from £1,000. All personal injury cases worth less than £50,000 had to be brought in the county court. Both the county court and the High Court had jurisdiction over any other tort or contract case. There was no longer a fixed maximum limit for cases heard in the county court, nor a minimum one for the High Court. In general though, cases worth less than £25,000 would be commenced in the county court, and cases worth more than £50,000 in the High Court; for actions falling between £25,000 and £50,000, the proper court would depend on the complexity and importance of the case.

Problems with the civil justice system before April 1999

Ess. Cases
p. 342

Lord Woolf was appointed by the previous Conservative Government to carry out a far-reaching review of the civil justice system. In *Access to Justice: Final Report*, published in 1996, he stated that a civil justice system should:

- be just in the results it delivers;
- be fair in the way it treats litigants;
- offer appropriate procedures at a reasonable cost;
- deal with cases with reasonable speed;
- be understandable to those who use it;
- be responsive to the needs of those who use it;
- provide as much certainty as the nature of particular cases allows;
- be effective, adequately resourced and organised.

Lord Woolf concluded that the system at the time failed to achieve all those goals. It is possible that this failure is inevitable, as some of the aims conflict with others. A system based on cost-efficiency alone would make it difficult to justify claims for comparatively small sums, yet these cases are very important to the parties involved, and wide access to justice is vital. Promoting efficiency in terms of speed can also conflict with the need for fairness. Making the courts more accessible could lead to a flood of cases which would make it impossible to provide a speedy resolution and keep costs down. One practical example of the conflict between different aims is that the availability of legal aid to one party, one of the aims of widening access to justice, can put pressure on the other side if they are funding themselves, and so clash with the need for fairness.

In addition, changes made to the civil justice system may have effects outside it – making it easier to bring personal injury actions, for example, could push up the costs of insurance, and it has been suggested that in the US this has led to unwillingness on the part of doctors to perform any risky medical treatment.

It is impossible to resolve all of these conflicts and a successful legal system must simply aim for the best possible balance. Lord Scarman has commented:

> To be acceptable to ordinary people, I believe [the] legal process in litigation must be designed to encourage, first, settlement by agreement; secondly, open and speedy trial if agreement is not forthcoming. In other words, justice, not truth is its purpose. It is against the criteria of justice and fairness that the system must be assessed.

In the final analysis, it is for the Government to decide the balance they wish to strike, and how much they are prepared to spend on it. While conflicting interests may mean it is impossible to achieve a civil justice system that satisfies everyone, there were serious concerns that the civil justice system before April 1999 was giving satisfaction to only a small minority of users for a range of reasons which will be considered in turn.

Too expensive

Research carried out for Lord Woolf's review found that one side's costs exceeded the amount in dispute in over 40 per cent of cases where the claim was for under £12,500. The simplest cases often incurred the highest costs in proportion to the value of the claim.

Because of the complexity of the process, lawyers were usually needed, making the process expensive. The sheer length of civil proceedings also affected the size of the bill at the end.

Lord Woolf has said that, 15 years before, his report would not have been necessary, because most lawyers made their money from other work, such as conveyancing, seeing litigation as a loss-maker that they would only undertake reluctantly. But, with the huge increase in the number of lawyers combined with the recession in the property market at the end of the 1980s, lawyers suddenly found that litigation could generate a steady income. He found that costs were now so high that even big companies were wary, with some preferring to fight cases in New York.

Delays

The Civil Justice Review observed that the time between the incident giving rise to the claim and the trial could be up to three years for the county courts and five for the High Court. Time limits were laid down for every stage of an action but both lawyers and the courts disregarded them. Often time limits were waived by the lawyers to create an opportunity to negotiate, which was reasonable, but the problem was that there was no effective control of when and why it was done.

According to the Civil Justice Review, long delays placed intolerable psychological and financial burdens on accident victims and undermined the justice of the trial, by making it more difficult to gather evidence which was then unreliable because witnesses had to remember the events of several years before.

Injustice

Usually an out-of-court settlement is negotiated before the litigants ever reach the trial stage. Excluding personal injury cases, for every 100,000 writs issued before 1999, fewer than 300 actually came for trial. An out-of-court settlement can have the advantage of providing a quick end to the dispute, and a reduction in costs. But out-of-court settlements can be unfair – see the discussion on this subject at p. 554.

The adversarial process

Many problems resulted from the adversarial process which encouraged tactical manoeuvring rather than cooperation. It would be far simpler and cheaper for each side to state precisely what it alleged in the pleadings, disclose all the documents they held, and give the other side copies of their witness statements. Attitudes did appear to be slowly changing, with a growing appreciation that the public interest demanded justice be provided as quickly and economically as possible. Some of the procedural rules, for example on expert witnesses, were changed and there was less scope for tactical manoeuvring.

Emphasis on oral evidence

Too much emphasis was placed on oral evidence at trial. This may have been appropriate when juries were commonly used in civil proceedings, but in the twentieth century much of the information the judge needed could be provided on paper and read before the trial. Oral evidence slowed down proceedings, adding to cost and delays.

The civil justice system after April 1999

On 26 April 1999 new Civil Procedure Rules and accompanying Practice Directions came into force. The new rules apply to any proceedings commenced after that date. They constitute the most fundamental reform of the civil justice system of the twentieth century, introducing the main recommendations of Lord Woolf in his final report, *Access to Justice*. He described his proposals as providing 'a new landscape for civil justice for the twenty-first century'.

The Woolf Report was the product of two years' intensive consultation, and was written with the help of expert working parties of experienced practitioners and academics. The recommendations of the Report received universal support from the senior judiciary, the Bar, the Law Society, consumer organisations and the media. In 1996, Sir Richard Scott was appointed as Head of Civil Justice with responsibility for implementing the reforms. The Civil Procedure Act 1997 was passed to implement the first stages of the Woolf Report. Following their election into office, the Labour Government set up their own review of the civil justice system and of Lord Woolf's proposed reforms. They quite reasonably wanted a second opinion before adopting the policies of their predecessors on those issues. The review was chaired by Sir Peter Middleton and took four months to complete. The final report was essentially in favour of implementation of Lord Woolf's proposals. His report placed an emphasis on the financial implications of the proposals and in particular the opportunities for cost-cutting. In November 1998, an intensive period of training for judges and court staff began, to prepare them for the changes, whilst the Treasury made available an additional £2 million to implement the reforms.

The reforms aim to eliminate unnecessary cost, delay and complexity in the civil justice system. The general approach of Lord Woolf is reflected in his statement: 'If "time and money are no object" was the right approach in the past, then it certainly is not today. Both lawyers and judges, in making decisions as to the conduct of litigation, must take into account more than they do at present, questions of cost and time and the means of the parties.' Lord Woolf suggested that the reforms should lead to a reduction in legal bills by as much as 75 per cent, though it might also mean some lawyers would lose their livelihoods.

The ultimate goal is to change fundamentally the litigation culture. Thus, the first rule of the new Civil Procedure Rules lays down an overriding objective which is to underpin the whole system. This overriding objective is that the rules should enable the courts to deal with cases 'justly'. This objective prevails over all other rules in case of a conflict. The parties and their legal representatives are expected to assist the judges in achieving this objective. The Woolf Report had heavily criticised practitioners, who were accused of manipulating the old system for their own convenience and causing delay and expense to both their clients and the users of the system as a whole. Lord Woolf felt that a change in attitude among the lawyers was vital for the new rules to succeed. According to r. 1.1(2):

> Dealing with a case justly includes, so far as is practicable –
> (a) ensuring that the parties are on an equal footing;
> (b) saving expense;
> (c) dealing with the case in ways which are proportionate –
>   (i) to the amount of money involved;
>   (ii) to the importance of the case;
>   (iii) to the complexity of the issues; and
>   (iv) to the financial position of each party;
> (d) ensuring that it is dealt with expeditiously and fairly; and
> (e) allotting to it an appropriate share of the Court's resources, while taking into account the need to allot resources to other cases.

The emphasis of the new rules is on avoiding litigation through pre-trial settlements. Litigation is to be viewed as a last resort, with the court having a continuing obligation to encourage and facilitate settlement. Lord Woolf had observed that it was strange

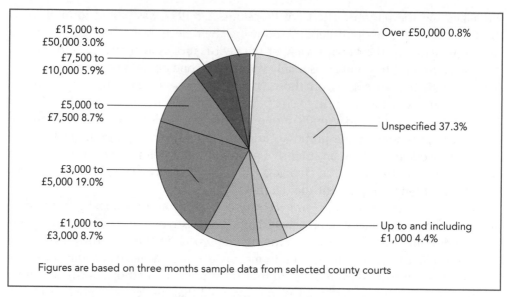

Figure 22.2 County Court claims issued by amount of claim, 2005

Source: Judicial Statistics Annual Report 2005 (revised), p. 44

that, although the majority of disputes ended in settlement, the old rules had been mainly directed towards preparation for trial. Thus the new rules put a greater emphasis on preparing cases for settlement rather than a trial.

The new approach to civil procedure will now be examined in more detail.

Civil Procedure Rules

The Lord Chancellor appointed the Civil Procedure Rules Committee to produce and maintain one unified procedural code for both the county court and the High Court. This produced the new Civil Procedure Rules which came into force in April 1999 and replaced the Rules of the Supreme Court and the County Court Rules. The new rules are simpler than their predecessors, providing a broad framework of general application rather than detailed rules covering every contingency. These framework rules are then fleshed out by a number of Practice Directions. There has been an attempt to write the rules in plain English, replacing old-fashioned terminology with more accessible terms. Lord Woolf hoped that the change in language would help to support a change in attitude, away from a legalistic, technical interpretation of words designed to give one party an advantage over their opponent, towards an attitude which was open and fair according to the overriding objective of the new rules.

While the new rules introduce some radical changes to the civil justice system, they also inherit much from the old system. In outline the procedure is as follows. Before proceedings are commenced, claimants should send a letter to defendants warning them that they are considering bringing legal proceedings. Proceedings should be brought within a fixed period (usually six years) from when the claimant suffered the harm. This period is known as the limitation period, and is laid down in the Limitation

Act 1980. This area of the law has proved particularly problematic for people who have suffered sexual abuse while they were children. It was pointed out in **Ablett *v* Devon County Council** (2000) that:

> It is the nature of abuse of children by adults that it creates shame, fear and confusion, and these in turn produce silence. Silence is known to be one of the most pernicious fruits of abuse. It means that allegations commonly surface, if they do, only many years after the abuse has ceased.

In **A *v* Hoare** (2008) the House of Lords tried to avoid injustice by allowing a woman who had been raped in the 1970s by a serial rapist who had subsequently won the lottery in 2004, to bring a successful case for damages against her attacker.

Almost all proceedings start with the same document called a claim form. This replaces the writ for the High Court and the summons for the County Court, and other specialist documents. The procedure for starting an action is thus undoubtedly simpler than under the old system. The claim form informs the defendant that an action is being brought against them. When claimants are making a claim for money, they must provide a statement as to the value of the claim in the claim form.

The Practice Direction supplementing Part 7 of the new Civil Procedure Rules (*How to start proceedings – the Claim Form*) specifies in which court proceedings should be started. For non-personal injury actions, a claim may be started in the High Court where the claimant expects to recover more than £15,000. For personal injury actions, a claim can only be started in the High Court where the claimant expects to recover at least £50,000 for pain, suffering and loss of amenity.

The claim form is served on the defendant to a case. The methods of service have been liberalised to reflect modern modes of communication, including the use of fax and e-mails. Service will normally be carried out by the court through postage by first-class post, unless a party notifies the court that they will serve the documents. Defendants must acknowledge service. The claimant (known before 1999 as the plaintiff) must then serve on the defendant the particulars of claim (previously called the statement of claim in the High Court).

The defendant should respond within 14 days by either filing an acknowledgement of service or a defence with the court. If the defendant fails to do either of these within that period of time, the claimant can enter judgment in default against the

Table 22.1 Changes in terminology

Old term	New term
Writ	Claim form
Discovery	Disclosure
Plaintiff	Claimant
Statement of claim	Particulars of claim
Payment into court procedures	Part 36 procedures

defendant (r. 12.3). The mechanics of pleading a defence are now regulated more strictly. Defendants may no longer simply deny an allegation, but must state their reasons for the denial and, if they intend to put forward a different version of events from that given by the claimant, then they must state their own version.

If the defendant files a defence, the court will serve an allocation questionnaire on each party (r. 24.4(1)). This is designed to enable the court to allocate each claim to one of the three tracks discussed at p. 544.

The disclosure procedures (previously known as discovery) are then followed, as discussed on p. 547. Either party may seek more details from the other, through a 'request for information'. This procedure merges the old system of interrogatories and requests for further and better particulars.

At any stage of the proceedings the parties can enter into 'without prejudice' negotiations to try to settle the dispute out of court. The without prejudice rule makes all negotiations genuinely aimed at settlement, whether oral or in writing, inadmissible in evidence at any subsequent trial. The rule lets litigants make whatever concessions or admissions are necessary to achieve a compromise, without fear of these being held against them if negotiations break down and the case goes to court. It is hoped that this will help and encourage the parties to settle their disputes early.

If defendants wish to settle a claim they can simply make a written offer to settle at any time including before legal proceedings have commenced. This is known as a Part 36 offer. An accepted offer must then be paid by the defendant within 14 days. A Part 36 offer can be withdrawn after 21 days. If the case is not settled out of court, the case proceeds to trial. If the claimant fails to receive an award which is more advantageous than an earlier Part 36 offer, then they will not receive any of their legal costs from the date that the offer was made, even though they have technically won the case.

KEY CASE

In **Carver v British Airways Authority** (2008) the claimant had suffered a minor injury and the British Airways Authority (BAA) had promptly accepted that they were liable for the accident but there was a dispute as to how much damages should be paid. BAA made a Part 36 payment of £4,000. The claimant failed to respond to this offer and the case proceeded to court. At court the claimant received £51 more than the Part 36 payment and wanted the defendant to pay their legal fees of over £80,000. The Court of Appeal held that the award of damages was not actually 'more advantageous' than the earlier offer, because this was not purely a financial calculation; courts also had to weigh in the balance the fact that going to court is time-consuming, expensive and stressful. The claim was for a relatively small sum and no reasonable litigant would have gone to trial for an additional £51. The court therefore rejected the claim that the defendant should pay the claimant's legal costs after the date of the Part 36 offer.

> In determining whether a Part 36 payment is more advantageous than the final award the court will not purely make a financial calculation, but it will also bear in mind that going to trial is time-consuming, expensive and stressful.

The different formal documents are described as the statement of case, while in the past they were called the pleadings. All statements of case must be verified by a statement of truth. This is a statement signed by the claimant (or their legal representative), in the following words: 'I believe that the facts stated in these particulars of claim are true.' The purpose of such a statement is to prevent a party from putting in facts for purely tactical purposes which they have no intention of relying upon. If a party makes a false statement in a statement of case verified by a statement of truth, the party will be guilty of contempt of court (r. 28.14).

Either party can apply for a summary judgment on the ground that the claim or defence has no real prospect of success. The court can also reach this conclusion on its own initiative.

The emphasis of the new procedural rules is to encourage an early settlement of proceedings. A MORI poll of 100 solicitors carried out in 2000 found that 76 per cent of solicitors believed that the reforms had increased the chances of an early settlement. The majority felt that the reforms had cut the amount of litigation. Between May 1999 and January 2000 there was a 25 per cent reduction in the number of cases issued in the county courts compared with the same period the previous year.

Pre-action protocols

The pre-trial procedure is, perhaps, the most important area of the civil process, since few civil cases actually come to trial. To push the parties into behaving reasonably during the pre-trial stage, Lord Woolf recommended the development of pre-action protocols to lay down a code of conduct for this stage of the proceedings. Ten pre-action protocols have been produced so far which cover such areas of practice as personal injury, medical negligence and housing. They were developed in consultation with most of the key players in the relevant fields, including legal, health and insurance professionals. The Civil Justice Council is currently producing a general protocol to cover all those cases that are not caught by the existing protocols.

Pre-action protocols are a major innovation and aim to encourage:

- more pre-action contact between the parties;
- an earlier and fuller exchange of information;
- improved pre-action investigation;
- a settlement before proceedings have commenced.

They strive to achieve this through establishing a timetable for the exchange of information, by setting standards for the content of correspondence, providing schedules of documents that should be disclosed along with a mechanism for agreeing on a single joint expert. The pre-action protocols seek to encourage a culture of openness between the parties. This should lead to the parties being better informed as to the merits of their case so that they will be in a position to settle cases fairly, so reducing the need for litigation. If settlement is not reached the parties should be able to proceed to litigation on a more informed basis. Pre-action protocols should also enable proceedings to run to timetable, and efficiently, if litigation proves to be necessary.

Compliance with a pre-action protocol is not compulsory but, if a party unreasonably refuses to comply, then this can be taken into account when the court makes orders for costs. It may be that these protocols will need 'sharper teeth' in order to be effective.

A Practice Direction on pre-action conduct has also been issued by the Civil Justice Council giving general guidance on how the parties should behave at the early stages of litigation. The Practice Direction seeks to encourage the parties to settle their claim out of court. A letter before claim must be sent and responded to within a reasonable time. This must be acknowledged within 14 to 90 days depending on the complexity of the dispute. The parties must attempt to resolve the dispute through alternative dispute resolution.

Alternative Dispute Resolution

At various stages in a dispute's history, the court will actively promote settlement by Alternative Dispute Resolution (ADR). For a detailed discussion of ADR in the English legal system see p. 621. There is a general statement in the new rules that the court's duty to further the overriding objective by active case management includes both encouraging the parties to use an alternative dispute resolution procedure (if the court considers that appropriate) and facilitating the use of that procedure (r. 1.4(2)(e)). Also, when filling in the allocation questionnaire, the parties can request a one-month stay of proceedings while they try to settle the case by ADR or other means (r. 26.4). The parties will have to show that they genuinely attempted to resolve their dispute through ADR and have not just paid lip service to the ideal, as has been the tendency in the past.

Case management

This is the most significant innovation of the 1999 reforms. Case management means that the court will be the active manager of the litigation. The main aim of this approach is to bring cases to trial quickly and efficiently. Traditionally it has been left to the parties and their lawyers to manage the cases. In 1995, the courts had made a move towards case management following a Practice Direction encouraging such methods, but it was only with the new Civil Procedure Rules that case management came fully into force. The new Rules firmly place the management of a case in the hands of the judges, with r. 1.4 emphasising that the court's duty is to take a proactive role in the management of each case. The judges are given considerable discretion in the exercise of their case management role. Lord Woolf does not feel that this will undermine the adversarial tradition, but he sees the legal professions fulfilling their adversarial functions in a more controlled environment.

Once proceedings have commenced, the court's powers of case management will be triggered by the filing of a defence. When the defence has been filed and case management has started, the parties are on a moving train, trial dates will be fixed and will be difficult to postpone, and litigants will not normally be able to slow down or stop unless they settle. The court first needs to allocate the case to one of the three tracks:

Claim No.

Does, or will, your claim include any issues under the Human Rights Act 1998? ☐ Yes ☐ No

Particulars of Claim (attached)(to follow)

Statement of Truth
*(I believe)(The Claimant believes) that the facts stated in these particulars of claim are true.
*I am duly authorised by the claimant to sign this statement

Full name

Name of claimant's solicitor's firm

signed _____ position or office held _____
*(Claimant)(Litigation friend)(Claimant's solicitor) (if signing on behalf of firm or company)
*delete as appropriate

Claimant's or claimant's solicitor's address to which documents or payments should be sent if different from overleaf including (if appropriate) details of DX, fax or e-mail.

Claim Form

In the

Claim No.

SEAL

Claimant

Defendant(s)

Brief details of claim

Value

Defendant's name and address

	£
Amount claimed	
Court fee	
Solicitor's costs	
Total amount	
Issue date	

The court office at

is open between 10 am and 4 pm Monday to Friday. When corresponding with the court, please address forms or letters to the Court Manager and quote the claim number.
N1 Claim form (CPR Part 7) (10.00)   Printed on behalf of The Court Service

Figure 22.3 A claim form

Source: Court service website at www.mcsi.gov.uk

the small claims track, the fast-track or the multi-track (r. 24.6(1)), which will deter-mine the future conduct of the proceedings. To determine which is the appropriate track the court will serve an allocation questionnaire on each party. The answers to this questionnaire will form the basis for deciding the appropriate track. When consider-ing the allocation questionnaire, the judge will determine whether a case should be subject to summary judgment, or whether a stay of proceedings should be given for alternative dispute resolution; and, if neither of these matters applies, whether there should be an allocation hearing called or whether the matter can be the subject of a paper determination of the allocation to a particular track.

The three tracks

The court allocates the case to the most appropriate track depending primarily on the financial value of the claim, but other factors that can be taken into account include the case's importance and complexity (r. 26.6). Normally:

- small claims track cases deal with actions with a value of less than £5,000 (or £1,000 for personal injury cases);
- fast-track cases deal with actions of a value between £5,000 and £25,000;
- multi-track cases deal with actions with a value higher than £25,000.

The three tracks will now be considered in turn.

The small claims track

The handling of small claims is largely unchanged by the Woolf reforms. In the small claims track, directions will be issued for each case providing a date for the hearing and an estimate of the hearing time, unless the case requires a preliminary hearing appoint-ment to assist the parties in the conduct of the case. This track was previously known as the small claims court, though it was never actually a separate court, but a procedure used by county courts to deal with relatively small claims. It was introduced in response to a report from the Consumers' Association in 1967 claiming that county courts were being used primarily as a debt collection agency for businesses: 89.2 per cent of the summonses were taken out by firms and only 9 per cent by individuals, who were put off by costs and complexity.

Established in 1973, this special procedure aims to provide a cheap, simple mech-anism for resolving small-scale consumer disputes. Disclosure is dispensed with and, if the litigation continues to trial, it is usually held in private rather than in open court. The hearing is simple and informal, with few rules about the admissibility or presenta-tion of evidence. No experts may be used without leave. It is usually a very quick process, with 60 per cent of hearings taking less than 30 minutes. Costs are limited except where, by consent, a case with a financial value such that it would normally be allocated to the fast-track was allocated to the small claims track. The procedure is designed to make it easy for parties to represent themselves without the aid of a lawyer, and legal aid for representation is not available. Under the Lay Representatives (Rights of Audience) Order 1992 made under s. 11 of the Courts and Legal Services Act 1990, a party can choose to be represented by a layperson, though the party must also attend.

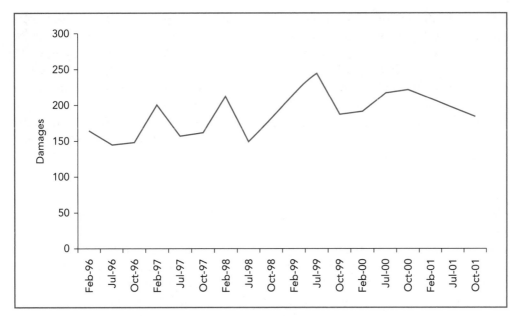

Figure 22.4 Small claims – average time from issue to hearing

Source: Civil Justice Reform Evaluation Further Findings (2002) [Figure 22.12]

The fast-track

Fast-track cases will normally be dealt with by the county court. Upon allocation to the fast track the court gives directions for the management of the case, and sets a timetable for the disclosure of documents, the exchange of witness statements, the exchange (and number) of expert reports, and the trial date or a period within which the trial will take place, which will be no more than 30 weeks later (compared to an average of 80 weeks before 1999).

A Practice Direction gives an example of a typical timetable that a court may give:

- disclosure: 4 weeks;
- exchange of witness statements: 10 weeks;
- exchange of experts' reports: 14 weeks;
- hearing: 30 weeks.

Although the parties can vary certain matters by agreement, such as disclosure or the exchange of witness statements, the rules are quite clear that an application must be made to court if a party wishes to vary the date for the trial.

Under this track the maximum length of the trial is normally one day. The relevant Practice Direction states that the judge will normally have read the papers in the trial bundle and may dispense with an opening address. Witness statements will usually stand as evidence in chief. Oral expert evidence will be limited to one expert per party in relation to any expert field and expert evidence will be limited to two expert fields.

In an attempt to keep lawyers' bills down, fixed costs for 'fast-track' trials have been introduced, but the introduction of pre-trial fixed costs has been delayed until additional information is available to inform the development of the revised costs regime. Lord Woolf had recommended that there should be a £2,500 limit on costs for fast-track cases (though clients could enter into a written agreement to pay more to their solicitors). Apart from the trial itself, litigants are still committing themselves to open-ended payment by the hour, which Lord Woolf described as being equivalent to handing out a blank cheque. He observed: 'If you and I are having our house repaired, we don't do it on a time and materials basis, because we know it will be a disaster. There is no incentive for the builder to do it in the least time and do it with the most economical materials.'

The multi-track

Upon allocation to the multi-track, the court can give directions for the management of the case and set a timetable for those steps to be taken. Alternatively, for heavier cases, the court may fix a case management conference or a pre-trial review or both. Unlike the fast-track, the court does not at this stage automatically set a trial date or a period within which the trial will take place. Instead it will fix this as soon as it is practicable to do so. Thus, this track offers individual case management with tailor-made directions according to the needs of the case. The High Court only hears multi-track cases.

A proactive approach

Gone are the days when the court waited for the lawyers to bring the case back before it or allowed the lawyers to dictate without question the number of witnesses or the amount of costs incurred. In managing litigation the court must have regard to the overriding objective, set out in Part 1, which is to deal with cases justly. To fulfil this key objective of the reformed civil justice system, the court is required to:

- identify the issues at an early stage;
- decide promptly which issues require full investigation and dispose summarily of the others;
- encourage the parties to seek alternative dispute resolution where appropriate;
- encourage the parties to cooperate with each other in the conduct of the procedures;
- help the parties to settle the whole or part of the case;
- decide the order in which issues are to be resolved;
- fix timetables or otherwise control the progress of the case;
- consider whether the likely benefits of taking a particular step will justify the cost of taking it;
- deal with a case without the parties' attendance at court if this is possible;
- make appropriate use of technology;
- give directions to ensure that the trial of a case proceeds quickly and efficiently.

A lot of the preliminary hearings, such as allocation hearings and case management conferences, are now dealt with by the judge over the telephone, rather than people having to attend court. This saves time and money by taking advantage of modern technology.

Disclosure

Before the 1999 reforms, disclosure was known as 'discovery'. The procedure used to involve each party providing the other with a list of all the documents which they had in relation to the action. The parties could then ask to see some or all of this material. The process could be time-consuming and costly. Pre-action disclosure was also available in claims for personal injury and death. Lord Woolf recommended that disclosure should generally be limited to documents which were readily available and which to a 'material extent' adversely affected or supported a party's case, though this could be extended for multi-track cases. This change would have altered significantly the disclosure process and risked going against the philosophy of openness between the parties generally advocated by Lord Woolf. He also favoured extending pre-action disclosure to be available for all proceedings and against people who would not have been parties to the future proceedings. However, the new Civil Procedure Rules are actually very similar to the old rules. These require the disclosure of documents on which they rely or which adversely affected or supported a party's case. It is not necessary for this impact to be to a 'material extent'. As under the old rules, additional disclosure will be ordered where it is 'necessary in order to dispose fairly of the claim or to save costs'. The availability of pre-action disclosure was not extended despite the fact that the Civil Procedure Act 1997 provided for its extension. The pre-action protocols are designed to ensure voluntary disclosure is made between likely parties. It seems that the Government wishes to see how the pre-action protocols operate in practice before implementing such changes.

Sanctions

Tough rules on sanctions give the courts stringent powers to enforce the new rules on civil procedure to ensure that litigation is pursued diligently. The two main sanctions are an adverse award of costs and an order for a case or part of a case to be struck out. These sanctions were available under the old rules, but the novelty of the new regime lies in the commitment to enforce strict compliance. There is an increasing willingness of the courts to manage cases with a stick rather than a carrot. The courts can treat the standards set in the pre-action protocols as the normal approach to pre-action conduct and have the power to penalise parties for non-compliance.

One of the most significant changes to the civil system made by the Woolf reforms concerned the approach to legal costs. Under the old system there was a basic principle that the loser paid the winner's costs. This principle was only departed from in exceptional circumstances. Although this principle still exists under the new system, it is now treated only as a starting point which the court can readily depart from. Where a party has not complied with court directions, particularly as to time, they can be penalised by being ordered to pay heavier costs, or by losing the right to have some or all of their costs paid.

A party who fails to comply with the case timetable or court orders may have their claim struck out. The court has power to strike out a party's statement of case, or part of it, where there has been a failure to comply with a rule, Practice Direction or court order (r. 3.4). This power can be exercised on an application from a party, or on the court's own initiative. Mere delay will be enough in itself to deprive a party of the power to bring or defend an action.

It is up to the defaulting party to apply for relief from sanctions using the procedure contained in r. 3.9. This is dramatically different from the previous state of affairs where a party in default of a court order was not the subject of any sanction unless the innocent party brought the matter to the court's attention.

Where, during the trial, any representative of a party incurs costs as a result of their own improper, unreasonable or negligent conduct they will not receive payment for those wasted costs. A wasted costs order is essentially a power to 'fine' practitioners who incur the disapproval of the court.

KEY CASE

Some guidance as to the court's approach to the use of sanctions was provided by the Court of Appeal in **Biguzzi v Rank Leisure plc** (1999). Giving the court's judgment, Lord Woolf commented:

> Sanctions should be imposed for delay in civil proceedings, though in many cases it will not be proportionate to strike out the case.

> The fact that the judge has [the power to strike out a claim] does not mean that in applying the overriding objective the initial approach will be to strike out the statement of case. The advantage of the CPR over the previous rules is that the court's powers are much broader than they were. In many cases there will be alternatives which enable a case to be dealt with justly without taking the draconian step of striking the case out.

Lord Woolf warned against a lax approach since this could lead to a return to the previous culture of regarding time limits as being unimportant. However, he went on to state:

> There are alternative powers which the courts have which they can exercise to make it clear that the courts will not tolerate delays other than striking out the case. In a great many situations those other powers will be the appropriate ones to adopt because they produce a more just result.

This judgment was considered by the Court of Appeal in **UCB Corporate Services v Halifax (SW) Ltd** (1999) where it stated:

> It would indeed be ironic if as a result of the new rules coming into force and the judgment of this court in the **Biguzzi** case, judges were required to treat cases of delay with greater leniency than they would have done under the old procedure. I feel sure that that cannot have been the intention of the Master of the Rolls in giving judgment in the **Biguzzi** case. What he was concerned to point out was that there are now additional powers which the court may and should use in the less serious cases. But in the more serious cases, striking out remains the appropriate remedy where that is what justice requires.

Court fees

Court fees have been increased significantly over the last two decades. The aim is that civil courts should be self-financing and managed according to business principles. The Labour Government has introduced a 'pay-as-you-go' system, which requires parties to pay for each stage of a civil action, with the costs obviously mounting if a party chooses to proceed all the way to a trial. The aim is both that the courts should be self-financing and that people should be encouraged to settle.

The increased court fees have been criticised on the ground that they will deter many lower-income households from pursuing reasonable claims for justice. Some observers point out that payments are not made by members of the public at the point of use in the education and health systems and that justice can be seen as being just as important as those services. The former head of the civil justice system, Sir Richard Scott, has warned that justice should be accessible and that:

> The policy fails to recognise that the civil justice system is, like the criminal justice system, the bulwark of a civilised state and the maintenance of order within that state. People have to use the civil courts. They can't engage in self-help in a way which would lead to chaos.

The civil justice watchdog, the Civil Justice Council, has called upon the Government to abandon its policy of making litigants pay almost the full cost of the civil courts through fees. It has stated: 'access to the civil courts must be seen as providing a social and collective benefit, as well as a service to the individual citizen'.

Money Claim Online

In 2002 Money Claim Online (MCOL) was established. It provides a debt recovery service over the Internet for sums up to £100,000. The debts might be for unpaid goods or services, or rent arrears, for example. Claimants can issue money claims via the Internet at **www.moneyclaim.gov.uk**. Fees are paid electronically by debit or credit card. The defence can use the online service to acknowledge service and file a defence. Most debt claims are undefended and if no defence is filed then the claimant can apply online for a judgment and enforcement. The parties can use the website to check the progress of their case, such as whether a defence has been filed. The service is available 24 hours a day, seven days a week. The new service has proved very popular with creditors, who have issued thousands of claims to date using the new service.

TOPICAL ISSUE

Opening up the family courts

There has been some controversy over whether the family courts have been too secretive. In the past the majority of family proceedings were held in private but in April 2009 the court rules were changed to try to encourage greater transparency and openness while still protecting rights to privacy, particularly of any children involved in

22

The civil justice system

the proceedings. While the media were keen for this reform to be introduced, the majority of judges, lawyers and local authority employees were opposed to this change.

The debate regarding the working of the family courts stems from the concern of fathers who feel that they have been treated unfairly by the courts. They have argued that the legal system has been biased in favour of mothers when determining such issues as access to their children and financial contributions. Some fathers managed to get support for their cause in the media, but there were suggestions that actually the public were not able to get a full picture of the case, because many of the court proceedings took place in private; so journalists might not be aware of good reasons why access to the father's children was being restricted, such as that he had been violent in the past. These issues raised the question of whether the public would have a better understanding of the court proceedings if they were open to the public. A balance needs to be achieved between the public's interest, and the interests of the children in a case. This balance has been highlighted where children have been taken into care by social services when there has been a suspicion of abuse and the family have claimed their innocence. While the family are free to speak to the media and put their side of the case, the social services have an obligation to respect the privacy of the children and fear that the public are getting a very one-sided perspective of the case.

In the light of these debates, the Government issued a consultation paper on whether the court privacy rules should be reformed. The paper was entitled *Confidence and Confidentiality: Improving Transparency and Privacy in Family Courts* (2006) and looked at how to find the delicate balance between the need for a transparent and open justice system while maintaining an individual's right to privacy. The aim was to increase public understanding and confidence in the legal process. However, research carried out by the academic Dr Julia Brophy – *Openness and Transparency in Family Courts: Messages from Other Jurisdictions* (2007) – found that in countries where there is more media access, such as Australia, there is no evidence of greater public understanding of the legal process.

Following strong opposition to the suggestions in this first consultation paper, a second consultation paper was published: *Confidence and Confidentiality: Openness in Family Courts – A New Approach* (2007). The Ministry of Justice issued its final report *Family Justice in View* in 2008.

Under the new scheme for family courts introduced in April 2009 the media now have access to all family proceedings except adoption cases and those concerned with judicially assisted conciliation or negotiation. Once the conciliation element of a hearing is complete and the judge is adjudicating upon the issues between the parties, journalists should be allowed to attend. Journalists must show a valid press card to have access to the court. At any stage of the proceedings the court may direct that a journalist cannot attend if this is necessary in the interests of a child, to protect the parties or witnesses, to enable the orderly conduct of proceedings or to prevent the obstruction of justice. No information must be published which would identify any child involved in court proceedings. The Government intends to include a statutory framework determining access to the family courts in the Improving Schools and Safeguarding Children Bill, which it intends to introduce into Parliament during the 2009/10 parliamentary session.

The media have inevitably been pushing for increased access to the family courts but, in practice, they will only be interested in reporting a narrow range of family cases, particularly celebrity divorces. Most family cases are of interest to nobody apart from the parties themselves (and perhaps a few nosy neighbours). Restrictions to media access to divorce courts were introduced in 1926 because of the lurid details of divorce cases then appearing in the press. It has to be remembered that the priority of the media is not to behave responsibly but to make money. In practice, it may be that the risk of media exposure will prompt a greater number of out-of-court settlements, as a person's desire to keep their personal lives private outweighs their desire to achieve the best possible outcome for themselves in a case.

Photo 22.2 A stunt at Buckingham Palace by the campaign group Fathers 4 Justice
Source: Scott Barbour/Getty Images

Criticism of the civil justice system

Costs

There is growing concern that Lord Woolf's reforms increased rather than reduced costs. *The Woolf Network Questionnaire* (2002) suggests that the cost of engaging in civil litigation has not been reduced by the civil justice reforms. The chair of the City of London Law Society said in 2008 that Lord Woolf's reforms had 'backfired'. The pre-action protocols combined with case management may have front-loaded costs onto cases which would have settled anyway before reaching court. While in the past lawyers could keep their early costs down while waiting to see if the case would settle, this is not possible when pre-action protocols and case management directions need to be complied with. There has been an increasing problem that after a legal dispute has been resolved, the parties then enter into separate litigation as to the amount of legal costs that should be paid by the losing party – known as satellite litigation.

As a result, the senior judge who is the president of the civil courts (the Master of the Rolls) has asked another judge, Lord Justice Jackson, to carry out an independent review of civil litigation costs. His final report is expected to be published at the end of 2009. In his interim report he has drawn attention to the cost-shifting rule (under which the loser pays the winner's costs) which causes particular complications where there is a conditional fee agreement. He appears to favour a one-way cost-shifting rule, particularly for personal injury claims. Under this if the defendant lost, he would pay the claimant's costs, but if the claimant lost, each side would bear its own costs. While this might appear unfair to the defendant, it would mean that after-event insurance where there are conditional fee agreements would no longer be necessary. The risk is that a one-way cost-shifting rule may encourage the pursuit of weak claims and claimants may not be motivated to settle their claims. Lord Justice Jackson is considering restricting the recoverability of costs incurred during the pre-action protocol period and limiting the duty of disclosure. He has suggested that the success fee and the cost of after-event insurance should not be recoverable by the winning party, but should be paid out of the winner's award of damages. He has also proposed that Lord Woolf's original idea of fixed costs being charged by lawyers for the whole of fast-track cases (not just the trial) should be implemented so that lawyers will not be able to choose themselves how much it is appropriate to charge for work on each case. He has noted that Germany has a system of fixed costs which works well in practice.

In many cases, especially those involving personal injury, the defendant's costs, and sometimes those of the claimant, will be paid by an insurance company – for example, the parties in a car accident are likely to have been insured and professionals such as doctors are insured against negligence claims. As Hazel Genn's 1987 study showed, where only one party is insured, this can place great pressure on the other, unless they have been granted state funding. The insured side may try to drag out the proceedings for as long as possible, in the hope of exhausting the other party's financial reserves and forcing a low settlement.

Professor Zander (2004) has argued that in many civil cases the claimant wins and the defendant is an insurance company who currently pays the claimant's costs. If, in future, the court can only order the loser to pay fixed and fairly low costs, then the claimant's lawyers will not be able to claim back everything that it was in fact necessary to spend on the case in order to win. He predicts that, as a result, either the work will not be done or the client will have to pay for it out of their damages. Either way, justice will not have been served.

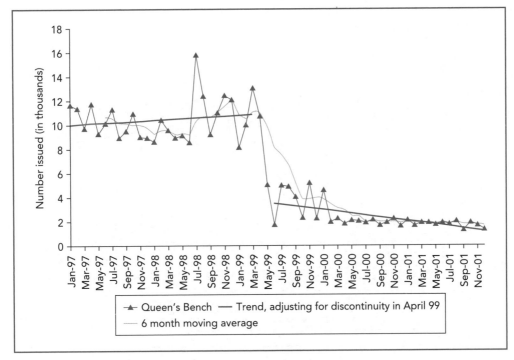

Figure 22.5 Claims in the Queen's Bench Division of the High Court

Source: Civil Justice Reform Evaluation Further Findings (2002) [Figure 2]

Standards

A pilot simulation carried out by civil litigators on behalf of the old Lord Chancellor's Department to try to predict the impact of the Woolf reforms on the civil justice system was not encouraging (*Report of the Fast Track Simulation Pilot* (1998)). Those involved expressed the fear that pressures on practitioners in terms of both time and costs might lead to corner-cutting, devolution of cases to less experienced fee earners, insufficient time for proper investigation of the claim, and the incurring of irrecoverable costs. They worried too that the openness that Lord Woolf was so keen to encourage as a fundamental principle underlying his reforms might be prejudiced by the 'fear factor'. In other words, solicitors might be secretive during the early stages of the litigation so as to avoid client criticism and potential negligence claims; and be reluctant to tell a client about the weakness of a case.

Enforcement

The enforcement of judgments continues to be a problem. Research carried out by Professor John Baldwin (2003) of Birmingham University has highlighted this weakness in the civil justice system. He concluded that the difficulties with enforcing civil judgments were leaving many claimants disillusioned with the legal system. The danger is that if the system of enforcement is inadequate creditors will look to other methods of securing payment. Provisions are contained in the Tribunals, Courts and

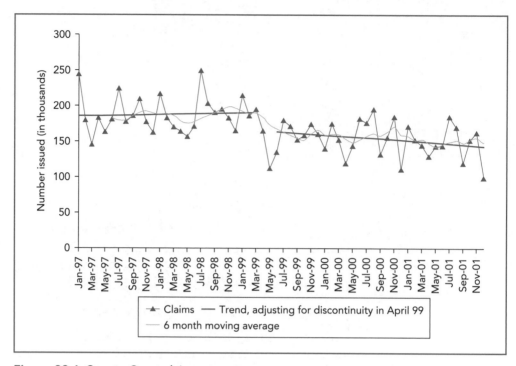

Figure 22.6 County Court claims

Source: Civil Justice Reform Evaluation Further Findings (2002) [Figure 1]

Enforcement Act 2007 which aim to improve the arrangements for the enforcement of judgments.

Out-of-court settlements

The *Judicial Statistics* show that there has been a significant drop in the number of cases reaching the courts since the Woolf reforms were introduced. In 1995 over 150,000 claims were commenced in the High Court. By 2007, the number had fallen to 64,000. The number of claims issued in the county courts has also dropped significantly in recent times. In 1998 the number of claims issued nationally was over 2,200,000 but by 2005 the number of annual claims had fallen to less than 1,900,000. This drop is partly due to the favourable economic climate, and 2006 saw a slight increase in the number of claims being brought as the economic climate turned sour with the global credit crunch starting to bite.

The use of pre-action protocols and claimant offers to encourage pre-trial settlements has diverted cases from being litigated in the courts. As a result only 8 per cent of cases listed for trial settle at the trial, while 70 per cent settle much earlier. The reforms put considerable emphasis on the use of out-of-court settlements, which can have the advantage of providing a quick end to the dispute, and a reduction in costs. For the claimant, a settlement means they are sure of getting something, and do not have to risk losing the case altogether and probably having to pay the other side's costs as well as their own. But they must weigh this up against the chances of being awarded a better

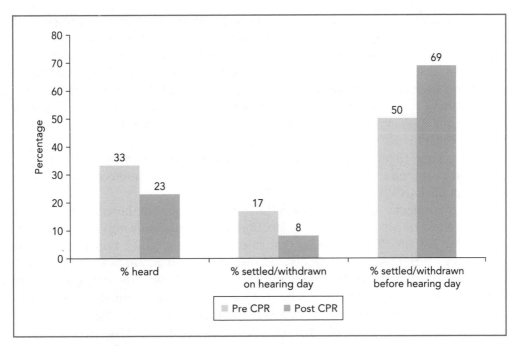

Figure 22.7 Comparison of disposal of 'Fast Track' cases
Source: Civil Justice Reform Evaluation Further Findings (2002) [Figure 6]

settlement if the case goes to trial and they win. The defendant risks the possibility that they might have won and therefore had to pay nothing, or that they may be paying more than the judge would have awarded if the claimant had won the case, against the chance that the claimant wins and is awarded more than the settlement would have cost.

The high number of out-of-court settlements creates injustice, because the parties usually hold very unequal bargaining positions. In the first place, one party might be in a better financial position than the other, and therefore under less pressure to keep costs down by settling quickly.

Secondly, as Galanter's 1984 study revealed, litigants can often be divided into 'one-shotters' and 'repeat players'. One-shotters are individuals involved in litigation for probably the only time in their life, for whom the procedure is unfamiliar and traumatic; the case is very important to them and tends to occupy most of their thoughts while it continues. Repeat players, on the other hand, include companies and businesses (particularly insurance companies), for whom litigation is routine. They are used to working with the law and lawyers and, while they obviously want to win the case for financial reasons, they do not have the same emotional investment in it as the individual one-shotter. Where a repeat player and a one-shotter are on opposing sides – as is often the case in personal injury litigation, where an individual is fighting an insurance company – the repeat player is likely to have the upper hand in out-of-court bargaining.

A third factor was highlighted by Hazel Genn's 1987 study of negotiated settlements of accident claims. She found that having a non-specialist lawyer could seriously prejudice a client's interests when an out-of-court settlement is made. A non-specialist may be unfamiliar with court procedure and reluctant to fight the case in court. They may, therefore, not encourage their client to hold out against an unsatisfactory settlement. Specialist lawyers on the other side may take advantage of this inexperience, putting on pressure for the acceptance of a low settlement. Repeat players are more likely to have access to their own specialist lawyers, whereas, for the one-shotter, finding a suitable lawyer can be something of a lottery, since they have little information on which to base their choice.

Clearly, these factors affect the fairness of out-of-court settlements. In court, the judge can treat the parties as equals, but for out-of-court negotiations one party often has a very obvious advantage.

The Government's first evaluation of the new Civil Procedure Rules has found that overall the reforms have been beneficial: *Emerging Findings: an early evaluation of the Civil Justice Reforms* (2001). It seems that cases are settling earlier, rather than at the door of the court. Lawyers and clients are now regarding litigation as a last resort, and making more use of alternative methods of dispute resolution. The pre-action protocols have been a success. Their effect has been to concentrate the minds of defendants and make them deal properly with a claim at the early stages rather than months after the issue of proceedings (conditional fee agreements could also be an explanation for this). While generally cases are being heard more quickly after the issue of the claim, small claims are taking longer. But the picture is not quite as straightforward as it looks. Lawyers know that as soon as they issue the claim form they will lose control of the pace of the negotiations and are going to be locked into timetables and procedures which they may find burdensome as well as costly. There is evidence that lawyers are therefore delaying issuing the claim. It is not yet clear whether litigation has become

Ess. Cases
p. 349 → cheaper. The report quotes practitioners who believe the front-end loading of costs caused by the pre-action protocols means that overall costs have actually gone up.

In their research paper, *More Civil Justice: The Impact of the Woolf Reforms on Pre-action Behaviour* (2002), the Law Society and the Civil Justice Council assessed the success of the new pre-action procedures. Most of the respondents were positive about their introduction. In particular, personal injury practitioners and insurers have welcomed the additional information the protocol requires to be disclosed during the early stages of proceedings, as it facilitates early settlement.

The latest research into the civil justice system, *The Management of Civil Cases: The Courts and the Post-Woolf Landscape* (2005), concludes that the reforms have led to a better litigation culture. They have significantly reduced the amount of litigation going to court from 2.2 million cases in 1997 to 1.5 million cases in 2003. However, costs have increased, they have become front loaded (in other words, more costs are incurred at the earlier stages of the litigation process) and the cost of each case is higher overall.

Court-appointed experts

Court-appointed experts may tend to increase cost in that the parties will often still employ their own experts.

Small claims track

The small claims procedure is an important part of the civil procedure system, involving around 80,000 actions each year. The procedure is quicker, simpler and cheaper than the full county court process, which is helpful to both litigants and the over-worked court system. It gives individuals and small businesses a useful lever against creditors or for consumer complaints. Without it, threats to sue over small amounts would be ignored on the basis that going to court would cost more than the value of the debt or compensation claimed. Public confidence is also increased, by proving that the legal system is not only accessible to the rich and powerful. The academic, Professor John Baldwin, has carried out research into the small claims track, *Lay and Judicial Perspectives on the Expansion of the Small Claims Regime* (2002). He noted that the official statistics show that the recent rises in the small claims limit have not led, as many feared, to the county courts being inundated with new cases. There has only been a slight increase in the number of small claims cases. Most small claims litigants involved in relatively high value claims are satisfied with the experience. However, there are long-standing concerns about the small claims procedure, which have not been tackled by the 1999 reforms. Small claims are not necessarily simple claims; they may involve complex and unusual points of law. Is the small claimant entitled to be judged by the law of the land or by speedier, more rough-and-ready concepts of fairness?

The Consumers' Association magazine, *Which?*, is of the view that the small claims procedure is not simple enough. It reported in 1986 that the process was still 'quite an ordeal', and the level of formality varied widely. The submissions of both the National Consumer Council and the National Association of Citizens' Advice Bureaux to the Civil Justice Review echoed this feeling. The Civil Justice Review recommended that court forms and leaflets should be simplified. The system is still largely used by small businesses chasing debtors, rather than by the individual consumer for whom it was set up. A consultation paper was issued in 1995 suggesting that, in limited cases, the judge might be given the power to award an additional sum of up to £135 to cover the cost of legal advice and assistance in the preparation of the case. If this reform were to be introduced it might assist individual consumers to bring their cases.

There are also problems with enforcement. A survey by the old Lord Chancellor's Department in 1986 found that 25 per cent of parties were failing to get the payment owed to them from the defendant following a successful application. A report by the Consumers' Association (November 1997) suggests that many people using the small claims procedure are being denied justice because of slow and inefficient enforcement procedures. The court is not responsible for enforcement, which is left to the winning party to secure. The report found that only a minority of defendants paid up on time and that after six months a substantial minority of people still had not paid their debts. Baldwin concluded that the enforcement problem was so serious that it threatened to undermine the small claims procedure itself by deterring people from using it.

The Government considered raising the financial level of personal injury cases that can be considered by the small claims procedures from £1,000 to £5,000. The Better Regulation Taskforce (an independent advisory body established in 1997) published a report *Better Routes to Redress* (2004). This suggested that the Government should consider raising the limits for personal injury cases to bring them into line with most other civil claims, which can already be considered by the small claims court when they involve claims of up to £5,000. The Taskforce suggested that the reform would 'increase access to justice for many as it will be less expensive, less adversarial and less stressful'. The Government is concerned that procedures and costs should be proportionate to the size of the claim.

At the moment most personal injury cases are heard under the fast-track procedure, which means costs can be recovered and lawyers can represent clients on a no win no fee basis. If the financial limits were changed about 70 per cent of personal injury cases would be heard by the small claims procedure. On the small claims track, court costs cannot be recovered and lawyers are not able to represent clients on a no win no fee basis. Litigants would therefore frequently be forced to represent themselves. The Association of Personal Injury Lawyers has argued that personal injury cases are complex and people want and need the help of a lawyer to prepare their case. The person being sued is likely to have been insured and will benefit from the specialist help of the insurer's lawyers.

Baldwin's research concluded that the informal small claims procedures inevitably involve a sacrifice in the standards of judicial decision-making. He questioned whether this could be justified in claims involving more than the existing financial limits.

The Civil Justice Council spent three years looking at the funding of civil claims and how to keep costs in proportion. In 2005 it published its report, *Improved Access to Justice – Funding Options and Proportionate Costs* (2005). It recommends that the small claims track limit for personal injury cases should be retained at £1,000. It considers that the fast-track limit for personal injury cases should be increased from £15,000 to £25,000, though parties could opt to have their cases on this track for claims up to £50,000.

The Government issued a consultation paper on this subject in 2007. It considers whether fast-track cases should be brought within fixed time limits and with fixed recoverable costs being payable to lawyers, rather than lawyers being paid by the hour for their work. For example, insurers would have three weeks to investigate road traffic claims and admit or deny liability, while the claimant solicitors would only carry out urgent investigations at this stage, to try to keep costs down.

In 2008, the Government announced that, following this consultation process, it had decided to raise the fast-track financial limit for personal injury cases to £25,000. A new streamlined procedure would be introduced for road traffic accident claims worth between £1,000 and £10,000.

The Government has decided against raising the small claims limit to £5,000 because this would not be in the interests of consumers.

TOPICAL ISSUE

Compensation culture

There has been some concern that the UK might be developing a compensation culture, which has historically been associated with the US. A compensation culture implies that people with frivolous and unwarranted claims bring cases to court with a view to making easy money. The phenomenon of a more litigious society can be interpreted in two very different ways. It can be seen as a good thing because more people are asserting their rights and obtaining stronger legal protection. At the same time it can be seen as a bad thing because the law is pushing people into relationships which lack trust and creating confrontational communities.

The Lord Chancellor has concluded that the UK does not have an unhealthy compensation culture (accident claims actually fell by 10 per cent in 2004), but the increased number of threats to sue and the resulting fear of being sued is having a negative effect on people's work and behaviour, and this trend needs to be reversed. In 2004 he commented:

> If you have a genuine claim – where someone else is to blame – you should be able to get compensation from those at fault. This is only fair. The victim or taxpayer shouldn't have to pay out where someone else is to blame. But there is not always someone else to blame. Genuine accidents do happen. People should not be encouraged to always 'have a go' however meritless the claim. The perception that there is easy money just waiting to be had – the so called 'compensation culture' – creates very real problems. People become scared of being sued; organizations avoid taking risks and stop perfectly sensible activities. It creates burdens for those handling claims and critically it also undermines genuine claims.

The Compensation Act 2006 contains provisions to encourage the courts to consider whether a successful negligence claim in a particular case might prevent a desirable activity, such as a school trip, from taking place in future.

The Government is concerned that the problems relating to a compensation culture are being aggravated by the unscrupulous sales tactics of some claims management companies, which encourage people who have suffered minor personal injuries to bring litigation. Advertisements are frequently broadcast on television, asking the viewers if they have suffered an accident in the last three years. A report on the issue, *Better Routes to Redress*, was published in 2004. This recommended that stronger guidelines regarding appropriate advertisements needed to be issued, and the claims management companies needed to be more carefully regulated. However, it did feel that these companies and advertisements should be allowed to continue, as they helped improve access to legal services by spreading information about the services available and the ways that these could be paid for. The Government has decided that claims management companies need to be regulated and relevant provisions are contained in the Compensation Act 2006.

The insurers, Norwich Union, have suggested a radical solution to the compensation culture, of abolishing all claims for under £1,000 (*A modern compensation system: moving from concept to reality* (2004)). The Law Society has rejected this suggestion, pointing out that denying people their right to seek compensation for claims under £1,000 would prevent the courts from getting to the root cause of injuries and falsely assumes that a loss of £1,000 is a trivial matter.

The Bar Council is concerned that plans to allow private companies to own law firms (see p. 216) would fuel the move towards a compensation culture, as such companies would seek to grow demand for legal services to increase profits. The legal sector could as a result become more commercialised, with franchising, national brand-building and more television advertising.

ss. Cases p. 352 →

22

The civil justice system

Professor Zander's concerns

Professor Zander (1998), a leading academic, felt that the reforms were fundamentally flawed, rather than prone to temporary hiccups, and was very vociferous in expressing his opposition to the reforms prior to their implementation. He is reported to have said that they amounted to taking a sledgehammer to crack a nut. Below is an analysis of the main concerns he has expressed.

The causes of delay

Lord Woolf's view was that the chief cause of delay was the way the adversarial system was played by the lawyers. Zander has criticised this analysis, pointing out that it is only supported by 'unsubstantiated opinion' rather than real evidence, despite the fact that it forms the basis for most of the subsequent proposals. By contrast, Zander has drawn attention to research carried out for the Lord Chancellor's Department in 1994 into the causes of delay. It identified seven causes: the type of case; the parties; the judiciary; court procedures; court administration; the lawyers (mainly due to pressure of work, inexperience or inefficiency); and external factors such as the difficulty of getting experts' reports, including medical reports. Of these seven factors, the last two factors were felt to be the most significant. Not all the reasons for the delay were the fault of the system: for example, in some cases it may be necessary to wait for an accident victim's medical condition to stabilise in order to assess the long-term prognosis. Accident victims in particular often do not seek legal advice until some time after the accident has occurred.

Clearly, if Lord Woolf has wrongly diagnosed the causes of delay it is unlikely that his reforms will resolve these problems. The *Judicial Statistics* published in 2002 show that, in the High Court, the time taken between issue and trial has gone up to 173 weeks, but delays have been reduced in the county court, where the average time from issue to trial fell from 640 days in 1997 to 500 in 2000–01.

Case management

Zander feels that court management is appropriate for only a minority of cases and that the key is to identify these. He has remarked that judges do not have the time, skills or inclination to undertake the task of case management. The court does not know enough about the workings of a solicitor's office to be able to set appropriate timetables. In addition, litigants on the fast-track may feel that the brisk way in which a three-hour hearing deals with the dispute is inadequate. Most will not feel that justice has been done by a short, sharp trial with restricted oral evidence and an interventionist judge chivvying the parties to a resolution of their dispute.

A move towards judicial management has already been seen in the US, Australia and Canada. A major official study was published by the Institute of Civil Justice at the Rand Corporation in California (Kakalik *et al.*, 1996). This research was not available to Lord Woolf while he was compiling his report. The study was based on a five-year survey of 10,000 cases looking at the effect of the American Civil Justice Reform Act 1990. This Act required certain federal courts to practise case management. Judicial case management has been part of the US system for many years so that, compared with

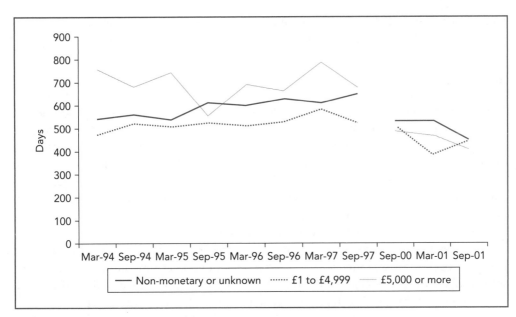

Figure 22.8 Trials – average time from issue to trial by claim value

Source: Civil Justice Reform Evaluation Further Findings (2002) [Figure 10]

this country, the procedural innovations being studied operated from a different starting point.

The study found that judicial case management did lead to a reduced time to disposition. Its early use yielded a reduction of one-and-a-half or two months to resolution for cases that lasted at least nine months. Also, having a discovery timetable and reducing the time within which discovery took place both significantly reduced time to disposition and significantly reduced the amount of hours spent on the case by a lawyer. These benefits were achieved without any significant change in the lawyers' or litigants' satisfaction or views of fairness.

On the other hand, case management led to an approximate 20-hour increase in lawyer work hours overall. Their work increased with the need to respond to the court's management directions. In addition, once judicial case management had begun, a discovery cut-off date had usually been established and lawyers felt an obligation to begin discovery on a case which might be settled. Thus, the Rand Report found that case management, by generating more work for lawyers, tended to increase rather than reduce costs.

The Rand Report noted that the effectiveness of implementation depended on judicial attitudes. Some judges viewed these procedural innovations as an attack on judicial independence and felt that it emphasised speed and efficiency at the possible expense of justice. The Report concluded, among other things, that judicial management should wait a month after the defence has been entered in case the action settles.

In research carried out for the Law Society, *The Woolf Network Questionnaire* (2002), 84 per cent of solicitors questioned said they thought the new procedures were quicker and 70 per cent said they were more efficient than the old ones. Greater use of telephone case management conferences was cited as leading to greater efficiency.

Sanctions

Procedural timetables for the fast-track are, according to Professor Zander, doomed to failure because a huge proportion of firms, for a range of reasons, will fail to keep to the prescribed timetables. This will necessitate enforcement procedures and sanctions on a vast scale which, in turn, will lead to innumerable appeals. Sanctions will be imposed that are disproportionate and therefore unjust, and will cause injustice to clients for the failings of the lawyers. Furthermore, if the judges did impose severe sanctions when lawyers failed to comply with timetable deadlines, it would usually be the litigants rather than the lawyers who would be penalised.

Professor Zander has pointed to the courts' experience of Ord. 17 under the old County Court Rules as evidence that lawyers are not good at time limits and sanctions were unlikely to change that. Under that order an action would be automatically struck out if the claimant failed to take certain steps within the time limits set by the rule. From its introduction in 1990 until 1998, roughly 20,000 cases had been struck out on this basis, leaving 20,000 people either to sue their lawyers for negligence or to start all over again. In relation to Ord. 17, the Court of Appeal stated in **Bannister** v **SGB plc** (1997):

> This rule has given rise to great difficulties and has generated an immense amount of litigation devoted to the question whether a particular action has been struck out and if so, whether it should be reinstated. In short, the rule has in a large number of cases achieved the opposite of its object, which was to speed up the litigation process in the county courts.

There is the danger that, if the court does not exercise its power temperately and judiciously then, in its eagerness to dispose of litigation, it will actually generate more litigation. This danger is particularly acute where the court exercises powers on its own initiative. If, for example, the court moves to strike out a statement of case on its own initiative, the likely result is that the party affected will apply to have its case reinstated; and if, in fact, it was not a suitable case for striking out, unnecessary cost and delay will be the result.

There is a risk that unrealistic trial dates and timetables will be set, particularly in heavy litigation, at an early stage, and of the judges insisting on their being adhered to thereafter, regardless of the consequences.

In the research for the Law Society, *The Woolf Network Questionnaire* (2002), some solicitors said they were reluctant to apply for sanctions against those who did not stick to the pre-action protocols. This was because they felt that the courts were unwilling to impose sanctions for non-compliance in all but the most serious cases, judges were inconsistent in their approach to sanctions and an application for sanctions was likely to cause more delays and additional costs.

Reform

Clearly the civil justice system underwent significant reforms in 1999, but further reforms could be made.

TOPICAL ISSUE

Road traffic accidents

The Government intends to introduce a streamlined claims system for personal injury cases following road traffic accidents for between £1,000 and £10,000 where the defendant does not dispute liability and the only dispute is with regard to how much damages should be paid. A consultation paper on the subject was published in 2007 entitled *Case Track Limits and the Claims Process for Personal Injury Claims*. The scheme is expected to be introduced in 2010 and will handle 70 per cent of all road accident claims. The aim is to provide a swift and cheap resolution procedure. The process is divided into three stages. The first stage involves the issuing of the claim and the defence response. Stage two is the effort to settle the case and stage three is the court hearing. There will normally only be a paper hearing of the case, though the parties will have the right to request an oral hearing. The whole process should normally be completed within three months. The parties will use standard template documents, they will be entitled to use lawyers, but only fixed costs will be payable.

Integration

A proposal to integrate the High Court and the county court to produce a simpler system was considered by the Gorell Committee on county court procedure back in 1912, but rejected, mainly on the grounds that hearing big cases in the county courts would prejudice the handling of smaller ones.

The proposal was also considered by the Civil Justice Review, which pointed out that the two-court system was inflexible, making it difficult to make rational allocations of judges' and administrators' time between the different courts. Consequently, some courts have much longer delays than others. In a unified court, all cases would start in the same way and be allocated to different sorts of judges on the basis of their complexity. Judges could be sent where they were needed most, and some higher level judges could be based outside London.

The recommendation was supported by solicitors, advice centres and consumer organisations but strongly opposed by barristers and judges, for rather unattractive reasons. Barristers feared that solicitors would have greater rights of audience in the unified court and that the London Bar would lose business to provincial solicitors; High Court judges thought that the proposals would reduce their standing and destroy their special way of life, especially if they were expected to be based for long periods of time in the provinces.

In the end the Review rejected the idea of a unified court, on the grounds that there was no general support for it, the financial implications were uncertain, a unified court would require major legislation and a lengthy implementation period and it might have adverse effects on the standing of the High Court judiciary. But the former Head of Civil Justice, Sir Richard Scott VC, has predicted that ultimately the High Court and county courts will merge.

Ess. Cases
p. 350 ➡

The Government looked again at this issue in a consultation paper, *A Single Civil Court?* (2005). That report considered abolishing the county courts, while giving the High Court a wider jurisdiction to hear all civil cases at first instance. The Government is concerned that it is inefficient and costly for the Courts Service to administer two separate civil court systems. The President of the Courts of England and Wales asked a senior judge, Sir Henry Brooke, to look at whether the civil courts should be unified, but he concluded in 2009 that they should not.

Changed court jurisdiction

Civil court proceedings are cheaper than High Court proceedings and the Government is considering whether more cases should be heard by the county court. A consultation paper, *Focusing Judicial Resources Appropriately* (2005), proposed that all civil and family cases should begin at the 'lowest appropriate level' (the county court or the magistrates' court), unless the lawyers in the case successfully argue that exceptional features in the case mean that it needs to be heard in the High Court.

An inquisitorial system

In theory, the civil justice system could move to an inquisitorial system, in which the judge would take a more investigative role and the two parties would be required to cooperate by revealing all their evidence to each other. Tactics would become less important and, since delay is often a part of these tactics, the whole process could be speeded up. Some would suggest that this system might also be fairer, since being able to afford the best lawyer would be less important.

In fact, a full change away from the adversarial system seems extremely unlikely, but there have been proposals for such movement in certain areas: the Civil Justice Review suggested that a paper adjudication scheme might be considered for handling certain claims, which would move to an oral hearing only if the adjudicator felt there were difficulties which made one necessary. The procedure would be compulsory for road accidents and claims under £5,000 and could also be used in other cases where the parties agreed. This idea has been opposed by both the National Consumer Council and the National Association of Citizens' Advice Bureaux, on the ground that those who could afford a skilled lawyer to draft their papers would have too much of an advantage. Some of the Woolf proposals also favour a move towards an inquisitorial approach and a less aggressive form of litigation.

Progress towards full pre-trial disclosure of evidence, and the fact that Small Claims Court arbitrators now take a more interventionist approach, can be seen as moves towards a more inquisitorial system.

Reform of compensation for personal injury

Tort law dictates that the victims of an accident (other than industrial accidents, which are covered by a compensation scheme) can get compensation only if they can prove that the harm caused to them was somebody else's fault. The result of this is that individuals with identical injuries may receive hundreds of thousands of pounds in compensation, or nothing more than state benefits, depending not on their needs but on whether they can prove fault – often very difficult to do conclusively. In many cases, the state has to spend money, in the form of legal aid, but if the case is lost, the only person to benefit from that expenditure is the lawyer. Because of this, it is often suggested that the tort action for personal injury should be abolished and the financial savings should be used to provide improved welfare benefits for all those injured by accidents. New Zealand has adopted such an approach and established a no fault system of compensation.

The National Health Service Redress Act 2006 contains provisions for a quick and simple process for compensating people with small claims (up to £20,000) against the NHS. The Act introduced a scheme overseen by the NHS Litigation Authority and cases are dealt with outside the courts. A more open approach is being fostered, so that NHS staff are encouraged to report mistakes, taking the onus off patients to initiate claims. In a particular case financial compensation may not be appropriate, but patients could still be provided with an explanation, apology and remedial care. Patients are able to withdraw from the scheme if they decide they would rather take their claim to court. But if they do withdraw from the scheme, they may find that legal aid is not available for legal proceedings. If patients accept an offer of redress then they waive their right to bring subsequent legal proceedings. Before the scheme was introduced, over three-quarters of claims valued between £10,000 and £15,000 cost more to settle than the amount awarded. The government's aim is to compensate more victims of clinical negligence, more quickly, on a less adversarial basis, at a lower administrative cost. While the National Health Service Redress Scheme provides an alternative to the court procedures for smaller claims, it is still necessary for claimants to have been the victim of conduct 'qualifying liability in tort' under s. 1(2) of the 2006 Act. Thus the scheme is not introducing a no-fault system of compensation.

Modernisation

The Government issued a consultation paper, *Modernising the Civil Courts* (2001). This looked at the possibility of applying the same developments in technology to the Courts Service that have been applied to the private sector, such as retail banking. Unfortunately, insufficient money has been invested in developing the IT system that a modern court system requires and so the current IT resources are inadequate. The senior judiciary are concerned that lack of investment in the civil courts is putting at risk London's status as an international centre for commercial litigation. The Master of the Rolls has stated: 'Our civil justice system must keep abreast of technological developments that are happening elsewhere.'

Answering questions

1 **To what extent has the adoption of the Woolf reforms changed the nature of the civil justice process?** *London External LLB*

This is the type of topical examination question which is likely to be popular with examiners for the next few years. Before you launch into answering this question, you need to decide what line of argument you are going to take. There are two lines of argument possible, which will both be equally correct provided you back up your arguments with facts. You could either take the view that the Woolf reforms made changes to the civil justice system but have not changed the 'nature' of those proceedings, or you could argue that the changes have been so fundamental that they have changed the very nature of the civil justice process. It is up to you which line of argument you take.

The reforms would have changed the nature of the proceedings if they had made them more inquisitorial rather than adversarial (see p. 425). Lord Woolf certainly hoped to change the litigation culture, so that through the use of pre-action protocols there would be a greater openness between the parties and more emphasis on early settlement of cases. The recent research into the civil justice reforms show that these goals have been achieved, though there has not been a significant shift towards alternative dispute resolution (see p. 631).

2 **(a)** **Discuss the advantages and disadvantages of the civil court system.**

(b) **What new reforms might further improve the civil justice system?**

(a) The capacity of the traditional civil courts to resolve disputes in a manner that is efficient, economic and speedy is an issue of enduring concern. You could point out that while the courts themselves have remained the same in recent years, the procedures practised within them have changed dramatically. With the introduction of the Woolf reforms it is difficult to assess at the moment how successful these reforms have been. You could discuss the weaknesses that had existed (see p. 534) and you could mention Zander's concerns that these reforms will not put an end to these problems (see p. 560). When looking at the advantages of the current system, you could mention the status of the judiciary in our society, the general belief in judicial impartiality, the certainty provided by the use of precedent (discussed at p. 33) and the structure of appeals to remedy mistakes (see p. 586).

(b) You could point out that major reforms were only just introduced in April 1999, and it might be wise to wait and see how far these reforms will prove to be effective before giving judgment on what should be done next. But possible reforms are discussed at p. 563. You could also consider whether a reversion to the pre-1999 position might be desirable. Using material from Chapter 25, you might discuss how far alternative methods of dispute resolution should replace the civil system.

3 Reforms to the civil justice system introduced after Lord Woolf's review and report, *Access to Justice* (1996), were aimed at eliminating unnecessary cost, delay and complexity from the system. Briefly explain what the main reforms were. In your view, have these reforms achieved their intended aims?

You should begin by explaining why the review was commissioned; outline Lord Woolf's recommendations and how these were implemented. You could explain the Civil Procedure Rules and mention the overriding objective (p. 537). You could discuss the pre-action protocols, case management and the three-track system (p. 544). The evidence to date is that the reforms have been beneficial, though they may not have achieved the original aims. This may be because of the constant amendments; problems with enforcement; and because the rules are not simple enough. You should also mention Professor Zander's concerns here (p. 560), then finish with the suggestions for further reform (p. 563).

4 Why has the small claims court proved so popular?

The small claims route in the county court was originally established in 1973 to provide a method of resolving small debt disputes and consumer claims without disproportionate expense, risk or complexity. Now, it is embodied in the small claims track of the county court and currently deals with claims valued at less than £5,000 (£1,000 for personal injury claims). Although included in the Woolf reforms, the small claims system has remained significantly unchanged by them. The small claims track remains attractive to individuals and small businesses as it discourages the formality of the full court (with the need for disclosure and the use of expert evidence), encourages lay representation (state funding for representation is not available), and most hearings are concluded within 30 minutes. A further advantage is that costs are not usually awarded, and so an individual may proceed without fear that failure would result in an adverse costs order.

However, there are problems: the value of a claim may not reflect the underlying complexity, and the limit for personal injuries is very low.

In some respects the small claims system may have been a victim of its own success, as the Government has on occasion considered whether the financial limits could be raised to increase the number of cases heard in this way. The academic John Baldwin, among others, has argued quite forcefully that the small claims track is good at what it is currently doing, but because of its limitations it would not be appropriate to extend it to financially more important and potentially more complex cases.

Summary of Chapter 22: The civil justice system

Civil courts
There are two main civil courts which hear civil cases at first instance. These are the county courts and the High Court.

The civil justice system before April 1999
Before the implementation of the Woolf reforms, there were two separate sets of civil procedure rules for the county courts and the High Court and Court of Appeal. The system was heavily criticised for being too expensive and slow.

The civil justice system after April 1999

In April 1999 new Civil Procedure Rules and accompanying Practice Directions came into force. The new rules introduce the main recommendations of Lord Woolf in his final report, *Access to Justice*. The reforms aim to eliminate unnecessary cost, delay and complexity in the civil justice system. The ultimate goal is to change fundamentally the litigation culture. Thus, the first rule of the new Civil Procedure Rules lays down an overriding objective which is to underpin the whole system. This overriding objective is that the rules should enable the courts to deal with cases justly. The emphasis of the new rules is on avoiding litigation through pre-trial settlements.

Civil Procedure Rules

For non-personal injury actions, a claim may be started in the High Court, where the claimant expects to recover more than £15,000. For personal injury actions a claim can only be started in the High Court where the claimant expects to recover at least £50,000.

Pre-action protocols

To push the parties into behaving reasonably during the pre-trial stage, pre-action protocols have been developed. These lay down a code of conduct for this stage of proceedings.

Alternative dispute resolution

At various stages in a dispute's history, the court will actively promote settlement by alternative dispute resolution (ADR).

Case management

Case management has been introduced, whereby the court plays an active role in managing the litigation. To determine the level and form of case management, cases have been divided into three types:

- small claims track;
- fast-track; and
- multi-track.

Sanctions

The courts now have tough powers to enforce the new rules on civil procedure to ensure that litigation is pursued diligently.

Criticism of the 1999 reforms

The 1999 reforms were generally well received, though Professor Zander has been a vociferous critic of the changes, suggesting that they would not succeed in reducing delays and expense.

Reading list

Baldwin, J. (1997) *Small Claims in County Courts in England and Wales: The Bargain Basement of Civil Justice?* Oxford: Clarendon Press.

Baldwin, J. (1998) 'Small claims hearings: The interventionist role played by district judges', 17 *Civil Justice Quarterly* 20.

Baldwin, J. (2002) *Lay and Judicial Perspectives on the Expansion of the Small Claims Regime*, London: Lord Chancellor's Department.

Baldwin, J. (2003) *Evaluating the Effectiveness of Enforcement Procedures in Undefended Claims in the Civil Courts*, London: Lord Chancellor's Department.

Barton, A. (2001) 'Medical litigation: who benefits?', *British Medical Journal* 322, 1189.

Galanter, M. (1984) *The emergence of the judge as a mediator in civil cases*, Madison: University of Wisconsin.

Genn, H. (1987) *Hard Bargaining: Out of Court Settlement in Personal Injury Actions*, Oxford: Clarendon Press.

Genn, H. (1997) 'Understanding civil justice', 50 *Current Legal Problems* 155.

Jolowicz, J. (1996) 'The Woolf Report and the Adversary System', 15 *Civil Justice Quarterly* 198.

Lord Chancellor's Department (2002) *Further Findings: A Continuing Evaluation of the Civil Justice Report*, London: Lord Chancellor's Department.

Morris, A. (2007) 'Spiralling or Stabilising?: The Compensation Culture and Our Propensity to Claim Damages for Personal Injury', 70 *Modern Law Review* 349.

Pleasence, P. (2004) *Causes of action: civil law and social justice*, London: HMSO.

Woolf, Lord Justice H. (1996) *Access to Justice*, London: Lord Chancellor's Department.

Woolf, Lord Justice H. (2008) *The Pursuit of Justice*, Oxford: Oxford University Press.

Zander, M. (1997) 'The Woolf Report: Forwards or Backwards for the New Lord Chancellor?' 17 *Civil Justice Quarterly* 208.

Zander, M. (1998) 'The Government's plans on civil justice', 61 *Modern Law Review* 382.

Zuckerman, A. (1995) 'A Reform of Civil Procedure – Rationing Procedure Rather than Access to Justice', 22 JLS 156.

Zuckerman, A. (1996) 'Lord Woolf's Access to Justice: Plus ça change . . .' 59 *Modern Law Review* 773.

Reading on the Internet

www The report of the Constitutional Affairs Select Committee, *Family Justice: the Operation of the Family Courts Revisited* (2007), is available at:
http://www.parliament.the-stationery-office.co.uk/pa/cm200506/cmselect/cmconst/cmconst.htm

The consultation paper *Confidence and Confidentiality: Openness in Family Courts – A New Approach* (2007) is available on the website of the Ministry of Justice at:
http://www.justice.gov.uk/publications/cp1007.htm

The research of Dr Julia Brophy, *Openness and Transparency in Family Courts: Messages from other Jurisdictions* (2007), is available on the website of the Ministry of Justice at:
http://www.justice.gov.uk/docs/consult-family-courts.pdf

The consultation paper *Case track limits and the claims process for personal injury claims* (2007) is available on the website of the former Department for Constitutional Affairs at:
http://www.dca.gov.uk/consult/case-track-limits/cp0807.pdf

The consultation paper *Confidence and Confidentiality: Improving Transparency and Privacy in Family Courts* (2006) is available on the website of the former Department for Constitutional Affairs at:
http://www.dca.gov.uk/consult/courttransparencey1106/consultation1106.pdf

The research *The Management of Civil Cases: The Courts and the Post-Woolf Landscape* (2005) is available on the Department for Constitutional Affairs' website at:
http://www.dca.gov.uk/research/2005/9_2005_summary.pdf

The report of the Civil Justice Council, *Improved Access to Justice – Funding Options and Proportionate Costs* (2005), is available at:
http://www.costsdebate.civiljusticecouncil.gov.uk

The research *Emerging Findings: an early evaluation of the Civil Justice Reforms* (2001) is available on the Department for Constitutional Affairs' website at:
http://www.dca.gov.uk/civil/emerge/emerge.htm

Lord Woolf's final report, *Access to Justice,* is available on the Department for Constitutional Affairs' website at:
http://www.dca.gov.uk/civil/final/index.htm

The website for Money Claim Online can be found at:
http://www.moneyclaim.gov.uk/csmco2/index.jsp

A useful source of information about court matters is the Court Service Annual Report at:
http://www.hmcourts-service.gov.uk

Visit www.mylawchamber.co.uk/ElliottELS to access multiple-choice questions, flashcards and practice exam questions to test yourself on this chapter.

23

Tribunals

This chapter discusses:

- the history of tribunals;

- tribunals today following the Tribunals, Courts and Enforcement Act 2007;

- tribunal procedure, composition and status;

- the employment tribunals;

- the availability of appeals and judicial review; and

- the advantages and disadvantages of the tribunal system.

Introduction

Many claims and disputes are settled not by the courts, but by tribunals, each specialising in a particular area. The tribunal system handles over a million cases each year.
Although tribunals have often been seen as an unimportant part of the legal system,
this caseload clearly shows that they are now playing a major role. Employment
Tribunals are probably the best-known example, but there are many others, dealing
with subjects ranging from social security and tax to forestry and patents. Not all are
actually called tribunals – the category includes the Criminal Injuries Compensation
Authority, which assesses applications for compensation for victims of violent crime.
The majority deal with disputes between the citizen and the state, though the Employment Tribunal is an obvious exception.

Tribunals are generally distinguished from the other courts by less formal procedures, and by the fact that they specialise. However, they are all expected to conduct
themselves according to the same principles of natural justice used by the courts: a fair
hearing for both sides and open and impartial decision-making.

History

Tribunals were in existence as long ago as 1799, but the present system has really
grown up since the Second World War. The main reason for this was the growth of

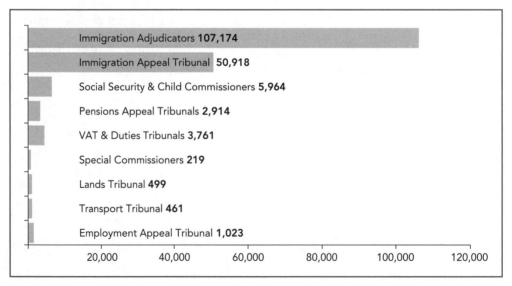

Figure 23.1 Tribunals: cases received, 2004

Source: Judicial Statistics Annual Report 2005, p. 106

legislation in areas which were previously considered private, and therefore rarely addressed by the state, such as Social Security benefits, housing, town and country planning, education and employment.

This legislation gave people rights – to a school place, to unemployment benefit, or not to be unfairly sacked, for example – but its rules also placed limits on these rights. Naturally, this leads to disputes: employer and employee disagree on whether the latter's dismissal was unfair under the terms of the legislation; a Social Security claimant believes he or she has been wrongly denied benefit; a landowner disputes the right of the local authority to purchase her field compulsorily.

Given the potentially vast number of disputes likely to arise, and the detailed nature of the legislation concerning them, it was felt that the ordinary court system would neither have been able to cope with the workload, nor be the best forum for sorting out such problems, hence the growth of tribunals.

As well as the administrative tribunals dealing with this kind of dispute, there are domestic tribunals, which deal with disputes and matters of discipline within particular professions – trade unions and the medical and legal professions all have tribunals like this. The decisions of these tribunals are based on the particular rules of the organisation concerned, but they are still required to subscribe to the same standards of justice as the ordinary courts and, in the case of those set up by statute, their decisions can be appealed to the ordinary courts – as can those of most administrative tribunals.

The Franks Report

In 1957, the Franks Committee investigated the workings of tribunals. It reported that the tribunal system was likely to become an increasingly important part of the legal system, and recommended that tribunal procedures should be marked by 'openness, fairness and impartiality'. Openness required, where possible, hearings in public and explanations of the reasoning behind decisions. Fairness entailed the adoption of clear procedures, which allowed parties to know their rights, present their case fully, and be aware of the case against them. Impartiality meant that tribunals should be free of undue influence from any Government departments concerned with their subject area. The Committee was particularly concerned that tribunals were often on Ministry premises, with Ministry staff.

The Committee also recommended the establishment of two permanent Councils on Tribunals, one for England and Wales and one for Scotland, to supervise procedures. A Council was subsequently set up (with a Scottish committee), consisting of 10–15 members. It reviewed and reported on the constitution and workings of certain specified tribunals, and was consulted before any changes to their procedural rules were made. It also considered and reported on matters referred to it concerning any tribunal. However, it had no firm say in any of these matters, and could not overrule any decisions. Its functions were only advisory – it had little real power, and could not reverse or even direct further consideration of individual tribunal decisions. The Council was, therefore, a watchdog with no teeth. In 1980, it put forward a report asking for further powers, but these were not granted.

Reforming the tribunals

Ess. Cases
p. 361 → Tribunals have recently been the subject of a major reform with the passing of the Tribunals, Courts and Enforcement Act 2007. This piece of legislation followed a lengthy review of the tribunal service undertaken by the Government. First, in 2000, the Government asked Sir Andrew Leggatt, a retired Lord Justice of Appeal, to look at the tribunal service. This was the first systematic examination of tribunals since the Franks Report in 1957. He was asked to look at the funding and management of tribunals, their structure and standards, and whether they complied with the Human Rights Act 1998.

Leggatt issued a consultation document in which he agreed with the Franks Committee that the main characteristics required of tribunals are fairness, openness and impartiality, though he saw openness and impartiality as components of the over-arching requirement of fairness. The Review proposed certain benchmarks against which the achievement of fairness could be tested. These benchmarks included the following:

- independence from sponsoring departments;
- an accessible and supportive system;
- tribunals exercising a jurisdiction suitable for the area that each is intended to cover;
- simple procedures;
- effective decision-making;
- ensuring that the decision-making process is suitable for the type of dispute;
- providing proportionate remedies;
- speed in reaching finality;
- authority and expertise appropriate for their task; and
- cost-effectiveness.

Ess. Cases
p. 357 → The final report of the Review, *Tribunals for Users: One System, One Service*, was published in 2001. Of the 70 different administrative tribunals in England and Wales, it found that their quality varied 'from excellent to inadequate'. It identified some significant weaknesses in the tribunal system. In particular, it was concerned that the tribunals were not always accessible or user-friendly, they were not independent from the Ministries whose decisions were the subject of the tribunal work and the tribunal system lacked coherence. These criticisms will be considered in turn.

The Leggatt Review criticisms

Lack of accessibility

The Franks Committee recommendation that tribunals should be 'open' requires more than just a rule that hearings should usually be held in public; it also demands that citizens should be aware of tribunals and their right to use them. In cases where the dispute is between a citizen and the Government, the citizen will usually be notified of procedures to deal with disputes, but in other cases more thought needed to be given to publicising citizens' rights.

Not user-friendly

The tribunals were originally intended to be user-friendly, providing easy access to justice. Over time many had become increasingly like courts and it is difficult as a result for claimants, without professional legal help, to take their case to a tribunal.

Dependent

The relevant Ministry responsible frequently provided the administrative support for the tribunal having jurisdiction over its decisions, selected the tribunal members, paid their fees and expenses and laid down the tribunal procedures. This meant that tribunals neither appeared to be, nor were in fact, independent. Responsibility for tribunals and their administration should not lie with those whose policies or decisions it is the tribunals' duty to consider. Otherwise, for users every case is an 'away game'. Such arrangements could be the subject of a successful challenge under Art. 6 of the European Convention on Human Rights, which guarantees the right to a fair trial.

Lack of coherence

Each tribunal had evolved as a solution to a particular problem, adapted to one particular area of law. Most tribunals were, therefore, entirely self-contained and operated separately from each other, using different practices and procedures. The result was a system that lacked coherence and which was not providing a uniformly high standard of service.

The Review proposals

The Review concluded that the tribunals had to be rationalised and modernised, and that a radical approach was both necessary and justified. The main proposal of the Review was that a single Tribunal Service should be established which would be responsible for the administration of all the tribunals. According to the Review, this would achieve efficiency, coherence and independence. Any citizen who wished to apply to a tribunal would simply have to submit their case to the Tribunal Service and the case would be allocated to the appropriate tribunal. This would be a considerable advance in clarity and simplicity for users and their advisers. The single system would enable a coherent, user-focused approach to the provision of information which would enable tribunals to meet the claim that they operate in ways which enable citizens to participate directly in preparing and presenting their own cases.

The Review hoped that a Tribunal Service would raise the status of tribunals, while preserving their distinctness from the courts. It could also yield considerable economies of scale, particularly in relation to the provision of premises for all tribunals, common basic training and the use of information technology. It would provide a single point of contact for users, improved geographical distribution of tribunal centres, common standards, an enhanced corporate image and a greater prospect of job satisfaction for employees on account of the size and coherence of the Tribunal Service.

The Review recommended that the Tribunal Service should be an executive agency of the Lord Chancellor's Department (now the Ministry of Justice). It considered that the independence of tribunals would best be safeguarded by having their administrative support provided by this Department with its extensive experience of managing courts.

Tribunals today

Ess. Cases
p. 360
→ Following the Leggatt Review, the Government issued a White Paper, *Transforming Public Services: Complaints, Redress and Tribunals* (2004), containing significant plans to reform the tribunal system. Many of these reforms are now contained in the Tribunals, Courts and Enforcement Act 2007. Before that Act was passed, tribunals had been created by individual pieces of primary legislation, without any overarching framework. The reforms amount to the establishment of an administrative legal system which can be compared to that found in many European countries.

Part 1 of the Act now creates a new, simplified statutory framework for tribunals. The Leggatt Review had recommended that there should be a single Tribunal Service and the Act moves in this direction by creating two new, generic tribunals: the First-tier Tribunal and the Upper Tribunal. The Upper Tribunal is primarily, but not exclusively, an appellate tribunal from the First-tier Tribunal. The Act gives the Lord Chancellor power to transfer the jurisdiction of existing tribunals to the two new tribunals. Schedule 6 to the 2007 Act lists the tribunals which it is intended will be abolished and their jurisdiction transferred to one of the two new tribunals. These tribunals consist of most of the tribunals that have been administered by central Government. The Act provides for the establishment of 'chambers' within the two tribunals so that the many jurisdictions that will be transferred into the tribunals can be grouped together appropriately. To date, four chambers have been set up in the First-tier Tribunal:

- the Social Entitlement Chamber;
- the Health, Education and Social Care Chamber;
- the War Pensions and Armed Forces Compensation Chamber; and
- the Tax Chamber.

Two further chambers are planned: the General Regulatory Chamber and the Land, Property and Housing Chamber. There will be about 60 hearing centres around the country so that many of the cases will be heard locally rather than in London.

The Upper Tribunal currently has three chambers:

- the Administrative Appeals Chamber;
- the Finance and Tax Chamber; and
- the Lands Chamber.

Each chamber is headed by a Chamber President and the tribunals' judiciary is headed by a Senior President of Tribunals. The Senior President is a new office and he or she is the judicial leader of the tribunal system.

Some tribunals have been excluded from the new structures because of their specialist nature and tribunals run by local government have not been included for the time being while further consideration is given to their financial situation. The Employment Tribunals (discussed below) and the Employment Appeal Tribunal will keep their separate identity, though they will share the administrative arrangements of the new tribunals. These two tribunals have been retained because of the nature of the cases that come before them, which involve one private party against another, unlike most other tribunals which hear applications from citizens against decisions of the state.

All the tribunals that fall within the responsibility of central government will increasingly be administered by a centralised Tribunal Service, which was established in 2006 and is an executive agency of the Ministry of Justice. This Tribunal Service is not identical to the one envisaged by Leggatt, but it provides a framework in which the administrative reforms envisaged by Leggatt can be introduced.

The Council on Tribunals has been abolished and replaced by the Administrative Justice and Tribunals Council, which has been given a broader remit than its predecessor. The new Council has a similar role of supervising the tribunals to the old Council, but in addition the new Council has responsibility for keeping the administrative justice system as a whole under review. It is required to consider and advise the Government on how to make the system more accessible, fair and efficient. It is of a comparable size to the old Council of between 10 and 15 members appointed by the Lord Chancellor and Ministers from the devolved administrations in Scotland and Wales.

Tribunal procedure

Until 2007 the tribunals all had their own rules of procedure. Under the 2007 Act a new Tribunal Procedure Committee has been established with responsibility for tribunal rules of procedure. It has produced a unified set of procedural rules for the tribunals, which are heavily influenced by the civil procedural rules introduced by Lord Woolf (see p. 536). For example, the new rules contain a similar overriding objective.

Composition

Most tribunals consist of a legally trained chairperson, and two lay people who have some particular expertise in the relevant subject area – doctors sit on some cases in the Health, Education and Social Care Chamber, for example, and representatives of both employees' and employers' organisations in the Employment Tribunal. The lay members take an active part in decision-making. The legally trained members now have the title of 'judge' under the Tribunals, Courts and Enforcement Act 2007 and their independence is protected by the Constitutional Reform Act 2005.

Tribunals composed entirely of lay people are considered to have been less effective than those with a legally qualified chairperson.

Employment Tribunals

Employment Tribunals provide one example of a powerful tribunal playing a central role in today's society. The role of Employment Tribunals has altered radically since they were first established in 1964. The number of applications has risen dramatically, so that in 2001 there were 130,408 applications. The procedure is quicker than the civil courts, with 75 per cent of cases being heard within 26 weeks of receipt, and only 4 per cent of cases are appealed. A MORI users' survey in 2002 found that both applicants and respondents were satisfied that cases were dealt with impartially and professionally. However, research into the Employment Tribunals has been carried out for the employers' organisation, the Confederation of British Industry (CBI). This research, *Restoring Faith in Employment Tribunals* (2005), concluded that employers lacked confidence in the Employment Tribunal system and often chose to settle weak and vexatious claims to avoid using it. Among the 450 employers polled, the research found that all firms with fewer than 50 staff settled every claim, despite advice that they would win almost half the cases. Most employers felt that the tribunal system had become too adversarial and legalistic, no longer satisfying the original idea that tribunals should hold quick, informal hearings.

Appeals and judicial review

Historically, there was no uniform appeals procedure from tribunals and there was no absolute right of appeal from a tribunal, though most did allow some right of appeal. An example of where there was no right of appeal was the Vaccine Damage Tribunal, set up under the Vaccine Damage Payments Act 1971 to assess claimants' rights to damages for disabilities caused by a vaccination. The Tribunals and Inquiries Act 1992 provided for appeals to the High Court on points of law from some of the most important tribunals. These appeals are heard by the Queen's Bench Division. However, appeals to the High Court are expensive, complex and time-consuming, and are therefore inconsistent with the basic aims of tribunals. Some tribunal appeals could only be made to the relevant Minister, who could hardly be seen as a disinterested party.

In addition to appeal rights, decisions of tribunals are sometimes subject to judicial review on the grounds that they have not been made in accordance with the rules of natural justice or are not within the powers of the tribunal to make (see p. 607). The controlling effect of the potential for judicial review is limited by the fact that it cannot consider the merits of decisions and that, where wide discretionary powers are given to a Minister, Government department or local authority, the court will find it difficult to prove that many decisions are outside those powers.

The Tribunals, Courts and Enforcement Act 2007 now provides a unified appeal structure for the tribunal system. Under the Act, in most cases, a decision of the First-tier Tribunal may be appealed to the Upper Tribunal and a decision of the Upper Tribunal may be appealed to the Court of Appeal. The grounds of appeal must relate to a point of law. The rights to appeal may only be exercised with permission from the tribunal being appealed from, or the tribunal or court being appealed to. It is hoped that this simplified appeal structure will enable the law to develop more consistently.

It is also now possible for the Upper Tribunal to deal with some judicial review cases which would in the past have been dealt with by the High Court. The Upper Tribunal has this jurisdiction only where a case falls within a class specified in a direction given by the Lord Chief Justice or transferred by the High Court. It is possible that in the future all judicial review cases could be heard by the Upper Tribunal which would be a logical way to develop the new administrative legal system.

Advantages of tribunals

Speed

Tribunal cases come to court fairly quickly, and many are dealt with within a day. Many tribunals are able to specify the exact date and time at which a case will be heard, so minimising time-wasting for the parties.

Cost

Tribunals usually do not charge fees, and each party usually pays their own costs, rather than the loser having to pay all. The simpler procedures of tribunals should mean that legal representation is unnecessary, so reducing cost, but that is not always the case (see below).

Informality

This varies between different tribunals, but as a general rule, wigs are not worn, the strict rules of evidence do not apply, and attempts are made to create an unintimidating atmosphere. This is obviously a help where individuals are representing themselves. A risk of the reforms introduced by the 2007 Act is that the tribunal system may become increasingly formal, particularly now cases are heard by judges.

Flexibility

Although they obviously aim to apply fairly consistent principles, tribunals do not operate strict rules of precedent, so are able to respond more flexibly than courts.

Specialisation

Tribunal members already have expertise in the relevant subject area, and through sitting on tribunals, are able to build up a depth of knowledge of that area that judges in ordinary courts could not hope to match.

Relief of congestion in the ordinary courts

If the volume of cases heard by tribunals was transferred to the ordinary courts, the system would be completely overloaded.

Awareness of policy

The expertise of tribunal members means they are likely to understand the policy behind legislation in their area, and they often have wide discretionary powers which allow them to put this into practice.

Privacy

Tribunals may, in some circumstances, meet in private, so that the individual is not obliged to have their circumstances broadcast to the general public (but see the first disadvantage below).

Disadvantages of tribunals

Despite the improvements made to the tribunal system by the Tribunals, Courts and Enforcement Act 2007, problems still remain with the tribunal system:

Lack of openness

The fact that some tribunals are held in private can lead to suspicion about the fairness of their decisions.

Unavailability of state funding

Full funding from the Legal Services Commission is available for only a small number of minor tribunals. Tribunals are of course designed to do away with the need for representation, but in many of them the ordinary individual will be facing an opponent with access to the very best representation – an employer, for example, or a Government department – and this clearly places them at a serious disadvantage. Even though the procedures are generally informal compared with those in ordinary courts, the average person is likely to be very much out of their depth, and research by Genn and Genn in 1989 found that much of the law with which tribunals were concerned was complex, and their adjudicative process sometimes highly technical; individuals who were represented had a much better chance of winning their case.

There is, however, some dispute as to the desirability of such representation necessarily involving lawyers; although in some cases this will be the more appropriate form of representation, there are fears that introducing lawyers could detract from the aims of speed and informality. If money for tribunal representation were to become available, it may be better spent on developing lay representation, such as that offered by specialist agencies like the UK Immigration Advisory Service, or the Child Poverty Action Group, who can develop real expertise in specific areas, as well as general agencies such as the Citizens' Advice Bureaux.

Answering questions

1 Sir Andrew Leggatt carried out a review of tribunals for the Lord Chancellor's Department. In his report, *Tribunals for Users – One System, One Service* (2001), he painted a picture of an incoherent and inefficient set of institutions which provided a service to the public which was well short of what people are entitled to expect. Do you agree with Sir Andrew Leggatt and, if so, will the reforms contained in the Tribunals, Courts and Enforcement Act 2007 be sufficient?

You need to show a detailed knowledge of both Sir Andrew Leggatt's Review and the 2007 Act. The criticism that the old tribunal system lacked coherence is discussed at p. 575. You could also point out that inefficiency and incoherence were not the only criticisms thrown at the old system. You could then look at the reforms introduced by the 2007 Act and consider whether these will create a more coherent and efficient system. In particular you would want to discuss the establishment of a single Tribunal Service and the First-tier tribunal and the Upper Tribunal. You could note that the Tribunal Procedure Committee has produced a unified set of procedural rules. You could also note the improvements to the appeal system. However, there are still a large number of tribunals that do not fall within the new tribunal arrangements, particularly local government tribunals. Even within the generic First-tier tribunal and Upper Tribunal there are individual Chambers which could be allowed to develop in very different ways.

2 Evaluate the role of tribunals in the English legal system.

You can begin by considering the role of tribunals. You should point out that they do vary widely, but broadly their job in the legal system can be said to include providing justice in a quick, inexpensive and accessible way, making independent decisions in disputes between the citizen and the state, putting into effect the policy behind legislation, and taking pressure off the courts. You then need to assess how well tribunals do these jobs.

The following are points you might mention:

- Speed – they are quicker than courts, but since the Franks Committee have adopted more court-like procedures, which may slow things down.
- Cost – some charge no fees, and costs are not usually awarded against a losing party as they would be in a court. However, the need for representation, and the fact that legal aid is not available, may eradicate these advantages for some.
- Accessibility – procedures are usually simpler than in courts but, again, the fact that representation is allowed means that powerful litigants will be represented, so less powerful ones are disadvantaged by representing themselves.
- Independence – though this has improved, there are still criticisms (see p. 575).

23

Tribunals

- Helping the citizen to assert rights against the state – this may be compromised by lack of independence, and also the problems with legal aid, putting the individual at a disadvantage.
- Effecting policy – tribunals do often have wider discretionary powers than courts.
- Taking pressure off the courts – you could point out the vast numbers of cases which arise in the kinds of matters dealt with by tribunals.

3 Tribunals play a significant role in deflecting disputes away from the traditional court system. This may be particularly true following the Leggatt recommendations and the Government's response thereto. Discuss with particular reference to:

(a) the advantages and disadvantages of the tribunal system; and

(b) the provisions for appeal and review of tribunal decisions.

The question clearly provides the structure for the answer. You should begin by explaining what tribunals are and what they do. This will lead you to the advantages and disadvantages of the tribunal system (p. 579). It is because of these disadvantages/criticisms that Sir Andrew Leggatt was asked to review the tribunal system. He made his recommendations in his 2001 report *Tribunals for Users: One System, One Service* in which he highlighted the defects and made a number of recommendations. The Government responded to these in the Tribunals, Courts and Enforcement Act 2007. This Act provides for appeals and review of tribunal decisions (p. 578).

Summary of Chapter 23: Tribunals

Introduction
Tribunals are generally different from ordinary courts because of their less formal procedures and the fact that they are very specialist.

History
Tribunals were in existence as long ago as 1799, but the present system has really grown up since the Second World War.

The Franks Report
In 1957 the Franks Committee investigated the workings of tribunals. It recommended that tribunal procedures should be marked by 'openness, fairness and impartiality'. Following the Committee's report, the Council on Tribunals was established.

Reforming the tribunals
Tribunals have recently been the subject of a major reform with the passing of the Tribunals, Courts and Enforcement Act 2007. This piece of legislation followed a lengthy review of the tribunal service undertaken by the Government. First, in 2000, the Government asked Sir Andrew Leggatt, a retired Lord Justice of Appeal, to look at the tribunal service. The report of the Review, *Tribunals for Users: One System, One Service*, was published in 2001. It identified some significant weaknesses in the current system. In particular, it was concerned that the tribunals were not always accessible or user-friendly,

they were not independent from the Ministries whose decisions were the subject of the tribunal work and the tribunal system lacked coherence. The Review concluded that the tribunals had to be rationalised and modernised.

Tribunals today

Following the Leggatt Review, the Government issued a White Paper, *Transforming Public Services: Complaints, Redress and Tribunals* (2004), containing significant plans to reform the tribunal system. Many of these reforms are now contained in the Tribunals, Courts and Enforcement Act 2007. Part 1 of the Act creates a new, simplified statutory framework for tribunals. The Act establishes two new, generic tribunals: the First-tier Tribunal and the Upper Tribunal. The Upper Tribunal is primarily, but not exclusively, an appellate tribunal from the First-tier Tribunal. The Act provides for the establishment of 'chambers' within the two tribunals so that the many jurisdictions that are being transferred into the new tribunals can be grouped together appropriately. The tribunals' judiciary is headed by a Senior President of Tribunals.

The Council on Tribunals has been replaced by the Administrative Justice and Tribunals Council, which has been given a broader remit.

Tribunal procedure

Under the 2007 Act, a new Tribunal Procedure Committee has been established with responsibility for tribunal rules of procedure.

Composition

Most tribunals consist of a legally trained chairperson, and two lay people who have some particular expertise in the relevant subject area.

Status

Tribunals are generally regarded as inferior to the ordinary courts.

Employment Tribunals

Employment Tribunals provide one example of a powerful tribunal playing a central role in today's society.

Appeals from tribunals

Historically there was no uniform appeals procedure from tribunals, though most did allow some right of appeal. Improvements to the appeal system have been made by the Tribunals, Courts and Enforcement Act 2007.

Advantages of tribunals

The advantages of tribunals include:

- speed;
- cost;
- informality;
- flexibility;
- specialisation;
- relief of congestion in the ordinary courts;
- awareness of policy; and
- privacy.

Disadvantages of tribunals

The disadvantages of tribunals include:

- lack of openness; and
- unavailability of funding from the Legal Services Commission.

Reading list

Department for Constitutional Affairs (2004) *Transforming Public Services: Complaints, Redress and Tribunals*, London: Stationery Office.

Dickens, L. (1985) *Dismissed: A Study of Unfair Dismissal and the Industrial System*, Oxford: Blackwell.

Genn, H. and Genn, Y. (1989) *The Effect of Representation at Tribunals*, London: Lord Chancellor's Department.

Reading on the Internet

www   The Report of the Review of tribunals by Sir Andrew Leggatt is available on:
http://www.tribunals-review.org.uk

The website of the Tribunal Service is available at:
http://www.tribunals.gov.uk/

The Tribunals, Courts and Enforcement Act 2007 is published on the website of the Office for Public Sector Information at:
http://www.opsi.gov.uk/acts/acts2007/20070015.htm

The explanatory notes to the Tribunals, Courts and Enforcement Act 2007 are published on the website of the Office of Public Sector Information at:
http://www.opsi.gov.uk/acts/acts2007/20070015.htm

Visit www.mylawchamber.co.uk/ElliottELS to access multiple-choice questions, flashcards and practice exam questions to test yourself on this chapter.

mylawchamber
controlled support for legal education

24 Appeals and judicial review

This chapter discusses:

- appeals in civil law cases from the county court and the High Court;

- appeals in criminal law cases from the magistrates' court and the Crown Court;

- the Criminal Cases Review Commission;

- the powers of the prosecution to appeal following an acquittal;

- the role of the Privy Council;

- criticism and reform of the appeal system; and

- the process of judicial review.

Appeals

The appeals system provides a way of overseeing the lower courts, and has two basic functions:

- Putting right any unjust or incorrect decisions, whether caused by errors of fact, law or procedure. An error of fact might be that a victim was stabbed with a knife rather than a broken bottle; an error of law might be that the judge has wrongly defined an offence when explaining to the jury what needs to be proved; and an error of procedure means that the trial has not been conducted as it should have been.
- Promoting a consistent development of the law.

Judicial review is not technically an appeal, though it is a way of reviewing the decisions of courts and tribunals as well as the decisions of the executive. It will be considered after the appeals system.

Appeals in civil law cases

Civil appeals may be made by either party to a dispute. The Government has been concerned at the increasing number of appeals being brought in civil proceedings. In 1990 there were 954 appeals heard and 573 applications outstanding. By 1996, 1,825 appeals were heard and 1,288 applications were outstanding. There has also been a slight increase in the number of appeals following the passing of the Human Rights Act 1998. A review of the Civil Division of the Court of Appeal was undertaken by a Committee chaired by Sir Jeffrey Bowman. It produced a report in the spring of 1998. A number of problems were identified as besetting the Court of Appeal. In particular, the court was being asked to consider numerous appeals which were not of sufficient weight or complexity for two or three of the country's most senior judges, and which had sometimes already been through one or more levels of appeal. Additionally, existing provisions concerning the constitution of the court were too inflexible to deal appropriately with its workload. Recommendations were made, designed to reduce the delays in the hearing of civil appeals, and the Government accepted many of its proposals. The Access to Justice Act 1999 introduced some significant reforms to the civil appeal process. By 2003 the number of civil appeals had been reduced to 1,075.

In the past permission was required for most cases going to the Civil Division of the Court of Appeal, but not elsewhere. Following the Access to Justice Act 1999, court rule 52 requires permission to appeal to be obtained for almost all appeals. This permission can be obtained either from the court of first instance or from the appellate court itself. Permission will be given where the appeal has a realistic prospect of success or where there is some other compelling reason why the appeal should be heard. More stringent conditions are applied for the granting of permission to appeal case management decisions. The main situation where permission to appeal is not required is where the liberty of the subject is at stake: for example, following the rejection of a *habeas corpus* application. The general rule is that appeal lies to the next level of judge in the court hierarchy.

The Access to Justice Act 1999 provides that in normal circumstances there will be only one level of appeal to the courts. Where the county court or High Court has already reached a decision in a case brought on appeal, there will be no further possibility for the case to be considered by the Court of Appeal, unless it considers that the appeal would raise an important point of principle or practice, or there is some other compelling reason for the Court of Appeal to hear it. Thus in future second appeals will become a rarity. Only the Court of Appeal can grant permission for this second appeal.

In the Court of Appeal cases are normally heard by three judges, but following the Access to Justice Act 1999 some smaller cases can be heard by a single judge.

Civil appeals will normally simply be a review of the decision of the lower court, rather than a full rehearing, unless the appeal court considers that it is in the interests of justice to hold a rehearing. The appeal will only be allowed where the decision of the lower court was wrong, or where it was unjust because of a serious procedural or other irregularity in the proceedings of the lower court.

From the county court

Appeals based on alleged errors of law or fact are made to the Civil Division of the Court of Appeal. Appeals from a district judge's decision normally go first to a circuit judge and then to the High Court (though exceptionally they will go to the Court of Appeal instead of the High Court).

The Court of Appeal does not hear all the evidence again, calling witnesses and so forth, but considers the appeal on the basis of the notes made by the trial judge, and/or other documentary evidence of the proceedings. Written skeleton arguments should normally be provided to the court so that oral submissions can be kept brief to save time and costs.

The Court of Appeal may affirm, vary (for example, by altering the amount of damages) or reverse the judgment of the county court. It is generally reluctant to overturn the trial judge's finding of fact because it does not hold a complete rehearing. As the trial judge will have had the advantage of observing the demeanour of witnesses giving their evidence, the Court of Appeal will hardly ever question his or her findings about their veracity and reliability as witnesses. From the Court of Appeal, there may be a further appeal to the Supreme Court, for which leave must be granted.

Judicial review by the High Court is also possible.

From the High Court

Cases started in the High Court may be appealed to the Civil Division of the Court of Appeal. The case is examined through transcripts rather than being reheard, as above. From there, a further appeal on questions of law or fact may be made, with leave, to the Supreme Court.

The exception to this process is the 'leapfrog' procedure, provided for in the Administration of Justice Act 1969. Under this procedure, an appeal can go directly from the High Court to the Supreme Court, missing out the Court of Appeal. The underlying rationale is that the Court of Appeal may be bound by a decision of the Supreme Court (or former House of Lords), so that money and time would be wasted by going to the Court of Appeal when the only court that could look at the issue afresh is the Supreme Court. In order to use this procedure, all the parties must consent to it and the High Court judge who heard the original trial must certify that the appeal is on a point of law that either:

(a) relates wholly or mainly to the construction of an enactment or of a statutory instrument, and has been fully argued in the proceedings and fully considered in the judgment of the judge in the proceedings; or

(b) is one in respect of which the judge is bound by a decision of the Court of Appeal or of the Supreme Court (or former House of Lords) in previous proceedings, and was fully considered in the judgments given by that Court (as the case may be) in those previous proceedings (s. 12(3)).

The trial judge has a discretion whether or not to grant this certificate, and there is no right of appeal against this decision. If a certificate is granted, leave will still need to be obtained from the Supreme Court. Even if that leave is obtained, the appellant might decide that it has been given on such restrictive terms that it would prefer to follow the ordinary appeal procedure rather than go ahead with a leapfrog appeal: **Ceredigion County Council *v* Jones** (2007).

From the civil jurisdiction of the magistrates' court

Appeals concerning family proceedings go to the Family Division of the High Court. From there, appeal with leave lies to the Court of Appeal and the Supreme Court. Appeals on licensing matters are heard by the Crown Court.

It is also possible for the magistrates to state a case (see p. 589) and for judicial review to be applied.

Appeals in criminal law cases

Significant reforms have been introduced to the criminal appeal system in the light of heavy criticism following some high-profile miscarriages of justice. The appeal process is supposed to spot cases where there have been wrongful convictions at an early stage so that the injustice can be promptly remedied. A wrongful conviction could arise because of police or prosecution malpractice, a misdirection by a judge, judicial bias, or because expert evidence, such as forensic evidence, was misleading. Sadly, the Court of Appeal in particular failed in the past to detect such problems and this led to demands for reform. The Criminal Appeal Act 1995 was therefore passed to make major amendments to the criminal appeal procedure.

From the magistrates' court (criminal jurisdiction)

There are four routes of appeal:

1 The magistrates can rectify an error they have made under s. 142 of the Magistrates' Courts Act 1980, as amended by the Criminal Appeal Act 1995. The case is retried before a different bench where it would be in the interests of justice to do so and the sentence can be varied.

2 A defendant who has pleaded not guilty may appeal as of right to the Crown Court on the grounds of being wrongly convicted or too harshly sentenced. Only appeals against sentence are allowed if the defendant pleaded guilty. The appeal has to be made within 28 days of the conviction. These appeals are normally heard by a circuit judge sitting with between two and four magistrates (not those who heard the original trial). Each person's vote has the same weight except where the court is equally divided when the circuit judge has the casting vote.

   The court will rehear the facts of the case and either confirm the verdict and/or sentence of the original magistrates, or substitute its own decision for that of the lower court. It can impose any sentence that the magistrates might have imposed – which can occasionally result in the accused's sentence being increased.

3 Alternatively, either the prosecution or the accused may appeal on the grounds that the magistrates have made an error of law, or acted outside their jurisdiction. The magistrates (or the Crown Court when hearing an appeal from the magistrates) are asked to 'state the case' for their decision to be considered by the High Court. This is, therefore, known as an appeal by way of case stated. In **R** *v* **Mildenhall Magistrates' Court, ex parte Forest Heath DC** (1997) the Court of Appeal held that magistrates could refuse to state a case if they feel that the application is frivolous, which they defined as 'futile, misconceived, hopeless or academic'. They must inform the defendant why they have reached this conclusion.

   Appeals by way of case stated are heard by up to three judges of the Queen's Bench Division and the sitting is known as a Divisional Court. The court can confirm, reverse or vary the decision; give the magistrates their opinion on the relevant point of law; or make such other order as it sees fit, which may include ordering a rehearing before a different bench.

4 The Criminal Cases Review Commission can refer appeals from the magistrates' court to the Crown Court. This body is discussed in more detail from p. 601 onwards. In fact, only 5 per cent of new cases received by the Commission since 1997 have been against convictions by the magistrates.

If an appeal has been made to the Crown Court, either side may then appeal against the Crown Court's decision by way of case stated. If a party has already appealed to the High Court by way of case stated they may not afterwards appeal to the Crown Court.

From the Divisional Court there may be a further appeal, by either party, to the Supreme Court, but only if the Divisional Court certifies that the question of law is one of public importance and the Supreme Court or the Divisional Court gives permission for the appeal to be heard.

Criminal cases tried by magistrates are also subject to judicial review.

In practice, appeals from the decisions of magistrates are taken in only 1 per cent of cases. This may be because most accused plead guilty and, since the offences are relatively minor and the punishment usually a fine, many of those who pleaded not guilty may prefer just to pay up and put the case behind them, avoiding the expense, publicity and embarrassment involved in an appeal.

A Home Office report (Taylor, *Cautions, Court Proceedings and Sentencing in England and Wales 1996* (1997)) found that the introduction of the right of magistrates to reopen cases to rectify their own mistakes by the Criminal Appeal Act 1995 had led to a significant reduction in both the number of appeals and the proportion of successful appeals. The number of appeals against conviction had fallen by 28 per cent from 14,100 in 1995 to 10,100 in 1996. The proportion of successful appeals – in other words, where the conviction was quashed or a retrial ordered – had fallen during the same period from a success rate of 41 per cent to 33 per cent.

From the Crown Court

There are three types of appeal for cases tried in the Crown Court.

1 An appeal on grounds that involve the facts, the law, or the length of the sentence can be made to the Court of Appeal. The accused must get leave to appeal from the trial judge or the Court of Appeal. A sentence cannot be imposed that is more severe than that ordered by the Crown Court. An appeal against sentence will only be successful where the sentence is wrong in principle or manifestly severe; the court will not interfere merely because it might have passed a different sanction.

   While only the accused can appeal to the Court of Appeal, from there either the accused or the prosecution may appeal on a point of law to the Supreme Court, provided that either the Court of Appeal or the Supreme Court grant permission for the appeal and that the Court of Appeal certifies that the case involves a matter of law of general public importance. The Royal Commission on Criminal Justice 1993 (set up after the release of the Birmingham Six) recommended that this latter requirement should be abolished.

2 The Criminal Appeal Act 1995 established the Criminal Cases Review Commission (CCRC), following a proposal made by the RCCJ. This body is not a court deciding appeals, rather it is responsible for bringing cases, where there may have been a miscarriage of justice, to the attention of the Court of Appeal if the case was originally heard by the Crown Court (or the Crown Court if the case was originally heard by a magistrates' court). Either a person can apply to the Commission to consider their case or the Commission can consider it on their own initiative if an ordinary appeal is time barred. The Commission can carry out an investigation into the case, which may involve asking the police to re-investigate a crime. Before making a reference the Commission is able to seek the Court of Appeal's opinion on any matter.

   The decision as to whether or not to refer a case will be taken by a committee consisting of at least three members of the Commission. It can make such a reference in relation to a conviction where it appears to them that any argument or evidence, which was not raised in any relevant court proceedings, gives rise to a real possibility that the conviction would not be upheld were the reference to be made. A reference

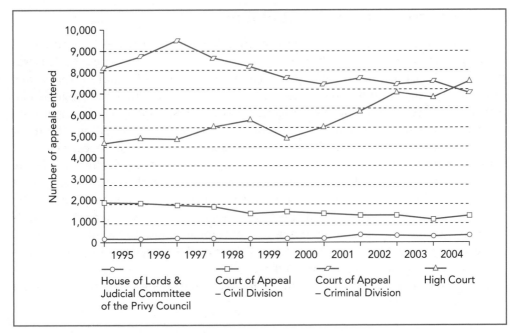

Figure 24.1 Appellate Courts: Appeals entered, 1995–2005

Source: Judicial Statistics Annual Report 2005, p. 6

in relation to a sentence will be possible if 'any argument on a point of law, or any information' was not so raised and, again, there is a real possibility that the conviction might not be upheld. Where the Commission refers a conviction or sentence to the Court of Appeal it is treated as a fresh appeal and the Commission has no further involvement in the case. Following the Criminal Justice and Immigration Act 2008, when a case is referred to the Court of Appeal by the Commission, the appeal can be dismissed if the only ground for allowing the appeal would have been because there has been a development in the law since the date of the conviction and in ordinary circumstances an application to appeal out of time would be rejected.

The Commission is based in Birmingham and consists of no fewer than 11 members, at least a third of whom are lawyers and one will have knowledge of the criminal justice system in Northern Ireland. They are appointed by the Queen on the advice of the Prime Minister.

3 Following the Access to Justice Act 1999, appeals by way of case stated have been introduced from the Crown Court to the High Court. Before these were only available from the magistrates' court. The Law Commission has issued a consultation paper – *The High Court's Jurisdiction in Relation to Criminal Proceedings* (2007) – in which it recommends that the appeal process should be simplified. It suggests that appeals (and judicial review hearings) from the Crown Court should no longer be heard by the High Court, but instead all appeals should be heard by the Court of Appeal.

Second appeal to the Court of Appeal

In exceptional circumstances the Court of Appeal will be prepared to hear an appeal twice, in other words an appeal from its own earlier decision in the same case. This was decided in the landmark case of **Taylor** *v* **Lawrence** (2002). The Court of Appeal had dismissed the first appeal, which had been based on the fact that the judge at first instance had been a client of the claimants. After that first appeal, the appellant then discovered that the judge had not been asked to pay for work carried out the night before the case went to court. When this came to light the Court of Appeal ruled that it would hear a second appeal. The Court of Appeal laid down guidelines for future cases on when it would be prepared to hear a second appeal in the same case. It must be clearly established that a significant injustice has probably been done, the circumstances are exceptional and there is no alternative effective remedy. There is no effective remedy if leave would not be available for an appeal to the Supreme Court. Leave to appeal would not have been given in **Taylor** *v* **Lawrence** because the case was not of sufficient general importance and merit.

The approach taken by the court in **Taylor** *v* **Lawrence** is now contained in Civil Procedure Rule 52.17.

Procedure before the Court of Appeal

Whichever appeal route is taken to reach the Court of Appeal, once the case is before the court it is dealt with under the same procedure which will now be considered.

Admission of fresh evidence

Unlike an appeal from the magistrates' court to the Crown Court, the Court of Appeal in criminal cases does not rehear the whole case with all its evidence. Instead, it aims merely to review the lower court's decision. This is at least partly because the Court of Appeal is reluctant to overturn the verdict of a jury, apparently fearing that to do so might undermine the public's respect for juries in general.

The Court of Appeal can admit fresh evidence 'if they think it necessary or expedient in the interests of justice' (Criminal Appeal Act 1968, s. 23(1)). In deciding whether to admit fresh evidence they must consider whether:

- the evidence is capable of belief;
- the evidence could afford a ground for allowing the appeal;
- the evidence would have been admissible at the trial; and
- there is a reasonable explanation why it was not so adduced.

In addition, under the 1995 Act, the Court of Appeal can direct the Criminal Cases Review Commission to investigate and report on any matter relevant to the determination of a case being considered by the court. Thus, the Court of Appeal has a radical new power to seek out new evidence themselves, something that no other criminal court in England currently has been able to do, due to our traditional adversarial procedures.

At one time, the Court of Appeal considered new evidence in the light of the effect it might have had on the decision of the jury; but, in **Stafford *v* DPP** (1973), Viscount Dilhorne said that if the court was satisfied that there was no reasonable doubt about the guilt of the accused, the conviction should not be quashed even though the jury might have come to a different view; the court was not bound to ask whether the evidence might have led to the jury returning a verdict of not guilty. The judges are, therefore, replacing the jury's opinion with their own, which is viewed by some as weakening the right to trial by jury. This approach of second-guessing the outcome of jury deliberations has been criticised by the European Court of Human Rights in **Condron *v* United Kingdom** (2000). The case of **Stafford *v* DPP** was reconsidered in **R *v* Pendleton** (2002). **Stafford *v* DPP** was not overruled but its interpretation needs to be reconsidered in the light of the later case. In 1986 Donald Pendleton was convicted of murdering a newspaper seller 15 years earlier. In 1999 the Criminal Cases Review Commission referred Mr Pendleton's conviction back to the Court of Appeal. The principal basis for the reference was that fresh evidence was available from an expert forensic psychologist to the effect that the appellant had psychological vulnerabilities, which raised serious doubts about the reliability of his statements to the police. The Court of Appeal both received this evidence and accepted the opinion of the expert. However, the appeal was dismissed on the ground that the conviction was safe because the fresh evidence did not put a 'flavour of falsity' on the content of the interviews. His further appeal to the House of Lords was allowed.

While **Stafford** was not overruled, the House stated that the Court of Appeal had to remember that it was a court of review and that the jury were the judges of fact. The Court of Appeal therefore had to bear in mind:

> that the question for its consideration is whether the conviction is safe and not whether the accused is guilty . . . It will usually be wise for the Court of Appeal, in a case of any difficulty, to test their own provisional view by asking whether the evidence, if given at the trial, might reasonably have affected the decision of the trial jury to convict. If it might, the conviction must be thought to be unsafe.

The appeal was allowed because the Court of Appeal had strayed beyond its role of simply reviewing the trial court's decision, and had come perilously close to considering whether the appellant in its judgment was guilty.

The case of Hanratty was referred to the Court of Appeal in 2002 by the Criminal Cases Review Commission (**R *v* Hanratty** (2002)). Hanratty had been convicted of murder and was later executed. A campaign was subsequently launched to establish his innocence. The Court of Appeal ordered that the body of the defendant be exhumed and samples of his DNA obtained. The prosecution made an application under the Criminal Appeal Act 1968, s. 23 to be allowed to submit fresh evidence consisting of the DNA analysis of evidence collected at the time of the murder. The defence argued against this application primarily on the basis that there was a risk that the evidence had been contaminated after the defendant's arrest. The prosecution's application was successful. The defendant's DNA was found on some of the evidence collected at the time of the murder and Hanratty's appeal was rejected.

Outcome of the appeal

The appellate court can allow the appeal, dismiss it or order a new trial. Under s. 2 of the Criminal Appeal Act 1968 (as amended by the 1995 Act) an appeal should be allowed if the court thinks that the conviction 'is unsafe'. There is conflicting case law as to whether, if a person is found to have had an unfair trial under Art. 6 of the European Convention on Human Rights, this will automatically mean that the conviction is unsafe and should be quashed. Some English judges prefer the view that if the defendant is clearly guilty their conviction should be upheld as safe even if the trial was unfair. This seems to conflict with the view of the European Court of Human Rights, which suggested in **Condron** *v* **UK** (2000) that the conviction should always be quashed if there has been an unfair trial. The Court of Appeal may order a retrial where it feels this is required in the interests of justice. It will only do so if it accepts that the additional evidence is true but is not convinced that it is conclusive – in other words, that it would have led to a different verdict.

TOPICAL ISSUE

The double jeopardy rule

In the past there was a general rule that once a person had been tried and acquitted they could not be retried for the same offence, under the principle of double jeopardy. The rule aimed to prevent the oppressive use of the criminal justice system by public authorities. Following the unsuccessful private prosecution of three men suspected of killing Stephen Lawrence, the judicial inquiry into the affair recommended that the principle of double jeopardy should be abolished. It proposed that the Court of Appeal should have the power to permit prosecution after acquittal 'where fresh and viable evidence is presented'.

The Home Secretary referred the matter to the Law Commission. This body recommended that the double jeopardy rule should be limited. Under their recommendation, it would have been possible to retry someone acquitted of murder if new evidence was later discovered which made the prosecution case substantially stronger and the new evidence could not have been obtained before the first trial.

Sir Robin Auld's *Review of the Criminal Courts* (2001) also recommended that the double jeopardy rule should be abolished but for a wider range of offences.

The Criminal Justice Act 2003, s. 75 has now abolished the double jeopardy rule. The Act introduces an interlocutory prosecution right of appeal against a ruling by a Crown Court judge that there is no case to answer or any other ruling made before or during the trial that has the effect of terminating the trial. A retrial is permitted in cases of serious offences where there has been an acquittal in court, but compelling new evidence subsequently comes to light against the acquitted person. Twenty-nine serious offences are listed in a Schedule to the Act, and are most of the offences which carry a maximum sentence of life imprisonment. This is wider than the recommendations of the Law Commission and Sir Robin Auld. The consent of the Director of Public Prosecutions is required to reopen investigations and to apply to the Court of Appeal.

The first person in 800 years to be tried and convicted for a crime he was previously cleared of was a man called William Dunlop. He had been tried twice for the murder of Julie Hogg in 1989, but at these two earlier trials the jury were unable to reach a verdict and he had been formally acquitted at the end of the second trial. When new evidence arose he was prosecuted again following the abolition of the double jeopardy rule and he pleaded guilty.

Certain other exceptions to the double jeopardy rule also existed prior to the 2003 Act:

- The prosecution can state a case for consideration of the High Court following the acquittal of a defendant by the magistrates' court. This is restricted to a point of law or a dispute on jurisdiction.
- The prosecution can also, with leave, appeal to the Supreme Court against a decision of the Court of Appeal.
- The Criminal Justice Act 1972 gives the Attorney General powers to refer any point of law which has arisen in a case for the opinion of the Court of Appeal, even where the defendant was acquitted. Defendants are not identified (though they may be represented) and their acquittal remains unaffected even if the point of law goes against them – so this procedure is not, strictly speaking, an appeal. The purpose of this power is to enable the Court of Appeal to review a potentially incorrect legal ruling before it gains too wide a circulation in the trial courts.
- The Criminal Justice Act 1988 enables the Attorney General to refer to the Court of Appeal cases of apparently too lenient sentencing, including cases where it appears the judge has erred in law as to their powers of sentencing. Leave from the Court of Appeal is required. The Court of Appeal may quash the sentence and pass a more appropriate one. This is the first time that the prosecution is involved in the sentencing process. The provision was enacted in response to the Government's view that public confidence in the criminal justice system was being undermined by unduly lenient sentences, which had been given much publicity by the tabloid press.
- The Criminal Procedure and Investigations Act 1996 created a power to order a retrial where a person has been convicted of an offence involving interference with, or intimidation of, a juror, witness or potential witness, in any proceedings which led to an acquittal.

It is unlikely that the abolition of the double jeopardy rule breaches the European Convention as Art. 4(2) expressly allows an appellate court to reopen a case in accordance with domestic law 'if there is evidence of new or newly discovered facts'.

Advances in DNA profiling have provided a new impetus for cases to be reopened and fresh criminal proceedings to be brought.

24

Appeals and judicial review

The Supreme Court

The Supreme Court is the highest national appeal court for both civil and criminal matters. It was established in 2009 following the abolition of the House of Lords by the Constitutional Reform Act 2005 (see p. 13).

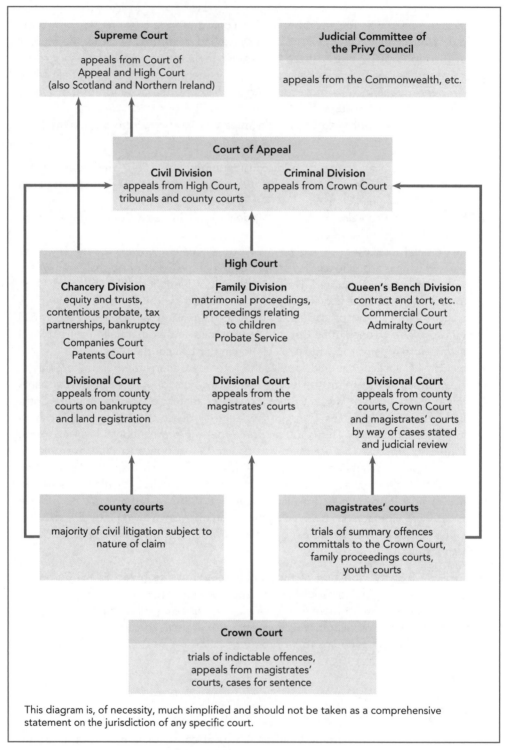

Figure 24.2 An outline of the court structure in England and Wales

Source: Judicial Statistics Annual Report 2004, p. 3

Privy Council

The Judicial Committee of the Privy Council hears:

- appeals from Commonwealth countries such as the Bahamas and Jamaica;
- appeals from Overseas Territories, such as the Falkland Islands and Gibraltar; and
- appeals from disciplinary proceedings by professional bodies and the courts of the Church of England.

The jurisdiction of the Privy Council has reduced over the years. Certain independent Commonwealth countries, including Australia, India, Malaysia, Nigeria, Pakistan and Singapore, have chosen to stop sending their final appeals to London. Most recently, a Caribbean Court of Justice has been established in Trinidad to hear final appeals from certain Caribbean islands. Many of these countries have retained the mandatory death penalty by hanging for the crime of murder. The Privy Council had been seen locally as an obstacle in the desire to execute those on death row. A landmark ruling by the Privy Council in London in 1993 stated that keeping someone on death row for more than five years was cruel and inhumane. Since then, defence lawyers have often managed to get death sentences reduced to life in prison by pursuing an appeals process that went beyond the five-year limit. The Privy Council was also viewed as a relic of the colonial past.

Criticism and reform of the appeal system

A Supreme Court

Under provisions contained in the Constitutional Reform Act 2005, the House of Lords has been abolished and replaced by a Supreme Court. This reform is discussed in detail at p. 13.

Do we need a second appeal court?

Do we need two courts with purely appellate jurisdiction? Could the Supreme Court be abolished altogether, leaving the Court of Appeal as the final appellate court? Efforts to abolish the third tier of appeal date back over 100 years – in fact the Judicature Act of 1873 contained a section which did just that, but was never brought into force. The following are some of the arguments on both sides.

For abolition

- The Court of Appeal should be sufficient; a third tier is unnecessary and illogical. A.P. Herbert (1966) points out that giving appellants the chance to get their case decided by two appellate courts is like having one's appendix taken out by a distinguished surgeon and then being referred to another who might confirm the first surgeon's decision, but might just as easily recommend the appendix be replaced! Reversing legal decisions might not pose the same practical problems as medical ones but, nevertheless, it may seem odd that the decisions of the eminent judges in the Court of Appeal can be completely overturned by the Supreme Court.

● It allows a litigant with the support of a minority of judges to win. Take the example of a litigant losing a civil case, appealing to the Court of Appeal and losing, but finally winning in the Supreme Court. Counting all the judges involved together, they may have had six against them (the original trial judge, the three judges hearing the case in the Court of Appeal, and two out of five in the Supreme Court). Yet, if three judges in the Supreme Court are in their favour, they win the case overall, even though twice as many judges supported their opponent.

● It adds cost and delay to achieving a decision. Usually, QCs are instructed in appeals to the Supreme Court, substantially increasing costs, and extra time is taken up. This can add to emotional stress and financial hardship for one or both litigants.

● The former House of Lords has failed to make any adequate contribution to the development of the criminal law. This point is made by the eminent criminal law specialists J.C. Smith (Smith and Hogan, 2002) and Glanville Williams and those criticisms are likely to be equally valid for the Supreme Court. Unlike the Court of Appeal, the House of Lords had no specialist divisions, and criticisms of the quality of their decisions in criminal appeals may stem from this. Glanville Williams (1983) points out that: 'It is particularly inapt that a Chancery judge should have the casting vote in the House of Lords in a criminal case, as Lord Cross did in **Hyam**.' He also suggests that the age of judges in the House of Lords is a problem, since old men are 'often fixed in their opinions' and 'tend to ignore the opinions of others'; this may be true, but the judges of the Court of Appeal are hardly in the first flush of youth either.

Part of the problem relates to the strict conditions for appealing to the old House of Lords (and the new Supreme Court), which meant that few criminal cases got there, and the Law Lords actually had very little chance to make notable contributions to this area of the law. In 2009 Lord Judge suggested that the new Supreme Court should not hear criminal appeals, but this suggestion has not gained general support.

● The House of Lords tended to side with the establishment, and usually the Government. This is the argument advanced by Griffith (1997, see p. 26), but there is little evidence to suggest that the Court of Appeal would be very different in this respect if it became the highest court.

● The Supreme Court offers nothing beyond finality, and that could be more efficiently achieved without it. Jackson (1989), an academic in the field, examined the 15 appeals made to the House of Lords in 1972, and found that eight involved Government departments or national authorities and five were disputes between commercial concerns. He deduced that, in the case of both Government departments and commercial concerns, the reason for taking the case to the House of Lords was nothing more than the fact that it is the final court.

In the case of Government departments, where judicial decisions appear to obstruct them, their object is to remove that obstruction; appeal to the Supreme Court may achieve this but, if not, the matter can be put right by legislation. However, they must have the final decision of the judiciary before this can happen, and must therefore go to the Supreme Court – not because of any innate quality of its decision-making, but simply because it is the final court. Jackson felt that the commercial cases were also likely to be based on the pursuit of finality. If this is correct, abolishing the Supreme Court would enable finality to be achieved more quickly and cheaply.

Against abolition

- Its small membership allows the Supreme Court to give a consistent leadership that the Court of Appeal, with its much greater number of judges, could not, and therefore to guide the harmonious development of the law. Louis Blom-Cooper QC (1972) has argued that, especially since the Practice Direction of 1966 allowing the third-tier appeal court to overrule its own decisions, the senior judges are in a unique position to be able to reform the law from the top. The much larger size of the Court of Appeal, and its division into different divisions, means there would always be a danger of different divisions within it applying different views of the law.
- The combination of the two appellate courts allows the majority of appeals to be dealt with more quickly than the Supreme Court could hope to deal with them, while still retaining the smaller court for those matters which require further consideration, and for promoting consistent development of the law.
- The Supreme Court plays a valuable role in correcting decisions by the Court of Appeal. In 2007 the then House of Lords heard 58 decisions, of which 40 per cent were successful.
- The former House of Lords made some important contributions to the development of our law, including making marital rape a crime – in **R v R** (1991) – and confirming the restricted scope of parental rights in a modern society in **Gillick v West Norfolk and Wisbech AHA** (1985).

24

Appeals and judicial review

TOPICAL ISSUE

Procedural irregularities

In his *Review of the Criminal Courts* (2001), Sir Robin Auld highlighted the difference between a conviction which was unsafe, in the sense that it was incorrect (or lacked supporting evidence), and one which was unsatisfactory because something had gone wrong in the trial process. He queried whether in the latter situation the conviction should be quashed. In September 2006, the Government issued a consultation paper, *Quashing convictions – report of a Review by the Home Secretary, Lord Chancellor and Attorney General*. This paper reviewed the legal test used by the Court of Appeal to quash criminal convictions. When the Government published the Criminal Justice and Immigration Bill this initially contained provisions adopting Sir Robin Auld's recommendations on this subject. The Bill provided that 'a conviction is not unsafe if the Court of Appeal are satisfied that the appellant is guilty of the offence'. The Court of Appeal judges would have allowed an appeal against conviction 'where they think that it would be incompatible with the appellant's Convention Rights to dismiss the appeal'. Thus, as initially drafted, the Bill would have altered the test applied by the Court of Appeal when considering appeals against conviction. A conviction would not have been found unsafe if the Court of Appeal was satisfied that the appellant was

▶

guilty of the offence. If it appeared to the Court of Appeal, in determining an appeal, that there had been serious misconduct by any person involved in the investigation or prosecution of the offence, the court could refer the matter to the Attorney General.

These provisions in the Bill were highly controversial and the subject of considerable criticism. In the light of such strong opposition the Government removed these provisions from the Bill before the Criminal Justice and Immigration Act 2008 was passed. In support of the failed reform, the Government had argued that to acquit defendants where the Court of Appeal considered they were guilty was itself an injustice to the victim and the public, because the guilty were being allowed to walk free without punishment; their convictions were being quashed 'on a technicality'. In its consultation paper, the Government observed, 'if the system or those who operate it are at fault it is they and not the public who should be punished or required to learn lessons, if appropriate'.

On the other hand, critics of the proposed reform, such as the academic Ian Dennis (2006), had argued that it would remove an important safeguard in the criminal justice system, which effectively discourages abuse of procedural rules by representatives of the state, such as the police or prosecution. They argued that a conviction is fundamentally unsatisfactory if it is gained in breach of the rule of law and to uphold such a conviction itself undermines the rule of law. They questioned whether the public would be happy to see the criminal courts appear to sanction a flagrant illegality by an agent of the state. The Court of Appeal does not rehear the evidence of a case and is not therefore in a strong position to reach a view on whether a person is innocent or guilty. Alternative sanctions of, for example, the police for procedural irregularities have not always proved effective. Alarmingly, in **R (on the application of Mullen)** v **Secretary of State for the Home Department** (2004) the Government seemed to view unlawful rendition – when a person is removed from a country without following the lawful procedures – as a mere technicality, yet this constituted a major violation of an individual's human rights.

The single test for quashing convictions

Before the Criminal Appeal Act 1995, there used to be three grounds on which the Criminal Division of the Court of Appeal could allow an appeal. These were where the court thought that:

- the jury's verdict was unsafe and unsatisfactory; or
- there was an error of law; or
- there was a material irregularity in the course of the trial.

The old law was criticised by the Runciman Commission on the basis that it was unnecessarily complex and that the different grounds for quashing a conviction overlapped. For example, it felt that there was no real difference between the words 'unsafe' and 'unsatisfactory'. In the light of this criticism the law has been reduced by the Criminal Appeal Act 1995 to a single test that the court thinks the conviction is unsafe. This is narrower than that recommended by the Runciman Commission as it had favoured a retrial where the conviction 'may' be unsafe. The Law Society, the

Bar, Liberty and JUSTICE all unsuccessfully called on the Government to follow the RCCJ's proposal. The Government's expressed view was that any such doubt implied by the concept of 'may be unsafe' was already implicit in the idea of a conviction being 'unsafe'.

Government Ministers insisted that the effect of the new law was simply to restate or consolidate the existing practice of the Court of Appeal. However, the pressure group JUSTICE, has criticised the new single test on the basis that there is a danger it will be interpreted more narrowly than the previous tests.

Michael Zander (one of the Commissioners and a leading academic on the English legal system), along with one other Commissioner, disagreed with the final proposal (Zander, 1993). They took the view that where there had been serious police malpractice then the conviction should always be quashed to discourage such conduct, and to prevent the police believing that they could benefit in terms of getting convictions by such behaviour. This is a situation where, under the old law, the Court of Appeal might have stated that the conviction was safe but it would be quashed because it was unsatisfactory. This route is no longer open to the court.

Lord Woolf on appeals

With regard to civil appeals, Lord Woolf (1996) has recommended the introduction of a system where cases could be referred to the Court of Appeal or House of Lords (now the Supreme Court) in order to ensure the proper development of the law. This would be appropriate where the lower court has reached an unsatisfactory decision but where no appeal has been brought or is possible.

ss. Cases
p. 405 →

The Criminal Cases Review Commission

The CCRC was established to replace the old s. 17 procedure contained in the Criminal Appeal Act 1968 and repealed in 1995. Under the old procedure, the Home Secretary could refer a case that had been previously heard in the Crown Court to the Court of Appeal, despite the fact that the normal time limit for appeals had expired or an unsuccessful appeal had already been heard. The Home Secretary had considerable discretion whether or not to make this referral: the statute simply required a reference to be made 'if he thinks fit'.

There were serious difficulties with the s. 17 procedure. The Home Secretary only usually referred cases where new evidence had come to light, and which were continuing to attract media comment and public concern long after the trial had taken place. Each year there were about 730 applications to the Home Office and its equivalent in Northern Ireland, but only 10–12 of those cases were actually referred to the Court of Appeal.

Problems with the process were highlighted by such cases as the Birmingham Six and the Tottenham Three, where references were only ordered after years of persuasion and publicity. The original appeal of the Birmingham Six was rejected in 1976. It was not until 1987 that the Home Secretary referred their case back to the Court of Appeal, though that appeal was rejected. Three years later, he again referred the case to the Court of Appeal and this time the Director of Public Prosecutions did not resist the application so that the court had little choice but to allow the appeal and quash the convictions.

The Court of Appeal showed a general reluctance to allow s. 17 appeals in cases where it had already dismissed an appeal, and in fact appeared to dislike s. 17 referrals generally: in the first (unsuccessful) s. 17 appeal from the Birmingham Six, the court stated that: 'As has happened before in references by the Home Secretary to this court, the longer the hearing has gone on the more convinced this court has become that the verdict of the jury was correct.' As MP Chris Mullins's book (1990) on the Birmingham Six points out, this seemed to be a thinly veiled message to the Home Secretary that referring such cases was a waste of time.

A further problem was that, once the reference was made, the appeal was governed by the Criminal Appeal Act 1968, and the expense and responsibility of preparing the appeal lay with the defendant, who would probably be in prison and have been there for quite some time. Legal aid might be available but investigation in these circumstances would be difficult.

It has been hoped that the CCRC will mark a considerable improvement on the old s. 17 procedure, but concerns have already been expressed about the new arrangements. One problem with the Commission is that, while it is predicted more cases will reach the Court of Appeal than they did under the s. 17 procedure, one of the weaknesses with that procedure was that even when the case was referred to the Court of Appeal the convictions were often upheld, even though later it was acknowledged that there had been a miscarriage of justice. Thus, cases such as the Birmingham Six had to be repeatedly referred back to the Court of Appeal before they would eventually overturn the original conviction. In that case the appeal was allowed on the basis that there was 'fresh' evidence as to the police interrogation techniques and the forensic evidence. In reality this evidence had, in essence, been before the Court of Appeal in 1987; the difference was that the court was forced to accept that the evidence raised a lurking doubt in 1991. Only if the other provisions are adequate to improve the Court of Appeal process will the same problems be avoided. An alternative solution would have been to give the Commission the power to decide appeals themselves.

The pressure group, JUSTICE, has criticised the fact that the CCRC has no power to assign in-house staff as investigating officers. It has argued that without this power the Commission could not guarantee the independence of an inquiry. The CCRC has no independent powers to carry out searches of premises, to check criminal records, to use police computers, or to make an arrest. To do this they would have to appoint someone who had these powers, usually a police officer. The fact that investigations carried out on behalf of the CCRC will be by the police has caused concern. Many allegations of a miscarriage of justice involve accusations of malpractice by the police. Experience of police investigations into the high-profile miscarriages of justice suggest that these are not always effective, with a tendency for the police to close ranks and try to protect each other. JUSTICE has also questioned the independence of the organisation as its members are Government appointees.

Over a third of applications made to the Criminal Cases Review Commission are concerned with murder convictions and a quarter relate to sex offences. In 2006–07, there were 1,051 applications made to the Commission, of which 38 were referred to an appeal court. Of these referrals, 70 per cent of the appeals were successful and led either to a conviction being quashed or a sentence being reduced.

Derek Bentley's appeal

One of the first referrals made by the Criminal Cases Review Commission concerned Derek Bentley. He had been involved with a friend in an unsuccessful burglary. This had resulted in a police chase when his friend had pointed a gun at a police officer and Derek Bentley had said 'let him have it', at which point the friend shot and killed the officer. Derek Bentley was convicted as an accomplice to the murder. He appealed but his appeal was rejected and he was hanged in January 1953.

The circumstances of his conviction gave rise to a long campaign by his family and numerous representations were made to the Home Office. He was given a royal pardon in 1993 but this was in respect of the sentence only. The family continued their campaign for the conviction itself to be quashed and in 1998 the CCRC referred the case to the Court of Appeal, which quashed the conviction. They found that the conviction was unsafe because of a defective summing-up by the trial judge to the jury, which had included such prejudicial comments about the defence case that Bentley had been denied a fair trial. This was a notable high-profile success for the CCRC.

The CCRC has found the main reasons for it to refer cases back to the courts are:

- Prosecution failings (such as breach of identification and interview procedures or the use of questionable witnesses).
- Scientific evidence (such as DNA and fingerprint evidence).
- Non-disclosure of evidence.
- New evidence (such as alibis, eye-witnesses or confessions).

There is a problem of funding submissions to the Commission. At the moment the Legal Services Commission only pays for two hours of a solicitor's time, which is insufficient for the preparation of such an application. As a result, more than 90 per cent of applicants are not represented by a solicitor.

Jill Dando's murder

Jill Dando was a successful television presenter who worked for the BBC. She was shot dead outside her home in London in 1999. Barry George was convicted of her murder. Part of the evidence against Barry George was that a single microscopic particle of gun shot residue was found in his coat pocket. After his conviction witnesses came forward stating that armed police officers had been present when he was arrested. The police denied this, but if it was true then the gun shot residue could have come from the police rather than from the murder. His conviction was referred to the Court of Appeal by the Criminal Cases Review Commission and his conviction was quashed in 2007 and a retrial ordered. He was acquitted by the jury at his retrial.

▮ Reluctance to overturn jury verdicts

The Court of Appeal seems to feel that overturning jury verdicts weakens public confidence in the jury system, and it is therefore very reluctant to do it. This view was spelt out during the final, successful appeal of the Birmingham Six in 1991, in which the Court of Appeal stated:

> Nothing in s. 2 of the Act, or anywhere else obliges or entitles us to say whether we think that the appellant is innocent. This is a point of great constitutional importance. The task of deciding whether a man is innocent or guilty falls on the jury. We are concerned solely with the question whether the verdict of the jury can stand.
>
> Rightly or wrongly (we think rightly) trial by jury is the foundation of our criminal justice system . . . The primacy of the jury in the criminal justice system is well illustrated by the difference between the Criminal and Civil Divisions of the Court of Appeal . . . A civil appeal is by way of rehearing of the whole of the case. So the court is concerned with fact as well as law . . . It follows that in a civil case the Court of Appeal may take a different view of the facts from the court below. In a criminal case this is not possible . . . the Criminal Division is perhaps more accurately described as a court of review.

The case of Winston Silcott illustrates the dangers. He had been convicted in 1985 of murdering PC Blakelock during the Tottenham riots. The offence had been committed by a group of 30 people. Six had gone on trial and only three were convicted, including Silcott. The only evidence against Silcott was a statement he was alleged to have made: 'You won't pin this on me . . . nobody will talk', which he had not signed. Despite these obvious weaknesses in the case, his conviction was initially upheld by the Court of Appeal and was only overturned in 1991.

The major problem with the appeal court's approach is that in many cases the fault lies not with the decision-making powers of the jury, but in the evidence presented to them. Where a jury has not seen all the evidence, or where the evidence it has heard has been falsified by the police (as was alleged in some of the well-known miscarriages of justice), or where the jury has in any other way failed to have the case properly presented to it, overturning the verdict should not automatically be viewed as a criticism of its ability to make correct decisions. A better way to demonstrate confidence in the jury system might be to order a retrial with a new jury.

The Runciman Commission concluded that the Court of Appeal should show greater willingness to substitute its judgment for that of the jury. They pointed out that in gauging the evidence juries could make errors, particularly in a high-profile case in which emotions run high. The trial of Winston Silcott is a classic case in point. The Criminal Appeal Act 1995 aims to instigate a change of philosophy in this regard, particularly through the changes to the rules on the admissibility of fresh evidence.

Up to 1995 the Court of Appeal was able to conclude that even if there was found to have been a material irregularity in the trial they could still uphold the conviction if they felt that no miscarriage of justice had occurred. This was known as 'applying the proviso' but the relevant statutory provision has now been repealed, which may lead to a greater willingness to overturn a jury verdict.

Admission of fresh evidence

Until 1995, s. 23 of the 1968 Act, as well as giving the court a discretion to admit new evidence, imposed a duty on the court to receive fresh evidence where it was 'likely to be credible'. In practice, the Court of Appeal was very reluctant to admit fresh evidence, despite the apparently broad drafting of the legislation. One of the reasons for the court's approach was that they were unwilling to turn what was supposed to be a process of review into a full rehearing. But, in effect, defendants could be punished and denied the right to a fair hearing for omissions caused by their lawyers' incompetence, the underfunding of the legal aid system, or the prosecution's obstructiveness. The RCCJ concluded that the statutory powers to admit fresh evidence were sufficient; the problem was that in practice they were being given too narrow an interpretation. Thus, they encouraged the Court of Appeal to take a more flexible approach.

Now the appeal court merely has a discretion to receive fresh evidence where 'it is capable of belief'. At the time of the amendment it was suggested this provided a wider discretion for the court in the interests of justice. Unfortunately, this does not seem to be reflected in the Court of Appeal's interpretation of the provision. In **R v Jones (Steven Martin)** (1996) the appellant had been convicted of his wife's murder and, on appeal, he had applied for the court to receive fresh expert evidence from three forensic pathologists. While on the facts of the case the evidence was allowed, the court stated that in general only new factual evidence as opposed to expert evidence would normally be admitted, noting that the test for admissibility was more appropriate to such evidence as one could rarely consider expert evidence as 'incapable of belief'. This case shows that the legislative amendment to s. 23 may have actually accentuated the problems of the Court of Appeal refusing to admit fresh evidence.

Lord Devlin, in his book *The Judge* (1979), criticised the Court of Appeal's decision in **Stafford v DPP** to follow its own view of whether new evidence makes a conviction unsafe (or unsatisfactory), rather than assessing the effect such evidence might have had on the trial jury. He felt that this involves judges in findings of fact, a function that properly belongs to the jury. The jury ends up playing a subordinate part in the verdict, since it has not heard all the evidence. He believes the change from assessing the possible effect of new evidence on the trial jury has not been sanctioned by Parliament and is an attack on the jury system.

Unwillingness to order retrials

Many have argued that the Court of Appeal should use its power to order retrials more often. The number of such retrials grew from three in 1990 to 23 in 1992, though they remain rare.

Lord Devlin has argued, as stated above, that a retrial should be ordered wherever fresh evidence could have made a difference to the verdict – the original verdict being clearly unsatisfactory since it was given without the jury hearing all the evidence.

Opponents argue that it may be unfair to the accused to reopen a decided case, and that a second trial cannot be a fair one, especially if some time has passed and/or the case has received a lot of publicity. But, as Lord Devlin argues, this does not stop retrials being ordered where the jury has failed to agree a verdict, nor are prosecutions necessarily stifled because witnesses have to speak of events many years before. In fact, at the same time as the Birmingham Six were told that a retrial 13 years after the original one was inappropriate, the Government was debating the prosecution of war criminals, some 44 years after the end of the Second World War. Shortly after the Six's unsuccessful appeal, an IRA man was brought to trial on charges dating back 13 years.

As far as publicity is concerned, the second jury may well know of the defendant's record and have noted other adverse publicity, as well as knowing that the defendant has already been convicted on a previous occasion for the crime. On the other hand, in all the high-profile miscarriages of justice, no further publicity could have affected the attitudes of potential jurors more than that surrounding the original offences and trials.

Many wrongful convictions result from mistaken identity, and it is difficult for the Court of Appeal, which does not usually re-examine witnesses, to assess the strength of such evidence. Retrials might be the best way of dealing with this problem. A general power to order a retrial could also be a way of convicting offenders who escape on a technicality first time round, and might be a more obviously just solution than applying the old proviso, or letting such defendants go free, which has a negative effect on the public, the jury and the victim. However, it could also subject genuinely innocent defendants to a second ordeal.

It has been suggested that wider use of retrials would 'open the floodgates' to a deluge of appeals, yet this does not appear to be a problem in other countries with wider powers of retrial, including Scotland. In any case, Lord Atkin has pointed out, 'Finality is a good thing but justice is better.'

The Runciman Commission considered the issue and concluded that the Court of Appeal should use the power to order a retrial more extensively.

Reluctance to address faults in the system

The problems outlined above can be seen as symptomatic of a more general reluctance to uncover the extent of miscarriages of justice in our system. This attitude was typified by Lord Denning's speech in **McIlkenny v Chief Constable of the West Midlands** (1980), the case in which the police successfully appealed against a civil action, brought against them by the Birmingham Six, in respect of injuries sustained after their arrest. Lord Denning said:

> If the six men win, it will mean that the police were guilty of perjury, that they were guilty of violence and threats . . . and that the convictions were erroneous . . . the Home Secretary would have either to recommend that they be pardoned or he would have to remit the case to the Court of Appeal . . . This is such an appalling vista that every sensible person in the land would say 'It cannot be right that these actions should go any further'.

The implication was that, even if the men were innocent, the damage such a revelation could do to confidence in the justice system meant it was better not known.

Judicial review

The system of judicial review by the High Court oversees the decisions of public bodies and officials, such as inferior courts and tribunals, local councils, and members of the executive including police officers and Government Ministers. Cases are heard by the Queen's Bench Division. Certain public bodies are exempt from judicial review. For example, in **R v Parliamentary Commissioner for Standards, ex parte Al Fayed** (1998) the Court of Appeal ruled that the Parliamentary Commissioner for Standards could not be subjected to judicial review. One of the functions of the Commissioner is to receive and, where appropriate, investigate complaints from the public in relation to the conduct of Members of Parliament. Mohammed Al Fayed, the owner of Harrods, had made such a complaint that Michael Howard, while Home Secretary, had received a corrupt payment. The complaint had been investigated and then rejected and Al Fayed had sought judicial review of this decision. The Court of Appeal ruled that the Parliamentary Commissioner for Standards operated as part of the proceedings of Parliament and its activities were non-justiciable. This is because of the principles of the separation of powers discussed at p. 3.

Unlike the appeal process, judicial review does not examine the merits of the decision. It can only quash a decision if the public body had no power to make it, known as *ultra vires* (*ultra* is Latin for 'beyond' and *vires* is Latin for 'powers'). There are two forms of *ultra vires*: procedural *ultra vires* and substantive *ultra vires*.

Procedural *ultra vires*

Where there has been procedural *ultra vires* it is often said that there has been a breach of natural justice. This means either that the body reaching the particular decision complained of was biased, or that procedures had been unfair. These requirements have been bolstered by Art. 6 of the European Convention on Human Rights which lays down the right to a fair and impartial hearing.

Bias

In **Dimes v Grand Junction Canal Proprietors** (1852), a dispute about land, Lord Chancellor Cottenham found in favour of the canal company. It was then discovered that he owned several thousand pounds worth of shares in Grand Junction Canal Proprietors, and the decision was set aside. This was the principle that was applied in the litigation concerning the extradition of Pinochet, the former dictator of Chile. In those proceedings the House of Lords had handed down a judgment that Pinochet could be extradited to Spain. It was subsequently discovered that one of the judges, Lord Hoffmann, had links with Amnesty International, a human rights organisation that was involved in the proceedings. Because the process could as a result be viewed as unfair, the House of Lords reopened the case and gave a fresh judgment several months later. Note, there is no need to prove the decision was in fact biased, only that there is a financial interest or some other reason why bias is likely – this is on the

Ess. Cases
p. 98

grounds that justice must be seen to be done as well as actually be done – R *v* Bow Street Metropolitan Stipendiary Magistrate, ex parte Pinochet Ugarte (No. 2) **(1999).**

Following the **Pinochet** decision a series of cases has arisen where a litigant has challenged the impartiality of the judge. In **Director General of Fair Trading *v* Proprietary Association of Great Britain** (2001) the Court of Appeal amended the test for bias. It stated that the court should:

- ascertain all the circumstances that had a bearing on the suggestion that the tribunal was biased;
- ask whether those circumstances would lead a fair-minded and informed observer to conclude that there was a real possibility that the tribunal was biased.

Unfairness

In **R *v* National Lottery Commission, ex parte Camelot Group plc** (2000) the National Lottery Commission had established a competition for the award of a new licence to operate the National Lottery. The Commission received bids from Camelot and The People's Lottery (TPL). After a long evaluation process and with only one month of Camelot's existing seven-year licence left to run, the Commission announced that neither bid met the statutory criteria for granting a licence. It declared that the competition was at an end, and stated that it would establish a new procedure under which it would negotiate exclusively with TPL for one month.

Camelot commenced judicial review proceedings, claiming that the Commission's decision to operate this new procedure was unfair. The court accepted that the Commission had tried to be fair. It had decided to negotiate only with TPL because it believed that the deficiencies in TPL's bid (unlike Camelot's) were capable of being addressed within the time constraints. Despite this, the court found that the decision to negotiate exclusively with TPL had been 'conspicuously unfair to Camelot' and was therefore unlawful.

Substantive *ultra vires*

This occurs where the content of the decision was outside the power of the public body that made it. Sometimes legislation may make it clear what the limits on the public body's powers are. Thus, the limits on the magistrates' jurisdiction are clearly laid down in legislation. If a magistrates' court decides to hear a case which is indictable only, and should therefore have been heard in the Crown Court, the magistrates' decision can be ruled *ultra vires* and quashed.

Often, however, the legislation does not lay down clear limits on the public body's powers. For example, the legislation might simply say that the Minister can appoint 'who he thinks fit'. If the Minister then appoints someone who is totally unqualified for the job, it is very difficult for the court to prove that the Minister did not think he was fit for the job. To get round some of the problems caused by broadly drafted powers such as these, the courts are prepared to imply certain limitations on the official's power even where they are not laid down by the relevant legislation.

Wednesbury unreasonable

A decision will be held to be outside the public body's power if it was so unreasonable that no reasonable public body could have reached the decision. This is known as the Wednesbury principle and was laid down in **Associated Provincial Picture Houses Ltd** v **Wednesbury Corporation** (1948).

> A decision is *ultra vires* if it is so unreasonable that no reasonable public body could have reached the decision.

Lord Diplock described such an executive decision in **Council of Civil Service Unions** v **Minister for the Civil Service** (1984) as 'a decision which is so outrageous in its defiance of logic or of accepted moral standards that no sensible person . . . could have arrived at it'.

In **R** v **Chief Constable of Sussex, ex parte International Trader's Ferry Ltd** (1998) lorries carrying livestock for export required police protection from animal rights protesters in order to gain access to the ferries. The Chief Constable decided to reduce the protection to certain days of the week due to insufficient police resources. The ferry company sought judicial review of this decision but it was held by the Court of Appeal and the House of Lords that the decision was not unreasonable.

If a decision interferes with fundamental human rights then the court applies a more stringent test in determining whether the decision was reasonable. The relevant test is whether a reasonable body could, on the material before it, have reasonably concluded that such interference was justifiable. The more substantial the interference with human rights, the more the courts require by way of justification before they are satisfied that a decision is reasonable. **R** v **Lord Saville of Newdigate, ex parte B** (1999) arose from the events of 'Bloody Sunday' when 13 people were killed and many others injured when British soldiers opened fire on a demonstration in Northern Ireland. In 1972 the Widgery tribunal was set up to inquire into the incident. The majority of soldiers giving evidence in that inquiry were allowed to remain anonymous. The subsequent report was criticised and eventually in 1998 a further inquiry was set up presided over by Lord Saville. In May 1999 the Ministry of Defence asked the tribunal to permit military witnesses to give their evidence again without disclosing their names, primarily on the grounds that such disclosure would endanger their lives as they would be exposed to the threat of revenge attacks by terrorist organisations. While the tribunal accepted that anonymity would not prevent it from discovering the truth, it refused to grant this request. An application was then made to the High Court by soldiers who had fired live bullets on 'Bloody Sunday' for judicial review of the tribunal's decisions, contending that it was unreasonable. The High Court accepted that the tribunal's decision potentially interfered with fundamental human rights, those rights being the rights to life, safety and to live free of fear. The question for the court was, given the tribunal's clear finding that anonymity would not impede it in its fundamental task of discovering the truth, could a reasonable tribunal conclude that the additional degree of openness to be gained by disclosure of the names of the 17 soldiers who fired the shots amount to so compelling a public interest as to justify subjecting the soldiers and their families to a significant danger to their lives. The authorities established that where fundamental human rights might be affected by a decision of a public authority, the law gave those rights precedence. The law was that such rights were to prevail unless either the threat that they would be infringed was slight or there was a compelling reason why they should yield. The High Court found that the tribunal had not accorded the applicants' fundamental human rights the required weight. The tribunal's decision was quashed and a subsequent appeal to the Court of Appeal was dismissed.

Irrelevant considerations

If the court concludes that a public body took into account irrelevant considerations then its decision may be quashed. For example, in **R v Somerset County Council, ex parte Fewings** (1995) Somerset County Council passed a resolution prohibiting stag hunting on its land. The ban was challenged on the ground that it was acting outside its statutory authority; the power under s. 120(1)(b) of the Local Government Act 1972, to manage its land for the benefit of the authority's area, did not extend to banning stag hunting on the ground that it was cruel or unethical. The Court of Appeal held that the ban was illegal. It found that, while the assertion that hunting was cruel was not a completely irrelevant consideration when exercising its discretion, the council may have given undue weight to the moral question concerning the desirability of hunting, at the expense of the statutory requirement to manage the land for the benefit of the authority's area.

Improper purpose

The idea of a body acting outside its powers has been extended to include abusing those powers by using them for an improper purpose. In **R v Derbyshire County Council, ex parte Times Supplements** (1990), *The Times* challenged Derbyshire County Council's decision to withdraw its advertising for educational appointments from *Times* publications, after the *Sunday Times* had printed two articles accusing the council of improper and legally doubtful behaviour. The Divisional Court held that the council's decision had been motivated by bad faith and vindictiveness, and was therefore an abuse of power.

Fettered discretion

Where the public body does have a discretion, that is to say a choice, they must exercise that choice. In **British Oxygen Co v Minister of Technology** (1971) a scheme had been set up where grants towards capital expenditure (the purchase of large pieces of machinery, etc.) by industry could be awarded from the Ministry of Trade at the Ministry's discretion. The Ministry developed a rule that grants would not be given for machinery costing less than £25. The British Oxygen Company had spent over £4 million on gas cylinders which cost £20 each. They applied for a grant to assist with the expenditure and, applying this blanket rule, the Ministry rejected their application. On appeal, the House of Lords concluded that a public body with a general legislative discretion was only allowed to develop such internal policies if it was prepared to listen to arguments for the exercise of individual discretion in particular cases.

In **R *v* Southwark London Borough Council, ex parte Udu** (1995) the applicant had obtained a law degree from South Bank University. The applicant applied to his local authority for a discretionary maintenance award in order to study the Legal Practice Course at the College of Law to qualify as a solicitor. The authority rejected the application in accordance with its policy of not providing grants for study at private institutions. The application for judicial review was dismissed. The authority could have a policy on the award of postgraduate grants provided it was rational and flexible and rejected the argument that the result of the policy was that only children of wealthy parents could enter the legal profession.

Error on the face of the record

Where the decision-making body's own record of the proceedings reveals it has made a mistake concerning the law, the decision may be quashed.

Proportionality

The case law of the European Court of Human Rights and the European Court of Justice will only allow a public body to use discretionary powers to do what is proportionate to the end to be achieved. In other words, they will not allow a public body to cause a greater degree of interference with the rights or interests of individuals than is required to deal with the state's objectives.

Traditionally, the English courts have been reluctant to adopt this test of proportionality, for fear that it can amount to the judges taking decisions instead of the executive, with judges starting to look at the factual merits of a particular decision. They have preferred to use the more restrictive test of reasonableness.

The courts are now prepared to apply the proportionality test to determine the legality of the actions of public authorities where these:

● are regulated by European law;
● touch on rights protected by the European Convention on Human Rights.

Remedies

In addition to any of the ordinary civil law remedies of damages, an injunction, or a declaration, the High Court may order a public law remedy only available through the judicial review proceedings. These remedies are often called prerogative orders, and three such remedies exist:

Quashing order

This order used to be called *certiorari*. It quashes (nullifies) an *ultra vires* decision. For example, it might be used to quash the refusal to pay child benefit. It is not available against the Crown, but usually a declaration in that situation will be sufficient.

Mandatory order

This is an order to do something and might be used, for example, to force a local authority to produce its accounts for inspection by a local resident, or to compel a tribunal to hear a previously refused appeal. A mandatory order is not available against the Crown. Often an applicant will seek both a quashing order and a mandatory order. A quashing order could quash an *ultra vires* decision and a mandatory order could compel the public body to decide the case according to its legal powers.

Prohibiting order

This can order a body not to act unlawfully in the future. Thus, while a quashing order quashes decisions already made, a prohibiting order prevents a decision being made which, if made, would be subject to a quashing order. For example, it can prohibit an inferior court or tribunal from starting or continuing proceedings which are, or threaten to be, outside their jurisdiction, or in breach of natural justice.

The former Labour leader Michael Foot made an unsuccessful application for a prohibiting order in **R v Boundary Commission for England, ex parte Foot** (1983). He had challenged the recommendations of the Boundary Commission on amendments to the boundaries of electoral constituencies, as he thought they were unjust. His application was rejected.

▨ Discretion

All the prerogative remedies are discretionary, so even if an applicant proves that the public body behaved illegally, the court can still refuse a remedy. Thus, in deciding whether to grant a remedy, the court should take into account whether it would be detrimental to good administration. If an alternative remedy is available, such as through the appeals process or a specialised tribunal, the court is unlikely to grant a prerogative order. Examples of other factors that might influence their use are consistency with other cases, the nature of the remedy sought, delay, and the motive of the applicant.

▨ Procedure

Part 54 of the Civil Procedure Rules lays down the procedures to be followed for judicial review. The rules contain safeguards to protect public authorities from unreasonable or frivolous complaints and to prevent abuse of the legal process.

Time limit

An application should normally be made within three months of the date when the grounds for the application arose. Even where the application is made within this time, if the court concludes that it was not made promptly it may still not be allowed. On the other hand, the court has a discretion to allow applications made outside the three-month time limit if there was good reason for the delay.

Leave

Before the case can be heard, leave must be obtained from a single judge in the High Court. To obtain leave, the applicants must prove that they have an arguable case. This is quite a low threshold, but the aim is to sift out very weak cases at an early stage to avoid too much unnecessary inconvenience to the administration.

Locus standi

The applicant must have 'a sufficient interest in the matter to which the application relates'. They must, therefore, have a close connection with the subject of the action. This is known as *locus standi*. Again, this rule aims to prevent time being wasted by vexatious litigants or unworthy cases. The issue can be considered both when leave is sought and at the main hearing.

KEY CASE

An important case on the subject of *locus standi* is **R v Inland Revenue Commissioners, ex parte National Federation of Self-Employed and Small Businesses** (1982), often called the Fleet Street Casuals case. An application for judicial review had been made by a taxpayers' association. They wanted to challenge an agreement that had been made by the Inland Revenue to waive the income tax arrears for 6,000 freelance workers in the newspaper printing industry, based at the time in Fleet Street, if they declared their earnings fully in the future. The House of Lords held that the applicant lacked *locus standi*. In deciding whether there was *locus standi* the merits of the case could be taken into account and the case had no merit as the Inland Revenue had no duty to collect every penny of tax due. The taxpayers' association did not have a sufficient interest in other taxpayers' affairs.

> In determining whether a party has *locus standi* to bring judicial review proceedings, the court can take into account the merits of a case.

Since the Fleet Street Casuals case the concept of *locus standi* has been broadened to include some interest and pressure groups. The Attorney General always has *locus standi*. If a party has failed to prove *locus standi* the Attorney General can choose to permit the action through a proceeding known as a 'relator action'. Under this mechanism the action officially proceeds under the Attorney General's name.

There is limited discovery of documents and cross-examination is only allowed in certain circumstances.

Where an application for judicial review is refused by the Divisional Court, application may be made to the Court of Appeal, which, if it accepts that the case should be heard, may refer it back to the Divisional Court, or conduct the hearing itself. Decisions made in a judicial review case may be appealed to the Court of Appeal, and from there to the Supreme Court.

Criticisms of judicial review

Problems with control of wide discretionary powers

While the courts have been prepared to imply certain limits to apparently broad discretionary powers of public bodies, it is still very difficult for such powers to be controlled. The Housing Act 1980, for example, empowers the Secretary of State for the Environment to 'do all such things as appear to him necessary or expedient' to enable council tenants to buy their council houses. In 1982, the then Secretary of State decided that this allowed him to take the sale of council houses out of the hands of local authorities who were not proceeding with such sales as quickly as he wished, and in **R v Secretary of State for the Environment, ex parte Norwich City Council** (1982), the courts had to agree. The powers granted were so wide that very little could be considered *ultra vires*.

Strictness of 'Wednesbury principles'

As Geoffrey Robertson points out in his book *Freedom, the Individual and the Law* (1993), the very narrow test of unreasonableness severely limits the court's power to supervise the executive. For example, in **R v Ministry of Defence, ex parte Smith** (1995) the applicants had been dismissed from the armed forces because they were homosexuals and sought judicial review of the Ministry of Defence's policy of banning homosexuals. The ban was held to be legal as it was not Wednesbury unreasonable; the decision was not completely irrational even if the reasons for the ban did not appear convincing. This illustrates how weak the test renders judicial review for protecting fundamental human rights. The approach of the English courts was subsequently heavily criticised by the European Court of Human Rights on the basis that the test of unreasonableness was set too high (**Smith and Grady v United Kingdom** (1999)).

From time to time the courts have toyed with the idea of adopting the principle of proportionality as a ground for judicial review. This principle, which is recognised by the administrative law of many European countries, would allow a decision to be struck down on the grounds that, although not irrational on Wednesbury terms, it is out of proportion to the benefit it seeks to obtain, or the harm it wishes to avoid – in other words, where a sledgehammer is being used to crack a nut. Clearly, this would provide a wider test than the Wednesbury principle and could lead to more decisions being struck down.

The idea of proportionality as a criterion for judicial review has been mentioned in **Council of Civil Service Unions v Minister for the Civil Service** (1984). It was also raised in **R v Secretary of State for the Home Department, ex parte Brind** (1991), where journalists unsuccessfully sought to challenge the Home Secretary's ban on broadcasting direct interviews with members of the IRA and other groups from Northern Ireland. In both cases the courts felt it was not open to them to accept it as a criterion at the time, but indicated that case-by-case development might eventually bring it into consideration.

When the courts are considering European law in the domestic context they are prepared to take into account the issue of proportionality. In **R v Chief Constable** of Sussex, ex parte International Trader's Ferry Ltd (1997) – discussed at p. 609 – the House of Lords made direct reference to the concept of proportionality. One of the basic precepts of Europe is free movement of goods. But this free movement can be restricted on the grounds of public policy. To fall within this concept the authority's conduct must have been proportionate to the risk involved. This required a balance to be reached between the restriction on the fundamental freedom, the right of local residents to protection from crime and disorder and the right to hold lawful demonstrations. On the facts the House of Lords held the particular decision to have been lawful.

Political nature of decisions

The nature of cases brought under judicial review means they inevitably become political at times. Critics, notably Griffith (1997), have noted that the judiciary seem more reluctant to interfere in decisions made by the executive where the executive concerned is a Conservative one. Cases such as **R v Boundary Commission for England, ex parte Foot** (1983) mentioned at p. 612 would support this argument.

Restrictions on applications

The procedural limitations on applications for judicial review can be seen as necessary to safeguard good administration from unnecessary distractions, vexatious litigants and busybodies. One of the advantages of the judicial review procedure is that it is relatively quick and if the volume of cases were increased this would cease to be true. On the other hand, they can also be seen as ways to discourage ordinary people from seeking to challenge Government or other authorities. There is no leave requirement for ordinary civil proceedings. It could be argued that the current time limits are too short and the courts' discretion is too vague so that sometimes justice is not done.

The concept of national security

Some have criticised reliance on the requirements of national security to inhibit judicial review of Government decisions. In **Council of Civil Service Unions v Minister for the Civil Service** (1984), the Civil Service union challenged the Government's decision to ban employees of Government Communications Headquarters (GCHQ, the Government intelligence centre, which monitors communications from abroad and ensures security for UK military and official communications) from membership of trade unions. The Divisional Court upheld the complaint on the ground that the decision had been made unfairly, since the unions had not even been consulted. On appeal, the Government argued that its decision had been motivated by considerations of national security, because the centre had been disrupted by industrial action some years earlier. Despite the fact that this argument had not been advanced in the initial proceedings, and that a no-strike agreement was offered by the union, the House of Lords overturned the original decision and upheld the ban. The Government was not required to prove that the ban was necessary, or even justifiable in the interests of security; only that the decision had been motivated by national security concerns.

Similarly, in **R** *v* **Secretary of State for the Home Department, ex parte Hosenball** (1977), Mark Hosenball, an American journalist, was made the subject of a deportation order on the ground that his presence in the UK was not conducive to the public good. He challenged the order on the basis that he had been given no details of the case against him so that the rules of natural justice had not been followed. The Court of Appeal held that, although the proceedings had been unjust, the rules of natural justice were not to be applied to deportation decisions made on grounds of national security.

As Geoffrey Robertson (1993) points out, where national security is invoked, the courts are reluctant to assess the strength of evidence presented, even to assert whether decisions made on such grounds were made rationally. He alleges that, so long as there appears to be some evidence of national security concerns, however slight or dubious, the courts will take a 'hands-off' approach. Obviously this problem occurs in only a minority of cases but, as the above examples show, they may be those which affect fundamental civil liberties.

Answering questions

1 **Assess the impact of the Criminal Cases Review Commission on the appeal process.**

You could start your essay by stating what the Commission is, and looking at the reasons for its creation – what were the problems with criminal appeals? You could mention the role that these problems played in the well-known miscarriages of justice – these are highlighted in the section on criticisms in this chapter, while the stories of some of the miscarriages of justice are told in more detail in Chapter 18.

Then move on to look in detail at the Commission itself; its membership, function and powers. One of the points you might want to make is that it is not an appeal court as such, but can merely refer cases for appeal, and that it replaces the old s. 17 procedure under which the Home Secretary referred cases back to appeal. You are asked to assess its impact; this essentially means considering how far it is solving the problems it was set up to address. In answering this, you should highlight ways in which it is an improvement on the previous situation – the problems with the s. 17 procedure are relevant here for example – and also any criticisms which can be made of it. You could point to the successful appeal in Derek Bentley's case (see p. 603), but that there is now a serious backlog of cases that is rapidly growing.

2 **Martin is due to be tried at Margate Crown Court for robbing £10,000 from a newsagent.**

(a) Following his conviction, advise Martin about how he can appeal against his conviction.

(b) Could the prosecution bring an appeal?

(c) Critically analyse the current appeal system.

(a) The appeal route is first to the Court of Appeal. The information required for this part of the answer is contained under the heading 'From the Crown Court' at p. 590. Note that reaching the Court of Appeal via the Criminal Cases Review Commission is an exceptional procedure.

There is then a further appeal possible to the Supreme Court. Following the Access to Justice Act 1999, he could also make an appeal by way of case stated to the High Court.

(b) Here you should discuss the material contained under the Topical Issue, 'The double jeopardy rule', at p. 594.

(c) The material contained in the section 'Criticism and reform of the appeal system' at p. 597 is relevant to this part of the answer. In particular, you would want to discuss how far the Criminal Cases Review Commission is more satisfactory than the old s. 17 procedure, the rules on the admission of fresh evidence and the whole debate surrounding the House of Lords and its replacement by a Supreme Court.

3 In 2007 a statute was passed authorising local authorities to make laws to 'ensure the safe use of pedestrianised areas'. The statute expressly stated that representatives of interested groups had to be consulted before any delegated legislation was passed. The local authority consulted market stall holders about passing legislation regulating street musicians. Following this consultation process a bye-law was made requiring all street musicians to have a licence and to perform on designated platforms. Eight months after the legislation had been passed, only classical musicians had been granted a licence. When Mary, a punk rocker who had frequently played in a town centre subway, applied for a licence, her application was rejected on the ground that she was too noisy. Her appeal was rejected by a committee established by the local authority to hear complaints. Mary subsequently discovered that the president of the committee was related to a successful street musician who had been granted a licence. Advise Mary about how she can challenge the behaviour of the local authority.

The Act of Parliament was a parent Act which gave the local authority the power to make delegated legislation. Mary can challenge the actions and decisions by which she has been deprived of her chance to earn money through the system of judicial review. In order to bring such proceedings, she would have to satisfy the strict procedural rules discussed from p. 612 onwards, and in particular the rule on *locus standi*. As Mary has lost her livelihood due to the local government's conduct, a court would rule that she did have *locus standi* to bring the proceedings.

Mary can found her challenge on two grounds: that the delegated legislation was made in breach of the law and that the decision of the committee had breached the law. Looking first at the delegated legislation, the relevant material on this issue can be found at p. 85. The delegated legislation could be challenged as invalid on the basis of procedural *ultra vires*. It would be claimed that the proper procedures were not followed in its creation. The parent Act required that the local authority consult representatives of all interested parties before making the delegated legislation. Mary could argue that though representatives of market stalls were consulted, the street musicians or their representatives had not been consulted.

Looking secondly at the decision of the committee, Mary could argue that there was substantive *ultra vires*. In particular she could argue that it had been made for an improper purpose as there is a suggestion that the decision may have been taken to favour certain kinds of musicians, perhaps from personal motives. Another line of argument would be that a policy appears to have been adopted to exclude musicians who did not play classical music. Thus, it may be that the local authority has fettered its discretion to grant licences.

Mary could also point to procedural *ultra vires* on the basis that the rules of natural justice had been violated. There is a strong possibility of bias in the decision-making process, as the president of the committee either has a personal financial interest (through his relative) or is likely to favour the local authority decision because of his concern for his relative's livelihood.

Finally you could point to the different remedies available under these procedures, especially quashing orders, mandatory orders (to compel further decision-making that is free of the illegality) and damages.

4 **In criminal appeals to the Court of Appeal, does the fact that the court will only hear fresh evidence in limited circumstances disadvantage the appellant?**

You might start by setting out the routes by which a criminal appeal reaches the Court of Appeal (pp. 588–92). Of particular relevance are appeals from the Crown Court because in these cases – subject to the provisions of the Criminal Appeal Act 1968, s. 23(1) – the Court of Appeal does not hear the whole case with all its evidence.

It could be argued that this disadvantages the appellant because judges could usurp the role of the jury (see **Condron** (2000), **Pendleton** (2002) and **Stafford** (1973) p. 593). You could say something brief about the role of the jury here. You would also need to discuss the implications of Art. 6 of the European Convention on Human Rights (see p. xxx, and refer back to Chapters 15 and 16).

5 **To what extent is judicial review an alternative to an appeal from a lower civil court?**

Many statutes will give a litigant the right to appeal to at least one court on specified grounds, although this may be subject to having permission to appeal. Appeals lie to the Court of Appeal from the county court and High Court, although an appeal from a district judge usually lies to a circuit judge; and in all cases a further appeal may be made to the House of Lords. In all cases, the appeal court will not rehear all the evidence but examine the trial judge's notes or formal transcripts of the case before the lower court, and may affirm, reverse or vary the lower court's judgment.

In contrast, the High Court exercises judicial review over the decision of various bodies (including inferior courts) to ensure compliance with the rules on *ultra vires*. Procedural *ultra vires* is where the lower court has not acted in accordance with natural justice and substantive *ultra vires* is where the court acts outside its powers. The remedy will usually be to correct the procedural defect rather than address the substance or merits of the case.

Summary of Chapter 24: Appeals and judicial review

Appeals in civil law cases

Following the report of Sir Jeffrey Bowman into the Civil Division of the Court of Appeal in 1998, the Access to Justice Act 1999 introduced some significant reforms to the civil appeal process. The Access to Justice Act provides that in normal circumstances there will be only one level of appeal.

From the county court

Appeals based on alleged errors of law or fact are made to the Civil Division of the Court of Appeal. Appeals from a district judge's decision normally have to go first to a circuit judge and then to the High Court.

From the High Court

Cases started in the High Court may be appealed to the Civil Division of the Court of Appeal.

Appeals in criminal cases

From the magistrates' court (criminal jurisdiction)

There are four routes of appeal:

- the magistrates can rectify an error they have made;
- a defendant who has pleaded not guilty may appeal as of right to the Crown Court on the grounds of being wrongly convicted or too harshly sentenced;
- either the prosecution or the accused may appeal to the High Court on the grounds that the magistrates have made an error of law or acted outside their jurisdiction; and
- the Criminal Cases Review Commission can refer appeals from the magistrates' court to the Crown Court.

From the Crown Court

There are three types of appeal from the Crown Court:

- an appeal to the Court of Appeal;
- an application to the Criminal Cases Review Commission; and
- an appeal by way of case stated from the Crown Court to the High Court.

Powers of the prosecution following acquittal

The general rule is that once a person has been tried and acquitted, he or she cannot be retried for the same offence, under the principle of double jeopardy. Major exceptions have now been developed.

Criticism and reform of the appeal system

The appeal system has been the subject of considerable criticism. There has been concern over the working of the Criminal Cases Review Commission. The Court of Appeal has been criticised for being reluctant to overturn jury verdicts, admit fresh evidence and order retrials. The Government has abolished the House of Lords and replaced it with a new, independent Supreme Court. The provisions for this reform were contained in the Constitutional Reform Act 2005.

Rejected reforms in the Criminal Justice and Immigration Bill would have altered the test applied by the Court of Appeal when considering appeals against conviction. Clause 26 of the Bill originally provided that 'a conviction is not unsafe if the Court of Appeal are satisfied that the appellant is guilty of the offence'.

Judicial review

The system of judicial review by the High Court oversees the decisions of public bodies and officials. There are two forms of *ultra vires*:

- procedural *ultra vires*; and
- substantive *ultra vires*.

Remedies

Three possible remedies can be ordered:

- quashing order;
- mandatory order;
- prohibiting order.

Reading list

Blom-Cooper, L. (1972) *Final Appeal: A Study of the House of Lords in its Judicial Capacity*, Oxford: Clarendon Press.

Bowman, Sir J. (1997) *Review of the Court of Appeal (Civil Division)*, London: Lord Chancellor's Department.

Cooper, S. (2009) 'Appeals, Referrals and Substantial Injustice', [2009] *Criminal Law Review* 152.

Dennis, I. (2006) 'Convicting the guilty: outcomes, process and the Court of Appeal', *Criminal Law Review* 955.

Elks, L. (2008) *Righting Miscarriages of Justice? Ten Years of the Criminal Cases Review Commission*, London: Justice.

Law Commission (2007) *The High Court's Jurisdiction in Relation to Criminal Proceedings*, Law Com CP 184, London: Law Commission.

Leigh, L.H. (2008) 'Injustice Perpetuated? The Contribution of the Court of Appeal', 72 *Journal of Criminal Law* 40.

Malleson, K. (1993) *A Review of the Appeal Process* (Royal Commission on Criminal Justice Research Series No. 17), London: HMSO.

Malleson, K. and Roberts, S. (2002) 'Streamlining and Clarifying the Appellate Process', *Criminal Law Review* 272.

Nobles, R. and Schiff, D. (2005) 'The Criminal Cases Review Commission: Establishing a Workable Relationship With the Court of Appeal', [2005] *Criminal Law Review* 173.

Owers, A. (1995) 'Not Completely Appealing', 145 *New Law Journal* 353.

Pattenden, R. (2009) 'The Standards of Review for Mistake of Fact in the Court of Appeal, Criminal Division', [2009] *Criminal Law Review* 15.

Plotnikoff, J. and Wilson, R. (1993) *Information and Advice for Prisoners about Grounds for Appeal and the Appeal Process* (Royal Commission on Criminal Justice Research Study No. 18), London: HMSO.

Spencer, J.R. (2006) 'Does our present criminal appeal system make sense?' *Criminal Law Review* 677.

Reading on the Internet

www   Any developments in the establishment of a Supreme Court are likely to be signalled on the Ministry of Justice website at:

http://www.justice.gov.uk

The annual report of the Criminal Cases Review Commission is published on the Commission's website at:

http://www.ccrc.gov.uk/publications/publications_get.asp

The consultation paper *Quashing Convictions – Report of a Review by the Home Secretary, Lord Chancellor and Attorney General* (2006) is available on the website of the Home Office at:

http://www.homeoffice.gov.uk/documents/cons2006-quashing-convictions2

Visit www.mylawchamber.co.uk/ElliottELS to access multiple-choice questions, flashcards and practice exam questions to test yourself on this chapter.

25

Alternative methods of dispute resolution

This chapter considers the alternatives to courts. In particular, it looks at:

- the problems with court hearings;

- the three main alternative dispute resolution (ADR) mechanisms;

- examples of ADR; and

- advantages and disadvantages of using ADR.

Introduction

Court hearings are not always the best way to resolve a dispute, and their disadvantages mean that, for some types of problem, alternative mechanisms may be more suitable. The main uses of these at present are in family, consumer, commercial, construction and employment cases but, following Lord Woolf's reforms of the civil justice system, these alternative mechanisms should play a more important role in solving all types of civil disputes. Civil Procedure Rule 1.4 requires the court to undertake case management which is stated to include:

> (2)(e) encouraging the parties to use an ADR procedure if the Court considers that appropriate and facilitating the use of such procedure;
> (f) helping the parties to settle the whole or part of the case.

In addition, Civil Procedure Rule 26.4 allows the court to grant a stay for settlement by ADR or other means either when one or all of the parties request this, or when the court considers this would be appropriate. If a party fails to use ADR where the court thinks this would have been appropriate then it can be penalised through a costs order (Civil Procedure Rule 44.5).

KEY CASE

In **Halsey** v **Milton Keynes General NHS Trust** (2004) the Court of Appeal held that the courts do not have the power to force parties to try ADR, as this might amount to a breach of a person's right to a fair trial under Art. 6 of the European Convention on Human Rights.

> The courts do not have the power to force parties to try ADR.

> It is one thing to encourage the parties to agree to mediation, even to encourage them in the strongest terms. It is another to order them to do so. It seems to us that to oblige truly unwilling parties to refer their disputes to mediation would be to impose an unacceptable obstruction on their right of access to the Court.

By contrast, in many other countries, such as the USA and Australia, the courts are prepared to force the parties to try ADR.

Problems with court hearings

Alternative methods of dispute resolution have become increasingly popular because of the difficulties of trying to resolve disputes through court hearings. Below are some of the specific problems posed by court hearings.

The adversarial process

A trial necessarily involves a winner and a loser, and the adversarial procedure combined with the often aggressive atmosphere of court proceedings divides the parties, making them end up enemies even where they did not start out that way. This can be a disadvantage where there is some reason for the parties to sustain a relationship after the problem under discussion is sorted out – child custody cases are the obvious example but, in business too, there may be advantages in resolving a dispute in a way which does not make enemies of the parties. The court system is often said to be best suited to areas where the parties are strangers and happy to remain so – it is interesting to note that in small-scale societies with close kinship links, court-type procedures are rarely used, and disputes are usually settled by negotiation processes that aim to satisfy both parties, and thus maintain the harmony of the group.

Technical cases

Some types of dispute rest on detailed technical points, such as the way in which a machine should be made, or the details of a medical problem, rather than on points of law. The significance of such technical details may not be readily understandable by an ordinary judge. Expert witnesses or advisers may be brought in to advise on these points, but this takes time, and so raises costs. Where detailed technical evidence is at issue, alternative methods of dispute resolution can employ experts in a particular field to take the place of a judge.

Inflexible

In a court hearing, the rules of procedure lay down a fixed framework for the way in which problems are addressed. This may be inappropriate in areas which are of largely private concern to the parties involved. Alternative methods can allow the parties themselves to take more control of the process.

Imposed solutions

Court hearings impose a solution on the parties which, since it does not involve their consent, may need to be enforced. If the parties are able to negotiate a settlement between them, to which they both agree, this should be less of a problem.

Publicity

The majority of court hearings are public. This may be undesirable in some business disputes, where one or both of the parties may prefer not to make public the details of their financial situation or business practices because of competition.

Alternative dispute resolution mechanisms

Where, for one or more of the reasons explained above, court action is not the best way of solving a dispute, a wide range of alternative methods of dispute resolution (often known as ADR) may be used. Three main forms of ADR can be identified: arbitration, mediation and conciliation:

- **Arbitration** is a procedure whereby both sides to a dispute agree to let a third party, the arbitrator, decide. The arbitrator may be a lawyer, or may be an expert in the field of the dispute. He or she will make a decision according to the law and the decision is legally binding.
- **Mediation** involves the appointment of a mediator to help the parties to a dispute reach an agreement which each considers acceptable. Mediation can be 'evaluative', where the mediator gives an assessment of the legal strength of a case, or 'facilitative', where the mediator helps the parties to find a settlement that is in all the parties' best interests. When a mediation is successful and an agreement is reached, it is written down and forms a legally binding contract unless the parties state otherwise.
- **Conciliation** is similar to mediation but the conciliator takes a more interventionist role than the mediator in bringing the two parties together and in suggesting possible solutions to help achieve an agreed settlement. The term conciliation is gradually falling into disuse and the process is regarded as a form of mediation.

One of the simplest forms of ADR is, of course, informal negotiation between the parties themselves, with or without the help of lawyers – the high number of civil cases settled out of court are examples of this. Formal schemes include the Advisory, Conciliation and Arbitration Service (ACAS) which mediates in many industrial disputes and unfair dismissal cases; the role of Ombudsmen in dealing with disputes in the fields of insurance and banking, and in complaints against central and local government and public services; the work done by trade organisations such as the Association of British Travel Agents (ABTA) in settling consumer complaints; inquiries into such areas as objections concerning compulsory purchase or town and country planning; the conciliation schemes offered by courts and voluntary organisations to divorcing couples; and the arbitration schemes run by the Chartered Institute of Arbitrators for business disputes. We will look at some of these in more detail below. Though procedural details vary widely, what they all have in common is that they are attempting to provide a method of settling disagreements that avoids some or all of the disadvantages of the court system listed above.

The Government is keen to promote ADR. It has set up a working party to draw up plans to increase awareness of the availability of ADR and intends to launch a wide-ranging awareness campaign. As part of the Government's commitment to promote alternative

Ess. Cases
p. 414 → dispute resolution, Government legal disputes will be settled by mediation or arbitration whenever possible. Government departments will only go to court as a last resort.

Figure 25.1 The ABTA logo

Source: Association of British Travel Agents

Pressure to use ADR

Following the Woolf reforms of the civil justice system (see p. 536), the Civil Procedure Rules positively encourage the use of ADR. The pre-action protocols direct the parties to consider ADR. When filling out the Allocation Questionnaire, the parties are invited to apply for a one-month stay of proceedings in order to explore settlement through ADR. Active case management under Civil Procedure Rule 1.4 involves '. . . encouraging the parties to use an alternative dispute resolution procedure if the court considers that to be appropriate and facilitating the use of such procedure . . .'. The courts will order a stay of the proceedings for ADR if the parties request it.

The Court of Appeal is now prepared to punish parties who refuse to use ADR by depriving them of costs, even if they are successful in the action: **Dunnett *v* Railtrack plc** (2002). A party may turn down an opponent's offer to mediate with impunity if it can satisfy the court that it has compelling reasons for doing so. Thus, in **Hurst *v* Leeming** (2002) the court held that when mediation can have no real prospect of success a party may, with impunity, refuse to proceed to mediation.

Examples of ADR

Following are some examples of ADR being used in practice.

Conciliation in unfair dismissal cases

A statutory conciliation scheme administered by ACAS operates before cases of unfair dismissal can be taken to an employment tribunal. ACAS conciliation officers talk to both sides with the aim of settling the dispute without a tribunal hearing; they are supposed to procure reinstatement of the employee where possible, but in practice most settlements are only for damages.

A conciliation officer contacts each party or their representatives to discuss the case and advise each side on the strength or weakness of their position. They may tell each side what the other has said, but if the case does eventually go to a tribunal, none of this information is admissible without the consent of the party who gave it.

Evaluation

The success of the scheme is sometimes measured by the fact that two-thirds of cases are either withdrawn or settled by the conciliation process. However, this ignores the imbalance in power between the employer and the employee, especially where the employee has no legal representation – the fact that there has been a settlement does not necessarily mean it is a fair one, when one party is under far more pressure to agree than the other. Dickens's 1985 study of unfair dismissal cases found that awards after a hearing were generally higher than those achieved by conciliation, implying that employees may feel under pressure to agree to any settlement. The study suggested that the scheme would be more effective in promoting fair settlements – rather than settlement at any price – if conciliation officers had a less neutral stance and instead tried to help enforce the worker's rights.

TOPICAL ISSUE

Mediation in divorce cases

In many ways, the court system is an undesirable forum for divorce and its attendant disputes over property and children, since the adversarial nature of the system can aggravate the differences between the parties. This makes the whole process more traumatic for those involved, and clearly is especially harmful where there are children. Consequently, conciliation has for some time been made available to divorcing couples, not necessarily to get them back together (though this can happen), but to try to ensure that any arrangements between them can be made as amicably as possible, reducing the strain on the parties themselves as well as their children.

The Family Law Act 1996 makes changes to the divorce laws and places a greater emphasis on mediation. The Act requires those seeking public funds for representation in family proceedings to attend a meeting with a mediator to consider whether mediation might be suitable in their case.

In divorce cases generally, success depends on the parties themselves and their willingness to cooperate. The parties may find that meeting in a neutral environment, with the assistance of an experienced, impartial professional, helps them communicate calmly, and can make the process of divorce less painful for the couple and their children, by avoiding the need for a court battle in which each feels obliged to accuse the other of being unfit to look after their children – a battle which can be as expensive as it is unpleasant, at a time when one or both parties may be under considerable financial strain.

A three-year study undertaken as a pilot scheme for the new reforms found that eight out of ten couples reached agreement on some issues through mediation, and four in ten reached a complete settlement. However, the Solicitors' Family Law Association points out that because men are usually the main earners in a family, and women's earning abilities may be limited by the demands of childcare, women may need lawyers to get a fair deal financially; in fact the Association says the reforms may well turn out to be 'a rogue's charter for unscrupulous husbands'.

Trade association arbitration schemes

The Fair Trading Act 1973 provides that the Director-General of Fair Trading has a duty to promote codes of practice for trade associations, which include arrangements for handling complaints. So far, more than 20 codes have received approval from the Office of Fair Trading (OFT), and there are many other voluntary schemes not yet approved. Many include provisions for an initial conciliation procedure between consumers and retailers or suppliers in case of complaints, often followed by independent arbitration if conciliation fails.

One of the best-known examples is that set up by the Association of British Travel Agents (ABTA) which, in the case of disputes between tour operators and consumers, offers impartial conciliation. If this fails, disputes may be referred to a special arbitration scheme – about half of all claims referred to it succeed, though not always winning the amount originally claimed.

Evaluation

The best of the schemes offer quick, simple dispute resolution procedures, but standards do vary – the National Consumer Council has reported that some are very slow, and there is some concern about the impartiality of arbitrators. These problems could be addressed relatively easily, but the main drawback is the diversity of the codes, and widespread ignorance of their existence, not only among consumers but even among some of the retailers covered by them! Tighter controls by the OFT and better publicity could make them much more useful mechanisms.

Commercial arbitration

Many commercial contracts contain an arbitration agreement, requiring any dispute to be referred to arbitration before court proceedings are undertaken – the aim being to do away with the need for going to court. Arbitrators may have expertise in the relevant field, and lists of suitable individuals are kept by the Chartered Institute of Arbitrators. The parties themselves choose their arbitrator, ensuring that the person has the necessary expertise in their area and is not connected to either of them. Once appointed, the arbitrator is required to act in an impartial, judicial manner just as a judge would, but the difference is that they will not usually need to have technical points explained to them, so there is less need for expert witnesses.

Disputes may involve disagreement over the quality of goods supplied, interpretation of a trade clause or point of law, or a mixture of the two. Where points of law are involved the arbitrator may be a lawyer. The Arbitration Act 1996 aims to promote commercial arbitration by providing a clear framework for its use. It sets out the powers of the parties to shape the process according to their needs, and provides that they must each do everything necessary to allow the arbitration to proceed properly and without delay. It also spells out the powers of arbitrators, which include limiting the costs to be recoverable by either party and making orders which are equivalent to High Court injunctions if the parties agree. Arbitrators are also authorised to play an inquisitorial role, investigating the facts of the case – many of them are, after all, experts in the relevant fields.

Arbitration hearings must be conducted in a judicial manner, in accordance with the rules of natural justice, but proceedings are held in private, with the time and place decided by the parties. The arbitrator's decision, known as the award, is often delivered immediately, and is as binding on the parties as a High Court judgment would be, and if necessary can be enforced as one.

The award is usually to be considered as final, but appeal may be made to the High Court on a question of law, with the consent of all the parties, or with the permission of the court. Permission will only be given if the case could substantially affect the rights of one of the parties, and provided (with some exceptions) that they had not initially agreed to restrict rights of appeal. The High Court may confirm, vary or reverse the award, or send it back to the arbitrator for reconsideration.

Evaluation

Arbitration fees can be high, but for companies this may be outweighed by the money they save through being able to get the problem solved as soon as it arises, rather than

Table 25.1 Commercial Court mediation statistics

	Apr 98-Mar 99	Apr 99-Mar 00	Apr 00-Mar 01	Apr 01-Mar 02
Number of commercial mediations	190	462	467	338
% referred by courts	not known	19%	27%	31%

Source: *Civil Justice Reform Evaluation Further Findings* (2002) [Figure 8].

having to wait months for a court hearing. The arbitration hearing itself tends to be quicker than a court case, because of the expertise of the arbitrator – in a court hearing time and therefore money can be wasted in explanation of technical points to the judge.

Privacy ensures that business secrets are not made known to competitors. Around 10,000 commercial cases a year go to arbitration, which tends to suggest that business people are fairly happy with the system and the more detailed framework set out by the 1996 Act has supported the use of arbitration. Arbitration has proved popular in international disputes because it does not have the national ties of one of the parties national courts.

Commercial Court ADR scheme

The Commercial Court has taken a robust approach to the use of ADR. Since 1993, it issues ADR orders for commercial disputes regarded as suitable for ADR. It requires each party to inform the court by letter what steps were taken to resolve the case by ADR and why those efforts failed. This has been the subject of research by the academic,

Ess. Cases p. 416

Hazel Genn, which was published in 2002 – *Court-based ADR Initiatives for Non-Family Civil Disputes: the Commercial Court and the Court of Appeal*. ADR was undertaken in a little over half of the cases in which an ADR order had been issued, though the research found that the take-up was increasing in recent years.

Of the cases in which ADR was attempted, 52 per cent settled through ADR, 5 per cent proceeded to trial following unsuccessful ADR, 20 per cent settled some time after the conclusion of the ADR procedure, and the case was still live or the outcome unknown in 23 per cent of cases. Among cases in which ADR was not attempted following an ADR order, about 63 per cent eventually settled. About one-fifth of these said that the settlement had been as a result of the ADR order being made. However, the rate of trials among the group of cases not attempting ADR following an ADR order was 15 per cent, compared with only 5 per cent of cases proceeding to trial following unsuccessful ADR.

ADR orders were generally thought to have had a positive or neutral impact on settlement. Orders can have a positive effect in opening up communication between the parties, and may avoid the fear of one side showing weakness by being the first to suggest settlement.

The Court of Appeal mediation scheme

In 1996 the Court of Appeal established a voluntary mediation scheme. Cases are not individually selected, but, with the exception of certain categories of case, a standard letter of invitation is sent to parties involved in appeals. Since 1999, parties refusing to mediate have been asked to give their reasons for refusal. If both parties agree to mediate, the Court of Appeal arranges mediations and mediators provide their services without charge. This scheme was also the subject of Hazel Genn's research that was published in 2002.

Between November 1997 and April 2000, 38 appeal cases were mediated following agreement by both sides. When the scheme had the benefit of a full-time manager, there was a significant increase in the proportion of cases in which both sides agreed to mediate.

About half of the mediated appeal cases settled either at the mediation appointment or shortly afterwards. Among those cases in which the mediation did not achieve a settlement, a high proportion (62 per cent) went on to trial. This suggests that there are special characteristics of appeal cases that need to be considered in selecting cases for mediation. Blanket invitations to mediate, particularly with an implicit threat of penalties for refusal, may not be the most effective approach for encouraging ADR at appellate level. There was some concern that clients felt they were being pushed into mediation and sometimes being pressured to settle. Although solicitors generally approved of the Court of Appeal taking the initiative in encouraging the use of ADR in appropriate cases, it was felt that there was a need for the adoption of a more selective approach, such as that being used in the Commercial Court.

Advantages of ADR

Cost

Many procedures try to work without any need for legal representation, and even those that do involve lawyers may be quicker and therefore cheaper than going to court.

In 1998, Professor Hazel Genn carried out research into a mediation scheme at Central London County Court. The scheme's objective was to offer virtually cost-free, court-annexed mediation to disputing parties at an early stage in litigation. This involved a three-hour session with a trained mediator assisting parties to reach a settlement, with or without legal representation. The scheme's purpose was to promote swift dispute settlement and a reduction in legal costs through an informal process that parties might prefer to court proceedings. Professor Genn's research did not find clear evidence that mediation saved costs. The overall cost of cases which were settled through mediation was significantly less than those which were litigated; but where mediation was used and the parties failed to reach an agreement, and then went on to litigate, it was possible for costs to be increased.

Accessibility

Alternative methods tend to be more informal than court procedures, without complicated rules of evidence. The process can therefore be less intimidating and less stressful than court proceedings.

Speed

The delays in the civil court system are well known, and waiting for a case to come to court may, especially in commercial cases, add considerably to the overall cost, and adversely affect business.

The research carried out by Professor Genn (1998) found that mediation was able to promote and speed up settlement. The majority (62 per cent) of mediated cases settled at the mediation appointment.

Expertise

Those who run alternative dispute resolution schemes often have specialist knowledge of the relevant areas, which can promote a fairer as well as a quicker settlement.

Conciliation of the parties

Most alternative methods of dispute resolution aim to avoid irrevocably dividing the parties, so enabling business or family relationships to be maintained.

Customer satisfaction

The research by Hazel Genn (2002) found that ADR generally results in a high level of customer satisfaction.

Problems with ADR

Imbalances of power

As the unfair dismissal conciliation scheme shows, the benefits of voluntarily negotiating agreement may be undermined where there is a serious imbalance of power between the parties – in effect, one party is acting less voluntarily than the other. Hazel Genn (2009) has also pointed out that the diversion of a case into alternative dispute resolution often amounts to removing the case from the state sector into the private sector. The priority of the private sector is normally profit not justice:

> The push for less law is supported by the growing ADR profession which professes a mission to rid society of conflict but which is more interested in the profits to be made from large commercial dispute settlement than the small change of the county courts.

Lack of legal expertise

Where a dispute hinges on difficult points of law, an arbitrator may not have the required legal expertise to judge although a legal expert can be appointed to advise an arbitrator if necessary.

No system of precedent

There is no doctrine of precedent, and each case is judged on its merits, providing no real guidelines for future cases. While arbitrators have a duty to apply the law contained in court judgments, the decisions of the arbitrators themselves do not act as precedents.

Enforcement

Decisions not made by courts may be difficult to enforce. While an arbitration award can be enforced just like a judgment, to enforce a mediation settlement a party may need to go to court to obtain a judgment which can then be enforced.

Low take-up rate

There is a relatively low take-up rate for ADR, and the numbers have not increased as much as expected following the introduction of the Woolf reforms. Research carried out for the Government, *Further Findings: A Continuing Evaluation of the Civil Justice Reforms* (2002), has found that after a substantial rise in the first year following the introduction of the Civil Procedure Rules 1998, there has been a levelling off in the number of cases in which alternative dispute resolution is used.

Hazel Genn's research (2002) found that outside commercial practice, 'the profession remains very cautious about the use of ADR. Positive experience of ADR does not appear to be producing armies of converts.' She looked at the reasons why parties choose not to use ADR. For the Commercial Court ADR scheme, the most common reasons given for refusal to mediate were:

- a judgment was required for policy reasons;
- the appeal turned on a point of law;
- the past history or behaviour of the opponent.

The most common reasons given for not trying ADR following an ADR order in the Court of Appeal were:

- the case was not appropriate for ADR;
- the parties did not want to try ADR;
- the timing of the order was wrong (too early or too late); or
- there was no faith in ADR as a process in general.

In addition, Professor Hazel Genn has suggested that following the Woolf reforms the increased number of pre-trial settlements might mean that fewer people feel the need for ADR in 'run of the mill' cases. The research concluded that an individualised approach to the direction of cases towards ADR is likely to be more effective than general invitations at an early stage in the litigation process. This would require the development of clearly articulated selection principles. The timing of invitations or directions to mediate is crucial. The early stages of proceedings may not be the best time, and should not be the only opportunity to consider using ADR.

The future for ADR

Although ADR appears to meet many of the principles for effective civil justice, the proportion of people with legal problems who choose to use ADR has remained very low, even when there are convenient and free schemes available. It is not altogether clear why this is so. Professor Genn's research (1998) found that in only 5 per cent of cases did the parties agree to try mediation, despite vigorous attempts to stimulate demand. It was least likely to be used where both parties had legal representation.

At present, many of those contemplating litigation will go first to a solicitor and Professor Genn's research shows widespread misunderstanding about mediation processes amongst solicitors. Many did not know what was involved and were therefore not able to advise clients on whether their case was suitable for any form of ADR, or the benefits that might flow from seeking to use it. Solicitors were apprehensive about showing weakness through accepting mediation in the context of traditional adversarial litigation. Litigants were also hostile to the idea of compromise, particularly in the early stages of litigation.

It is likely that in the future ADR will play an increasingly important role in the resolution of disputes. It is already widely used in the US where the law frequently requires parties to try mediation before their case can be set down for trial. It is generally accepted that the UK will see a similar expansion in the use of ADR, as both the courts and the legal profession begin to take ADR more seriously than they once did. Following Lord Woolf's reforms of the civil justice system, the new rules of procedure in the civil courts impose on the judges a duty to encourage parties in appropriate cases to use ADR and to facilitate its use. Parties can request that court proceedings be postponed while they try ADR and the court can also order a postponement for this reason. Backing up this position is the fact that the Government has said, in the explanatory notes to the Access to Justice Act 1999, that in time they hope to extend public funding increasingly to cover the use of ADR.

Answering questions

1 Do you think that the courts offer the best means of solving disputes?

Your introduction might mention the fact that although courts are accepted as a means of resolving disputes, there are some types of dispute where they are not helpful, and so other methods of dispute resolution have developed. You can then examine the disadvantages of courts as means of dispute resolution, and then relate these disadvantages to the types of dispute where courts have not been found to offer the best solution.

You could then go through the four types of alternative dispute resolution we have examined, pointing out why they have advantages over the court system for those types of dispute. In this essay you could also look at tribunals (see Chapter 23), and examine how and why they provide a useful alternative to courts.

You might then discuss some of the disadvantages of alternative methods of dispute resolution, pointing out the kinds of case for which these disadvantages might make them unsuitable. Your conclusion might simply point out that courts may provide the best way of solving some disputes, but be unhelpful in others.

2 **Should people be obliged to use ADR before being allowed to pursue their case in court?** *LLB*

This question requires a discussion of the strengths and weaknesses of ADR and the benefits and disadvantages of automatic referral to ADR. Recent research by, for example, Hazel Genn, could be discussed. Relevant cases discussed on p. 625 could also be considered.

3 **Compare and contrast arbitration, mediation and conciliation as effective methods of ADR.**

All three of these methods of ADR are commonly used to resolve commercial and consumer disputes away from the ordinary domestic courts. The use of each form of ADR is normally voluntary and the results binding only if so agreed in advance (e.g. through a contract which provides for binding arbitration) or subsequently incorporated into a binding agreement. Occasionally, a statute may require parties to use a form of ADR prior to, or as part of, the litigation process.

In arbitration, both sides agree to a third person deciding the dispute in a legally binding way. Arbitration is particularly popular in the commercial sector.

A mediator assists the parties to reach a mutually acceptable agreement, helps the parties to define the issues and may provide an 'external' assessment of the strength of each side's case. The parties then write down the agreement, once reached, for formal acceptance.

Whilst conciliation resembles mediation, the conciliator adopts a more active role. Because of the voluntary nature of mediation and conciliation, their effectiveness depends heavily upon the parties' desire to resolve the dispute.

4 **'Alternative Dispute Resolution (ADR) is an alternative means of resolving disputes without reference to the traditional court system.' Critically analyse this statement with particular reference to (i) the context in which ADR operates; and (ii) its non-enforceability.**

First of all, you must explain what ADR is and what its main forms take (p. 624). You then need to illustrate in what situations it is used (emphasising the fact that it is a civil law resolution that is encouraged in the Civil Procedure Rules 1998). So, for example, you could mention unfair dismissal cases; divorce cases; and the procedures for ADR as it is exercised in the Commercial Court.

Certainly ADR does have its advantages, but there are a number of problems which – in addition to its unenforceability – may explain why take-up is low. This then leads you into a discussion of its problems (including high fees; unwillingness to compromise; and possible pressure to settle).

Summary of Chapter 25: Alternative methods of dispute resolution

Introduction
Following Lord Woolf's reforms of the civil justice system, ADR should play a more important role in solving all types of civil disputes. ADR has become increasingly popular because of problems resolving disputes through court hearings.

Alternative dispute resolution mechanisms
Three main forms of ADR can be identified:

- arbitration;
- mediation; and
- conciliation.

Conciliation in unfair dismissal cases
A statutory conciliation scheme administered by the Advisory, Conciliation and Arbitration Service (ACAS) operates before cases of unfair dismissal can be taken to an employment tribunal.

Mediation in divorce cases
The Family Law Act 1996 has made changes to the divorce laws and places a greater emphasis on mediation.

Trade association arbitration schemes
The Fair Trading Act 1973 provides that the Director-General of Fair Trading has a duty to promote codes of practice for trade associations. Many include provisions for an initial conciliation procedure, often followed by independent arbitration if conciliation fails.

Commercial contracts
Many commercial contracts contain an arbitration agreement, requiring any dispute to be referred to arbitration before court proceedings are undertaken.

Commercial Court ADR scheme
Since 1993 the Commercial Court has issued ADR orders for disputes regarded as suitable for ADR.

The Court of Appeal mediation scheme
The Court of Appeal has a voluntary mediation scheme, under which a standard letter is sent to the parties inviting them to enter mediation.

Advantages of ADR
The advantages of ADR include:

- cost;
- accessibility;
- speed;
- expertise;

- conciliation of the parties; and
- customer satisfaction.

Problems with ADR

The problems with ADR are that:

- there may be a serious imbalance of power between the parties;
- an arbitrator may lack legal expertise;
- there is no system of precedent;
- enforcement may be difficult; and
- there is a low take-up rate.

The future of ADR

It is likely that in the future ADR will play an increasingly important role in the resolution of disputes.

Reading list

Alternative Dispute Resolution – A Discussion Paper (1999), London: Lord Chancellor's Department.

Boyron, S. (2006) 'The rise of mediation in administrative law disputes: Experiences from England, France and Germany', *Public Law* 230.

Evans, Sir A. (2003) 'Forget ADR – think A or D', *Civil Justice Quarterly* 230.

Fricker, N. and Walker, J. (1993) 'Alternative dispute resolution – State responsibility or second best?' *Civil Justice Quarterly* 29.

Genn, H. (1998) *The Central London County Court Pilot Mediation Scheme: Evaluation Report*, London: Lord Chancellor's Department.

Genn, H. (2002) *Court-based ADR Initiatives for Non-Family civil disputes: the Commercial Court and the Court of Appeal*, London: Lord Chancellor's Department.

Lightman, J. (2003) 'The Civil Justice System and legal profession – the challenges ahead', *Civil Justice Quarterly* 235.

Partington, M. (2004) 'Alternative Dispute Resolution: Recent Developments, Future Challenges', *Civil Justice Quarterly* 99.

Supperstone, M., Stilitz, D. and Sheldon, C. (2006) 'ADR and Public Law', *Public Law* 299.

Reading on the Internet

www

The research carried out by Professor Genn in 1998 on the mediation scheme at Central London County Court is available on the Department for Constitutional Affairs' website:
http://www.dca.gov.uk/research/1998/598esfr.htm

For information about ombudsman systems see the website of the British and Irish Ombudsman Association:
www.bioa.org.uk/youngpeople.htm

Visit **www.mylawchamber.co.uk/ElliottELS** to access multiple-choice questions, flashcards and practice exam questions to test yourself on this chapter.

25

Alternative methods of dispute resolution

CONCEPTS OF LAW

Part 5 seeks to encourage a profound analysis of the very concept of law. Up to now we have explored some areas of law and practice without questioning what law actually is and why it exists in society. In this Part we will seek to provide answers to the questions 'What is law?' and 'Why do we have law?'

26 Law and rules

This chapter looks at the distinction between legal rules and other types of rules by examining different academic theories on the subject. In particular it considers:

- the command theory developed by John Austin in the seventeenth century;

- Professor Hart's distinction between primary and secondary rules;

- Professor Dworkin's emphasis on legal principles;

- the natural law theory; and

- the importance that some writers have placed on the function of law.

Introduction

What is law? What do we mean when we say that something is the law? One answer is that a law is a type of rule, but clearly there are many rules which are not law: rules of etiquette, school or club rules, and moral rules, for example. One way to understand more about what law is, is to look at what distinguishes legal rules from other types of rules.

Austin: the command theory

The nineteenth-century writer John Austin, in his book *The Province of Jurisprudence Determined*, argued that law differed from other rules because it was the command of a sovereign body, which the state could enforce by means of punishment. The relevant sovereign body would vary in different countries; in Britain it was the Queen in Parliament, but in other countries it might be the monarch alone, or an emperor or president.

Austin's definition has fairly clear application to some areas of law, most obviously criminal law, where we are told we must do or not do certain things, with penalties for disobedience. But there are large areas which fall outside it. Contract law, for example, details the sanctions which can be imposed when contracts are broken, but it does not command us to make contracts in the first place. The law concerning marriage does not order anyone to marry; it simply sets out the conditions under which people may do so if they wish, the procedure they should follow to make the marriage legally valid, and the legal consequences of being married. The rules about marriage and contracts could be described as rules giving power, in contrast to the rules imposing duties which comprise criminal law; they have different functions, but both types are legal rules. As Professor Hart and other legal philosophers have pointed out, there are an enormous number of legal rules which neither make commands, nor impose sanctions. The complexity and variety of legal rules make it impossible to cover them all with the proposition that laws are commands.

Hart: primary and secondary rules

In his influential book *The Concept of Law* (1994, first published in 1961), Professor Hart attempted to link types of rules with types of legal systems. He divided legal rules into primary rules and secondary rules, and argued that the existence of secondary rules was a mark of a developed legal system.

Primary rules were described as those which any society needs in order to survive. These rules forbid the most socially destructive forms of behaviour – typically murder, theft and fraud – and also cover areas of civil law, such as tort. According to Hart, simple societies, which generally have a high degree of social cohesion, can survive with only these basic rules but, as a society becomes more complex, it will require what he described as secondary rules.

Secondary rules confer power rather than impose duties, and can be divided into three types: rules of adjudication, rules of change and rules of recognition.

Rules of adjudication

In simple societies, the primary rules can be applied and enforced by means of informal social pressures within the group; this works because the community is close-knit, and individuals rely on each other. As societies become larger and more complex, these bonds are broken, and social pressures will not be enough to shape behaviour. Therefore the community needs some means of giving authority to its rules, and the secondary rules of adjudication are designed to provide this. They enable officials (usually judges) to decide disputes, and to define the procedures to be followed and the sanctions which can be applied when rules are broken. Examples of secondary rules in our society are those which lay down what kind of issues can be decided by courts, who is qualified to be a judge and sentencing legislation for criminal cases; there are many more.

Rules of change

The second type of secondary rule is concerned with making new rules, both primary and secondary. A developed society will need these to respond to new situations – perhaps the clearest example in our society is the huge number of laws introduced over the last century as a result of the invention of motorised transport. Rules of change lay down the procedure to be followed in making new rules or changing old ones. In our system, the main rules of change are those concerning how legislation is made and how judicial decisions become part of the common law.

There are also rules of change concerning the power of individuals to produce changes in the legal relationships they have with others.

Rules of recognition

The fact that in simple forms of society rules are enforced by social pressure means that they are only binding if the community as a whole accepts them. Within a small-scale, close-knit community it will generally be obvious to all what the accepted rules are. In a more complex society, this is not the case; there may be many rules, some of them complex, and individuals cannot be expected to know them all. To minimise uncertainty, the developed society, according to Hart, develops rules of recognition, which spell out which of the many rules that govern society actually have legal force. As Hart explains, in the simpler form of society we must wait and see whether a potential rule gets accepted as a rule or not; in a system with a basic rule of recognition we can say before a rule is actually made that it will be valid if it conforms to the requirements of the rule of recognition.

Hart described the UK as having a single rule of recognition: what the Queen in Parliament enacts is law. This leaves out the issue of judge-made law; the difficulties in pinpointing exactly how precedent works mean that a rule of recognition is more difficult to specify here, but it would certainly be inaccurate to say that only what the Queen in Parliament enacts is law.

Dworkin: legal principles

Professor Dworkin (1986) rejects Hart's analysis of law as consisting purely of rules. He argues that the rich fabric of law contains not just rules, but a set of principles on which all legal rules are based. Dworkin defines rules as operating in an all or nothing manner, stating a particular answer to a particular question. Legal principles, on the other hand, are guidelines, giving a reason that argues in one direction, but does not dictate a decision. Take, for example, a hypothetical murder of a father by his son. One of the legal principles Dworkin advances is that no one should benefit from their own wrong, and this should clearly be taken into account in deciding this dispute. But it does not dictate a particular answer; there may be other aspects to the dispute which make other principles a stronger influence (perhaps the son killed in self-defence, for example). By contrast, a rule that no one can inherit property from a person they have murdered is clear-cut and straightforward in application: the son cannot inherit from his father.

Other differences between principles and rules, according to Dworkin, are that principles have a dimension of weight or importance – a suggestion of morality – that rules lack. Conflicts between principles can be weighed up by a judge, and the background guidance they give means that, even in hard cases, they should provide a fairly clear answer: if rules clash, a further rule will be needed to establish which should prevail (for example, the rule that if law and equity conflict, equity prevails). Finally, the strength of a principle can become eroded over time, whereas rules stand until they are removed.

The natural law theory

The theories of Austin (1954) and Hart (1963) attempt to define what law is, without examining what it says: they could be said to look at the outside appearance of law, rather than defining it by its content. This approach is called positivism. Another school of thought, the natural law theory, defines law by its content: only laws which conform to a particular moral code, seen as a higher form of law, can genuinely be called law. This natural law theory is discussed on p. 655.

The function of law

Some writers have taken the view that law is best understood by looking at the role it plays in society: what is it for? The following are some of the key theories in this area.

Social cohesion

The nineteenth-century French sociologist, Emile Durkheim (1983), looked at the issue of social cohesion, searching for what keeps a society together, and concluded that law played an important role in this area. He looked at the role of law in two contrasting types of society: the first a relatively simple, technologically undeveloped society; the second highly developed in terms of technology and social structure.

Durkheim argued that in the first type of society, the whole group would have clearly identifiable common aims, and would all work to achieve them: the interests of any individual within the group would be exactly the same as those of the group as a whole. A moral and legal code based on these aims would be recognised and accepted by all, and would keep the group working together. Durkheim called this mechanical solidarity. An individual who deviated from this code would be punished, and their punishment would reinforce the code by reflecting the group's disapproval of the wrongdoing.

According to Durkheim's analysis, as social groups become larger and more complex, developing links with other social groups, the interests of individual members become less closely linked to those of the group as a whole. To take a simple example, members of a forest tribe might hunt together to provide food for everyone, whereas in a developed society individuals and families look after their own interests. Social solidarity does not disappear but becomes based on increasing interdependence, which itself stems from the division of labour. Whereas, for example, in the small-scale society, each family would make its own bread, in the developed society this task is shared between farmer, flour mill, bakery and retailer, all dependent on each other and the consumer. This interdependence means that the individual has social importance in their own right, rather than occupying a social position simply as one member of the group.

Durkheim argued that these changes would be accompanied by a corresponding change in the type of law present in the society. Penal law would become less important and would increasingly be replaced by compensatory law, where the object is not to punish but to resolve grievances by restoring the injured party to the position they were in before the dispute arose. There would be less need for resolution of disputes between the individual and society, and more for those between individuals.

Durkheim's analysis has been criticised for overestimating the extent to which criminal law would decline and give way to compensatory law in an industrialised society: if anything, industrialised societies have increased the application of criminal law and, indeed, industrialisation has created new crimes, such as computer fraud and pollution. Anthropological studies have shown that he also underestimated the degree to which compensatory or civil law already exists in simple societies.

Survival

Professor Hart argues that the main function of law is simply to allow human beings to survive in a community. He suggests that there are certain truths about human existence which, without rules guiding our behaviour, would make life excessively dangerous. Each member of society has, more or less, the same physical strength and intelligence, and both our powers of self-restraint and willingness to help others are limited. We therefore all face the danger of attack from the others and competition for such resources as are available. Knowing this, any group of humans will soon recognise that it needs rules curbing individual desires and impulses. We realise that, if we attack people or take their goods when they are weak, the same could easily happen to us. To protect ourselves we must accept limitations on our behaviour. The alternative would be a degree of conflict that would make it impossible for the group to stay together, yet individual members might be even less safe if they had to face the world alone.

The realisation that we are not safe in the world alone and can only be safe in a community if there are rules of self-restraint, leads to the development of such rules, protecting the property and person of others. It also leads to acceptance of the idea that observance of the rules must be guaranteed by some kind of penalty directed against the rule-breaker. Hart maintains that such rules are the minimum necessary content of law in any society.

The maintenance of order

The German sociologist, Max Weber (1979), argues that the primary role of law is to maintain order in society. Law makes individuals accept the legitimacy of their rules, and gives them the power to make law and coerce individuals into obeying it. Without this coercive power, argues Weber, order could not be maintained.

This idea has enjoyed much political support as political parties, from either side of the spectrum, are keen to present themselves as promoting law and order. But Weber's view can be criticised as overestimating the role of law in keeping order. If he is to be believed, a relaxation of law would result in the immediate degeneration of society into chaos and disorder; but this ignores the many other factors which make our society relatively orderly. In many cases we obey the law not because it is the law, but because of social or moral pressures – we do not steal, for example, because we have been brought up to think stealing is wrong, not because we might be caught and punished for it. Similarly, we may obey moral or social rules as strictly as we obey legal ones – we are unlikely to find ourselves in court for swearing at the vicar, but few of us would do it because of strong social and moral pressures.

Critics argue that Weber's theory fails to allow for the fact that societies are not just a loose group of independent individuals; they have clear patterns of behaviour, relationships and beliefs, which differ from society to society. These are what hold society together and, while law is one aspect of them, it is not the only force for social cohesion. Other social institutions which promote cohesion include the family and schools, which transmit social standards to new generations; political institutions (Parliament, political parties); economic and commercial institutions (trade unions, manufacturers' associations, patterns of production and trade); and religious and cultural institutions (such as literature and the arts, the press, television and radio). All of these play a part in establishing social rules.

The importance of these social rules can be seen if we compare a human society to a group of animals. Like animals, we have instincts to eat, sleep and mate. But whereas animals do all these things in response only to instinct and opportunity, our behaviour is controlled, directly and indirectly, through moral standards, religious doctrines, social traditions and legal rules. For example, like animals we are born with a mating instinct but, unlike animals, human societies attempt to channel this instinct into a form of relationship which has traditionally been seen as offering benefits for society: heterosexual marriage. As we have said, there are no legal rules commanding people to marry, but there are a great many social and moral pressures upholding heterosexual marriage as the desired form of relationship; the predominant religion in our history upholds it, and alternatives, such as homosexual relationships or heterosexual couples living together without marriage, have traditionally been seen as immoral and socially unacceptable. It can be argued that these pressures have, in the past, operated just as forcefully as laws do in other areas, though they now appear to be breaking down.

Balancing different interests

The US jurist, Roscoe Pound (1968), saw law as a social institution, created and designed to satisfy human wants, both individual and social. Pound identified different interests in society, including individual, domestic, property, social and public interests. He argued that the law's main aim was to secure and balance these different and often competing interests.

Where interests on a different level conflicted – such as individual interests conflicting with social interests – they could not be weighed against each other, but where there is a conflict between interests on the same level, they must be weighed against one another with the aim of ensuring that as many as possible are satisfied.

'Law jobs'

Karl Llewellyn (1962) was a member of the US realist school of thought which, like the positivists, is concerned with what law is, rather than what it ought to be. Working with Hoebel, an anthropologist, Llewellyn studied American Indian groups and, from this research, constructed a theory of 'law jobs' to explain the social functions of law.

Llewellyn's theory is that every social group has certain jobs which need to be done for it to survive, and law is one of the main ways in which these jobs are done. The jobs include preventing disruptive disputes within the group; providing a means of resolving disputes which do arise; allocating authority and providing mechanisms for constructing relationships between people, including ways of adjusting to change. Although these jobs are common to all societies, the ways in which the jobs are done will vary from society to society. For example, the allocation of authority in a simple society might be done by basic rules on electing or appointing a chief while, in a more complex society, this job can be done by a constitution.

Robert Summers (1992) has also looked at law in terms of the various jobs it does for society, and identified five main uses of law: putting right grievances among members of a society; prohibiting and prosecuting forbidden behaviour; promoting certain defined activities; conferring social and governmental benefits, including education and welfare; and giving effect to private arrangements, such as contracts. Although their theses are different, both Llewellyn and Summers look at law in its social context, in contrast to writers such as Austin who believe rules, including legal rules, can be analysed without reference to their settings.

Exploitation

A radical alternative to the views of writers such as Durkheim and Weber is put forward by Karl Marx (1933). Durkheim and Weber disagreed about the precise functions of law, but they accepted the idea that law must in some way be of benefit to society as a whole. Marx, however, rejected the idea that there was a common interest in society which law could serve. He argued that society was composed of classes whose interests were fundamentally opposed to each other. Law, Marx maintained, was not made in the interests of society as a whole, but in the interests of the small group which dominates society; through law (and other social institutions, such as religion), this group is able to exploit the working class, which Marx called the proletariat.

Later Marxist writers, such as Althusser and Gramsci, have developed this thesis. They argue that the ruling class controls the ideology of society, including the beliefs and ideas which shape it. This ideology is expressed through social institutions such as the school, the family, religion and the law. By shaping the way in which people see the world around them, the ruling class is able to ensure that the working class see their exploitation as natural, as the only way things could be, rather than as the oppressive state of affairs that Marxists see. This minimises their resistance.

Law is seen as an important part of this process. Because, for example, the law protects private property, we come to view private property and all its implications as natural and inevitable. Take, for example, the acceptance of profit. If someone pays £100 for a set of raw materials, and pays an employee £100 to turn those materials into goods which they then sell for £600, it is quite acceptable in our society for the employer to keep the profit, because they purchased both the raw materials and the employee's labour. Clearly, an acceptance of people making a profit out of another's labour is fundamental to acceptance of the capitalist system as a whole, and the legal doctrine of private property is the basis of this acceptance. But Marxists point out that the situation can be looked at in another way, as the employer stealing from the worker the added value their labour gives to the raw materials. The fact that we would not usually think to see it this way is, Marxists say, because we see it through a capitalist ideology, and law plays a fundamental role in upholding this ideology.

Marx believed that law was only needed because of the fundamental clash of interests between those of the ruling class and those of the proletariat; once society was transformed by communism, these divisions would no longer exist, and law would wither away.

Why are laws obeyed?

Austin thought laws were obeyed because of the threat of sanction and out of a habit of obedience to the state. Hart rejects this explanation, arguing that acceptance of a rule is more important than possible sanctions. As well as the external aspect of obedience – recognition of the validity of the rule, and a potential sanction – Hart argues that there is an internal process, which inclines us to obey because we consider it right and proper to do so. Hart suggests that if a law is not internalised, an individual will feel no obligation to obey it. In our system there are many examples of laws which for some reason widely fail this internalisation test: parking offences, speeding, tax evasion and drug legislation are obvious examples of laws which large numbers of people apparently feel no real compulsion to follow. He suggests that in order for law to promote social cohesion in a simple society with only primary rules, members must not only obey those rules, but also consciously see them as common standards of behaviour, breaches of which can legitimately be criticised: in other words, they internalise all the rules, following them not just because they are rules, but because they consider it right to do so. But, in a more developed legal system like ours, Hart believes individuals need not internalise every rule. It is clearly desirable for them to internalise as many as possible, but, failing this, the necessary functions can be served by officials internalising the rules and, thereby, becoming committed to their maintenance.

Fear and internalisation

If we obey laws because we internalise them, what makes us internalise some rules and not others? One theory, put forward by Professor Olivecrona (1971), suggests that fear is a strong motivation. He points out that we are all aware from childhood of the consequences of breaking rules and, as a result, we experience a tension between temptation to break rules and fear of punishment. Olivercrona suggests that the human mind cannot accommodate such tension indefinitely, and so we gradually adjust psychologically to accept conformity to rules as a means of getting rid of the fear of punishment; eventually we do not believe we are acting out of fear at all, we have just become used to keeping the rules.

Perhaps because of the efficacy of this process, many writers have suggested that law can be used to shape moral and social ideas. Aristotle suggested that law could be used to educate citizens, commenting that 'Legislators make citizens good by forming their habits.' More recently, Lord Simon of Glaisdale has observed that law still has an educative function, which it exercises when certain conduct becomes stigmatised by becoming illegal.

On the other hand, social pressures can often bring about changes in conduct which legal rules have been unable to do. A recent example is that of drink-driving. At one time this offence was seen as being in a similar category to speeding or parking offences; it was against the law, but many still saw it as acceptable. Now, as a result of social pressures, partly driven by public information campaigns, it is viewed as highly anti-social behaviour, and the law is apparently more widely obeyed.

26

Law and rules

Answering questions

1 '. . . a law is a type of rule, but clearly there are many rules which are not law.' Discuss.

In essence, this simply requires an analysis of what rules are and what law is (possibly by reference to its functions: pp. 642–6), referring to the authors mentioned in this chapter (in other words, Austin, Hart and Dworkin). It will also require knowledge of the natural law theory (see Chapter 27, p. 655) in order to discuss the quotation comprehensively.

2 **Is it possible to live in a society without law?**

This type of question allows many different approaches, all of which could be very successful. One approach would be to use the material under the heading 'The function of law' at p. 642. You could consider each theory in turn and consider whether, if that theory is right, there would be a society without law. For example, Durkheim suggests that law achieves social cohesion, without law you could only have a primitive society and not a technologically advanced society, while Karl Marx considers that law is merely a tool for exploitation and that without law we could enjoy a much healthier society.

Summary of Chapter 26: Law and rules

One way to understand more about what law is, is to look at what distinguishes legal rules from other types of rules.

Austin: the command theory
The seventeenth-century writer John Austin argued that law differed from other rules because it was the command of a sovereign body, which the state could enforce by means of punishment.

Hart: primary and secondary rules
Professor Hart divided legal rules into primary rules and secondary rules, and argued that the existence of secondary rules was a mark of a developed legal system. Primary rules were described as those which any society needs in order to survive. Secondary rules confer power rather than impose duties, and can be divided into three types:

- rules of adjudication;
- rules of change; and
- rules of recognition.

Dworkin: legal principles
Professor Dworkin argues that the rich fabric of law contains a set of principles on which all legal rules are based. Legal principles are guidelines, giving a reason that argues in one direction, but does not dictate a decision.

The natural law theory
The natural law theory defines law by its content: only laws which conform to a particular moral code, seen as a higher form of law, can genuinely be called law.

The function of law
Some writers have taken the view that law is best understood by looking at the role it plays in society.

Social cohesion
The nineteenth-century French sociologist Emile Durkheim looked at the issue of social cohesion, searching for what keeps a society together, and concluded that law played an important role in this area.

Survival

Professor Hart argues that the main function of law is simply to allow human beings to survive in a community.

The maintenance of order

The German sociologist Max Weber argued that the primary role of law is to maintain order in society.

Balancing different interests

The US jurist Roscoe Pound saw law as a social institution, created and designed to satisfy human wants, both individual and social.

'Law jobs'

Karl Llewellyn's theory is that every social group has certain jobs which need to be done for it to survive, and law is one of the main ways in which these jobs are done.

Exploitation

Karl Marx argued that society was composed of classes whose interests were fundamentally opposed to each other. Law, Marx maintained, was not made in the interests of society as a whole, but in the interests of the small group which dominates society; through law (and other social institutions, such as religion), this group is able to exploit the working class.

Why are laws obeyed?

Austin thought laws were obeyed because of the threat of sanction and out of a habit of obedience to the state. Hart argues that there is an internal process, which inclines us to obey because we consider it right and proper to do so.

Fear and internalisation

If we obey laws because we internalise them, what makes us internalise some rules and not others? One theory, put forward by Professor Olivecrona, suggests that fear is a strong motivation.

Reading list

Austin, J. (1954) *The Province of Jurisprudence Determined*, London: Weidenfeld & Nicolson.

Durkheim, E. (1983) *Durkheim and the Law*, Oxford: Robertson.

Dworkin, R. (1977) *Taking Rights Seriously*, London: Duckworth.

Dworkin, R. (1986) *Law's Empire*, London: Fontana Press.

Hart, H.L.A. (1994) *The Concept of Law*, Oxford: Clarendon Press.

Llewellyn, K. (1962) *Jurisprudence: Realism in Theory and Practice*, Chicago: University of Chicago Press.

Marx, K. (1933) *Capital*, London: J.M. Dent.

Olivecrona, K. (1971) *Law as Fact*, London: Stevens.

Pound, R. (1968) *Social Control Through Law*, Hamden: Archon Books.

Twining, W. and Miers, D. (1991) *How To Do Things With Rules*, London: Weidenfeld & Nicolson.

27 Law and morals

This chapter discusses:

- the relationship between law and morality;
- the evolution of law and morality;
- differences between law and morality;
- whether law and morality should be separate; and
- the impact of morality on law as seen through the work of the Human Fertilisation and Embryology Authority.

Introduction

Morals are beliefs and values which are shared by a society, or a section of a society; they tell those who share them what is right or wrong. In our society, moral values have been heavily influenced by the dominant religion, Christianity, though this is not our only source of moral values.

Debates about morals and morality often centre around sexual issues, such as sex outside marriage, homosexuality and pornography. But moral values also shape attitudes towards money and property, gender roles, friendship, behaviour at work – in fact it is difficult to think of any area of our lives where morality has no application. Mary Warnock (1986), an academic who has been involved in inquiries into issues of moral concern, says: 'I do not believe that there is a neat way of marking off moral issues from all others; some people, at some time, may regard things as matters of moral right or wrong, which at another time or in another place are thought to be matters of taste, or indeed to be matters of no importance at all.' However, she points out that in any society, at any time, questions relating to birth and death and to the establishing of families are regarded as morally significant. These can perhaps be regarded as core moral issues.

As Warnock has observed, moral attitudes tend to change over time. It is only within recent decades, for example, that the idea of couples living together without marriage has become widely accepted; even now acceptance is not total, but a generation or so ago it would have been unthinkable. Similar shifts have taken place with regard to homosexuality and women's liberation.

The French sociologist, Durkheim (1983), has highlighted the fact that in a modern, developed society it is difficult to pinpoint a set of moral values shared by all. In less developed societies, such as small tribal groups, Durkheim argued that all the members of the group are likely to share a moral code; but, in a technologically advanced society such as our own, where individuals differ widely in social status, income, occupation, ethnic background and so on, its members are unlikely to share identical moral values, even if they largely agree on some basic points. For example, most people in the UK agree that it is usually wrong to kill or steal, but there is much less consensus on whether it is wrong to take drugs, have abortions, experiment on animals or help a terminally ill person to die. Even on the basic crimes of theft and murder, some people will see these as always wrong, while others will believe there are situations in which they may be justified; among the latter, there will be disagreement as to what those situations are.

Criminologist Jock Young (1971) has pointed out that much depends on the standpoint of the observer, and how they see the norms of society. Looking at attitudes to illegal drug use, Young has observed that to those who see society's rules as based on a moral consensus, drug-taking was against that moral consensus, so those who indulged in it were therefore maladjusted and sick. But, if society's rules on deviant behaviour are seen simply as a yardstick of what that particular society considers normal, drug-taking is neither necessarily deviant nor necessarily a social problem: it is merely deviant to groups who condemn it and a problem to those who wish to eliminate it. What is being made is simply a value judgement, and values vary between people and over time.

27

Law and morals

Law and morality

Both law and morals are normative; they specify what ought to be done, and aim to mark the boundaries between acceptable and unacceptable conduct. While moral rules tend not to be backed by the obvious sanctions which make some legal rules enforceable, they are often reinforced by pressures which in some cases may be as strong, if not stronger: the disapproval of family and friends, loss of status and being shunned by the community are powerful disincentives against immoral conduct. Of course many types of undesirable behaviour offend against both moral and legal rules – serious crimes are obvious examples.

Both law and morals are often presented as if they were the only possible responses to social or political problems and crises, yet both vary widely between societies. For example, in our society, private property is such a basic doctrine that we readily condemn any infringement of our rights – legal and moral – to acquire, possess and enjoy our personal property. Stealing is seen as immoral as well as illegal. But in a society where property is held communally, any attempt by one individual to treat property as their own private possession would be regarded as every bit as immoral as we would consider stealing. The idea of private property is not a basic part of human nature, as it is often presented, but a socially constructed value. Our society has for centuries been based on trade, and this requires a basis of private property.

Some areas of law are explicitly presented as raising moral issues and, when these areas arise in Parliament, MPs are allowed to vote according to their own beliefs, rather than according to party policy. This is called a vote of conscience and was used, for example, when the issue of capital punishment was debated. However, the kinds of issue on which a vote of conscience would be allowed are not the only ones to which moral values apply: when MPs vote on tax changes, the welfare state, employment or any number of issues before Parliament in every session, they are voting on moral issues, because they are voting on the way a Government treats its citizens, and the way in which citizens are allowed to treat each other.

Similarly, some areas of law, such as criminal law, have obvious moral implications, but these are also present in areas where morality is less obvious. Tort law, for example, and especially negligence, is built around the principle that those who harm others should compensate for the damage done; that, as Lord Atkin noted in the famous case of **Donoghue v Stevenson** (1932), the biblical principle of 'love thy neighbour' must include 'do not harm your neighbour'. Similarly, contract, as Atiyah (1979) has pointed out, is based around the principle that promises should be kept. Even land law which, on the surface, appears to consist of technicalities far removed from elevated questions of morality, has enormous moral importance because it is upholding the whole notion of property and ownership. Take the question of squatting: the property owner has all the rights to begin with but, if the squatting continues for long enough, the squatter can gain some rights. Is it moral that the property owner should lose rights to someone acting illegally? On the other hand, is it moral that some should be homeless while others have property they can afford to leave empty?

In **Re A (Children) (Conjoined Twins: Surgical Separation)** (2001), the Court of Appeal expressly stated that it was 'not a court of morals but a court of law and our decisions have to be taken from a solid base of legal principle'. But, in reality, law and morals were closely interlinked in that case. It concerned the legality of an operation to separate conjoined twins. The operation would inevitably lead to the death of the weaker twin, but was the sole chance of saving the life of the stronger twin. The judgment of the court is based on the principle of the sanctity of life, which itself is a moral commitment.

Changes in law and morality

As we have observed, the moral values of a society tend to change over time; the same applies to its laws. In the UK, legal changes have tended to lag behind moral ones, coming only when the process of moral acceptance is well advanced. Thus, the law was changed in 1991 to make rape within marriage a crime, the House of Lords stating that the change was necessary because marriages were now seen as equal partnerships, in which the husband could no longer enforce rights to sex. This shift in attitude had taken place long before 1991, but the time-lag between moral change and legal change was fairly typical. Often it is the possession of effective political power which finally determines which and whose definition of morality is reflected in the law.

On the other hand, law can sometimes bring about changes in social morality. Troy Duster, in *The Legislation of Morality* (1970), traced the history of drug use and its legal control in the US from the end of the nineteenth century. At that time, drug addiction was commonly restricted to the middle and upper classes, who had become dependent on morphine through the use of patented medicines; despite the fact that these contained morphine, it was perfectly legal to buy and sell them. Addiction carried no social stigma. However, when certain drugs were made illegal under the Harrison Act 1914, such drugs began to be supplied by the criminal underworld. Dependency on drugs became associated with this underworld and with the lower classes who had most contact with it. This in turn led to social stigma. Interestingly, this stigma, which was in a sense created by legal controls, was partly responsible for the calls for greater legal controls on drug-taking which have been heard over the last two decades, as more and more young people become involved in the drug culture.

Academics from the Scandinavian realist standpoint, such as Olivercrona (1971), argue that our morality is created by the law, rather than the law emerging from our morality. Olivercrona suggests that law has an influence on us from our earliest days, helping to mould our moral views. From the start, parents and teachers tell us what we must and must not do and we quickly learn the consequences of disobedience.

Differences between law and morality

Although law and morality are clearly closely linked, there are certain ways in which they differ. Many types of behaviour exist which may be widely considered to be immoral, yet we would be very surprised to find laws against them: telling lies, for example. Equally, some forms of behaviour are illegal, but would not usually be described as immoral, such as parking on a yellow line. Then there are areas where the law shares morality's disapproval, but not so far as to prohibit the relevant behaviour. Adultery, for example, is not illegal in this country, but it has long constituted grounds for a divorce, an important legal step for individuals.

KEY CASE

The problem for the law in deciding whether to respond to appeals to morality is that there are very often conflicting moral views in a given situation. We can see this in the case of **Gillick v West Norfolk and Wisbech Area Health Authority** (1985). The claimant, Mrs Victoria Gillick, was a Roman Catholic. She objected to guidance given to doctors from the Department of Health and Social Security that, in exceptional cases, they could offer contraceptive advice and treatment to girls under 16, without parental consent. Mrs Gillick sought a declaration that these guidelines were illegal because they encouraged under-age sex.

> Children have the legal capacity to consent to medical treatment if they are sufficiently mature and intelligent to understand the nature and implications of the proposed treatment.

Mrs Gillick lost at first instance, won in the Court of Appeal and lost by a majority in the House of Lords. The House held that the guidelines were lawful because they concerned what were essentially medical matters. In this field, girls under 16 had the legal capacity to consent to a medical examination and treatment, including contraceptive treatment, as long as they were sufficiently mature and intelligent to understand the nature and implications of the proposed treatment. The majority, in reaching this conclusion, stressed they were merely applying the law as it stood rather than taking a moral standpoint; the minority referred to the kind of moral arguments Mrs Gillick had advanced. This does not mean that, in rejecting Mrs Gillick's view, the majority ignored morality, even though they claimed to be making an objective decision. It could be argued that if teenage girls were likely to have sexual intercourse anyway, preventing doctors from giving contraceptive help would simply increase the chances of unwanted pregnancies and it would, therefore, be moral to protect girls from that. Neither approach is objectively wrong or right; in this, as in many areas, there are opposing moral views.

Should law and morality be separate?

The view taken by Mrs Gillick would seem to suggest that if something is immoral it should also be illegal and, to the person who holds strong moral opinions, this may seem a natural conclusion. But there are problems with it. First, moral opinions, however strongly held, are just that: moral opinions. Mrs Gillick believes under-age girls should not be given contraception and many people agree with her, but many others disagree. Which group's moral opinions should be adopted by the law?

Even if there were complete consensus, the logistics of enforcing as legal rules all the moral rules of our society would present enormous problems. How would we pay for the necessary manpower, both for policing and prosecutions? What sanctions would be severe enough to compel obedience, yet not too severe for the nature of the offences? Making every immoral act also illegal seems both impossible and undesirable, yet law with no connection to morality might find it difficult to command much respect. There is still much debate as to how far law should reflect morality; the following are some of the key suggestions.

Natural law

Natural law theorists argue that law should strongly reflect morality. Though their specific theories differ, their shared premise is that there is a kind of higher law, known as the natural law, to which we can turn for a basic moral code: some, such as St Thomas Aquinas, see this higher law as coming from God, others see it as simply the foundations of a human society. The principles in this higher law should be reflected in the laws societies make for themselves; laws which do not reflect these principles cannot really be called law at all, and in some cases need not be obeyed. The campaign, during the 1980s, against payment of the Poll Tax on the grounds that it was unfair might be seen as an example of this kind of disobedience.

Different natural law theorists disagree as to the actual content of natural law, but it is usually felt to embody basic human rights which governments should respect. Bills of Rights, like that in the US Constitution, could be seen as embodying natural law principles. Professor Fuller, in *The Morality of Law* (1969), talked about law's inner morality which he formulated in terms of eight procedural requirements of a legal system:

1 Generality: there should be rules, not *ad hoc* judgments.
2 Promulgation: the rules should be made known to all those affected by them.
3 Non-retroactivity: rules should not have retrospective effect.
4 Clarity: rules should be understandable.
5 Consistency: rules should not conflict.
6 Realism: people should not be required to do the impossible.
7 Constancy: rules should not be changed so frequently that people cannot use them to guide their behaviour.
8 Congruence: the actual administration of the rules should coincide with the information available to the public about them.

Fuller claims that a legal system which fails in any one of these areas is not just a bad system, it is not a legal system at all. As an example, he gives the legal system of Nazi Germany: although laws were made by recognised methods, in Fuller's view the system's failure to meet the above criteria meant that those laws were not really law at all.

Utilitarianism

During the nineteenth century, the rise of science and the beginning of the decline in the social importance of religion meant that natural law theories declined. In their place the theory of utilitarianism grew up, apparently offering a rational and scientific theory of law. One of the best-known exponents of this theory is John Stuart Mill (1859). He argued that rather than society imposing morality on individuals, individuals should be free to choose their own conduct, so long as in doing so they did

27

Law and morals

not harm others or, if they did, that the harm done did not outweigh the harm which would be done by interfering with individual liberty.

The view that people should be left alone to do what they like so long as they do not harm others remains influential today, but it is open to criticism. First, the fact that someone's actions do not cause another direct and physical harm, in the way Mill envisaged, does not necessarily mean they do no harm at all. For example, opponents of pornography claim that while looking at pornography may not directly inspire individual users to rape, the fact that pornography is available and, to a degree, accepted, promotes the view that women are sexual objects which, in turn, promotes sexual violence against women.

Secondly, who counts as another? This issue is clearly at the heart of debates over abortion and experimentation on embryos: does harming an unborn child count as harming another person, and from what point? The fact that abortion is legal up until a certain stage in pregnancy suggests that the law sees this as the moment at which the foetus becomes another: many people believe that point is reached earlier in pregnancy, and those opposed to abortion believe it is at the time of conception. On the other hand, many people who support the law on abortion nevertheless disapprove of experiments on embryos, even though their views of abortion might suggest that the embryo is not another at this point.

Crimes without victims

Modern theories which subscribe, at least partly, to Mill's view of individual liberty have tended to focus on what are often called victimless crimes. Using the examples of drug use, homosexuality and abortion, all of which were illegal at the time in which he was writing, in *Crimes Without Victims* (1965), the academic Schur observes that the common characteristics of such crimes are that they involve no harm to anyone except the participants; they occur through the willing participation of those involved; and, as a result, there is no victim to make a complaint, rendering the law difficult to enforce. Schur argues that there is a social demand for these activities, which continues to be met despite illegality, through such means as back street abortions and black market drug supply. There is no proof that prohibition of such activities brought greater social benefits than decriminalisation, therefore there is no good reason to prohibit them.

As with John Stuart Mill, the main criticism of Schur's theory is his assertion that these activities harm no one who has not willingly taken part in them. Anti-abortionists would certainly dispute this as far as abortion is concerned. A further criticism is directed at the suggestion that participants join in these activities of their own free will; in the case of drug-taking, for example, that may be so at first, but can we really say that, once addicted, drug users take drugs of their own free will?

The Hart–Devlin Debate

The issue of whether or not law should follow morality was hotly debated during the late 1950s, when there was public concern about what was perceived to be a decline in sexual morality. The Government of the day set up a commission to look at whether the laws on homosexuality and prostitution should be changed, and much debate was triggered by publication of the commission's findings, known as the Wolfenden Report (1957). Central to this debate were the writings of the leading judge, Lord Devlin, who opposed the report's findings, and Professor Hart who approved of them.

The Wolfenden Committee recommended that homosexuality and prostitution should be legalised, with some restrictions. Its reasoning was based on the notion that some areas of behaviour had to be left to individual morality, rather than being supervised by the law. The purpose of the criminal law, said the report, was:

> to preserve public order and decency, to protect the citizen from what is offensive and injurious and to provide sufficient safeguards against exploitation and corruption of others especially the vulnerable, that is the young, weak in body or mind, inexperienced or those in a state of physical, official or economic dependence. The law should not intervene in the private lives of citizens or seek to enforce any particular pattern of behaviour further than necessary to carry out the above purposes.

The reasoning is very like that of Mill: leave people to make their own choices, so long as they do not harm others. The Committee therefore recommended that prostitution itself should not be an offence, since the individual ought to be allowed to choose whether to take part in it, but activities associated with prostitution which could cause offence to others (such as soliciting in the street) were still to be regulated by the law.

Lord Devlin was opposed to this approach. He argued that some form of common morality, with basic agreement on good and evil, was necessary to keep society together. This being the case, the law had every right – and in fact a duty – to uphold that common morality. He compared contravention of public morality to treason, in the sense that it was something society had to protect itself against. How are we to know what this public morality consists of? Devlin argued that we can judge immorality by the standard of the right-minded person, who could perhaps be thought of as the person in the jury box. Opinions should be reached after informed and educated discussion of all relevant points of view and, if there is still debate, the majority view should prevail, as it does in the ordinary legislative process.

In addition, said Devlin, there was a set of basic principles which should be followed by the legislature. First, individuals should be allowed the maximum of freedom consistent with the integrity of society, and privacy should be respected as much as possible. Secondly, punishment should be reserved for that which creates disgust among right-minded people, and society has the right to eradicate any practice which is so abominable that its very presence is an offence. Law-makers should be slow to change laws which protect morality. Thirdly, the law should set down a minimum standard of morality; society's standards should be higher.

Reaction to Devlin's thesis was mixed. Those who felt the Wolfenden Report had gone too far agreed with him, and there were many of them – the commission's recommendations seem rather tame now, but at the time they were ground-breaking. Others felt that his approach was out of step with the times. Hart, who was influenced by John Stuart Mill and, therefore, approved of the commission's approach, led this opposition. Hart argued that using law to enforce moral values was unnecessary, undesirable and morally unacceptable: unnecessary because society was capable of containing many moral standpoints without disintegrating; undesirable because it would freeze morality at a particular point; and morally unacceptable because it infringes the liberty of the individual. Devlin's response was that individual liberty could only flourish in a stable society: disintegration of our society through lack of a shared morality would, therefore, threaten individual freedom.

Hart pointed out that the standard of the right-minded person is a tenuous one. When people object to unusual behaviour, the response is not always prompted by rational moral objections, but often by prejudice, ignorance or misunderstanding. He gave four basic reasons why moral censure should not necessarily lead to legal sanctions. First, punishing the offender involves doing some harm to them, when they may have done no harm to others. Secondly, the exercise of free choice by individuals is a moral value in itself, with which it is wrong to interfere. Thirdly, this exercise of free choice can be valuable in that it allows individuals to experiment and learn. Finally, as far as sexual morality is concerned, the suppression of sexual impulses affects the development or balance of the individual's emotional life, happiness and personality and, thus, causes them harm. He objects strongly to the idea that the law should punish behaviour which does not harm others, but merely causes them distress or disgust by its very existence, even when conducted out of their sight: recognition of individual liberty as a value involves, as a minimum, acceptance of the principle that individuals may do what they want, even if others are distressed when they learn what it is that they do, unless, of course, there are other good grounds for forbidding it.

Judicial support for Devlin's view – and perhaps reaction against liberalising legislation – can be seen in some of the more high-profile cases which arose in its aftermath. In **Shaw v Director of Public Prosecutions** (1961), Shaw had published a booklet entitled *The Ladies' Directory*, which contained advertisements by prostitutes, featuring photographs and descriptions of the sexual practices they offered. He was convicted of the crime of conspiring to corrupt public morals, an offence which had not been prosecuted since the eighteenth century. The House of Lords upheld the conviction and, defending the court's power to uphold the recognition of such an antiquated offence, Viscount Simonds said: 'In the sphere of criminal law I entertain no doubt that there remains in the courts of law a residual power to enforce the supreme and fundamental purpose of the law, to conserve not only the safety and order but also the moral welfare of the State.' As an example of offences against this moral welfare, Viscount Simonds said:

> Let it be supposed that at some future, perhaps early, date homosexual practices between consenting adult males are no longer a crime. Would it not be an offence if, even without obscenity, such practices were publicly advocated and encouraged by pamphlet and advertisement?

This proved to be an uncannily accurate prediction: in 1967 the Sexual Offences Act was passed, which stated that homosexual acts between consenting adult males in private were no longer a criminal offence.

In **Knuller Ltd** *v* **Director of Public Prosecutions** (1972), the defendants were prosecuted for having published in their magazine, *International Times*, advertisements placed by readers inviting others to contact them for homosexual purposes. Once again, the charge was conspiracy to corrupt public morals and the court convicted. Lord Reid (who had dissented from the majority decision in **Shaw's** case, but felt that **Shaw** should still apply to avoid inconsistency) recognised that the 1967 Act legalised homosexual acts, but said:

> I find nothing in that Act to indicate that Parliament thought or intended to lay down that indulgence in these practices is not corrupting. I read the Act as saying that, even though it may be corrupting, if people choose to corrupt themselves in this way that is their affair and the law will not interfere. But no licence is given to others to encourage the practice.

More recent decisions still show judicial support for the Devlin viewpoint that some acts are intrinsically immoral, regardless of whether they harm others. In **R** *v* **Gibson** (1990), an artist exhibited earrings made from freeze-dried foetuses of three to four months' gestation. A conviction for the common law offence of outraging public decency was upheld. The appellants in **R** *v* **Brown** (1992) were homosexual men who had willingly participated in the commission of acts of sado-masochistic violence against each other, involving the use of, among other things, heated wires, stinging nettles, nails, sandpaper and safety-pins. Evidence showed that all the men involved had consented; although the activities were videotaped by the participants, this was not for any profit or gain; none of the injuries was permanent and no medical attention had been sought; the activities were carried out in private; and none of the victims had complained to the police. They were convicted of committing a range of offences against the person and appealed to the House of Lords, arguing that, since all the participants had consented and the activities took place in private, the law had no reason to intervene. Their convictions were upheld; by a majority, the House held that public policy demanded such acts be treated as criminal offences. This decision was subsequently approved by the European Court of Human Rights.

The Warnock Committee

Despite the debate between Devlin and Hart, their two views are not always as opposed as they may seem, and in practice both are influential: a Government commission, the Warnock Committee, incorporates features of both approaches in its reasoning. The Committee was set up by the Government to consider issues relating to scientific advances concerning conception and pregnancy. With the advent of *in vitro* fertilisation (the technique used to create test-tube babies) and other technological advances, new scientific possibilities have arisen. These include the possibility of creating embryos for use in medical experiments, sperm, egg and embryo donation by fertile men or women to those who are infertile, and the use of surrogate mothers – women who bear a child for another couple, using their own egg and the father's sperm. These practices raised a number of moral issues, including that of payment for surrogacy, and the parentage of children born from donated eggs and sperm.

27

Law and morals

The Committee's report, published in 1984, advised the setting up of an independent statutory body to monitor, regulate and license infertility services and embryo experiments. On the specific issues before them, they recommended that experiments on embryos up to 14 days old should be lawful; and that sperm, egg and embryo donation should be facilitated in that the babies born could be registered as the legitimate children of the non-contributing parent(s) on the birth certificate, and donors should be relieved of parental rights and duties in law. But surrogacy arrangements met with disapproval by the majority, who recommended that surrogacy agencies should be criminally prohibited, and private surrogacy arrangements between individuals should be illegal and unenforceable in the courts – although no criminal sanction would be imposed as it would be against the child's interests to be born into a family threatened by imprisonment. Many of the Committee's conclusions became law in the Human Fertilisation and Embryology Act 1990.

If we look at the reasoning behind the Committee's findings, we can see aspects of both Hart's utilitarian approach, and Devlin's upholding of common morality. In its conclusions on embryo research, it points out:

> We do not want to see a situation in which human embryos are frivolously or unnecessarily used in research but we are bound to take account of the fact that the advances in the treatment of infertility, which we have discussed in the earlier part of this report, could not have taken place without such research; and that continued research is essential, if advances in treatment and medical knowledge are to continue. A majority of us therefore agreed that research on human embryos should continue.

But this utilitarian approach is balanced against issues of morality.

> A strict utilitarian would suppose that, given procedures, it would be possible to calculate their benefits and their costs. Future advantages, therapeutic or scientific, should be weighed against present and future harm. However, even if such a calculation were possible, it could not provide a final or verifiable answer to the question whether it is right that such procedures should be carried out. There would still remain the possibility that they were unacceptable, whatever their long-term benefits were supposed to be. Moral questions, such as those with which we have been concerned are, by definition, questions that involve not only a calculation of consequences, but also strong sentiments with regard to the nature of the proposed activities themselves.

As the report shows, issues of law and morality cannot easily be separated into distinct theoretical approaches like those of Hart and Devlin; legislators in practice have to tread an uneasy path between the two.

TOPICAL ISSUE

Infertility treatment

Modern science has made major developments in helping women who in the past would have been unable to have children, but these developments have themselves given rise to fundamental moral dilemmas. A case that caused some controversy is that of **R v Human Fertilisation and Embryology Authority, ex parte Blood** (1997).

The husband of Diane Blood contracted meningitis and lapsed into a coma. Diane Blood asked for samples of his sperm to be collected for future use in artificial insemination. The samples were entrusted to a research trust for storage. The husband died and the Human Fertilisation and Embryology Authority prevented the research trust from releasing the samples from storage, on the ground that the written consent of the donor to the taking of his sperm had not been obtained as required by the relevant statute. The applicant sought judicial review of the Authority's decision. The Court of Appeal ruled that the applicant could have the sperm samples and undergo treatment for an artificially assisted pregnancy, provided she went abroad for the fertility treatment. The Authority's decision had been lawful under the terms of the statute but the circumstances were exceptional and had not been foreseen by Parliament when passing the regulatory legislation. Judicial discretion was sufficiently flexible to grant the remedy which the compassionate circumstances demanded, particularly as the legal situation had never before been explored.

In **Evans v Amicus Healthcare Ltd** (2004) Natalie Evans and her partner had no children and attended a fertility clinic for IVF treatment. During the course of treatment, it was discovered that Natalie had cancer in both her ovaries. Before her ovaries were removed, Natalie had some of her eggs fertilised with her partner's sperm and the resulting six embryos frozen. She and her partner had been engaged to be married, but they later split up and her partner wrote to the clinic stating that the embryos should now be destroyed. Natalie went to court to try to stop the embryos being destroyed as they were her only chance of having her own biological child. The Court of Appeal rejected her application. While it accepted that the destruction of the embryos was an interference with Natalie's private life under Art. 8 of the European Convention, it considered that this interference was necessary to respect the rights of her former partner. This seems quite a tough decision, as her former partner was able to have children with a future partner, but Natalie would not be able to, so perhaps the interference with her ex-partner's rights should have been justified to prevent the much greater interference with Natalie's rights.

Natalie took her case to the European Court of Human Rights, but again the European Court held there had not been any breach of the European Convention and rejected her application (**Evans v United Kingdom** (2007)).

27

Law and morals

The Human Fertilisation and Embryology Authority

The Human Fertilisation and Embryology Authority (HFEA) was set up in 1990. Areas of debate on morality and the need for law to prevent immorality have centred in recent years around scientific developments that the HFEA has to regulate. In the field of human genetics it is difficult for the law to keep up with the changes in scientific knowledge and the moral dilemmas to which these can give rise. The birth of Dolly, the cloned sheep, has caused particular concern. In January 1998 the Human Genetics Advisory Commission and the HFEA jointly published a consultation paper inviting views on various issues raised by cloning technology. The most troubling questions focused on the legality, ethics and practical consequences of human and reproductive cloning. The Authority's policy at the moment is not to license any research having reproductive cloning as its aim. The Human Reproductive Cloning Act 2001 was passed confirming this position.

The Human Genetics Advisory Commission has now recommended that controlled research using embryos (which are eggs that have been fertilised) should be allowed in order to increase understanding about human disease and disorders, and their treatment. It has recommended that reproductive cloning of human beings should remain a criminal offence. The Government has accepted these recommendations.

Another area of scientific activity that raises difficult moral questions concerns research which mixes human and animal tissue. This can take various forms:

- cybrids (where the nucleus of an animal egg is replaced with that from a human cell) – the resulting inter-species embryo is 99.9 per cent human;
- human transgenic embryos where a human embryo is altered by the introduction of animal genetic material;
- human–animal chimeras where a human embryo has been altered by the introduction of animal cells – chimeras can be made by fertilising an animal egg with human sperm.

There is public anxiety about such scientific developments, as these experiments evoke images of mad scientists creating half human/half animal monsters, such as the Minotaur – a half human/half bull monster from Greek mythology. There is also concern that these experiments fail to respect the moral status of human beings, including human embryos. HFEA has approved the creation of cybrids for research purposes by scientists at London University and the University of Newcastle. The creation of a cybrid involves the same cloning procedure that was used to create Dolly the sheep, but, instead of using cells from two animals of the same species, cells are used from two different species. The eggs are likely to come from farmyard animals, such as cows and sheep, since thousands of these animals are killed each day to be eaten. A key reason for using these eggs is simply that they are more easily available than human eggs. Two hundred and seventy sheep eggs were needed before the successful creation of Dolly the sheep.

Cybrid embryos will enable scientists to create cells useful for research into genetic diseases. It is hoped that this research could enable scientists in the future to grow tissues or organs that could replace damaged parts of the body of people suffering from such illnesses as spinal muscular atrophy, Alzheimer's disease or motor neurone disease. The recipient's immune system would not reject these transplants because they would be tissue compatible with the patient's body.

Another contentious issue is how far parents should be allowed to have 'designer babies' to provide living tissue to help cure a sibling. A high-profile case on this subject was that of **R (on the application of Quintavalle) v Human Fertilisation and Embryology Authority** (2005). The case concerned a young boy, Zain Hashmi, who had been born with a rare blood disorder. He would have died if he had not received stem cells from a compatible donor. These stem cells were taken from the umbilical cord of his healthy sibling, who had been conceived for this purpose. HFEA had licensed the procedure by which a genetically compatible embryo was selected for implantation in the body of the boy's mother. A pro-life campaigning organisation, Comment on Reproductive Ethics (CORE), had challenged the legality of HFEA's conduct, arguing that the procedure was opening the door to parents selecting 'designer babies' according to such criteria as sex, hair and eye colour. CORE's action succeeded in the High Court but the mother's appeal was successful before the Court of Appeal and the House of Lords. The House gave a purposive interpretation to the legislation containing HFEA's powers rather than a narrow literal reading, and thereby found that the Authority had the power to issue the licence. Zain Hashmi's life was saved both by the Law Lords and his 'saviour sibling', but CORE felt the medical procedure had been immoral.

In 2005 the House of Commons Science and Technology Select Committee published a review of the Human Fertilisation and Embryology Act 1990. The Department of Health issued a White Paper on the subject in 2006 and the Human Fertilisation and Embryology Act was passed in 2008. This Act replaces the provisions in the 1990 Act, updates and rationalises the law in this field to reflect developments in research and recent case law, and enshrines in the law some of the practices already adopted by HFEA and fertility clinics. It seeks to support medical research while respecting the dignity of human life and modern ethical values.

The Act extends the statutory storage period for embryos from five to ten years. If consent to storage and use of an embryo is withdrawn by one party, storage of the embryo will remain lawful for 12 months. This allows the parties time potentially to reach an agreement about the fate of the embryo after a relationship has broken down. Unfortunately, this will not resolve the type of problem that arose in the case of Natalie Evans where the parties were never able to reach an agreement. Sex-selection of an embryo for non-medical reasons is prohibited but is allowed in order to screen for gender specific diseases. The Act includes a 'saviour sibling' provision permitting the testing of embryos to establish whether the tissue from a child resulting from that embryo would be compatible for treating an existing sibling suffering from a serious medical condition.

The Act allows the creation of all three types of inter-species embryos: cybrids, human transgenic embryos and chimeras. They can be kept for a maximum of 14 days from the date of their creation. It is felt that this is both desirable and necessary for advanced medical research. A licence is necessary to carry out this type of research. Originally the Government had planned to ban such activities but it has been persuaded that the medical benefits outweigh any moral dilemma.

Other reforms in the Act aim to reflect changes in moral and social values. For instance, while the welfare of the child must be taken into account in cases of fertility treatment, the Act removes the reference to 'the need for a father' as a factor to be considered. Both partners in same-sex couples can be regarded as legal parents with parental responsibility, while in the past only the woman giving birth was regarded as the legal parent. The Act also introduces a new 'right to know' for children born as a result of fertility treatment who, on reaching majority, can apply for certain details of their biological origins.

27

Law and morals

Answering questions

1 Does morality play an important role in the development of the law?

A good start to this essay would be to define the meaning of morality – you could do this by contrasting moral rules with rules of law. Point out that, although morality is often talked of in connection with sexual issues, it is actually a much broader concept, covering many areas of law.

If you give morality this broad definition, you can argue that moral values have influenced most, if not all, areas of law, illustrating this point with areas of law you have studied in detail. For example, if you have studied contract law, you might consider the moral view which holds that some promises should be binding and others not; in criminal law, you could discuss the idea of *mens rea* as being indicative of moral fault, and the values behind some of the defences. You need to make this part of the essay quite detailed, giving specific examples from case and statute law which back up your points.

You might then go on to make the point that some areas of law seem to have an overtly moral content, but that here, again, morals are not absolute – the Gillick case is an example of a situation where the two sides each believed that their view represented morality.

Finally, you could discuss how far morality should influence the law, using the theoretical arguments of Devlin and Hart, and relating them to cases which you know, such as the case of **R v Brown** where criminal liability was imposed on homosexual sado-masochists.

2 Is civil disobedience ever justified?

In your introduction you could explain what is meant by civil disobedience and give recent examples of where the UK has seen such behaviour: for example, during the Poll Tax riots, the animal rights protests, the Greenham Common women and demonstrations against road developments in the interests of protecting the environment.

The material in the previous chapter under the heading 'The function of law' will be useful to answer this question. If you accept Marx's theory, the role of the law is to sustain the capitalist ideology and continue the oppression of the proletariat. If this is the case then civil disobedience would always seem to be justified as a means of ending that injustice and reaching the point when the law can 'wither away'. You could draw attention to the natural law theorists who mainly accept that laws failing to reach the standards of the higher, natural law are not laws at all and can, therefore, be disobeyed.

On the other hand, academics such as Durkheim and Weber would consider that obedience of the law is very important for the cohesion of society and the maintenance of order.

Finally you could consider some of the specific areas of our substantive law, such as the Criminal Justice and Public Order Act 1994 and the absence of an entrenched Bill of Rights and consider how far in the UK civil disobedience is justified.

3 How far should the law enforce morality?

This is a standard question on the relationship between law and morality and the central part of your essay would discuss the Hart–Devlin debate.

Summary of Chapter 27: Law and morals

Morals are beliefs and values which are shared by a society, or a section of a society; they tell those who share them what is right or wrong.

Law and morality

Both law and morals are normative; they specify what ought to be done, and aim to mark the boundaries between acceptable and unacceptable conduct. While moral rules tend not to be backed by the obvious sanctions which make some legal rules enforceable, they are often reinforced by pressures, such as the disapproval of family and friends.

Changes in law and morality

As we have observed, the moral values of a society tend to change over time; the same applies to its laws. In the UK, legal changes have tended to lag behind moral ones, coming only when the process of moral acceptance is well advanced. On the other hand, law can sometimes bring about changes in social morality.

Differences between law and morality

Although law and morality are clearly closely linked, there are certain ways in which they differ. Many types of behaviour exist which may be widely considered to be immoral, yet we would be very surprised to find laws against them: telling lies, for example. Equally, some forms of behaviour are illegal, but would not usually be described as immoral, such as parking on a yellow line. Then there are areas where the law shares morality's disapproval, but not so far as to prohibit the relevant behaviour.

Should law and morality be separate?

Making every immoral act also illegal seems both impossible and undesirable, yet law with no connection to morality might find it difficult to command much respect. There is still much debate as to how far law should reflect morality; the following are some of the key suggestions.

Natural law

Natural law theorists argue that law should strongly reflect morality. Though their specific theories differ, their shared premise is that there is a kind of higher law, known as the natural law, to which we can turn for a basic moral code.

Utilitarianism

One of the best-known exponents of this theory is John Stuart Mill (1859). He argued that, rather than society imposing morality on individuals, individuals should be free to choose their own conduct, so long as in doing so they did not harm others or, if they did, that the harm done did not outweigh the harm which would be done by interfering with individual liberty.

The Hart–Devlin Debate

The issue of whether or not law should follow morality was hotly debated during the late 1950s, when there was public concern about what was perceived to be a decline in sexual morality. The Government of the day set up a commission to look at whether the laws on homosexuality and prostitution should be changed, and much debate was triggered by publication of the commission's findings, known as the Wolfenden Report (1957). Central to this debate were the writings of the leading judge, Lord Devlin, who opposed the report's findings, and Professor Hart who approved of them.

The Warnock Committee

The Warnock Committee was set up by the Government to consider issues relating to scientific advances concerning conception and pregnancy. Many of the Committee's conclusions became law in the Human Fertilisation and Embryology Act 1990. If we look at the reasoning behind the Committee's findings, we can see aspects of both Hart's utilitarian approach, and Devlin's upholding of common morality.

The Human Fertilisation and Embryology Authority

The Human Fertilisation and Embryology Act 1990 created the Human Fertilisation and Embryology Authority (HFEA). This body regulates scientific practice involving human genetics. The Human Fertilisation and Embryology Act 2008 has now replaced the provisions in the 1990 Act. It aims to update and rationalise the law in this field to reflect developments in research and recent case law.

Reading list

Aquinas, St T. (1942) *Summa Theologica*, London: Burns Oates & Washbourne.

Devlin, P. (1965) *The Enforcement of Morals*, Oxford: Oxford University Press.

Duster, T. (1970) *The Legislation of Morality*, New York: Free Press.

Fenton, A. and Dabell, F. (2007) 'Time for change (1)', 157 *New Law Journal* 848.

Fenton, A. and Dabell, F. (2007) 'Time for change (2)', 157 *New Law Journal* 964.

Fuller, L. (1969) *The Morality of Law*, London: Yale University Press.

Hart, H.L.A. (1963) *Law, Liberty and Morality*, Oxford: Oxford University Press.

Lee, S. (1986) *Law and Morals*, Oxford: Oxford University Press.

Mill, J.S. (1859) *On Liberty*, London: J.W. Parker.

Schur, E. (1965) *Crimes Without Victims: Deviant Behaviour and Public Policy, Abortion, Homosexuality, Drug Addiction*, New York: Prentice-Hall.

Warnock, M. (1986) *Morality and the Law*, Cardiff: University College Cardiff.

Wolfenden, J. (1957) 'Report of the Committee on Homosexual Offences and Prostitution', Cm 2471, London: HMSO.

Reading on the Internet

www   The website of the Human Fertilisation and Embryology Authority is:
       http://www.hfea.gov.uk/cps/rde/xchg/hfea

Visit www.mylawchamber.co.uk/ElliottELS to access multiple-choice questions, flashcards and practice exam questions to test yourself on this chapter.

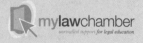

28

Law and justice

This chapter explores the concept of justice by looking at:

- the ideas of the Greek philosopher Aristotle;

- the theory of natural law;

- utilitarianism;

- the economic analysis of law;

- Professor John Rawls's theory of justice; and

- the communist views of Karl Marx.

Introduction

Achieving justice is often seen as one of the most basic aims of a legal system. When areas of that system go wrong, the result is often described as injustice: for example, when people are convicted of crimes they have not committed, as in the cases of the Tottenham Three and the Birmingham Six, we say that a miscarriage of justice has occurred. But what is justice, and what is its relationship with law? These questions have been addressed by writers throughout the centuries, and we will look at some of the most important views in this chapter.

Aristotle

The Greek philosopher Aristotle is responsible for some of the earliest thinking on justice, and his work is still influential today. He considered that a just law was one which would allow individuals to fulfil themselves in society, and distinguished between distributive justice and corrective justice.

Distributive justice was concerned with the allocation of assets such as wealth and honour between members of the community. Here the aim of justice was to achieve proportion, but this did not mean equal shares; Aristotle thought that individuals should receive benefits in proportion to their claim on those benefits.

Corrective justice, on the other hand, applies when a situation that is distributively just, is disturbed – for example, by wrongdoing. A judge should discover what damage has been done, and then try to restore equality by imposing penalties to confiscate any gain made by the offence, and compensate for any damage caused.

Natural law theories

Natural law theories assume that there is a higher order of law, and if the laws of society follow this order they will be just. Aristotle supported this view, and believed that the higher law could be discovered from nature; others, such as the medieval scholar St Thomas Aquinas, thought that the higher law derived from God.

For Aquinas, there were two ways in which law could be unjust. First, a law which was contrary to human good, whether in its form or in its result, was, according to Aquinas, not true law at all. However, such laws might still be obeyed if to do so would avoid causing social disorder. Secondly, a law which was against God's will, and therefore a violation of the natural law, should be disregarded.

Utilitarianism

The utilitarian movement, which includes such writers as Mill and Bentham, is based on the idea that society should work towards the greatest happiness for the greatest number, even if this means that some individuals lose out. Utilitarians assess the justice of rules (and therefore law) by looking at their consequences; in their view, if a rule maximised happiness or well-being or had some other desirable effect, for the majority, it was just. A law could therefore be just even if it created social inequalities, or benefited some at the expense of others, so long as the benefits to the many exceeded the loss to the minority.

The utilitarian approach can be criticised as focusing only on justice for the community as a whole, and leaving out justice for individuals.

The economic analysis of law

This approach has developed mainly in the US, and attempts to offer a more sophisticated alternative to utilitarianism. While the goal of utilitarianism was to promote the greatest happiness of the greatest number, it offered no reliable way of calculating the effect of a law or policy on this goal, or measuring the relative benefits.

The economic analysis takes the view that a thing has value for a person when that person values it; its value can therefore be measured by how much the person is prepared to pay for it, or what would be required to make them give it up. As we have seen, a conflict exists between the concerns of utilitarianism and individual justice, and the same conflict exists here. Take the example of an NHS doctor with a limited budget, faced with one person who needs a life-saving operation costing £100,000, and ten others who each need more minor operations costing £10,000 each. On the face of it, doing the ten operations clearly seems to produce benefit for a greater number at the same cost, and in this sense may be the best way to spend public money. But can we say that this solution offers the first person justice?

A common criticism of the economic analysis of law is that it favours a particular ideology, that of market capitalism. It is based on the idea that the prices at which goods and services are bought and sold are the direct result of the value placed on them by buyer and seller, and therefore the result of free will; it presumes that sellers cannot exploit buyers, because nobody would pay more for something than it was worth to them. Critics of this approach point out that, in practice, power in the marketplace is frequently unequal; a seller may have the monopoly on particular goods, or sellers may collude to keep prices high. Equally, the idea that a thing has value because a person wants it ignores the question of where the desire for that thing originates; expensive advertising campaigns may produce the desire for what they sell, but can we objectively say that such publicity gives them value? In the same way, people may take low-paid jobs, not because they agree with that valuation of their labour, but because there are no other jobs and they have no power in the labour market.

Rawls: *A Theory of Justice*

Professor John Rawls first presented his ideas in *A Theory of Justice* which was published in 1971, and amended them slightly in his later book, *Political Liberalism* (1972). He approaches the question of justice through an imaginary situation in which the members of a society are to decide on a set of principles designed to make their society just, and advance the good of all its members. He describes this initial debate as the original position. The individuals involved will hold their discussions without knowing what their own position in the society is to be – whether they will be rich or poor, of high or low social status, old or young, and what will be the economic or political situation in the society. This veil of ignorance is designed to ensure that the ideas put forward really are the best for all members of society, since nobody will be willing to disadvantage a section of the community if they might find themselves a member of it.

Rawls believes that the principles which would result from such a discussion would include an equal distribution of what he calls social primary goods: these are the things which individuals are assumed to want in order to get the most out of their own lives, including rights, powers and freedoms, and, in Rawls's later work, self-respect. In addition to this, there would be two basic principles. The first involves liberty: a set of basic liberties – including freedom of thought, conscience, speech and assembly – would be available to all. Each person's freedom would be restricted only where the restriction on them was balanced out by greater liberty for the community as a whole. So, for example, the liberty of a person suspected of crime could be restricted by police powers of arrest, since these would increase the freedom from crime of society as a whole. The second basic principle is based on equality. This covers both equality of opportunity – offices and positions within society should be open to all equally – and equality of distribution. Rawls envisages an equal distribution of wealth, with inequalities allowed only where necessary to help the most disadvantaged.

If a social order is just, or nearly just, according to these principles, Rawls argues that those who accept its benefits are bound to accept its rules as well, even if they may disapprove of some of them, provided that those rules do not impose heavy burdens unequally, nor violate the basic principles. Professor Rawls would support limited disobedience, where the basic principles are violated, other means of obtaining redress fail, and no harm is done to others.

Rawls's theory has been extensively criticised. The clearest problem is simply its artificiality, particularly that of the veil of ignorance. As Dworkin has pointed out, even if we accept the scenario Rawls creates, the fact that individuals accept certain principles when they do not know what their position in society will be, does not necessarily mean they will continue to live by them if they find themselves in a position to maximise their own advantage at the expense of others. Rawls's theory appears to view human beings as rather more perfect than they have in fact shown themselves to be.

Nozick and the minimal state

Robert Nozick's provocative essay, *Anarchy, State, and Utopia*, argues that, for a truly just society, the state should have the minimum possible right to interfere in the affairs of individuals; its functions should be limited to the basic needs, such as protecting the individual against force, theft and fraud, and enforcing contracts. Published in 1975, the essay revives a claim traditionally associated with the seventeenth-century writer John Locke, and has strong links with eighteenth-century individualism, and nineteenth-century *laissez-faire* capitalism.

Nozick's theory emphasises the importance of individual rights and, in particular, rights to property. He argues that the right to hold property is based on the way in which that property is obtained, either by just acquisition (such as inheritance) or just transfer (such as purchase from another), or by rectification of an unjust acquisition (for example, returning stolen property to its owner). Provided individuals have obtained their property in a just manner, the distribution of property throughout society is just; attempts to redistribute wealth are unjust because they interfere with the individual's right to hold justly obtained property. The state should, therefore, have no role in adjusting the distribution of wealth. In fact, Nozick rejects the idea that there are any goods belonging to society; goods belong only to individuals and the state has no right to interfere with them. Nozick's theories have been criticised, but they do reflect a growing disenchantment in Western society with the idea of redistributing wealth – in Britain we can see this in the emphasis placed by recent Governments on lowering taxes and expecting individuals to look after themselves, rather than taking taxes from the rich to help the poor.

28

Law and justice

Karl Marx

Marx held that it was impossible for a capitalist society to be just: such a society was organised with the aim of upholding the interests of the ruling class, rather than securing justice for all. For Marx, a just society would distribute wealth 'from each according to his capacity, to each according to his needs'; individuals should contribute what they can to society, and receive what they need in return. Marx's views are still influential, but the main criticism made of them is that so far no country has been able to put them into practice with sufficient success to bring about the fair society Marx envisaged.

Kelsen and positivism

For positivists, law can be separated from what is just or morally right. Parts of law may be based on, or incorporate ideas of, morality or justice, but this is not a necessary component of law; a law is still a law and should be obeyed even if it is completely immoral.

One of the best-known positivists is Kelsen, whose theories were first published in 1911, and further developed in his *General Theory of Law and State*, first published in 1945. Kelsen tried to develop a pure theory of law, to explain what law is rather than suggesting what it ought to be. He saw justice as simply the expression of individual preferences and values and, therefore, as an irrational ideal. Because of this, argued Kelsen, it is not possible scientifically to define justice.

Justice in practice

One of the most important aspects of the British legal system is parliamentary supremacy, which essentially means that Parliament is the ultimate law-maker, and can make or unmake any law it wishes. In most other developed countries, a written constitution sets down basic principles with which law should conform, and judges can strike down any legislation which conflicts with them. That is not the case in the UK; our constitution is unwritten and judges must apply the law that Parliament makes, even if they believe it is unjust. If Parliament wanted to make laws condemning all blonde women to death, banning old men from keeping pet dogs, or obliging parents to sell their eldest child into slavery, there would probably be political obstacles to doing so, but there would be no legal ones and judges would be obliged to apply the laws.

Clearly, this situation conflicts with the natural law approach we discussed earlier, where unjust laws were considered not to be true law and, in some circumstances, not to require application by the courts or obedience by the citizen. Arguments for a Bill of Rights, a statement of basic principles against which courts could measure legislation and strike down any in conflict with them, have something in common with the natural law approach, since they assume that some values are fundamental and those given the power to make law in a society should be bound to follow them, rather than being free to make any law they want.

As with most developed legal systems, ours is based on the idea that, to achieve justice, like cases must be treated alike – thus if two people commit a crime in identical circumstances, they should be punished in a similar way. This aim requires fixed rules, so that decision-makers base their verdicts on the application of those rules to the case before them, and not on arbitrary factors such as their own mood or what they personally think of the defendant. However, the downside of this approach is that fixed rules can make it difficult to do justice in individual cases. Take the crime of murder, for example: to commit a murder, a defendant must have intended to kill or to cause serious injury; if this intention is present, the motive for killing is largely irrelevant. While this promotes the idea of like cases being treated alike, allowing judges to opt out of assessing the pros and cons of different motives, which must of necessity involve personal views, it presents problems in individual cases – can we say it is just for someone who kills a terminally ill relative to spare them from pain to be treated in the same way as someone who kills another so they can rob them? They both have intention but are they equally blameworthy? Fixed rules can sometimes promote justice in the majority of cases at the expense of justice in the individual, out-of-the-ordinary one.

The problem of fixed rules preventing justice in individual cases was one which our legal system faced early on in its life, when the common law was first becoming established. Then the answer was to develop a special branch of law, equity, with the specific aim of providing justice in cases where the ordinary rules of law failed to do so. Equity is no longer a separate branch of law, but equitable principles are still important in some areas of the civil law, and allow the courts to use their discretion in order to do justice in individual cases. In the criminal law (though not for the offence of murder) discretion over sentencing can fulfil a similar role. The challenge is to maintain a balance between too much discretion, leading to the possibility of arbitrary decisions, and too little, leading to harsh results in individual cases.

Answering questions

1 Various writers, such as Aristotle, Mill, Bentham, Rawls, Nozick, Marx and Kelsen, have advocated individual theories of justice. Explain, evaluate and analyse three of these. Which theory do you prefer? Explain why.

The question, in effect, sets out the structure of the answer for you. All that is required is to look in depth at theories that explain 'justice' as advocated by three of the above philosophers. You will need to know what each theory is, in detail, in order to be able to express your preference, and be able to evaluate their strengths and weaknesses before you can come to a view.

Summary of Chapter 28: Law and justice

Achieving justice is often seen as one of the most basic aims of a legal system. When areas of that system go wrong, the result is often described as injustice. But what is justice, and what is its relationship with law? These questions have been addressed by writers throughout the centuries.

Aristotle
The Greek philosopher Aristotle considered that a just law was one which would allow individuals to fulfil themselves in society, and distinguished between distributive justice and corrective justice.

Natural law theories
Natural law theories assume that there is a higher order of law, and if the laws of society follow this order they will be just.

Utilitarianism
The utilitarian movement is based on the idea that society should work towards the greatest happiness for the greatest number, even if this means that some individuals lose out. Utilitarians assess the justice of rules (and therefore law) by looking at their consequences; in their view, if a rule maximised happiness or well-being or had some other desirable effect, for the majority, it was just.

The economic analysis of law

The economic analysis takes the view that a thing has value for a person when that person values it; its value can therefore be measured by how much the person is prepared to pay for it, or what would be required to make them give it up.

Rawls: *A Theory of Justice*

Professor John Rawls approaches the question of justice through an imaginary situation in which the members of a society are to decide on a set of principles designed to make their society just, and advance the good of all its members. He describes this initial debate as the original position. Rawls believes that the principles which would result would include an equal distribution of what he calls social primary goods. In addition to this, there would be two basic principles: liberty and equality.

Nozick and the minimal state

Robert Nozick argues that, for a truly just society, the state should have the minimum possible right to interfere in the affairs of individuals; its functions should be limited to the basic needs, such as protecting the individual against force, theft and fraud, and enforcing contracts.

Karl Marx

Marx held that it was impossible for a capitalist society to be just: such a society was organised with the aim of upholding the interests of the ruling class, rather than securing justice for all. For Marx, a just society would distribute wealth 'from each according to his capacity, to each according to his needs'; individuals should contribute what they can to society, and receive what they need in return.

Kelsen and positivism

For positivists, law can be separated from what is just or morally right. Parts of law may be based on, or incorporate ideas of, morality or justice, but this is not a necessary component of law; a law is still a law and should be obeyed even if it is completely immoral.

Reading list

Hayek, F. (1982) *Law, Legislation and Liberty: A New Statement of the Liberal Principles of Justice and Political Economy*, London: Routledge.

Kelsen, H. (1945) *General Theory of Law and State*, Cambridge, Mass: Harvard University Press.

Locke, J. (1967) *Two Treatises of Government*, London: Cambridge University Press.

Nozick, R. (1975) *Anarchy, State, and Utopia*, Oxford: Blackwell.

Rawls, J. (1971) *A Theory of Justice*, Oxford: Oxford University Press.

Visit www.mylawchamber.co.uk/ElliottELS to access multiple-choice questions, flashcards and practice exam questions to test yourself on this chapter.

Appendix: Answering examination questions

At the end of each chapter in this book, you will find detailed guidelines for answering examination questions on the topics covered. Many of the questions are taken from actual A-Level past papers, but they are equally relevant for candidates of all law examinations, as these questions are typical of the type of questions that examiners ask in this field.

In this section, we aim to give some general guidelines for answering questions on the English legal system.

Citation of authorities

One of the most important requirements for answering questions on the law is that you must be able to back up the points you make with authority, usually either a case or a statute. It is not good enough to state that the law is such and such, without stating the case or statute which says that that is the law. Some examiners are starting to suggest that the case name is not essential as long as you can remember and understand the general principle that the case laid down. However, such examiners remain in the minority and the reality is that even they are likely to give higher marks where the candidate has cited authorities; quite simply, it helps give the impression that you know your material thoroughly, rather than half-remembering something you heard once in class.

This means that you must be prepared to learn fairly long lists of cases by heart, which can be a daunting prospect. What you need to memorise is the name of the case, a brief description of the facts, and the legal principle which the case established. Once you have revised a topic well, you should find that a surprisingly high number of cases on that topic begin to stick in your mind anyway, but there will probably be some that you have trouble recalling. A good way to memorise these is to try to create a picture in your mind which links the facts, the name and the legal principle. For example, if you wanted to remember the contract law case of *Redgrave v Hurd*, you might picture the actress Vanessa Redgrave and the politician Douglas Hurd, in the situation described in the facts of the case, and imagine one of them telling the other the principle established in the case.

Knowing the names of cases makes you look more knowledgeable, and also saves writing time in the exam, but if you do forget a name, referring briefly to the facts will identify it. It is not necessary to learn the dates of cases though it is useful if you know whether it is a recent or an old case. Dates are usually required for statutes. Unless you are making a detailed comparison of the facts of a case and the facts of a problem question, in order to argue that the case should or could be distinguished, you should generally make only brief reference to facts, if at all – long descriptions of facts waste time and earn few marks.

When reading the 'Answering questions' sections at the end of each chapter in this book, bear in mind that, for reasons of space, we have not highlighted every case which you should cite. The skeleton arguments outlined in those sections *must* be backed up with authority from cases and statute law.

When discussing the English legal system, as well as citing relevant cases and statutes it is particularly important to cite relevant research and reports in the field being discussed. If there are important statistics in an area, being able to quote some of them will give your answers authority.

There is no right answer

In law exams, there is not usually a right or a wrong answer. What matters is that you show you know what type of issues you are being asked about. Essay questions are likely to ask you to 'discuss', 'criticise', or 'evaluate', and you simply need to produce a good range of factual and critical material in order to do this. The answer you produce might look completely different from your friend's but both answers could be worth 'A' grades.

Breadth and depth of content

Where a question seems to raise a number of different issues – as most do – you will achieve better marks by addressing all or most of these issues than by writing at great length on just one or two. By all means spend more time on issues which you know well, but be sure to at least mention other issues which you can see are relevant, even if you can only produce a paragraph or so about them.

Civil or criminal

In some cases, a question on the English legal system will require you to confine your answer to either the civil or criminal system. This may be stated in the question – for example, 'Discuss the system of civil appeals'. Alternatively, it may be something you are required to work out for yourself, as is often the case with problem questions. For example, a question might state:

Jane has been charged with criminal damage.
(a) How may she obtain legal aid and advice? and
(b) If convicted, to which courts may she appeal?

This question only requires you to discuss the legal aid and advice available in criminal cases, and the criminal appeals system; giving details of civil legal aid and the civil appeals system will waste time and gain you no marks, as would bringing the criminal appeals system into the previous question. Equally, where a question does not limit itself to either civil or criminal legal systems, you will lose marks if you only discuss one.

Because of this danger, it is a good idea to make a point of asking yourself before you answer any legal system question whether it covers just the civil legal system, just the criminal, or both.

The structure of the question

If a question is specifically divided into parts, for example (a), (b) and (c), then stick to those divisions and do not merge your answer into one long piece of writing.

Law examinations tend to contain a mixture of essay questions and what are known as 'problem questions'. Tackling each of these questions involves slightly different skills so we consider each in turn.

Essay questions

Answer the question asked

Over and over again, examiners complain that candidates do not answer the question they are asked – so if you can develop this skill, you will stand out from the crowd. You will get very few marks for simply writing all you know about a topic, with no attempt to address the issues raised in the question, but if you can adapt the material that you have learnt on the subject to take into account the particular emphasis given to it by the question, you will do well.

Even if you have memorised an essay which does raise the issues in the question (perhaps because those issues tend to be raised year after year), you must fit your material to the words of the question you are actually being asked. For example, suppose during your course you wrote an essay on the advantages and disadvantages of the jury system and then, in the exam, you find yourself faced with the question 'Should juries be abolished?' The material in your coursework essay is ideally suited for the exam question, but if you begin the main part of your answer with the words 'The advantages of juries include . . .', or something similar, this is a dead giveaway to the examiner that you are merely writing down an essay you have memorised. It takes very little effort to change the words to 'Abolition of the jury system would ignore certain advantages that the current system has . . .', but it will create a much better impression, especially if you finish with a conclusion which, based on points you have made, states that abolition is a good or bad idea, the choice depending on the arguments you have made during your answer.

During your essay, you should keep referring to the words used in the question – if this seems to become repetitive, use synonyms for those words. This makes it clear to the examiner that you are keeping the question in mind as you work.

Plan your answer

Under pressure of time, it is tempting to start writing immediately, but five minutes spent planning each essay question is well worth spending – it may mean that you write less overall, but the quality of your answer will almost certainly be better. The plan need not be elaborate: just jot down everything you feel is relevant to the answer, including case names, and then organise the material into a logical order appropriate to the question asked. To put it in order, rather than wasting time copying it all out again, simply put a number next to each point according to which ones you intend to make first, second and so forth.

Provide analysis and fact

Very few essay questions require merely factual descriptions of what the law is; you will almost always be required to analyse the factual content in some way, usually highlighting any problems or gaps in the law, and suggesting possible reforms. If a question asks you to analyse whether lay magistrates should be replaced by professional judges you should not write everything you know about magistrates and judges and finish with one sentence saying magistrates should/should not be kept. Instead you should select your relevant material and your whole answer should be targeted at answering whether or not magistrates should be kept.

Where a question uses the word 'critically', as in 'critically describe' or 'critically evaluate', the examiners are merely drawing your attention to the fact that your approach should be analytical and not merely descriptive; you are not obliged to criticise every provision you describe. Having said that, even if you do not agree with particular criticisms which you have read, you should still discuss them and say why you do not think they are valid; there is very little mileage in an essay that simply describes the law and says it is perfectly satisfactory.

Structure

However good your material, you will only gain really good marks if you structure it well. Making a plan for each answer will help in this, and you should also try to learn your material in a logical order – this will make it easier to remember as well. The exact construction of your essay will obviously depend on the question, but you should aim to have an introduction, then the main discussion, and a conclusion. Where a question is divided into two or more parts, you should reflect that structure in your answer.

A word about conclusions: it is not good enough just to repeat the question, turning it into a statement, for the conclusion. So, for example, if the question is 'Is the criminal justice system satisfactory?', a conclusion which simply states that the system is or is not satisfactory will gain you very little credit. Your conclusion will often summarise the arguments that you have developed during the course of your essay.

Problem questions

In problem questions, the exam paper will describe an imaginary situation, and then ask what the legal implications of the facts are – for example, 'Jane had suffered physical violence at the hands of her husband for many years. One day she lashes out and kills him. She is arrested by the police and later charged with murder. In which court will Jane be tried? If she is convicted to what court may she appeal?'

Read the question thoroughly

The first priority is to read the question thoroughly, at least a couple of times. Never start writing until you have done this, as you may well get halfway through and discover that what is said at the end makes half of what you have written irrelevant – or at worst, that the question raises issues you have no knowledge of at all.

Answer the question asked

This means paying close attention to the words printed immediately after the situation is described. In the example given above you are asked to advise about the courts and appeal procedure, so do not start discussing sentencing powers as this is not relevant to the particular question asked. Similarly, if a question asks you to advise one or other of the parties, make sure you advise the right one – the realisation as you discuss the exam with your friends afterwards that you have advised the wrong party and thus rendered most of your answer irrelevant is not an experience you will enjoy.

Spot the issues

In answering a problem question in an examination you will often be short of time. One of the skills of doing well is spotting which issues are particularly relevant to the facts of the problem and spending most time on those, while skimming over more quickly those matters which are not really an issue on the facts, but which you clearly need to mention.

Apply the law to the facts

What a problem question requires you to do is to spot the issues raised by the situation, and to consider the law as it applies to those facts. It is not enough simply to describe the law without applying it to the facts. So in the example given above it is not enough to write about the appeal procedure in general for civil and criminal cases; you must apply the rules of criminal appeal to the particular case of Jane. She has committed an indictable offence that would have been tried by the Crown Court so you are primarily concerned with appeals from the Crown Court to the Court of Appeal. Nor should you start your answer by copying out all the facts. This is a complete waste of time, and will gain you no marks.

Unlike essay questions, problem questions are not usually seeking a critical analysis of the law. If you have time, it may be worth making the point that a particular area of the law you are discussing is problematic, and briefly stating why, but if you are addressing all the issues raised in the problem you are unlikely to have much time for this. What the examiner is looking for is essentially an understanding of the law and an ability to apply it to the particular facts given.

Use authority

As always, you must back up your points with authority from case or statute law.

Structure

The introduction and conclusion are much less important for problem questions than for essay questions. Your introduction can be limited to pointing out the issues raised by the question, or, where you are asked to 'advise' a person mentioned in the problem, what outcome that person will be looking for. You can also say in what order you intend to deal with the issues. Your conclusion might simply summarise the conclusions reached during the main part of the answer, for example that Jane will be tried in the Crown Court and her main route of appeal will be to the Court of Appeal.

There is no set order in which the main part of the answer must be discussed. Sometimes it will be appropriate to deal with the problem chronologically, in which case it will usually be a matter of looking at the question line by line, while in other cases it may be appropriate to group particular issues together. Problem questions on the English legal system are often broken down into clear parts – a, b, c and so on – so the answer can be broken down into the same parts. Thus with the example about Jane the question was clearly broken into two parts, and so your question should deal with first the trial court and then with the issue of appeal.

Whichever order you choose, try to deal with one issue at a time – for example, finish talking about the trial court before looking at the issue of appeal. Jumping backwards and forwards gives the impression that you have not thought about your answer. If you work through your material in a structured way, you are also less likely to leave anything out.

Glossary

Administrative law. The body of law which deals with the rights and duties of the state and the limits of its powers over individuals.

Arraignment. The process whereby the accused is called to the Bar of the court to plead guilty or not guilty to the charges against him.

Bill of Rights. A statement of the basic rights which a citizen can expect to enjoy.

Case stated. Under the proceedings, a person who was a party to a proceeding before the magistrates (or the Crown Court when it is hearing an appeal from the magistrates) may question the proceeding of the court on the ground that there was an error of law or the court had acted outside its jurisdiction. The party asks the court to state a case for the opinion of the High Court on the question of law or jurisdiction.

Caution. 1. A warning to an accused person administered on arrest or before police questioning. Since the abolition, by the Criminal Justice and Public Order Act 1994, of the right of silence, the correct wording is: 'You do not have to say anything. But it may harm your defence if you do not mention when questioned something which you later rely on in court. Anything you do say may be given in evidence.'

2. A formal warning given to an offender about what he has done, designed to make him see that he has done wrong and deter him from further offending. This process is used instead of proceeding with the prosecution.

Certiorari. An order quashing an *ultra vires* decision.

Chambers. The offices of a barrister.

Community sentence. This means a sentence that will be served in the community.

Constitution. A set of rules and customs which detail a country's system of government; in most cases it will be a written document but in some countries, including Britain, the constitution cannot be found written down in one document and is known as an unwritten constitution.

Contingency fee. A fee payable to a lawyer (who has taken on a case on a 'no win, no fee' basis) in the event of his/her winning the case.

Convention. 1. A long-established tradition which tends to be followed although it does not have the force of law.

2. A treaty with a foreign power.

Corporation aggregate. This term covers groups of people with a single legal personality (e.g. a company, university or local authority).

Corporation sole. This is a device which makes it possible to continue the official capacity of an individual beyond their lifetime or tenure of office: e.g. the Crown is a corporation sole; its legal personality continues while individual monarchs come and go.

Counsel's opinion. A barrister's advice.

Custom. 'Such usage as has obtained the force of law' (**Tanistry Case** (1608)).

Ejusdem generis **rule.** General words which follow specific ones are taken to include only things of the same kind.

Equity. In law it is a term which applies to a specific set of legal principles which were developed by the Chancery Court and add to those provided in the common law.

Habeas corpus. This is an ancient remedy which allows people detained to challenge the legality of their detention and, if successful, to get themselves quickly released.

He who comes to equity must come with clean hands. This means that a claimant who has been in the wrong in some way will not be granted an equitable remedy.

He who seeks equity must do equity. Anyone who seeks equitable relief must be prepared to act fairly towards their opponent.

Indictable offences. These are the more serious offences, such as rape and murder. They can only be heard by the Crown Court. The indictment is a formal document containing the alleged offences against the accused, supported by brief facts.

Law Officers. They are the Attorney General and the Solicitor General.

Lawyer. This is a general term which covers both branches of the legal profession, namely barristers and solicitors, as well as many people with a legal qualification.

Leapfrog procedure. This is the procedure provided for in the Administration of Justice Act 1969, whereby an appeal can go directly from the High Court to the Supreme Court, missing out the Court of Appeal.

Natural law. A kind of higher law, to which we can turn for a basic moral code. Some, such as St Thomas Aquinas, see this higher law as coming from God; others see it simply as the basis of human society.

Noscitur a sociis. The meaning of a doubtful word may be ascertained by reference to the meaning of words associated with it.

Obiter dicta. Words in a judgment which are said 'by the way' and were not the basis on which the decision was made. They do not form part of the *ratio decidendi* and are not binding on future cases, but merely persuasive.

Parliament. Consists of the House of Commons, the House of Lords and the Monarch.

Per incuriam. Where a previous decision has been made in ignorance of a relevant law it is said to have been made *per incuriam*.

Plea bargaining. This is the name given to negotiations between the prosecution and defence lawyers over the outcome of a case: e.g. where a defendant is choosing to plead not guilty, the prosecution may offer to reduce the charge to a similar offence with a smaller maximum sentence in return for the defendant pleading guilty to that offence.

Practice Direction. An official announcement by the court laying down rules as to how it should function.

Prohibition. An order prohibiting a body from acting unlawfully in the future: e.g. it can prohibit an inferior court or tribunal from starting or continuing proceedings which are, or threaten to be, outside their jurisdiction, or in breach of natural justice.

Puisne judges. High Court judges are also known as puisne judges (pronounced puny) meaning junior judges.

Ratio decidendi. The legal principle on which a decision is based.

Relator action. A proceeding whereby a party, who has failed to prove *locus standi*, can choose to permit the action to be brought in the name of the Attorney General.

Small Claims Track. This is a procedure used by the county courts to deal with claims under £5,000.

Sovereignty of Parliament. This has traditionally meant that the law which Parliament makes takes precedence over that from any other source, but this principle has been qualified by membership of the EU.

Stare decisis. Abiding by precedent: i.e. in deciding a case a judge must follow any decision that has been made by a higher court in a case with similar facts. As well as being bound by decisions of courts above them, some courts must follow their own previous decisions.

Summary offences. These are most minor crimes and are only triable summarily in the magistrates' courts. 'Summary' refers to the process of ordering the defendant to attend court by summons, a written order usually delivered by post, which is the most frequent procedure adopted in the magistrates' court.

Ultra vires. Outside their powers.

Wednesbury principle. This principle, which was laid down in **Associated Provincial Picture Houses Ltd** *v* **Wednesbury Corporation** (1948), is that a decision will be held to be outside a public body's power if it is so unreasonable that no reasonable public body could have reached it.

Youth court. Young offenders are usually tried in youth courts (formerly called juvenile courts), which are a branch of the magistrates' court. Youth courts must sit in a separate courtroom, where no ordinary court proceedings have been held for at least one hour. Strict restrictions are imposed as to who may attend the sittings of the court.

Select bibliography

Abel, R. (1988) *The Legal Profession in England and Wales*, Oxford: Basil Blackwell.

Abel-Smith, B., Zander, M. and Brooke, R. (1973) *Legal Problems and the Citizen*, London: Heinemann-Educational.

Advice Services Alliance (2004) *The Independent Review of the Community Legal Service. The Advice Services Alliance's response to the Department for Constitutional Affairs' consultation on the recommendations made by Matrix Research and Consultancy*, London: ASA.

Alternative Dispute Resolution – A Discussion Paper (1999), London: Lord Chancellor's Department.

Anti-Social Behaviour Orders – Analysis of the first six years (2004), London: National Association of Probation Officers.

Aquinas, St T. (1942) *Summa Theologica*, London: Burns Oates & Washbourne.

Atiyah, P.S. (1979) *The Rise and Fall of Freedom of Contract*, Oxford: Clarendon Press.

Audit Commission (1996) *Streetwise: Effective Police Patrol*, London: HMSO.

—— (1997) *Misspent Youth: Young People and Crime*, London: Audit Commission Publications.

—— (2003) *Victims and Witnesses*, London: Audit Commission Publications.

—— (2004) *Youth Justice*, London: Audit Commission Publications.

Auld, Sir R. (2001) *Review of the Criminal Courts*, London: HMSO.

Austin, J. (1954) *The Province of Jurisprudence Determined*, London: Weidenfeld & Nicolson.

Austin, R. (2007) 'The New Powers of Arrest: *Plus ça Change*: More of the Same or Major Change?', [2007] *Criminal Law Review* 459.

Bailey, S. and Gunn, M. (2002) *Smith and Bailey on the Modern English Legal System* (2nd edn), London: Sweet & Maxwell.

Baldwin, J. (1992a) *The Role of Legal Representatives at the Police Station* (Royal Commission on Criminal Justice Research Study No. 2), London: HMSO.

—— (1992b) *Video Taping Police Interviews with Suspects: an Evaluation*, London: Home Office.

—— (1997) *Small Claims in County Courts in England and Wales: The Bargain Basement of Civil Justice?* Oxford: Clarendon Press.

—— (2002) *Lay and Judicial Perspectives on the Expansion of the Small Claims Regime*, London: Lord Chancellor's Department.

—— (2003) *Evaluating the Effectiveness of Enforcement Procedures in Undefended Claims in the Civil Courts*, London: Lord Chancellor's Department.

Baldwin, J. and McConville, M. (1979) *Jury Trials*, Oxford: Clarendon Press.

Baldwin, J. and Moloney, T. (1992) *Supervision of police investigations in serious criminal cases* (Royal Commission on Criminal Justice Research Study No. 4), London: HMSO.

Bar Council Working Party (2007) *Entry to the Bar: Working Party Final Report*, London: Bar Council.

Barton, A. (2001) 'Medical litigation: who benefits?' *British Medical Journal* 322, 1189.

Bell, J. and Engle, Sir G. (eds) (1995) *Statutory Interpretation*, London: Butterworths.

Bennion, F.A.R. (1999) 'A naked usurpation?' 149 *New Law Journal* 421.

—— (2005) *Statutory Interpretation*, London: Butterworths.

—— (2007) 'Executive estoppel: *Pepper v Hart* revisited' *Public Law* (2007) Spring 1.

Blom-Cooper, L. (1972) *Final Appeal: A Study of the House of Lords in its Judicial Capacity*, Oxford: Clarendon Press.

Bond, R.A. and Lemon, N.F. (1979) 'Changes in Magistrates: Attitudes During the First Year on the Bench' in Farrington, D.P. *et al.* (eds) (1979) *Psychology, Law and Legal Processes*, London: Macmillan.

Boon, A. and Levin, J. (2008) *Ethics and Conduct of Lawyers in the UK*, Oxford: Hart.

Booth, A. (2002) 'Direct effect', *Solicitors Journal* 924.

Bottoms, A.E. and Preston, R.H. (eds) (1980) *The Coming Penal Crisis: A Criminological and Theoretical Exploration*, Edinburgh: Scottish Academic Press.

Bowling, B. and Ross, J. (2006) 'The serious organised crime agency – should we be afraid?', *Criminal Law Review* 1019.

Bowman, Sir J. (1997) *Review of the Court of Appeal (Civil Division)*, London: Lord Chancellor's Department.

Boyron, S. (2006) 'The rise of mediation in administrative law disputes: Experiences from England, France and Germany', *Public Law* 230.

Brazier, R. (1998) *Constitutional Reform*, Oxford: Oxford University Press.

Bridges, L. and Cape, E. (2008) *CDS Direct: Flying in the Face of the Evidence*, London: Centre for Crime and Justice Studies at King's College London.

Bridges, L. and Choongh, S. (1998) *Improving Police Station Legal Advice: The Impact of the Accreditation Scheme for Police Station Legal Advisers*, London: Law Society's Research and Planning Unit: Legal Aid Board.

Bridges, L. *et al.* (2007) *Evaluation of the Public Defender Service in England and Wales*, London: Stationery Office.

Brophy, J. (2007) *Openness and Transparency in Family Courts: Messages from other Jurisdictions*, London: Ministry of Justice.

Brown, D. (1998) *Offending While on Bail*, Home Office, Report No. 72, London: Home Office.

Brown, D. and Neal, D. (1988) 'Show Trials: The Media and the Gang of Twelve' in Findlay, M. and Duff, P. (eds) *The Jury under Attack*, London: Butterworths.

Brown, D. *et al.* (1992) *Changing the Code: Police Detention Under the Revised PACE Codes of Practice*, Home Office Research Study No. 129, London: HMSO.

Brownlee, I. (2004) 'The statutory charging scheme in England and Wales: towards a unified prosecution system', *Criminal Law Review* 896.

Burney, E. (1979) *Magistrates, Court and Community*, London: Hutchinson.

Burns, S. (2006) 'Tipping the Balance', 156 *New Law Journal* 787.

—— (2008) 'An incoming tide', 158 *New Law Journal* 44.

Burrows, A. (2002) 'We Do This At Common Law But That in Equity', 22 *Oxford Journal of Legal Studies* 1.

Campbell, S. (2002) *A review of anti-social behaviour orders*, Home Office Research Study No. 236, London: Home Office.

Cape, E. (2007) 'Modernising Police Powers – Again?', [2007] *Criminal Law Review* 934.

Cape, E. and Young, R. (2008) *Regulation Policing: The Police and Criminal Evidence Act 1984 Past, Present and Future*, Oxford: Hart Publishing.

Carlen, P. (1983) *Women's Imprisonment: A Study in Social Control*, London: Routledge.

Carter, P. (2003) *Managing Offenders, Reducing Crime*, London: Strategy Unit, Home Office.

Carter, Lord (2006) *Legal aid: a market-based approach to reform*, London: Department for Constitutional Affairs.

—— (2007) *Securing the Future – Proposals for the efficient and sustainable use of custody in England and Wales*, London: Ministry of Justice.

Chalmers, J., Duff, P. and Leverick, F. (2007) 'Victim impact statements: can work, do work (for those who bother to make them)' [2007] *Criminal Law Review* 360.

Citizens' Advice Bureau (2004) *Geography of Advice*, London: Citizens' Advice Bureau.

—— (2005) *No win, no fee, no chance*, London: Citizens' Advice Bureau.

Constitutional Affairs Select Committee (2007) *Family Justice: the Operation of the Family Courts Revisited*, London: Stationery Office.

Consumer Council (1970) *Justice Out of Reach: A Case for Small Claims Courts: A Consumer Council Study*, London: HMSO.

Cooper, S. (2009) 'Appeals, Referrals and Substantial Injustice', [2009] *Criminal Law Review* 152.

Cotton, J. and Povey, D. (2004) *Police Complaints and Discipline, April 2002–March 2003*, London: Home Office.

Craig, P. and de Búrca, G. (2007) *EU Law: Text, Cases and Materials*, Oxford: Oxford University Press.

Cretney, S. (1998) *Law, Law Reform and the Family*, Oxford: Clarendon Press.

Criminal Justice: the Way Ahead (2001) Cm 5074, London: Home Office.

Cross, Sir R. (1995) *Statutory Interpretation*, London: Butterworths.

Cruickshank, E. (2007) 'Sisters in the Law', *Solicitors Journal* 1510.

Cutting Crime – Delivering Justice: Strategic Plan for Criminal Justice 2004–08 (2004) Cm 6288, London: Home Office.

Darbyshire, P. (1991) 'The lamp that shows that freedom lives – is it worth the candle?' *Criminal Law Review* 740.

—— (1999) 'A comment on the powers of magistrates' clerks', *Criminal Law Review* 377.

De Tocqueville, A. (2000) *Democracy in America* (George Lawrence, trans.; J.P. Mayer, ed.), New York: Perennial Classics.

Denning, A. (1952) 'The need for a new equity', 5 *Current Legal Problems* 1.

—— (1982) *What Next in the Law?* London: Butterworths.

Dennis, I. (2006) 'Convicting the guilty: outcomes, process and the Court of Appeal', *Criminal Law Review* 955.

Department for Constitutional Affairs (2004) *Broadcasting courts*, CP 28/04, London: DCA.

—— (2004) *Transforming Public Services: Complaints, Redress and Tribunals*, London: Stationery Office.

—— (2004) *The Independent Review of the Community Legal Service*, London: DCA.

—— (2005) *Supporting magistrates' courts to provide justice*, Cm 6681, London: Stationery Office.

—— (2006), *Delivering simple, speedy, summary justice*, 37/06, London: DCA.

Department for Trade and Industry (2004) *Fairness for All: A New Commission for Equality and Human Rights*, Cm 6185, London: Stationery Office.

Devlin, P. (1956) *Trial by Jury*, London: Stevens.

—— (1965) *The Enforcement of Morals*, Oxford: Oxford University Press.

—— (1979) *The Judge*, Oxford: Oxford University Press.

Dicey, A. (1982) *Introduction to the Study of the Law of the Constitution*, Indianapolis: Liberty Classics.

Dickens, L. (1985) *Dismissed: A Study of Unfair Dismissal and the Industrial System*, Oxford: Blackwell.

Director General of Fair Trading (2001) *Competition in professions*, OFT 328, London: OFT.

Doak, J. (2008) *Victims' Rights, Human Rights and Criminal Justice: Reconceiving the Role of Third Parties*, Oxford: Hart Publishing.

Dodgson, K. *et al.* (2001) *Electronic monitoring of released prisoners: an Evaluation of the Home Detention Curfew Scheme*, London: Home Office.

Dow, J. and Lapuerta, C. (2005) *The benefits of multiple ownership models*, available on the former Department for Constitutional Affairs website at: http://www.dca.gov.uk/legalsys/dow-lapuerta.pdf.

Duff, A., Farmer, L., Marshall, S. and Tadros, V. (2007) *The Trial on Trial (Volume 3): Towards a Normative Theory of the Criminal Trial*, Oxford: Hart Publishing.

Durkheim, E. (1983) *Durkheim and the Law*, Oxford: Robertson.

Duster, T. (1970) *The Legislation of Morality*, New York: Free Press.

Dworkin, R. (1977) *Taking Rights Seriously*, London: Duckworth.

—— (1978) 'Political judges and the rule of Law', 64 *Proceedings of the British Academy* 259.

—— (1986) *Law's Empire*, London: Fontana Press.

Edwards, I. (2002) 'The Place of Victims' Preferences in the Sentencing of "Their" Offenders', *Criminal Law Review* 689.

Elks, L. (2008) *Righting Miscarriages of Justice? Ten Years of the Criminal Cases Review Commission*, London: Justice.

Ellis, T. and Hedderman, C. (1996) *Enforcing Community Sentences: Supervisors' Perspectives on Ensuring Compliance and Dealing with Breach*, London: Home Office.

Enright, S. (1993) 'Cost effective criminal justice', 143 *New Law Journal* 1023.

Epstein, H. (2003) 'The liberalisation of claim financing', 153 *New Law Journal* 153.

Evans, R. (1993) *The Conduct of Police Interviews with Juveniles*, London: HMSO.

Evans, Sir A. (2003) 'Forget ADR – think A or D', *Civil Justice Quarterly* 230.

Fenton, A. and Dabell, F. (2007) 'Time for change (1)', 157 *New Law Journal* 848.

—— (2007) 'Time for change (2)', 157 *New Law Journal* 964.

Field, S. (2008) 'Early Intervention and The "New" Youth Justice: A Study of Initial Decision-Making', [2008] *Criminal Law Review* 177.

Findlay, M. (2001) 'Juror comprehension and complexity: strategies to enhance understanding', 41 *British Journal of Criminology* 56.

Fionda, J. (2006) *Devils and Angels*, Oxford: Hart Publishing.

Flood-Page, C. and Mackie, A. (1998) *Sentencing During the Nineties*, London: Home Office Research and Statistics Directorate.

Freeman, M.D.A. (1981) 'The Jury on Trial', 34 *Current Legal Problems* 65.

Fuller, L. (1969) *The Morality of Law*, London: Yale University Press.

Galanter, M. (1984) *The emergence of the judge as a mediator in civil cases*, Madison: University of Wisconsin.

Genn, H. (1982) *Meeting Legal Needs? An Evaluation of a Scheme for Personal Injury Victims*, Oxford: SSRC Centre for Socio-Legal Studies.

—— (1987) *Hard Bargaining: Out of Court Settlement in Personal Injury Actions*, Oxford: Clarendon Press.

—— (1998) *The Central London County Court Pilot Mediation Scheme: Evaluation Report*, London: Lord Chancellor's Department.

—— (2002) *Court-based ADR Initiatives for Non-Family Civil Disputes: the Commercial Court and the Court of Appeal*, London: Lord Chancellor's Department.

—— (2009) *Judging Civil Justice* (Hamlyn Lectures 2008), Cambridge: Cambridge University Press.

Genn, H. and Genn, Y. (1989) *The Effect of Representation at Tribunals*, London: Lord Chancellor's Department.

Goriely, T. and Gysta, P. (2001) *Breaking the Code: The Impact of Legal Aid Reforms on General Civil Litigation*, London: Institute of Advanced Legal Studies.

Green, P. (ed.) (1996) *Drug Couriers: A New Perspective*, London: Quartet.

Griffith, J.A.G. (1997) *The Politics of the Judiciary*, London: Fontana Press.

Grout, Paul A. (2005) *The Clementi Report: Potential Risks of External Ownership and Regulatory Responses – A Report to the Department for Constitutional Affairs*, London: Department for Constitutional Affairs.

Gudjonsson, G.H. (1992) *The Psychology of Interrogations, Confessions and Testimony*, Chichester: Wiley.

Hailsham, Lord (1989) 'The Office of Lord Chancellor and the Separation of Powers', 8 *Civil Justice Quarterly* 308.

Hale, Sir M. (1979) *The History of the Common Law of England*, Chicago: University of Chicago Press.

Halliday, J. (2001) *Making Punishment Work, Report of the Review of the Sentencing Framework for England and Wales*, London: Home Office.

Hamer, D. (2009) 'The Expectation of Incorrect Acquittals and the "New and Compelling Evidence" Exception to Double Jeopardy', [2009] *Criminal Law Review* 63.

Hart, H.L.A. (1963) *Law, Liberty and Morality*, Oxford: Oxford University Press.

—— (1994) *The Concept of Law*, Oxford: Clarendon Press.

Hayek, F. (1982) *Law, Legislation and Liberty: A New Statement of the Liberal Principles of Justice and Political Economy*, London: Routledge.

Hedderman, C. and Hough, M. (1994) *Does the Criminal Justice System Treat Men and Women Differently?* London: Home Office Research and Planning Unit.

Hedderman, C. and Moxon, D. (1992) *Magistrates' Court or Crown Court? Mode of Trial Decisions and Sentencing*, London: HMSO.

Herbert, A. (2003) 'Mode of trial and magistrates' sentencing powers: will increased powers inevitably lead to a reduction in the committal rate?' *Criminal Law Review* 314.

Herbert, A.P. (1966) *Wigs at Work*, London: Penguin.

HM Inspectorate (1999) *Police Integrity: Securing and Maintaining Public Confidence*, London: Home Office Communication Directorate.

Hohfeld, W.N. and Cook, W.W. (1919) *Fundamental Legal Concepts as Applied in Judicial Reasoning*, London: Greenwood Press.

Holland, L. and Spencer, L. (1992) *Without Prejudice? Sex Equality at the Bar and in the Judiciary*, London: Bar Council.

Home Office (1990) *Crime, Justice and Protecting the Public*, Cm 965, London: HMSO.

—— (1998) *Violence: Reforming the Offences Against the Person Act 1861*, London: Home Office.

—— (2001) *Criminal Justice: The Way Ahead* (Cm. 5074), London: Stationery Office.

—— (2003) *Statistics on Race and the Criminal Justice System*, London: Home Office.

—— (2003) *Statistics on Women and the Criminal Justice System*, London: Home Office.

—— (2004) *Are Special Measures Working? Evidence from surveys of vulnerable and intimidated witnesses*, Home Office Research Study 283, London: Home Office.

—— (2004) *Modernising Police Powers to Meet Community Needs*, London: Home Office.

—— (2004) *One Step Ahead: A 21st Century Strategy to Defeat Organised Crime*, London: Stationery Office.

—— (2005) *Exclusion or Deportation from the UK on Non-conducive Grounds*, London: Home Office.

—— (2006) *Making Sentencing Clearer*, London: Home Office.

—— (2006) *Rebalancing the Criminal Justice System in Favour of the Law-Abiding Majority*, London: Home Office.

—— (2007) *Asset Recovery Action Plan*, London: Home Office.

Home Office Research Development and Statistics Directorate (2000) *Jury Excusal and Deferral* (Research Findings No. 102) London: Home Office.

Honess, T., Charman, E. and Levi, M. (2003) 'Factual and Affective/Evaluative Recall of Pretrial Publicity: Their Relative Influence on Juror Reasoning and Verdict in a Simulated Fraud Trial', 33 (7) *Journal of Applied Social Psychology* 1404.

Hood, R., Shute, S. and Seemungal, F. (2003) *Ethnic Minorities in the Criminal Courts: perceptions of fairness and equality of treatment*, London: Lord Chancellor's Department.

Horowitz, I. and Fosterlee, L. (2001) 'The effects of note-taking and trial transcript access on mock jury decisions in a complex civil trial', 25 *Law and Human Behaviour* 373.

Horowitz, M.J. (1977) 'The Rule of Law: An Unqualified Good?', 86 *Yale Law Journal* 561.

House of Lords Parliamentary Committee (2007) *Relations Between the Executive, the Judiciary and Parliament*, London: Stationery Office.

Hucklesby, A. (2004) 'Not necessarily a trip to the police station: the introduction of street bail', *Criminal Law Review* 803.

Hutton, Lord (2004) *Report of the Inquiry into the Circumstances Surrounding the Death of Dr David Kelly C.M.G.*, London: Stationery Office.

Hynes, S. and Robins, J. (2009) *The Justice Gap: Whatever Happened to Legal Aid?* London: Legal Action Group.

Idriss, M. (2004) 'Police perceptions of race relations in the West Midlands', *Criminal Law Review* 814.

Ingman, T. (2008) *English Legal Process* (12th edn), London: Blackstone Press.

Jackson, J. (2003) 'Justice for All: Putting Victims at the Heart of Criminal Justice?', 30 *Journal of Law and Society* 309.

Jackson, R.M. (1989) *The Machinery of Justice in England*, Cambridge: Cambridge University Press.

Jacobson, J. and Hough, M. (2007) *Mitigation: the role of personal factors in sentencing*, London: Prison Reform Trust.

Jeremy, D. (2008) 'The Prosecutor's Rock and Hard Place', [2008] *Criminal Law Review* 925.

Johnson, N. (2005) 'The training framework review – what's all the fuss about?' 155 *New Law Journal* 357.

Joseph, M. (1981) *The Conveyancing Fraud*, London: Woolwich.

—— (1985) *Lawyers Can Seriously Damage Your Health*, London: Michael Joseph.

Julian, R. (2007) 'Judicial Perspectives on the Conduct of Serious Fraud Trials', *Criminal Law Review* 751.

—— (2008) 'Judicial Perspectives in Serious Fraud Cases: The Present Status of and Problems Posed by Case Management Practices, Jury Selection Rules, Juror Expertise, Plea Bargaining and Choice of Mode of Trial', [2008] *Criminal Law Review* 764.

Kairys, D. (1998) *The Politics of Law: A Progressive Critique*, New York: Basic Books.

Kakalik, J. *et al.* (1996) *An Evaluation of Judicial Case Management Under the Civil Justice Reform Act*, California: Rand Corporation.

Kelsen, H. (1945) *General Theory of Law and State*, Cambridge, Mass: Harvard University Press.

Kennedy, H. (1992) *Eve was Framed: Women and British Justice*, London: Chatto.

King, M. and May, C. (1985) *Black Magistrates: A Study of Selection and Appointment*, London: Cobden Trust.

Law Commission (1976) *Criminal Law: Report on Conspiracy and Criminal Law Reform*, London: HMSO.

—— (1982) *Offences Against Public Order*, London: HMSO.

—— (1999) *Bail and the Human Rights Act 1998* (Report No. 157), London: HMSO.

—— (2006) *Post-Legislative Scrutiny*, Cm 6945, London: HMSO.

—— (2007) *The High Court's Jurisdiction in Relation to Criminal Proceedings*, Law Com CP 184, London: Law Commission.

Law Society (2008) *Conditional Fees: A Guide to CFAs and Other Funding Options*, London: Law Society.

Laws, J. (1998) 'The limitations of human rights', *Public Law* 254.

Lawson, C.M. (1982) 'The family affinities of common law and civil law legal systems', 6 *Hastings International Comparative Law Review* 85.

Lee, S. (1986) *Law and Morals*, Oxford: Oxford University Press.

Legal Services Commission (2007) *Best Value Tendering for Criminal Defence Services*, London: Legal Services Commission.

Leigh, A. *et al.* (1998), *Deaths in Police Custody: Learning the Lessons*, London: Home Office.

Leigh, L. (2008) 'Injustice Perpetuated? The Contribution of the Court of Appeal', 72 *Journal of Criminal Law* 40.

Leigh, L. and Zedner, L. (1992) *A Report on the Administration of Criminal Justice in the Pretrial Phase in London, France and Germany*, London: HMSO.

Leng, R. (1993) *The Right to Silence in Police Interrogation* (Royal Commission on Criminal Justice Research Study No. 10), London: HMSO.

Lester, A. (1984) 'Fundamental Rights: The United Kingdom Isolated?' *Public Law* 46.

Levi, M. (1988) 'The Role of the Jury in Complex Cases' in Findlay, M. and Duff, P. (eds) *The Jury under Attack*, London: Butterworths.

—— (1992) *The Investigation, Prosecution and Trial of Serious Fraud*, London: HMSO.

Levitsky, J. (1994) 'The Europeanization of the British Legal Style', 42 *American Journal of Comparative Law* 347.

Lidstone, K. (1984) *Magisterial Review of the Pre-Trial Criminal Process: A Research Report*, Sheffield: University of Sheffield Centre for Criminological and Socio-Legal Studies.

Lightman, J. (2003) 'The Civil Justice System and legal profession – the challenges ahead', *Civil Justice Quarterly* 235.

Llewellyn, K. (1962) *Jurisprudence: Realism in Theory and Practice*, Chicago: University of Chicago Press.

Lloyd-Bostock, S. (2007) 'The Jubilee Line jurors: does their experience strengthen the argument for judge-only trial in long and complex fraud cases', *Criminal Law Review* 255.

Locke, J. (1967) *Two Treatises of Government*, London: Cambridge University Press.

Lord Chancellor's Department (1998) *Determining Mode of Trial in Either Way Cases*, London: Lord Chancellor's Department.

—— (2000) *The House of Lords: Completing the Reform*, Cm 5291, London: Stationery Office.

—— (2002) *Further Findings: A Continuing Evaluation of the Civil Justice Reforms*, London: Lord Chancellor's Department.

—— (2003) *Delivering Value for Money in the Criminal Defence Service*, Consultation Paper, London: Lord Chancellor's Department.

MacCormick, N. (1978) *Legal Rules and Legal Reasoning*, Oxford: Clarendon.

The Macpherson Report (1999) Cm 4262-I, London: HMSO.

Maine, Sir H. (2001) *Ancient Law*, London: Dent.

Mair, G. and May, C. (1997) *Offenders on Probation* (Home Office Research Study No. 167), London: HMSO.

Making Simple CFAs a Reality (2004), London: Department for Constitutional Affairs.

Malleson, K. (1993) *A Review of the Appeal Process* (Royal Commission on Criminal Justice Research Series No. 17), London: HMSO.

Malleson, K. (1999) *The New Judiciary – The Effect of Expansion and Activism*, Aldershot: Ashgate.

Malleson, K. and Roberts, S. (2002) 'Streamlining and Clarifying the Appellate Process', *Criminal Law Review* 272.

Mansfield, M. (1993) *Presumed Guilty: The British Legal System Exposed*, London: Heinemann.

Markus, K. (1992) 'The Politics of Legal Aid' in *The Critical Lawyer's Handbook*, London: Pluto Press.

Marsh, N. (1971) 'Law reform in the United Kingdom: A new institutional approach', 13 *William and Mary Law Review* 263.

Martinson, R. (1974) 'What Works? – Questions and Answers About Prison Reform', 35 *The Public Interest*, 22–54.

Marx, K. (1933) *Capital*, London: Dent.

Matthews, R., Hancock, L. and Briggs, D. (2004) *Jurors' Perceptions, Understanding, Confidence and Satisfaction in the Jury Systems: A Study in Six Courts*, London: Home Office.

Mayhew, L. and Reiss, A. (1969), 'The social organisation of legal contacts', 34 *American Sociological Review* 309.

McCabe, S. and Purves, R. (1972) *The Jury at Work: A Study of a Series of Jury Trials in which the Defendant was Acquitted*, Oxford: Blackwell.

McConville, M. (1992) 'Videotaping Interrogations: Police Behaviour On and Off Camera', *Criminal Law Review* 532.

McConville, M. and Baldwin, J. (1977) *Negotiated Justice: Pressures to Plead Guilty*, Oxford: Martin Robertson.

—— (1981) *Courts, Prosecution and Conviction*, Oxford: Oxford University Press.

McConville, M. and Hodgson, J. (1993) *Custodial Legal Advice and the Right to Silence* (Royal Commission on Criminal Justice Research Study No. 16), London: HMSO.

McConville, M., Sanders, A. and Leng, P. (1993) *The Case for the Prosecution: Police Suspects and the Construction of Criminality*, London: Routledge.

Mendelle, P. (2005) 'No detention please, we're British?' 155 *New Law Journal* 77.

Mill, J.S. (1859) *On Liberty*, London: J.W. Parker.

Millar, J., Bland, N. and Quinton, P. (2000) *The Impact of Stop and Search on Crime and the Community*, Police Research Series Paper 127, London: Home Office.

—— (2000) *Upping the PACE? An Evaluation of the Recommendations of the Stephen Lawrence Inquiry on Stop and Search*, Police Research Series Paper 128, London: Home Office.

Millett, L. (2000) 'Modern equity: a means of escape', *Judicial Studies Board Journal* 21.

Ministry of Justice (2007) *Confidence and Confidentiality: Openness in Family Courts – A New Approach*, London: Ministry of Justice.

—— (2007) *The Governance of Britain: A Consultation on the Role of the Attorney General* (2007) Cm 7197, London: Stationery Office.

—— (2007) *The Governance of Britain: Judicial Appointments*, London: Ministry of Justice.

—— (2008) *The Governance of Britain: Constitutional Renewal*, London: Ministry of Justice.

Mitchell, B. (1983) 'Confessions and police interrogation of suspects', *Criminal Law Review* 596.

Modernising Justice (1997) Cm 4155, London: Home Office.

Montesquieu, C. (1989) *The Spirit of the Laws*, Cambridge: Cambridge University Press.

Moore, R. (2003) 'The use of financial penalties and the amounts imposed: The need for a new approach', *Criminal Law Review* 13.

—— (2004) 'The methods for enforcing financial penalties: the need for a multidimensional approach', *Criminal Law Review* 728.

Moorhead, R. and Cape, E. (2005) *Demand Induced Supply? Identifying Cost Drivers in Criminal Defence Work*, London: Legal Services Commission.

Moorhead, R. and Cumming, R. (2008) *Damage-based Contingency Fees in Employment Cases: A Survey of Practitioners*, Cardiff Law School Research Paper No. 6, Cardiff: Cardiff University.

Moorhead, R. and Hurst, P. (2008) *Improving Access to Justice: Contingency Fees. A study of their operation in the United States of America*, London: Civil Justice Council.

Moorhead, R. *et al.* (2001) *Quality and Cost: Final Report on the Contracting of Civil, Non-Family Advice and Assistance*, London: Stationery Office.

Morgan, R. and Russell, N. (2000) *The Judiciary in the Magistrates' Courts* (Home Office RDS Occasional Paper No. 66), London: Home Office.

Morris, A. (2007) 'Spiralling or Stabilising? The Compensation Culture and Our Propensity to Claim Damages for Personal Injury', 70 *Modern Law Review* 349.

Moxon, D. (1985) *Managing Criminal Justice: A Collection of Papers*, London: HMSO.

Moxon, D. and Crisp, D. (1994) *Case Screening by the Crown Prosecution Service: How and Why Cases are Terminated*, London: HMSO.

Mullins, C. (1990) *Error of Judgement: The Truth About the Birmingham Bombings*, Dublin: Poolbeg Press.

Narey, M. (1997) *Review of Delay in the Criminal Justice System*, London: Home Office.

National Association of Citizens' Advice Bureaux (1995), *Barriers to Justice: CAB Clients' Experience of Legal Services*, London: NACAB.

—— (1999) *A Balancing Act: Surviving the Risk Society* London: NACAB.

National Audit Office (1999) *Criminal Justice Working Together*, London: Stationery Office.

—— (2003) *Community Legal Service: The Introduction of Contracting*, HC 89, 2002–03, London: HMSO.

—— (2005) *Facing Justice: Tackling Defendants: Non-attendance at Court* (HC1162), London: TSO.

—— (2006) *CPS: effective use of magistrates' court hearings*: London: Stationery Office.

New Zealand Law Commission (2001) *Juries in Criminal Trials*, Report 69, Wellington: New Zealand Law Commission.

—— (2006) *Sentencing Guidelines and Parole Reform*, New Zealand: New Zealand Law Commission.

Nobles, R. and Schiff, D. (2005) 'The Criminal Cases Review Commission: Establishing a Workable Relationship With the Court of Appeal', [2005] *Criminal Law Review* 173.

No More Excuses – A New Approach to Tackling Youth Crime in England and Wales (1998), London: Home Office.

Norwich Union (2004) *A modern compensation system: moving from concept to reality*, Norwich: Norwich Union.

Nozick, R. (1975) *Anarchy, State, and Utopia*, Oxford: Blackwell.

Nuttall, C., Goldblatt, P. and Lewis, C. (1998) *Reducing Offending: An Assessment of Research Evidence on Ways of Dealing with Offending Behaviour* (Home Office Research Study No. 187), London: Home Office.

Olivecrona, K. (1971) *Law as Fact*, London: Stevens.

Ormerod, D. (2003) 'ECHR and the Exclusion of Evidence: Trial Remedies for Article 8 Breaches?' *Criminal Law Review* 61.

Ormerod, D. and Roberts, A. (2003) 'The Police Reform Act 2002 – Increasing Centralisation, Maintaining Confidence and Contracting Out Crime Control', *Criminal Law Review* 141.

Owers, A. (1995) 'Not Completely Appealing', 145 *New Law Journal* 353.

Packer, H. (1968) *The Limits of the Criminal Sanction*, Stanford, California: Stanford University Press.

Pannick, D. (1987) *Judges*, Oxford: Oxford University Press.

Parliamentary Penal Affairs Group (1999) *Changing Offending Behaviour – Some Things Work*, London: Parliament.

Partington, M. (2004) 'Alternative Dispute Resolution: Recent Developments, Future Challenges', *Civil Justice Quarterly* 99.

Paterson, A. (1982) *The Law Lords*, London: Macmillan.

Pattenden, R. (2009) 'The Standards of Review for Mistake of Fact in the Court of Appeal, Criminal Division', [2009] *Criminal Law Review* 15.

Peach, Sir L. (1999) *Appointment Processes of Judges and Queen's Counsel in England and Wales*, London: HMSO.

Philips, C. (1981) *The Royal Commission on Criminal Procedure*, Cmnd 8092, London: HMSO.

Pickles, J. (1988) *Straight from the Bench*, London: Coronet.

Pleasence, P. (2004) *Causes of action: civil law and social justice*, London: HMSO.

Plotnikoff, J. and Wilson, R. (1993) *Information and Advice for Prisoners about Grounds for Appeal and the Appeal Process* (Royal Commission on Criminal Justice Research Study No. 18), London: HMSO.

Pound, R. (1968) *Social Control Through Law*, Hamden: Archon Books.

Quinton, P., Bland, N. and Miller, J. (2000) *Police Stops, Decision-making and Practice*, Police Research Series Paper 130, London: Home Office.

Quirk, H. (2006) 'The significance of culture in criminal procedure reform: why the revised disclosure scheme cannot work', *International Journal of Evidence and Proof 10 42*.

Race and the Criminal Justice System: an overview to the complete statistics 2003–2004 (2005) London: Criminal Justice System Race Unit.

Raine, J. and Walker, C. (2002) *The Impact on the Courts and the Administration of Justice of the Human Rights Act 1998*, London: Lord Chancellor's Department, Research Secretariat.

Ramsbotham, Sir D. (1997) *Women in Prison: A Thematic Review*, London: Home Office.

Rawls, J. (1971) *A Theory of Justice*, Oxford: Oxford University Press.

—— (1972) *Political Liberalism, John Dewey Essays in Philosophy*, New York: Columbia University Press.

Raz, J. (1972) 'The Rule of Law and its Virtue', 93 *Law Quarterly Review* 195.

Renton, D. (1975) *The Preparation of Legislation*, London: HMSO.

Renton, Sir David (1978) 'Failure to implement the Renton Report', Address by Right Honourable Sir David Renton QC, MP, to the Statute Law Society, 6 April 1978, available at http://www.francisbennion.com/pdfs/non-fb/1979/19k79–001-nfd-renton.pdf

Restorative justice: helping to meet local need (2004), London: Office for Criminal Justice Reform.

Review of the Crown Prosecution Service (The Glidewell Report) (1998) Cm 3960, London: HMSO.

Rippon, Lord (1992) *Making the Law. Report of the Hansard Society Commission on the Legislative Process*, London: Hansard Society.

Roberts, J. (2008) 'Aggravating and Mitigating Factors at Sentencing: Towards Greater Consistency of Application', [2008] *Criminal Law Review* 264.

Roberts, P. and Saunders, C. (2008) 'Introducing Pre-Trial Witness Interviews: A Flexible New Fixture in the Crown Prosecutor's Toolkit', [2008] *Criminal Law Review* 831.

Robertson, G. (1993) *Freedom, The Individual and The Law*, London: Penguin.

Rock, P. (2004) *Constructing Victims' Rights*, Oxford: Oxford University Press.

Roskill Committee (1986) *Report of the Committee on Fraud Trials*, London: HMSO.

Royal Commission for the Reform of the House of Lords, Report of the (2000) *A House for the Future*, Cm 4534, London: HMSO.

Royal Commission on Criminal Justice Report (1993), Cm 2263, London: HMSO.

Runciman, G. (1993) *Report of the Royal Commission on Criminal Justice*: London: HMSO.

Ryan, E. (2007) 'The unmet need: focus on the future', 157 *New Law Journal* 134.

Salter, M. and Doupe, M. (2006) 'Concealing the past? Questioning textbook interpretations of the history of equity and trusts', 22 *Liverpool Law Review* 253.

Sanders, A. (1993) 'Controlling the Discretion of the Individual Officer' in Reiner, R. and Spencer, S. (eds) *Accountable Policing*, London: Institute for Public Policy Research.

Sanders, A. and Bridge, L. (1982) 'Access to Legal Advice' in Walker, C. and Starmer, K. (eds) *Justice in Error*, London: Blackstone Press.

Sanders, A. *et al.* (1989) *Advice and Assistance at Police Stations and the 24 hour Duty Solicitor Scheme*, London: Lord Chancellor's Department.

Sanders, A., Hoyle, C., Morgan, R. and Cape, E. (2001) 'Victim Impact Statements: Don't Work, Can't Work', *Criminal Law Review* 447.

Scarman, L. (1982) *The Scarman Report: The Brixton Disorders, 10–12 April, 1981*, London, Penguin Books.

Schur, E. (1965) *Crimes Without Victims: Deviant Behaviour and Public Policy, Abortion, Homosexuality, Drug Addiction*, New York: Prentice-Hall.

Sentencing Commission Working Group (2008) *A Structured Sentencing Framework and Sentencing Commission*, London: Ministry of Justice.

Shapland, J. (2008) *Does Restorative Justice Affect Reconviction?*, Ministry of Justice Research Series 10/08, London: Ministry of Justice.

Sherman, L. and Strang, H. (2007) *Restorative Justice: The Evidence*, London: The Smith Institute.

Skryme, Sir T. (1979) *The Changing Image of the Magistracy* (2nd edn, 1983), London: Macmillan.

Smedley, N. (2009) *Review of the Regulation of Corporate Legal Work*, London: Law Society.

Smith and Bailey: see Bailey, S. and Gunn, M. (2002) *Smith and Bailey on the Modern English Legal System* (2nd edn), London: Sweet & Maxwell.

Smith, D. and Gray, J. (1983) *Police and People in London* (The Policy Studies Institute), Aldershot: Gower.

Smith, J.C. and Hogan, B. (2002) *Criminal Law*, London: Butterworths.

Smith, R. (1998) *Legal Aid Contracting: Lessons from North America*, London: Legal Action Group.

Smith, R. (2007) 'Ever decreasing circles', 157 *New Law Journal* 1437.

Smith, R. *et al.* (2007) *Poverty and Disadvantage among Prisoners' Families*, London: Joseph Rowntree Foundation.

Spencer, J.R. (2006) 'Does our present criminal appeal system make sense?' *Criminal Law Review* 677.

Stern, V. (1987) *Bricks of Shame: Britain's Prisons*, London: Penguin.

Steyn, J. (2001) '*Pepper* v *Hart*: A Re-examination', *Oxford Journal of Legal Studies* 59.

Summers, R. (1992) *Essays on the Nature of Law and Legal Reasoning*, Berlin: Duncker & Humblot.

Supperstone, M., Stilitz, D. and Sheldon, C. (2006) 'ADR and Public Law', *Public Law* 299.

Susskind, R. (1996) *The Future of Law*, Oxford: Oxford University Press.

Susskind, R. (2008) *The End of Lawyers? Rethinking the Nature of Legal Services*, Oxford: Oxford University Press.

Tain, P. (2003) 'Master of the game?' *Solicitors Journal* 192.

Tata, C. *et al.* (2004) 'Does mode of delivery make a difference to criminal case outcomes and clients' satisfaction? The public defence solicitor experiment', *Criminal Law Review* 120.

Taylor, R. (1997) *Cautions, Court Proceedings and Sentencing in England and Wales 1996*, London: Home Office.

Thomas, C. (2008) 'Exposing the Myths of Jury Service', [2008] *Criminal Law Review* 415.

Thomas, C. and Balmer, N.J. (2007) *Diversity and Fairness in the Jury System*, London: Ministry of Justice.

Thomas, D. (1970) *Principles of Sentencing: The Sentencing Policy of the Court of Appeal Criminal Division*, London: Heinemann.

—— (2004) 'The Criminal Justice Act 2003: Custodial sentences', *Criminal Law Review* 702.

Tonry, M. (1996) *Sentencing Matters*, Oxford: Oxford University Press.

Twining, W. and Miers, D. (1991) *How To Do Things With Rules*, London: Weidenfeld & Nicolson.

Vennard, J. (1985) 'The Outcome of Contested Trials' in Moxon, D. (ed.) *Managing Criminal Justice*, London: HMSO.

Vennard, J. and Riley, D. (1988a) 'The use of peremptory challenge and stand by of jurors and their relationships with trial outcome', *Criminal Law Review* 723.

—— (1988b) *Triable Either Way Cases: Crown Court or Magistrates' Court?* London: HMSO.

Vogt, G. and Wadham, J. (2003) *Deaths in custody: redress and remedies*, London: Liberty.

Wade, Sir W. (2000) 'Horizons of horizontability', 116 *Law Quarterly Review* 217.

Wakeham, Lord (2000) *A House for the Future*, Cm 4534, London: HMSO.

Waldron, J. (1989) *The Law*, London: Routledge.

Walker, C. (2008) 'Post-Charge Questioning of Suspects', [1998] *Criminal Law Review* 509.

Warnock, M. (1986) *Morality and the Law*, Cardiff: University College Cardiff.

Wasik, M. (2008) 'Sentencing guidelines in England and Wales – state of the art?' *Criminal Law Review* 253.

Weber, M. (1979) *Economy and Society*, Berkeley: University of California Press.

Weinreb, L. (2004) *Legal Reason: The Use of Analogy in Legal Argument*, Cambridge: Cambridge University Press.

White, P. and Power, I. (1998) *Revised Projections of Long Term Trends in the Prison Population to 2005*, London: Home Office.

White, P. and Woodbridge, J. (1998) *The Prison Population in 1997*, London: Home Office.

White, R. (1973) 'Lawyers and the Enforcement of Rights' in Morris, P., White, R. and Lewis, P. (eds) *Social Needs and Legal Action*, Oxford: Martin Robertson.

Whittaker, C. and Mackie, A. (1997) *Enforcing Financial Penalties*, Home Office Research Study 165, London: Home Office.

Williams, G. (1983) *Textbook of Criminal Law*, London: Stevens and Sons.

Willis, J. (1938) 'Statute interpretation in a nutshell', 16 *Canadian Bar Review* 13.

Windlesham, Lord (2005) 'The Constitutional Reform Act 2005: Ministers, judges and constitutional change, Part 1', *Public Law* 806.

Wolfenden, J. (1957) 'Report of the Committee on Homosexual Offences and Prostitution', Cmnd 2471, London: HMSO.

Woodhead, Sir P. (1998) *The Prison Ombudsman's Annual Report*, London: Home Office.

Woodhouse, D. (2007) 'The Constitutional Reform Act 2005 – defending judicial independence the English way' 5 (1) *International Journal of Constitutional Law* 153.

Wooler, S. (2006) *Review of the Investigation and Criminal Proceedings Relating to the Jubilee Line Cases*, London: HM Crown Prosecution Service Inspectorate.

Woolf, Lord Justice H. (1995) *Access to Justice: Interim Report to the Lord Chancellor on the Civil Justice System in England and Wales*, London: Lord Chancellor's Department.

—— (1996) *Access to Justice*, London: Lord Chancellor's Department.

—— (2008) *The Pursuit of Justice*, Oxford: Oxford University Press.

Yarrow, S. (1997) *The Price of Success: Lawyers, Clients and Conditional Fees*, London: Policy Studies Institute.

Young, J. (1971) *The Drugtakers: The Social Meaning of Drug Use*, London: Paladin.

Young, S. (2005) 'Clementi: in practice', 155 *New Law Journal* 45.

Young, W. and Browning, C. (2008) 'New Zealand's Sentencing Council', *Criminal Law Review* 287.

Your Right to Know (1997) Cm 3818, London: HMSO.

Zander, M. (1988) *A Matter of Justice*, Oxford: Oxford University Press.

—— (1993) *Note of Dissent, Report of the Royal Commission on Criminal Justice* (Cmnd 2263), London: HMSO.

—— (1998) 'The Government's plans on civil justice', 61 *Modern Law Review* 382.

—— (2000) 'The complaining juror', 150 *New Law Journal* 723.

—— (2001a) 'Should the legal profession be shaking in its boots?' 151 *New Law Journal* 369.

—— (2001b) 'A question of trust', *Solicitors Journal* 1100.

—— (2004) *The Law-Making Process*, London: Butterworths.

—— (2005) 'The Prevention of Terrorism Act 2005', 155 *New Law Journal* 438.

—— (2006) 'Mission Impossible', 156 *New Law Journal* 618.

—— (2007a) 'Carter's wake (1)', 157 *New Law Journal* 872.

—— (2007b) 'Carter's wake (2)', 157 *New Law Journal* 912.

—— (2007c) 'Full speed ahead?' 157 *New Law Journal* 992.

—— (2007d) 'Change of PACE' 157 *New Law Journal* 504.

—— (2008) 'What's the rush?', 158 *New Law Journal* 7317.

Zander, M. and Henderson, P. (1993) *Crown Court Study*, London: HMSO.

Zuckerman, A. (1995) 'A Reform of Civil Procedure – Rationing Procedure Rather Than Access to Justice', 22 *Journal of Legal Studies* 156.

Index

Terms in **bold** indicate glossary entries.